DATE DUE	

"Race," Rights and the Law in the Supreme Court of Canada

Historical Case Studies

JAMES W. ST. G. WALKER

The Osgoode Society for Canadian Legal History
and Wilfrid Laurier University Press

© 1997 The Osgoode Society for Canadian Legal History
and Wilfrid Laurier University Press
Printed in Canada

ISBN 0-88920-306-7

Printed on acid-free paper

Cover design by Leslie Macredie using a photograph of the Gibson Block,
Edmonton, Alberta. The photograph shows the building as it still existed when it
was photographed by Peter Macklon in the late 1970s or 1980.

Canadian Cataloguing in Publication Data

Walker, James W. St. G., 1940-
"Race," rights and the law in the Supreme Court of Canada

Co-published by the Osgoode Society for Canadian
Legal History.
Includes index.
ISBN 0-88920-306-7 (pbk.)

1. Race discrimination – Law and legislation –
Canada – Cases. 2. Race discrimination –
Law and legislation – Canada – History – 20th
century. 3. Canada. Supreme court. I. Osgoode
Society for Canadian Legal History. II. Title.

KF4395.W34 1997   342.71'0873   C97-931762-2
KF4483.C58W34 1997

This book has been published with the help of a grant from the Humanities and Social Sciences Federation of Canada, using funds provided by
the Social Sciences and Humanities Research Council of Canada.

Contents

Foreword

THE OSGOODE SOCIETY FOR CANADIAN LEGAL HISTORY

The purpose of the Osgoode Society for Canadian Legal History is to encourage research and writing in the history of Canadian law. The Society, which was incorporated in 1979 and is registered as a charity, was founded at the initiative of the Honourable R. Roy McMurtry, a former attorney general for Ontario, now Chief Justice of Ontario, and officials of the Law Society of Upper Canada. Its efforts to stimulate the study of legal history in Canada include a research support program, a graduate student research program and work in the fields of oral history and legal archives. The Society publishes volumes that contribute to legal-historical scholarship in Canada, including studies of the courts, the judiciary and the legal profession, biographies, collection of documents, studies in criminology and penology, accounts of significant trials and work in the social and economic history of the law.

Current directors of the Osgoode Society for Canadian Legal History are Jane Banfield, Tom Bastedo, Brian Bucknall, Archie Campbell, Susan Elliott, J. Douglas Ewart, Martin Friedland, Charles Harnick, John Honsberger, Kenneth Jarvis, Allen Linden, Virginia MacLean, Wendy Matheson, Colin McKinnon, Roy McMurtry, Brendan O'Brien, Peter Oliver, Paul Reinhardt, Joel Richler, James Spence and Richard Tinsley.

The annual report and information about membership may be obtained by writing: The Osgoode Society for Canadian Legal History, Osgoode Hall, 130 Queen Street West, Toronto, Ontario M5H 2N6.

Professor James Walker is a distinguished historian who has made a substantial contribution to understanding the role of minority groups, especially aboriginal populations and those of African ancestry, in the Canadian past. The present study is a culmination of years of thought and research in this critical area. *"Race," Rights and the Law in the Supreme Court of Canada: Historical Case Studies* is a superb analysis of how the Canadian judicial system dealt with four cases where "race" and "law" intersected: *Quong Wing v. The King* (1914); *Christie v. York Corporation* (1939); *Noble and Wolf v. Alley* (1950); and *Narine-Singh v. Attorney General of Canada* (1955).

Professor Walker himself aptly notes that the events described in this book will "challenge many Canadians' image of our national history and character, and the nature of our justice system." But these events are on the whole encouraging and even inspirational, revealing how minority Canadians confronted restrictions in the past despite institutional barriers.

The book also illustrates the rich possibilities of using case law to illuminate Canadian social history and the value of understanding the context of the times in interpreting court decisions. Not least impressive is how surefootedly Professor Walker, without formal legal training, has tackled and understood legal issues of great complexity and subtlety. *"Race," Rights and the Law* achieves new standards of legal-historical analysis in Canada. It will be of great interest to scholars of law and history and to all those concerned with building a Canadian future worthy of those who challenged racial disadvantage in the past.

R. Roy McMurtry
President

Peter N. Oliver
Editor-in-Chief

Preface

Racism is a hot and handy target. We recoil when accused of it, whether at the expense of Aboriginals, Jews, immigrants or Blacks, or in its more cultural anti-French, anti-English forms in Canada. Virtually no Canadian openly condones such beliefs or any acts based on them. Yet, we live in a country whose history remains full of words and deeds rooted in presumptions of racial superiority-inferiority.

If we are to avoid leading unexamined lives, then the need for a definition of racism, in legal and in popular parlance, becomes all the more urgent. That is why James Walker's cool, complex, vivacious reconstruction of these four case histories, analyzed within their well-documented social contexts, demands our full attention. And that is also why Wilfrid Laurier University Press and The Osgoode Society deserve Canada's gratitude for courageously publishing what some may think is an examination of our legal-judicial culture that is best left unacknowledged.

Each case came before the Supreme Court of Canada and was resolved there. The two that could have been appealed further to England's Judicial Committee of the Privy Council were not. Each dramatically illustrated Canadian racism in action. Two plaintiffs challenged legislated racism, in 1912 and 1955; and two cases arose out of custom-based civil actions of private discrimination, in a public establishment (1939) and in a restrictive, private property covenant (1950). If the issue in each case had been put to a referendum, Walker's evidence leaves little doubt that a majority of Canadian voters at each case's time would have allowed the racism. The juridical path proved equally accommodating, because in each case Canada's highest court effectively left racism where legislation and common practice placed it.

But that was there and then, and we are here and now. If we cannot avoid having our own judgments about these cases, and about the men who prosecuted, defended and judged them, where then does James Walker's book locate itself, and its readers, regarding the Canadian legal system's treatment of racism? The short answer is in Walker's method. He takes his reader beyond the judges' formalistically reported reasons for judgment, beyond the courts' bureaucratic case files, back to each case's local origins and the bits and pieces of primary, archival evidence that produced patterns of facts, unique to each case's social context but common to the racism that created and sustained all four cases. Walker's view of the role of law in these cases follows that of Clifford Geertz: that law is not organic or autonomous but "genuinely situated in a social context," all around us in the forms of explicit rules, judgments and habituated norms of behaviour.

In his opening chapter, racism is defined and located as consistent with much of the science, sociology, even theology that prevailed in popular and academic circles during the first half of the twentieth century. Racism in these four cases was a social construct, an asserted truth about civilized v. primitive cultures, that made law into an instrument which privileged those of European origins who controlled it. Thus, racism often had less to do with skin colour, more to do with hostility to cultural differences and to prospects of assimilation. Professor Walker makes clear how pervasive was the public policy protecting racism in the 1914-55 period, and how thoroughly private citizens, often without malice, practised it. He then traces how historians from past to present have also constructed racism, ending with his own rejection of it.

Professor Walker's book holds special appeal to anyone concerned for Canada's constitutional, political, social and moral values. To those who think that the Charter of Rights and Freedoms and social progress have remedied racism, Professor Walker ends with "apprehensions" and "reflections": about the historicist who rationalizes past laws that condoned racism as relatively right for that era, and about the presentist who recognizes those past laws as wrong because present laws and values are right. The result is a book that will be a double clarion to all Canadians, to be vigilant in making our legal culture express our highest aspirations, especially when judging the mere mortals we employ to operate it, and to understand how our legal system actually works, especially when recognizing and correcting its misjudgments.

DeLloyd J. Guth
Faculty of Law, University of Manitoba

Acknowledgments

Early in 1988 I entered the Supreme Court of Canada building in Ottawa to seek the advice of the Consultant Curator, DeLloyd Guth, for a research project I then had under way. By the time I emerged several enlightened hours later Professor Guth had recruited me to write an article for a book of thematic essays to be published by the Supreme Court of Canada Historical Society. My contribution was to be a piece of about 30 to 40 pages on the Court's "race" decisions. It did not seem too daunting a task at the time. As my research progressed it became apparent to me that a single article would not convey the impact of the several important decisions I was uncovering. Fortunately DeLloyd Guth's project was expanding as well, and we decided that I would write an entire volume for a series he would edit on Supreme Court history. Over the years that followed DeLloyd and I were in frequent contact as I struggled and drafted chapters, and his advice was often decisive in the shaping of the project. But before my volume could appear the series was obliged for financial reasons to discontinue, and I had to find a new publisher. Though he is no longer listed as its editor I am delighted that Professor Guth has been invited to contribute a preface to the present publication, for he has been intimately involved since its inception.

In its early stages I believed I could proceed with this project at minimal expense, but travel costs in particular began to mount as I discovered more and more pertinent archival collections that had to be visited, and more surviving participants who should be interviewed. At that crucial moment Judy Young, then Multicultural Program Director in the federal Multicultural Department, lent her assistance so that I was able to obtain a grant to continue with the research in a more appropriately thorough fashion. I am grateful to her and to the Multicultural Department for their essential support. Some of the material that now appears in chapters 3 and 4 had been collected under a previous grant from the Social Sciences and Humanities Research Council of Canada for a project on "The Movement for Racial Equality in Postwar Canada," and I am pleased to express my appreciation for that assistance as well.

It is not possible to pursue historical research without the professional assistance of archivists and librarians, and I gratefully record my debt to dozens of them from coast to coast in Canada. A few, in my view, went beyond their formal responsibilities to take a personal interest in my project, to discuss my progress and problems in research, to draw my attention to records that I would otherwise have missed, to make me aware of potential subjects for interview. In the National Archives of Canada, Myron Momryk and Lawrence Tapper fell easily into this category, as did Stephen Speisman and Howard Markus in the Ontario Jewish Archives in Toronto and Allan Dunlop in the Public Archives of Nova Scotia. In my home library at the University of Waterloo, Diane Fitz-Patrick and Susan Moskal regularly and generously exceeded their job descriptions in helping me find obscure materials. Permission to conduct research in restricted archival collections was kindly extended by John Brewin, Daniel G. Hill, Kalmen Kaplansky and Walter Tarnopolsky. Constance Backhouse graciously shared some of her own research on topics of our mutual interest.

As I have indicated in my Introduction, this project and its resulting publication have been immeasurably enriched by my interviews with people who were directly involved in the stories I was pursuing. I am grateful to them all, and they are warmly acknowledged in my endnotes. Once again it is the case that among my benefactors in this category there were some who offered much more than their reminiscences, providing me with documentation in their personal possession, advice and commentary on the direction of my research, introductions to other participants; some even read and criticized portions of the manuscript. I am pleased to acknowledge such extraordinary contributions from Vivien Mahood Batke, Carrie Best, Hugh Burnett, Jack Desmond, Stanley G. Grizzle, Donna Hill, Kalmen Kaplansky, Ben Keyfetz, Ted King, Anne and Eddie Packwood and Ted and Marion Richmond.

Once I had a manuscript in hand I continued to require professional assistance. As will be immediately apparent to most readers, I am not a lawyer. One of the reasons this project lasted so many years was that I had to teach myself some rather basic law, even how to read a case report, before I could immerse myself in a more familiar archival environment. Inevitably, I sometimes got it wrong. For reading a large manuscript and offering advice on legal or human rights issues I thank sincerely Arthur Drache, Doug Ewart, Augie Fleras, Alain Goldschlager, Karin MacHardy, Jim Phillips, Patricia Roy, David Schneiderman and Paul Winn. The manuscript was submitted to several anonymous reviewers whose commentary directed me towards improvements in my final draft. They rest unknown and therefore unsung, but by no means unappreciated. It is customary to absolve critics of any responsibility for the end product, and this is especially necessary since there remained some areas of disagreement with certain of my reviewers. They will recognize passages where I have taken their advice, and others where I have reinforced my original interpretation in response to their commentary. Peter Oliver of the Osgoode Society and Sandra Woolfrey of Wilfrid Laurier University Press picked up this orphaned project at just the right time and have marshalled it to its ultimate, publishable version. This book has been published with the help of a grant from the Humanities and Social Sciences Federation of Canada, using funds provided by the Social Sciences and Humanities Research Council of Canada. Finally recognition is due to Stephanie, Timothy, Marcus, Julian, Paulette and Nathaniel Walker, whose familial interruptions drive me to distraction just often enough to keep me sane.

"RACE," RIGHTS AND THE LAW IN THE SUPREME COURT OF CANADA

Historical Case Studies

Invitation

The cases described in this book will challenge many Canadians' image of our national history and character, and the nature of our justice system. We tend to seek distinctions between ourselves and Americans, and both "race" and "law" feature strongly in the comparisons that we draw in our own favour. In the first instance, Canadians perceive themselves to be tolerant of racial and cultural diversity, to possess a history of equal treatment towards all, to have avoided the syndrome of racism so evident south of the border.[1] As a case in point, Canadians have the Underground Railroad era, when oppressed American slaves were welcomed and protected against marauding slave-catchers and legal extradition attempts by the American government. In a 1990 survey more Canadian high school students could identify the Underground Railroad than John A. Macdonald or the date of Confederation.[2] A 1993 televised "Heritage Moment" sponsored by the C. R. Bronfman Foundation presented a one-minute vignette illustrating 19th-century white Canadians delivering a grateful black fugitive to freedom and equality. These characteristics have been incorporated into the Canadian identity: asked in a 1989 survey which word best described the "ideal Canadian," Canadians put "tolerant" in first place. (Americans in the same survey picked "independent minded" for themselves.)[3]

The notes to the Invitation are on pages 346-47.

In a very real sense this is our "national dream," and it is attributed to our nonviolent history and our respectful attitude toward peace and order, our dedication to the rule of law.[4] It is frequently remarked that Americans elect their judges or subject them to public confirmations where they are required to pander to current fashion. Canadian judges, on the other hand, are appointed by the appropriate authorities because they are learned in the law and equipped to select the right law for any occasion. Canadians therefore have faith in their law and their judicial system, that the principles of justice will be administered fairly and equally. Canada's response to the Tienanmen Square massacre and reports of widespread human rights abuses in China was to give grants to Chinese scholars to study the Canadian justice system.[5] On 19 February 1981 MP Serge Joyal, co-chair of the constitutional committee, introduced the Charter of Rights and Freedoms to the House of Commons on a note resonant with this imagery:

Canada is a dream; a dream of equality, a dream of liberty, a dream in which the right to be different is guaranteed in the basic law, in which the rights of Canadians as Canadians, because they belong to this country, are the same everywhere, whether they are men or women, native or from mother countries, or whether they are immigrants full of hope who have just arrived dreaming of liberty and justice.[6]

The project set for this book is to engage in some detailed historical case studies where "race" and "law" intersected, to test the "Canadian dream" against specific incidents from our past and in particular to explore the role of the Supreme Court of Canada in effecting the dream. Four cases have been selected for intimate study, representing different Canadian minority groups from different regions and periods, addressing distinct issues within the general theme: *Quong Wing v. The King* (1914); *Christie v. York Corporation* (1939); *Noble and Wolf v. Alley* (1950); and *Narine-Singh v. Attorney General of Canada* (1955).

Quong Wing, a naturalized Canadian born in China, owned a cafe in Moose Jaw, Saskatchewan. In 1912 the Saskatchewan legislature passed an act to prevent "Chinamen" from hiring or managing white females, and Quong Wing was charged under the provincial act for employing two white waitresses. He refused to pay his fine, and appealed his conviction by the local magistrate on the grounds that the federal *Naturalization Act* guaranteed his equal rights.

Fred Christie was a Montreal chauffeur and hockey fan. Before a 1936 game he entered the York Tavern, located inside the Forum, and ordered beer for himself and two friends. The waiter explained that house policy prevented him from serving "Negroes," so Fred Christie sued the tavern for damages, claiming it as a right to be served equally in a public establishment.

Beach O' Pines is a Lake Huron summer home development. Under a covenant attached to the original titles, no "person of the Jewish . . . or coloured race or blood" could rent or purchase land within the development area. Bernard Wolf, a Jew, purchased a cottage from Annie Maude Noble in 1948, but the restrictive covenant was invoked by the other owners to invalidate the sale. Mr. Wolf proceeded with his purchase, bringing the covenant before the scrutiny of the courts.

In 1953 Harry Singh, a Trinidadian of East Indian ancestry, sought to join the Canadian army. When he presented himself at the Toronto immigration office, he was served with a deportation notice stating that he was excluded from Canada as a member of "the Asian race," though the *Immigration Act* had eliminated "race" as a ground of admissibility in 1952. He turned to the courts when the minister of Immigration refused his appeal.

Quong Wing challenged the constitutionality of racial discrimination, Fred Christie objected to a widespread practice of private business, Bernard Wolf disputed the validity of a legal instrument dependent for enforcement on the courts, and Harry Singh protested a bureaucratic interpretation of parliamentary intent. For all four the legal issue was "race" and its meaning in Canadian law. For all four, constituent organizations rallied behind the challenger and financed appeals to the Supreme Court of Canada, rendering the cases symbolic as community causes. These cases have been deliberately selected and are not presented as random or representative "samples" in the normal use of the term. All have been significant for their subsequent use as judicial precedent or their effect upon policy changes through legislative enactment. They are offered as "keys" to the Canadian dream in the first half of the 20th century, as aids to understanding the meaning of "race" in the lives of Canadians, the operation of the law as an instrument for social equality and the often-hidden history of the minority experience in Canada.

A court decision, particularly in the nation's highest court, settles a specific dispute, but it also establishes principles and sets rules for future conduct. Decisions are perpetuated through their use as precedents or interpretations in subsequent cases, they influence the way the law is to be administered by state authorities and they set the standard which a law-abiding population uses to measure its behaviour. Case law, therefore, has a shaping influence on the conditions that exist in society and becomes in effect part of the social circumstances within which further incidents and disputes will be defined. An analysis of case law can illuminate the rules for "race relations" in Canada and, of equal interest, efforts to change them. From the vantage point of people who fought against it, a reader may experience a sense of what racial disadvantage was like, how the law was perceived as an ally in the struggle and how resolutions produced in court affected minority communities.

Attitudes and policies toward "race" in Canada were not static; they participated in the general cultural developments with which they were entwined. There was, for example, an apparent watershed, even a "paradigm shift," during and just after World War II. Almost every commentator on Canadian human rights policy mentions it; *Drummond Wren*, described in chapter 4, is often designated as the point where the turn became legally manifest. The nature of the "shift" and how Canadian courts were involved in it can be discerned not only through *Drummond Wren* itself but in other cases dealing with racial issues in the same period. Over the half century examined in the book there was a profound change in the conceptualization of "rights," not just that certain things became "rights" and other things lost that status, but a change in perspective over time, so that the interpretation even of who had a right and how it should be exercised was redefined. As a single example, in the *Quong Wing* case a provincial law was passed to prevent Chinese men from employing white women. This was challenged as a restriction on the right of a Chinese Canadian to employ whomever he chose; it was defended as a province's legitimate right to protect white women. No record exists of any legal contention that the law restricted the right of white women to choose their own employment. To understand the perspective expressed in these arguments would be to gain insight not only into the racial stereotypes of 1914 but into the operation of "common sense" on the perception of problems and, consequently, on the choice of solution. Every one of the cases has equivalent opportunities.

Unless it behaved differently toward "race" questions than otherwise, these four case studies should also lend insight into the functioning of the Supreme Court of Canada and perhaps even the functioning of "the law." The cases grant an occasion to see whether judges really did simply apply existing rules, or whether they participated in the making of the law. Judges themselves urgently disclaimed any innovative role, but that is one of the assumptions that can be tested against actual cases. At the same time the cases allow an impression of how legal issues were conceptualized in order to make them amenable to judicial resolution, how the "pith and substance" was extracted and interpreted. If the outcome in each case was not inevitable, as it rarely was, then some consideration of alternative choices and why they were not taken might enlighten the decision that was in fact reached.

One route to follow would be to examine dissenting opinions (they exist for three of the four cases): if the conclusion was foregone, how could some judges learned in the law and steeped in their own historical context arrive at decisions so different from their colleagues? Do individual judges make a difference after all? Two of Canada's most renowned jurists, Lyman Poore Duff and Ivan Rand, can be observed at work in these cases. Ten present or future chief justices, obviously persons of learning and influence, sat on one or more, and two other future chief justices, John Cartwright and Bora Laskin, were connected as counsel. They offer an array of talent upon which to test theories of judicial personality. Were any special interests being served through these decisions, and was there any reason why Supreme Court justices might ally with certain ones over others? Were power struggles identifiable, over which judges acted as mediators? Was it simply that "community standards" were being interpreted according to the honest understanding of the judges? Are there signs of an "implied Bill of Rights" discernible in these cases? Did the abolition of appeals to the Privy Council make any difference to Canadian enthralment with British standards? Two of the cases occurred before and two after the change in 1949, making it possible to form some observations.

More generally still, judicial decisions can provide a fruitful research resource for the social history of Canada, especially for those groups or issues which are underrepresented in the more standard sources. Legislatures operate by majority rule, reflecting the outlook and aspirations of the dominant elements in society. In court, where each side is given an opportunity to present an argument, the articulation of minority concerns and goals becomes possible. Court provides a forum where an injured party can challenge a law or a contract, even a social convention or a bureaucratic practice, as the case studies exemplify. Invisible policies were made visible and documents were generated and preserved for historical analysis. The challenge as defined by the appellant, and the response of opposing interests, were assessed by the courts in the light of precedent and fashioned for future application. By definition, those who challenged prevailing conditions were people who did not accept the status quo. This provides an opening to evaluate the notion of "multiple trajectories" in Canadian history through these tales of resistance to the "common sense" of their own times. Entire communities stepped in to support these different visions, demonstrating the extent of the discontent and a willingness to participate in change. In the files of the Supreme Court of Canada, case law and social history converge.

Each of chapters 2 to 5 begins with an incident or situation that led to the Supreme Court case as described in the case files. This is followed by a historical exploration of the conditions that allowed this incident to happen, the policy context and the cultural environment. Then comes a more specific discussion of the legal instruments, both legislation and case law, which contributed to the incident and the eventual decision. Although the outcome is never in doubt, it is hoped that readers will be given enough legal information to assess the eventual judgment in terms of the available options. The narrative will then proceed through the lower courts and eventually to the Supreme Court of Canada, examining the arguments put before the judges as well as their final decision. Where there has been critical comment a canvassing of scholarly opinion upon the case will be presented, both contemporary and retrospective, to give readers different insights and, perhaps, more foundation upon which to build their own evolving analysis of the procedures under observation. Once made, the Court's decision will be appraised for its impact on the development of "race relations" in Canada (its social legacy) and its implications for an understanding of Canadian society and history (its theoretical, or interpretive, legacy). Finally the selected case will be pursued as a precedent in subsequent court cases (its legal legacy). This post-decision examination, of the case as ongoing legacy, is intended to give the benefit of hindsight in weighing the issues that were at stake, and above all to illuminate the Supreme Court decision as process. Only through placing each case on a historical continuum can it be recognized not just as a product but as an agent, as an active participant in the creation of the legal and social strata supporting current laws, attitudes and choices.

Chapter 1 offers an "Orientation" to the conventional wisdom or prevailing discourse about "race" and the law, the common sense and the public policy that lent context to the events unfolding through the four case studies. This orientation is intended to illustrate the cultural package, the loosely bound but widely accepted network of assumptions, which contained Canadian law and society at the time each decision was made. Included is an indication of scientific opinion as well as common understanding, with hints that specialized theories did in fact break into public discourse at least occasionally. The second section of chapter 1, "Approaching the Bench," is primarily for non-lawyers. It is intended as a quick and convenient passage into the mechanical operations of the courts and how a Supreme Court of Canada decision was reached, the technical apparatus brought into play in each of the subsequent cases. Section 3, "Approaching the Past," is a discussion of developments in social and legal history and in the study of "race relations." It is presented with the intent of assisting readers to analyze the cases for themselves and to assess the analyses contained in chapters 2-5. Readers concerned with history as a discipline may find it interesting to identify the emerging historiographical trends that have influenced this book. Besides, it can be therapeutic to recognize that our current "approach" is situated on a trend and is not some final revelation. This section is also intended for non-historians. People often take for granted that there will be more than one interpretation of most legal issues – and hence the need for courts to settle disputes – but they assume when it comes to historical issues that there is a correct version which any industrious historian must be able to discover. "Approaching the Past" can be regarded as a review of the evolving common sense about our own history, the things we take for granted, the cultural web we wear without always being conscious of it. But if a survey of scholarly methodology seems uninviting, Section 3 can be skipped, or perhaps postponed until after the four cases have been examined. It should become more apparently relevant once chapter 6 is reached, where the implications of the entire sequence of cases will be evaluated for the lessons they offer to legal and social theorists as well as to practitioners in Canadian courts and classrooms, and ultimately to the citizen concerned about justice in Canada. Finally an "Afterword" surveys developments in Canadian law and public policy since the cases occurred, and discusses the impact of our current system of rights guarantees on "race relations" in Canada. If, as the "Afterword" suggests, the problems have not yet been eliminated, then our attention to circumstances seems to be of more than academic interest.

Each chapter in this book, therefore, pays a great deal of notice to "context," but context is not in itself an explanation: it is something that needs explaining. The goal has been to facilitate a reader's understanding of what these four cases "meant" in their own times, a prerequisite for deciding what they might mean for our own. The research path taken in pursuit of this objective began with the individual case files located in the bowels of the Supreme Court of Canada, or for *Quong Wing* in the National Archives next door,[7] and proceeded through the records of the various courts where the four cases were heard en route to Ottawa. Sometimes the Supreme Court of Canada dossiers contained complete transcripts from original hearings, and there were often hundreds of pages of additional information deemed pertinent by the lawyers arguing the case. But the case files alone did not hold enough information, or the right kind of information, to acquire a sense of the context in which the cases were disputed and decided. Since legislation featured in all the decisions, and in two cases recent legislative changes had precipitated the court challenge,[8] recourse was had to any relevant statutes and also to debates of the legislatures during their enactment to help discern their intent. Departmental records of the government agencies administering the laws in question were examined, for in its application a law is often made more clear than in parliamentary debate. Official documentation provided a certain kind of context, but for the more general discourse of the period, the "cultural formation" of which the cases were a part, contemporary newspapers, magazines and popular literature, even speeches and pamphlets, proved to be fruitful. Memoirs were useful for evoking the tenor of an era, however self-interested the author. To learn about the judges involved, about contemporary modes of judicial expression, any hints about "common sense" as seen from the bench, a wide range of case reports was examined, even if they had no obvious connection to racial issues. Census data and other statistical reports built impressions of the broader picture, to help in assessing the significance to contemporaries of incidents that might be regarded differently today. Archival research was especially valuable. Some participants themselves have left personal documents which were not included in the case files preserved by the Supreme Court of Canada. The lawyers involved have sometimes left records of their own, which were broadly useful even when they referred to different cases. Local records turned up details about participants that helped portray the life behind the litigant, such as background information on Chinese in Moose Jaw or blacks in Montreal. Most abundant were the records of community and advocacy organizations. Each court challenge studied here was taken up by an association of some kind, and for three of the four cases there are extensive archival papers available for consultation.[9]

To supplement the written record, interviews were sought with living persons connected with the incidents or with the associations and communities that became involved. Direct participants were found for every case but *Quong Wing*. Their memories were a fertile source of details unpreserved elsewhere, but most vital were their reminiscences about characters, feelings, motives and disappointments. They made the notion of "multiple trajectories" a concrete reality, for here were people whose vision of society differed from that of the mainstream. Besides being the most interesting and enjoyable research experience, interviews offered an opportunity to record perspectives that might otherwise be lost. "Documents" are literally created in the course of an interview. Equally significant, the interview format suggested a model of inquiry to be carried into the analysis of written documents as well, an engagement, as it were, in a dialogue with every source of information. This approach had the advantage of treating each document not just as a subjective source but as a source of subjectivity. In the final analysis this book is about subjectivity, about common sense, and about the participation of the courts in generating and applying common sense through the law of Canada, as revealed in four cases singled out for that purpose.

Despite the challenge the following stories present to our national image, they are on the whole encouraging and even inspirational. They are, above all, Canadian stories: the heroes are unsung and the achievements undramatic, the approach is cautious and the demeanour always polite. Quintessentially Canadian, it might be said. Quite apart from any historical lessons that may be derived from them, these are fascinating episodes from Canada's past and they deserve to be told.

1

Orientation

1. "RACE" AND THE LAW

Common Sense

In 1900 a prominent English scholar and humanitarian, Gilbert Murray, expressed a sentiment that was then unchallengeable:

There is in the world a hierarchy of races. . . . [Some] will direct and rule the others, and the lower work of the world will tend in the long run to be done by the lower breeds of men. This much we of the ruling colour will no doubt accept as obvious.[1]

It was indeed "obvious," for wherever one looked in the world white people were ruling over others. Although themselves colonials, in a world divided by colour Canadians could identify with the ruling "race" and with the imperial mission. At a 24th of May speech in Toronto in 1914, R. B. Bennett explained to his fellow Canadians why "we" were ruling over places such as India and Egypt:

We are there because under the Providence of God we are a Christian people that have given the subject races of the world the only kind of decent government they have ever known [applause] . . . and you and I must carry our portion of

---

The notes to this chapter are on pages 347-59.

that responsibility if we are to be the true Imperialists we should be.... An Imperialist, to me, means a man who accepts gladly and bears proudly the responsibilities of his race and breed [applause].[2]

Canadians did not invent "race": it was the product of a global paradigm emerging from European expansion and conquest. In the vast imperial structures that were created, the world itself became a system in which different peoples were assigned particular economic functions consequent upon their local resources, their power to resist, their geographical location, and ultimately their potential contribution to the enrichment of Europe. Human beings inherit various genetic characteristics from their parents which determine such phenotypes as skin colour, hair texture and facial structure. Only in certain historical circumstances are these visible features responsible for the assignment of people into groups for social or economic purposes. In ancient Europe, for example, physical differences were noticed and recorded, but they did not govern the roles people played in society.[3] The expansion of Europe into regions with populations bearing dramatically different physical features led to a global stratification of conqueror and conquered, superior and subordinate, by which was created, through military and political means, an observable coincidence between phenotype and social position. The fact that phenotypes are indelible and heritable meant that any individual's position was immediately recognizable and that it would be passed from one generation to the next. Physical features had been rendered significant; persons who were grouped according to phenotype shared with members of the same group not only physical characteristics but functional characteristics as well, particularly social and economic, and a common relationship with members of other groups. Nineteenth-century Europe's attempt to explain these readily observable structural distinctions produced the doctrine that inherited physical attributes were indicative of immutable behavioural traits which suited different people for different roles. Thus was "race" produced.

By the late 19th century a racial typology existed across the world. Positions in the structure had been set and were being accepted as "natural," and elaborate scientific doctrines were being developed to explain a phenomenon which had evolved circumstantially. Canadians accepted the racial explanation, along with the functional aspects of European supremacy. It was "common sense." It did not need to be examined or proved, for it was self-evident. Pierre Bourdieu has commented that "common sense speaks the clear and simple language of what is plain for all to see."[4] In an essay entitled "Common Sense as a Cultural System," Clifford Geertz maintained that common sense is not "rational," it is "not a fortunate faculty, like perfect pitch"; rather, "it is a special frame of mind," "a cultural system" which reveals "a loosely connected body of belief and judgment."[5] The sense of "race" shared by Canadians in the decades surrounding the *Quong Wing* decision was such a system. It was assumed that "races" were evolutionary units, fixed in their physical and behavioural characteristics. These units were destined to compete at the group level, for their interests, dictated by biology, were inherently in conflict. Some "races," it was thought, bore characteristics that were unsuitable as foundation stock for the fledgling Dominion of Canada. Physically, some "races" could never adjust to the Canadian climate. Furthermore those same "races" were not equipped to participate in Canada's democratic government and free institutions. If admitted to full participation, they would unwittingly subvert those institutions and ruin them for everyone else. An increasing concern in the early 20th century was sexual morality. "Races" less evolved than the Anglo-Saxon were more likely to be driven by base instinct; their presence would not only contaminate the "moral fibre" of the new nation but would pose a specific threat to white women whose health and safety were essential to the future of the Anglo-Saxon "race" in Canada, leading to "race degeneration."[6] "Races" who did not possess the appropriate characteristics, or who could not readily gain them through assimilation, would endanger the nation.

The prevailing common sense about "race" permeated a book written in 1909 by James S. Woodsworth, superintendent of the Methodist All People's Mission in Winnipeg and later to become first leader of the Co-operative Commonwealth Federation. Though it expressed a generous compassion towards new immigrants and revealed its author's experience in Winnipeg's North End immigrant communities, *Strangers within Our Gates, or Coming Canadians* presented and perpetuated the assumption that "race" determined human behaviour. In Woodsworth's scheme, adopted from leading American commentators of the day, very fine lines divided the different racial categories, making Czechs more intelligent than Slovaks, Magyars less industrious than Slavs, northern Italians more independent-minded than southern. Woodsworth's concern was to ensure the eventual assimilation of these disparate European types into the Anglo-Saxon mainstream of western Canada. The alternative was "race" conflict and ultimately "race suicide" for the Anglo-Saxons, who would be degraded to the level of the lowest immigrants. For some "races," however, the gulf was too wide to make assimilation possible. "The Mongolians, the Hindus, and the negroes" would remain forever distinct, creating a "fatal barrier" to the development of a Canadian nation. The only solution was to exclude this kind of immigrant completely.[7] A more succinct version of the same common sense appeared in a petition organized by the Edmonton Board of Trade in April 1911 to demand the exclusion of African-American migrants: "It is a matter of common knowledge that it has been proved in the United States that negroes and whites cannot live in proximity without the occurrence of revolting lawlessness, and the development of bitter race hatred."[8] In April 1914 the Vancouver City Council passed a resolution calling for the removal of Chinese pupils from the public schools because "association of the two races must result in a condition detrimental to the future welfare of our children who have nothing to gain, either mentally or morally, by daily association with Orientals."[9]

Parliamentary debate was equally specific. Prime Minister Sir Wilfrid Laurier confessed that "racial antagonism" was irreconcilable and "amalgamation" with Asians was "neither possible nor desirable."[10] Nanaimo MP Ralph Smith discovered a "universal principle" of struggle that was part of the human condition, illustrated "not only in the conflict of man against man but of race against race."[11] His colleague R. G. Macpherson from Vancouver told the House of Commons that "the oriental and the Caucasian" could never co-exist in Canada. "It is just as impossible to do this as to mix oil and water."[12] Duncan Ross, from Yale-Cariboo, traced racial antagonism to the biblical Noah, whose sons were assigned different roles on earth by "an all-wise though inscrutable Providence"; being divinely ordained, "race prejudice ... will continue to exist for all time."[13] Mr. Ross quoted the *Edinburgh Review* on the insurmountable differences fixed in the Asian soul:

Should they, conceivably or inconceivably, adopt Christianity, they will produce an entirely different sort of Christian; should they break themselves into the Roman character, they will still read life from right to left. We shall never be able to foretell their mental processes more accurately than those of the cat upon the hearth-rug, even had we as favourable opportunities for study.[14]

Unassimilable "races," such as Asians and Africans, were considered "dangerous to Canadian interests," a threat to "the life of this democracy," perpetually and inconvertibly "alien." An article by Hilda Glynn-Ward from the Vancouver *World* was read into *Hansard*:

Between the Orient and the Occident there is more than a mere ocean, there is a great divide, intangible and insurmountable. The leopard cannot change his spots any more than a white man can be orientalized or an oriental be brought to live by the customs and laws of the European. The morals of the one are neither worse nor better than the other; but they are different.[15]

In 1922 Prime Minister Mackenzie King drew an analogy to "Gresham's law of the precious metals": "the baser metal tended to drive the finer metal out of circulation." The same thing would happen if lower "races" were allowed to mingle freely in Canada; Anglo-Saxons would be debased. Opposition Leader Arthur Meighen concurred. For certain "races," "their temperaments, their habits and their very natures are such that assimilation with our people is an impossibility. Assimilation is always an impossibility where marriage itself is forbidden by the very essence of the fact." It was essential for the future of Canada "that we maintain here our racial purity."[16]

These were not intended to be inflammatory remarks, or populist appeals to the fears of Anglo-Canadians; J. S. Woodsworth and the parliamentarians were reflecting, and often quoting, the most advanced scientific opinions of their time. Then in the 1930s scientific orthodoxy began to shift. The definition of "race" as a biological category lost its precision. American sociologist Robert Park taught that a division of labour imposed by the dominant party created the situation of competition and conflict, resulting in group interests and group consciousness. For the sake of preserving their advantages, the dominant party established fixed structures of privilege and disadvantage according to racial categories.[17] Swedish economist and sociologist Gunnar Myrdal, whose research team produced a massive study of "race relations" in the United States, proposed that centuries of discrimination, not "nature," must be held responsible for the distinct characteristics demonstrated by black and white Americans. Far from being insurmountable, according to Myrdal, the observable differences could be eliminated if only American ideals of democracy and equality were applied indiscriminately.[18]

At the very least, this emerging scientific opinion caused confusion about the meaning of "race" both as a biological term and as a social category. In 1938 John Murray Gibbon published *Canadian Mosaic: The Making of a Northern Nation*, inspired by the "racial problems" then being manifest in Europe which made it imperative that Canadians "should examine the progress being made in the amalgamation of their own and other racial groups in the new democracy of the Dominion."[19] Gibbon took racial differences for granted, but attributed them to cultural habits as well as to biology. His colour illustrations of different ideal "types" – Scots-Canadian, Dutch-Canadian, Hebrew-Canadian – depended as much on ethnic costume as on physical features. Gibbon's goal was to celebrate those differences and to show how the different types all contributed something positive to Canadian society. The assimilation of the Canadian-born generation, in the most important characteristics, was a well-established trend, while the preservation of Old World folkways, music and dance merely enriched the Canadian "mosaic." Although he considered only immigrants of European origin, Gibbon's analysis represented a notable movement away from the views offered by Woodsworth only 30 years before.

The biological-cultural ambiguity found in Gibbon was found as well in a study of the 1931 census on "Racial Origins and Nativity of the Canadian People." This commissioned study, written by economics professor W. Burton Hurd and published in 1942, was intended "to measure the progress of assimilation and to discover and evaluate the forces which are working toward that end."[20] Like Gibbon, Hurd both acknowledged and demonstrated the prevailing lack of confidence in biological "race." In his Introduction, Hurd wrote that the term "nativity" presented no problem, but "Unfortunately the same can not be said of the term 'racial origin.'" He elaborated:

In a strictly biological sense, the term "race" signifies a subgroup of the human species related by ties of physical kinship. Scientists have attempted to divide and subdivide the human species into groups on the basis of biological traits, such as shape of the head, stature, colour of skin, etc., and to such groups and to such only, would the biologist apply the term "race." The use of the term, however, even in this strictly scientific sense is neither definite nor free from confusion, for there is no universally accepted classification. Furthermore, the identification of certain types of culture with definite biological types has led inevitably to the result that, even in the hands of the ethnologist, the term "race" has acquired a cultural as well as a biological implication.

Hurd went on to explain that most modern nations were composed of different "races"; even the "English type, if such exists in the biological sense, is the product of the commingling of perhaps half a dozen primitive stocks." "Racial origin" must therefore have both biological and cultural meaning, and the relative importance of each "is not subject to quantitative measurement." "One merely follows popular usage in employing the terms," he admitted. "Such usage is familiar to the public in general, and only when our 'origin' classifications follow such lines can they be collected by a census, be understood by the people or have any significance from the practical standpoint of the development of a Canadian nation."[21] Data on racial origin were useful as a measurement of immigration and as a means of monitoring the pace of assimilation, but Hurd also offered statistics by "race" for such things as criminal activity, illiteracy and insanity, and his "index of segregation" implicitly attributed segregation to the initiative of the segregated group. "Immigrants from Scotland show the least tendency to segregate," he observed. "The Japanese show the greatest tendency to segregate."[22] In a final demonstration of the ambiguity surrounding racial terminology, Hurd cited the instructions given to enumerators for the 1931 census:

A person whose father is English and whose mother is French will be recorded as of English origin, while a person whose father is French and whose mother is English will be recorded as of French origin, and similarly with other combinations. In the case of the aboriginal Indian population of Canada, the origin is to be traced through the mother. . . . The children begotten of marriages between white and black or yellow races will be recorded as Negro, Chinese, Japanese, Indian, etc., as the case may be.[23]

Under the *Indian Act*, native Indian status was traced through the father. Census and Act were contradictory.

Once again, parliamentary debate offered a confirmation that common sense about "race" was in a state of flux. About the time that Fred Christie was refused service in the York Tavern and launched his court challenge, Canada's representative to the League of Nations was quoted as saying "that we did not have any minority problems in Canada."[24] Not long afterwards Prime Minister King told the House:

The problem is not one of inferior or superior races. It is not a racial problem at all. The problem is one of different civilizations, of different economic structures in the different countries. As long as there are those differences there is bound to be unrest as a consequence of immigration which leads to unfair and undue competition on the part of those who have lower standards of living and who may not assume the same measure of responsibility with regard to their citizenship as do the citizens of the country to which they come. I think it is from that broad point of view, that this question must be faced.[25]

Economic competition had long been regarded as a consequence of racial difference, but the prime minister seemed to be giving it causal significance. Mr. King's own certainty about the meaning of biological "race," as expressed in 1922, had apparently come unstuck.

This direction in thinking about "race" was being reinforced both by scholarly analyses and by the reverberations from World War II. Psychologists began to theorize that the tendency to discriminate was a characterological defect to be found and explained within the discriminatory individual, rather than a symptom of group competition. John Dollard developed a "frustration-and-aggression" hypothesis in 1937,[26] in which he proposed that accumulated resentment can turn into aggression against "acceptable" targets such as racial minorities, compensating for feelings of individual powerlessness. Psychological explanations were made more attractive by the horrors of war, when many people found it impossible to accept that "normal" individuals could have perpetrated the Holocaust. The most elaborate interpretation was developed by Theodor Adorno and his colleagues at Frankfurt, who discovered what they called "the authoritarian personality."[27] They too attributed discrimination to the dysfunctional individual harbouring suppressed anger from childhood, but to suit the image of the Nazi functionary the same individual had to remain respectful and subservient toward authority figures. The Frankfurt scholars identified an "F-scale," which purported to measure submission to authority above coupled with aggression towards those who are below. Other psychological explanations retained the focus on the prejudiced individual, but enhanced the part played by social context. Since prejudice is so widespread, to the point of orthodoxy in some settings, it must be explicable as a learned behaviour.[28]

Franz Boas, who led the attack on old concepts of the meaning of "race," wrote in 1936: "We talk glibly of races and nobody can give us a definite answer to the question what constitutes a race."[29] This view, considered radical in the 1930s, gained universal endorsement in the UNESCO Statement on Race issued on 18 July 1950, in the midst of the Supreme Court of Canada's deliberations over Noble and Wolf. In clause 14 of the Statement, the scientists assembled by UNESCO in Paris maintained that

for all practical purposes "race" is not so much a biological phenomenon as a social myth. The myth of "race" has created an enormous amount of human and social damage. In recent years it has taken a heavy toll in human lives and caused untold suffering. It still prevents the normal development of millions of human beings and deprives civilization of the effective co-operation of productive minds.[30]

Canada was not exempt from the impact of the "war conscience" and the emergence of a new common sense linking racism to inhuman atrocities. Of most significance in attracting Canadian attention to the "race" issue was the treatment of Japanese Canadians at the hands of their own democratic government. In 1942, when more than 20,000 Japanese Canadians were displaced from their homes in British Columbia, most Canadians were prepared to accept this extreme measure in the face of an alleged threat during wartime. Public opinion was far less tolerant of the goverment's decision in 1944 to disfranchise the Japanese Canadians who had been moved to other provinces where, until this time, they would have been entitled to vote. Letters and petitions from outraged citizens, church groups and civil liberties organizations flowed to Ottawa. In the House of Commons, Liberal Arthur Roebuck described racial equality as one of the main principles of Liberalism, yet a Liberal government was disfranchising certain citizens on grounds of "race." "To my untutored mind, to my simple way of thinking, that is race discrimination," Roebuck charged. "If you keep that up, it will not be long before Canada will be Hitlerized."[31] North Battleford MP Denise Nielsen insisted that "Race discrimination is a fascist trend which should have no place in our country."[32] Acadia's Victor Quelch agreed. "We are not fighting to-day merely to defeat Germany and Japan; we are fighting in defence of definite principles. We are fighting for a peace based on justice, and justice must be granted to minorities as well as to majorities. It seems to me that this legislation is a negation of the declaration of principles contained in the Atlantic charter."[33] Though the controversial measure was passed, the identification of racial discrimination with the wartime enemy had been established in the prevailing rhetoric.

Discrimination was being viewed as aberrational, and "new eyes," as the Vancouver *Sun* put it, were seeing Canadian minorities in an entirely different light.[34] "What is plain for all to see," in Bourdieu's phrase, was undergoing profound change. Not just racial discrimination but "race" itself came under attack in parliament. In 1952, not long before Harry Singh walked into the Immigration Office in Toronto, Winnipeg North MP Alistair Stewart denounced the government for using the word "race" in immigration regulations and the census because "it is a word which had very little scientific validity."[35] The discourse of scientists seemed to be en route to the conventional wisdom in Canada, settling the ambiguity about "race" and consigning racial discrimination to the realm of the unacceptable and the aberrational. By 1956 the popular magazine *Saturday Night* was instructing its readers on "The Myth of White Supremacy," explaining that "So far as anyone can tell, all the evidence shows that, within the limits of normality, there is no relation between the character of the mind and either brain weight, brain shape, cranial capacity or anything physical that we can measure." Racial prejudices, the article continued, "are attitudes that have to be cultivated for they do not grow naturally in the young human mind."[36]

Throughout the period under study, that is the first half of the 20th century, Canadians also held a "common sense" view of their judicial system, a "frame of mind" concerning the nature and meaning of law and the courts and what they were supposed to do in a parliamentary democracy. Its fundamental principle was a belief in "rule of law." In a mechanical sense this meant that judges applied the law to particular cases and that everyone in society was subject to the same law. Judges must therefore not only be learned in the law, they must be absolutely impartial in administering it. To ensure judicial impartiality in the application of the law, courts did not themselves initiate proceedings. Cases were brought before them by the contending parties, and the adversary process provided each party with a full opportunity to develop legal arguments on its own behalf for the judges to weigh. Judges served as neutral arbiters in a concrete dispute; their judgment was an adjudication between two contesting arguments, following their interpretation of the appropriate law relevant to the case at hand. The judges then wrote a legal decision in which they set out not only the result but the reasoning behind it. They clarified the meaning of the disputed law, articulating its underlying principles and, especially in an appellate court, thereby establishing guidelines for future application in comparable cases.

This procedural format emanated from an understanding that an objective judiciary "discovers" the applicable law. Judges did not insert their personal views or decide what the law ought to be, according to this theory, they simply administered and enforced the law as it was. In 1923 Justice Anglin of the Supreme Court of Canada, soon to become chief justice, defined the judicial process as a search for fixed rules, as in the natural sciences. "Our common object is to make the administration of justice as nearly certain and scientific as it is possible that any human institution can become."[37] Although politicians made the law, its explication was entrusted to apolitical judges unaffected by immediate pressures or the balancing of divergent interests. Judges would determine the intent or legislative purpose of any statute, and they would ensure that established principles were incorporated into their interpretation of what the law was saying in any particular set of circumstances. Central to this procedure was the doctrine of *stare decisis*, by which courts followed prior decisions or precedents relevant to the case before them. *Stare decisis* promoted adherence to the rule of law by limiting the individual judges' interpretive scope; they must follow the established authorities, the guidelines produced by their predecessors. Capricious decisions were avoided, and the public could have some reasonable confidence that a sitting judge would not suddenly move in an arbitrary direction. This meant that the law was generally stable and predictable, and as a consequence that change was very gradual.[38]

Also fundamental to the legal context during the period under study was the current understanding of how the *British North America Act* affected judicial interpretation. According to the Preamble of the Act, the new Dominion of Canada was invested with "a Constitution similar in Principle to that of the United Kingdom." On the one hand this meant that the rights of the subject as evolved through legislation and the common law would operate in Canada as in Britain, and the courts would protect those traditional rights against encroachment. On the other hand the British constitution incorporated the principle of parliamentary sovereignty: the elected representatives of the people could "make or unmake any law whatever," as A. V. Dicey explained in 1885.[39]

In Britain there was only one parliament, but in Canada, by that same *BNA Act*, parliamentary authority was divided between federal and provincial legislatures, both of them elected by the people and both of them inheriting the Westminster mantle. What the *BNA Act* had to do was distribute parliamentary sovereignty between the two legislative levels, primarily through sections 91 and 92 which delineated those powers exclusive to either the central parliament or the provincial legislatures.[40] In 1912, just as Quong Wing's case was beginning to work its way through the courts, the Privy Council ruled that "whatever belongs to self-government in Canada belongs either to the Dominion or to the provinces within the limits of the British North America Act."[41] This "principle of exhaustive distribution of legislative powers" was the application in Canada of parliamentary sovereignty, as adapted to the requirements of a federal system.[42] Canadian decisions could be appealed to the Privy Council in London where the sovereignty of parliament was taken for granted and, in addition, where constitutional interpretations tended to favour provincial over federal authority in disputed areas of law.[43] Although it would be argued that there had historically existed "a convention against exercise of parliamentary power to abrogate the common law principles which the courts have developed," and in particular a "received convention of legislative restraint where civil liberties are concerned,"[44] the regnant orthodoxy in the early decades of the 20th century was neatly expressed by Justice W. R. Riddell of the Ontario Supreme Court:

Parliament can do everything but make a woman a man and a man a woman. . . . An Act of Parliament can do no wrong though it may do several things that look pretty odd. . . .

The Legislature within its jurisdiction can do everything which is not naturally impossible, and is restrained by no rule human or divine. . . .

But while we do not allow a court to set aside legislation as unwise or unjust, opposed to natural justice or what not, it is sometimes necessary for the Courts to enquire whether the particular legislation of Dominion or Province comes within the ambit of powers conferred by the British North America Act.[45]

When a legislative act was challenged the Canadian judiciary, following the Privy Council example, tended to limit its investigation to the determination of whether the legislature passing the act was operating within its jurisdiction under the *BNA Act*. In the absence of explicit guarantees, claims to racial equality had to be expressed in terms recognizable to contemporaries, and legal arguments had to be organized under principles which the courts of the time felt themselves equipped to consider.

Such was the "cultural system" that existed in Canada surrounding the significance of "race," the propriety of racial discrimination, and the function of the courts. The extent to which this context affected the legal deliberations instigated by Quong Wing, Fred Christie, Bernard Wolf and Harry Singh is a major question for the case studies that follow.

Public Policy

In 1938 the German government sought advice on the introduction and implementation of racially discriminatory legislation. One of the places they turned to was Canada. On 14 March the German consul-general in Ottawa, Dr. H. U. Granow, wrote to the Department of External Affairs for an account of federal or provincial laws which "make race (racial origin) of a person a factor of legal consequence." Herr Granow went on to specify his interest in "laws governing the exercise of civil and political rights, the marriage, the illegitimate sexual relations, the exercise of a profession, the administration of schools and universities, and the immigration" with any provisions depending on "race or colour."[46] It took O. D. Skelton of External Affairs until 27 June to compose a reply. Following a small flurry of letters to different departments, Mr. Skelton told the Germans "that the laws of the Dominion and of the provinces do not make the race of a person a factor of legal consequence." The only exceptions, the letter continued, were some immigration laws and "certain provincial laws affecting Asiatics"; otherwise there were "special provisions" for native Indians but they were "protective rather than restrictive" and in any case Indians were free at any time to "assume the legal status of other Canadians."[47]

Undersecretary Skelton's reply was not entirely candid. It is true that there was no national policy coordinating "race" as a "factor of legal consequence," but there was an inherent logic connecting federal and provincial legislation. By the *BNA Act* civil rights were a provincial concern, whereas aliens and naturalization were federal matters.[48] The constitutional division of power shaped many of the "race-related" policies introduced by provincial legislatures and led the provinces to articulate their restrictions in explicitly racial terms to apply to the Canadian-born, for to apply them only to the alien or naturalized subject would be to invade federal jurisdiction and risk disallowance. The Canadian political structure also translated local and provincial concerns to the federal level, so that national policies affecting immigration, military service and the franchise, to offer some outstanding examples, could be determined by regional interests.

Canada also operated in an imperial context, as part of an empire that justified its existence by its contribution to human equality and progress. Colonial Secretaries insisted that the Empire was free of racial distinctions, at the same time urging Canadian governments to disguise their discriminatory restrictions behind tactical euphemisms such as literacy tests in a European language. Specific British and imperial interests added restraints to Canada's available policy options. Anglo-Japanese treaties guaranteeing personal movement and reciprocal rights forced Canada to modify several policies aimed at Japanese Canadians. Renegotiation of the so-called "Unequal Treaties" between Britain and China in the 1920s brought imperial pressure to bear upon policies toward Chinese in Canada. India's loyalty to the Empire could not be undermined by thoughtless decisions in Ottawa or the provincial capitals. At the same time Canada was watching other countries design policies to maintain white exclusivity: American, Australian and South African legislation restricting immigration and limiting civil rights served as an inspiration and a conscious example for the framing of Canadian policies toward minority "races."[49]

Within this general environment it is possible to identify policies that trespassed on each of the areas mentioned in Herr Granow's letter. In the "civil and political" category, regulations were developed to exclude unsuitable persons from the rights, privileges and duties normally accompanying Canadian birth or naturalization. In one of its first acts after Confederation, the BC legislature in 1872 disfranchised Chinese in the province, adding Japanese and East Indians in 1895 and 1907, respectively, as their numbers began to warrant similar attention. Saskatchewan followed BC's example and disfranchised Chinese residents in 1908. Since the federal franchise derived from provincial qualifications, persons barred by a province were automatically denied the federal vote. Many other rights and privileges depended upon being on the provincial voters' list as well, including the right to public office, jury service, employment in the public service and the practice of law.[50] Without any direct reference, these regulations greatly extended the distinctions imposed on grounds of "race." In the case of native Indians, explicit legislation at both the federal and provincial levels denied them the vote.[51] Emphasizing their lower-class citizenship, when World War I broke out young men of native Indian, African and Asian origin were at first rejected as volunteers by the Canadian Expeditionary Force, on the grounds that their racial qualities made them inadequate soldier material. In late 1915 native Indians began to be recruited, initially in separate Indian units, and in 1916 a segregated battalion was formed for black volunteers. Although individuals were admitted to regular fighting units on the discretion of their commanders, only Japanese Canadians were widely acceptable as front-line soldiers, and their recruitment began only in 1916 in the midst of a recruitment crisis.[52]

Rules governing "marriage" and "sexual relations" were rampant through various versions of the *Indian Act*,[53] though Mr. Skelton would undoubtedly explain that they were "protective rather than restrictive." Otherwise the most overt barriers within this category were provincial laws banning the employment of white women by Chinese Canadian men, as in the case of *Quong Wing* in 1914, designed to eliminate sexual exploitation. Legally enforced residential and recreational segregation, however, sometimes had the prevention of sexual contact as an admitted motive.[54]

Most elaborate were pieces of legislation restricting economic activity on racial grounds, expressing an underlying principle that certain "races" were permitted in Canada only to perform certain chores. A racially defined and usually unskilled "caste" was created and maintained by policies limiting the kinds of employment legally available, or imposing prohibitive conditions to discourage employers from hiring minority group members. British Columbia introduced racially specific laws prohibiting Asian Canadians from employment on public works or in underground mines, from the purchase of Crown lands, and even from cutting timber on Crown property. Liquor licences, in exclusively provincial jurisdiction, were withheld from Asians and native Indians in British Columbia, and hawkers' licences carried differential fees depending on the "race" of the applicant.[55] The federal government restricted fishing licences to Japanese Canadians in the 1920s, with the ultimate intention of driving them out of the fisheries.[56] Less directly, an early form of "contract compliance" was employed to ensure that private contractors working on provincial or federal government projects in BC would not hire Asians. And quite apart from its own enforcement of employment discrimination, the federal government permitted discriminatory practices by private and Crown corporations and by the civil service.[57] During the Depression unemployed Chinese Canadians in Alberta received less than half the relief payment accorded to whites.[58]

In many parts of Canada access to "schools and universities" was governed by "race." In order to enforce their attendance at residential industrial schools, native Indian children were denied the right to attend provincial schools near their homes.[59] In both Nova Scotia and Ontario the segregation of black schoolchildren was established by law in the 19th century and those laws still existed at the time of the Granow inquiry. Nova Scotian legislation further limited the educational benefits of black children by requiring schools with provincial subsidies (including all black schools) to employ teachers with nothing higher than a fourth-class certificate. "De facto" separate schools existed for black children in New Brunswick, Saskatchewan and Alberta, supported, but not created, by provincial laws and policies. Several attempts were made to legislate segregated schools for Asian children in British Columbia. The law condoned the widespread use of quotas for the admission of Jewish students to universities, especially in Ontario and Quebec.[60]

Mr. Skelton was required to admit that "some immigration laws" contained provisions making "the race of a person a factor of legal consequence." The 1869 *Immigration Act*, anticipating only British applicants, was silent on the racial issue; by 1910, experience having revealed the error of this expectation, the Act specified "race" as a ground for admission or exclusion. This was not soon enough for British Columbia, the province chosen by most Asian immigrants. Victoria passed a series of provincial acts banning or limiting Asian immigration, but until the completion of the railroad Ottawa disallowed the exclusion of Chinese labour. Finally in 1885 the federal government passed its own act to discourage the Chinese, imposing a $50 head tax on new arrivals from China. Under continual pressure from BC governments and MPs, parliament increased the head tax to $100 in 1900 and $500 in 1903, and in 1923 passed the *Chinese Immigration Act* which virtually ended Chinese admission until after World War II.[61]

Certain other immigrants, though considered just as unsuitable, could not be treated so abruptly as the Chinese. Japan was Britain's Pacific ally, and Japan itself was ready to protest any perceived insult to its dignity as a rising global power. BC's persistent restrictions on Japanese immigrants were as persistently disallowed by Ottawa, usually citing imperial interests. Only when frustrations erupted in a public riot in 1907, directed against Chinese and Japanese districts in Vancouver, was the Laurier government embarrassed into action. A "Gentleman's Agreement" was negotiated with Japan whereby the number of emigrants permitted to leave for Canada was voluntarily limited.[62] India, as part of the Empire, presented its own complications. The failure of negotiated limitation led to Canada's unique contribution to euphemistic legislation: the "continuous journey rule." By order-in-council the federal government stipulated that all immigrants must arrive by an unbroken journey from their country of origin.[63] Since no direct travel connections existed with India, Indian migration was eliminated without any specific racial references to disrupt imperial relations. Similarly, restraints operated against an explicit exclusion of African Americans, for despite its domestic treatment of black citizens the United States was not content to see them openly insulted by a neighbouring country. American influence was reinforced by the presence in Nova Scotia and southwestern Ontario of African-Canadian voters who objected to any policy directed against black immigrants. Instead, immigration officials engaged in a campaign to discourage African-American applicants, and rejected them on medical or other grounds rather than "race." An order-in-council was passed in 1911 to impose a one-year ban upon black immigration, but its implementation proved unnecessary as the informal measures achieved the desired purpose.[64] In these various ways, each one designed to meet specific circumstances, policies excluded immigrants deemed unassimilable. By the 1930s practically no persons of African or Asian origin were entering Canada.

Public policy, whether implemented through openly debated legislation or more surreptitious regulations, can be recognized as the practical application of common sense. It was also a reinforcement, legitimizing common attitudes with the dignity of the law. Legal barriers against Asian immigration, for example, would be a none-too-subtle signal to Canadians that the Asians in their midst were not worthy of equal respect. This cycle of reinforcement was also visible in native Indian policy. The "special provisions" for Indians in Canadian law identified by Mr. Skelton were not entirely as he represented them in his response to the German consul-general. "Protection" was undoubtedly a feature of federal policy, though even at its most innocent this suggests a relationship of inequality, but from the very beginning of a formal policy in 1763 "protection" meant "control." By Royal Proclamation and by instructions sent to Governor James Murray, Indians were permitted to trade only with government-approved white men, use of alcohol was regulated, credit and debt were allowed only under the strictest supervision, and Indian land could be purchased exclusively by the Crown.[65] In the name of protecting Indians against unscrupulous whites, the law prevented Indians from selling their land or trading their goods or entering a contract with persons of their choice; it kept them dependent on the Crown. By the time of Confederation the assimilation of the Indian population was the avowed purpose of native policy, while the *British North America Act* granted responsibility for "Indians, and lands reserved for Indians" to the federal parliament.[66] The first consolidated *Indian Act* in fulfilment of this responsibility was passed in 1876, and it contained at least in embryo the characteristics that would dominate native policy until World War II.[67]

The 1876 Act outlined the steps to be taken by an Indian who wished to become enfranchised; that is, in Skelton's term, to "assume the legal status of other Canadians." First the individual had to be "sober and industrious" and had to convince his local Indian agent that he was qualified for the franchise. If convinced, the agent gave the applicant a ticket for a parcel of reserve land. After three years of successful cultivation, the Indian would receive personal title to this land. There followed an additional three-year period during which the applicant had to demonstrate "good behaviour," and if he passed this probationary term satisfactorily he ceased to be an Indian and became an ordinary Canadian.[68]

For those who remained Indians, the federal government assumed control, or at least supervision, of their local affairs, ostensibly to further the project of gradual assimilation. Traditional leaders were replaced by elected chiefs and band councils. This was intended to give Indians experience with democratic processes, but since those elected could be deposed on grounds of intemperance, immorality, dishonesty or incompetence, the band leadership remained dependent on the good will of the Indian agent.[69] An assimilationist motive also lay behind the stipulation that an Indian woman who married a non-Indian man automatically lost her band membership and her Indian status, theoretically becoming an independent Canadian, but it amounted to a direct government imposition in total disregard of individual wishes.[70] Many native cultural practices, notably the west coast "potlatch" and prairie dances, were outlawed because they perpetuated traditional mores and impeded the kind of sobriety and industry considered a prerequisite for full membership in Canadian society.[71] To accelerate assimilation, attendance at residential schools was made compulsory for Indian children.[72] Finally, admitting the failure of contradictory policies, the government actually implemented compulsory enfranchisement in 1920 for those whom the Indian agent considered suitable. This policy was withdrawn in the face of Indian objections in 1922, but it reappeared in somewhat softer terms in 1933 in a mockery of the principle that enfranchisement represented self-reliance.[73]

Other components of the 1876 Act and its many amendments were overtly controlling, with no pretence of preparation for democratic citizenship. The very definition of who was an Indian, and therefore who was eligible for band membership, treaty considerations, residence on reserves, and so on, was the privilege of the federal government.[74] Intimate details of daily life were subject to government control: who could consume alcohol and under what conditions, sexual morality, responsibility for deserted families, recreation in poolrooms or pubs, the use of band money raised through the sale of goods or services, the dispensation of personal estates and the appointment of executors; Indians could even be forced to go to the hospital against their will if the agent felt it to be in their best interests. Indian land, as specified in the BNA Act, came under especial scrutiny. Indians could not sell or lease their land, but the government could do so on their behalf, even without their consent. The presence on reserves of non-Indians or Indians from other bands was severely regulated, and even the traffic passing through a reserve was a matter for government regulation. Sanitary provisions on reserves were dictated from Ottawa. In case a band did not like what the federal authorities had done in any instance, the *Indian Act* was amended in 1927 to prohibit Indians from hiring lawyers to press any claims against the government.[75] None of these conditions could reasonably be expected to promote self-reliance and some regulations, indeed, seemed deliberately designed to *retard* Indian progress towards independence. When prairie Indians became successful agriculturalists in the late 19th century, for example, and began selling their surplus produce into local markets, the government introduced a "permit system" whereby Indians' ability to sell their produce was restricted. At the same time Indians were effectively prevented from utilizing mechanized farm equipment, thus seriously limiting their ability to engage in efficient modern agriculture.[76] Of course not all these regulations were put into effect at the local level,[77] but their existence even in potential is a powerful representation of majority Canadian attitudes towards the native people and their apparent incapacity to manage their own affairs. The syndrome represented in Canadian Indian policy could not have been established except as part of the evolving common sense about "race" and imperial responsibility that infused Western culture in the late 19th and early 20th centuries.

But, as was discussed above, the assumptions about "race" and racial discrimination began to change not long after the exchange of letters between Messrs. Granow and Skelton in 1938. When the War began in 1939 the military rejected black volunteers, as had been the case in World War I. A Special Committee on Orientals in BC concluded in October 1940 that both Chinese and Japanese should be excluded from the armed services, and a 1943 federal interdepartmental committee decided that East Indians must not be conscripted and could be accepted as volunteers only if they assimilated to Anglo-Canadian dress and dietary standards.[78] Eventually these barriers would be lowered in the face of overseas military requirements. When called to serve, East Indian and Chinese Canadians took advantage of the opportunity to point out that their citizen's duty to fight in defense of democracy was not matched by a citizen's right to participate in democratic elections in Canada. At the same time African and Jewish Canadians protested racially discriminatory hiring practices in defense industries, and although private employers remained free to discriminate, the government itself eliminated "race" as an employment criterion in 1942.[79]

Following the unsuccessful campaign over the disfranchisement of Japanese Canadians in 1944, the public conscience was again aroused against the government's attempt to deport certain Japanese Canadians to Japan after the War. A broad coalition of Canadian groups, led by the Co-Operative Committee on Japanese Canadians, eventually forced the plan's abandonment by the federal government in 1947.[80] Encouraged, university students demonstrated against Toronto facilities that discriminated against blacks; the Committee for the Repeal of the Chinese Immigration Act united labour and church groups behind the Chinese Canadian demand for reform; public opinion polls began to show majorities in favour of enfranchising East Indians and Chinese. There was a new concept dawning in international thought, of "human rights" as a distinct entity with universal applicability. Canadian policy had not recognized this concept early in the War, but through its participation in UN declarations Canada was accepting the international intention to promote fundamental rights. This was reflected in Canada's first *Citizenship Act*, passed in 1946, which represented the notion that Canadian citizens must share equally in all rights and duties, that there could be no legal distinctions between Canadians on racial or any other grounds. There was, in short, a new Canadian self-image, a new and less restrictive meaning to the very term "Canadian."[81]

Racial disadvantage, as it was understood to exist, would have to be addressed. In 1947 Parliament repealed the discriminatory *Chinese Immigration Act* and enfranchised East Indian and Chinese Canadians; in 1949 the final legal restrictions were removed from Japanese Canadians. A revised *Indian Act* in 1951 allowed greater autonomy to Indian bands, ended compulsory enfranchisement, and eliminated the increasingly offensive term "Indian blood" from the requirement for Indian status. In 1960 native people became eligible to vote in federal elections.[82] But generally there was no sense of urgency to legislate change. The existing "British freedoms" were understood to protect minorities once the few overt exceptions were removed from public policy, and those ideals also served to restrain legislative interference which could restrict the white majority's freedom of thought, speech and association. The minorities themselves, however, remained dissatisfied. They formed pressure groups, produced briefs to provincial cabinets, and conducted educational campaigns through union locals and church groups. By the late 1940s public opinion polls showed a majority of Canadians in favour of legislation protecting individuals against religious or racial discrimination, demonstrating political support to encourage provincial legislatures to act.[83]

As a consequence of these campaigns, prohibitory policies were declared, making racially specific practices illegal. The *Fair Employment Practices* and *Fair Accommodations Practices Acts*, passed in Ontario in 1951 and 1954 respectively and soon emulated by the other provinces, contained in their preambles the absolute statement that racial discrimination was contrary to public policy.[84] By the legislation passed in the 1950s, "race" was eliminated as a legitimate reason to distinguish people's rights and access to public facilities. There was, however, one major exception: access to the country itself. When the *Chinese Immigration Act* was repealed in 1947 Prime Minister King made his "classic" statement on Canadian immigration policy, declaring that "the people of Canada do not wish, as a result of mass immigration, to make a fundamental alteration in the character of our population." Assimilation, or rather the presumed inability of certain peoples to assimilate, remained the guiding criterion.[85] Continuing international pressures, especially from the "new Commonwealth," brought forth gestures of equality, such as the decision in 1951 to admit an annual quota of immigrants from India, Pakistan and Ceylon. Campaigns for further reform achieved one apparently significant change in 1952 when the *Immigration Act* eliminated the term "race" as a condition for immigration, substituting the new term "ethnic group."[86] It seemed to be a victory for the newly emerging common sense.

2. APPROACHING THE BENCH

The *British North America Act* authorized the federal parliament to establish a "General Court of Appeal for Canada,"[87] but provincial (especially Quebec) opposition delayed the introduction of a *Supreme Court of Canada Act* until 1875. The Court first met in 1876. It was not, however, a court of "final" appeal, for parliament decided to honour the traditional right of the British subject "of going to the foot of the Throne for redress,"[88] which in practical terms meant that decisions could be appealed to the Judicial Committee of the Privy Council in London. The Court would also continue the Canadian practice of following the common law precedents established in Britain, with those of the Privy Council regarded as binding. Since the French Civil Law Code prevailed in Quebec, the Supreme Court of Canada would sit as a civil law court when hearing private law appeals from that province, though once made a Court decision would be accepted by Quebec courts over the provisions of the Code. For this reason the *Supreme Court Act* required one third of the justices to come from Quebec. Originally this was two of the total of six judges. The Quebec quota remained unchanged when the bench was increased to seven in 1927, but became three of nine when the Court grew again in 1949. (Regional distribution of judges appointed from other provinces was based on political considerations and was not required by the Act). Despite the high public profile and undoubted prestige of the Supreme Court of Canada today, throughout much of the period covered in this book the Court operated in relative obscurity. Not only could its decisions be appealed higher but appellants could bypass it altogether and go directly from a provincial court to the Privy Council. This discouraged many prominent lawyers from accepting appointment to the Supreme Court of Canada, so that elevation to the Dominion's highest tribunal tended to become a patronage appointment for political allies of the current prime minister. In 1949 appeals to the Privy Council were abolished, opening the possibility that a more vigorous and more Canadian tradition might be launched.[89]

The Supreme Court of Canada hears appeals under both federal and provincial jurisdiction, and in both the public and private realms of law. Two of the case studies in this book will be public (where one party to the dispute is a government), and two private (where both parties are private). Apart from the provision that the government may refer a question to the Court for an advisory opinion, disputes arrive via provincial courts of appeal or, with the consent of both parties, directly from the court of original jurisdiction.[90] During the era under study, a capital criminal case or a civil suit for more than $10,000 had an automatic right of appeal; otherwise a dissatisfied litigant applied for "leave to appeal" before a panel of judges, and if they decided that the case or the issues it represented were sufficiently important they permitted it to proceed as an appeal case. The appellant would then be required to post a bond, to cover court costs in case the appeal failed. Most of the time, therefore, the Court was addressing a concrete dispute which had already been heard (usually twice) before at lower levels, which had already been recognized as significant, and with litigants capable of posting a fairly substantial bond. The Court did not have to give reasons for rejecting or accepting a case for appeal.

Under the adversary system, it was the contestants who presented the facts and precedents to the Court. This was done through a written *factum*, prepared by each party's lawyer, containing their argument and the relevant case law. The appellant also filed an appeal or pleading, stating the explicit objections in law to the lower court decision (the "grounds") and the purpose of the appeal. Either side could also submit supporting documentation, and the decisions or transcripts of the cases giving rise to the appeal were placed before the Court. A panel of judges (usually four or five for the period under study) was assigned by the chief justice to consider the case. They read the appellant's *factum* first, then the respondent's, followed by the pleadings and the trial and provincial appeal court materials. At an appointed time the parties met before the judges at the Supreme Court building in Ottawa for a public hearing. Each party beginning with the appellant made an oral presentation, summarizing or emphasizing the most significant points from their *factum*. Since the judges were already familiar with the basic arguments from their preliminary reading, they may have isolated certain issues for detailed consideration or prepared questions for the lawyers. The hearing, therefore, could be a lively exchange, as judges challenged and prompted the contenders to develop their arguments further. Traditionally the judges were supposed to keep an open mind until the hearing was completed, but the nature and direction of the questioning sometimes suggested that minds had been made up on the basis of the written submissions or on the individual judges' legal outlook. A hearing was usually completed in a single sitting, but sometimes the lawyers' statements or the questioning from the bench would extend a case over two or more days.

Following the hearing the judges formulated their decision. Typically, when these four cases were being considered, each judge made an individual decision on the case; though they regularly consulted, and judges would sometimes concur in the reasoning articulated by a colleague, there was no formal conference or assignment of writing a majority decision as there is today. In reaching their decision they relied on the arguments presented by or extracted from the litigants, applying certain fundamental precepts. In any dispute involving the interpretation of a statute, one precept was that the judges must determine and respect the "intent" of Parliament in passing the law. In doing so they were discouraged from consulting the "parliamentary history" of the act, that is the things said about it or changes made to it during parliamentary debate and in committee, on the theoretical ground that judges were to discern the meaning from the statute itself and from the purpose it was designed to meet, for in the product as passed by Parliament was distilled the will of the majority. Still a statute may be ambiguous, and for it to reach the Court at all there must be at least two possible interpretations. Judges would decide which meaning was appropriate through the context (the "surrounding circumstances") of its passage or, since only part of a statute was usually in dispute, through the context of the statute as a whole. In the final analysis judges could apply the "plain-meaning rule": how would the language of the act be construed by the "average reasonable person," for in a democracy this must have been what Parliament intended it to mean. Justice Lyman Duff put it succinctly in 1935: "The duty of the court in every case is loyally to endeavour to ascertain the intention of the legislature, and to ascertain that intention by reading and interpreting the language which the legislature itself has selected for the purpose of expressing it."[91] Another fundamental precept was *stare decisis*, so that common law precedents must be followed if the circumstances or legal principles were the same. In a disputed case the facts would rarely be identical, and almost always the contending lawyers could find precedents implying directly opposite conclusions. It fell to judges, therefore, to interpret the underlying principles informing the precedent. For this they would look to the reasoning behind the earlier decision, the *ratio decidendi*, to determine its relevance to the current case. If they found that it did not fit, the precedent could be "distinguished," to show that it was sufficiently different that it need not be followed.[92]

When the issues seemed clear enough, when the language was plain or the precedent exact, the judges could announce their decision from the bench. More often they would retire and each judge would independently write a decision based on his interpretation of the statutory and case law, or concur in that of a colleague. The tendency was for each judge to recount the facts of the case and the results in the lower courts, before giving his own decision and the reasons for it. Written decisions were therefore often lengthy and repetitious. If a majority of the judges agreed on a decision, even if their reasons were different from one another, that was the ruling of the Court. This was a frequent occurrence, and will be reflected in several of the following case studies. It seems anomalous, since it is not only the decision itself but the reasoning behind it that entered posterity as a precedent. The *ratio decidendi*, according to the doctrine of *stare decisis*, contained the underlying principles of law, the "rule," that could be applied in subsequent cases. In effect, multiple and even contradictory reasons created a choice for future judges in applying the precedent. *Stare decisis*, in these circumstances, would be less restrictive (and predictive) than it might at first seem. The results, including the written decisions and a summary giving the basic facts and the important principles, were finally published in *Supreme Court Reports*, usually six months or so after the decision came down, and would be available to every judge and lawyer in Canada.

3. APPROACHING THE PAST

Over a three-year period, from 1987 to 1990, the Gitksan and Wet'su-wet'en people of British Columbia argued a claim for more than 50,000 square kilometres in the Skeena River district, in a case known as *Delgamuukw v. BC*.[93] Chief Justice Allan McEachern's weighty *Reasons for Judgment* appeared in 1991, deciding against the native land claim. While the *Delgamuukw* decision contains a great deal about aboriginal rights in Canada, it also illustrates the absolute significance of historical theory, or the historian's approach to the past, in determining the meaning of the past and even in deciding what happened in the past. Of additional importance for this book, Chief Justice McEachern demonstrated that historical interpretation can be directly implicated in judicial decision-making.

In his *Reasons* the chief justice announced that courts of law usually cannot consider "subjective considerations," such as native oral histories or even anthropological reconstructions of community traditions. Rather, "cases must be decided on admissible evidence."[94] What he considered admissible evidence, untainted by subjectivity, became clear as he concluded his comment on the various kinds of evidence presented to him during the long trial:

Lastly, I wish to mention the historians. Generally speaking, I accept just about everything they put before me because they were largely collectors of archival, historical documents. In most cases they provided much useful information with minimal editorial comment. Their marvellous collections spoke for themselves.[95]

The interpretation of native life accepted by Judge McEachern showed the Indian cultures as weak, dependent and unable to adapt to the progress brought by European settlers. Their displacement, in other words, was inevitable. This view did once prevail as orthodoxy in Canadian historical writing,[96] but more recent research using a broader range of source material has suggested that, on the contrary, native cultures did develop rational strategies for adapting to the European presence and in many cases were so successful that they offered economic competition to white traders and farmers. Their ultimate collapse as independent societies and their continuing dependency grew not from some inherent weakness but from government policies, some deliberately designed to impede their competitiveness.[97] The fact that Chief Justice McEachern's historical content is not entirely up-to-date is not, however, the most significant point to be made. Far more important is his methodological assumption, first that historical documents "speak for themselves" and secondly that the historian's role is to collect those documents and thus uncover a past which is preserved intact and waiting to be excavated from the archival record. The judge's approach to history corresponds to a historical theory and method known as "positivism."

Historians have traditionally been reluctant to discuss theory, partly because the kind of models used by social scientists can seem trivial and partly because almost any empirical study reveals the impossibility of determining general laws applicable to every circumstance. Historical research forces a consideration of detail, by which every case is seen to be a special case. But historical writing is not simply the narration of discovered facts: to order events in a coherent narrative is necessarily to suggest their meaning; in effect, historians create history. In the interest of becoming more self-consciously aware of what the historical process entails, historians are belatedly entering the theoretical debates, subjecting their activities to critical reflections, and assessing the theoretical frameworks for their potential usefulness.

Developments in Social History

"Positivism" was a product of the Victorian era with its faith in science and its belief in a universe directed by cause-and-effect which could be uncovered and explained. Thus could it be insisted that "the study of history is a study of causes" which begins with "the selection and marshalling of facts."[98] The sequence was rendered coherent for a reader through a logical narrative, a "plot," which both described and explained what happened.[99] The story tended to be about governments and states, leaders and elites, and historical writing was categorized according to periods rather than subject matter or approach. When G. M. Trevelyan described "social history" in 1944 as "the history of a people with the politics left out,"[100] he implied that it was something marginal to the more meaningful course of events.

Thirty years later social history had moved from the margins to a dominant position in North American history departments,[101] and in the process it had become a far more complex discipline than Trevelyan had indicated. Following the example of the French Annales historians,[102] and British Marxists such as E. P. Thompson,[103] the "new" social history was characterized both as a subject matter and as a method. The focus of attention shifted from kings and parliaments to disempowered groups and those features of their lives which did not belong to the political elite: kinship and family, local customs and festivals, the private existence at the core of people's lives but on the periphery of politics. Fernand Braudel took historical study beneath politics, to the long-term historical forces established by geography and traced by economic and demographic trends (*la longue durée*), and to the medium term (*conjoncture*) whose fluctuations over 25 or 50 years establish social relationships and community structures. These two levels of analysis, Braudel taught, reveal the profound influences upon human life and history. The third level, "events" (*événements*) in the political and cultural sphere, Braudel presented as "surface disturbances, crests of foam that the tides of history carry on their strong backs."[104] From Braudel and his *Annales* colleagues came an insistence upon "total" history, upon society as an "integrated organism": one event, one institution, one individual cannot be studied in isolation from the broader systems and trends that make it functional and therefore understandable. The works of E. P. Thompson demonstrated how to write "history from below" or "from the bottom up," to recover histories hitherto left unstudied.[105] Whereas Trevelyan could reconstruct a kind of social life from literary evidence, "ordinary" people did not usually leave similar records and in any case they proved relatively meaningless given the new social history agenda. But as members of groups which had been and could be counted, ordinary people provided a statistical record that could be squeezed for meaning. The social history "movement" had a sophisticating effect upon the discipline as a whole. It encouraged detailed research, and avoided conceptual leaps beyond the available evidence in offering causes or conclusions. It also extended the reach of historians beyond elites to groups and to areas of life never before given any attention. Finally, the new social history enticed historians of all persuasions to declare their interpretive orientations and to identify according to their methodological approach, burying at last the pretence that historians merely recovered and described the past.[106]

By the 1980s a younger generation of social historians became impatient with the limitations of statistical method and the analysis of socioeconomic factors, and turned their attention towards culture and group consciousness. This shift in focus required further methodological adaptation, away from an affinity with sociology and economics toward anthropology and literature.[107] One of the influences effecting this turn was Michel Foucault. Though neither Marxist nor *Annaliste*, and not even calling himself a social historian,[108] Foucault nevertheless marked the conceptual orientation of recent social history writing through the challenges he launched at the assumptions and implications of what was becoming "mainstream" social history.

Foucault denied the possibility of writing "total history." The social and economic structures supposedly underlying historical reality were to Foucault not fixed entities amenable to historical analysis as conventionally understood, but "discursive formations," themselves historically contingent and constantly changing. At the centre of Foucault's explanation was this notion of discourse, of discursive networks and the power of words and of those who control them. For example, his first major book confronted the changing and contingent history of "madness"[109] in which, as he later explained, "the question was to know how and why madness, at a given moment, had been problematized through a certain institutional practice and a certain apparatus of knowledge."[110] Madness is undoubtedly a state of mind, but of whose mind: the person designated "mad" or the party doing the designating? Foucault set out to understand "the problem that madness posed to others."[111] By focusing historical attention on "discourse," Foucault revealed the fundamental role of words in societal relationships. The generators of discourse, the producers of designation, are in control of truth itself, for truth and fact do not exist independently but are products created within a discourse that is inherently neither true nor false.[112] He told an interviewer that

A few years ago, historians were very proud to have discovered that they could write not only the history of battles, of kings and institutions, but also of the economy. Now they're all dumbfounded because the shrewdest among them learned that it was also possible to write the history of feelings, of behaviors and of bodies. Soon they'll understand that the history of the West cannot be disassociated from the way in which "truth" is produced and inscribes its effects.[113]

Foucault also challenged historians' quest for "origins," a concept that implies a "cause." Instead he looked for "beginnings" in moments of change and differentiation, which may happen accidentally or coincidentally, and he traced the subsequent "genealogies" which derived from them.[114] What his exploration was intended to reveal was an analyzable series of discursive forms and the relationships among them. In the process he undermined the principle that society itself is the reality to be studied, and he threatened the confidence of the quantifiers and objectifiers who presumed to find meaning and direction merely by recounting sets of numbers.

Perhaps more directly influential than Foucault in "turning" history toward the preoccupations and methods of anthropology and literature was the American anthropologist Clifford Geertz. Geertz, like Foucault, reacted against "trying to explain social phenomena by weaving them into grand textures of cause and effect," a process he derided as "laws-and-causes social physics."[115] And like Foucault he emphasized that social analysis was necessarily partial and incomplete:[116] there could be no realistic aspiration for totality, for no one method or even any one discipline could supply the answers needed for a general explanation.[117] Instead, Geertz advocated and demonstrated an "interpretive turn" toward the discovery of meaning within specific institutional and cultural formulations.[118] To accomplish this, he maintained, scholars must examine "the ways in which the world is talked about – depicted, charted, represented – rather than the way it intrinsically is."[119] Human behaviour is "saying something," to which the analyst must listen and then construct a "reading" just as if it were a literary text.[120] To accomplish this the scholar must be "actor-oriented,"[121] seek "the meaning particular social actions have for the actors whose actions they are,"[122] and try to enter "the conceptual world in which our subjects live so that we can, in some extended sense of the term, converse with them."[123]

Geertz's great influence upon recent scholarship in a range of different disciplines comes not just from his theoretical orientation but from his methodological precision. This can most readily be characterized by the terms he has used as titles for two of his most seminal works, "local knowledge" and "thick description," both of which suggest a method as well as a theory. Things can be understood (can *only* be understood) in "local frames of awareness,"[124] so the route to understanding is through the analysis of local examples, "a series of concrete analyses."[125] This demands "microscopic" attention to intimate detail, not to find "the world in a teacup,"[126] for there is no microcosm representing typical human experience, but to discover the "orienting notions"[127] which can provide a key to that particular culture. Geertz endorsed particularism, for it is in the "thick description" of observable phenomena that meaning is discovered.[128] This model, of interpreting meaning rather than assigning causes, was readily adaptable by historians seeking to restore explanation to a social history that was losing its purposive sense.

The old, pre-social history paradigm of "reality and representation"[129] was left further behind; cause-and-effect determinism fell more deeply under suspicion.[130] Direct historical enquiry into culture and cultural phenomena proliferated, shifting the emphasis away from the structural analyses that had characterized both the *Annales* and the Marxist models. After a brief absence politics were restored to the historian's legitimate concern, but in a new and more sophisticated fashion following Foucault's insights into power relations. It was not elections and legislatures that attracted attention but patterns of influence and authority which permeate culture in all its manifestations.[131]

The result, not surprisingly, was a different kind of social history, called the "newer social history" by Natalie Zemon Davis as distinguished from the "classic social history" of the 1960s and 1970s. Methodologically one of its characteristics was a return to events, to "telling events" which speak beyond themselves to exemplify social processes and cultural understandings.[132] The preferred unit of study was typically a local one, a "singled-out case," which could be teased for meaning to offer a *key to* an entire period or phenomenon. It was a "subject-centred" approach, concentrating on "micro-units" and "lived experience." It was also "actor-centred," seeking to assign meaning to the expressions of the past as understood by contemporaries and acknowledging that people play an active role in making their own history and defining their own culture. This could be an individual actor or a community, a "being-in-common" and its network of relationships. And the "newer" version of social history revived narrative presentation, the "thick" narrative in Geertzian terms which combined description and analysis of cultural meaning.[133]

In the newer social history there is contained an acknowledgment that history is plural, that there can be no definitive interpretation, that historical vision is fragmented and that some of the stories, as told, are mutually contradictory. Stories that have been deliberately excluded and groups that have been ignored are now receiving attention and challenging the predominance of the reigning versions, and of the groups who produced those versions. This has generated a critical attention to what it is historians are doing, a self-conscious consideration of the effects of historical writing, resulting in the theoretical debates which have resonated through history departments and journals in the past few years.[134] The respectful acknowledgment of plurality has also demanded and legitimized a plurality of strategies. Many types of research materials, analytical approaches and methods of inquiry can co-exist peacefully now that the notions of "master story" and "grand explanation" have been abandoned.

Developments in Legal History

Comparable trends occurred in the study of legal history, though they have not been entirely parallel. Laws change over time, and one's approach to legal history depends on one's understanding of the nature of law. Where legal historians look for change, how they measure it and explain it and even how they define it, connects directly to their underlying theory of law.

As legal studies became professionalized in British and American universities, there was a movement to provide student lawyers with historical training particularly suited to their needs as future practitioners. Legal history was designed for lawyers. Lawyers' history not unnaturally took a common law approach: begin with a current problem, and then look for precedents to support the present case. This promoted a focus on case law, and encouraged an impression that legal history was continuous and cumulative, following an internal dynamic of its own. The notion that history was evolutionary, that the purpose of the past was to provide the present moment, fitted in with the 19th century "Whig" interpretation of history; that is, what now exists is good, natural and normal, and the historian's task is to discover the stages that led up to it.[135] For reasons of its own, "lawyers' history" retained a Whig-like orientation for an extra century. Partly those reasons were methodological. An exclusive reliance upon case law sources lent an organic design to the development of the law; viewed in isolation, the law seemed to grow naturally. Other reasons were more theoretical. The separate existence of an autonomous law was an accepted concept: if law exists as an entity, then obviously it can and must be studied on its own terms. In fact it would be fair to say that the autonomous, organic quality of the law was deemed to be responsible for the authority of the law. Legal decisions were legitimate precisely because judges were consulting an objective table of legal answers honed by history. In Darwinian orthodoxy, the laws that survived must be the fittest. Legal historical method meshed completely with this theory, one reinforcing the other.[136] The product was something Robert Gordon has termed "internal legal history":

The internal legal historian stays as much as possible within the box of distinctive-appearing legal things; his sources are legal, and so are the basic matters he wants to describe or explain. . . . Legal scholars not only took the boxful of legal things as their exclusive subject-matter, but whenever possible adduced as factors explaining the development of legal things only *other* legal things. The rule seemed to be: stay inside the box. . . . [137]

This kind of history was ultimately no more satisfying than social history when it was defined as "history with the politics left out"; significant questions could not always be answered without reference to social context and the social effects of the law. As Graham Parker has suggested, "To teach the lessons of history from this viewpoint is like trying to plant cut flowers."[138] The scholar chiefly associated with the escape from the box into "external" history is the American J. Willard Hurst. In several major books published in the 1950s and early 1960s,[139] Hurst pioneered a more inclusive methodology in legal history – examining the context in painstaking detail – and he developed a new theoretical perspective from which to interpret the relationship between law and society. Hurst proposed that law, and indeed the legal order, is an expression of prevailing social values, and in incorporating those values law functions to direct social change. In other words, change originates outside the law; law is contingent upon social context. For legal historiography Hurst offered a convincing demonstration of the value of including contextual evidence in explaining changes in the law. The notion that law operated in isolation was undermined.

A historical understanding that law is contingent upon social context, or "historicism," meant a transformation in the approach to law itself. In the wake of the historicist challenge, two main intellectual orientations emerged. One of these was to assimilate the new methodology into orthodox common law theory: as society outgrows certain legal expressions designed for earlier times, the law adapts to meet the needs of the new circumstances. Legal anomalies do not long persist; law and society march forward in mutual support of each other.[140] This perspective would tend to promote satisfaction with the nature and pace of legal change. An alternative theoretical response, often known as "instrumentalism," promoted profound dissatisfaction with existing law. Instrumentalists argued that the law "adapts" to social conditions according to deliberate efforts of special interests. The directive function of the law is not part of a benign evolutionary process but an "instrument" in the hands of the ruling elite.[141] One of instrumentalism's leading practitioners, Morton Horwitz, has described his kind of legal history as "essentially destabilizing and subversive,"[142] whereas he characterized traditional "lawyers' history" as an attempt "to pervert the real function of history by reducing it to the pathetic role of justifying the world as it is."[143] Though very different in their explanations, and in their implications, these developments in historicism shared a vision of "what happened," and both schools could therefore be regarded as members of the "Hurstian" family. Recent developments in legal theory also recognize

Hurst as a parent, but new lines of descent from completely new disciplinary sources are also discernible.

One of those influential lines passed through Clifford Geertz, whose contribution to social history has already been described. Geertz taught that human experience is understood, expressed and explained through "local knowledge." That is, humans perceive their reality translated by the structures and commonplaces of their immediate culture. According to Geertz, law participates in this kind of cultural and institutional process.[144] He pointed out that by "law" is meant both a set of normative ideas and a structure of decision procedures, for pervading sensibilities and broad principles must work themselves through an actual case in a real court. Law is a cultural system, a frame of mind and a framework. "Legal facts," he went on, "are made, not born, are socially constructed"; facts are not "discovered" somewhere out there in nature but are "produced" in a legal system.[145] To make it workable in a courtroom, an event or dispute has to be rendered into fact, and this happens via a set of rules and procedures which are culturally relevant. From this theoretical position it is not possible to describe law as contingent upon specific events or social developments. Geertz explicitly rejected "a social-echo view of legal process";[146] law does not "reflect" society or adapt to a "normative consensus."[147] Nor is this perspective compatible with instrumentalism, for law is not about social control or promoting the interests of dominant classes.[148] Geertz proposed a grander vision, "an approach to adjudication that assimilates it not to a sort of social mechanics, a physics of judgment, but to a sort of cultural hermeneutics, a semantics of action."[149]

A key to understanding Geertz's explanation is the concept of "legal sensibility." Every culture has one, not adjacent to or supportive of or emanating from the society, but as an essential, integral and active part of the society. Law and society cannot be separated. Law is local knowledge.[150] Geertz concluded that legal sensibilities "do not just regulate behavior, they construe it."[151] Legal systems are wound in culture. Law is not simply contextualized wisdom: law and context are part of the same cultural process.

The insights Geertz brought from interpretive anthropology were not in the direct Hurstian line of descent, but they were not entirely isolated from other streams of thought. Michel Foucault also argued that the history of law and the history of society are not separate developments which occasionally overlap and influence one another, nor even two streams deriving from "some common matrix," but rather, he suggested,

"both derive from a single process of 'epistemologico-juridical' formation."[152] Or as E. P. Thompson concluded more colourfully after examining the role of law in 18th-century England:

I found that law did not keep politely to a 'level', but was at *every* bloody level; it
was imbricated within the mode of production and productive relations themselves (as property-rights, definitions of agrarian practice) and it was simultane-
ously present in the philosophy of Locke; it intruded brusquely within alien
categories, reappearing bewigged and gowned in the guise of ideology; it danced
a cotillion with religion, moralizing over the theater of Tyburn; it was an arm of
politics and politics was one of its arms; it was an academic discipline, subjected
to the rigor of its own autonomous logic; it contributed to the definition of the
self-identity both of rulers and of ruled; above all, it afforded an arena for class
struggle, within which alternative notions of law were fought out.[153]

These influences have intersected with a new intellectual movement
known as "critical legal studies." Fundamental to the theoretical
approach of this movement is a perspective upon legal history that oblit-
erates the "box" altogether; the "new legal history," or "critical legal history," is neither "internal" nor "external" but "integrated," in a
recognition that a new form of posing questions about legal development is required.[154] There are many implications from this philosophical
orientation, and indeed many different paths are being followed under
the general heading of "critical legal history,"[155] but there is a Geertz-like
quality linking them to a focus on law as culture.

The new scholarship is at base a new theory of the law and its role in
society, but like every shift in theoretical perspective it is having an
impact on historical interpretation.[156] The organic, autonomous, evolutionary image of law is under attack, and therefore the notion of "contingency" has had to change. Laws are not contingent as meaning reflective
of discrete events or influences, but rather "constitutive": law is "omni-
present in the very marrow of society"; a law is not only a product of
prevailing consciousness but helps to reproduce it by confirming it.[157]
Law as captive instrument is also transcended in the sense that it "helps
to create the conceptual universe shared by all parties to the struggle";[158]
it is the dominant ideology, and not the dominant party, to which the
legal instruments conform. And when law is genuinely situated in a
social context "it varies with variations in that context" and straddles
multiple trajectories.[159] There is nothing automatic or predictable about
developments in the law, for it participates in the same turmoil as every

other aspect of human history. Enigmas posed by critical legal scholars are transforming the study of legal history as much as the study of law.

One very recent trajectory to emerge from Critical Legal Studies itself is a movement known as Critical Race Theory. Primarily a method for effecting reforms in American civil rights and equal opportunity law, Critical Race Theory is also challenging traditional historical explanations for such landmarks as *Brown v. Board of Education*, the school desegregation decision in 1954, and the *Civil Rights Act* of 1964. The movement insists that racism is inherent in American society and that the white majority tolerates reform only when its own interests converge with those of African Americans. Contextual analysis is therefore a fundamental requisite for Critical Race Theorists, and a host of new interpretations is now emerging on the history of "race" in America. Interestingly, the model of presentation most often adopted for these interpretations is intensely narrative and subject oriented.[160]

"Race" and "Race Relations"

When prevailing opinion accepted the existence of discrete, naturally existing biological units who competed at the group level, scholarly attention concentrated upon the physical aspects of "race": the object of inquiry was to determine racial characteristics that motivated a distinctive kind of "relations," and that could help to illuminate the nature of their interaction.[161] As the idea of "race" as a biological category lost scientific credibility, replaced by "race" as a socio-political construct, the concern was to discover how the *relationship* determined *"race,"* rather than vice versa, and emphasis therefore shifted toward social analysis of dominant and subordinate groups divided by colour.[162] Psychological explanations, at first focusing upon pathological individuals, moved towards an analysis of the acquisition of stereotypes and how they connect with discriminatory social conditions,[163] defining a circular dynamic not unlike the one described by Gunnar Myrdal: prejudice leads to discrimination and subsequent disadvantage, which in turn justifies the prejudice.

It is apparent that virtually all scholarly lines were converging upon "society." The directing notion was that, on the basis of perceived attributes, real groups had been established with substantive boundaries between them and consequently with genuinely different interests and a particular set of problems. The study of "race relations," Michael Banton suggested, should be about "the creation, maintenance and change of such boundaries"; the field was "defined by its problems."[164] Since the object was to study "process" – of inequality, injustice, domination and oppression, and the erection of structural systems to facilitate and perpetuate them – the analytical orientation of "race relations" scholars tended overwhelmingly to be historical.[165]

One of the earliest and most influential of the new approaches was the theory of pluralism as established by M. G. Smith and elaborated by Leo Kuper and others. A "plural society," as the name suggests, is ethnically heterogeneous, but specifically it is one organized according to the principle of "differential incorporation." Typically in a colonial situation, people are incorporated into the social and economic structure according to their ethnicity and colour, and political and juridical provisions are designed to maintain those positions. Thus there are distinct status groups, or "estates," characterized phenotypically, culturally and politically. The process of differential incorporation during colonization assigns group membership before class roles have developed. Competition and conflict occur not between classes but between racial "estates," shaped by their position in the plural hierarchy. "Race" becomes responsible for economic role rather than vice versa, and a "plural society" exists in which phenotypically distinguishable groups have different positions in the economic and political order.[166]

A similar result is explained somewhat differently by the "internal colonialism" approach. Robert Blauner sought to understand why some American ethnic groups assimilated after the immigrant generation and others did not. Like Smith, he discerned "differential incorporation" in the way such groups as native Indians, African slaves and Chinese migrants were assigned their domestic status, and he noted that it parallelled the way conquered populations were treated in the European overseas empires. The colonial structures thus established were not surmountable on an individual basis, and so the internal colony was perpetuated over the generations.[167] Michael Hechter called this "a cultural division of labour,"[168] a concept he found more compatible with Marxism than "pluralism" because in this model the cultural distinctions were seen as being superimposed upon pre-established class lines, through segregation and differential treatment. If assimilation was assumed to be the norm, as in the case of European immigrants, it was possible to conclude that separate cultural development for unassimilated groups was consequent upon class division rather than vice versa.

Another Marxist-compatible approach to have attracted much attention is the "split labour market" theory originated by Edna Bonacich.

She was struck by the observation that "racism so often has taken the form of keeping a group in a subordinate position for purposes of exploitation,"[169] but unlike the orthodox Marxists she recognized that white labourers were often the most racist element in society. She hypothesized that in a situation where an ethnic minority was vulnerable to accepting a lower wage than majority workers, a three-way conflict was produced among business and the two labour groups in which employers sought to replace the more expensive with the cheaper workers, and the majority workers, to prevent undercutting, would either seek to exclude the cheaper competition altogether or to isolate it in certain "caste" positions. This might mean lower pay for performing the same work or, more likely, relegation to the lowest paid and least skilled employment categories. For Bonacich the capitalists provoked the resulting ethnic antagonism through an initial differential in the price of labour, but based on an ideology of laissez faire rather than an ideology of "race." It was the white workers, through their voting power, who enlisted the state apparatus in the struggle to preserve their advantages.[170] Adherents to split labour market theory are satisfied that it explains not only ethnic antagonism but the increase of racism in industrial societies, despite capitalism's interest in hiring the cheapest workers whatever their colour.

Most of these theories identified certain common elements in the history of "race relations," such as the centrality of colonialism, differential assignment to labour, the significance of political and legal systems in structuring inequality so that it became self-perpetuating, the cumulative nature of barrier construction. Consideration of these components brings an awareness of the universality of the "race" experience in the modern world. Even if no single theory adequately explains the Canadian experience, together they offer useful analytical questions and a reminder that events in any one time or place must be understood against a much broader pattern.

Applications

There are strategic and tactical lessons that might be drawn from recent historiographical developments in order to formulate some operational principles to guide this examination of the Supreme Court of Canada. At the most broadly strategic level, Canadian racial practice can be approached as something coming from a long-term momentum, a very *"longue durée"* shaken into life by European overseas expansion and the transatlantic slave trade. Global "pluralism" dictated differential access to power and resources on the basis of "race"; specific roles were assigned according to imperial patterns of incorporation. What occurred in Canada can therefore be understood not as an "origin," requiring site-specific causal explanation, but as a "beginning" in this country of a local career, a "genealogy," of a supra-national phenomenon. The approach, then, would be towards an analysis of how the global paradigm was articulated in Canadian terms, of how a universal idea became "local knowledge." Rather than treating the Canadian events as aberrations, they can be understood as participants in a widespread cultural system. Attention is drawn to a process whereby a certain ideology or power relationship became "normative"; it described a "reality" which was accepted as "truth," as "common sense," and therefore not even requiring analysis or proof. The strategic message would be to include contemporary discourse as a subject for analysis, to discern what was common sense and how experience was interpreted. Ideas about "law" and "race" were embedded in the same cultural framework. The challenge is to seek connections, exchanges and developments over time, the dynamic context to "events" which cannot be understood in isolation.

There are some tactical suggestions accompanying these strategic considerations. If the past is a conversation, then it is necessary to find a way of listening in. Natalie Davis has suggested that there are "telling" events, incidents that "speak" beyond themselves, making it possible to hear the "voice" of the past.[171] This gives tactical value to the "singled-out case" which is "key to" a particular historical condition. As Davis and Geertz among others have demonstrated, the actor-oriented micro-study grants access into the deeper workings of society, providing data that can be interpreted for meaning about the context, the dynamic within which the individual case was manifest.[172] The structures, for long the target of historical inquiry, become understandable at the human level, where they impact upon an individual life. Legal records can be instrumental in providing the "telling" case and in producing the data that preserve the "voice" to which historians can listen. From a historical perspective "race relations" in Canada have not produced an abundance of personalized records or statistics for convenient analysis, so that some Canadians deny that there is any history of "race" or racism in this country. To employ the device of the "singled-out case" on the analysis of court cases, to listen to the voices made audible through the Supreme Court of Canada, therefore emerges not only as legitimate but especially appropriate in the circumstances.

There is a corollary. To listen to the voices of the past, and to understand what they are saying, it is imperative to approach with an attitude of respect, acknowledging their sincerity. Sometimes, it's true, modern observers do know certain things about the past that were obscured to contemporaries, but they also carry concepts, values and "common sense" of their own which come between them and the experience of the people they study historically. Differences can seem like moral deficiencies, past lives less complicated than the present. "Presentism" is the term used for a perspective that judges the past in terms of the present, as if other ages should have had a supra-historical sensitivity that is absent today. Beliefs have changed, and so have myriad behaviours connected to them. It is not productive to isolate statements about "race" and listen to them alone. On the other hand a condescending attitude toward the past may impose an amoral relativism upon the decisions of former generations. To say that whatever they did must have been right implies that they had no choices, that they were incapable of discerning differences or the impact of their own actions. A respectful attitude includes a recognition that there were multiple trajectories, that group interests and personal positions affected choices then as now.

This is not only a tactic to take *into* historical study but a benefit to be taken *from* it. In the course of examining the following cases, readers will become increasingly aware of how "race" was instituted in Canadian society and, especially, of how it has changed over time. The ideas, the practices, the implications of "race" were not a consistent package handed down intact from generation to generation. The four cases demonstrate that racism – the ideology of "race" – was intimately attached to and dependent upon the society that produced it. It was indeed a child of its times. This would suggest that any racism existing today is a manifestation of our own society. The study of "race" in Canada's past is not an exercise in assigning blame, but in understanding historical processes from which we are not exempt.

2

Quong Wing v. The King

1. THE LEGISLATION

On 5 March 1912 the Saskatchewan legislature passed *An Act to Prevent the Employment of Female Labour in Certain Capacities.*[1] Threatening a fine of up to $100 or two months in jail, the Act specified that

No person shall employ in any capacity any white woman or girl or permit any white woman or girl to reside or lodge in or to work in or, save as a *bona fide* customer in a public apartment thereof only, to frequent any restaurant, laundry or other place of business or amusement owned, kept or managed by any Japanese, Chinaman or other Oriental person.

Attorney General W. F. A. Turgeon explained that the Act would not go into force until 1 May to give affected businessmen the opportunity to dispose of any white female help.[2]

Immediately Chinese and Japanese residents in Saskatchewan registered their protests. A Japanese restaurant owner in Moose Jaw complained the day the law was passed that it constituted an "insult to the honour of Japan" and argued that at the very least it should be amended to exclude Japanese: their numbers in Saskatchewan were too few to pose a threat, and they were generally not found in the restaurant or laundry businesses.[3] Japanese Consul Y. A. Hori travelled from Vancou-

The notes to this chapter are on pages 359-77.

ver to Regina to deliver a personal protest to the attorney general, claiming that the new legislation contravened treaty provisions between the empires of Great Britain and Japan, affirmed by the Canadian government in 1907, guaranteeing reciprocal rights and freedoms.[4] The federal government was inclined to support this interpretation of the treaty, and there were in fact only 57 Japanese in the province at that time. The Saskatchewan legislature therefore agreed to amend the Act by striking out the terms "Japanese" and "or other Oriental person." The retraction came too late to avert the prosecution under the original wording, in August 1912, of a recent Japanese immigrant named Yoshi who employed three white waitresses in the Saskatoon restaurant he ran with his wife. When the revised Act came into effect in January 1913, however, it ensured there would be no further repercussions for Mr. Yoshi by adding a clause to the effect that "The said Act shall be construed as though the said words struck out by subsection (1) hereof had never been contained therein."[5]

This meant that the provision against white female employment now applied only to Chinese. In early 1912 China was still in the midst of a political revolution at home, and although the Chinese community held a mass meeting of protest in Moose Jaw on the eve of the law's implementation, and a letter from Sun Yat Sen to a local Chinese leader promised Chinese government action if the law were enforced, Consul Yang Shu-Wen was unable to register his official objections as effectively as his Japanese counterpart. Consul Yang did not make a personal visit to Saskatchewan, and by the time he asked the federal government to disallow the Act he was advised that the one-year disallowance period had already passed. There was in any case no comparable treaty status for Chinese in Canada, and no strategic reason to assuage the honour of the Chinese Empire. The Chinese interdiction therefore remained in place.[6] But the Chinese diplomat continued to complain, and Chinese residents of Saskatchewan sent delegations to Regina declaring that the female labour law was a disgrace to the Chinese nationality. Finally in 1919 Saskatchewan Premier W. M. Martin conceded. A new *Act to Prevent the Employment of Female Labour in Certain Capacities* was passed stating only that

No person shall employ any white woman or girl in any capacity requiring her to reside or lodge in or to work in any restaurant or laundry without a special licence from the municipality in which such restaurant or laundry is situated, which licence the council of every municipality is hereby authorised to grant.

The racial reference was omitted, and a grateful Yang Shu-Wen registered his cordial thanks to the people of Saskatchewan.[7]

An episode had apparently ended satisfactorily. Diplomatic niceties had been restored. But while the Act had contained its explicit Chinese prohibition, a Moose Jaw restaurant owner named Quong Wing had been charged and fined $5 by a local magistrate. His appeal, which went eventually to the Supreme Court of Canada in 1914, gave Canada's highest tribunal its first opportunity to examine legislation with an overtly racial intent. The decision upheld a province's right to pass racially discriminatory legislation as long as it did not exceed provincial jurisdiction under the *British North America Act*, and came to be regarded as a basepoint from which to measure the evolution of egalitarian principles in Canadian law.[8]

If the Saskatchewan legislature seemed so conciliatory as to amend the law after a few diplomatic protests, thereby apparently acknowledging an error or at least a lack of conviction, was the Supreme Court reacting precipitously in a situation that really did not deserve such attention? A closer analysis of that era suggests that in fact the Court was reflecting widely held values and attitudes, and that Saskatchewan's gesture towards equality in 1919 was no more than cosmetic. In its *Quong Wing* decision the Supreme Court of Canada acknowledged that the Chinese presence was perceived as a "problem," whose features and whose implicit threats could be recognized even in remote Moose Jaw of 1912.[9]

At the time of the 1911 census there were 957 Chinese in Saskatchewan, a number larger than that of any other "visible" group apart from native Indians but hardly significant in a total provincial population of 492,432. What was deemed significant was not the numbers but the rate of growth. Since 1901 Saskatchewan had experienced an overall population growth of over 400 percent, the largest rate in Canada both proportionally and in absolute numbers. Saskatchewan knew it was a new and growing society, and was conscious that some controls had to be set over the kind of person permitted to join it. In this context a Chinese increase of over 2,300 percent, from 41 persons in 1901, could indeed be regarded as cause for concern. The local *Evening Times* estimated that there were "more than 500" Chinese in Moose Jaw in 1911, a situation that was "viewed with alarm by very many people." This number was probably an exaggeration, since the official census recorded only 268 Chinese in Moose Jaw District. Still, this represented the largest concentration in Saskatchewan and, after Winnipeg and Calgary, the third largest across the Canadian prairies.[10]

The Chinese community of Moose Jaw did not resemble the city's other ethnic groups. Since the population was almost exclusively male, there were few Chinese families and fewer children in the local schools. Social contact was virtually non-existent, and even economic integration was minimal. Some of the men worked as labourers in a white-owned abattoir, a few were domestic servants in white homes, but most were self-employed or worked in Chinese-owned enterprises. There were in 1912 more than 25 Chinese laundries and 10 restaurants in Moose Jaw, and several hotels or rooming houses. Chinese homes and businesses were concentrated along River Street West, where Moose Jaw's version of Chinatown existed. Discouraged from mixing with the white residents, the Chinese men largely kept their own company, forming several fraternal organizations where Chinese cultural practices and social relationships could be maintained. Their political attention focused upon China itself, and the raising of funds to support Sun Yat Sen's republican movement. About 100 had been converted to Christianity, but they worshipped in a separate Chinese congregation, Zion Methodist, founded in 1912 by Pastor Yip Sam. The pastor also conducted evening English language classes in the River Street home of merchant Yip Foo, considered Moose Jaw's "leading Chinaman." A separate Chinese cemetery had been founded in 1911.[11]

As was often the case in different parts of Canada, Moose Jaw's Chinatown was located in one of the least desirable sections of the city. River Street was separated from the main residential areas by the business district, and this degree of remoteness combined with the proximity of the CPR station gave the street a certain attraction for businesses anxious to avoid public scrutiny. With the cooperation of the city's police force, Moose Jaw's River Street harboured brothels and bootleggers and effectively became the red-light district for Regina, less than 45 miles away along the CPR. According to one contemporary journalist, "You came out of the Moose Jaw station, turned left on River Street, and you could have been in New Orleans."[12] The north side of River Street contained an assortment of gambling dens, drinking joints and hotels worked by up to 100 prostitutes in the summer season. The south side of the street was occupied by Chinatown. Police Chief W. P. Johnson, "the wealthiest policeman in the West," conducted regular raids along River Street, allegedly for tribute and perhaps to reassure the respectable citizens that the law was being upheld. An inordinately large number of the raids were aimed at the Chinese fraternal organizations on the south side of the street, where gambling and opium smoking, both practices brought from China, were among the most prevalent social activities.[13] China-town's association with drugs and gambling and its neighbourhood with the city's sin centre gave the Chinese community itself an aura of immorality, and a stereotype was sustained of the "Chinaman" as invet-erate gambler, drug addict and procurer of prostitutes. As such the Chi-nese were an apparent threat to the white men who might become their customers, and more ruinously to white women who could be corrupted into prostitution. In introducing the Female Labour Bill, Attorney Gen-eral Turgeon explained that "Its purpose was . . . to suppress what had become a menacing feature of the white slave traffic," and though on third reading he admitted that some "Oriental" businesses were run in a proper manner, still he insisted the Bill was necessary "to prevent a cer-tain state of affairs which frequently results from the employment of white women in establishments conducted by Chinamen, Japs and other Orientals."[14] No figures were given on the frequency of this state of affairs, presumably because none were available. Although several mod-ern commentaries claim that the *Female Labour Act* was inspired by a sex-ual attack by a Chinese restaurateur upon his white employee, contemporary Saskatchewan newspapers mentioned no precipitating incident.[15] The attorney general, like the rest of the white population at the time, seems to have formed an opinion based on stereotype rather than fact, i.e., that Chinese would corrupt white women if permitted the opportunity. Consul Yang Shu-Wen lamented this implication. "I find the Act is based on the protection of morality of white women," he wrote to the federal justice minister. "This something is still *ridicurous* to me, because morality, as I think, is more or less a self-restraining nature sub-ject to no violence and influence at all."[16]

The consul's views, however, were in the minority; the assump-tions expressed in the Saskatchewan legislature were widely shared. In February 1913 Manitoba passed an identical Act to Saskatchewan's 1912 version (including the Japanese reference),[17] and in May 1914 Ontario amended its *Factory, Shop and Office Building Act* by adding a clause to the effect that "No Chinese person shall employ in any capacity or have under his direction or control any female white person in any factory, restaurant or laundry."[18] By this time the Chinese consulate was mobi-lized and arrangements were made to prevent the Manitoba and Ontario laws from being proclaimed.[19] This did not prevent some Ontario munic-ipalities from restricting the employment of white females in Chinese restaurants, apparently in the belief that the amendment had in fact been proclaimed as passed.[20]

In British Columbia the Royal Commission on Labour, reporting in 1914, declared that although they had no evidence that Chinese proprietors in the province employed any white women, "such employment must have a demoralizing influence" if it did exist and recommended legislation to forbid it. In 1919 the BC legislature duly amended its *Municipal Act* with a clause duplicating Saskatchewan's revised version (applying to Chinese only).[21] Provincial police officer Thomas Parsons assured his attorney general that "Apart from its 'race bearing' – the employment of Caucasian by Mongolian – there is no doubt white women introduced to Orientals through this medium succumb to both immorality and narcotics."[22] Submitting in turn to Chinese diplomatic pressure, BC brought in a *Women and Girls' Protection Act* in 1923 which omitted the specific racial reference but required local police officials to determine whether each instance of the employment of females by Chinese was "advisable in the interests of the morals of such women and girls." As a unique elaboration, BC included native Indian women in its restriction.[23]

In British Columbia, as indeed in Saskatchewan under its 1919 Act, the omission of the term "Chinese" was not intended to impede the enforcement of the prohibition. As the *Regina Daily Post* announced on 17 January 1919, the amendment requiring a municipal licence for the employment of white women in restaurants or laundries meant that "The power to prevent the employment of white women by Chinese will therefore rest with the local councils." Attorney General Turgeon was quoted as saying that Chinese diplomatic objections had caused the change in wording, but that "The government desired to maintain the same law." Whatever euphemisms or generalities might appear in the amended legislation, it is therefore clear that Chinese were the intended target, and the Supreme Court's *Quong Wing* decision more directly represented the intention of the legislature.

2. THE CHINESE PROBLEM

This observation may absolve the Supreme Court from any charge of holding peculiar racist tendencies, but it still begs the question of how provincial legislatures arrived at the conclusion that Chinese in Canada needed special regulation. The "beginning" of anti-Chinese feeling in Canada dates virtually from their first arrival in 1858 with the discovery of gold on the Fraser River and the migration of thousands of fortune hunters from California. Few of the Chinese among them were actually miners, but the mining camps offered innumerable employment opportunities as cooks, laundrymen and general labourers. By 1860 there were over 4,000 Chinese on Vancouver Island and the British Columbia mainland, most engaged in unskilled ancillary enterprises generated by the gold mining industry. As individual claims gave out and white prospectors moved on to richer fields, Chinese would often take over the depleted mine, content with a more modest return for their efforts. Already the notion that Chinese would work for less was becoming familiar on the West Coast.[24]

By the mid-1860s the gold rush had subsided, and many Chinese left the country. Those who stayed sought employment in the newly developing coal mines, in fishing and salmon canneries, as farm labourers and domestic servants. Numbers remained small until CPR contractor Andrew Onderdonk, following the example of the Northern and Southern Pacific Railways, began importing Chinese labourers to build his line through the Rocky Mountains. Beginning with a few hundred experienced construction workers from the United States, Onderdonk moved on to chartering shiploads of unskilled labourers from China. Between 1881 and 1885 Onderdonk brought over 15,000 Chinese to British Columbia, many of them contracted to gang bosses who permitted them the merest subsistence living. In a BC white population of only 35,000 the Chinese proportion was noticeable, as were their living and working conditions. Once again the completion of the railway meant the departure of numbers of the Chinese workers, but thousands remained (the 1891 census showed over 9,000). Most were labourers, though increasing numbers founded businesses as grocers, shopkeepers, market gardeners, and especially laundrymen and restaurateurs. Many migrated back along the railway line they had constructed, settling in railway towns across the prairies and further east. The first Chinese laundry was established in Moose Jaw in 1889, typical of what was happening all along the frontier as a white male society looked to others for cooking, washing and the performance of similar household chores. The Chinese stepped into the opportunities thus created. In 1891, 98 percent of Canada's Chinese were located in British Columbia. By 1911 this had decreased to 70 percent, with the remainder moving increasingly into the small towns of the prairies. Not all were CPR veterans. Between 1891 and 1910 over 50,000 Chinese entered Canada, though more than half of them returned to China or crossed to the United States so that the 1911 census recorded a total of only 27,774. The migrants from China, with very few exceptions, originated in a small region of Kwangtung Province southeast of Canton. They were members of poor peasant families, sent abroad to join uncles and cousins already here, expected to submit the fruits of their labour back to the family at home and, eventually, to retire in peace in their Kwangtung villages.[25]

For the Chinese themselves, then, Canada represented a source of income to which they could migrate temporarily. Few would have considered striking permanent roots in this alien and often hostile land.[26] Wherever the Chinese migrated in the late 19th century the pattern was similar: Chinese were attracted by an economic opportunity, engaged in hard labour for low pay, and moved home or on to another opportunity. To ensure their onward movement, California, New Zealand, and the Australian and South African colonies passed a range of laws making it difficult for Chinese to settle. Their strange living habits, their association with a "backward" homeland, and their readiness to accept minimal wages all provoked a negative reaction from the fledgling communities of the Anglo-Saxon diaspora. The experience elsewhere was becoming known in Canada even as the first Chinese were arriving. The *Victoria Gazette* in March 1859 warned that the Chinese in Australia and California had done more harm than good: "They are, with few exceptions, not desirable as permanent settlers in a country peopled by the Caucasian race and governed by civilized enactments. No greater obstacle to the coming of the class of immigrants needed in British Columbia could be devised, than the presence of Chinamen in large numbers."[27] Twenty years later a select committee of the BC legislature confirmed this fear by reporting that the 6,000 Chinese in the province were virtually held in slave labour, the women were all prostitutes and there existed "an inconquerable and not unreasonable prejudice" against them on the part of the "free members" of the community. In the federal House of Commons restrictive laws of the Australian type were urged upon Canada. The prime minister himself was moved to make a statement in Parliament in 1882:

I share very much the feeling of the people of the United States and the Australian colonies against a Mongolian or Chinese population in our country as permanent settlers. I believe that it is an alien race in every sense, that would not and could not be expected to assimilate with our Aryan population, and therefore, if the temporary necessity had been overcome and the railway constructed across the continent with the means of sending the European settlers and labourers into British Columbia, then it would be quite right to join to a reasonable extent in preventing the permanent settlement in this country of Mongolian, Chinese or Japanese immigrants. . . . At present it is simply a question of alternatives: either you must have this labour or you cannot have the railway.[28]

Macdonald's brief pronouncement encapsulated opinion towards the Chinese at that time, and implicitly identified the fundamental Chinese characteristic: their definition as cheap labour. This definition developed from various and complex influences. As Europe industrialized and modernized and extended its imperial will over much of the world, China came increasingly to represent everything Europe was not, and wanted not to be: changeless, corrupt, effete, despotic. For Europe, China was constructed as a negative, against which Europe's own identity was rendered positive.[29] This cultural legacy supplied a prism through which Canadians and other Westerners would view China and the Chinese people. Circumstances in beleaguered China disposed young men to seek opportunities abroad, and though overseas opportunities might be meagre for those lacking industrial skills they still appeared greater than anything available at home.[30] China's place in the evolving global economic system in the late 19th century disposed receiving societies to assign the migrants to the least attractive physical labour. The Chinese workers, accustomed to subsistence conditions and unencumbered by wives or children, acquiesced in a level of comfort that white Canadian families would not contemplate. Limited material expectations meant, consequently, that the Chinese could accept low rates of pay and still have a small surplus to send home. These factors combined to direct Chinese workers toward employment categories with the lowest pay and the least power to bargain for improvements. The specific structuring of Chinese employment in Canada further accentuated these limitations. Most Canadian employers acquired Chinese workers through a Chinese contractor, who provided labourers at a prearranged rate and often managed them on the job. Such a system worked most efficiently with highly disciplined gangs employed at low-skilled tasks; it did not facilitate workplace integration, the acquisition of skills or consideration of individual personalities.[31]

International stereotypes were thus replicated locally, and the image of China was translated to local experience. Accompanying it was the ideology of "race," which explained Chinese habits of life and labour according to their genetic inheritance. It was accepted as scientific that "race" characteristics were fixed and would determine an individual's behaviour throughout life. As Prime Minister Macdonald's statement illustrates, the Chinese were perceived as utterly and permanently *alien*, too remote from Anglo-Saxons in culture and physique ever to assimilate or even to live in harmony. They were simply not the stuff wanted to populate a new land. "The main objection to the Chinese is that they are not of our race and cannot become a part of ourselves," the Senate was told in 1886. "We cannot build up a homogeneous people in Canada with races of that description, a population totally alien to ours."[32]

Canadian labour was the group most concerned with the presence of a perpetual underclass, for it suggested direct competition for certain jobs and indirect pressure keeping wages generally low. In 1878 BC's first trade union, the Workingmen's Protective Association, came into being explicitly for "the mutual protection of the working class of British Columbia against the great influx of Chinese."[33] As industry enjoyed its protective tariffs, labour needed protection from cheap imported workers. Canadian labour generally was becoming more self-conscious and militant, and manifestos denouncing the employment of Asians became common features in the struggle for better wages and working conditions.[34] There were boycotts organized against companies hiring Chinese workers, campaigns to convince consumers to buy only union-made products, pressure on governments to outlaw Chinese labour from certain fields, mining for example, and to insert "white labour clauses" in government contracts, and finally demands to exclude Chinese immigrants altogether.[35] In periods of scarce employment all immigrants offered competition, but Chinese were perceived as a special case. As the *BC Trades Unionist* explained, "Admitting that European immigration, as it has developed, constitutes a problem demanding immediate attention, it is after all a problem of quantity, whereas Asiatic immigration is distinctly a problem of quality."[36]

Although employment segregation and the contract system meant that direct competition for "white jobs" was not widespread, conflict flared when employers used Chinese as strikebreakers, and when economic displacement forced white workers downwards into the employment levels occupied by Chinese.[37] Such instances seemed proof that the Chinese presence was damaging the interests of white labour. In British Columbia, where the concentration of Chinese was becoming the cause of considerable alarm, the provincial legislature passed a series of laws in 1884 prohibiting further Chinese immigration, imposing a $10 head tax on those already there, and preventing them from acquiring Crown lands.[38] The Preamble to the *Act to Regulate the Chinese Population* neatly summed up the attitudes in BC:

The coming of Chinese to British Columbia largely exceeds that of any other class of immigration, and the population so introduced are fast becoming superior in number to our own race; are not disposed to be governed by our laws; are dissimilar in habits and occupation from our people; evade the payment of taxes justly due to government; are governed by pestilential habits; are useless in instances of emergency; habitually desecrate graveyards by the removal of bodies therefrom; and generally the law governing the whites is found to be inapplicable to Chinese, and such Chinese are inclined to habits subversive of the comfort and well-being of the community.[39]

Given the perceived need for Chinese labour in the construction of the railway, the federal government disallowed British Columbia's immigration restrictions,[40] but it did establish a Royal Commission to examine the Chinese phenomenon on the West Coast. Chaired by federal Secretary of State J. A. Chapleau and BC Supreme Court Justice John H. Gray, the commission first heard evidence in California, where the "Oriental question" had been an issue for a longer time, and then travelled to BC to meet members of the provincial and municipal governments, representatives of large and small business, labour unionists and concerned citizens. The commissioners discovered in BC a racially stratified labour market, in which skilled work went to whites and menial work to Chinese. Chinese were paid less, even in those instances where they were doing the same job: skilled whites averaged $3.50-4.50 per day, unskilled whites $2-2.50 and Chinese $1. In their submission to the commission the Nanaimo Knights of Labor stated that

All history proves that a free, manly, intelligent, and contented laboring population, is the foundation and the source of prosperity of any and every nation, and essential to the stability of free, popular institutions. . . . Now, Chinese labor is confessedly of a low, degraded, and servile type, the inevitable result of whose employment in competition with free white labor is to lower and degrade the latter without any appreciable elevation of the former. Their standard of living is reduced to the lowest possible point, and, being without family ties, or any of those institutions which are essential to the existence and progress of our civilization, they are enabled to not only live but to grow rich on wages far below the lowest minimum at which we can possibly exist. They are thus fitted to become all too dangerous competitors in the labor market.[41]

The commissioners concluded, however, that because of the segregated nature of the workplace lower Chinese wages did not in fact create unfair competition for white workers. On the contrary, Chinese labour was judged to have been absolutely essential to the material prosperity of the province, doing jobs for which white labour was often unavailable. As one employer argued, "I do not see how people would get on here at all without Chinamen. They do, and do well, what white women can not do, and do what white men will not do."[42] Organized labour's hostility, several witnesses pointed out, had been artificially provoked by politicians seeking to win the "labouring class vote."[43] Even when praising the Chinese presence, however, the commission *Report* acknowledged the inferiority of Chinese as human beings. As Justice Gray explained:

It is fortunate that, in a young and sparsely settled Province, this cheap labour can be obtained, for it enables those whose minds are capable of higher development and whose ambition looks to more enobling industry – to follow pursuits in which they will rise rather than toil and slave in grovelling work, which wears out the body without elevating the mind.[44]

The commission also heard evidence on the dress, hairstyles, religious traditions and moral standards of the Chinese migrants, which most witnesses accepted as external expressions of inherent character traits. The provincial surveyor-general proposed:

We want here a white man's community, with civilized habits and religious aspirations, and not a community of "Heathen Chinee" who can never assimilate with us, or do ought to elevate us, and who can be of no possible use to a state in any capacity other than that of drawers of water and hewers of wood.[45]

Commissioner Chapleau admitted that since "the Chinese [are] a non-assimilable race, clearly marked off from white people by color and national and race characteristics, their presence in a country is not unattended with disadvantages." Still he concluded that their "labor is a most efficient aid in the development of a country, and a great means to wealth" and besides, "the statements as to their bad moral effect on the community are grossly exaggerated. In fact their morality is not lower than that of the same classes of other nationalities."[46]

The Royal Commission *Report* of 1885 clearly did not accept the dangers attributed to the Chinese presence. Justice Gray even protested that "It is something strange to hear the strong, broad-shouldered race, superior physically and mentally, sprung from the highest types of the old and new world, expressing a fear of competition with a small, inferior and comparatively speaking, feminine race."[47] And yet both commissioners felt compelled to recommend restrictions against further Chinese immigration. With the railway nearing completion their labour was no longer necessary, and the prejudices of the white population were such that future development could actually be retarded unless the whites' anxieties were put to rest.[48] "There seems to be an instinctive feeling of preference for whites, independent of any reasoned opinion respecting their merits or demerits as compared with Chinamen," Chapleau wrote, and in Parliament he lamented, "The fact is that we are naturally disposed, through inconscient prejudices, to turn into defects even their virtues."[49] It fell to Chapleau to introduce the government's Bill to Restrict and Regulate Chinese Immigration to the House of Commons following the submission of his *Report*. In recommending the imposition of unique barriers against one group of people, he explained:

it is a natural and well-founded desire of British subjects, of the white population of the Dominion, who come from either British or other European States and settle in this country, that their country should be spoken of abroad as being inhabited by a vigorous, energetic and white race of people.[50]

The reality of racial character, of fixed and insurmountable differences, was accepted absolutely by the Royal Commission and by the government of Canada, even though no convincing evidence had been offered. It was a matter of "common sense." While some witnesses argued that the Chinese could continue to be useful, none contended that they should or could become permanent members of Canadian society. The Chief Justice of British Columbia, Sir Matthew Begbie, articulated the common sense of 1885: "The Chinaman is in every respect the reverse of the European except that he is a man."[51]

The *Chinese Immigration Act* of 1885 placed a special tax of $50 on every Chinese person entering Canada, and set shipping conditions intended to make it more expensive to transport people from China.[52] The minister for trade and commerce, Sir Richard Cartwright, explained the apparent anomaly of a racially based law in a democratic society: "It appears to me, although it may be said that this practice of taxing Chinamen is opposed to British practice . . . to a very considerable extent the instinctive feeling which prevails in British Columbia has its origin in a wholesome feeling of self-preservation."[53] Liberal Prime Minister Wilfrid Laurier later addressed the same dilemma in equivalent terms. Though "one of the most tolerant of all races," Anglo-Saxons shared "an invincible repugnance to the people of the Mongolian races." "That is the fact," Laurier continued, "and we have to reckon with it. I say at once that it will not do for this Government, or for any Government, to ignore it; on the contrary, the Government is quite prepared to recognize it and to deal with it accordingly."[54] It was legitimate for a democratic government to respond to the needs of the voters. On this authority, in the face of complaints that the $50 tax was becoming decreasingly effective, Parliament increased the Chinese tax to $100 in 1900 and appointed a new Royal Commission to investigate "Oriental" immigration to Canada.

Commissioners Roger Chute, Christopher Foley and Daniel Munn found a situation more desperate than in 1885. The threats perceived primarily by organized labour in 1885 were recognized much more broadly in the white population by the end of the century. Despite the head tax the number of Chinese in the province had grown from 6,000 to 16,000, and there were an additional 6,000 Japanese who had migrated in the same period. Employment segregation and wage differentials for ordinary labourers were still firmly entrenched – in the logging camps, for example, Japanese received $1 per day, Chinese $1.25 and whites from $2.25 to $3.75 – and the contract system still supplied gangs of unskilled labour. "Each performed specific jobs for different rates of pay," the commissioners reported.[55] And there were still defenders of the employment of Asian labour. The manager of one colliery insisted that Chinese workers *upheld* white wages, since "The cost of production would be greater without the Chinese. . . . [Their absence] would compel us to reduce the white man's wage."[56] Exclusion from various occupations had, however, produced a significant shift in Chinese employment patterns: whereas in 1885 only 3 percent of Chinese had been in business for themselves, by 1901 that figure was over 25 percent, leading non-Chinese merchants and farmers to fear the effect of Chinese competition.[57] The consensus among the witnesses, and accepted as valid by the commissioners, was that the Chinese impact was "deadly" and their lurking presence in the economy undermined the white working-class family. With their "customs, habits and modes of life fixed and unalterable," the Chinese formed "a community within a community, separate and apart, a foreign substance . . . a people that cannot assimilate." Their sanitary habits were "a continual menace to health," morally "their effect upon the rest of the community is bad," they were unsuited to democratic laws and institutions and could never "become citizens in the sense of the term as we understand it." Discovering "entire unanimity" on this point, the commissioners concluded that the Chinese "are so nearly allied to a servile class that they are obnoxious to a free community and dangerous to the state."[58]

The equivocations of the 1885 commissioners were not echoed in the 1902 *Report*: there were no reservations or excuses softening the conclusion that Asians were a negative factor in the Canadian body politic. Nor was it only in British Columbia that such an impression prevailed. These were, after all, federal investigations, their reports were presented to the House of Commons in Ottawa, their evidence was given national circulation, their conclusions entered the national discourse, and ultimately they produced federal legislation. Commenting on the 1902 *Report*, the *Canadian Annual Review* argued that Canada was becoming "flooded with an undesirable class of people, non-assimilative and most detrimental to the wage earning class."[59] In the next session of Parliament the government increased the head tax to a more effective $500, anticipating that no Chinese labourer could ever afford to pay it. This met with the approval of *Saturday Night* magazine, published in Toronto, which advised its readers in 1906:

This is a white man's country and white men will keep it so. The slant-eyed Asiatic, with his yellow skin, his unmanly humility, his cheap wants, would destroy the whole equilibrium of industry. He would slave like a Nubian, scheme like a Yankee, hoard like the proverbial Jew. Turn these people loose in a country like ours and they would make progress like a pestilence. Race prejudice! This is race prejudice of course. . . . Let them swarm in once and the yellow stain on the country will be one that cannot be rubbed out. We cannot assimilate them. They are an honest, industrious, but hopelessly inferior race.

When a BC reader wrote in to insist that Chinese labour was a valuable asset, *Saturday Night's* editor responded in a subsequent issue:

The employers in British Columbia are favorable to the admission of Chinese because these yellow fellows are great workers, cheap, docile, reliable. . . . They are an inferior race of men like the Africans, who were brought over in thousands to the Southern States and now constitute a serious and permanent danger to the neighboring republic. . . . Yellow men would be more dangerous than black ones, for the latter were frivolous and trifling, while the former are industrious, plodding, patient. . . . These people will not possess value as citizens, and when once fastened on the country will retard its development.[60]

Though perhaps the most organized voice, white labour was not the only element in Canadian society demanding restrictions upon Chinese by the early years of the 20th century, and wage competition was not the exclusive complaint. Alarm was raised over alleged "filth" and "depravity" in the overcrowded Chinese residential quarters. "[W]hat can we expect but vice unspeakable," Emily Murphy demanded, when Chinese were allowed "to swarm in filthy hovels and to burrow like rats in cellars."[61] Danger was perceived in eating groceries raised by Chinese market gardeners contaminated by "filth"; it was even argued that in Chinese laundries "the dainty garments of white women puddled around in suds that reeked with dirt."[62] The *Calgary Herald* reported in 1910:

Chinese, when they come to reside in a place ought to be treated the same as an infectious disease or an isolation hospital. They live like rabbits in a warren and 30 of them crowd into where 5 white people would ordinarily reside.

They have not the first idea of cleanliness or sanitation. Everywhere they go they are undesirable citizens and furnish a problem to the municipality.[63]

No doubt images from late-19th-century China fed such stereotypes, nowhere more clearly than in a Vancouver *World* story in 1912 on that city's Chinatown, which began:

Conditions prevailing in the cities of China are familiar topics of the returned missionary, who will dwell at length upon the awful condition of the slums, the armies of the unwashed, and the prevalence of vice in the shape of opium smoking and gambling, in the empire across the seas. Would you believe that the same condition of affairs is in existence in the city of Vancouver, in our Chinatown...?[64]

The association of Chinese with gambling, opium and vice was universally made. In 1902 the *Regina Standard* decried the moral degeneracy caused by narcotics use, tracing its supply to the Chinese community. The *Saskatoon Phoenix* in 1907 concluded that opium destroyed moral as well as physical and mental health. A *Calgary Herald* reporter toured his city's Chinatown in 1909 and described for his readers the extensive gambling, prostitution and use of opium that went on there. Thousands of young men, the Trades and Labour Congress lamented, "can lay their ruin to the Chinese who taught them the terrible habit of opium smoking."[65] An unsubstantiated but widely disseminated report from Winnipeg in 1911 claimed that most brothels were operated by Chinese or Japanese, a conclusion accepted by delegates to a National Council of Women convention in London, Ontario, in 1912.[66] The Women's Christian Temperance Union and the Women's Institute warned particularly that women would be enticed into Chinese dens, addicted to opium and held in prostitution. Reports came from Lethbridge and Saskatoon that young girls were becoming addicts and prostitutes under Chinese auspices, recruited right off the streets.[67] The Methodist Church listed Chinese restaurants as "dangerous places" for white women.[68] In Toronto the Vigilance Committee circulated a broadside urging "strenuous efforts to break up Chinese dens of infamy, kept for the purpose of ruining young Canadian girls."[69] "Entrapment" of white women foolish enough to work in Chinese restaurants or laundries, or even to visit them as customers, became an accepted scenario in the popular imagination.[70] In September 1911 the Toronto magazine *Jack Canuck* located the "Yellow Peril" in the city's laundries:

The bland smiling Oriental and his quaint pidgeon English does not *appear* very formidable to the young woman who enters his store for the weekly wash. She does not notice the evil lurking in the almond eyes as she accepts the silk handkerchief or other trifling Oriental knick knack.[71]

One labour official warned that not even home was safe, for Chinese house servants were adulterating their employers' food with drugs, "thus placing the female members of the household at their disposal and unscrupulous will."[72] This assault upon white womanhood was attributed to the lascivious urges of the Chinese libido, but it was also alleged that the Chinese were deliberately setting out to undermine the "superior white race" through an attack on its moral fibre.[73] Emily Murphy believed that both Chinese and "Negroes" were trying to bring about "the downfall of the white race," and the spread of opium and prostitution was motivated by "their desire to injure the bright-browed races of the world."[74]

3. RESTRICTION AND REGULATION

The experience of the Chinese community in Moose Jaw was typical of what was happening across Canada, and especially in British Columbia where the largest number resided: Chinese were excluded from political participation, confined to a narrow sector in the economy, and harassed and rejected in their daily encounters with white Canadians. Theatres, dance halls, swimming pools and hotels regularly refused admission to Chinese patrons. There were several attempts in Vancouver and Victoria to segregate Chinese schoolchildren to prevent them from contaminating the morals of white pupils.[75] Occasionally the urge to isolate the Chinese was expressed through physical violence. In Timmins, Ontario, in the first decades of the 20th century, it was reported, Chinese people could not walk in the streets without having things thrown at them. In Winnipeg, Chinese restaurants would be vandalized, just for "fun." More seriously, white construction workers attacked a Chinese camp near Lytton, BC, because, they believed, the Chinese were stealing white jobs. In the melee two Chinese were murdered. A fully fledged riot broke out in Vancouver in 1887 when hundreds of whites converged on the Chinese district, chased the people out of town and looted and burned their belongings. The allegation, again, was that Chinese were taking jobs which belonged properly to whites. In 1892, 300 whites attacked Calgary's Chinese, attributing to them a recent smallpox epidemic. There were scattered outbursts of vigilante activity directed towards forcing Chinese out of town in Slocan Valley, Atlin, Salmo and Penticton, BC, and in Whitehorse, Yukon, between 1898 and 1906. Mobs demolished Chinese restaurants in Lethbridge in 1907.[76]

Violence was therefore no stranger to the Chinese when Canadian history's largest race riot occurred in Vancouver in 1907. The issue was Chinese and Japanese immigration. The federal government had denied an appeal that summer from organized labour to halt Asian immigration, and a restrictive immigration law passed by the provincial legislature was reserved by Lieutenant-Governor James Dunsmuir (whose Wellington colliery was a large employer of Asian labour), and was subsequently disallowed by Ottawa. Feeling betrayed by their governments and threatened by a rumoured influx of new Asian immigrants, Vancouver workers formed an Asiatic Exclusion League and planned a mass rally for the evening of 7 September. A crowd approaching 10,000 people gathered at city hall, where speakers representing business and the churches as well as labour denounced "Orientals" and demanded government action. Dunsmuir was burned in effigy. Though no violence was apparently intended towards the Chinese that evening, Chinatown was only a block away from the huge demonstration and some of the mob strayed there. A window was broken, and the sound of violence inspired more. Sticks and stones were picked from the streets and hurled at Chinese homes and businesses. Fires were started. For four hours mob members ravaged Chinatown, and then moved on to the Japanese district. Forewarned, the Japanese were able to organize in self-defense. Virtually all of the personal injuries sustained that night occurred during the exchange with the Japanese. No one, fortunately, was killed, but an international incident had been created. The Japanese consulate was in constant contact with the Laurier government throughout the riot and its aftermath. The prime minister issued an immediate apology to the Japanese Empire and sent W. L. Mackenzie King, the deputy minister of Labour, to investigate the causes of the riot, to assess the damages to Japanese property, and to arrange compensation. No thought was given to the Chinese, who had in fact suffered much greater losses than the Japanese, until the Colonial Office, engaged in negotiating compensation for some Britons in China, pressured Laurier to settle the Chinese damages as well. Mackenzie King heard the Chinese claims eight months later, in May 1908. In the end $9,175 compensation was paid to Japanese claimants and $26,990 to Chinese.[77]

The Vancouver riot of 1907 was the culmination of a "constitutional tango" between Ottawa and Victoria on the issue of Asian immigration.[78] Beginning in 1884 British Columbia passed nine immigration acts restricting Asian immigration; under the authority of the *BNA Act* the federal government disallowed eight, and the lieutenant-governor reserved one in 1907.[79] At first, as has been seen, Ottawa was motivated by the perceived need for Chinese labour on the railroad. Anglo-Japanese treaties in 1894 and 1905 provided that "subjects of the two High Contracting Parties shall have full liberty to enter, travel or reside in any part of the dominions and possessions of the other Contracting Party,"[80] and this was interpreted by the federal government, as well as by London and Tokyo, to preclude specific restrictions against Japanese. The "tango" effect emerged from the fact that a provincial law was in effect *until* it was declared invalid, a period that could last a year or more. Prime Minister Laurier advised the BC government "that if they were to restrict their action to Chinese immigration, that if they were to except Japanese immigrants from their legislation, we would not interfere, leaving them to exercise their own will in regard to Chinese immigration."[81] On the West Coast, however, Japanese were regarded as an equivalent threat, at least, and the legislature persistently restricted both Chinese and Japanese in the face of federal disallowance. The "Gentleman's Agreement" negotiated with Japan in 1907-8 limited the number of emigrants leaving Japan to 400 per year.[82] China declined to enter a similar agreement, but the federal government had been convinced by the 1902 Royal Commission *Report* to keep in place effective barriers against Chinese immigration. BC no longer found it necessary to produce legislation of its own.[83]

In the meantime thousands of Chinese had arrived, but they were not to be allowed to become a part of Canadian society. British Columbia joined Confederation in 1871; at the very first session of the provincial legislature, in 1872, Chinese were disfranchised even if they became British subjects and, in a symbolic gesture, Chinese were excluded from registering their vital statistics.[84] When disfranchisement on racial grounds was questioned, the *Provincial Elections Act* clarified its definition: "The expression 'Chinaman' shall mean any native of the Chinese Empire or its dependencies not born of British parents, and shall include any person of the Chinese race, naturalized or not."[85] Under BC law, disqualification from the franchise also meant exclusion from public office and from jury service, and since the provincial voters' list was adopted for federal elections, the federal franchise was lost de facto. Prime Minister Macdonald explained the federal position to the House of Commons in 1885:

The Chinese are foreigners. If they come to this country, after three years residence, they may, if they choose, be naturalized. But still we know that when the Chinaman comes here he intends to return to his own country; he does not bring his family with him; he is a stranger, a sojourner in a strange land, for his own purposes for a while; he has no common interest with us, and while he gives us his labour and is paid for it, and is valuable, the same as a threshing machine or any other agricultural implement which we may borrow from the United States on hire and return it to the owner on the south side of the line; a Chinaman gives us his labour and gets his money, but that money does not fructify in Canada; he does not invest it here, but takes it with him and returns to China; and if he cannot, his executors or his friends send his body back to the flowery land. But he has no British instincts or British feelings or aspirations, and therefore ought not to have a vote.[86]

Saskatchewan, the only other province overtly to disfranchise the Chinese, did so in 1908 as Chinese numbers crept into the hundreds.[87]

It is arguable that at the time these provisions were enacted, few Chinese would have been interested in the vote. Of more immediate concern were restrictions on employment explicitly aimed at removing Chinese from competition. Certain disabilities came circumstantially, by making the franchise a qualification for eligibility. Hand-logging, for example, was reserved for provincial voters in British Columbia, as were the professions of law and pharmacy.[88] Other restrictions were undisguised. By the *Coal Mines Regulation Act* of 1877, BC made it illegal for a Chinese to "occupy any position of trust or responsibility in or about a mine."[89] This was amended in 1890 to give it broader effect: "No boy under the age of twelve years, no woman or girl of any age, and no Chinaman shall be employed in or allowed to be for the purposes of employment in any mine to which this Act applies underground."[90] An *Alien Labour Act* in 1897 and a series of *Labour Regulation Acts*, aimed at prohibiting the employment of Chinese and Japanese in certain undertakings, were disallowed by the federal government as contrary to the terms of the Anglo-Japanese Treaty.[91] As an alternative, the province passed orders-in-council in 1902 making it necessary to insert an employment clause in all Crown leases. The standard wording was: "Provided always, that these presents are upon the express condition that no Chinese or Japanese shall be employed in or about the said premises or any part thereof."[92] In a province where logging and mining were the major industries, these lease restrictions were widely effective. Railway construction was reserved for white workers by the *Subsidized Works Labour Regulation Act* of 1902, which denied right of way over provincial lands to any company or person who did not enter an agreement "as to the employment of labour upon or in connection with said railway or other work, upon such terms and conditions as to the Lieutenant-Governor-in-Council shall seem meet and proper."[93] Similarly the *Railway Assessment Act* was amended in 1908, exempting railway companies from certain taxes provided that no aliens were employed or, if they were absolutely essential to the project, the alien workers must be "paid such rates of wages as may be currently payable to white workingmen, labourers and servants engaged in similar occupations in the district in which such railway is constructed and operated."[94] In 1904 BC Supreme Court Justice Martin listed 22 provincial acts restricting Chinese, passed since 1884.[95]

Such elaborate restrictions applied only in British Columbia, where Chinese sought employment in the resource industries, though in 1918 a United Mineworkers delegation asked Alberta's Premier Steward to eliminate Asians from all aspects of the mining industry. The premier acknowledged his government's opposition to Asian labour, but claimed it was beyond provincial authority to ban their employment.[96] In other parts of Canada Chinese were not perceived as an equivalent threat, being largely engaged in personal service, laundries and restaurants. Yet even in these relatively petty enterprises, discriminatory taxes and restrictions were imposed. British Columbia amended the *Municipalities Act* in 1885, authorizing local councils to levy semi-annual licensing fees of $75 for operating a laundry. Vancouver passed a by-law in 1900 prohibiting laundries where water was sprayed from the mouth while ironing, a typical practice of the Chinese laundryman, and a Sunday observance by-law was enforced against Chinese laundries, the only ones operating on Sundays. Toronto brought in a 1902 regulation imposing oppressive "sanitation" requirements on laundries, intended to make it more difficult for Chinese proprietors, and in 1903 Kamloops declared Chinese laundries a public nuisance. Calgary city council passed a motion in 1904 asking "That the City Clerk prepare a by-law, to prohibit any more Chinese laundries," and Lethbridge in 1906 placed a $100 tax on laundries operated by Chinese. Hamilton, Ontario, restricted Chinese laundries to certain limited neighbourhoods in 1911. Quebec put a provincial licence fee on all laundries not run by women, charitable societies or incorporated companies, leaving basically the Chinese liable to pay.[97] Manitoba amended its *Factories Act* in 1916 to restrict the hours and conditions of labour in "any laundry operated or owned by Chinese."[98]

4. LITIGATION

Not all these enactments went unchallenged. In fact an impressive body of case law was built up and the Chinese litigants enjoyed considerable success. In the process, however, racial differences were recognized judicially, as they were in legislation, and "race" became a constitutional category assigned to provincial jurisdiction by the arbiters of Canadian justice.

In 1878 BC passed *An Act to Provide for the Better Collection of Provincial Taxes from Chinese*, requiring every Chinese over the age of twelve to take out a licence every three months at a cost of $10. Any Chinese not having such a licence in his possession, and any person employing an unlicenced Chinese, would be fined $100 or imprisoned for two months. Tai Sing took the Act before the courts as a test case on behalf of a dozen fellow Chinese merchants in Victoria. Since there was no explicit guarantee of Chinese rights available to support their claim, Tai Sing and his colleagues cast their argument as a division of powers issue, contending the Act was *ultra vires* the provincial legislature as dealing with trade and commerce, as an interference with aliens, and as interfering with the powers and duties of the Dominion government arising under treaties between Great Britain and China.[99] Justice John Hamilton Gray agreed S91 ss2 of the *BNA Act* gave to the Dominion Parliament the regulation of trade and commerce, and ss25 that of naturalization of aliens. "It is plain, therefore, the local Legislature can legally pass no Act interfering with the regulation of either the one or the other," Gray concluded, and he perceived that "the object of this Act is not so much to prevent the evasion of the payment of taxes by the Chinese, as to prevent their living or carrying on business in this country."[100] It was equally clear to Gray that treaties of 1858 and 1860, imposed upon the Chinese by British envoys seeking trading opportunities for Britons, granted permission to the subjects of each empire to travel, work and trade in the other. Section 137 of the *BNA Act* gave Ottawa "all powers necessary or proper for performing the obligations of Canada, or of any province thereof, as part of the British Empire, towards foreign countries arising under treaties between the Empire and such foreign countries." Justice Gray therefore had no difficulty in pronouncing the *Chinese Tax Act* unconstitutional and void. But his explanation reached beyond the division of powers, and suggested that a case could be made on the basis of Chinese rights:

Sumptuary Laws affecting the domestic and personal habits of a people, where not necessary for the prevention of crime, the preservation of public health, or purposes of morality, have always been considered objectionable. To enact that employment shall not be given to classes, except on hazardous and ruinous terms, is practically prohibiting intercourse with the particular class specified. If you cannot deal or trade with a man, but at the risk of a penalty far exceeding the value of the service, that dealing or trading will be put an end to. . . .

The Act, exceptional in its nature as to one class of foreigners, bristles with imprisonment and hard labour, and places the frightful power of conviction and punishment in the hands of any Justice of the Peace throughout the country, at the instance of a Collector whose interest it may be to gratify the promoters of the Act. . . .

It was not intended to collect revenue, but to drive the Chinese from the country. . . . [101]

The British Columbia legislature tried again with the *Chinese Regulation Act* of 1884, containing provisions for an annual $10 licence fee and penalties against unlicenced Chinese or their employers, and adding special sanitary conditions for any building occupied by Chinese. Wing Chong of Victoria was fined for not having a licence in his possession, and challenged his conviction before Justice Henry Pellew Crease of the BC Supreme Court. Wing Chong's lawyers pressed the *Tai Sing* precedent, arguing that this tax exceeded provincial powers. Attorney Montague Drake, however, also inserted the argument that "the imposition of the $10 tax was invalid because of inequality. . . . [I]rrespective of constitutional limitation a particular class of citizens could not be burdened for the advantage of others."[102] In his decision Justice Crease seemed to accept the point that the Act offended the Chinese as well as the federal government. "On applying to the preamble," he wrote, "we find that it looks like a bill of indictment as against a race not suited to live among a civilized nation." Indeed, he found that the preamble "describes the Chinese in terms which, I venture to think, have never before in any other country found a place in an Act of Parliament."[103] While he applied the *Tai Sing* decision and declared the act *ultra vires* as trespassing on federal jurisdiction, Crease added:

if such a law can be tolerated as against Chinese, the precedent is set, and in time of any popular outcry can easily be acted on for putting any other foreigners or even special classes among ourselves, as coloured people, or French, Italians, Americans or Germans, under equally the same law.[104]

These dicta from Gray and Crease had not, however, established that an underlying discriminatory purpose should be regarded as sufficient grounds for invalidating any act of the legislature. In 1896 BC's *Coal Mines Regulation Amendment Act* of 1890 was referred to the provincial Supreme Court sitting in full court to determine the validity of the prohibition against "Chinamen" from working underground.[105] Justice Walkem, who as provincial premier had authored the 1878 Act annulled in *Tai Sing v. Maguire*, held that the issue was one of mine safety: "The object of the Act before us is to regulate the working of coal mines, and not to define the rights or disabilities of aliens. The latter subject, as dealt with in the Act, is merely incidental to the main object of the Act. In my opinion the Act is within the competence of the Legislature."[106] Justice Drake, with Justice McColl concurring, looked beneath the safety euphemism to the more realistic issue of economic competition, and this they found acceptable. Justice Drake wrote:

The restriction, apparently, was imposed on the ground that by the employment of Chinese the wages of the white labourer were reduced, and that involves the larger question of right of employer and employee to absolute freedom of contract. It is a clear principle of law that the employer of labour may engage whom he pleases and that an employee is free to contract for his labour with whom and at what rate and upon what terms he chooses. But the Legislature has imposed a restriction on this freedom of contract; a restriction which may be supported on the ground that it deals with property and civil rights and is a merely local matter.[107]

Even if it is discriminatory both against Chinese and the mine owners, Justice Drake concluded, "this is not a case affecting trade and commerce, but a question of property and civil rights, and regulations of a particular business hitherto untouched by Dominion legislation." To distinguish this decision from his argument as attorney in *Wing Chong*, Drake contended that both *Wing Chong* and *Tai Sing* had "turned on the subject of special taxation imposed on the Chinese; and, although, *incidentally*, the powers of the Provincial and Dominion Legislatures were discussed, the points decided are no guide to the present case."[108] The *Coal Mines Act* was upheld unanimously.

Justice Drake's apparent attempt to minimize the significance of the constitutional issue in the two earlier cases notwithstanding, the principle connecting these apparently contradictory decisions was in fact the distribution of powers in a federal system. The discriminatory provisions challenged in *Tai Sing* and *Wing Chong* were deemed to trespass on federal ground as determined by the *BNA Act* S91 ss2 and ss25, and S137. The *Coal Mines Act* was upheld even though it was acknowledged to be discriminatory because it was judged to concern the regulation of industrial safety, freedom of contract and property and civil rights, all of which fell properly within the provincial jurisdiction. This rehearsal helps to reconcile two other decisions, taken by the Judicial Committee of the Privy Council, which were to feature powerfully in the Quong Wing case. What the judges were trying to decide was whether the determining principle in a given act placed it in federal or provincial control.

The first of these precedents arose out of the coal mines regulations just described. John Bryden, a shareholder in the Union Colliery Company and son-in-law of its founder Robert Dunsmuir (and brother-in-law of the current principal owner James Dunsmuir), instituted an action in the BC Supreme Court for an injunction restraining the company from employing Chinese underground, which it had continued to do in defiance of the 1890 law. The provincial attorney general, aware that the suit was a collusive attempt to force a reconsideration of the 1896 *Coal Mines* decision, became a party to the litigation as intervenant. The case on appeal was heard by the Judicial Committee of the Privy Council in July 1899.[109] The appellants, reviving the equality theme raised in *Tai Sing* and *Wing Chong*, contended that the *Coal Mines Act* "disabled Chinamen for the exercise of the ordinary right, preserved to all others, to earn their bread by their labour, for no other reason than that of their origin."[110] But in delivering the judgment of the court Lord Watson rejected the issue of discrimination and focussed on the distribution of powers:

In so far as they possess legislative jurisdiction, the discretion committed to the parliaments, whether of the Dominion or of the provinces, is unfettered. It is the proper function of a court of law to determine what are the limits of the jurisdiction committed to them; but, when that point has been settled, courts of law have no right whatever to inquire whether their jurisdiction has been exercised wisely or not.[111]

Having established the nature of the contest, Lord Watson noted that the *BNA Act* S91 ss25 gave exclusive authority over "naturalization and aliens" to the federal parliament, and he found that

the leading feature of the enactments consists in this – that they have, and can have, no application except to Chinamen who are aliens or naturalized subjects, and that they establish no rule or regulation except that these aliens or naturalized subjects shall not work, or be allowed to work, in underground coal mines within the Province of British Columbia.

Their Lordships therefore concluded: "the whole pith and substance of the enactments . . . consists in establishing a statutory prohibition which affects aliens or naturalized subjects, and therefore trench upon the exclusive authority of the Parliament of Canada."[112]

The anti-Chinese restriction was declared illegal. Union Colliery had won, but its strategic partner, John Bryden, was required to pay costs. To reimburse him, his brother-in-law James Dunsmuir had the pay of each Chinese worker at Union Colliery docked 50 cents per month until the costs were recovered.[113]

The second and apparently contradictory case was provoked by a naturalized subject of Japanese origin, Tomey Homma (or Tomekichi Honma as he is remembered in the Japanese Canadian community), who sought to be registered on the BC voters' list in October 1900. The Vancouver Collector of Voters refused because S8 of the *Provincial Elections Act* stated that "No Chinaman, Japanese or Indian shall have his name placed on the register of voters for the electoral district, or be entitled to vote at any election."[114] Chief Justice McColl, hearing Homma's appeal sitting as a County Court judge, decided that the *Bryden* judgment bound him to find in favour of the naturalized subject, and he allowed Homma's appeal with costs.[115] He added that

the residence within the Province of large numbers of persons, British subjects in name, but doomed to perpetual exclusion from any part in the passage of legislation affecting their property and civil rights would surely not be to the advantage of Canada, and might even become a source of national danger.[116]

When the full BC Supreme Court upheld McColl's decision,[117] British Columbia appealed to the Privy Council in 1902.[118] In this judgment the Empire's highest tribunal repeated Lord Watson's disclaimer that the courts might serve as a legal conscience, for "the policy or impolicy of such an enactment as that which excludes a particular race from the franchise is not a topic which their Lordships are entitled to consider."[119] Lord Halsbury, delivering the judgment, distinguished Homma's case from *Bryden*:

That case depended upon totally different grounds. This Board, dealing with the particular facts of that case, came to the conclusion that the regulations there impeached were not really aimed at the regulation of coal mines at all, but were in truth devised to deprive the Chinese, naturalized or not, of the ordinary rights of the inhabitants of British Columbia and, in effect, to prohibit their continued residence in that province, since it prohibited their earning their living in that province. It is obvious that any such decision can have no relation to the question whether any naturalized person has an inherent right to the suffrage within the province in which he resides.[120]

The Canadian *Naturalization Act*, Lord Halsbury explained, did not grant the right of suffrage in any province. Furthermore "In the history of this country the right to the franchise has been granted and withheld on a great number of grounds, conspicuously upon grounds of religious faith."[121] British Columbia, therefore, could legally exclude an alien from the franchise if it wished. Two further points were made. Since the provincial act excluded Japanese on grounds of "race," it meant that it really had nothing to do with alienage or naturalization. "A child of Japanese parentage born in Vancouver City is a natural-born subject of the King, and would be equally excluded from the possession of the franchise."[122] And finally, the *BNA Act* gave the federal government authority to determine what shall constitute alienage or naturalization, "but the question as to what consequences shall follow from either is not touched." A province, therefore, could legitimately decide what privileges should or should not be attached to naturalization.[123] Tomey Homma lost. A full elaboration of the meaning of *Tomey Homma* and *Bryden*, and of any contradictions between them, would await Quong Wing.

5. DEFENDING THE FAMILY

There was a pervasive sense of threat in turn-of-the-century Canada. The increasing movement from farm to city, from agriculture to industry, had an impact on work and family patterns that seemed to indicate an impending collapse of traditional roles and relationships. Moral decline was apparent in a rising divorce rate, family desertion and prostitution. Unfamiliar values and lifestyles brought by an unprecedented wave of immigration shook the confidence of Victorian Canada and introduced household practices that could prove to be as infectious as the diseases that often accompanied them. Civilization rested on the strength of the family, its bedrock institution; an undermining of family life presaged the collapse of the entire social structure.[124]

The challenge inspired a response. To defend civilization the family must be defended, and the key to a healthy family was its mother. Woman's biological function made her the physical vessel of future civilization, and biology equipped her for this role by making her the natural repository of civilized standards. Female virtue, acknowledged as biologically appropriate, became sound public policy as well: for the sake of the community and its succeeding generations, the position of wife and mother must be preserved and enhanced. According to Emily Murphy, a leading articulator of the female sphere, "a good man must perforce be a father to his wife as well as a husband"; it was his responsibility to ensure the effective functioning of her maternal destiny.[125] Female reformers did not want to change woman's nurturing role but to extend it, beyond the confines of a single household, so that her maternal instincts would benefit the community at large.[126] The National Council of Women of Canada, founded in 1893, declared in its constitution:

We, Women of Canada, sincerely believing that the best good of our homes and nation will be advanced by our own greater unity of thought, sympathy, and purpose, and that an organization of women will best conserve the greatest good of the Family and the State, do hereby band ourselves together to further the application of the Golden Rule to society, custom and law.[127]

Local Councils of Women were established across Canada, formed by an affiliation among existing women's organizations, to implement "feminine influence over all the operations of society."[128]

Many items on the agenda of the new women's movement were long-standing concerns applied to a national scale: childcare, health and sanitation, domestic training for young women.[129] Others were products of more recent anxieties. Prostitution, for example, had been accepted in frontier Canada as a "necessary social evil" whose chief danger had been to the health and hygiene of the customers. In the context of the late 19th century, however, prostitution was redefined as a threat to the family, through the moral corruption of men and above all for the degradation of the prostitutes themselves. As women, prostitutes were inherently innocent and asexual, potential mothers seduced from their maternal path by evil men. Women did not choose to become prostitutes but were entrapped into "white slavery" and exploited by vicious pimps.[130] Women's missionary societies, the National Council of Women of Canada, the Women's Christian Temperance Union, the Young Women's Christian Association, all indicated the "traffic in white slavery" as a target for urgent reform. Immigration, similarly, was an issue generated in the context of the times. Unassimilated and unassimilable newcomers threatened the public standards of behaviour demanded by the maternal reformers. More significantly, the reproduction of the Anglo-Saxon "race" could be thwarted by the indiscriminate mixture of white Canadian women with foreigners.[131]

Although the home was "our divinely appointed place," according to the WCTU, the challenge of mothering an entire nation required considerable engagement in public affairs, for "It is only by legislation that the roots of great evils can be touched."[132] Where "moral suasion" failed, "legal suasion" would have to rule.[133] The issues selected for maternalistic intervention generally had a connection to family protection. Prohibition, the most outstanding example, would obviate masculine weakness for alcohol, redirect men's efforts to the economic support of their families, and preserve victimized wives and children from alcohol-induced violence or neglect.[134] The WCTU and the NCWC were among the organizations calling upon the government to exclude Asian immigrants because of their alleged moral deficiencies.[135] Increasingly stringent penalties were demanded for male customers, procurers or economic beneficiaries of female prostitution.[136] Despite "a virtual explosion" of criminal sanctions against the "debauching of innocent women" at the end of the 19th century,[137] the state's reluctance to impose the full agenda encouraged women's organizations, hesitantly at first, to espouse the suffragist crusade for female enfranchisement. The NCWC declared that it was the disintegration of the traditional family that led women to seek participation in public life.[138] As Nellie McClung put it: "Women have cleaned up things since time began; and if ever women get into politics there will be a cleaning-out of pigeon-holes and forgotten corners, on which the dust of years has fallen, and the sound of the political carpet-beater will be heard in the land."[139] To preserve the maternal influence, to defeat the threat to civilization, women's issues would have to become national issues.

The maternal reformers were generally middle class, with no economic reason to enter the workforce themselves. They proposed no programs that would have encouraged women's economic independence from men, sharing the prevailing ideology that biological differences determined "separate spheres" for men and women. By strengthening the family unit, they hoped, the providing male would fulfil his economic function to the benefit of his dependent wife and children, and rather than economic opportunity they sought aid for widows or deserted mothers left without a male provider. It was acknowledged that some women had to work, but this would be temporary, pre-marital or at least pre-maternal, and should not normally become a "career." Woman's only worthy career was as a mother, and "Where the mother works, the baby dies," affirmed Dr. Helen MacMurchy in her 1910 "Report on Infant Mortality in Toronto."[140] Yet the number of single women working for wages was increasing with urbanization, arousing concerns for their physical and moral safety against threats that might affect their later careers as mothers. Even white-collar work, it was feared, could provoke nervous disorders that might be passed along to future offspring and lead ultimately to "race degeneration."[141] The maternal reformers therefore added protective legislation for female workers to their national agenda.[142]

Organized labour and the middle-class women's movement shared a fundamental concept: the Canadian working man must be paid a "family wage." If a man was paid adequately, his wife would not need to work and possibly bring her motherhood into danger. On the other hand if women did work they would contradict the argument for a family wage and their workplace competition could drive down wages for male providers. As the factory system became prevalent in Canadian industry, employers often found that they could replace skilled workers with mass production techniques employing the unskilled at lower rates of pay. Organized labour's early campaigns were to ensure that these developments should not destroy the family wage, and one part of the strategy was to restrict the employment of "cheap labour" who were often recruited among the groups least concerned for, or strong enough to demand, a family wage: temporarily employed single women, children, alien sojourners. At first the TLC platform called bluntly for "abolition of . . . female labour in all branches of industrial life, such as mines, workshops, factories, etc." This was amended, following the example of the American Knights of Labor, to demand "equal pay for equal work" on the assumption that an employer would not hire inferior labour if there was no economic advantage in doing so. A third tactical development was the insistence upon "the protection of women who enter industries . . . (with the view of their responsibility towards the nation, as the mothers of our future citizens). . . ." Female employment, the TLC advised the federal government, must be contingent upon an investigation to determine the working conditions, and if they were inappropriate either women should not be hired or special facilities for female workers must be provided.[143]

Economic concern for a family wage and moral concern for women's safety coincided completely, and both reinforced the notion of female dependency and vulnerability. Workplace renovations and restrictions would raise the effective cost of female workers so that employers would be disinclined to hire them and the separate spheres could be preserved. It would be impossible for later generations to segregate motives or isolate self-interest in the demand for female protection. Helena Gutteridge, leading BC female activist and women's labour organizer, sought to encourage women's employment opportunities, yet she insisted in 1914: "Short hours are far more essential to women than they are to men. . . . The injurious physical and mental effects of such work are plainly visible . . . and the rapid aging of the working women has its injurious effects on the next generation."[144] Biology was at the basis of the distinctions, and all women required protection. The minister of Labour made no qualifications for class or background, though his imagery was decidedly middle class, when he told a Montreal audience in 1914: "The great aim of labour legislation is the establishment of the home on a solid basis. Every effort must be made to keep the mother in the home, she being the natural and primary factor in education and in the development of good citizenship."[145] This is not to suggest that class barriers were being eliminated, for the maternal reformers left their own domestic servants outside the protective ring on the grounds that domestic work, even on behalf of others, was natural for women. When male labour representatives wanted to establish a minimum weekly wage of $16.50 for female workers, the Vancouver Local Council of Women recommended it be set at $5 "to be fair to employers as well as the employee."[146] But because their vulnerability was an aspect of their biological condition, and they had the same responsibility toward future generations, working-class women had to be covered by the middle-class protective net. Few middle-class daughters would have sought employment in the industrial occupations subject to the most stringent restrictions. Class and gender interests were indistinguishable in an ideology of biological determinism. Gender defined the type of work available, the conditions of labour, the rate of pay, the acquisition of skills, just as did class, age and "race."

As female participation in the workforce grew, factory acts were passed in the various provinces protecting women from hazardous tasks and providing for their special needs as workers.[147] Hours of labour were limited and night work was banned, proper dining and dressing rooms were required, leaves for pregnant and nursing mothers were established. Women were not permitted to serve alcohol in many provinces, or to work in labour camps.[148] Even shops were required to have seats for female employees, lest a day spent waiting on the public have a detrimental physical effect, and female clerks could not be employed after 6 pm.[149] Pensions were granted to widows, deserted wives or any woman whose husband was "so physically disabled that he is unable to support his family," and minimum wages were introduced for female employees.[150] Moral protection followed a parallel path. The Criminal Code in 1892 created a special offence to punish an employer or manager who seduced a female employee under his direction. At first specifying only factories, mills and workshops, the offence category was extended to shops and stores in 1900 and to all places of work in 1920.[151]

This legislative direction was launched and sustained without any specific reference to "race," but racial assumptions lent certain implications to its application. Most fundamentally, women were the bearers of the "white race" and the preservation of the latter required the protection of white women from, *inter alia*, racial impurities. There were no Canadian laws against intermarriage, but there were occasional proposals to make it illegal, and gender-specific legislation against inter-racial mixing was certainly compatible with prevailing ideology. *Saturday Night* magazine published a front-page editorial entitled "Girls Be Careful Whom You Marry" which warned Canadian (white) women against marriage to "a Chinaman, Hindu, Moslem or African Negro." American state laws prohibiting intermarriage were praised and Canadians were urged to emulate their fine example, for "nothing short of a legal embargo can possibly accomplish the desired end, which is, of course, the total elimination of such unions in this country.... [Since] such marriages place their white participants and the offspring under various social disadvantages, as well as being distinctly undesirable from the point of view of the State, the Federal Government would do well to prohibit them altogether."[152]

Contemporary stereotypes made Chinese particularly liable to disfavour in this regard. Among the images brought back by Western missionaries and travellers in China was one of a wretchedly low condition of women in that civilization. Female infanticide, concubinage and polygamy, the apparent enslavement and sale of young women, attracted the particular distaste of the Canadian maternal reformers who expressed concern that the Chinese example could seduce Canadian males "away from higher Anglo-Saxon standards."[153] In Canada, too, Chinese men were alleged to be buying and selling Chinese women, and Chinese house-servants in Chinese homes were regularly referred to as "slave girls" by the white women reformers.[154] These manifestations were confirmation of the society-wide belief in Chinese moral inferiority, and aroused an interventionist response from Canadian women. For example in 1909, when Chinese merchants in Victoria hired some white female students as English-language instructors for their children, the Local Council of Women asked city council to pass an emergency by-law to prevent it.[155]

The idea of using the state to legislate morality in general, and the protection of white women in particular, was an established component of "common sense" by the first decade of the 20th century. Carried by a women's movement awakened to the threat against the Anglo-Saxon family and the special role of women in defending it, the protective impulse meshed with the economic interests of organized labour, the chivalric ideals of white manhood, and biological orthodoxy as applied to both "race" and gender characteristics.

6. THE MORAL CRUSADE

Organized reformism had already identified the Chinese opium den as a moral problem when deputy labour minister William Lyon Mackenzie King went to Vancouver in 1908 to investigate Chinese losses from the previous year's riot. Two Chinese opium merchants submitted claims of $600 for damaged stocks and loss of business, alerting King to the extent of their traffic. On questioning the merchants further, King was astounded to learn that the majority of their customers were white people. Historically opium use had not been a concern in Canada. Babies were put to sleep on syrups containing opium, doctors prescribed opiates for asthma and appendicitis, coughs and nerves, epilepsy and diarrhoea. In

1907, 44 tons of opium were imported into Canada, mostly for accepted medical purposes. The "indiscriminate use of opium" had long been associated with Chinatown in the public eye, but King's revelation provided documentary evidence that the practice was seeping into the white population. Supported by the "better class" of Chinese merchants in Vancouver, who publicly regretted the damage opium abuse was causing to "the social, physical and moral condition of both Chinese and Europeans," King announced that "We will get some good out of this riot yet" and launched a special inquiry into the West Coast opium industry. His report, *The Need for the Suppression of the Opium Traffic in Canada*, was submitted in July 1908, recommending that the importation or manufacture of opium be outlawed "save in so far as may be necessary for medicinal purposes." Three weeks later Canada became the first Western nation to prohibit the production or sale of opium for recreational use. Raids were thereupon conducted on opium dens across British Columbia and in Calgary, Saskatoon, Winnipeg and Toronto.[156]

As Canada's resident expert on opium, and a Member of Parliament since 1908, Mackenzie King was selected as Canadian representative to an international convention on opium in Shanghai in 1909. Awakened to the international dimensions of moral degeneracy, and prompted by cries from the Canadian West for stricter enforcement, King urged the federal government in 1910 to appoint a Royal Commission to examine the opium phenomenon more fully. With that report in hand, King introduced a new Act in 1911 to make opium possession a criminal offense and to increase police powers of search and seizure. Included in the legislation was a "reverse onus" provision, to relieve the state of the necessity of proving that an accused was knowingly in possession of the narcotic. This provision allegedly tempted police into planting evidence during Chinatown raids. That Chinese were the intended objects of punishment was explicitly mentioned in the House of Commons, and the form for reporting convictions was divided into columns for "Chinese" and "Others." Hundreds of convictions showed that the riot was beginning to render its benefits.[157]

The Trades and Labour Congress took some satisfaction from the opium measures, having since its 1890 Convention drawn attention to the corruptions wreaked upon society by Chinese drug-peddlers, including the enticement of white women into prostitution through the use of drugs. The TLC was Canada's most consistent lobby urging state intervention to control the Chinese. Its *Platform of Principles* listed "Exclusion of all Orientals" as an organizational goal, and it was instrumental in having the head tax imposed as a discouragement to immigration (though its recommendation of a $1,000 tax was never accepted). The TLC passed various resolutions opposing the employment of Chinese in competition with whites and proposing enforcement of stricter health regulations on Chinese laundries.[158] Then at the 1911 annual convention in Guelph, Ontario, a new issue appeared on the agenda:

Whereas it has come to light from time to time, especially in our coast cities, that Orientals employing white girls have used their positions as employers to seduce and destroy all sense of morality by the use of drugs and other means, bringing them down to the lowest depths of humanity; therefore, be it resolved, that this Congress impress on the Federal Government the necessity of passing legislation making it a criminal offence for Orientals to employ white girls in any capacity.[159]

This was the first time such a proposal was made publicly, though it did represent a logical extension from, or combination of, the movements for economic restriction and moral protection.

The TLC in Saskatchewan was in a militant mood, especially during a major organizing drive between 1908 and 1911. In an agricultural province with little secondary industry, only 5,008 out of a total work force of 208,600 were unionized by 1912, but they tended to be the skilled craftsmen whose cooperation was most essential to the construction boom accompanying Saskatchewan's phenomenal population growth. A wave of strikes in 1910 demonstrated the power of worker solidarity to the workers themselves and to their employers. With the assistance of the Regina Board of Trade, employers promoted the immigration of unskilled workers from Britain to undermine the unions, contributing to a further outburst of labour militancy in 1912.[160] In the midst of this turmoil, on 6 February 1912, the TLC provincial Executive Committee had its annual meeting with the Saskatchewan government. Present were James Somerville, William McAllister, G. H. Merlin and John McGrath for the TLC, and for the government Acting Premier J. A. Calder, Municipal Affairs Minister A. P. McNab and Labour Bureau Superintendent Molloy. *Inter alia*, the TLC delegation requested "An Act prohibiting the employment of white girls or females by Orientals in restaurants, laundries, etc.," further to the 1911 Convention resolution.[161]

Within just three weeks *An Act to Prevent the Employment of Female Labour in Certain Capacities* was introduced in the Saskatchewan legislature. Although the TLC delegation was the immediate occasion for this development, organized labour was not the only constituency demanding restraints on the Chinese community. The Saskatchewan Social and Moral Reform Council, established in 1907 primarily as a temperance organization, was also expressing concern about the potential dangers to white women from Chinese employers. The Reformers were advised by a "prominent citizen" that

Through the three prairie Provinces and British Columbia these Oriental almond-eyed anthropoids own a large proportion of our eating houses, and are found working side by side with white women in almost all of our hotels and restaurants. In Western Canada our sisters, even our mothers, are working under these harpies and with them for sixteen and sometimes as many as eighteen hours a day. To my certain knowledge many of them afterwards go down into the underworld to suffer a fate worse than death. You who make a business of combatting social evils must take this one into consideration speedily. Each day's delay means scores of Canadian women lost to decency, and shames our country in the eyes of all moral nations.[162]

Besides all the major churches, temperance societies and women's organizations, the Council included representatives from the Retail Merchants' Association, which had its own campaign to impose restrictions – for example, early closing regulations – upon Chinese businesses whose lack of Sunday observance and family responsibility allegedly gave them an unfair competitive advantage over white Christian businessmen. Owners of steam laundries added the complaint that they had to abide by a set of stringent sanitary regulations while Chinese hand laundries were left unregulated. Labour, business, religion and women reformers combined to convince the Saskatchewan government of the necessity for the *Female Labour Act*.[163]

The Saskatchewan delegates received the wholehearted congratulations of their brothers at the next Convention in September 1912. The only other provincial executive to raise the issue with its government that year was Manitoba's, and they received a polite rejection. Encouraged by the Saskatchewan example, the 1912 Convention resolved "that our executives be instructed to again call for Legislation on this matter in all unprotected Provinces."[164] Subsequent annual meetings learned that Manitoba, Ontario and British Columbia had seen fit to accept the TLC's recommendations and to introduce legislation modelled after Saskatchewan's.[165]

7. CHINESE RESPONSE

One recent article on Chinese in Canada lists "avoidance," "fatalism," "acceptance," "sojourner attitude" and "social segregation" as examples of the "coping behavior of Chinese in Canada," characteristics that explain their "failure to mobilize collectively" in opposition to discrimination. Another recent account has a section entitled "Avoidance and Self-withdrawal as Coping." These and similar themes seem to dominate much of the literature on the Chinese response to white Canadian attitudes and actions.[166] There is certainly ample evidence to suggest that Chinese did tend to seek each other's company both organizationally and residentially, and to establish "ethnic" businesses in a narrow occupational range, but the accompanying image of retreat and passivity is not justified.

The Chinese consistently had the lowest percentage of naturalized subjects for any ethnic group in Canada. In 1911 fewer than 10 percent of Chinese in Canada were naturalized, and this declined to less than 5 percent in the 1921 census, indicating that the attractions of a Canadian identity were not great.[167] Commissioner Gray included an explanation for this phenomenon in the 1885 *Report*: "By provincial legislation in British Columbia and the general hostility towards them, the Chinese are practically prohibited from becoming attached to the country. They are made, so far as provincial legislation can go, perpetual aliens."[168] The difficulties recognized by Justice Gray were not limited to British Columbia, especially as numbers of Chinese moved east of the Rockies following completion of the railway. No doubt the absence of citizenship rights and other exclusionary practices did discourage naturalization, but for Japanese the corresponding naturalization figures were almost 25 percent in 1911 and over 33 percent in 1921. Since the Japanese suffered equivalent hostility and legal disabilities in Canada, with the exception of the entry tax, the Chinese rejection of naturalization must have reflected some additional aspect of the Chinese experience in Canada.

The Chinese-Canadian community was not "normal" in the sense of containing a distribution by age and sex. In the 1911 census there were 279 Chinese males for every Chinese female, by far the greatest imbalance in Canada at that time and a decided contrast to the Japanese.[169] This was not entirely a matter of choice. The escalating head tax made it unlikely that a poorly paid Chinese worker could afford to bring his family to Canada. On the other hand it might be noted that Chinese owners of small businesses in Canada did bring sons, nephews and cousins to work in their laundries and restaurants, all of whom were liable to head taxes, and wives could have been brought under similar circumstances since, presumably, a wife could be sufficiently productive in a restaurant or market gardening operation to justify payment of the tax. Clues to a non-economic reason behind the absence of Chinese women surfaced in the 1902 Royal Commission *Report*. A Vancouver merchant explained the attitude of the majority of his compatriots: "A large proportion of them would bring their families here, were it not for the unfriendly reception they got here during recent years, which creates an unsettled feeling."[170] A market gardener spoke on his own behalf: "I have been here 12 years.... My wife and two children are in China.... I would like to bring my children here.... The people in this country talk so much against the Chinese that I do not care to bring them here."[171] The head tax was merely symptomatic of Canadian discrimination, and it was partly to protect their families that Chinese men decided not to expose them to life in Canada.

It is suggested that the dynamics of the Chinese community were strongly influenced by the fact that it was populated, by and large, by adult males who retained their political and citizenship links with China. Being without a family, they gathered together in their non-working hours for company and comfort, forming an array of fraternal, clan and locality-of-origin associations which sustained Chinese language, iden-tity and the observance of traditional customs. Being without Canadian citizenship, the politics of the homeland or the local affairs of Chinatown dominated discussion. Gambling and opium use were part of the culture they brought with them, no doubt enhanced by the absence of immediate family involvements, further distinguishing them from other ethnic groups. Their associations took on many of the functions of the extended family back home, providing lodgings, recreational facilties, employment assistance, emergency relief, funerals.[172] Chinese isolation cannot be understood simply as "coping" with discrimination, but also as a conse-quence of transplanting a particular demographic slice from an intricate and integrated homeland civilization.

The Chinese movement into "ethnic" businesses has also been described as a "retreat" from competition with whites.[173] The centrifugal force of white hostility was undoubtedly the fundamental factor, but it must be remembered that most Chinese arrived in Canada with the skills and work experience of a rural village in China's southern rice-produc-ing region. There was no obvious Canadian employment sector for which they were prepared, though many brought local market-trading experience and a tradition of launching small enterprises on borrowed or pooled capital.[174] They moved into areas where they perceived a need, for example in laundries and restaurants, and for which very little capital investment was required. Partnerships of kin- or locality-related men could consolidate their meagre savings, share in the labour, live in a room behind the business space: they were, in effect, making their own jobs and providing their own homes, and the kind of work they performed – cooking and cleaning – was similar to the domestic service of many of their colleagues directly employed by whites. While census statistics show that industrial occupations declined while service occupations increased over time, the vast majority was always engaged in unskilled labour even in such "industrial" categories as railway construction or mining. But the "escape" into "ethnic" business never enabled them to avoid conflict with whites, and if that were the chief motivation they would soon have learned that it was ineffective. The Canada-wide movement to restrict Chinese laundries, already described, meant that the laundry business provided no safe haven from white discrimination. Nor, beginning with the TLC resolution of 1911, did restaurants provide such a haven.

Obviously the life of the Chinese in Canada was one of struggle. Their concentration in ethnically defined associations and ethnically stereotyped businesses need not, however, be interpreted exclusively as a liability, for the resulting social bonds also offered some strengths. The manner in which those strengths were employed should dispel any notions of Chinese passivity, and help put Quong Wing in a more realistic context. The first community-wide Chinese organization to be formed in Canada was the Chinese Consolidated Benevolent Association, founded in Victoria in 1884. Its immediate inspiration was the set of discriminatory laws and taxes enacted in BC that year, and the Association's first object was to mobilize the Chinese in a united protest movement. The CBA also established a set of rules and enforcement procedures to control the crime, prostitution and extortion which were increasing in Victoria's Chinatown, and to provide for the settlement of disputes within the community. It served as a quasi-government for the Chinese membership and represented Chinese interests to the mainstream society. Until the establishment of an official Chinese consulate in 1908, it was the CBA and its branches that served in an equivalent capacity.[175]

With or without CBA coordination, there was a pattern of refusing to acquiesce in oppression and restriction. Discrimination was often confronted through boycotts and strikes. When British Columbia introduced its licensing enactment in 1878, Chinese refused to pay the tax and went on a five-day strike as well as hiring a lawyer to help petition the provincial legislature. Similarly there were frequent work stoppages during the construction of the CPR to protest pay delays or aggressive foremen, and Chinese laundrymen declined to pay Victoria's $75 semi-annual laundry licensing fee in 1886. Another Victoria move in 1893, to regulate Chinese residential densities, was met with Gandhi-like resistance: a refusal to pay the fines and the acceptance, instead, of a jail sentence in the hope of clogging the system. To enforce the campaign, the CBA paid each person jailed a $10 reward, while those who paid the city's fine were punished with an additional $10 fine to the CBA. When Victoria tried to establish a separate school for Chinese children, they boycotted the school until they were readmitted to the regular system. Following the 1907 Vancouver riot Chinese withdrew their services as domestics in homes and hotels and closed their shops to reinforce a claim for compensation. Proposed by-laws against Chinese laundries in Calgary and Montreal were successfully opposed by CBA delegations. Most effective, of course, were appeals to the courts. Though by no means an unbroken string of success, the tactic of challenging discriminatory laws had established an encouraging record long before 1912.[176]

8. QUONG WING AND QUONG SING

The appearance of the *Female Labour Act* provoked a defiant response from the Chinese community in Saskatchewan. A mass meeting was held in Moose Jaw, home to the province's largest Chinese population, where the Act's implications were discussed and a decision was made to continue the employment of white women and to fight a test case pending diplomatic action by the Chinese government.[177] They did not have long to wait. On 20 May 1912 Moose Jaw police chief Walter P. Johnson sent constable W. W. De Rossiter to visit two Chinese-owned establishments where he confidently expected to find white female employees, the CER Restaurant and the Royal Restaurant and Rooming House.[178]

The CER Restaurant at the corner of Main and Manitoba Streets in Moose Jaw had been owned since about 1904 by Quong Wing, formerly of the "Empire of China" and a British subject since 1905.[179] For more than a year before the new Act came into effect, Quong Wing (or "Charlie" as he was known locally) employed Nellie Lane and Mabel Hopham as waitresses. This was a reasonably typical prairie operation in 1912, except that Quong Wing was a naturalized British subject at a time when only about 5 percent of Saskatchewan's Chinese had taken out naturalization. Quong Wing also seems to have been a Christian.[180] Quong

Wing's neighbour on River Street West and proprietor of the Royal, Quong Sing, was also a naturalized British subject and even more unusually had brought his wife and three children to live with him in Moose Jaw. At the Royal Rooming House, upstairs from the restaurant, Quong Sing employed Annie Hartman as a chambermaid.[181] On receiving De Rossiter's eyewitness report that three white women were being employed by "Chinamen" contrary to law, Chief Johnson swore a complaint against Quong Wing and Quong Sing before Magistrate W. F. Dunn the very next day, 21 May 1912.

A week later, on 27 May, Quong Wing and Quong Sing appeared in Magistrate Dunn's court to answer the charge. Because of the approach taken by defence attorney Netson R. Craig, the court hearing turned into a discussion on the criteria for "race" categorization acceptable in Canada at that time. Mr. Craig, who often appeared on behalf of Moose Jaw's Chinese community, challenged the very concept of "race," forcing witnesses to explain what they meant by the term "Chinaman" and how a Chinese person was different from any other person. If "Chinese" did not signify citizenship or allegiance, Craig wanted to know, just what significance did it have? The responses he evoked displayed the conventional wisdom that racial categories were both real and obvious. "Chinamen" could be identified by their appearance, their language and above all, by the "common sense" of the observer. Secondarily, Netson Craig challenged the vulnerability and dependency of white women and their need for protection against Chinese, and in this he had the apparent agreement of the three female employees who were called as witnesses. The defence case was therefore a sophisticated attack upon the principles underlying the *Female Labour Act*. Other parties in the court, and the Moose Jaw *Evening Times*, regarded it rather as a source of amusement. It was funny because it did not make "sense" to them.

Acting for the Crown that day was William Grayson, and he proceeded first against Quong Wing. S. R. McClure was appointed stenographer, to take a shorthand account of everything said in court. Grayson's first witness, Chief Walter Johnson, established that Quong Wing was the owner of the CER Restaurant.

Q. What nationality is he?
A. A Chinaman.
Q. He is of the Oriental Race?
A. Yes sir.

To Grayson's question "Have you seen any White women in the Restaurant kept by him?" Chief Johnson identified two persons sitting in the court, "The lady with the blue sweater and the one with roses in her hat." Netson Craig then cross-examined:

Q. I suppose you have never been in the Orient, Chief?
A. No. . . .
Q. Your knowledge of Chinamen you have gained in Moose Jaw?
A. I have seen them before that I think.
Q. But your knowledge of whether a man is a Chinaman or not is simply that you have heard someone else call him a Chinaman. You never saw a man standing on Chinese soil in your life, or a man you could swear of your own knowledge was born there?
A. No.
Q. Or a man you could swear of your own knowledge was an Oriental?
A. I will swear that Quong Wing is a Chinaman.
Q. That they call him a Chinaman?
A. That will do. . . .
Q. You are not a professional Ethnologist. ·
A. No. . . .
Q. Do you know the difference between a Chinaman and any other man. Is there any difference between a Chinaman and any other man?
A. I know the difference when I see them.
Q. You think you could swear to the difference between a Chinaman and a Japanese, for instance, if you had not seen them before and did not know which was which.
A. I HAVE seen this man before Mr. Craig.
Q. Yes, you have. To cut the matter short, you won't pledge yourself though that that man is a Chinaman absolutely. You think he is a Chinaman, because he has always been known as such to you.
A. There is no doubt in my mind Mr. Craig; I don't wish to evade your question, there is no doubt that he is a Chinaman. . . . He has always been known here, I have known him for six years, known him as a Chinaman. . . .

Alerted to Craig's line of questioning, Grayson pressed his next witness, Constable De Rossiter, "Of what nationality is Quong Wing?" "To the best of my knowledge and belief he is a Chinaman." "You have no doubt about that have you?" "No sir." Again Netson Craig challenged the witness's ability to identify a "Chinaman:"

Q. Your grounds for swearing that Quong Wing is a Chinaman are the same as the Chief's?

A. I am swearing on my own knowledge based on my own knowledge and belief.

Q. You cannot swear where he was born, nor where he came from to this country?

A. No.

Q. Nor what country he owes allegiance to?

A. He didn't come from the same country as I did.

Q. I don't know about that, and I don't know who is to be congratulated. You don't know what authority he owes allegiance to?

Mr. Grayson: Perhaps he is Scotch.

Q. You don't know that country he came from nor what country he owes allegiance to?

A. No Mr. Craig I do not.

Apparently to add scientific authority to Quong Wing's identification as Chinese, Grayson called Frank Cartledge, Moose Jaw's official Health Inspector, who swore that the accused was Chinese on the grounds that "He is similar to other Chinamen that I have seen in appearance" and he spoke the Chinese language. Craig tried to evoke more precision from the witness:

Q. What is a Chinaman, Mr. Cartledge?

A. I should say a native of China.

Q. What is a native of China?

A. A man born there, his parents being Chinese.

Q. Say a British Subject or Consul at Hong Kong has a White wife, who has a child that child would be a Chinese. . . .

A. It could not be Chinese. . . .

Q. You don't know Quong Wing's parents?

A. No.

Q. You don't know where he was born in China?

A. No.

A prominent member of the Chinese community and pillar of the Chinese Methodist congregation, Yip Foo, was in court that day, as a friend of the accused and, as a restaurant owner himself, one materially interested in the outcome. To his surprise Yip Foo was called as a witness for the prosecution to establish Quong Wing's "race." Yip Foo admitted that he was himself Chinese. Grayson then asked "What is Quong Wing?" and Yip Foo answered "He Chinese too." Craig remained persistent, however, and extracted from Yip Foo an admission that he had not known Quong Wing in China and could not swear from personal knowledge that he was born there or that his parents were Chinese, leading Craig to conclude that Yip Foo could not "really swear whether he is Chinese or not." Yip Foo concurred.

Grayson's next witness, the employee Nellie Lane, was decidedly reluctant to implicate her employer. Grayson asked:

Q. What Nationality are you.
A. I am English.
Q. No Chinese about you?
A. Cheshire.
Q. I thought so.
A. You bet. . . .

Confirming that she had worked in the CER Restaurant for the past twelve months, Mrs. Lane was asked:

Q. Who paid your wages?
A. Charlie – Quong Wing, and he always paid me to the day too.
Mr. Grayson: I am not disputing that, I know he is a very fine gentleman who pays his way. . . .
Q. What Nationality is Quong Wing?
A. Well I treat him as myself.
Q. I know, but what is he?
A. I don't know what he was only what people have told me.
Q. What is he Mrs. Lane.
A. I could not tell you.
Q. What language does he speak?
A. He can speak two, he can speak English and he can speak Chinese.
Q. Is he English?
A. No, he is not English, but I could not tell you where he came from, it would be hard for me to say, but he is as good as me and all.

Under cross-examination by Netson Craig, Nellie Lane admitted that she could not distinguish the Chinese language from German "or any foreign language," and she continued to insert positive comments about her working life with Quong Wing.

Q. You have been working for him for twelve months.

A. Yes, and never worked for a better master, he pays me to the day and has an honest living.

Q. Respectable?

A. Yes, they call him Chinese, he is as good as me.

Q. You have no fault to find with him at all?

A. No fault whatever.

The second employee, Mabel Hopham, confessed to Mr. Grayson that Quong Wing was "Chinese I guess," but to Mr. Craig that she could not recognize the Chinese language and had no idea of his birthplace or parentage.

The case for the prosecution was now closed. Craig produced Quong Wing's Naturalization Certificate which declared that its bearer, Quong Wing, "has become naturalized as a British subject, and is, within Canada, entitled to all political and other rights, powers and privileges, and is subject to all obligations to which a natural born British subject is entitled or subject within Canada."

On this Netson Craig rested the case for the defence. Magistrate Dunn, however, was unimpressed with the statement on the Certificate, and unconvinced by Craig's attempt to cast doubt on Quong Wing's racial identity. He concluded "on the evidence"

1. That the accused Quong Wing was born in China and of Chinese parents. . . .

4. That on the said 20th day of May 1912 the said accused had in his employ as waitresses in the said restaurant one Mabel Hopham and one Nellie Lane, and that the said Mabel Hopham and Nellie Lane are white women.

He thereupon determined that Quong Wing was in violation of the *Female Labour Act* and fined him $5, though he specified that the accused would not be held responsible for costs.[182] The Moose Jaw *Evening Times* confirmed the magistrate's conclusion in an amused report of the trial. "Is anyone in Moose Jaw really certain that the many Chinese in the city are really Chinamen? . . . For a time Hong's [sic] nationality was uncertain, some venturing he was Scotch. At last the court decided after much legal sparring that Hong was a 'Chink' absolutely."[183]

The trial of Quong Sing, which followed immediately, continued in an identical manner. Prosecution witnesses stated their belief that the accused was Chinese, but did not know where he was born or to which country he owed his allegiance. The chambermaid Annie Hartman added that she had no complaints against her employer. "He has used you all right." "Yes sir." When Craig introduced Quong Sing's Naturalization Certificate, however, it was discovered that it was made out in the name of "Quon Sing," and Quong Sing had to be sworn as a witness to identify it as belonging to him. Given the opportunity, Grayson asked:

Q. Where were you born?
A. Hong Kong.
Q. You are a Chinaman.
A. Yes.

Craig leapt in:

Q. By being a Chinaman, what do you mean?
A. I was born in China.
Q. That is what you mean.
A. Yes.
Q. Under that certificate what are you to that country.
A. I am English.
Q. A British Subject.
A. Yes.

The racial strategy seemed lost, but the resourceful Craig found another target for his attack on the conceptual validity of "race": he moved "For dismissal on the grounds that there is no proof that the woman employed is a white woman or girl." This won him even less attention than his challenge to the identity of Quong Wing and Quong Sing. Stenographer McClure noted simply that Craig's motion was "Overruled," with no further comment or discussion. The "race" of Annie Hartman was beyond dispute.[184] Quong Sing was found guilty and fined $5, without costs.

Given that the fine could have been $100 each, that a refusal to pay meant two months in jail, and that costs were normally assigned against those convicted in magistrate's court, the Messrs Quong might have been expected to express their gratitude to Magistrate Dunn and humbly pay their $5. This would have accorded with the enduring stereotype of the retiring Chinese avoiding conflict. But they did not pay. Instead they engaged Wellington B. Willoughby, Netson Craig's senior partner, establishment figure and leader of the Conservative Opposition in the Saskatchewan legislature, to appeal their conviction to the Saskatchewan

Supreme Court.[185] On 30 May they announced their intention to appeal, and on 12 June they each posted a bond of $200 and registered their desire "to question the said conviction on the ground that it is erroneous in point of Law and in excess of jurisdiction."[186] Responding on behalf of the attorney general, barrister Jasper Fish stated "that important, intricate and difficult questions affecting the validity of a statute of the province of Saskatchewan will be raised and will be decided on or after the hearing of this matter," and so requested a delay while more details could be sought from the convicting magistrate. Dunn's reply was immediate. After setting out the facts in the case and Mr. Willoughby's objections, Dunn respectfully "submitted for the judgment of this honourable Court" the following questions:

1. Whether the premises described as being the place in which the alleged white women worked is included in the Act under which the information was laid.

2. Whether any offence under the said Act is disclosed.

3. Whether the accused, being a naturalized British subject, is one of the persons prohibited by the Act from employing female labour.

4. Whether the said Act under which the said information was laid is ultra vires.

5. Whether the conviction was in excess of the jurisdiction of the [Magistrate's] Court.[187]

The issue of "race" and the validity of racial classification raised by Netson Craig was replaced by the question of jurisdiction. "Race" had been assumed: Quong Wing and Quong Sing were Chinese, Annie Hartman, Mabel Hopham and Nellie Lane were white; the difference was both obvious and sufficiently significant to justify legal distinctions, but who should make those distinctions had to be decided.

The Supreme Court of Saskatchewan sitting *en banc* heard the joint appeal on 1 March 1913, and delivered judgment on 9 July.[188] Present were Chief Justice Haultain and Justices Newlands, Lamont and Brown, with Willoughby and Fish for the appellants and Crown respectively.[189] Reviewing the questions submitted by Magistrate Dunn, the Chief Justice set out that the only real question for the court was whether the *Female Labour Act* was within the competency of the Saskatchewan legislature, and that would depend upon the construction of the *BNA Act* Sections 91 and 92. The provincial Act, he observed, imposes upon Chinese owners and keepers of hotel, restaurant and other business property special disabilities and restrictions, not only with regard to the labour they employ but also with regard to the public they serve. It also puts a practical prohibition on the employment of any Chinaman as the manager of any business in which female employees are required. A Chinaman who wishes to invest in business property must do so with the full knowledge that his only possible tenant will be persons who are willing to carry on a business which can only employ coloured female labour, and, in the case – say – of a hotel, can only accommodate coloured female guests.[190]

Weighing *Bryden* and *Tomey Homma*, Haultain concluded that

Both the reasoning and the decision in *Union Collieries v. Bryden*, in my opinion, apply to the enactment now under consideration. The regulations which are here impeached are not really aimed at the regulation of restaurants, laundries, and other places of business and amusement or of the employment of female labour, but were devised to deprive the Chinese, whether naturalized or not, of the ordinary rights of the inhabitants of Saskatchewan. The right to employ, the right to be employed, the right to own property and to own, manage or conduct any business without being subjected to unequal and discriminatory restrictions, are just as truly ordinary rights of the inhabitants of Saskatchewan as the right to work.

The act, therefore, was *ultra vires* of the legislature and the conviction must be reversed.[191]

Justice Lamont differed, at great length. "The wisdom or unwisdom, the justice or injustice, of provincial legislation, or the fact that it discriminates against one person or set of persons and in favour of another person or set of persons is excluded from our consideration," he reasoned. "The only matter for inquiry is as to the legislative competence of the Provincial Legislature to pass the Act impeached."[192] Admitting that certain restrictions were imposed on Chinese, Justice Lamont found that they fell within "property and civil rights" or "local works and undertakings" which belonged to the province under *BNA Act* S92 ss13 and ss10 respectively. *Bryden* could be distinguished because the employment of white women was not *necessary* for a Chinese to carry on his business. *Tomey Homma* showed that once an alien became naturalized he passed out of the jurisdiction of the Dominion parliament. The Saskatchewan Act would be invalidated, therefore, only if it interfered with the alien's right to become naturalized, not merely the consequences of naturalization once effected. Applying the "pith and substance" rule, or what he called "the predominating aspect," Lamont concluded that

the Act was passed in the interests of morality and for the protection of white women, and not for the exclusion of Chinese or preventing those who are still aliens from becoming naturalized subjects.... In this aspect the legislation impeached amounts to no more than police regulations and as such is within the legislative competence of the provincial legislature.[193]

The conviction, obviously, should be affirmed.

Justice Brown, with Justice Newlands concurring, was also prepared to acknowledge that "the legislation prevents a Chinaman as such from being employed in many positions of trust and responsibility, it handicaps him in carrying on legitimate business, and it greatly limits the uses to which he may put his property." But examining the "pith and substance" he found that the act could not be considered a "statutory prohibition against Chinamen" as defined by *Bryden*, for "the sum and object of this legislation is to prevent white women from coming, through employment, lodging, work, or otherwise, under the control or influence of any Chinaman."[194] Advising that the appeal should be dismissed, Justice Brown added

It is surely competent for the province to legislate for the protection of any class of its citizens – in this case white women and girls – such legislation being in the nature of police regulations and if in so doing the ordinary rights of another class – in this case Chinamen – are affected, even seriously affected, that will not, in my judgment, in view of what has been laid down by the Privy Council, make the legislation *ultra vires* of the province. We, of course, have nothing to do with the policy or impolicy of the legislation; that is a matter entirely for the legislature.[195]

Chief Justice Haultain was a minority of one.[196] Quong Wing and Quong Sing lost. The assumption that Chinese were a threat to white womanhood (a point not even argued by Jasper Fish, who relied on *Tomey Homma* to make his case), was implicit in the decision, for otherwise the "pith and substance" to that effect could not have been taken seriously. Only the chief justice saw this as a ruse, though even its euphemistic value would reveal its credibility at that time. Fifty years of associating Chinese with drugs, disease and immorality had reached a point of fruition.

9. *QUONG WING v. THE KING*

But if one set of Chinese stereotypes had been confirmed, Quong Wing continued to challenge another. He immediately announced his intention to appeal to the Supreme Court of Canada. Exactly why his case was selected rather than Quong Sing's is not recorded,[197] but it is evident that this was a deliberate test of the law and Quong Wing had the support of the Chinese community. The $500 bond, required of all Supreme Court appellants, was posted on 12 August 1913 by Quong Wing himself with Yip Foo and another Moose Jaw restaurant owner, Chan Dou. Meanwhile the Chinese Benevolent Association headquarters in Victoria was conducting a fundraising campaign amongst Chinese across Canada, eventually sending a total of $1,175 to Regina to help finance the attack on the female labour law.[198] The Trades and Labour Congress traced the challenge to "certain property interests" who were encouraging Chinese to violate the act, but they were left unidentified.[199] Presumably the "property interests" would have been the wealthier class of Chinese merchants since, unlike the Union Colliery case, there was no group of white employers whose interests would have been at stake. Later the TLC reported that "Chinese representatives" had taken the matter through the courts.[200] This probably referred to the CBA, though the TLC may have suspected that the Chinese government's representative in Ottawa, Yang Shu-Wen, took a hand in the case.

And so Quong Wing, thousands of miles from his Canton birthplace, proprietor of a tiny cafe, a man whose personal resources must have been extremely limited, found himself confronting the government of Saskatchewan on behalf of Chinese rights in Canada. The day after bond was posted, attorney Wellington B. Willoughby launched the appeal with an affadavit swearing "That the Appellant is dissatisfied . . . and wishes to have the decision of the Court of Saskatchewan, En Banc, reversed."[201] The appellant's *factum* was prepared by G. F. Henderson of MacCracken, Henderson, Greene and Herridge. Jasper Fish continued to represent the attorney general of Saskatchewan. Grounds for the appeal were that "the learned Judges erred in finding that the aim of the said Act was not to deprive the Chinese, whether naturalized or not, of the ordinary rights of the inhabitants of Saskatchewan," and they erred further

in finding that the subject matter of the said Act fell exclusively in the classes of subjects assigned by Section 92 of the *BNA Act* to the province and did not interfere with the authority of the Parliament of Canada to legislate on "trade and commerce" or "aliens and naturalization" or other subjects reserved exclusively by the *BNA Act* to the Parliament of Canada.[202]

The battle waged in each *factum* was the battle between the *Bryden* and *Tomey Homma* precedents. At issue was not simply the position of Chinese in Canada, but the apparent constitutional conflict between those two Privy Council decisions.

"The outstanding question on appeal is as to the constitutionality of the Statute in question," Henderson began. His argument was that Quong Wing's case fell entirely within the *Bryden* precedent: by establishing regulations applicable to operating a business, the Saskatchewan Act trespassed on federal authority over trade and commerce; by applying those regulations only to Chinese, it trespassed upon federal authority over aliens and naturalization. The coal mine regulations invalidated in *Bryden* were determined to be truly aimed at prohibiting Chinese from earning a living. The Saskatchewan law, Henderson submitted, more severely restricted Chinese from earning a living than had BC's coal mines law. Agreeing that, following *Tomey Homma*, a naturalized alien could not claim the franchise as a right, Henderson contended that "The right to engage in business, on the other hand, is a right which is clearly included in the wide terms of the Naturalization Act." The handicap imposed by the Saskatchewan Act would "neutralize" every advantage of naturalization and this, surely, was an infringement upon federal jurisdiction. Henderson concluded by proposing that the term "Chinaman" used in the Act could not have been intended to include naturalized subjects, and so "the present appeal should be allowed upon the short ground that the Appellant is not within the purview of the Act."[203]

In writing the respondent's *factum* Jasper Fish quite naturally relied on *Tomey Homma*. In order to fall within the federal authority over aliens and naturalization, a statute "must deal with aliens as such" and not simply have an effect upon aliens. Innumerable provincial laws, dealing with everything from mortgages to factory conditions, have an effect upon aliens, but no one would seriously challenge their validity. The female labour law came legitimately under the *BNA Act* S92 ss13, giving property and civil rights to the province, and ss8, dealing with municipal institutions, as "a necessary incident of the police power." Submitting, finally, that "the regulation of places of business and resorts kept, owned or managed by Chinese independent of nationality may very properly be considered necessary to the welfare of women and girls in Saskatchewan," Fish pointed out that the regulation was similar to any existing provincial factory act which insisted upon "proper accommodation and conveniences for the sexes, and upon supervision in the same interest and the keeping of proper hours."[204]

The Supreme Court of Canada, consisting of Chief Justice Sir Charles Fitzpatrick and Justices F. A. Anglin, L. H. Davies, Lyman Duff and John Idington, heard the case on 12 February 1914 and issued their decision just 11 days later, less time than usual in that period. The chief justice, a former solicitor general and Justice minister in the Laurier government, was most impressed with Jasper Fish's closing argument. In a brief written decision, Sir Charles found that the act was passed "in the interest of the morals of women and girls in Saskatchewan."

There are many factory Acts passed by provincial legislatures to fix the age of employment and to provide for proper accommodation for workmen and the conveniences of the sexes which are intended not only to safeguard the bodily health, but also the morals of Canadian workers, and I fail to understand the difference in principle between that legislation and this.[205]

Provinces, he wrote, were empowered to authorize disciplinary regulations over the opening hours of taverns and to prevent disorder on Sundays, and they were equally empowered to restrict the employment of women and girls under certain conditions. "The difference between the restrictions imposed on all Canadians by such legislation and those resulting from the Act in question is one of degree, not of kind."[206] He recommended against the appeal.

Justice Davies, with Justice Anglin concurring, treated the violation of Chinese rights more seriously than did his senior colleague, but he maintained that "The question on this appeal is not one as to the policy or justice of the Act in question, but solely as to the power of the provincial legislature to pass it."[207] Reviewing both *Bryden* and *Tomey Homma*, as the chief justice had not done, Davies found that the "pith and substance" of the act was "the protection of white women and girls," and this put it squarely within provincial jurisdiction.[208] "There is no inherent right in any class of the community to employ women and children which the legislature may not modify or take away altogether."[209] Since "the prohibition is a racial one" it dealt with property and civil rights, not alienage or naturalization. The Act "was not aimed at any class of Chinamen, or at the political status of Chinamen, but at Chinamen as men of a particular race or blood,"[210] and this made Quong Wing's naturalized status irrelevant to the question. Davies and Anglin recommended against the appellant.

Lyman Duff, though born in Ontario, had made his career in British Columbia and was a BC Supreme Court judge before his appointment to Ottawa. Of all the judges he was therefore most sensitive to Western feelings about the Chinese, and he explained:

In the sparsely inhabited Western provinces of this country the presence of Orientals in comparatively considerable numbers not infrequently raises questions for public discussion and treatment, and, sometimes in an acute degree, which in more populated countries would excite little nor no general interest.

In such circumstances, he suggested, the "pith and substance" of the Saskatchewan legislature's intentions must be understood as the best interests of white women and of local relations between Europeans and Orientals. It was not, simply, a prohibition against Chinese as was considered in *Bryden*. The act did not prevent Chinese from engaging in business, for the employment of white women was not "a necessary condition" for operating a laundry or restaurant.[211] But the "decisive point," as far as Justice Duff was concerned, was that the act "applies to persons of the races mentioned without regard to nationality." Duff came the closest among his colleagues to offering a legal definition of "race," and for this he had recourse to "the *common understanding* of the words," entirely denying the line of argument pursued by Netson Craig in Moose Jaw:

The terms Chinaman and Chinese, as generally used in Canadian legislation, point to a classification based upon origin, upon racial or personal characteristics and habits, rather than upon nationality or allegiance. . . . Indeed, the presence of the phrase "other Oriental person" seems to make it clear, even if there could otherwise have been any doubt upon the point, that the legislature is not dealing with these classes of persons according to nationality, but as persons of a certain origin or *persons having certain common characteristics and habits* sufficiently indicated by the language used.

Lord Watson, in the *Bryden* decision, had maintained that the mining regulations had "no application except to Chinamen who are aliens or naturalized subjects." As had Justice Davies, Duff noted that since the female labour law applied to all Chinese, Lord Watson's stricture could not be applied.[212] Duff could not therefore find any parallel between Quong Wing and *Bryden*. Instead, the interpretation of provincial powers must follow the definition laid down by Lord Halsbury in *Tomey Homma*. He sided with Fitzpatrick, Davies and Anglin in rejecting the appeal.

Justice John Idington, at 74 the oldest member of the Court, was the only one to discern a different pith and substance in the Saskatchewan law: "The Act, by its title, refers to female labour and then proceeds to deal only with the case of white women. In truth, its evident purpose is to curtail or restrict the rights of Chinamen."[213] Placing his faith in the *Naturalization Act* and the rights of a British subject, he argued

that the highly prized gifts of equal freedom and equal opportunity before the law, are so characteristic of the tendency of all British modes of thinking and acting in relation thereto, that they are not to be impaired by the whims of a legislature; and that equality taken away unless and until forfeited for causes which civilized men recognize as valid. For example, is it competent for a legislature to create a system of slavery and, above all, such a system as applied to naturalized British subjects? This legislation is but a piece of the product of the mode of thought that begot and maintained slavery; not so long ago fiercely claimed to be a laudable system of governing those incapable of governing themselves.[214]

The Dominion government could veto the Saskatchewan Act as guarantor of the equality of freedom and opportunity contained in the federal *Naturalization Act*, or, indeed, the courts could strike it down. Certain "political rights" may be limited by a province, but "the other rights" of a British subject "do not so clearly fall within the powers of the legislatures to discriminate . . . as between classes or sections of the community." Alluding to *Bryden* and *Tomey Homma*, Justice Idington suggested that neither supplied a conclusive authority to be followed in this case, but of the two he found *Bryden* to be more relevant.[215] Still, his decision rested upon the concept of naturalization. Before an applicant could be naturalized, he must have lived in Canada for three years and show himself to be a person of good character throughout that time. By allowing Quong Wing to become naturalized, Canada had certified him to be a man of good character and worthy of equal treatment with other British subjects as assured by the *Naturalization Act*. Referring to the female labour law, Idington exclaimed: "Indeed, in a piece of legislation alleged to have been promoted in the interests of morality, it would seem a strange thing to find it founded upon a breach of good faith which lies at the root of nearly all morality worth bothering one's head about."[216] The Act, then, could not possibly apply to a naturalized person. Whether it were judged to be *ultra* or *intra vires* in general terms, Quong Wing's sta-

tus as a naturalized subject protected him from this or any other discriminatory act and his appeal should be allowed.

Quong Wing had lost again, decisively this time for his application to
appeal to the Judicial Committee of the Privy Council was rejected.[217]
Given the circumstances of the time the wonder is not that four justices
decided against him, but that one found in his favour. The majority was
prepared to accept a restriction on civil rights because it did not specifically trench upon federal authority. Only John Idington contended that
equality was a national issue and must be upheld by the Dominion government in fulfilment of its responsibilities under the *Naturalization Act*
and the broad powers awarded under Section 91 of the *BNA Act*.[218] To
the modern reader several things are remarkable. One is the frequency
with which senior jurists disclaimed any responsibility to examine the
justice of a legislative act. Another is the ironic fact that a law based upon
racial discrimination, applying to all members of a given "race" whether
Canadian- or foreign-born, was more acceptable than a law construed to
apply only to aliens and naturalized subjects. A third point would probably be the readiness with which the majority accepted Saskatchewan's
moral imperative to protect white females from the undisputed dangers
posed by Chinese males. Finally, since *Quong Wing* dealt with an
employment issue, the lay reader might incline to find it closer to *Bryden*
than *Tomey Homma* and therefore conclude that even within its own narrow terms, the Supreme Court should have granted Quong Wing's
appeal.

The confusion has been widely shared. As early as 1915 the Trades and
Labour Congress attempted to reconcile *Bryden* with *Quong Wing*, and
found that class interests explained the apparent anomaly. Under *Bryden*,
white employers could hire Chinese workers to compete with white
workers. Under *Quong Wing* the Chinese employer could not hire white
workers, which might enable him to compete with white employers. In
the TLC's own words:

the provinces have the right to prevent the employment of certain people by certain other people and the provinces have not the right to prevent the employment of certain people by certain other people – the provinces have the right to
prevent the employment by certain Asiatics of people in certain circumstances,
but the provinces have not the right to prevent the employment by certain people
of Asiatics in certain circumstances. . . . In the one case it is the welfare and interests of the workers that are at stake, in the other the interests of the employers.[219]

The most thorough scholarly discussion of the decision came from Walter Tarnopolsky, who concluded that the pith and substance of the Saskatchewan Act was not genuinely to protect white females but to deprive Chinese of their livelihood. Since there were no Chinese women available to hire, and it could not reasonably have been expected that Chinese would employ white men in their laundries and restaurants, the effect of the law must have been to drive Chinese out of business. Tarnopolosky added that *Tomey Homma* was not an adequate precedent for *Quong Wing*, as it dealt only with certain consequences of naturalization, specifically the franchise, and was no more inclusive of all such consequences than *Bryden* was of all the consequences of naturalization or alienage. Though today the franchise is regarded as a right, in 1914 it was still a privilege. *Bryden*, however, referred to the right of every Canadian resident to earn a living.[220] Thus it was preferable, according to Professor Tarnopolsky, to apply the *Bryden* precedent and find for Quong Wing.

10. EXPLANATIONS

Although subsequent generations of lawyers have largely treated *Quong Wing* as a division of powers decision, it must also be recognized that in 1914 the Supreme Court of Canada pronounced on the legality of racial inequality. The judges were directly confronted with the issue of discrimination and invited to overrule the Saskatchewan law not just because it fell in this or that subsection of the *BNA Act* but because it violated Quong Wing's "right" to freedom from discrimination. In his very first ground for appeal submitted to the Supreme Court of Canada, Quong Wing charged that the *Female Labour Act* deprived him as a Chinese of the "ordinary rights of inhabitants of Saskatchewan." Saskatchewan Chief Justice Haultain, in his minority decision, had already recognized that Quong Wing must be accorded those "ordinary rights" "without being subjected to unequal and discriminatory conditions." At the Supreme Court of Canada, four of the five justices wrote or concurred in opinions which acknowledged that Quong Wing's civil rights were affected, and three upheld it precisely because it was *racially* discriminatory. The question of jurisdiction was of course central to the Supreme Court of Canada (and the Saskatchewan Supreme Court) decisions, but the judges were not unaware of the impact their ruling would have on the rights of Chinese in Canada. This was quite apparent to contemporaries: the Chinese Benevolent Association perceived a threat to the rights of Chinese Canadians and sponsored Quong Wing's challenge; the federal government, whose jurisdiction was supposedly being tested, did not intervene, send money, offer advice or become involved in any way. And, while parliamentary supremacy was understood in 1914, John Idington was one who acknowledged that this implied certain restraints and responsibilities when he wrote that "equal freedom and equal opportunity before the law . . . are not to be impaired by the whims of a legislature." As if in anticipation of Section 1 of the Charter of Rights and Freedoms,[221] Justice Idington added that equality rights should not be "taken away unless and until forfeited for causes which civilized men recognize as valid." It becomes possible to recognize racial discrimination as the question, and division of powers as the means to articulate the answer. If Idington's implied Bill of Rights was too radical, *Bryden* was available to squelch a law that was openly discriminatory. Why, then, did the Supreme Court of Canada support this racially discriminatory law, and were the Court's reasons the same as those of the Saskatchewan legislature in passing the act in 1912?

Morality featured prominently in the contemporary explanations offered by the Saskatchewan attorney general and by the courts, and some modern sources contend that the entire episode was prompted by a specific sexual assault. The most comprehensive survey of Chinese history in Canada accepts that the law was a response to an incident in which a Chinese restaurant owner had assaulted a white female employee in 1912.[222] A 1973 "Study of the Chinese Community in Moose Jaw" locates the alleged assault in that city, accounting for the law itself and for its first prosecution in Moose Jaw, and this is supported by a major history of Chinatowns in Canada published in 1988.[223] This explanation seems unlikely, however. There was an assault case reported in the local press, in which Alfred Essrey charged Charlie Quong for throwing him physically out of the kitchen at the Royal restaurant. Mr. Essrey had gone there to fetch a pork chop for his Sunday breakfast. The newspaper account added that "bad blood" existed between Essrey and the Chinese community since he "reprimanded a Chinaman for assaulting his sweetheart who was a waitress in the Royal restaurant" the previous week. Magistrate Dunn dismissed the case.[224] An earlier charge against Charlie Chow, alleged to have indecently assaulted a young white girl in the CER restaurant, was similarly dismissed.[225] Even if these allegations were true, they did not arouse enough attention to provoke a response like the *Female Labour Act*. They were not even reported in the Regina or Saskatoon newspapers. There is no published report of the criminal conviction of a Chinese in Saskatchewan on any sex-related charge in the first two-and-a-half decades of the 20th century. References to Chinese morality during the legislative debate on the Act were extremely vague and no specifics were cited. Quong Wing himself cannot have been implicated in any incident. At his trial his female employees insisted that he was "respectable," and prosecutor Grayson volunteered, "I know he is a very fine gentleman."[226] One cannot believe that the Moose Jaw Chinese community and the national Chinese Benevolent Association would have made a test case based on a man guilty of the very thing the law was supposed to prevent. Nor can one suppose that the police and courts would have overlooked a guilty example to prosecute a man whose personal record was unblemished. Supposing an assault did occur, it was never *used* to support the passage of the Act or the case against Quong Wing. Above all, the 1911 TLC resolution calling for restrictions on Chinese employers was passed before the assault is even alleged to have occurred. To the extent that morality was an issue it was tied to a much more general perception of Chinese as a threat and white women as vulnerable, rather than to any actual perpetrator and victim.

More often, commentators have concluded that "economic reasons" were behind the Saskatchewan law, with morality providing a convenient excuse.[227] Even the Trades and Labour Congress, the bill's immediate sponsor, soon became convinced that it represented a conspiracy by legislatures and courts to inhibit workers' rights and to enhance the position of employers.[228] The economic motive has often been used to explain legislated restrictions in British Columbia: the instruments of the state, it is contended, deliberately enforced a split labour market and undermined the competitive capacity of small Chinese enterprises in order to distract white labour and to profit white business.[229] The application of this kind of explanation to Saskatchewan, however, is far less apparent. The government had reason to gratify organized labour in 1912, in a situation of labour tension, but the provincial TLC was agitating against *British* immigration at that time for reasons of economic self-interest;[230] Chinese labour was already "ghettoized" and posed no perceptible threat to white wages. On the contrary, if Chinese were driven out of their restaurant and laundry businesses they would be *more* likely to come into conflict and competition with white labour. Nor was there in Saskatchewan a class comparable to the BC mine owners who might be motivated by a desire to exploit any Chinese labour displaced from self-employment by laws attacking restaurants and laundries. The only Saskatchewan constituency that might have benefited economically from the Act was small business, specifically the non-Chinese owners of competing laundries and restaurants.[231] Such individuals did participate in the Social and Moral Reform Council, which had supported passage of the Act in 1912, but so did the churches, women's organizations, dental and medical associations, teachers and lawyers. Saskatchewan legislators cannot have been blind to the economic impact of their Act,[232] but white restaurant owners were hardly conspicuous in the reform campaign or, for that matter, in the economy. If economic motives were present, they too must have been related to a general perception rather than an immediate threat.

Legally the Supreme Court did not need to decide as it did. No immoral incident served as a precipitating event. Economically there was no apparent urgency to disarm Chinese competition. The situation existing about the year 1914 fails to deliver a convincing explanation for the Saskatchewan Act or the Supreme Court decision. They must be understood, first, in the context of a momentum already established, which was producing increasing animosity towards Chinese because of dangers they seemed to pose to the welfare of white Canadians. In addition, any trends of which the *Quong Wing* decision formed a part can only be revealed through the history of subsequent developments relating to Chinese in Canada. The history to which *Quong Wing* belongs neither began nor ended in 1914. What happened after 1914 is equally essential to any explanation.

Judicial developments, to take one obvious example, confirmed the movement away from *Bryden* and indicated that *Quong Wing* was a stage rather than an end in a process. Depriving Chinese of their means of subsistence, denied by *Bryden* and accepted by *Quong Wing* only in disguise, became an admitted principle in 1923. Reference has already been made to BC orders-in-council in 1902 permitting Crown leases only upon the provision that Chinese and Japanese must not be employed on or in connection with the lease thus granted. In 1913 the Dominion Parliament ratified an Anglo-Japanese treaty which stated, in part, that subjects of each contracting party "shall in all that relates to the pursuit of their industries, callings, professions, and educational studies be placed in all respects on the same footing as the subjects of the most favoured nation."[233] Since treaty obligations are federal under the *BNA Act*, Ottawa seemed bound to disallow the discriminatory provincial orders. A referral to the BC Court of Appeal in 1920[234] produced the opinion that the provincial orders were *ultra vires*, whereupon the BC legislature passed an *Oriental Orders in Council Validation Act* which was, in turn, referred to the Supreme Court of Canada.[235] Justice Idington argued that *Quong Wing* must logically lead to a decision in favour of the province,[236] and Justice Brodeur agreed that, insofar as Chinese were concerned, *Quong Wing* would make the Act *intra vires*. But Brodeur joined the majority in finding the exclusion of Japanese to be clearly within federal authority and so the Act as a whole was invalidated.

The question reached the Judicial Committee of the Privy Council in 1923 via an action by Brooks-Bidlake and Whittal, Limited, whose timber licence was cancelled by provincial authorities because the company employed Chinese and Japanese labour on its Crown lease.[237] The Privy Council upheld the cancellation because the province was authorized to set conditions on its own property (timber leases), and secondly, since the company had employed both Chinese and Japanese any conflict with the *Japanese Treaty Act* was irrelevant: the anti-Chinese condition having been broken was alone sufficient cause to rescind the lease. The right of a province to pass a racially discriminatory act within its legislative fields was firmly upheld, even if it threatened the livelihood of the "races" involved. Though *Quong Wing* was not cited in *Brooks-Bidlake*, it is apparent that the Privy Council was giving its retroactive approval to the spirit of the Supreme Court's 1914 decision.

Legislative developments confirmed the same trend. In 1922 the House of Commons debated the proposition that

in the opinion of this House, the immigration of oriental aliens and their rapid multiplication is becoming a serious menace to living conditions, particularly on the Pacific Coast, and to the future of the country in general, and the Government should take immediate action with a view to securing the effective restriction of future immigration of this type.[238]

Although the $500 head tax had been immediately effective in discouraging Chinese immigration, it had also made the contracting system unprofitable since a contractor would have to advance such a large sum to procure entry for each labourer. With the "middleman" removed and labour supplies reduced, wages for Chinese in Canada began to increase, and as they reached an average of $60 or $70 per month it became feasible for an individual already in Canada to assist the immigration of a relative and for the new immigrant to repay the tax in about two years. From only eight individuals in 1904, Chinese immigration numbers rose to 7,445 in 1913 and then, after a wartime interruption, reached 4,333 in 1919. The consequence was renewed pressure on Parliament to find a new measure to exclude Chinese immigration, and ultimately to enact the *Chinese Immigration Act* of 1923,[239] which abolished the head tax but which banned all Chinese from entering Canada except students, merchants, diplomats and Canadian-born returnees.

Under the new Act merchants lost the privilege of bringing in their wives and minor children, a change which indicates that the admission of the merchants, like the diplomats and students, was based on the assumption that they would not become permanent residents of Canada. When the government's bill reached the Senate, Wellington B. Willoughby, now a senator from Moose Jaw, moved an amendment to permit Chinese merchants to bring their families. "[I]n the interest of the comity of nations and for the sake of preserving the moral position of the Chinamen in the country, it might be wise to grant this privilege. We all recognize that among the best Chinamen the family tie is one that is regarded sacredly."[240] The reaction to Senator Willoughby's suggestion was universally hostile. In a characteristic response, Senator Robert F. Green from Victoria commented:

The mind of the Chinaman is absolutely different from the mind of the ordinary white man. You cannot in any possible way find out just how the Chinese mind works. It is very true that in a way the Chinese are good citizens. They make good domestic servants and faithful workers, but they will never help us to build up a Canada of which we will be proud. Anyone who knows the Chinese knows perfectly well that our race will never intermarry with them nor assimilate them. . . . They practise polygamy, and when a Chinaman has several wives, how are you going to single out one and say that she may come in and the others may not? I hope, hon. gentlemen, you will protect us from this evil and let the Bill go through as it stands.[241]

In the total absence of support from his colleagues Willoughby withdrew his amendment and the government's *Chinese Immigration Act* passed intact.

That same year parliament passed a consolidated *Opium and Narcotic Drug Act*[242] incorporating recent amendments which dramatically increased the penalties for possession of opium, including whipping and deportation. Public and parliamentary opinion had been moved in this direction by a book published in 1922 by Magistrate Emily Murphy, *The Black Candle*, consisting in part of articles written for *Maclean's* magazine in 1920. Murphy's primary target was the Chinese opium user, though she also referred frequently to "blackamoors" or "gen'lemen of color," and their most heinous crime was the entrapment of white women into addiction and prostitution. The book's photographs showed white women in compromising positions with Asian or African men, and Murphy noted meaningfully that more than 75 percent of all drug arrests involved Chinese suspects.[243] Warning white women in particular to beware of association with Chinese, Murphy exclaimed "Yes! it is quite certain we do not understand these people from the Orient, nor what ideas are hid behind their dark inscrutable faces."[244]

The sentiments behind these enactments were expressed more specifically in the refinement and prosecution of laws prohibiting Chinese from employing white females. In 1919 Saskatchewan dropped its explicit reference to Chinese from the *Female Labour Act*, but the intention was that municipalities should refuse licences to Chinese establishments applying to employ white women.[245] In August 1924 Yee Clun applied to the Regina city council for a licence to employ white women in his restaurant and rooming house, claiming that because of the new *Chinese Immigration Act* there was a shortage of Chinese males available to hire.[246] Council deferred the application until its next meeting, allowing the women's reform movement in Regina to mobilize its opposition. The WCTU convened a special meeting to pass a resolution that "it was not in the best interests of the young womanhood of the city to grant the request," and representatives were assigned to attend the next council meeting to oppose Yee Clun's licence.[247] The Women's Labor Council and the Local Council of Women also voted to oppose this and any licence for a Chinese to employ a white woman.[248] When council met two weeks later about 20 women were present. The leader of the Women's Labor League delegation warned that "Employment of white women by Chinese might lead to mesalliances," and that Regina's claim to be "Queen City of the West" could be corrupted to "queer city of the west."[249] Another deferral postponed consideration until the October council meeting, where a lawyer hired by the Local Council of Women quoted Emily Murphy to illustrate the dangers of opium and entrapment waiting for white women in Chinese restaurants. In the face of such opposition, council ignored the advice of its own solicitor and rejected Yee Clun's application.[250] With the support of the Regina Chinese community Yee Clun thereupon sued the city.[251]

In the Saskatchewan Court of King's Bench, Justice Philip Mackenzie heard council members admit that their reason for refusing Yee Clun's licence was that he employed "a number of Chinamen on his premises" and "they feared that such employees would constitute a menace to the virtue of white women."[252] Justice Mackenzie found this a fallacious argument for, he reasoned, had Yee Clun employed "an equal number of white men" rather than Chinese, "the menace to the virtue of the white women might well be greater ... since there would exist no racial antipathy to be overcome between them and the white men."[253] He concluded "that the council really refused the licence in this case upon racial grounds," and since the 1919 amendment had explicitly eliminated "race," "It would be strange if the municipalities to which has been delegated authority of granting such special licences could now go on and maintain the discriminatory principle which the Legislature had been at such pains to abolish."[254] He therefore ordered that the licence be granted to Yee Clun. But Justice Mackenzie's impeccable logic caused him to misread the legislature's intent.[255] Soon after the *Yee Clun* decision, and to avoid its repetition, the Saskatchewan legislature amended the *Female Employment Act* so that a city council could refuse a licence at its own discretion without giving any reasons, and to remove any licence already granted.[256] The legislature's intent, unchanged since 1912, was made quite clear.

British Columbia had also removed the explicit racial qualification from its 1923 *Women and Girls' Protection Act*, but to acquire a licence owners had to satisfy the police that no threats to the morals of white (or native Indian) women lurked on the premises. The law was indifferently enforced until the mid-1930s, when a violent crime involving a Chinese suspect and a white female victim prompted Vancouver city officials to begin warning Chinese restaurants that they must dismiss their white female employees or lose their licences. In September 1937 Vancouver council suspended the licences of three Chinese cafes when it was discovered that they continued to employ white waitresses. The owners, one of whom was president of the Chinese Benevolent Association, threatened to sue, but a compromise was reached whereby the Chinese agreed to fire the waitresses and drop the court action and the city would restore the licences. The former waitresses, whose own jobs had disappeared in the course of these negotiations, appeared before city council on 12 October 1937 to plead for the restoration of their jobs. "We must live and heaven knows if a girl is inclined to go wrong she can do it just as readily on Granville Street as she can down here [in Chinatown]," they argued. Denying the validity of the threat to their morals, the waitresses alleged that racial discrimination underlay the city's action. Mayor George Miller declared, "It is ridiculous to suggest that there was racial discrimination," and the women's plea was rejected.[257] A year later another Chinese restaurant was discovered with a white waitress and its licence was suspended, being restored only after the waitress was fired.

Chief Constable W. W. Foster was asked to conduct an investigation into whether employment by Chinese was a verifiable threat to women's morals. In his March 1939 report Chief Foster wrote: "In view of the conditions under which the girls are expected to work it is almost impossible for them to be so employed without falling victims to some form of immoral life."[258] Early in 1943 the League of Women Voters asked Vancouver city for a by-law to prohibit Chinese from employing white women. Mayor Cornett replied that a by-law was not necessary because "there was a gentleman's agreement with the proprietors of Chinese cafes not to hire white girls."[259]

The most bizarre developments in the same direction occurred in Ontario. When the *Act to Amend the Factory, Shop and Office Building Act*, containing the anti-Chinese clause, was given assent on 1 May 1914, its enforcement was held in abeyance by Section 2 (2), which declared that the law "shall not come into force until a day to be named by proclamation of the Lieutenant-Governor-in-Council."[260] Acting Premier J. J. Foy explained to a TLC delegation that because Saskatchewan's Act had been appealed to the Privy Council (as was then believed), Ontario would not proclaim its own version until and unless a favourable decision was received from London.[261] In the event the Privy Council refused to hear the case, the "bring forward" signal was not triggered, and Ontario's law lay unproclaimed or at least unacknowledged for over a decade.[262] Then in 1927 Ontario consolidated its laws in the *Revised Statutes of Ontario* which were, according to custom, proclaimed as a body. Included was RSO 1927 c. 275, *The Factory, Shop and Office Building Act*, Section 30 of which outlawed the employment of white women by Chinese.

On 22 August 1928 the *Toronto Star* announced in a heading that "White Girls Cannot Work for Orientals." The accompanying story explained that Mayor Sam McBride had "received many letters from citizens asking that the provision in the Statutes prohibiting this be enforced," and that his worship would "set in motion the machinery of the law." Nine days later, amidst reports that Chinese were actually being prosecuted, Consul Chow Kwo Hsien wrote to Premier Howard Ferguson protesting the act as "inconsistent with Anglo-Saxon sense of justice and fairplay" and adding a threat that Ontario's intransigence "might be followed by retaliatory measures in China."[263] No satisfactory answer was received, and a personal visit with the premier and attorney general failed to produce any amendment.[264] Chow then contacted Ottawa asking for a federal disallowance since the Ontario Act was contrary to treaties between Great Britain and China.[265] Federal mandarins were impressed with the consul's determination "to agitate this matter to the fullest extent of his power." The deputy minister of Justice wrote to his Ontario counterpart: "it seems to me extraordinary that a section which the Legislature declared should not come into force until proclaimed should be brought into force by the mere fact that the Commissioners included it in the revision."[266] The Ontario attorney general was prepared only to promise "to do our best to see that prosecutions are not instituted against Chinese for past offences if the Chinese will obey the law in the future."[267] A solicitor engaged by the Chinese consulate, urging federal disallowance, wrote that in 1914 Chinese restaurants had "operated as gambling houses and opium dens," but there had been no allegations of a similar nature since that time. "No one even noticed" the law until August 1928.[268]

Press reaction was mixed. *Labour* pronounced that organized labour "has long sought this regulation and it expects the Ontario government to enforce the law."[269] The Toronto *Globe,* in an editorial entitled "End this Stupid Statute," reiterated its longstanding position "that indiscriminate mixing of different colours and races is criminally unwise," but on the other hand "To lump all Chinese . . . as a class of invariable moral degenerates is . . . hideously unjust." The telling point for the *Globe* was that Britain was at that moment renegotiating "the miscalled unequal treaties which were designed to secure fair play for British subjects in China." At this delicate moment Ontario's "pinpricks" could upset the Chinese; the Nationalist foreign minister had already protested, and retaliation must not be ruled out. Since the law was never intended, and was only "included by oversight" in the 1927 revision, the *Globe* called for its withdrawal.[270]

Between these two positions fell an article in the December 1928 *Chatelaine.* Announcing that "The old problem of the employment of white women by Chinese establishments has come up again, brought to light by a no less portentous occurrence than an error in the setting of the statute books of Ontario!,"[271] the article presented comments representing different points of view. A report from the National Council of Women's Committee on Trades and Professions for Women outlined the various provincial restrictions and concluded,

The bar raised by the statute is not for the purpose of discriminating against an Oriental race but inasmuch as Orientals have not Oriental women in this country and as naturally an employee is more or less under the control of her or his employer, this Act protects the white girls and is passed for their protection only.

The NCWC committee turned up no evidence of actual harmful treatment, however, and added that waitresses were more likely to be annoyed by their white patrons than by Chinese employers. The *Chatelaine* reporter commented that in circumstances where a white patron was "intent on mischief," the Chinese employer would be unable to "surround female employees with security and good influences" because the white man would never "respect the authority of a Chinaman." A missionary to the Toronto Chinese community scoffed at the idea that Chinese could be a threat since their civilization instilled profound respect for law and order, and he mentioned that the white waitresses whom he had interviewed in Toronto "feel no need of protection and resent interference with their liberty of action." Magistrate Helen Gregory MacGill approved of the protection of women, but thought it wrong to single out a particular "race" as the source of danger. The *Chatelaine* article, too, accepted the premise that Canadian women required "moral as well as industrial protection," and did not so much object to the legislation as complain that it did not go far enough to secure its stated purpose. What was needed, according to *Chatelaine*, was a proper national program addressing the "growing problem" of "women placed in circumstances prejudicial to their welfare." "A scattered bit of provincial legislation here and there, discriminating against one race, will do little to remove undesirable conditions in any quarter."

The federal government considered its options. Because the offending statute was part of the RSO, already proclaimed and in force, it would be necessary to disallow the entire body of Revised Statutes and this would leave the province of Ontario lawless. Disallowance was therefore not a serious consideration.[272] China pressured London to lean on Ottawa to coerce Toronto into cancelling the law.[273] External Affairs and the federal Department of Labour did a study.[274] The Chinese consul visited the acting prime minister, Ernest Lapointe, on two occasions.[275] Eventually Ontario found a compromise: the Act would not be cancelled, but it would be put back on the shelf. The Ontario legislature amended the Act, reinstating the subsection which provided that the Chinese restriction "shall not come into force until a day to be named by the Lieutenant-Governor by his proclamation," and gave it retroactive effect from 31 December 1927 when the Revised Statutes were proclaimed.[276] The undersecretary of state for External Affairs advised the Chinese government "according to the amendment made recently by the Ontario Legislature, the prohibitive clause can only be made effective by Proclamation and until and unless a Proclamation has been issued it is not in force."[277]

This may have settled the international controversy, but complaints that Toronto police continued to prosecute Chinese under the retracted law were still being reported in October 1929.[278]

It is apparent that the public, press, courts, legislatures and law-enforcement agencies of Canada continued to perceive Chinese as a threat, and continued to countenance discriminatory restrictions against them. The *Quong Wing* decision was not an aberration, and not a product of a particular coincidence of circumstances. The forces opposed to the Chinese culminated not in 1914 but in 1923, the year of *Brooks-Bidlake* and of the new *Chinese Immigration Act* which effectively ended further Chinese immigration until its repeal in 1947. In Moose Jaw itself the sentiments perceptible in Quong Wing's prosecution would climax on 7 June 1927, when Canada's first and largest Ku Klux Klan Konclave burned a 60-foot cross on Caribou Street and a crowd of 10,000 heard demands that River Street be cleaned up and Moose Jaw made safe for Anglo-Saxon Protestants. "One flag, One language, One race, One religion, Race purity and Moral rectitude" was the cry, and to that end an immediate ban on marriage between white women and "Negroes, Chinese or Japanese." The Klan donated a ward for the Moose Jaw hospital, and to it was affixed a plaque dedicating it to "Confederation . . . Our Public Schools, Law and Order, Separation of Church and State, Freedom of Speech and Press, White Supremacy."[279]

It may be instructive to examine the impact of these restrictions and popular attitudes upon the Chinese themselves. In the first place, the Chinese population of Canada continued to grow as, in particular, did that of Saskatchewan. The 1921 census showed 36,924 Chinese, 2,613 of them in Saskatchewan (of whom only 39 were female), a provincial increase of almost 200 percent during a period for most of which an explicit anti-Chinese law was in force. By 1931, the rate of growth slowed by the 1923 immigration act, Canada had 40,254 Chinese and Saskatchewan 3,221. Especially interesting is the continued Chinese trend toward the hotel, restaurant and laundry industries. In 1921, 50 percent of Saskatchewan Chinese were employed in restaurants (as owners, cooks or waiters); in 1931 this had increased to 70 percent. Most of the remainder were owners or employees of laundries and hotels/rooming houses; 90 percent of Chinese men and 100 percent of Chinese women in Saskatchewan were engaged in typical (or stereotypical) service industries in 1931.[280] This was occurring despite the existence of laws and licensing restrictions that prevented Chinese from hiring white women. The restrictions obviously were not sufficient to discourage Chinese from entering the targeted industries or to drive them out of the province. Even Quong Wing, whose personal discouragement must have been considerable, remained in Moose Jaw in his restaurant. In 1915 both he and Quong Sing were among the 25 board members of the newly incorporated "Eastern Club."[281] In May 1916 Jasper Fish was still trying to collect for costs incurred by the Crown in the Saskatchewan Supreme Court: Justice Brown, with Justice Newlands concurring, had recommended "The appeal in each case should, therefore, be dismissed, with costs," Chief Justice Haultain wished the magistrate's conviction to be reversed, and Justice Lamont affirmed the conviction without mentioning costs. The formal judgment did not provide for costs, and Mr. Fish sought "to have the said omission corrected." There is no record that Quong Wing ever paid.[282]

The question remains whether this subsequent history can help to interpret the 1914 decision, or perhaps vice versa. One thing that seems to emerge is that the "economic or moral" distinction is too simple. If the motivation were purely economic, then surely the failure of the "white female" tactic to limit Chinese restaurants and laundries must have prompted a more effective method; yet none was attempted. Instead, laws which clearly did not impede the spread of Chinese laundries and restaurants were more urgently enforced, often at the insistence of white women's organizations with no possible economic benefits to themselves. *Brooks-Bidlake* had an openly economic purpose: the restrictions on BC Crown leases, upheld by the Privy Council, pretended no other goal than the exclusion of Chinese and Japanese from certain fields of employment. But the employment, and the fear, of Chinese labour did not occur in isolation; they were connected to a conceptual climate that allowed Chinese workers to be rendered a separate category at all, "cheap" or otherwise. *Quong Wing* and *Brooks-Bidlake*, *Bryden* and *Tomey Homma* were not contradictions or coincidences but glimpses of a common phenomenon. White females, too, constituted a distinct category, whose unique characteristics required special consideration. The moral issue was dependent on a "natural" female condition of vulnerability, and a specific Chinese threat could not have survived, in the absence of any real incidents, without a belief in that general condition.

There were many identifiable historical circumstances contributing to the Quong Wing episode: imported prejudices, economic interests, cultural differences, geographical isolation, social movements. By overlapping the histories of two of the human categories, "race" and gender, *Quong Wing* revealed that there was something connecting those ingredients, making them meaningful and consistent, making "sense." That was an underlying understanding of human behaviour as biologically driven, a world view receptive to interpreting differences as permanent and to accommodating differential legal treatment for the allegedly discrete units of humanity. A person's "race" could account for simpler wants and for a "servile" personality, which in turn caused that person to accept lower wages and hence present a threat to members of more "civilized races." A person's "race" accounted for the "instinct" for democratic institutions or for despotisms of the Oriental type, and hence could present a threat to Canadian democracy. A person's "race" was indelible, and if lower "races" were allowed to pollute the higher, through intermarriage or seduction, the result would be the weakening of the superior strain. Male and female gender characteristics were similarly perceived to be fixed and natural, and to require distinctive treatment. Companies like Union Colliery and Brooks-Bidlake did not deny the conventional belief in "race" by seeking to hire Chinese and Japanese; on the contrary, they affirmed it and merely sought to profit by it. Note that even Justice Philip Mackenzie, who decided in favour of Yee Clun's licence to employ white women, assumed that a "racial antipathy" would protect white women from succumbing to the seduction of Orientals. BC attorney general Alex Manson encapsulated this world view when he told the provincial legislature in 1922:

the real objection to [the Oriental] and the one that is permanent and incurable is that there is an ethnological difference which cannot be overcome. The two races cannot mix and I believe our first duty is to our own people. . . . It is a matter of our own domestic affairs that we should endeavour to protect the white race from the necessity of intermingling with Oriental blood, and I think we have every warrant for fighting to prevent a situation that will inevitably result in race deterioration.[283]

Scholars of "race" who concentrate on British Columbia may conclude that the "Oriental menace" was the combination of locally explicable circumstances and events. Because *Quong Wing* was launched in Saskatchewan and confirmed in Ottawa, where those or similar events had far less purchase, the decision requires a confrontation with forces at work across Canada which cannot be explained in terms of self-interest, fear of being overwhelmed numerically, industrial relations or site-specific stereotypes. When placed in a longer-term and a national context, *Quong Wing* reveals the existence of a broad sensibility that to admit Chinese and similar minorities was to risk Canada's future as a free British democracy where equality of opportunity and an honest reward for hard work could be the guarantee of every citizen. The Supreme Court in 1914, sharing that vision of Canada and victim to that ideology of "race," could justify its decision according to the moral standards then intact. John Idington had the same vision for Canada, but he recognized, in terms readily acceptable to the modern reader, that racial inequality would in itself undermine the democratic future of Canada. In 1914, he was in the minority.

Fifteen years after *Quong Wing*, the Saskatchewan government established a Royal Commission on Immigration and Settlement to set priorities for the future population of the province. In its 1930 Report the Commission revealed that a biological world view continued to shape public policy: "We desire only those racial elements that can make a contribution to our common citizenship, and keep alive the proud traditions and high respect for law which have characterized at all times the British race."[284]

11. *QUONG WING* AS PRECEDENT

For the social historian, *Quong Wing* is most significant for the insight it provides into the history of racial attitudes in Canada, and the support lent to those attitudes by Canadian public institutions. Yet as a legal precedent *Quong Wing* has not featured in "race-related" cases. After the *Japanese Treaty Act* decisions early in the 1920s,[285] it has been used virtually exclusively in cases with a constitutional implication, and used in ways remote from anything contemplated by the Moose Jaw restaurant keeper when he resisted a discriminatory law by challenging its constitutionality. *Quong Wing* has helped to convict a Winnipeg dance hall owner on a gambling charge,[286] keep non-resident Americans from buying certain properties in Prince Edward Island,[287] confirm the legality of Nova Scotia's film censorship board,[288] uphold British Columbia's *Holiday Shopping Regulation Act*,[289] close a "biotherapy clinic" in Montreal[290] and allow a PEI couple convicted of welfare fraud to stay out of jail.[291] In every instance *Quong Wing* was enlisted to determine whether a particular law was within the jurisdiction of the body that passed it. This subsequent legal career lends credibility to the interpretation of *Quong Wing* as a division of powers case, and perhaps has helped to obscure its original role in racializing Canadian law. One of those later cases elicited an interesting comment from Chief Justice Bora Laskin, in which he seemed to declare that the Privy Council's *Bryden* decision was wrong:

I would not myself have thought that the mere prohibition against employment of Chinese persons in underground mining could be taken to be a general prohibition against their earning a living in British Columbia and, however distasteful such legislation was, that it was beyond provincial jurisdiction.[292]

Although he refrained from approving *Quong Wing* explicitly, still the chief justice's comment suggested that his predecessors in 1914 were correct to sustain a provincial law, however distasteful, that fell within provincial jurisdiction. The implications Justice Idington had found in the "ordinary rights" of a British subject had not prevailed.

The provincial laws restraining Chinese men and white women from working together have all been repealed.[293] For the Canadian courts *Quong Wing* has ceased to have any relationship to "race" or even to morality; rather, it helps to define a specific corner of provincial jurisdiction and this gives it a continuing utility. To the lay person it may be interesting to find that a decision which had the effect of upholding racial inequality should still be employable in constitutional cases. The explanation lies exactly in the fact that *Quong Wing* has been divorced from the "race" issue; it has laid divergent trails for jurists and historians. But while *Quong Wing* has long since lost its racial implications, this does not mean that racial discrimination disappeared from Canadian society or the courts. Another and even more overtly racial question would be brought before the Supreme Court of Canada in 1939, in *Christie v. York Corporation.*

3

Christie v. York Corporation

1. THE INCIDENT

The characteristics that Canadians often associated with Chinese, and that were used to justify discriminatory treatment, could not be applied to African Canadians. Black people were not "aliens," either legally or culturally. They did not live in male enclaves or indulge in suspicious pastimes. They did not speak a foreign language or owe allegiance to a foreign state. They were not exotic or inscrutible in their dress, diet or religion. On the contrary, people of African descent had been in Canada for generations, lived in family units, attended Christian churches, spoke English and/or French, fought on behalf of king and empire in every war since the American Revolution and publicly comported themselves according to the norms established by the majority society. The only significant distinguishing characteristic was colour. And yet African Canadians were subjected to restrictions in employment, housing, education, services and recreation. Chiefly they were set apart and kept down, marginalized as neighbours, as employees and as citizens. With only a few exceptions the law did not *impose* segregation and inequality on African Canadians; rather, the law upheld the right of Canadian individuals, organizations and institutions to discriminate on grounds of "race." The most significant statement in support of this situation came from the Supreme Court of Canada in the case of *Christie v. York*.[1]

The notes for this chapter are on pages 378-94.

Fred Christie was a black man, a chauffeur by occupation, a member of the Union (United) Church, a resident of Montreal for over 20 years when the incident in question occurred. A tall man with a fit and healthy demeanour, impeccably clean and well-dressed, Mr. Christie is described as having the deportment of a gentleman and an impressive manner in his carriage and speech. In complexion he was pale brown.[2] Born in Jamaica in 1902, he migrated to Montreal as a teenager at the end of World War I. His Jamaican accent had long since been modified, but its legacy was a precise way of speaking which added to his courtly and dignified air. Among his Canadian acquisitions was a passion for the sport of ice hockey. He had a season ticket to a box seat at the Montreal Forum, and he rarely missed a game.[3]

In the spring of 1936 the York Tavern moved from its previous location into the ground floor of the Montreal Forum. To announce its move the tavern took out newspaper advertisements and displayed a large sign inviting the public to visit its new premises and taste its wares. Fred Christie and his friends had often enjoyed a glass of beer in the old York Tavern, which had been located just to the north of the largest concentration of black population in Montreal. The new location, however, brought with it a new policy: management instructed the staff that under no circumstances were "Negroes" to be served.[4]

On the evening of Saturday July 11, 1936, Mr. Christie and two friends, Emile King and Steven St. Jean, entered the Forum to attend a hockey game. Mr. King was a Texas-born African American who had lived in Montreal for 19 years and was employed as a butler. Mr. St. Jean was a French-Canadian salesman. They often attended athletic events together. At Christie's invitation the three friends decided to stop for a beer before the game. He had no reason to suspect that they might be unwelcome. A waiter approached and Fred Christie placed a 50-cent piece on the table, politely ordering "three steins of beer." The waiter responded, "Gentlemen, I am very sorry I cannot serve colored people." Mr. Christie asked, "Why? Since when?" "It is an order from the manager," he was told. Incredulous, Christie demanded an interview with the manager. First to arrive was bartender George Gressie, who confirmed that ever since the tavern opened in the Forum its policy had been to refuse service to black people. Christie insisted on seeing someone more senior, and eventually assistant manager Roméo Lajoie was brought to the table. Quietly and politely, so that neighbouring tables could not overhear, Mr. Lajoie explained to the party that even had he wanted to, he was not permitted by the York Corporation's regulations to accommodate "colored" men in the tavern. "Is that the only reason?" Christie asked. "Yes," said Lajoie. His demeanour slipping, Christie stalked to a pay telephone just outside the tavern and called the police. Apparently anticipating some disorder, the two constables who responded were less than tactful, alerting the crowd of 70 patrons to the dispute at the Christie table. In the presence of the police witnesses Mr. Christie again insisted on being served. Mr. Lajoie repeated his polite refusal one last time. The policemen, whose impatience was directed more at Christie than Lajoie, said there was absolutely nothing they could do. They left, followed by Fred Christie and his two friends.[5]

Fred Christie and Emile King were no strangers to racial discrimination, but they were outraged by this incident. Like most other African Canadians in Montreal, they had learned which shops and theatres to avoid, which jobs were unavailable, which residential districts would exclude them. But when they expected service, in an establishment so publicly located, they felt betrayed and humiliated. The "colour line" had advanced toward them, or so it seemed, and they decided it was time to fight back.[6] Confident that they had an absolute right to equality and insulted at the inferiority implied by their rejection, Christie and King decided to sue the York Tavern for the humiliation they had suffered.[7]

2. "JIM CROW" IN CANADA

An 1891 magazine article predicted that "to the end of time Africa will bless Canada for the refuge and home given to her children in that period of their trouble and trial."[8] New World slavery was undoubtedly a period of trouble for the children of Africa, but Canada's innocence was less obvious than the quotation might suggest. Between 1628 and the first decade of the 19th century, approximately 3,000 people of African origin were held as slaves in what is now Canada, their status duly noted in the legal documents of the times.[9] As late as 1808 the Nova Scotia Assembly debated a "Bill for regulating Negro Servitude," prompted by a petition from slave owners seeking to confirm the legality of slavery.[10] Nor did the extinction of slavery bring equality to Canada's black population. In his classic description of American racial segregation, *The Strange Career of Jim Crow*, C. Vann Woodward identified the areas of life where legalized segregation tended to apply following the end of slavery in the United States. He listed "churches and schools," "housing and jobs," "eating and drinking," "public transportation," "sports and recreations," "hospitals, orphanages, prisons and asylums" and, in death, "funeral homes, morgues and cemeteries."[11] In virtually every one of these areas of life and death, African Canadians too experienced exclusion and separation from mainstream institutions, amounting to a Canadian version of "Jim Crow."

Canada's free black community dates from the American Revolution, when British officials promised freedom and equality to rebel-owned slaves who joined the Loyalist cause. Over 3,500 black Loyalists were transported to the Maritimes during the British evacuation from the new republic in 1783. They were settled on the fringes of larger white towns, close enough to offer their daily labour yet far enough to maintain social distinctions. The legacy of slavery consigned them to a labouring and service role, and they would never receive the recognition and rewards as Loyalists that their service during the war had earned them.[12] They were joined during the War of 1812 by more than 2,000 other former American slaves, known as the black Refugees, who similarly had fled to the British upon a wartime promise of land and freedom.[13] In their segregated settlements the free African Canadians continued to experience a barrier defined by their colour, doomed to menial employment, denied access to public institutions, locked in poverty. Discrimination and disadvantage were mutually reinforcing, as the consequences of restricted opportunity were attributed to racial inferiority.

Elsewhere in Canada the patterns of black settlement were less abrupt than in the Maritimes, but the "refuge and home" eulogized in 1891 were never untarnished. Tens of thousands of fugitive American slaves migrated to Ontario in the decades leading up to the American Civil War; almost 1,000 others moved from California to Vancouver Island. Social separation and economic deprivation destroyed the dreams of the American runaways who crossed the border expecting a sanctuary not just from slavery but from the inequalities imposed by racism. Approximately three quarters of them returned to the American South after Emancipation.[14] It was not until the new century that black migration to Canada was resumed. Between 1900 and 1912 about 1,300 blacks from Oklahoma settled in Alberta and Saskatchewan, but rejection and harassment ensured that the renewed movement was brief.[15]

Throughout the period when white Canadians prided themselves for offering a haven to African Americans, negative stereotypes rendered a positive reception virtually impossible. In 1815 the Nova Scotian Assembly observed the arrival of the black Refugees "with concern, and alarm," and passed a resolution "to prohibit the bringing any more of these people, into this Colony." Their reason, the resolution explained, was that the proportion of Africans already in this country is productive of many inconveniences; and that the introduction of more must tend to the discouragement of white labourers and servants, as well as the establishment of a separate and marked class of people, unsuited by nature to this climate, or to an association with the rest of his Majesty's Colonists.[16]

Apart from the implication that African people must be labourers and servants, a direct product of black slavery, the resolution reveals an acceptance of the notion that blacks and whites were separate classes who could not suitably associate with one another. Such ideas prevailed throughout British North America. The Upper Canadian Assembly received petitions as early as 1830, when the "Underground Railroad" was just beginning, calling for restrictions on black settlement in the province because of the African Americans' alleged degradation and defects of character.[17] During American Reconstruction, between 1865 and 1877, Canadian newspapers regarded the Southern experiment in racial equality with an interest, and often a horror, that directly reflected the conventional wisdom. Reconstruction was doomed to failure because of the former slaves' inherent laziness. "If they work at all, they will do just enough to secure themselves from starvation," proclaimed a typical editorial. As natural servants, black people could not operate without white direction. Careful supervision was required as well to curb the "animal passions" of African sexuality which could burst forth in "demoniacal rage and lust." Above all, the "instinctive feelings of repugnance" that whites naturally held toward blacks made "mixing and even association" of whites and blacks unthinkable.[18]

What was true in the United States must be true in Canada. Writing in the popular *Canada and Its Provinces* series, Superintendent of Immigration W. D. Scott maintained that "The negro problem, which faces the United States and which Abraham Lincoln said could be settled only by shipping one and all back to a tract of land in Africa, is one in which Canadians have no desire to share."[19] Or as the Toronto *Mail and Empire* bluntly asserted, "If negroes and white people cannot live in accord in the South, they cannot live in accord in the North."[20] These and similar attitudes existed quite independently of personal experience. When 16 black men arrived in Virden, Manitoba, in the summer of 1908 they found "the farmers in the neighbourhood have a strong objection to the employment of coloured labour."[21] Despite the fact that no black people had ever been through Virden before, the mayor explained that "farmers' wives are afraid of them."[22] The most dramatic expression of similar sentiments came from the Edmonton chapter of the Imperial Order of the Daughters of the Empire. In March 1911 the chapter met in emergency session to consider "the influx of Negroes" from Oklahoma then in progress. They sent a petition to Immigration Minister Frank Oliver:

We view with alarm the continuous and rapid influx of Negro settlers into Northern Alberta and believe that their coming will bring about serious social and political conditions.

This immigration will have the immediate effect of discouraging white settlement in the vicinity of the Negro farms and will depreciate the value of all holdings in such areas.

We fear that the welcome extended to those now coming will induce a very large black population to follow them.

The problems likely to arise with the establishment of these people in our thinly populated province must be plain to all, and the experience of the United States should warn us to take action before the situation becomes complicated and before the inevitable racial antipathies shall have sprung up.

We do not wish that the fair fame of Western Canada would be sullied with the shadow of Lynch Law but we have no guarantee that our women will be safer in their scattered homesteads than white women in other countries with a Negro population.

We would therefore urge upon the Government the need for immediate action and the taking of all possible steps to stop Negro immigration into Alberta.[23]

In line with the same sexual mythology, Mrs. Isobel Graham, described as a "Manitoba suffragist," wrote in the *Grain Growers' Guide* of 3 May 1911 that atrocities would inevitably be committed by African-American immigrants against white Canadian women, and warned that lynching and even burning at the stake would become necessary.[24] Dr. Ella Synge, speaking on behalf of prairie women, pointed to "the enormous increase in outrages on white women that has occurred" in South Africa as a result of liberal British policies, and predicted that "the finger of fate is pointing to lynch law which will be the ultimate result, as sure as we allow such people to settle among us."[25]

When members of parliament raised the concerns of their African-Canadian constituents that black immigrants were being excluded on grounds of colour, the federal government denied that any policy existed to refuse entrance on grounds of "race, colour, or previous condition of servitude," but Minister Frank Oliver admitted that

there are many cases where the admission or exclusion of an immigrant depends on a strict or a lax interpretation of the law, so that if the immigrant is of what we would call the desirable class it may be that they are administered laxly, and if he is of the presumably less desirable class then they are administered more restrictedly.[26]

When the minister rejected the suggestion, being proposed in the popular press, that a restrictive head tax be imposed to discourage black immigration, MP William Thoburn from the Ontario riding of Lanark cried out in the House of Commons: "I would like to ask the government if they think it in the interests of Canada that we should have negro colonization in our Canadian Northwest? Would it not be preferable to preserve for the sons of Canada the lands they propose to give to niggers?"[27]

Sentiments such as these readily explain the substantial extent of racial segregation in Canada. The most significant area of separation, at least in legislative terms, was in education.[28] In Nova Scotia the *Education Act* of 1836 permitted local commissioners to establish separate schools for "Blacks or People of Colour."[29] Since the black schools were irregularly funded by special legislative grants and charitable donations, teachers and equipment were inevitably inferior and educational quality suffered. Black parents organized protests against the limitations placed upon their children, culminating in an 1883 petition campaign demanding the full integration of provincial schools. This precipitated a debate in the legislature, resulting in amendments to the *School Act* in 1884 and a partial but significant victory for African Canadians. The revised Act continued to permit school commissioners to establish segregated facilities, but added that "colored pupils shall not be excluded from instruction in the public school in the section or ward where they reside."[30] In the city of Halifax this provision gained African-Canadian youths access to secondary education for the first time. A later section of the 1884 Act was less helpful, stipulating that no school receiving special aid could hire a teacher with anything higher than a fourth-class certificate.[31] Since every all-black school in the province at that time received provincial aid, this ensured that they would be served by the most poorly qualified teachers. Separate must also be inferior, according to Nova Scotian law.

Ontario's *Common School Act* of 1850 allowed 12 or more heads of family to request a separate black school.[32] The intention of the Act may have been to permit black families to opt for their own school, but in practice

12 white family heads could request separate schools for black children. Under this legislation segregated education was imposed in most Ontario districts with a sizeable African-Canadian population. Several court cases refined the administration of the segregated schools. In *Washington v. The Trustees of Charlotteville* Chief Justice John Beverley Robinson ruled that where no separate school existed, black children must be admitted to the common school with white children.[33] In a second case immediately afterwards, however, Robinson decided that if a black school had been established in the school district, even if it was as far as four miles away from their homes, black children could be forced to attend the segregated facility.[34] The trustees in Chatham exploited this ruling to create a separate school district comprising every black family wherever they lived in the town, but this practice was rendered illegal in *Simmons v. Chatham* in 1861 when the chief justice concluded that such subjective school section boundaries were too uncertain to be administered effectively.[35] In 1864 the courts found that when a separate school fell into disuse the black children thus displaced should be accepted in the nearest common school.[36] Under this principle, parental actions, including the withholding of school taxes, led gradually to the closing of most separate black schools and the integration of the children, though the segregation provision remained in the Ontario legislation until repealed in 1964.[37] In New Brunswick, where *de facto* separate schools served all-black communities, the law recognized but did not require the separate education of black children;[38] on the prairies, though the law was silent on the question, African-Canadian children were frequently rejected from public schools because of their colour.[39]

The separation accepted in education was acceptable too in many other areas of life, though not with the support of positive legislation. Early African-Canadian settlers in Ontario were moved to declare "our perfect contentment with our political condition, living, as we do, under the influence of free and equal laws, which recognize no distinction of colour in the protection which they afford and the privileges which they confer."[40] But "legal equality" would not mean freedom from racial restriction and exclusion in Canada. Ida Greaves was not far from the mark when she wrote in 1929, "the Negro has exactly the same rights as anybody else until he tries to use them, then he can be quite legally restrained."[41] Legally acceptable racial segregation had a long and full history in Canada before Fred Christie ever set foot in the York Tavern. The barriers were by no means absolute, but across Canada from Halifax to Victoria there were establishments normally open to the public where

African Canadians were refused admission. Segregation in housing, employment, restaurants and bars, transportation, recreation, hospitals, orphanages and cemeteries – every one of Vann Woodward's "Jim Crow" categories – had its Canadian example.[42]

Most Canadian cities had a district where the majority of black residents lived, with boundaries enforced by racially restrictive covenants or more usually by consent among white homeowners and real estate agents. As the *Windsor Herald* explained to black citizens in that city:

If a certain locality is prohibited, let them avoid it, as they will experience no difficulty in finding places for settlement; but if they endeavor to force themselves into positions where they are not wanted, under the idea that the British constitution warrants them in so doing, they may discover in the end that the privileges which they now enjoy will become forfeited.[43]

In 1920 four black families moved into the Victoria Park district of Calgary, where no black people had lived before. A petition was organized and signed by 472 of the district's 670 households, asking city council to relocate the black families and to restrain any further purchases. Calgary council had little experience with this kind of issue – there were only 70 African Canadians in the city and none had caused any "trouble" before – and so after a brief debate the city clerk was instructed to write to 16 other Canadian cities for guidance from those more experienced:

Would you be so kind as to inform me by return mail as to any legislation that might be in effect in your municipality segregating the residences of negroes to any particular district or districts. Further, if there is any legislation preventing negroes from locating in your City at all.

This last request is prompted by a statement which has been made to the effect that such legislation does exist in certain municipalities in Canada.[44]

There were no such by-laws in Canada in 1920,[45] though several respondents (including Windsor's city clerk) volunteered that black people tended to live in concentrated areas anyway. Nevertheless it is surely significant that Calgarians assumed examples must exist, and were ready to implement legal segregation in their city. In fact Calgary solved its problem in the typical Canadian fashion: whites resident in Victoria Park agreed to sell no more homes to blacks, and the blacks there agreed to sell their homes only to white purchasers.[46]

Employment discrimination was widespread, encompassing the civil service as well as the private sector.[47] African Canadians complained that public transportation and accommodations were denied to them without legal recourse. When a black man was physically ejected from the Mansion House hotel in London, Ontario, and sought a warrant against the owner from a local magistrate, it was the black man who found himself convicted of assault.[48] *Saturday Night* magazine expressed no sympathy when Toronto's Queen's Hotel barred the Rev. C. O. Johnson, declaring that "In Canada there is no active prejudice against the colored race" and black people were never affronted "except when they forget that no well-bred person will endeavour to force himself into a place where he is not wanted."[49] An Edmonton newspaper reported in 1912:

Irate Negroes were turned down services in two hotels. They ask, "Have Edmonton bartenders the right to draw the colour line?" The attorney general's department said while it gives the hotel keeper the right to sell liquor, "it cannot compel him to sell to anyone if he does not wish to do so."[50]

Only a few days after Fred Christie's ordeal in Montreal, *Saturday Night* took editorial note of a black singer denied access to the dining room in the Toronto hotel where she was a guest. "[T]he situation in Canada, with regard to discrimination against colored persons in public hostelries, is little if at all better that it is in [the United States]," the magazine admitted, though blame was placed on Americans who "dictate their policies" when they patronized Canadian hotels. While this was acknowledged to be "an intolerable anomaly in a free, liberal and supposedly Christian country," no legal solution was offered.

The only feasible way of dealing with the situation appears to be the establishment of international clubhouses in the larger urban centres in which foreigners of any race, color, religion or political philosophy, provided that they are personally acceptable, will be admitted to the full enjoyment of all privileges.[51]

Canadian theatres frequently had separate seating for black patrons, and this could be enforced by mob violence on occasion: a riot erupted in the Empress Theatre in Victoria when a group of prominent African-Canadian citizens took seats in the dress circle, contrary to local convention.[52] In Windsor, Ontario, the Palace Theatre maintained a "Crow's nest" for black customers; Loew's (later the Capital) had its "Monkey cage." These practices were still in existence when the York Tavern incident occurred.[53] Ontario's deputy attorney general explained in a letter to Stephen Leacock in 1929 that

Coloured people have exactly the same rights as others in the matter of public places of entertainment, but as the obligation of a proprietor to sell seats in his theatre or meals in his restaurant does not ordinarily exist, he can refuse to sell to Negroes if he pleases, just as he could refuse to sell to any other person or class of people, as long as the refusal is not accompanied by insult or violence.[54]

Across Canada hospitals typically would not accept African Canadians as nurses, black doctors were denied hospital privileges in several cities, and in at least one Edmonton hospital blacks were not even received as patients in the 1920s and 1930s.[55] A separate orphanage was established in Nova Scotia for African-Canadian children in 1921.[56] Black veterans of World War I were buried in a segregated section of Camp Hill cemetery in Halifax,[57] and the Nova Scotia municipality of St. Croix had a by-law passed in 1907, still enforced as late as 1968, excluding African Canadians from burial in the local cemetery.[58]

White reluctance to associate intimately with African Canadians extended even into the emergency conditions of World War I. The appeal to save the Empire and democracy in the fall of 1914 did not carry any colour implications, but black volunteers were systematically rejected by recruiting officers. Many protested, convinced that a contribution to the war effort would earn the gratitude and respect of the white majority. From Saint John came a letter to the governor general: "I beg to call your attention to the fact that Colored men of good repute have been denied the chance of enlistment in the Forces for overseas service etc. on the ground of Color."[59] The Hamilton black community advised the minister of militia that virtually every eligible young man had sought to enlist, but had been

turned down and refused solely on the ground of color or complexional distinction; this being the reason given on the rejection or refusal card issued by the recruiting officer.

As humble, but as loyal subjects of the King, trying to work out their own destiny, they think they should be permitted in common with other peoples to perform their part, and do their share in this great conflict.[60]

Similar letters were received from every part of Canada in 1914, 1915 and 1916. "It is certainly shameful and insulting to the Race," one such letter concluded.[61] Vancouver's chief recruiting officer complained that "Coloured candidates are becoming insistent, and I should like to know what course I am to pursue."[62]

Militia headquarters had an issue on its hands, and several queries were sent to regional and unit commanders to determine their attitudes. In typical replies, the Victoria district commander reported that black enlistment "would do much harm, as white men here will not serve in the same ranks with negros [sic] or coloured persons,"[63] and from the East Coast that whites would withdraw if blacks were accepted, as "neither my men nor myself, would care to sleep alongside them, or eat with them, especially in warm weather."[64] The issue became especially insistent after a group of Toronto blacks formed a platoon of their own and offered it to Militia Minister Sam Hughes. Every commanding officer in the military district administered from Toronto was canvassed to find a battalion willing to accept the African-Canadian platoon in the spring of 1916. Some replies were simple: "I have no desire to have a coloured platoon in my Battalion"; "I would object very strongly to accepting the Platoon mentioned." Some sought to blame their reluctance on the prejudices of the common soldiers: "it would seriously affect our recruiting"; "it would cause great dissatisfaction among the men now enlisted." Some even attempted humour: "Thank goodness, this battalion is over strength and does not need a 'colored' platoon, nor even a colored 'drum-major'!"; the Canadian Highlanders suggested coyly that "these men would not look good in kilts." At a time when Prime Minister Borden had committed Canada to the daunting task of keeping 500,000 men in the battlefields, not a single battalion would take a black platoon.[65]

The policy set by the militia council was that "coloured men can be enlisted in any Overseas Unit provided that the Commanding Officer is willing to accept them, but it is not thought desirable, either in the interests of such men themselves or of the Canadian Forces, that Commanding Officers should be forced to take them."[66] But when black Nova Scotians gained the ear of several prominent Nova Scotian politicians, including Fleming McCurdy, John Stanfield and Robert Borden, Chief of General Staff Willoughby Gwatkin was ordered to conduct a study and report on the feasibility of African-Canadian enlistment. His reply encapsulates the feelings prevalent in 1916:

Memorandum on the enlistment of negroes in Canadian Expeditionary Force.

1. Nothing is to be gained by blinking facts. The civilized negro is vain and imitative; in Canada he is not being impelled to enlist by a high sense of duty; in

the trenches he is not likely to make a good fighter; and the average white man will not associate with him on terms of equality. Not a single commanding officer in Military District No. 2 is willing to accept a coloured platoon as part of his battalion; and it would be humiliating to the coloured men themselves to serve in a battalion where they were not wanted.

2. In France, in the firing line, there would be no place for a black battalion, C.E.F. It would be eyed askance; it would crowd out a white battalion; it would be difficult to reinforce.

3. Nor could it be left in England and used as a draft-giving depot; for there would be trouble if negroes were sent to the front line for the purpose of reinforcing white battalions; and, if they are good men at all, they would resent being kept in Canada for the purpose of finding guards, etc.

4. It seems, therefore, that three courses are practicable:
   (a) As at present, to allow negroes to enlist, individually, into white battalions at the discretion of commanding officers.
   (b) To allow them to form one or more labour battalions. Negroes from Nova Scotia, for example, would not be unsuitable for the purpose.
   (c) To ask the British Government if it can make use of a black battalion, C.E.F., on special duty overseas (e.g. in Egypt): but the battalion will not be ready before the fall, and, if only on account of its relatively extravagant rates of pay, it will not mix well with other troops.

5. I recommend courses (a) and (b).[67]

Convinced by Gwatkins' option (b), the militia council voted just three days later to establish a black labour unit, the Nova Scotia No. 2 Construction Battalion, with authority to recruit black men from all across Canada.[68] But while African Canadians were at last acceptable into the Canadian Expeditionary Force, if only in the traditional and stereotypical role of labourers, social distance had still to be maintained. Most astonishingly, the black battalion was transported overseas in 1917 in a separate troop ship to avoid "offending the susceptibility of other troops," and it was actually recommended, though not accepted, that their ship should not join a regular convoy but should cross the submarine-infested Atlantic on its own.[69] Once overseas and engaged in their duties, the men of the No. 2 were segregated in the camp cinema, were provided with their own "coloured chaplain," were treated in a separate hospital wing when ill or wounded, and were incarcerated in a separate punishment compound when they misbehaved.[70] Back in England after the

Armistice and awaiting return transport to Canada, a sergeant from the No. 2 arrested a white man and placed him "in charge of a colored escort" en route to the camp jail. White soldiers unwilling to contemplate such an insult attacked the black party, provoking a riot between white and black soldiers throughout the camp.[71] Their efforts during the War had not won respect for black Canadians.

Separation and subordination were to be maintained, by violence and intimidation where necessary. Probably the most dramatic example of community action to enforce "Jim Crow" occurred in Oakville, Ontario, on 28 February 1930. Ira Johnston, described in the press as a "coloured man" or a "Negro" aged 30, became engaged to marry 20-year-old Isabella Jones who bore the description "white girl" ("Johnston," the *Toronto Daily Star* reported, "is a fine-looking man and nearly white"). The pending marriage caused much talk among the neighbours, since it was widely considered improper to mix "races" in this way. Miss Jones' mother tried to prevent the match, applying to the police and an Oakville magistrate for legal intervention and then, when she learned that no law prevented her daughter from marrying a black man, she wrote to the Ku Klux Klan for assistance. Meanwhile Mr. Johnston had difficulty finding a minister who would perform the marriage, though he had received a valid marriage licence, and so late in February Miss Jones moved in with Mr. Johnston, still unmarried. The Klan kept watch, and on Friday 27 February learned that Mr. Johnston had arranged with the pastor of the African Methodist Episcopal Church to conduct the marriage on 2 March. This precipitated what the Klan called its first "direct action" in Canada on the night of 28 February. About 75 Klansmen, most of them from Hamilton, Ontario, travelled by car to Oakville where they marched through the streets in their hooded uniforms, burned a large cross at Main and Third Streets in downtown Oakville in the presence of hundreds of spectators, and then went in pursuit of the offending couple. They were found at the home of Ira's aunt, where they were playing cards at about 11 pm. Isabella was told to get in a Klansman's car, and when Ira "asked what authority they had for taking her away" they made no reply "but closed the door and drove off." Isabella was taken to her mother's home, where before witnesses she swore to have nothing to do with Ira Johnston again. At Mrs. Jones' request, the Klan took Isabella to a Salvation Army hostel for safekeeping. Returning to "interview" Ira further on his transgression, the Klansmen surrounded the house and burned another cross on the front lawn. Ira's mother explained that he had gone out in search of his fiancée, whereupon "the spokesman told me that if Ira, my son, was ever seen walking down the street with a white girl again the Klan would attend to him." As they were leaving town the Klan cavalcade was intercepted by Police Chief David Kerr. He recognized many of them, for they had removed their masks, and he appeared to approve when they told him everything that had happened.[72]

The following day Oakville Mayor A. B. Moat told the press: "Personally I think the Ku Klux Klan acted quite properly in the matter. The feeling in the town is generally against such a marriage. Everything was done in an orderly manner. It will be quite an object lesson." Chief Kerr, explaining why he did not arrest anyone, said, "They used no force nor did they create a disturbance of any kind. . . . The conduct of the visitors was all that could be desired." But the Ontario black community was outraged. An "indignation meeting" was held in Toronto, and black leaders called upon the attorney general to investigate the incident and prosecute the guilty. Their rights as British subjects were being violated, they claimed; in the recent War they had served their king and empire for the sake of upholding rule of law, and now a disorderly mob was taking the law into its own hands. A black Baptist minister said, "I hold no brief for the promiscuous intermingling of the races. But I am unalterably opposed to the substitution of the purely authorized law enforcement agencies by such an intolerant organization as the Ku Klux Klan." Rabbi Maurice Eisendrath of Holy Blossom Synagogue joined the protest, claiming that the official apathy served as condonement for the Klan's illegal act. The attorney general agreed. Charges were laid against four of the Klansmen for having their faces "masked or blackened, or being otherwise disguised, by night, without lawful excuse." Only one of the four, Hamilton chiropractor William A. Phillips, was found guilty and fined $50. Phillips appealed his sentence and the Crown cross-appealed. Klan spokesman Dr. Harold Orme insisted that "Our only interest in race matters is that we want our country kept pure from contamination by mixed marriages." The "mixture of blood," according to the Klan, created "fiery, subnormal people to whom most of the violent crimes could be traced." Chief Justice Mulock decided, however, that "The motive of the accused and his companions is immaterial." They had taken "illegal interference" with the liberty of the young woman. "Their action was unlawful and it is the duty of this Court to pronounce the appropriate punishment." The court upheld Phillips' conviction and increased his penalty to three months in jail. Unrepentant, Phillips declared that he was "happy to serve a term in prison for such a cause as this," and the Klan issued a statement that all its members were ready and willing to sacrifice themselves for Christianity and the flag. Even Isabella said she felt sorry for Phillips. "He thought he was doing me a kindness. I have a letter that he sent me containing good advice. I don't like to think of him having to go to jail." In an editorial the Toronto *Globe* expressed what may have been majority opinion on the subject. The Klan was denounced for taking the law into its own hands, for intimidation of a fellow-subject, for its un-British conduct committed in secrecy. But the editorial concluded: "The work the nocturnal visitors did at Oakville in separating a white girl from a colored man may be commendable in itself, and prove of benefit, but it is certain that the methods were wrong."[73]

3. THE MONTREAL COMMUNITY

The historical pattern in Montreal reflected the national experience for African Canadians. There were black slaves in Montreal at its foundation in 1641, and from then until the Conquest more than 600 slaves resided in the city and its environs. Slavery was an acceptable and respectable institution in the ancien régime: Mother Marie-Marguerite d'Youville, founder of the Sisters of Charity, was one of Montreal's more prominent slaveholders, a fact that did not interfere with her canonization in 1990.[74] Undoubtedly the slave who left her mark most emphatically on Montreal history was Marie-Joseph-Angélique, who in April 1734 set fire to her mistress' home to distract attention from an attempt to escape. The fire spread, destroying 46 houses and the Hôtel-Dieu. Following a highly publicized trial and unsuccessful appeal, the 25-year-old slave was hanged in Montreal's public square, her body burned and her ashes thrown to the winds.[75]

The legal status of slavery was confirmed by an order signed by Intendant Jacques Raudot on 13 April 1709 clarifying title to Panis (native Indian) and African slaves held in the colony. Apparently some *habitants* were encouraging slaves to leave their masters on the pretext that slavery was illegal. Raudot declared slaves to be the property of the persons who bought them, and announced a fine of 50 livres for anyone assisting a runaway.[76] In 1734 Intendant Gilles Hocquart ordered the militia to arrest runaway slaves, and two years later introduced a complicated procedure to register manumissions in an effort to discourage masters from freeing their own slaves. Voluntary manumissions, Hocquart noted, were causing confusion, making it "necéssaire de fixer d'une manière invariable l'état des esclaves."[77] When Montreal fell to the British in 1760,

Article 47 of the Capitulation provided that slaves should remain the property of their masters, as before:

[L]es nègres et panis des deux sexes resteront en leur qualité d'esclaves en la possession des français et canadiens à qui ils appartiennent; il leur sera libre de les garder à leur service dans la colonie ou de les vendre; ils pourront aussi continuer à les fair lever dans la réligion catholique.[78]

The day after the capitulation the governor of Montreal wrote to the commandant at Detroit, explaining that although he had been required to surrender to General Amherst he had managed to do so "à des conditions très avantageuses pour les colons. . . . En effet ils conservent le libre exercise de leur réligion, et sont maintenus en leur possessions de leurs biens...; ils conservent leurs Nègres et Panis."[79] As a Missouri judge would point out a century later,

the 47th article is not only a clear recognition of the existence of slavery [in Montreal], but of the value of the interests connected with it. Only the most prominent objects seem to have engaged the attention of the retiring governor, for he secures nothing for his master's subjects but their religion and their slaves.[80]

The new British rulers had, in any case, no intention of challenging slavery. General James Murray, the first English governor, wrote to a friend in New York in November 1763:

I must most earnestly entreat your assistance, without servants nothing can be done. Had I the inclination to employ soldiers, which is not the case, they would disappoint me, and Canadians will work for nobody but themselves. Black slaves are certainly the only people to be depended upon.

Murray went on to ask his friend to buy him some slaves in New York, and added: "You may buy for each a clean young wife, who can work and do the female offices about a farm. I shall begrudge no price...."[81] A few free black Loyalists landed in Lower Canada, but they were far outnumbered by the approximately 300 slaves brought by white Loyalist masters. In 1783 the Montreal press carried an advertisement announcing

TO BE SOLD

A Negro Wench about 18 years of age, who came lately from New York with the Loyalists. She has had the Small Pox – The Wench has a good character and is exposed to sale only from the owner having no use for her at present. Likewise to be disposed of a handsome Bay Mare.[82]

A Bill introduced in the Lower Canada legislature in 1793 "tendant à l'abolition de l'esclavage" was tabled by a decisive vote of 28 to 3.[83] Advertisements for the sale of slaves were published in Montreal at least until 1805, at which time there were about 150 slaves in the city.[84]

As slavery died out in Lower Canada in the 19th century, former slaves and their descendants either moved away or lost their identity. In the 1871 census there were only 72 persons of African descent dispersed throughout Montreal, and there was no identifiable "black community" when the city again became a destination for black migrants in the 1880s. The American Pullman Company already used black porters and waiters on its continental service, and when Montreal was connected with New York and Boston in 1886, and became the eastern Canadian headquarters for both the CPR and the Grand Trunk, the practice spread across Canada. Canadian railway agents were sent to the major American urban centres and to campuses of black colleges in the South to recruit African Americans as porters and waiters. They were housed in Montreal and travelled from coast to coast serving white passengers. Initially a community of temporary male sojourners, by the 1890s many railway workers were beginning to settle in Montreal and to bring their families. Their commitment to Montreal was later enhanced by the establishment of the headquarters there for the Order of Sleeping Car Porters, for CNR employees, and the Porters' Mutual Benefit Association for those working on the CPR.[85]

To this initial core of American railway workers there was added a small but increasing flow of young black men from rural Ontario and Nova Scotia seeking work on the Pullman cars. Most were not considered sophisticated enough for this kind of service, but they could become red caps in Windsor Station or shoeshiners or elevator operators. Those who found jobs brought their families and settled permanently in Montreal. West Indians, too, were attracted to the opportunities of Montreal. Though white passengers might regard their porters and waiters as menial servants, for African Canadians in the early 20th century railway work was stable, reasonably well-paid and generally the most satisfactory kind of employment available. The Montreal black community grew from 293 persons in the 1911 census to 928 in 1921 and 1,202 in 1931, with men and women gradually coming into balance.[86] Because of rampant housing discrimination in most districts of Montreal,[87] the blacks inhabited a fairly defined area close to the Canadian National and Canadian Pacific railway yards. Although African Canadians were not a majority in this area, and some resided outside it (including Fred Christie, who participated in a small black movement to Verdun in the mid-1920s), this neighbourhood constituted the physical community of black Montreal with St. Antoine Street as its main thoroughfare. The area was characterized by poor quality housing and low rents, but physical proximity fostered the development of black community institutions and a sense of identity. The African Canadians of Montreal tended to stay in their own neighbourhood for shopping and recreational purposes as well. In most other parts of the city, hotels, restaurants and stores regularly refused service to black customers, and even some churches rejected black members.[88]

The most significant discrimination experienced by black people in Montreal was in employment. Even those Americans and West Indians who arrived with skills discovered that they could not find appropriate jobs, either because employers preferred to hire whites or because the American-affiliated unions would not admit them to membership.[89] Apart from the railroads, their chief employer, African-Canadian men could get work as dishwashers, janitors and, occasionally, as unskilled or semiskilled factory and construction hands.[90] Because wages were low, both adult partners were required to work in order to support a family, with almost all the women working as domestic servants in white homes.[91] Montreal hospitals would not train or employ black nurses for, as one priest explained, "les malades ne voudront certainement pas recevoir les soins d'une noire."[92] Even the railways were no safe place for black men. In the 1920s black waiters in the dining cars were replaced by whites, first on the CPR and then on the CN.[93] The sleeping-car porter's position remained black, but regardless of qualifications or length of service a black porter could not be promoted to sleeping-car conductor, a post reserved for whites.[94]

The situation in Montreal was perceived by many African Canadians to be worsening in the years following World War I.[95] Quebec as a society was experiencing disruption from an economic recession beginning in 1920, and social dislocation caused by rapid industrialization and urbanization. The sense that the French Canadian equilibrium was being upset by alien forces, coming from outside the francophone community, provoked a resurgence of nationalism and an articulated resentment against "foreigners."[96] In this respect Quebec was not unique: nativist movements swept across Canada in the 1920s, and south of the border the

Americans shared the experience of "the tribal twenties."[97] Still the nativist phenomenon in Quebec had its own special features. One was the intimate link, indeed the identification, between the Roman Catholic Church and Quebec nationalism, which rendered any non-Catholic virtually ineligible for inclusion. Another was the appeal to history, the glorification of the struggle against a hostile nature and overwhelming enemies which had produced a singular people, specially adapted to conditions in Quebec. Combined, these features created a sense of divine mission, a "social priesthood," to which the French-Canadian nation had to be faithful.[98] This nationalist spirit was epitomized in the teachings of the priest and historian Lionel Groulx. The first professor of Canadian history at the University of Montreal, Groulx presented Canadian history as a contest between "races": on the one side "a stock that is more princely than any on earth. We are of a divine race, we are the sons of God"; on the other "barbarians," aliens, the forces of cosmopolitanism and "hermaphroditism."[99] Above all, Groulx exhorted the French-Canadian people, "rester d'abord nous-mêmes." As editor of the nationalist journal *L'Action Française*, he wrote in 1921:

it is this rigorously characterized French type, dependent upon history and geography, having ethnical and psychological hereditary traits, which we wish to continue, on which we base the hope of our future; because a people, like all growing things, can develop only what is in itself, only the forces whose living germ it contains.[100]

To protect the French-Canadian nation, Groulx warned against foreign corruptions, from intermarriage to American movies and magazines.[101]

An economic element was present in French-Canadian nationalism throughout the 1920s, but it was accentuated in the 1930s as a result of the Great Depression, when the ethnic conflict became identified in economic terms. *L'Action Française*, which had ceased publication in 1928, was succeeded in 1933 by *L'Action Nationale* and a program of economic nationalism symbolized by the slogan "Achat Chez Nous." This "campaign of commercial chauvinism"[102] was most obviously directed against Jewish shopkeepers, but a participant explained to the sociologist Everett C. Hughes that it targeted anyone who was not French and Catholic: "he could be a Chinaman or a Negro."[103] The cultural homogeneity demanded by Groulx had produced "un courant de pensée hostile à la présence de non-francophones, et notablement de Juifs, au sein des institutions et services de la majorité."[104] Jews were included within a generalized xenophobia, as revealed in André Laurendeau's explanation of 1930s Quebec antisemitism as "revulsion directed against *foreigners*."[105] Black people, mostly migrants from the United States, West Indies or Nova Scotia, were outsiders by virtue of their origin, their language and their religion. Some French-Canadian shopkeepers even grew reluctant to serve black customers and personal association, always remote, became less likely than ever.[106] It was during the 1930s that Montreal hospitals began refusing black medical students as interns, leading the McGill University Faculty of Medicine to make an arrangement with Howard University for African Canadians to serve their internships in Washington, D.C.[107] In 1936, the year Fred Christie tried to enter the York Tavern, Maurice Duplessis led his Union Nationale party to electoral victory on a platform of nationalism. These developments did not produce a Montreal that was more discriminatory than British Columbia or southwestern Ontario, for example, but they did serve notice to African Canadians that the situation in Montreal was worsening and it was time to take a stand.

This was the context of open suspicion and occasional hostility within which Montreal's African-Canadian population sought to survive as a community. In the early decades of the century the community produced institutions and societies to serve the needs of its own members. Most important was Union Church, founded in 1907 and affiliated to the Congregational Church until 1925 when it joined the United Church of Canada. Other black churches existed, introduced by American immigrants, but Union Church on Delisle Street would become the mother institution for the entire community.[108] The two porters' organizations provided recreational facilities at their headquarters, and there was a host of smaller social or mutual benefit associations and athletic clubs.[109] The largest secular organization was the Universal Negro Improvement Association. Marcus Garvey, its Jamaican founder, visited Montreal in 1917, and a formal UNIA branch was organized in 1919. Openly political and directed at instilling pride in black hearts and dignity in black lives, the UNIA enlisted hundreds of African Canadians in Montreal in the 1920s. Sunday morning was devoted to church; Sunday afternoon belonged to the UNIA with meetings at Liberty Hall, speeches extolling the virtues of black independence, debates, dances and picnics.[110]

Despite poverty and rejection it was a vital, vibrant community, and never more so than during the tenure of the Rev. Charles Este as pastor of Union Church. Este arrived in Montreal from Antigua in 1913, hoping to find work on the railroad, but was forced instead to become a shoe-shiner at a hotel. Night school courses over many years prepared him to enter the Congregational seminary, and in 1925 he became the minister at Union Church. Charles Este was the unrivalled spiritual leader of black Montreal, and he also had considerable influence in secular affairs. He campaigned vigorously for African-Canadian employment opportunities and admission to training programs. In 1927 Este founded the Negro Community Centre, located at first in the basement of Union Church, as a focal point for black social life and community consciousness. During the Depression, when many other organizations drifted or declined and even the UNIA went into hibernation, the Centre and its parent church provided the energy and the confidence to enable the community to survive.[111]

It was to this community that Fred Christie turned for support. Many of its members had grown to believe that nothing could be done about discrimination; Christie's defiance was regarded as unusual, curious and thrilling, and attracted widespread attention among African Canadians.[112] A group of men responded to Christie's challenge by forming "The Fred Christie Defence Committee." The Committee was chaired by Dr. Kenneth Melville, professor of biology at McGill, and the vice-chair was Alfred Potter, a red cap. Treasurer was A. E. Smith, chief red cap for the CPR, and as publicity director they recruited E. M. Packwood, publisher of Montreal's only black newspaper, *The Free Lance: Afro-Canadian Weekly*. They opened a campaign office at 1314 St. Antoine Street, and organized a mass meeting at the UNIA Hall. Money flowed in, literally in nickels, dimes and quarters, collected in the black barbershops and newsstands, at Union Church and the campaign office. African-Canadian women organized a social evening at the Coloured War Veterans' Hall, with the proceeds going to the Christie fund. Through circular letters and "authorized collectors" almost every black family in Montreal learned of the campaign and made some small contribution. The red caps', CN and CP porters' associations pledged their formal support. Fred Christie had sparked a mass community crusade to confront the humiliations of racial discrimination. As the *Free Lance* editorialized: "Unless we are prepared to fight for equal treatment under the law of the land, we ought not and will not be regarded or treated as responsible citizens."[113]

4. ISSUES AND INITIATIVES

When a group of African Canadians asked the federal government in 1916 whether racially discriminatory practices were legal, the deputy minister of Justice had replied that legislation was silent on this issue.

"The remedy is in the courts."[114] It was therefore to the courts and the common law that the Christie Defence Committee had resort. As far as the Committee was concerned, the issue involved was simple: racial discrimination should not be permitted in a democratic society. For the courts, however, there were complications.

Since medieval times the common law of England had required an innkeeper to serve any traveller who applied for lodging and refreshment, subject only to limitations of space or some other reasonable excuse. Over the years certain kinds of behaviour on the part of the customer were deemed to constitute a reasonable ground for refusal, primarily drunkenness or other disorderly conduct. The particular tastes and preferences of the innkeeper could not be exercised.[115] The original principle was that a traveller was at the mercy of the innkeeper, perhaps literally for life or death in medieval conditions, and so in exchange for the right to engage in public business the innkeeper accepted the obligation to receive the public without discrimination. This same principle had been extended to other services, in particular to common carriers who could not refuse to carry a customer's goods without a lawful excuse. Both the innkeeper and the carrier were "common" in that they offered their services to anyone, without an explicit contract being required. Similarly, any business granted a state monopoly or position of privilege, by analogy, could not arbitrarily refuse service to a bona fide customer. This was articulated in Lord Hale's doctrine, which set out that enterprises (in this particular case a public wharf) which held an exclusive licence to provide a certain service must receive everyone, for they "are affected with a public interest, and they cease to be *juris privati* only."[116] Elaborating this principle, Chief Justice Holt ruled in 1701:

Where-ever any subject takes upon himself a public trust for the benefit of the rest of his fellow-subjects, he is *eo ipso* bound to serve the subject in all the things that are within the reach and comprehension of such an office, under pain of an action against him. . . . [O]ne that has made profession of a public employment, is bound to the utmost extent of that employment to serve the public.[117]

The issue before the court in Christie's case was therefore not the legality of discrimination per se, but the right of the York Tavern, as a licensed business offering to serve the public, to refuse service arbitrarily. Would Lord Hale's doctrine extend to a tavern in the province of Quebec?

The question was not without its Canadian precedents. On 11 March 1898 a black man named Frederick Johnson, who worked at Montreal's

Queen's Hotel as a bellhop, presented a coupon at the box office of the Academy of Music in exchange for two tickets for a theatrical performance the following evening. The clerk, believing Mr. Johnson must be on an errand for a white customer, gave over the tickets for seats 1 and 3 in row K of the orchestra. In fact, Johnson had received the coupon as a tip from a Mr. Swizzell, the manager of the touring theatrical group, who was staying at the Queen's Hotel. When Mr. Johnson and a black woman attended the theatre the next night, the usher refused to seat them in the orchestra section because of a house regulation restricting blacks to the dress circle only. Some commotion occurred as Johnson declined the offer of alternate seats in the dress circle, and he and his woman friend had finally to be ejected forcibly from the theatre. They took a cab to the Théâtre Français, where they were admitted to a performance. Then Mr. Johnson sued the Academy of Music for damages.

Justice John Sprott Archibald of the Quebec Superior Court agreed with Johnson and awarded him $50 damages for the humiliation, trouble and expense to which the Academy's action had subjected him.[118] Dismissing the theatre's claim that as a "high class" establishment its exclusive seating arrangement was reasonable, Justice Archibald articulated two fundamental questions raised by this case. First, could a theatre legally make "invidious regulations" restricting coloured persons to certain sections and, secondly, having exchanged the patron's pass for tickets to two actual seats, could the theatre refuse to admit him to those seats?[119]

In responding to his first question Justice Archibald gave a ringing denunciation of racial discrimination. The theatre's seating regulation, he maintained,

is undoubtedly a survival of prejudices created by the system of negro slavery. . . . Our constitution is and always has been essentially democratic, and it does not admit of distinctions of races or classes. All men are equal before the law and each has equal rights as a member of the community. . . . I should certainly hold any regulation which deprived negroes as a class of privileges which all other members of the community had a right to demand, was not only unreasonable but entirely incompatible with our free democratic institutions.[120]

On the second and more technical question Justice Archibald held that a theatre is essentially similar to a hotel, and just as a hotel is obliged to receive every traveller, so a theatre must accept every paying guest. The analogy was supported by the fact that both hotels and theatres require public licences and operate under municipal regulations; they are not therefore strictly private enterprises and are not free to discriminate among their customers. Furthermore, the theatre's advertising constituted an offer to the public to attend performances without distinction. Finally, since the theatre issued Mr. Johnson with tickets to seats K1 and K3 for 12 March 1898, refusal to grant those seats constituted a breach of contract.[121] The Academy of Music immediately launched an appeal.

The appeal decision was written by Justice Bossé of the Quebec Court of Queen's Bench.[122] The original award of $50 to Mr. Johnson was upheld, but the grounds were more limited than those assigned by Justice Archibald. On the point that as a publicly licensed enterprise the theatre could not discriminate in admitting members of the public to performances, Justice Bossé wrote on behalf of his colleagues that theatres did not bear the same obligations as hotels:

Nous n'adoptons pas ces raisons, non pas l'assimilation, pour la décision de la question, d'un théâtre à une auberge ou un hôtel.

L'hôtelier ou aubergiste est, par nos lois, soumis à des obligations spéciales nécessaires pour la securité et la santé des voyageurs.

Un théâtre est placé dans des conditions essentiellement différentes. Il n'y a plus la nécessité, mais simple question d'amusement. C'est une entreprise de commerce dans un but d'intérêt privé. . . . [123]

On the other hand, Mr. Johnson did have tickets for specific seats and therefore a contract existed between him and the Academy of Music. By refusing him admission to those seats the theatre had broken the contract and was liable for the damages.[124] The broader question – "si les noirs ont, en cette province, le même droit d'admission que les blancs" – was irrelevant to the case,[125] the court decided, but in dismissing Justice Archibald's reasoning the appeal decision undermined any general application of the non-discriminatory principle. That principle was sustainable only when an explicit contract existed.

"A few years later," Ida Greaves reports, a similar case occurred in Toronto. An African-Canadian mother "who looked white under the electric light" purchased a ticket for her darker-skinned son at a roller skating rink. The management refused to admit the son when he presented his ticket, so the mother sued for damages. In Divisional Court "the Judge held that the woman was damaged the price of the ticket," and the company owning the rink had to refund her 25 cents. No other damages were sustained "since they had a perfect right to refuse to sell the ticket."[126] A decision closer in principle to *Johnson* came in a British Columbia case in 1914, *Barnswell v. National Amusement Company*. Mr. Barnswell, a long-time resident of Victoria, purchased a ticket to the Empress Theatre in that city. He entered the lobby but was refused admission at the door of the auditorium because "there was a rule of the house that coloured people should not be admitted." Mr. Barnswell called the police, and a constable witnessed the theatre's insistence not to admit a black patron. When Mr. Barnswell continued to protest, the manager asked the policeman to remove him from the premises. Barnswell sued the theatre for damages for breach of contract and for assault.[127] In County Court the theatre admitted to damages only for the amount paid for the ticket, 10 cents, but Justice Peter S. Lampman decided that "the defendant broke its contract, and I have no doubt the plaintiff was humiliated."[128] Damages were fixed at $50, the same as in *Johnson*, though the Montreal case was not raised in argument. The Empress Theatre's appeal was heard in Vancouver in April 1915. Justice A. E. McPhillips declared in favour of the theatre, on the grounds that "it is in the public interest and in the interest of society that there should be law which will admit of the management of places of public entertainment having complete control over those who are permitted to attend all such entertainments."[129] His four colleagues on the appeal bench, however, dismissed the appeal because Mr. Barnswell's money had been accepted and he was already on the premises before being ejected. No reference was made in *Barnswell* to the issue of racial discrimination: the damages arose exclusively from breach of an established contract.

The limitations of the "contract" principle were made apparent in another Montreal theatre case in 1919. Loew's theatre was one of those known for its practice of seating black people only in the balcony. In 1917 Montreal blacks had formed the Coloured Political and Protective Association, intended to promote "racial advancement" through coordinated action, particularly at election times.[130] On 26 January 1919 the Association sent Messrs. Sol Reynolds and Norris Augustus Dobson and their wives to test Loew's theatre's seating policy. Mr. Reynolds purchased four general admission tickets at the box office, and proceeded with his companions to sit in the main orchestra section where there were many empty seats. When theatre staff insisted that they move to the balcony, Mr. Dobson protested loudly. All four African Canadians were then ejected from the theatre. Reynolds and Dobson entered suits for damages on the strength of *Johnson*.[131]

In Mr. Reynold's case Justice Thomas Fortin of the Superior Court awarded the plaintiff $10 damages, declaring

> In this country the colored people and the white people are governed by the same laws, and enjoy the same rights without any distinction whatever, and the fact that Sol Reynolds was a colored man offers no justification for Loew's Montreal Theatre Limited, refusing him admission to the orchestra chairs in its theatre after issuing to him a ticket for such seat and after acceptance of the same by its collector.[132]

The theatre argued that an admission ticket did not entitle Mr. Reynolds to a reserved seat but only to a seat on *either* the ground floor or mezzanine "as the management might desire and as the comfort and convenience of other patrons might demand." Furthermore there appeared on each ticket a printed condition: "The management reserves the right to refund the amount paid for this ticket and to revoke all privileges originally granted purchaser." But Justice Fortin ruled that the purchaser "had the option of choosing his own seat" and that the printed condition "can only justify such revocation before the contract is executed or in the course of execution. It cannot justify the revocation after the acceptance by the theatre's ticket collector." However in the companion suit brought by Mr. Dobson, Justice Fortin found rather ingenuously that Mr. and Mrs. Dobson were removed from the theatre not on grounds of colour but because they raised their protest "in such a tone of voice that attracted quite a large number of people and blocked the entrance way." This behaviour, according to the judge, was "unjustified," and overlooking the house rule on segregated seating which he had castigated in *Reynolds* he found the theatre had not violated the Dobsons' contract when it ejected them.[133]

Loew's theatre appealed the *Reynolds* decision to the Court of King's Bench. In a dissenting judgment Justice Henry-George Carroll held that a contract did exist between Reynolds and Loew's, giving the customer the right to sit where he chose. There was nothing distinctive about his ticket to indicate a limitation on the usual right to any seat in the house. He could only be denied a seat for a reasonable cause, such as drunkenness or disturbing behaviour; colour was not a valid reason for cancelling the contract. Reiterating Justice Archibald's 1899 denunciation of racial discrimination, Justice Carroll insisted that "Tous les citoyens de ce pays, blancs et noirs, sont soumis à la même loi et tenus aux mêmes obligations."[134] American cases brought by Loew's as precedents could not be applied, since American social conditions and consequent legislation authorizing discrimination did not exist in Canada. French legal precedents restricting access of certain classes of people had been obviated by the French Revolution. Reynolds, Carroll concluded, "a été gravement blessé" and must be awarded damages.[135]

The other four members of the appeal court decided in favour of the theatre, reversing Justice Fortin's decision. Reynolds' ticket was not for a specific seat; the theatre's discriminatory regulations were legal; it was Reynolds who rejected the seat offered him in the balcony and insisted on sitting in the orchestra section where he knew he was not allowed. Conditions were therefore quite different from the *Johnson* case, and Reynolds had no claim for damages.[136] Chief Justice Lamothe was most eloquent on behalf of the majority: since no explicit law stated otherwise, managers were authorized to set any rules for their own establishments, however arbitrary or discriminatory, provided they did not contravene good morals and public order.

En achetant un billet, Reynolds savait que ce billet lui donnait droit de prendre un siège aux endroits designés et non ailleurs. C'est donc délibérément qu'il s'est exposé au refus dont il se plaint dans son action. Il a voulu, malgré la règle, prendre place dans les fauteuils d'orchestre, endroit prohibé.

Aucune loi, dans notre province, n'interdit aux propriétaires de théâtres de faire une règle semblable. Aucun règlement municipal ne porte sur ce sujet. Alors, chaque propriétaire est maître chez lui; il peut, a son gré, établir toutes règles non contraires aux bonnes moeurs et à l'ordre public. Ainsi, un gérant de théâtre pourrait ne recevoir que les personnes revêtues d'un habit de soirée. La règle pourrait paraître arbitraire, mais elle ne serait ni illégal ni prohibée. Il faudrait s'y soumettre, ou ne pas aller à ce théâtre. Tenter de violer cette règle à l'aide d'un billet, serait s'exposer à l'expulsion, ce serait s'y exposer voluntairement.[137]

In 1916 the Ministry of Justice had advised African Canadians to seek redress in the courts, in the absence of positive law relating to discrimination. The Court of King's Bench was now declaring that in the absence of positive law, discrimination was legal. It was up to the proprietor to decide, on any basis he chose. As Justice Pelletier elaborated, the theatre could lose white patrons if blacks were admitted: "Il est prouvé que la présence des noirs dans les sièges d'orchestre empêche d'autres citoyens d'aller au théâtre et l'appelante n'est pas obligée de subir une perte de revenus qui résulte de ce fait."[138] Discrimination justified discrimination.

Another case to test the issue occurred in Ontario, where the distance from a proprietor's "duty to serve" was broadened by another significant step. On 20 July 1923 Mr. W. V. Franklin, a watchmaker and diamond specialist from the city of Kitchener, was visiting London, Ontario, and stopped at The Cave restaurant for lunch. When the waitress told him that "they did not serve coloured people," Mr. Franklin complained to the police and then returned to speak to the restaurant owner, Alfred Evans. Mr. Evans and his wife both repeated, in terms the court would later call "unnecessarily offensive," their absolute refusal to serve a black person on their premises. With the support of London's African-Canadian community and "some of London's foremost [white] citizens," and a fundraising campaign organized by the black newspaper *The Dawn of Tomorrow*, Mr. Franklin sued the Evanses "for the establishment of what he believes to be a right as a Canadian citizen." "I am not fighting," he insisted, "to soothe my own injured feelings. I am taking this stand for the benefit of all peoples of color, for generations of colored children yet unborn. Again, I want to prove to Mr. Evans and to all the world that the majesty of the British law will b[r]ook no prejudice."[139]

In 1899 Justice Archibald had found that a theatre, or any publicly licensed and regulated enterprise, had the same obligation to serve the public as a common innkeeper. The appeal court had narrowed this obligation to those occasions when a contract existed, at least in a theatre which offered amusement rather than an essential of life. In 1919 the definition of contract was made more specific, as was the right of a proprietor to set conditions, upon the terms of the service offered. Franklin's case seemed clearly distinct from *Reynolds*: a restaurant does provide an essential, and is far more analogous to the innkeeper's situation than is a theatre. Restaurants and inns are subject to similar licences and regulations. Mr. Franklin was indisputably a traveller and had been previously unaware of the restaurant's regulations. The Evanses had not simply set conditions but had refused to serve him any refreshment at all.

Justice Haughton Lennox sympathized with Mr. Franklin, whom he regarded as "a thoroughly respectable man," and he admitted to being "touched by the pathetic eloquence of his appeal for recognition as a human being, of common origin with ourselves."[140] Asked whether he had any ground for damages, Mr. Franklin told the court

Not in dollars and cents, but in humiliation and inhuman treatment at the hands of this fellow man, yes. Because I am a dark man, a condition over which I have no control, I did not receive the treatment I was entitled to as a fellow human being. God chose to bring me into the world a colored man, and on this account, defendent placed me on a lower level than he is.[141]

Yet Justice Lennox found himself required to decide in favour of the restaurant. There was, he explained, an "obvious dividing line" between a restaurant and an inn or hotel. That line, apparently, was the monopolistic nature of the innkeeper's licence:

[the] restaurant-keeper is not at all in the same position as persons who, in consideration of the grant of a monopoly or quasi-monopoly, take upon themselves definite obligations, such as supplying accommodation of a certain character, within certain limits, and subject to recognized qualifications, to all who apply.[142]

The fact that an enterprise was publicly licensed did not in itself carry any "duty to serve." Municipalities grant licences "partly for the purpose of regulating trade, but mainly for the purpose of producing a revenue. . . . [N]o limit is placed upon the number of licences issued." Butcher shops and department stores in London were also licensed, Justice Lennox reasoned, yet no one could deny the department store proprietor's right to refuse to sell his goods to any particular customer. The Canadian theatre cases – *Johnson, Barnswell* and *Reynolds* – might have suggested another analogy, but they were not considered by the court. Citing a series of British precedents, the judge concluded that a common innkeeper's duty could not be applied to other commercial enterprises.[143] Franklin's only consolation was that because of "the unnecessarily harsh, humiliating, and offensive attitude of the defendant and his wife toward the plaintiff," the action was dismissed without costs.[144] Had the refusal been expressed more politely, presumably, the costs would have been assigned against Mr. Franklin. Racial discrimination per se was legally acceptable.

5. LA QUESTION DE LA LIBERTÉ

In September 1936 the Christie Defence Committee engaged Lowell C. Carroll, an independent attorney and a scholar with publications in landlord and tenant law.[145] The York Tavern hired Brown, Montgomery and McMichael, a firm of 22 members including 12 KCs, with experience representing Loew's Theatre in its successful appeal against Reynolds.[146] They met before Mr. Justice Philippe Demers in the Quebec Superior Court in February 1937. Carroll argued that the tavern had a public licence and should therefore serve the public, and besides, by its general publicity advertising the sale of beer, it had offered an implicit contract which was broken when Christie's order was refused. Fred Christie was asked:

Q. Did you notice a large sign outside bearing the words York Tavern?
A. Yes.
Q. Was there anybody at the door to refuse your entrance?
A. No. . . .

Mr. Carroll pursued the same line when examining assistant manager Roméo Lajoie:

Q. Did you put any notice up that negroes were not to be sold beer?
A. No.
Q. Did you ever put a notice in the papers?
A. No.
Q. Did you ever advertise that in the newspapers generally or in the publicity for the tavern?
A. No.
Q. When the tavern was opened, was there any publicity in the newspapers?
A. Yes.
By the Court: Publicity to the effect that negroes were not admitted?
By Plaintiff's Counsel: No.
Q. That publicity, did it say negroes were not to be allowed to get beer?
A. No.
Q. It was unconditional.
By the Court: Do you hold a license by the Government to sell beer?
A. Yes.

Carroll argued further that Fred Christie and Emile King had been insulted and humiliated by the Tavern's refusal to serve them, and asked for $200 each in damages. Defendant's counsel Hazen Hansard picked at this contention in his cross-examination of Christie:

Q. [Y]ou complain of being exposed to ridicule and contempt, humiliation, pain and suffering, injury to reputation, damage to honour and sensibility and deprival of the pleasure of consuming beer with your friends at the time mentioned, and you say that is a value to you of at least a sum of two hundred dollars. Are you in a position to divide the two hundred dollars into those various allegations, or can we take it the real thing you are complaining about is the refusal to serve you with beer, and you want to find out what your rights are?

A. It is a very funny question.
Q. There is no catch in it, Mr. Christie. . . .
By Plaintiff's Counsel: All Mr. Hansard wants to know is, are those real damages or not?
A. Yes.

In response Hansard maintained that no humiliation had occurred because the tavern staff had behaved quietly and politely. He asked the waiter, René St. Jean:

Q. You heard the evidence given by Mr. Christie and Mr. King of your refusal to serve them was on the grounds that they were colored people, is that correct?
A. Yes. . . .
Q. Did any of the people there hear you say that?
A. No. . . .
By the Court: Didn't you think it was humiliating?
A. Well, if it is humiliating to them, then it is humiliating.
By the Court: You did it as quietly as possible?
A. Yes.
By the Court: You had your orders, and gave them politely?
A. Yes.

Hansard insisted that as "a private enterprise operated for gain" the tavern had the right to make any rules it deemed necessary to protect its business interests. Since it was not a restaurant or an inn, it was under no obligation to serve any member of the public. He asked Mr. Lajoie whether the tavern served any meals.

A. Just sandwiches.
Q. Are those sandwiches hot?
A. They are not made at the tavern, they are made at a restaurant, and we call for them when needed.

Finally, Hazen Hansard sought to prove that the discrimination practised by the York Tavern was commonplace among similar establishments. Since waiter René St. Jean had worked "in taverns and similar places" since 1907, with experience at the Russell House in Ottawa, the Senate restaurant and the Chateau Laurier, and at the CPR's Royal Alexandra Hotel in Winnipeg, Hansard claimed that he could properly be considered "an expert in tavern practice." St. Jean was asked:

Q. Are you able to say from your experience whether or not there is a prejudice amongst white people to be thrown amongst colored people?

A. In the places where I have worked, they did not care to receive colored people.

By the Court: They did not care?

A. No, they had a special place for them.

By the Court: Was it a bar?

A. Yes.

By the Court: Did you not admit them at the bar in any of those places?

A. No, Sir, we never saw one or served one either.

By Defendant's Counsel: Did you have any rule about admitting them?

A. If I remember rightly, at the Chateau Laurier we were told not to serve colored people. They had a special place for them, where the porters would go over to them and go right to that service bar.

By Plaintiff's Counsel: Was that rule well known to the porters?

A. Yes, because they all went there. . . .

By the Court: Did you refuse them at the Chateau Laurier?

A. I never had a chance to refuse them because they never came in there.

By Defendant's Counsel: Would the serving of negroes, in any numbers, in the York tavern, have any effect on the business of the tavern, are you able to say? . . .

By the Court: He never served them and cannot say what effect it would have. . . .

By Defendant's Counsel: Do you know whether or not there are taverns down on St. Antoine St., what might be said to be the negro quarter?

A. Yes, there is a tavern and a restaurant licensed there.

Q. And negroes may be served down there?

A. Yes, that is what I was told.

By the Court: That is not the question. It is a question of rights, that is if you have the right to refuse a man on account of his color. It is a question of law, not of evidence.

By Defendant's Counsel: The circumstances vary for different places.

By the Court: No, no circumstances, it is a question of law whether you have the right or not.

By Defendant's Counsel: I have another witness.

By the Court: I do not require to hear him.

By Defendant's Counsel: Your Lordship rules I cannot examine any more witnesses.

By the Court: It is not necessary.[147]

Philippe Demers' frequent interventions indicated that he was not impressed by the waiter's testimony, nor was he convinced by the legal precedents brought by the tavern, including *Loew's v. Reynolds* and *Franklin v. Evans*. Unfortunately for the tavern, Justice Demers stated, the previous cases occurred in circumstances where there was no law restraining the proprietor's liberty, but the Quebec *Licence Act* had a specific provision protecting the customer. According to Section 33 of that Act "no licensee for a restaurant may refuse, without reasonable cause, to give food to travellers." Section 19 defined a "restaurant" as "an establishment, provided with special space and accommodation, where, in consideration of payment, food (without lodging) is habitually furnished to travellers"; and a "traveller" was "a person who, in consideration of a given price . . . is furnished by another person with food or lodging or both."[148] In Justice Demers' view, beer is nourishment and should fall within the definition of food. "Quand je prends une verre de lait, une tasse de café, une verre de bière, je mange tout autant que lorsque je mâche du pain." Furthermore, sandwiches were available for purchase in the tavern. On both counts, then, the York Tavern must be considered a "restaurant." As persons seeking "food," Christie and King were definable as "travellers" under the *Licence Act*. This meant that the tavern's regulation was illegal, and the humiliation caused by the refusal of service must be compensated. Since Emile King had not actually placed an order or offered money, only Fred Christie was awarded damages: $25 plus costs.[149] The Montreal *Gazette* announced on its front page that "Court Bars Color Line": "Hotels and restaurants in the Province of Quebec have no right to discriminate between their guests and must serve anyone who pays. . . . The case established jurisprudence in the province."[150] But the *Gazette*'s excitement was premature, for the York Tavern appealed the Demers decision to the Court of King's Bench.

In presenting Christie's case this second time, Lowell C. Carroll reiterated his contention that when the patron accepted the tavern's offer to sell beer, a contract was completed and could only be broken for reasonable cause. He added that a tavern, like a restaurant or inn, was obliged to serve the public, and that discrimination was contrary to the Criminal Code. Four of the five King's Bench judges disagreed.[151] In the first place, the majority concluded, there was no contract. Justice Bond found that because Christie was immediately and politely informed that he could not be served, there was "no contract ever completed – no bargain struck."[152] Justice Barclay decided that the tavern's general advertisement announcing the sale of beer "does not constitute an offer to sell but is merely an invitation to buy."[153] There was therefore "no foundation for an action *ex contractu*."[154]

Turning more specifically to Justice Demers' Superior Court decision, the majority decided that a tavern was not governed by the same law as a restaurant. The Quebec statutes themselves made a distinction: in the *Alcoholic Liquor Act*,[155] under which taverns were licensed, "tavern," "restaurant" and "hotel" were all defined differently; the requirement in the *Licence Act* that restaurants and hotels must serve all travellers was significantly silent on taverns.[156] In any case, according to Justice St. Germain, no evidence had ever been offered to suggest that Christie was a genuine traveller and thereby entitled to service.[157] Just because food was available in the York Tavern did not in itself make it a restaurant; sandwiches were sent from a neighbouring establishment when a York customer placed an order, and even if beer had nutritive value Christie sought it only as a beverage.[158]

British and French cases were cited to indicate that no obligation required taverns to serve the public without discrimination. In British courts an "inn" had been defined concisely, excluding taverns from the duty to serve.[159] *Franklin v. Evans* was added to illustrate that British common law did not impose the innkeeper's responsibility on restaurants either.[160] In France the principle was that a proprietor's choice was only limited if public order required it or if the business enjoyed a monopoly or privilege, and neither of these conditions could be applied to the situation before the court.[161] Article 13 of the Quebec *Civil Code* invalidated any action which might contravene "the laws of public order and good morals," but the terms were left undefined.[162] In the opinion of the King's Bench majority, the York Tavern's action did not fall into this category. Nor did the court find that licensing restrictions constituted any infringement on the status of a tavern as a private enterprise: licences had as their object the raising of revenue; they did not create a condition of monopoly or privilege.[163] The public interest was not involved. "The fact that a tavern-keeper decides in his own business interests that it would harm his establishment if he catered to people of colour cannot be said to be an action which is against good morals or public order."[164]

For these various reasons, the Court concluded, no restraints existed on the right of the York Tavern to choose its own customers. Since there was no fault, there could be no liability for damages.[165] The fundamental issue in this case was "la question de la liberté": the freedom of a proprietor, in the absence of positive law, "d'entrer ou de ne pas entrer en relations d'affaires avec les personnes qu'il lui plaît."[166] The Court was "not called upon to express any opinion upon the abstract philosophical concept that all men are born equal," Justice Bond insisted, quoting Sir William Scott that "to vindicate the policy of the law is no necessary part of the office of a Judge."[167] "The function of this Court or of any court is to interpret the law as it is passed by the Legislature – not to change it or alter it or add to it," Justice Barclay added. "When a situation arises which is of public concern, then it is the Legislature and not the courts which should be called upon to remedy the situation."[168]

One judge saw the issue differently. In a thoroughly dissenting opinion, Justice Antonin Galipeault shifted the question of liberty from the proprietor to the patron. Christie was a British subject, a respectable citizen and personally well-behaved; he had a right to purchase a glass of beer in a public establishment such as a tavern.[169] Point by point Justice Galipeault found that the precedents argued in favour of Fred Christie. Contradicting his colleagues, he maintained that a contract did exist. In *Sparrow v. Johnson*, when the Court of King's Bench defined the sale of a theatre ticket as a contract, the judgment had been supported in part by the fact that "no notice of the existence or public announcement" of any racially restrictive policy had ever been made.[170] In *Loew's v. Reynolds*, the judgment had stressed that Reynolds did know of the theatre's restrictions before attempting to occupy a certain seat, and this exempted the theatre from the *Sparrow v. Johnson* precedent.[171] The *Loew's* decision, Justice Galipeault emphasized, had only permitted the theatre to seat black people in a designated section, not to exclude them entirely.[172] Much less so could a tavern exclude them. The numerous regulations imposed on a tavern made it effectively a monopoly or quasi-monopoly; licences were not for the unique purpose of revenue, but to control the numbers, locations and operating conditions of liquor outlets.[173] The *Alcoholic Liquor Act* repeatedly used the word "privilege" with reference to the sale of alcohol by licence, thus explicitly defining a tavern as a privileged enterprise.[174] The difference between a tavern, a hotel or a restaurant was one of degree; all three shared the same fundamental purpose and nature, and should all be subjected to the same responsibility to serve the public.[175] According to the wording in the *Licencing Act*, Christie qualified as a "traveller" and could legitimately expect to be served.[176] Justice Galipeault even agreed with Justice Demers that beer is a food.[177] If a hotel could not refuse lodging to a black man, and a restaurant could not refuse food, by what logic could a tavern refuse a glass of beer? "Est-il besoin d'un texte pour le tavernier? Était-il besoin d'un texte pour l'hôtelier et le restauranteur? J'estime que non."[178] As for the tavern's claim that it would lose business if black customers were served, Justice

Galipeault found that "un peu enfantin ou ridicule." A tavern is after all only a tavern, not a congregation or a club; clients come and go, and are not required to socialize with one another.[179] *Franklin v. Evans* had no relevance to Quebec, for it dealt with a restaurant and in Quebec a restaurant was required by legislation to be non-discriminatory. Had Justice Lennox heard that same case in Quebec he would certainly have decided that hotels, restaurants and taverns exercised a quasi-monopoly, rendered a public service, and were obliged not to discriminate.[180] It was necessary to push the proposition to the extreme: if a publicly licensed establishment could exclude African Canadians, why not Jews or Chinese or any other "race"? Why not members of certain religions, or persons who spoke certain languages? To support the York Tavern in its discriminatory policy would be tantamount to deciding "contre les bonnes moeurs, contre l'ordre public, contre le droit et la loi."[181]

Justice Galipeault's detailed arguments notwithstanding, the question of liberty was resolved in favour of the proprietor. The principle was reaffirmed that "in the absence of any specific law, a merchant or trader is free to carry on his business in the manner that he conceived to be best for that business."[182]

6. IN THE SUPREME COURT OF CANADA

The King's Bench decision was announced on 31 May 1938, and the Christie Defence Committee immediately launched a campaign to raise the $1,000 bond needed to carry an appeal to the Supreme Court of Canada. Committee chair Kenneth Melville wrote to the Montreal black community:

The recent decision rendered against Mr. Fred Christie of Montreal, in the case of the York Corporation versus Christie, makes it highly imperative that citizens of the Negro race unite solidly to protect themselves against this glaring support of the principle of racial discrimination in public places in Montreal.

To allow this case to be closed without any attempt to appeal this decision to the Supreme Court of Canada, would only tend to encourage further and more open discrimination against members of the Negro race, to encourage the disregard of public order, and indeed, to foster inter-racial discord.

The Appeal Requires Money. Accordingly, a committee of Negro citizens working at their request in conjunction with Mr. Christie, have decided to make an appeal to raise sufficient funds by voluntary contributions for this purpose. This committee feels firmly convinced that the Supreme Court of Canada will not uphold this malicious principle of racial discrimination, which is certainly contrary to British principles and traditions.[183]

The response was gratifying. "In the most enthusiastic demonstration of racial solidarity," the *Free Lance* reported, "local public opinion continues to crystalize in united support of the Christie Defence Committee."[184] By September, the impoverished community had scraped together the required bond money, only to learn that the Quebec Court of King's Bench dismissed Mr. Carroll's motion for leave to appeal to the Supreme Court. Carroll thereupon enlisted Section 41 of the *Supreme Court Act*,[185] which permitted direct appeal if the matter in controversy was deemed to be of sufficient general importance and if the future rights of the contesting parties might be affected. Leave to appeal was granted on 7 February 1939.[186]

Attorney Carroll prepared the Appellant's *Factum* around one central issue: racial discrimination was contrary to public order and good morals. Though the *Code* itself left these terms undefined, Carroll insisted that the Tavern's policy was a clear violation of the rule and must not be sanctioned by a court of law.

Quebec law is against any discrimination against a citizen on the ground of religion, language or colour. Bilingualism exists by law in Canada. All religions are free to practice their faiths, without control. All citizens are subject to taxation, without discrimination as to colour. The common law of Quebec is the free enjoyment by all its citizens of the facilities for education, nourishment and happiness which are available. It cannot be assumed from the fact that the legislature has, in the case of hotels and restaurants, taken care in dealing with their licences, to lay down a statutory obligation to receive, that this was expressly omitted in the case of a tavern. It was omitted because it was not thought necessary, in view of the monopolistic nature of a Quebec tavern, and its privileges under the law, that there would be any question of refusing its facilities to any citizen.

The York Tavern had put out advertisments in the press and in the streets inviting the general public. Nowhere was it stated or implied that black patrons were not welcome. Mr. Christie had frequently visited the tavern before, in its original location. Suddenly and without notice the policy had changed, excluding certain customers on grounds of colour alone.

If this ridiculous exclusion is sanctioned by law, it could be extended without limitation . . . until this country bristled with racial, religious and colour discriminations like certain European countries. A right to do so, particularly in the case of a Governmentally controlled monopoly, like a Quebec tavern, would certainly be against public order and good morals. Even in the southern United States the right to discriminate must be granted by statute.

The tavern's refusal to serve Christie "was a direct insult and slander, implying inferiority." For the suffering caused by this humiliation he deserved to be awarded damages. Although a group could not sue a slanderer for a racial insult, an individual could do so if the insult was directly applied to him. Mr. Christie's "gentlemanliness and conduct has not been impeached"; he was deemed "undesirable" only because of colour. According to *Loew's v. Reynolds* and other precedents, management could exclude the unruly and could make certain rules concerning dress requirements and seating arrangements,

But it could not make rules against public order and good morals, and it is respectfully urged that the respondent's rule, refusing negroes, even if it had been made public, which had not been done, was against public order and good morals, particularly in Canada and Quebec, part of an Empire teeming with various races, religions and colours.[187]

The Respondent's *Factum* was prepared by Montgomery, McMichael, Common and Howard, and argued before the Court by Hazen Hansard. There was no dispute over the facts; the tavern's case was that its action was permissible and reasonable, that

the refusal in question was made for purely business reasons on account of the prejudice generally held by white persons to drinking in company with negroes, and that refusal to serve negroes was common in the better class of establishments such as that operated by the Respondent.

The underlying principle was not racial discrimination but the freedom of a private business to choose its customers. "It is essentially a question of contract, and the merchant or trader, in the absence of special statutory provisions, is not under any duty to enter into a contractual relationship with anyone." In the case of Mr. Christie, no contract ever existed. "The Respondent refused to enter into a contract for the sale of the beer with the Appellant and, upon being pressed for a reason, gave as its reason the rule it had against serving negroes. The Appellant therefore was told the rule, and knew of it at all material times." The Respondent was not an innkeeper, obliged to supply the wants of travellers, but a merchant "free to deal or not as he may choose." The *Alcoholic Liquor Act* specified that "Any person in charge of a tavern . . . *may* sell therein beer by the glass"; the language was not compulsory but "purely permissive." The refusal was made "in the exercise of a right – *damnum absque injuria*." The

York did not enjoy a monopoly on the sale of beer, for there were taverns on St. Antoine Street where Christie could have been served. Numerous functions and enterprises required licences – the operation of a motor car, for example – and they did not thereby become monopolies. Throughout the incident tavern employees had behaved politely, quietly and inoffensively. No embarrassment or humiliation had occurred until the Appellant brought it upon himself by calling the police. "On the evidence of record therefore and apart from any question of right, the Appellant suffered no damages at the hands of the Respondent."[188]

The Supreme Court of Canada considered these arguments on 10 May 1939. It was a strong court, chaired by Chief Justice Sir Lyman Duff, who has been regarded as "the most influential member in the history of the Supreme Court of Canada"[189] and who was the only person on the bench to have heard the Quong Wing case 25 years previously. Also present were Justices Thibaudeau Rinfret and Patrick Kerwin, both of whom would later become chief justice (1944-54 and 1954-63, respectively), Oswald Crocket and Henry Davis. Their judgment was published on 9ˋDecember 1939.[190]

Justice Rinfret, appropriately a native of Montreal, delivered the decision for the majority. He accepted the evidence that York employees had behaved

quietly, politely, and without causing any scene or commotion whatever. If any notice was attracted to the appellant on the occasion in question, it arose out of the fact that the appellant persisted in demanding beer after he had been so refused and went to the length of calling the police, which was entirely unwarranted by the circumstances.[191]

"In considering this case," Justice Rinfret continued,

we ought to start from the proposition that the general principle of the law of Quebec is that of complete freedom of commerce. Any merchant is free to deal as he may choose with any individual member of the public. It is not a question of motives or reasons for deciding to deal or not to deal; he is free to do either. The only restriction to this general principle would be the existence of a specific law, or, in the carrying out of the principle, the adoption of a rule contrary to good morals or public order.[192]

The French principle of "la liberté du commerce" articulated this right explicitly, except in cases of privilege or monopoly, and it had been followed in *Loew's v. Reynolds* "where the facts presented a great deal of similarity with those of the present case." Another case "practically identical with the present one" was *Franklin v. Evans*, where Justice Lennox found that the English cases led to the same conclusion.[193] Reviewing the Demers decision, Justice Rinfret felt that it could only be supported if the Quebec *Licence Act* explicitly made it illegal for a tavern to refuse service without reasonable cause. No conditions existed justifying an exception on principle to "la liberté du commerce," for clearly "it cannot be argued that the rule adopted by the respondent in the conduct of his establishment was contrary to good morals or public order." Having thus summarily annihilated the theme of Carroll's *factum*, Justice Rinfret added "Nor could it be said, as the law stood, that the sale of beer in the province of Quebec was either a monopoly or a privileged enterprise."[194] A licence does allow certain government controls, but its main purpose is to raise revenue and it does not prevent the operation of a tavern as a private enterprise. "The only point to be examined," therefore, was whether the *Licence Act* could be applied. Such an examination led to the conclusion that "the appellant was not a traveller asking for food in a restaurant within the meaning of the statute. . . . According to the definitions, he was only a person asking for a glass of beer in a tavern."[195] The legislature had obliged restaurants and hotels to serve the public, but "no similar provision is made for taverns." The decision, in which Duff, Crockett and Kerwin concurred, was that "As the case is not governed by any specific law . . . it falls under the general principle of freedom of commerce; and it must follow that, when refusing to serve the appellant, the respondent was strictly within its rights."[196] Christie's appeal was dismissed with costs, by a count of four to one.[197]

The single dissenting voice belonged to Justice Henry Davis. He agreed that the Quebec *Licence Act* could not be applied to a tavern. He agreed as well that the primary question needing resolution was: "Has a tavern keeper in the province of Quebec under the special legislation there in force the right to refuse to sell beer to any one of the public?"[198] Thereafter Justice Davis' reasoning diverged from his colleagues. Since its first passage in 1921, the *Alcoholic Liquor Act*[199] had established state control over alcoholic beverages, including beer. The sale of beer by the glass with consumption on the premises was strictly limited to specially adapted and licensed establishments defined as taverns. The furniture and equipment required to qualify for a tavern licence were regulated, and the sale of beer was explicitly referred to as a "privilege" conferred by that licence. The hours and days when beer sales were permitted were set out in the Act. Most significantly, the Act listed specified classes who were not to be served alcoholic drinks, including those under the age of 18 years, convicted drunks, and persons individually prohibited by a decision of the Quebec Liquor Commission.[200] By a separate statute (the *Alcoholic Liquor Possession and Transportation Act*[201]), even the possession and transportation of alcohol, including beer, were placed under state control. The York Tavern had been granted a licence and was privileged, within this strict environment of control and regulation, to sell beer by the glass for consumption on the premises. But did this "special privilege" include "the right to pick and choose those of the public to whom he would sell?" The statute governing the licence already defined the persons to whom the licensee could not sell. Could the licensee impose a separate code of eligibility?[202]

Justice Davis reexamined the precedents to determine whether "freedom of commerce" was as encompassing as the King's Bench decision allowed. In *Loew's v. Reynolds*, for example, Justice Martin had said for the majority that "while it may be unlawful to exclude persons of colour from the equal enjoyment of all rights and privileges in all places of public amusement, the management has the right to assign particular seats to different races and classes of men and women as it sees fit." In *Franklin v. Evans*, Justice Lennox had concluded that English cases did not require a restaurant to serve without discrimination. One of the cases supporting this conclusion was *Sealey v. Tandy*,[203] in which a licensee (not a common innkeeper) was permitted to exclude a customer whom he did not wish to serve. But, Justice Davis pointed out, in the newest edition of Halsbury this case carried a footnote to the effect that "a victualler will be compelled to sell his victual if the purchaser has tendered him ready payment, otherwise not." A victualler, according to the dictionary, was "one who sells food or drink to be consumed on the premises."[204]

Justice Davis admitted that "The question is one of difficulty, as the divergence of judicial opinion in the courts below indicates," but considering the legislation establishing complete state control over alcohol, he concluded that taverns were not free to pick and choose their customers.

In the changed and changing social and economic conditions, different principles must necessarily be applied to the new conditions. It is not a question of creating a new principle but of applying a different but existing principle of the law. The doctrine that any merchant is free to deal with the public as he chooses had a very definite place in the older economy and still applies to the case of an ordinary merchant, but when the state enters the field and takes exclusive control of

the sale to the public of such a commodity as liquor, the old doctrine of the freedom of the merchant to do as he likes has in my view no application to a person
to whom the state has given a special privilege to sell to the public.

Since the Act already specified the various grounds for exclusion, it was
up to the legislature itself, not the licence holder, to enact any additional
ground such as colour, "race" or religion.[205]

Professor Melville's prediction was not fulfilled; the Supreme Court
had upheld the "malicious principle of racial discrimination" and the
Christie Defence Committee had to pay the York Tavern's legal costs.[206]
Fred Christie was personally humiliated and disillusioned by this
betrayal of what he had regarded as "British justice." A few months after
the Supreme Court decision was announced, Mr. Christie moved to the
United States and took up residence in Vermont.[207] The case attracted
very little public attention, despite its implications,[208] but lawyers reading the *Dominion Law Reports* were given an Editorial Note identifying
the significance of the *Christie* judgment:

This would appear to be the first authoritative decision on a highly contentious
question and is the law's confirmation of the socially enforced inferiority of the
coloured races. The principle upon which the judgment is based, though derived
from *Code* sources, will be found equally applicable to the common law. The
authorities are considered in *Franklin v. Evans*.[209]

Legal scholars have generally lamented the *Christie* decision, perceiv-
ing the same consequences as the editor of the *Dominion Law Reports*.
Some commentators have expressly found that the judgment was wrong;
others have merely regarded it as unnecessary. Closest to the event, and
most critical, was Bora Laskin. Commenting in 1940, Professor Laskin
wrote:

As between the majority's support of the doctrine of freedom of commerce and
Davis J's enunciation of a principle based on legislative assumption of control of
an industry the latter ought to be preferred, especially on grounds of policy and
where, as in this case, in the absence of a constitutional guarantee of equality of
treatment, the result would be the rejection by the courts of tendencies toward
discrimination. The principle of freedom of commerce enforced by the Court
majority is itself merely the reading of social and economic doctrine into law, and
doctrine no longer possessing its nineteenth century validity. With governmental
intervention in the control of certain industries and services in the public interest,

the courts may properly conclude that in the absence of legislative pronouncement there is to be no discrimination by government licensees against customers. . . . Where the government has established legislative control of products or services it seems more desirable to interpret the legislation as not permitting discrimination unless expressly providing therefor rather than as allowing licensees to discriminate unless expressly forbidden.[210]

Douglas Schmeiser has argued that the innkeeper principle could have been extended to cover this situation, had the Court chosen to do so,[211] and Henry Molot has challenged "the wisdom and validity" of the *Christie* judgment:

That a business can simply arrogate to itself and to its premises the immunity which reputedly shelters the private individual in his home . . . is belied by the recognition already given by common law and statute to the businessman's more vulnerable position vis-à-vis potential patrons: they are invitees, not trespassers.[212]

Walter Tarnopolsky, like Laskin, has found the dissenting opinion of Justice Davis to be most compelling.[213] For Ian Hunter, too, the decision could have been different. "The judiciary had not lacked opportunities to advance equality, but had preferred to advance commerce; judgments had adumbrated a code of mercantile privilege rather than a code of human rights."[214] Frank Scott regretted the majority judgment without implying that it was in error:

The freedom of commerce, it was said, enabled the tavern-keeper to choose his customers as he liked. The freedom of Christie from racial insult was not found to be protected by the law. . . . [O]ne kind of freedom conflicts with another. . . . The great principle of equality before the law must prevail at some point over the other value of freedom of commerce. . . . [T]he law as laid down in the Christie case should be changed.[215]

In a separate comment Professor Scott added that "In choosing the particular result in this case, the majority of the judges exercised a discretion that could as well have gone the other way."[216] The literature lacks absolutely any applause for Sir Lyman Duff and his Court in *Christie v. York*.

It would seem that, as in the case of *Quong Wing*, a different decision was at least possible in 1939. Two precedents were chiefly considered: *Loew's v. Reynolds* and *Franklin v. Evans*. *Loew's v. Reynolds*, however, contained two principal restrictions which limited its application as a precedent for *Christie*. One, as noted by Justice Davis, was Justice Martin's caution that total exclusion "may be unlawful." For him, it was only the assignment of *particular seats* that was clearly within the right of the proprietor.[217] Justice Pelletier seemed to accept the same narrower definition when he wrote: "Un propriétaire de théâtre a le droit de placer les spectateurs où il veut *dans des endroits*. . . ."[218] The second apparent restriction was the emphasis placed by the majority in the 1919 decision upon the fact that Sol Reynolds was aware of the theatre's discriminatory policy before he purchased his tickets. Chief Justice Lamothe began his statement by writing "En achetant un billet, Reynolds *savait*. . . ," and he concluded with "*Dans les circonstances* révélées par la preuve, Reynolds ne peut réclamer des dommages-intérêts."[219] Justice Pelletier distinguished *Sparrow v. Johnson* from *Loew's v. Reynolds* primarily because Johnson had been unaware of the theatre's regulations, whereas "Dans la présente cause, non seulement le demandeur connaissait ce règlement, mais il s'est rendu pour le défier et faire ce qu'il appelle un test case. . . . *Il résulte de tout cela* que le précédent de *Sparrow v. Johnson* n'est pas applicable."[220] Justice Martin's opinion was equally influenced by the fact that Reynolds "purchased his ticket with the knowledge of the existence of the rule of the theatre that he would not be seated where he asked to be seated, viz, in an orchestra seat, and this en vertu d'un règlement porte à sa connaissance. He could not successfully urge or contend that there was violation of any contractual right and he is not entitled to any damages."[221] The judgment summary in *Rapports Judiciaires de Québec* specifies both these qualifications: "a theatre may impose restrictions and make rules as to *the place which each person should occupy*," and "when a colored man bearer of a ticket of general admission, wants to take a seat in a part of the house *which he knows* is by a rule of the manager prohibited to colored persons, he cannot complain if he is refused. . . ."[222] The York Tavern was refusing service to Fred Christie, not simply assigning him a certain seat. Fred Christie was totally unaware of the York's rule, and had been served by the same management before the tavern moved into its Forum location. The cases could have been distinguished.

Nor is *Franklin v. Evans* entirely convincing. Justice Davis drew attention to the footnote which changed the application of *Sealey v. Tandy*, i.e., that a "victualler" must not discriminate against a customer who "tendered him ready payment." Since Justice Lennox found *Sealey* "decidedly pertinent" in dismissing Franklin's claim, that footnote could have affected his decision, and modified his statement that he could "find no authority directly in support" of Franklin.[223] In rendering the majority judgment at the Supreme Court, Justice Rinfret did not himself review the common law cases, but relied on Justice Lennox. This meant that *Barnswell*, for example, continued to be ignored, though it was a case where the plaintiff's admission to the premises before being refused further service was a decisive point. Most of the reasoning in *Franklin v. Evans* builds upon the distinction – "the obvious dividing line"[224] – between an inn and a restaurant. In developing this distinction, Justice Lennox lent great significance to the fact that a restaurant was not a "monopoly or quasi-monopoly."[225] For this to be a "distinction," then it must be assumed that an innkeeper *did* somehow enjoy a monopoly or quasi-monopoly, and this is what imposed the unique obligation to serve the public without discrimination. Yet nowhere did Justice Lennox or any of the cases he quoted specify that an innkeeper's licence gave monopolistic privileges. All the evidence Justice Lennox offered against regarding a municipally licensed restaurant as a monopoly could equally demonstrate that a municipally licensed inn was not a monopoly either. The innkeeper's "duty to serve" had much more complex origins than Justice Lennox implied, and since this duty had been amenable to application by analogy to common carriers and public wharves, there seems to be no "obvious dividing line" preventing its application to restaurants. At least there were some weaknesses in *Franklin v. Evans* which could have been exploited had the Supreme Court chosen to do so.

But of course the Supreme Court did not choose to do so. In considering the different principles involved, there was a direct confrontation between two sets of rights as then understood. It is only in retrospect that the rights of Fred Christie take obvious precedence. The right of association, for example, contains the right not to associate; the right of a customer to buy or not to buy was matched, with certain specified exceptions, by a proprietor's right to sell or not to sell. The fact that an alternative decision was possible in 1939, as every subsequent authority has maintained, serves to illustrate how context operates upon the judicial process. Although invited to do so by Lowell C. Carroll, the Court did not find racial discrimination to be contrary to good morals or public order. The very notion was summarily dismissed in a single sentence by Justice Rinfret.[226] Henry Davis, like John Idington in 1914, perceived a change in the context within which the law would be interpreted and applied. Increasing state intervention in public affairs would shift the balance of rights between proprietor and public, but on the eve of World War II that was not yet generally apparent.

7. AFTERMATH

Undoubtedly the Supreme Court opinion that racial discrimination was not immoral or damaging accurately reflected prevailing views on morality and public order. No one ever challenged the York Tavern's contention that white patrons preferred not to associate with blacks, and evidence at the trial indicated that this kind of prejudice was generally acceptable.[227] Prime Minister Mackenzie King noted his personal distress, about the same time as the *Christie* decision appeared, that Germans and English were killing each other. "It is appalling to think that in this way, the white stocks are making it possible for yellow men and the brown to inhabit the globe."[228] The prime minister notwithstanding, it was the War itself that initiated a process of change.

That change was by no means immediate; the public order assessed by the Court retained its acceptability well beyond the outbreak of hostilities in Europe. Employment discrimination, for example, was enforced by the National Selective Service, the government agency created to direct workers into appropriate employment for the effective prosecution of the war effort. The NSS used a registration form asking an employer's "requirements as to age, skill and race," and it honoured any employer's preference to exclude African Canadians. In fact NSS officers were not merely responsive to the stated prejudices of others: black applicants were simply assigned to stereotypical positions as domestic servants and unskilled workers. In many parts of the country black people were not even considered for employment in war munitions factories.[229] Under pressure from black groups in Toronto, Montreal and Windsor, the federal agency finally agreed in November 1942 to withdraw the offending questionnaire and to end any racial distinctions in its own job assignments. In its statement dated 14 November the NSS admitted that "discrimination impairs the war effort by preventing the most effective use of our total labour supply and tends . . . to defeat the democratic objectives for which we are fighting."[230]

The anomaly was not recognized by the NSS until the War was already three years old. Even more astonishing, for later generations, was the reluctance of the armed services themselves to accept African-Canadian recruits. RCAF regulations stated that "The following classes of men will not be eligible for enlistment . . . (c) Men who are not both of pure European descent and the sons of natural born or naturalized subjects."[231] In

1943 the "pure European descent" rule was dropped;[232] in certain instances prior to that some black volunteers were accepted for ground duties, but could not be appointed to commissioned rank or to air crew.[233] The navy's similar rule, that a recruit must be "of the white race," was not changed officially until June 1944, after the D-Day landing.[234] Meanwhile public advertisements urging enlistment in the air force and navy, like those of the York Tavern, made no reference to racial qualifications.[235]

As had happened in World War I, black Canadians volunteering to serve their country were told that they were not welcome. The army's official policy, once again, was that individual commanding officers must be free to accept or reject volunteers for any reason. The minister of national defence wrote to a leader of the Halifax black veterans: "I am sure that you will understand why we do not feel that we should interfere with this prerogative and I am sure you will equally recognize that racial questions have had no part in the establishment of it."[236] In a remarkable echo of the previous war, persistent attempts by black volunteers to enlist prompted a survey of unit commanders in Nova Scotia. Of 14 officers queried, all responded that black soldiers would be unacceptable: "would prejudice recruiting," "objection on part of white troops to coloured," "unit would disintegrate," were among the reasons offered.[237] Serious consideration was given to the establishment of a segregated labour battalion, but Ottawa headquarters rejected the idea.[238] In May 1941, in the midst of an urgent recruiting campaign which attracted numbers of prospective black volunteers, the Halifax district commander sought Ottawa's advice on "the question of the enlistment of Negroes." Recruitment regulations, he pointed out, suggested that any Canadian citizen who was "physically fit and in possession of the necessary educational qualifications" could join the army. He added reassuringly that "the local Negroes are of a low standard of education, which suggests the number of enlistments would not be large."[239] On 5 June 1941 Nova Scotian recruiters were advised that "provided they are physically fit and not illiterate," black personnel were eligible for enlistment.[240] If the rejection and segregation of African Canadians was acceptable in a time of national crisis, as the experience in the early years of the War would attest, the Supreme Court's 1939 refusal to enforce integration in a simple tavern can be recognized as consistent with Canadian morality at that time. Even after the dramatic changes brought about by the War – including not only a new sensitivity to the ideology of racism but the increasing involvement of the state in public affairs with the consequences foreseen by Justice Davis – racial equality was far from won. The experience of Johnson, Barnswell, Reynolds, Franklin and Christie continued to be true: black people themselves had to seize the initiative and claim their rights; sometimes they would be successful, and sometimes they would not.

Striking testimony to the vigour and legality of "Jim Crow" in postwar Canada, and to African Canadians' continuing determination to achieve equal rights, was provided by the case of Viola Desmond. Mrs. Desmond was a Halifax beautician who made tours to the smaller black communities in Nova Scotia to promote her line of beauty products and sometimes to do the hair of African-Canadian women. Her service was necessary because many white-operated beauty salons refused to accept black customers.[241] On one such trip to New Glasgow in November 1946, Mrs. Desmond attended a performance at the Roseland Cinema. She asked the ticket-seller for "one down, please," and proceeded to sit in the downstairs section of the theatre. The person collecting the tickets, however, informed her "this is an upstairs ticket, you will have to go upstairs." Coming from Halifax, Mrs. Desmond was not familiar with local practice that African Canadians such as herself were required to sit in the balcony. She attempted to exchange her ticket, but was told "I'm not permitted to sell downstairs tickets to you people." Aware now of the situation, Viola Desmond quietly but determinedly occupied a seat downstairs. Manager Henry MacNeil insisted that she move, indicating the notice on the back of the ticket reserving the right to refuse admission to anybody. When Mrs. Desmond expressed her conviction that the cinema had no right to discriminate against her, Mr. MacNeil sought the assistance of a policeman who was standing at the back of the cinema, watching the show on his supper break.

Unable to intimidate Mrs. Desmond into moving voluntarily, Mr. MacNeil and the policeman resorted to physical force. In her later testimony Mrs. Desmond referred to a "scuffle" in which her knee and hip were injured and her purse and one shoe were lost. Mr. Jack Desmond, Viola's widower, reports that his wife "put up a fight," though other family members claim that Mrs. Desmond's small stature and dignified demeanour did not make physical resistance likely. In any case, Mrs. Desmond was forcibly removed from her seat, carried by Mr. MacNeil and the policeman to a waiting taxi and taken to the police station where she was locked up overnight. The next morning, 9 November 1946, Magistrate Rod MacKay found Mrs. Desmond guilty of defrauding the province of Nova Scotia of one cent in sales tax: the upstairs price of 30 cents included two cents in tax, the downstairs price of 40 cents included three cents tax. By paying for an upstairs ticket and sitting downstairs Mrs. Desmond had failed to pay enough tax. She was fined $20 plus $6 costs. The costs were paid over to Mr. MacNeil.[242]

With the moral and financial support of the recently established Nova Scotia Association for the Advancement of Coloured People, Viola Desmond engaged Halifax lawyer F. W. Bissett to challenge the New Glasgow decision. Apparently as a strategy to undercut the legitimacy of the entire proceedings against his client, Mr. Bissett did not appeal Magistrate MacKay's specific ruling but instead applied for a writ of *certiorari*, arguing that Viola Desmond "was illegally and improperly convicted" and alleging "want of jurisdiction of the convicting magistrate for the reason that the evidence did not support the conviction." Justice Maynard B. Archibald of the Nova Scotia Supreme Court, however, dismissed this application on 20 January 1947 because "It is clear . . . that the magistrate had jurisdiction to enter upon his inquiry."

It was apparent at the argument that the purpose of this application was to seek by means of *certiorari* proceedings a review of the evidence taken before the convicting magistrate. It is obvious that the proper procedure to have had such evidence reviewed was by way of an appeal.

But the time for an appeal had passed, and *certiorari* was inappropriate.[243] Mr. Bissett appealed this ruling to the full bench of the Nova Scotia Supreme Court on 13 March, where he argued that "natural justice" had been denied to Mrs. Desmond. Following the precedents, and according to the fundamental purpose for the existence of *certiorari*, "There is a denial of justice where a person is convicted without evidence and the court will grant the writ [of *certiorari*] where an obvious injustice has been done, even though an appeal could have been taken."[244] But the court unanimously rejected the argument, ruling that "The defendant was convicted on a conviction good on its face and regular in form before a magistrate having jurisdiction."[245] Justice William Hall couched his decision in terms that showed he fully understood, and sympathized with, Mrs. Desmond's challenge to racial segregation, and seemed to regret that Bissett had not chosen a straightforward appeal.

Had the matter reached the Court by some method other than *certiorari*, there might have been opportunity to right the wrong done this unfortunate woman.

One wonders if the manager of the theatre who laid the complaint was so zealous because of a *bona fide* belief there had been an attempt to defraud the Province of Nova Scotia of the sum of one cent, or was it a surreptitious endeavour to enforce a Jim Crow rule by misuse of a public statute.[246]

New Glasgow's black newspaper, the *Clarion*, took Justice Hall's comment as a moral victory. "It would appear that the decision was the only one possible under the law. . . . [T]he reason for the decision lies in the manner in which the case was presented to court."[247] At least "Jim Crow" had been recognized and denounced.[248] But stories of discriminatory treatment in New Glasgow stores and restaurants continued to appear in the *Clarion*, increasing black citizens' frustration at the failure of the judiciary to protect them. In August 1947 editors Carrie Best and James Calvert Best launched a campaign for a municipal by-law authorizing council to suspend the licences of any establishment refusing service on grounds of colour.[249] Their model was a Toronto by-law requiring places of amusement licensed by the city to accept all customers regardless of "race, colour or creed," passed in response to public demonstrations after a skating rink ejected a boy simply because he was black.[250] No by-laws resulted in Nova Scotia, but the Desmond case and the *Clarion*'s editorials forced the provincial black population to recognize the weakness of the law as it stood and prompted the NSAACP to adopt a program aimed at legislative change rather than judicial enforcement of "rights" that turned out to be deficient.[251]

The route to desegregation through a municipal by-law, following the Toronto model, was attempted in several other Canadian cities. After widespread publicity was given to a refusal by Calgary hotels to accommodate African Canadians in early 1947, organized labour and the CCF joined the city's black community in demanding municipal action against discrimination. A motion was presented to council, but the city solicitor gave the opinion that since persons refused accommodation at a common inn or hotel had recourse to damages under the common law, no by-law was necessary. Any by-law reaching beyond hotels, for example to include taverns or other places of amusement, would be outside the authority of the council. Instead, Calgary mounted "an educational campaign to eradicate discrimination."[252] The campaign did not convince the manager of a local swimming pool, who admitted in 1948 that blacks were not permitted to swim there because "If too many Negroes came to swim no one else would want to use the pool and we would go out of business."[253] A Calgary dance hall barred blacks "because the parents of white girls attending dances there have objected."[254] Oshawa council, on the other hand, passed an anti-discriminatory by-law in December 1949, against the opinion of its city solicitor, who advised "I don't think the city has the power to legislate in such matters."[255] This same doubt had plagued the town council of Dresden, Ontario, where local African Canadians began pressing for a by-law to eliminate racial discrimination in 1947. Unsure of its authority, the council held a referendum in December 1949 asking Dresden citizens: "Do you approve of the Council passing a by-law licensing restaurants in Dresden and restraining the owner or owners from refusing service regardless of race, color or creed?" The vote was 517 to 108 against the by-law.[256]

Circumstances such as these, and in particular the continuation of blatant discrimination in Dresden, forced black people and their allies to move into the provincial arena to seek an end to racist practices. Ontario was first to provide a remedy through the *Fair Accommodations Practices Act* in 1954, which forbade racial discrimination in places to which the public was "customarily admitted."[257] Over the next decade most other Canadian provinces passed equivalent laws.[258] Quebec's *Hotels Act* was amended in June 1963 to similar effect.[259] It would no longer be possible for the York Tavern to refuse a black customer. Fred Christie's campaign, indirectly and eventually, seemed to be vindicated. And yet, late into the 1960s, housing discrimination remained prevalent in Montreal, and most African Canadians still resided in the vicinity of the railroad tracks and St. Antoine Street.[260] The situation would finally explode in 1969 when black and other students at Sir George Williams University occupied the computer centre to protest racial discrimination in their university and in the city generally. In the resulting publicity, far more attention was paid to the destruction of computer equipment than to the problems which had created the student frustration.[261] When, at a Liberal fundraising dinner in Montreal in 1975, Prime Minister Pierre Trudeau warned that racism threatened to appear in Canada, his Montreal audience shared the ignorance of their leader that he was speaking far too late.[262] Fred Christie might never have existed.

8. *CHRISTIE* AS PRECEDENT

But if Fred Christie was unknown to the public, the principles enunciated in his case survived in the courts of Canada. Less than six months after the Supreme Court's *Christie* decision, a case with almost identical circumstances occurred in Vancouver. A black man named Rogers and a white business colleague entered the Clarence Hotel on Seymour Street, which had recently undergone renovations and had reopened under new management. The new proprietor had taken out newspaper advertisements announcing this fact and inviting "our patrons" to see for themselves. Mr. Rogers and his friend, a partner in their shoe-repair business, had often had a beer in the Clarence Hotel under its previous owner, and had no reason to think he might be unwelcome now. Yet the new proprietor did refuse to serve Mr. Rogers, and stated that she did so only because she objected to his "race" and colour. Mr. Rogers' suit for damages against the hotel reached the British Columbia Court of Appeal in May 1940.[263]

Chief Justice MacDonald found the refusal of service "contrary to ethics and good morals," but regretfully he felt bound to follow the *Christie* precedent and refuse damages to Mr. Rogers. Justice Sloan agreed that *Christie* must be applied, thus giving the hotel a majority of the three-man court. They felt that the "freedom of commerce" principle articulated by the Supreme Court was not confined to Quebec. The Quebec *Licence Act* had substantially the same regulations as the BC *Government Liquor Act*,[264] and neither had any explicit provision inhibiting a proprietor's right to refuse service. The use of the Ontario case of *Franklin v. Evans* in its *Christie* judgment placed it "beyond question" that the Supreme Court intended the principle to apply everywhere in Canada.[265]

Justice Cornelius H. O'Halloran dissented. *Christie* was governed by the civil law of Quebec, and could not bind the courts of the common law provinces. According to the legal principles prevailing in British Columbia, Justice O'Halloran found three reasons to decide in favour of Mr. Rogers:

First, that it is contrary to common law to refuse service to a person solely because of his colour or race. Furthermore the appellant could not refuse the respondent without showing reasonable cause: in that *secondly*, she "held out" her premises to the public without reservation or limitation, as common and public refreshment rooms where beer might be purchased by the glass; and *thirdly*, the operation of beer parlours in this Province is "affected with a public interest," and is a "public employment" so as to displace any asserted common law right, if such existed in the appellant, to sell only to whom she would.[266]

Justice O'Halloran supported these contentions in a thorough canvas of common law cases. He insisted that "All British subjects have the same rights and privileges under the common law," and regretted that Justice

Lennox had overlooked "this elementary principle" in *Franklin v. Evans*.[267] Citing *Rothfield v. North British Ry Co*,[268] in which an Edinburgh hotel was required to pay damages for excluding a Jewish patron, Justice O'Halloran illustrated an explicit denial that "race and nationality" could be a reasonable cause to refuse service. The Clarence Hotel could refuse Mr. Rogers for reasonable cause, but obviously not simply because of his "race." The hotel's advertisements constituted "a general invitation" to patronize its beer parlour. Though *Rothfield* dealt with accommodation in what was legally a common inn, the British court's decision was based on the fact that it "held out" its services to the general public, and not on the innkeeper's duty to serve.[269] Finally, Lord Hale's doctrine of "public interest" must be applied, because the provincial legislature had eliminated "freedom of commerce" in beer and through its *Government Liquor Act* had "affected the sale of beer with a public interest."[270] For these various reasons the Clarence Hotel had no right to refuse Mr. Rogers.

We cannot consider the right of the beer parlour operator to refuse the respondent without also considering the right of the respondent to be served. Society is made up of individuals. The common law rights of each individual are necessarily limited by the manner in which their exercise affects the common law rights of other individuals. If the respondent had the right to be served (as he did from the general invitation to the public and the "holding out") it is repugnant to any sense of fair dealing to contend that he could be denied the right except for reasonable cause. It would be unreasonable and unjust; a clear invasion of his common law rights.[271]

The commentator in the *Canadian Bar Review* viewed the O'Halloran dissent as the most interesting part of the *Rogers* decision, but found it mistaken. Common law equality only meant entitlement to equal treatment "under the law or before the Courts or as against the Crown or government"; it had no application between private individuals. The comment also criticized Justice O'Halloran's "holding out" principle: "One might as well say that when a store advertises its wares it makes an offer which can be accepted by anyone who appears in response to the advertisement." On the other hand the *CBR* was impressed with O'Halloran's argument that a licensed beer parlour was "affected with a public interest" and should not therefore discriminate among its customers.[272] Douglas Schmeiser has taken a different line, criticizing Justice O'Halloran's use of the British precedents since each cited case applied to an innkeeper and not to a liquor establishment. Nor does Professor Schmeiser agree that Lord Hale's doctrine of public interest, as interpreted in subsequent British and American cases, affected a licensed tavern in BC. He concludes: "it must be recognized that no matter how socially desirable the view of O'Halloran J.A. might appear to be, there is little legal authority supporting it." Nevertheless Professor Schmeiser does agree with Justice O'Halloran that "There is nothing in the *Christie* case to indicate that the Supreme Court of Canada intended to lay down a rule binding in other provinces – in fact, the judgment points to the opposite conclusion."[273] The view that *Christie* applied only to Quebec, however, has not been sustained or even argued in other instances.

The federal government, certainly, concluded that *Christie* confirmed the right of taverns and restaurants across Canada to discriminate on grounds of "race." In 1943 Mr. Hugh Burnett, a carpenter from Dresden, complained to the minister of Justice that he had been refused service in a local restaurant because he was black. The deputy minister replied:

I beg to inform you that I have been requested to reply to your letter of July 17th complaining that the proprietor of a public refreshment parlour – Mr. Morley McKay – refused to permit you to buy refreshment in his establishment. This refusal was apparently based on the fact that you are a member of the negro race. A merchant or restaurant keeper is free to deal as he may choose with such members of the public as he may choose. This rule or principle, in certain circumstances such as you relate, is unfair or discriminatory in its effect; however, to adopt a law requiring a merchant or restaurant keeper to transact business with every member of the public who presented himself, since it would be entirely one-sided, might operate to the serious detriment of business. The principle of freedom of contract which I have mentioned has been recognized and accepted by the Supreme Court of Canada in a decision rendered as recently as 1939. This was on an appeal from the Court of Appeal of the Province of Quebec.[274]

In Calgary in 1947 City Solicitor D. S. Moffat, asked to comment on the legality of an anti-discrimination by-law, cited both *Christie v. York* and *Rogers v. Clarence Hotel* to conclude that with the sole exception of a common innkeeper, "The right to exclude any person from their premises is a civil right thus established by the Supreme Court of Canada and unless this were changed by a decision of the Privy Council or by Legislation it must stand as the law of this Province."[275] As has been noted previously, the *Dominion Law Reports* editors also assumed that *Christie* would "be found equally applicable to the common law."[276] Justice Rinfret, who wrote the *Christie* decision, would apparently have agreed. He wrote in his 1956 "Reminiscences" that in 29 years on the bench he had never found a single case where the application of common law and civil law would have yielded different results.[277]

Not only was *Christie* used to restrict the "duty to serve" exclusively to common innkeepers, but to limit its application to genuine travellers. On 13 May 1959 Mr. Ted King was trying to contact a friend who he believed was staying at Barclay's Motel on Macleod Trail in Calgary. He telephoned the motel to ask if his friend was registered there, describing him as "coloured." Proprietor John Barclay replied that he was not, and added "We don't allow coloured people here." Mr. King was one of the founders, and in 1959 was the president, of the Alberta Association for the Advancement of Coloured People. The purpose of this association was "to promote goodwill and to seek equality in social and civic activities throughout the province"; according to another charter member this included campaigning "to get rid of some obvious forms of racism."[278] Mr. Barclay's statement seemed to offer an opportunity to challenge one obvious form of racism. Mr. King and a black colleague, Mr. Harvey Bailey, drove to the motel and asked for accommodation. The "Vacancy" sign was posted outside. Mr. Barclay at first said the motel was full, but under questioning from Mr. King admitted that "We don't take coloured people." Mr. King then sued the motel for $500 damages, hoping to establish an exemplary precedent.[279]

In Calgary District Court Justice Hugh Farthing accepted the truth of Mr. King's charge of racial discrimination, but he decided that the motel was free to do so. Since Alberta had no regulation against discrimination, *Christie* and *Rogers* both indicated that freedom of commerce must allow John Barclay to select his own customers. Only an innkeeper was otherwise obligated, and Justice Farthing noted that an innkeeper was one who provided "lodging and food." No food was available at Barclay's Motel, and so it was not by definition an inn. Even if it had been, it would not be obliged to receive Ted King because he was not a bona fide traveller. King owned a home in Calgary, drove a car with a Calgary registration, and had taken no luggage to the motel. He admitted in court that he had gone to the motel "for purposes of investigation," to test its discriminatory policies. Judge Farthing dismissed Mr. King's action with costs, and added "in no uncertain terms" that he did not "appreciate" the way the case had been publicized in the press by Mr. King's lawyer, Tony Palmer.[280] The Alberta Supreme Court heard Ted King's appeal on 14 February 1961. No written reasons were offered, but all five justices of the Appellate Division held that King was not a traveller, and four of the five held further that the motel, which did not serve food, was not an "inn." The appeal, accordingly, was dismissed, and Mr. King received another lecture from the bench criticizing his attempt to use the courts to effect social change.[281] Shortly thereafter Alberta amended its *Innkeeper's Act* to remove the "food" requirement,[282] so that motels would be required to receive black travellers. The fundamental purpose of the AAACP action had been achieved, but not through the courts.

An interesting decision in Quebec confronted many of the same issues as *Christie* but did not, ironically, even mention that case. In April 1960 Mrs. Joseph, a black woman, made a deposit on a vacant apartment in Montreal and received the owner's verbal assurance, made by telephone, that she could rent the apartment. When she presented herself to sign the lease, however, the owner refused to confirm the agreement and explained "the reason is because you are coloured." Mrs. Joseph's suit for damages came before Justice André Nadeau in October 1965. In granting her damages, including interest from 1960, Justice Nadeau found that an oral contract could only be broken with a valid excuse, and this could not include "race." He concluded that racial discrimination was, in any case, contrary to good morals and public order:

Toute discrimination raciale est illégale parce que contraire à l'ordre public et aux bonnes moeurs; le geste discriminatoire posé par le locateur constitue une violation des règles couramment admises de la morale applicables à la vie en société; il est aussi de la catégoire des actes attentatoires à l'ordre public, étant de nature à troubler la paix dans la société.[283]

Justice Lamothe's denial in *Reynolds* that racial discrimination was contrary "aux bonnes moeurs et à l'ordre public,"[284] echoed by Justice Rinfret in *Christie*,[285] had finally been challenged by a Quebec court. At the time of Justice Nadeau's decision, Quebec did not have legislation covering discrimination in rental accommodation.

Christie's legal career was not yet terminated, though it moved through a phase that was remote from the issue of racial discrimination. A betting agency lost access to Ontario racetracks,[286] but General Electric was required to sell to an electrical contractor because no other suppliers were available in the market.[287] In the latter case Justice Nadeau explained that "Si répréhensible que fut la conduite du tavernier, il y avait tout de même d'autres alternatives qui s'offraient au client," and he disavowed the racial element in *Christie's* value as a precedent: "les standards de conduite de 1940 ont singulièrement évolué depuis, et que ce qui pouvait être acceptable à cette epoque ne le serait plus aujourd'hui, la notion d'ordre public évoluant avec le cours des ans."[288] Even in cases where the racial issue per se was not before the courts, it was deemed expedient to distinguish *Christie's* support for discriminatory behaviour as belonging to a particular time and place. The courts could, therefore, continue to recognize a general right of the freedom of commerce without perpetuating the right to discriminate on grounds of "race." By the 1970s public morality and positive legislation, as Justice Nadeau pointed out, had fundamentally undermined the legality of racial discrimination. One recent case to mention *Christie* does constitute an explicit allegation of racism, and while the different courts reached opposing decisions, the impact at all judicial levels was to confirm that racism should no longer be tolerated in Canadian law.

At issue was the claim of a South Asian woman, an experienced teacher with a PhD in mathematics, that Seneca College of Applied Arts and Technology refused to hire her on grounds of "race" and ethnic origin. Instead of filing a complaint under the *Ontario Human Rights Code*, Dr. Pushpa Bhadauria issued a writ for damages for discrimination and for breach of the *Code*. Justice Callaghan dismissed her action, finding that the *Code* itself established a remedy for her complaint and she therefore had no right to a civil action. The Ontario Court of Appeal saw otherwise.[289] The unanimous judgment of the court was delivered by Justice Wilson, who considered the question in two parts: was there a common law duty not to discriminate, which the College had breached, and secondly did a violation of the *Ontario Human Rights Code* give rise to a cause of action. Justice Wilson began her answer with a consideration of *Christie v. York* and *Rogers v. Clarence Hotel*, and was most impressed with Justice O'Halloran's dissenting opinion in the latter that the common law gave a right to equality. If so, she went on, there must be a common law remedy, as the British chief justice had enunciated in *Ashby v. White* in 1703.[290] Furthermore in 1945 Justice Mackay of Ontario had declared a racially restrictive covenant to be void as against public policy.[291] It did not require a positive law: the common law alone grants full protection against discrimination. Acknowledging that the matter was *res integra*, since no authorities directly recognized a tort of discrimination, Justice Wilson argued that the common law was not restricted by the existence of the *Ontario Human Rights Code*, which after all had not created but merely recognized the right of every citizen to freedom from discrimination. She therefore concluded that Dr. Bhadauria could sue the College, as a common law remedy to the breach of a common law right. The question of whether the *Code* itself gave rise to a civil cause of action was, in the circumstances, irrelevant.[292]

The case came before the Supreme Court of Canada in 1981.[293] Once again the decision was unanimous, but it was this time against Dr. Bhadauria's right to a civil claim. Chief Justice Bora Laskin, on behalf of the entire Court, found that "a refusal to enter into contract relations or perhaps, more accurately, a refusal even to consider the prospect of such relations has not been recognized at common law as giving rise to any liability in tort." *Christie* and the other cases brought by black Canadians had not revealed a common law right against discrimination; Justice O'Halloran's dissent was weakened by its reliance on *Rothfield*, a case involving an innkeeper's obligation, which was not applicable to other situations. The principle in *Ashby v. White* only applied if a right in fact existed. Justice Mackay's 1945 statement that racial discrimination was contrary to public policy, with which Chief Justice Laskin personally agreed, had not been upheld by the Ontario Court of Appeal or the Supreme Court of Canada in a 1950 property covenant case. While he commended Justice Wilson's "bold . . . attempt to advance the common law," Chief Justice Laskin decided that the common law route was "foreclosed by the legislative initiative which overtook the existing common law of Ontario and established a different regime which does not exclude the Courts but rather makes them part of the enforcement machinery under the *Code*."[294] Dr. Bhadauria's proper procedure was to lay a complaint under the *Code*, and seek compensation (i.e., damages) under its explicit provisions. The *Ontario Human Rights Code* contained a declaration that public policy was opposed to racial discrimination, and the *Code* also laid out the necessary procedures to enforce that policy. Justice Wilson's judgment was set aside, and Justice Callaghan's was restored: the remedy established in the *Code* was comprehensive and exclusive; there was no parallel remedy through a civil action.[295]

The Supreme Court did not weaken the prohibition of racial discrimination, it merely channelled the remedy through the provisions of the *Code* rather than through a civil suit for damages. For Dr. Bhadauria herself, any vindication of her rights and compensation for the damages she allegedly suffered would be determined if she laid a complaint before the Ontario Human Rights Commission. By 1981 the only dispute was over the means by which a complainant should seek to enforce his or her right to freedom from discrimination. The Supreme Court's *Bhadauria* decision, however, has the effect of lending retroactive approval to *Loew's v.*

Reynolds, Franklin v. Evans, Christie v. York, Rogers v. Clarence Hotel and *R. v. Desmond,* all of which occurred before human rights codes existed in Canada. Although Chief Justice Laskin did not deny the possibility that a common law right existed prior to the enactment of human rights legislation, he confessed that he had "some difficulty in understanding" Justice Wilson's claim that the *Code* "recognized" but did not "create" the right to freedom from discrimination. Indeed he implied that the *Code* had created rather than recognized that right by adding:

There is no gainsaying the right of the Legislature to establish new rights or to create new interests of which the Court may properly take notice and enforce, either under the prescriptions of the Legislature or by applying its own techniques if, on its construction of the legislation, enforcement has not been wholly embraced by the terms of the legislation.[296]

In the context this statement was meant to suggest that the legislation did provide for satisfactory enforcement; placed against Justice Wilson's pronouncement it suggests as well that the right was newly created. This impression is further reinforced by the distinction the chief justice drew between *Rogers v. Clarence Hotel* and *Rothfield*:

The common law of innkeepers' liability had, historically, developed along *different lines* from that respecting restaurants and taverns; keepers of common inns were under an obligation to receive travellers or intending guests, irrespective of race or colour or other arbitrary disqualification.[297]

Taverns, such as the York, had therefore not been under any such obligation.

Christie had survived another test.

4

Noble and Wolf v. Alley

1. EXCLUSIVE CLIENTELE

Almost half a century after it became the subject of a Supreme Court controversy for its restrictive policies, Beach O' Pines remains "exclusive" and "restricted." Visitors to this Lake Huron summer estate enter between stone pillars with notices marked "strictly private" and "no trespassing," past a guard-kiosk and barrier gate and along a roadway interrupted by speed bumps and stop signs every few hundred metres. The roadway passes handsome summer homes on large wooded lots, and ends at the border of the Pinery Provincial Park. About halfway through the estate there is a sign posted in front of one of the private cottages bearing a friendly but anomalous message of welcome: "Shalom." One wonders: is the irony intentional?

In the 1940s terms like "exclusive" and "restricted" had a specific meaning, an encoded message, and it was "No Jews Allowed." The message was prevalent throughout the resort areas of Canada in the early postwar years, a symptom of endemic discrimination against Jews in virtually every reach of Canadian society. In the summer of 1948 *Maclean's* magazine assigned a junior reporter named Pierre Berton to do a feature article on the phenomenon of Canadian antisemitism. Berton conducted interviews and collected statistics, and to enliven his story he engaged in a direct test. Two letters were sent to each of 29 summer resorts, one

---

The notes to this chapter are on pages 395-410.

using the name Marshall and the other Rosenberg. The Rosenberg letter was mailed a day earlier. Marshall received twice as many reservations as Rosenberg, including some from resorts who told Rosenberg they were already full and others who did not reply to Rosenberg at all. Pursuing this technique further, in the autumn Berton recruited two young women to pose as applicants for employment. One assumed the name of Greenberg, the other Grimes. Both had identical qualifications and experience as secretaries, for which there was a large demand at the time. Greenberg always answered an advertisement first, followed by Grimes a few minutes later. After 47 companies were called, Grimes had received 41 appointments for interview, Greenberg only 17. In 21 cases Greenberg was told the job was already filled, yet it was still available to Grimes only moments later. The reporter then called some of the companies to ask about their employment policies. He was told, among other things, that Jews did not have the right "temperament" for certain companies, that "they don't know their place" and simply that "we don't employ Jews."[1]

Pierre Berton was himself surprised and unsettled by what he had discovered. An acquaintance reported: "The investigation he undertook for the article convinced him of the seriousness of anti-Semitism in Canada, and as he put it, 'it was an eye-opener' to him. He feels the tendency is being accentuated rather than diminished, which is a somewhat discouraging view, to say the least."[2] The young writer's perception of a distressing "tendency" was accurate, though by 1948 antisemitism already had a long history in Canada.

The pioneers of the Canadian Jewish community had struggled against a variety of disabilities transported from Britain, until in 1832 they achieved their objective with the proclamation in Lower Canada of *An Act to Declare Persons Professing the Jewish Religion Intitled to All the Rights and Privileges of the Other Subjects of His Majesty in This Province.*[3] Introduced by Louis Joseph Papineau and the first of its kind passed by any jurisdiction in the British Empire, the Act ensured that there would be no further *de jure* discrimination against Jews. Its language also revealed that in 1832 Jews were recognized as British subjects who happened to profess a different faith. This accorded with the identity claimed by the Jews themselves, who were as proud of their British origin as any Loyalist. They were a small community, numbering scarcely more than 1,000 people in the first Dominion census in 1871, and well integrated into the commercial middle class of Anglo-Montreal and Toronto.[4]

Changes began in the 1880s with the initiation of Jewish immigration from eastern Europe. Yiddish-speaking, poor and uneducated, pos-sessing a culture distinctly non-British, bearing the painful memories of the horrifying pogroms perpetrated by Christian Europeans, the new immigrants clustered in the poorer districts of a few Canadian cities where they appeared to their neighbours to constitute an alien blot on the urban landscape. By the 1921 census there were over 125,000 Jews in Canada, and the remnant of the British middle-class pioneers had been overwhelmed by the character of the *shtetl* and *ghetto* of working-class eastern Europe.[5] In Montreal's St. Lawrence-Main neighbourhood, in Toronto's "Ward" around Bloor and Spadina and in Winnipeg's North End, the Jews survived as sweatshop labour and avoided the distaste of the mainstream population by staying close to home and creating their own cultural, charity and community associations.[6]

It was their Canadian-born and -educated children, usually, who con-fronted Christian Canada more directly by seeking better jobs and better homes in areas where Jews had seldom been met as equals. But the stereotype of the alien, annoying, clannish Jew, the rag-collector, the ped-lar, the seamstress, had already become established and the new genera-tion discovered that there were limits to their horizons in Canada. Indicative of mainstream sentiments was a Toronto *Telegram* allegation in September 1924: "An influx of Jews puts a worm next to the kernel of every fair city where they get a hold. . . . They are not the material out of which to shape a people holding a national spirit. They remain cosmopolitan. . . . Jews of all countries should be discriminated against as a race by a poll tax. . . ."[7] Employment discrimination became much more overt as Jews gained qualifications and attempted to move into dif-ferent endeavours from those occupied by their immigrant parents. In an effort to stem the flow, universities and professional schools set quotas upon their Jewish enrolment or refused Jewish students altogether. It was for these reasons that Canadian Jews tended to seek employment in Jewish-run enterprises or in the self-employing professions, such as medicine, dentistry and law, where they could serve a Jewish clientele.[8]

While these "tendencies" were already apparent by the 1920s, they were considerably accentuated during the 1930s. The Depression un-doubtedly had a serious impact on Jewish employment prospects, and it also encouraged a quest for scapegoats among those who could be cate-gorized as "foreigners," including Canadian-born Jews. In response many Jews became prominently involved in radical and left-wing orga-nizations, lending a subversive image to their entire community. The

Globe and Mail editorialized on 15 November 1937: "Although it cannot be said that a majority of Jews are Communists, the indications are that a large percentage, and probably a majority of Communists are Jews."[9] Most disturbingly, the rise of Hitler in Germany and international anti-semitic propaganda had the effect of legitimizing discriminatory and exclusionary practices directed against Jews in Canada.[10]

An increasingly hostile climate of opinion translated into disabilities imposed upon individual Jews, however talented or acculturated. In June 1934 Samuel Rabinovitch, who had topped his class at the Université de Montréal medical school, was accepted as an intern at the Hôpital Notre Dame. He was to join the staff on 15 June, but at midnight on the 14th all the interns at Notre Dame went out on strike in protest against being required to work with a Jew, and against imposing a Jewish physician upon Christian patients. They were joined in sympathy by the interns at four other Montreal hospitals, St. Jean-De-Dieu, Ste. Justine, Hôtel-Dieu and Miséricorde. Under this kind of pressure Dr. Rabinovitch resigned on 18 June, the hospital was saved from contamination and the nationalist journal *L'Action Nationale* applauded the interns' accomplishment. The Notre Dame incident was a dramatic expression of a sentiment common across Canada as Jewish nurses and doctors were denied hospital training or were accepted only under strict quotas – Toronto General Hospital, for example, was admitting only one Jewish intern per year at that time – forcing many aspiring Jewish physicians to do their internships in the United States and spawning the movement toward separate Jewish hospitals in Canada.[11] That same year of 1934 the University of Toronto Library School declined a Jew's application on the charitable grounds that upon graduation he would be unable to find a job and therefore "would spoil the placement record of the School."[12] Bora Laskin, who graduated as top student in law from the University of Toronto in 1933 and proceeded to graduate studies at Harvard, returned to Toronto in 1937 to find that no established law firm would hire him. Eventually applying to teach in the Faculty of Law at Toronto, Canadian-born Laskin required a testimonial letter from the department chair to the university president declaring that although "Laskin is Jewish he is a loyal, bright subject, loyal to our institutional traditions and forms of government. You may be assured that he will not disgrace the university."[13] Banks and financial institutions kept Jews only in the most junior positions, and there were no judges, few teachers or professors and almost no architects, engineers or chartered accountants who were Jews anywhere in Canada.[14]

And yet, despite these barriers, Jews continued to strive for educational and professional qualifications: in 1935-36 over 14 percent of Canadian medical students and 17 percent of dental students were Jews, yet Jews formed only 1.5 percent of the population.[15] Not surprisingly, the same attitudes that restricted their employment opportunities also produced resistance to their presence in residential districts and recreational facilities. As their attempts to gain access increased, owners and managers sought to deflect them with methods ranging from the subtle to the most blatant declarations of prejudice. Signs announcing "Gentiles Only" were commonplace, often placed in prominent locations. Others bore the insulting message "No Jews or Dogs Allowed." More polite, but equally effective, was the notice appearing at the entrance to St. Andrew's Golf Club in Toronto: "After Sunday, June 20 [1937], this course will be restricted to Gentiles only. Please do not question this policy."[16] Both English and French hotels in the Laurentians posted notices declaring that Jews would not be admitted. In the summer of 1939 the vicar of Ste. Agathe urged his flock not to rent their homes and cottages to Jews, and two days later his ecclesiastical superior announced the formation of a committee to monitor property sales in Ste. Agathe to prevent purchase by Jews.[17] One Montreal-area resort had a sign "Christians Only" at the entrance, but to be doubly effective an employee "walked along the beach with a megaphone, politely inquiring whether there was a Jew present despite the warning, and asking him to leave as quickly as possible."[18] Eschewing such directness, many more Canadian hotels, resorts and facilities utilized euphemisms like "selected" or "restricted clientele" in their advertising to convey the message that Jews could save themselves an unpleasant confrontation by staying away. The assault committed upon Jewish self-respect by such public notices rejecting their company is not difficult to imagine; equally powerful would be the impact imposed upon the minds of Christians whose attitudes would be shaped by the apparent universality and acceptability of anti-Jewish prejudice.

One indication of Canadian antisemitism in the 1930s was the almost total rejection of Jewish refugees from Nazi Europe. Of course Jews were not alone in being excluded as immigrants from Depression Canada, but as the Hitler regime increased its persecutions Canadians were aware that Jews were fleeing and that other countries were receiving them in much greater numbers. Canada's share of some 4,000 fugitive Jews compared unfavourably with the United States' 200,000, Britain's 70,000 or Australia's 15,000. At the Evian Conference in July 1938, convened to address the fugitive issue, Canada distinguished herself as a reluctant refuge. Even when the "Kristallnacht" slaughter in November 1938 aroused sympathy across Canada, evoking resolutions and petitions and editorials advocating a more generous policy toward Jewish refugees, the government decided that it was more politically advantageous to maintain the restrictions. The *Globe and Mail*, not given to liberal causes, was moved to utter its regret in an 18 November 1938 editorial that "The shock given to the civilized world by the latest demonstration of Nazi barbarity made not a dent in the complacency of Canada's government so far as the country can see." However the pressure upon the government, though intense, did not last long, and as Kristallnacht faded from the news so did the popular demand for a more liberal refugee policy.[19] In January 1939 MP Wilfrid Lacroix presented a petition to the House of Commons from the St. Jean Baptiste Society with over 127,000 signatures claiming that "the energy inspired by the instinct of self-preservation" led them to demand an end to "all immigration whatsoever and especially Jewish immigration."[20]

An even more frightening indication of the same sentiment was an apparent Canadian tolerance towards the domestic spread of fascism and the adoption of overt antisemitic rhetoric by mainstream institutions. This was especially the case in Quebec. As was discussed in the previous chapter, Quebec underwent a resurgent nationalism in the 1920s and 1930s, characterized by an attitude of exclusion against any who were not French and Roman Catholic. Québécois hostility towards Jews was part of a more general xenophobia of that period. It took on the specific language and style of antisemitism only when the European example and Nazi propaganda lent a kind of international validity to attitudes that were already prevalent.

An occasion for an expression of nationalist anxiety was presented in 1930 when the government of Premier Louis-Alexandre Taschereau drafted a bill to establish a separate Jewish school commission in Montreal. The Roman Catholic hierarchy strongly opposed the move, since it would introduce a non-Christian element into the Catholic-Protestant system of education, and popular sentiment was aroused against an alleged Jewish attempt to win "special privileges" for themselves, disrupting the historic English-French equilibrium. Any disturbance to the status quo was interpreted as a threat to French Canada's vulnerable position in an English-dominated confederation.[21] A political compromise was reached, affirming Jewish access to the Protestant system, but the schools controversy cast Jews as an enemy to French Catholic interests and provided a respectable platform for Montreal journalist and fascist propagandist Adrien Arcand. Arcand exploited the schools issue to alert nationalist Québécois to the "Jewish problem," alleging that the satanic Jews were embarked on a plot to crucify Christianity just as they had crucified Christ. Inspired by Hitler's success in Germany, in 1934 Arcand founded Le parti national social chrétien, patterned after the Nazis, which he used to promote stories of Jewish conspiracy and murder and to distribute racist literature originating in Germany.[22]

Arcand represented a "lunatic fringe," but a note of undisguised antisemitism resonated through the nationalist campaigns of the 1930s. "Achat chez nous," ostensibly a movement to encourage French Canadians to patronize French Canadian business, effectively became an anti-Jewish boycott endorsed by newspapers such as *L'Action Nationale* and *Le Devoir*, by Jeune-Canada and the St. Jean Baptiste Society, and by many clergy including the influential Abbé Lionel Groulx. Jews were an especial target because they were the largest and fastest-growing "alien" minority in the province (5.8 percent in Montreal by 1931),[23] and because their neighbourhood shops and businesses offered a readily available object for economic action. Lists of Jewish-owned businesses were distributed to facilitate their avoidance. Usually small retail shops were targeted, as accessible symbols of Québécois economic subservience, though the Jewish-owned Imperial Tobacco Company was also identified in a campaign beseeching French Catholics to "fumez Chrétien." Jewish businessmen were denounced not only as exploiters of their customers but as practitioners of fraud who undermined the system of honest Canadian commerce. If Quebec sought a villain for the economic dislocations of the 1930s, the "Achat chez nous" movement pointed to the province's Jewish community. When a rally was sponsored by Montreal Jews in April 1933 to protest the Nazi takeover in Germany, a counter-rally was held by the nationalist Jeune-Canada organization where speakers blamed Jews for their own persecution in Germany or insisted that tales of Nazi atrocities were a fabrication of Jewish press barons. Jeune-Canada, with echoes in *Le Devoir*, suggested that Jewish immigration must cease and that Jewish citizens of Canada should be disfranchised to diminish their potential damage to Canadian Christian society. As André Laurendeau said at the Jeune-Canada rally, "Les Israélites aspirent – tout le monde sait cela – au jour heureux où leur race dominera le monde."[24]

Through Arcand's agency, but also independently, Nazi-like organizations appeared in other parts of Canada as well. William Whitaker and A. F.

Hart Parker founded the Nationalist Party of Canada in Winnipeg, and used their *Canadian Nationalist* newspaper to propagate antisemitic venom. An Ontario branch of Arcand's National Social Christian Party was established in Ontario in 1937, promoting a boycott of Jewish stores in Toronto, and in July 1938 there was even a national fascist convention held in Toronto's Massey Hall with no apparent interference from the authorities.

The Nazi example provoked, or at least gave form to, several outbreaks of violence against Jews and Jewish property. Most notorious was the so-called Christie Pits riot of August 1933, when swastika banners and anti-Jewish taunts led to six hours of violent conflict between Jewish and Christian youths in Toronto. Along the eastern beaches of the city that same summer, swastikas and Nazi slogans were painted and Jewish bathers were physically attacked. A synagogue was set ablaze during a sabbath service in a resort district near Montreal in the summer of 1937, the culmination of a harassment campaign which featured swastikas and Nazi paraphernalia and the desecration of synagogues.[25]

The outbreak of war squelched any further public expressions of Nazism and postponed the refugee issue, but the old prejudices remained. Certain units in the Canadian forces rejected Jewish volunteers, leading some young Jews to disguise their background upon enlistment.[26] A Quebec cabinet minister informed the Assembly that his own son had become ill as a consequence of being examined by a Jewish physician when he volunteered for army service, and complained that "Our children were thrown into the hands of infamous Jewish examiners who regaled themselves on naked Canadian flesh."[27] The National Selective Service discriminated against Jews as well as blacks in assigning Canadians to work in the war industries and essential services. Although this practice was ordered to be changed in November 1942, an interpretive circular was issued on 9 December 1943, advising NSS officers across the country to use "good sense" and not to take the non-discriminatory policy "literally" by sending applicants to jobs "where it may not be practical to employ certain types."[28] Official attitudes towards "race" were apparently as confused during the war as ever. The 1941 census listed "Jewish" as a "Racial Origin," as had every census since 1901, while an explanatory note advised that

In actual census practice, the criterion on which the racial origin classification is based varies for different groups. The Indian, Eskimo, Negro, Hindu, Chinese, and Japanese races are segregated on the basis of colour; with the Jewish, the criterion is mainly [*sic*] religion; with the Ukrainian, language.[29]

Of Canada's 170,241 Jews enumerated by "race" in 1941, only 168,585 were shown as Jewish by religion, lending further confusion to the definitional criteria employed by census personnel and public alike. What exactly was a Jew was obviously uncertain, at least insofar as the Christian majority was concerned; it was certain only that associating with Jews, on the job or at the beach or even in the streets, was something to be avoided if possible. In a Gallup Poll taken at mid-war in 1943, Canadians listed Jews in third place after Japanese and Germans as the people who should be rejected as immigrants to Canada.[30]

Enormous changes in both policy and practice would eventually occur, but they were by no means automatic in the wake of the War. Typical employment application forms continued to ask for racial origin and religion, and if it was later discovered that a Jew was hired either by inadvertence or misrepresentation, he or she could be fired.[31] Quotas and restrictions were maintained, with even public employers such as the City of Toronto refusing to hire Jews in certain positions, including the police force and the transit commission.[32] In a postwar Gallup Poll, Canadians moved Jews to second place, behind Japanese but this time ahead of Germans, on the list of most undesirable immigrants.[33] Surveys in 1947 and 1950, similar to the one undertaken by Pierre Berton for Maclean's, confirmed that most summer resorts upheld an "exclusive clientele" policy which translated into an exclusion of Jews.[34]

Residential separation was maintained through a device known as the racial restrictive covenant. There were covenants made as agreements among owners of adjacent properties, binding themselves and their successors not to sell or rent to members of certain "races," and there were covenants placed in deeds by land companies and developers restricting ownership according to racial origin. Once instituted, both types were legally registered and could be enforced by the courts. In Nova Scotia covenants were most often directed against blacks, in British Columbia against Asians.[35] In central Canada, while persons of African or Asian origin were not exempted from such restrictions, covenants usually specified Jews among the rejected categories. In an extremely elaborate version, attached to a deed for Lake Huron cottage lots registered in Sarnia in 1946, it was specified that the properties must not be

transferred by sale, inheritance, gift or otherwise, nor rented, licensed to or occupied by any person wholly or partly of negro, Asiatic, coloured or Semetic [sic] blood, nor to any person less than four generations removed from that part of Europe lying south of latitude 55 and east of longitude 15 east. Relationship, however slight, to any class forbidden as aforesaid shall be deemed sufficient to prevent transfer to or occupancy by such person, it being the intention that the occupation of the lands in the subdivision and beach aforesaid shall be restricted to persons of northern and western European descent, other than Jews.[36]

It was therefore neither unusual nor illegal when a property developer known as the Frank S. Salter Company included a restrictive covenant in the deeds of individual cottage lots being laid out in the Beach O' Pines subdivision on the shores of Lake Huron. Each deed, registered in the County of Lambton in January 1933, contained the requirement that

the Grantee for himself, his heirs, executors, administrators and assigns, covenants and agrees with the Grantor that he will carry out, comply with, and observe, with the intent that they shall run with the lands and shall be binding upon himself, his heirs, executors, administrators and assigns, and shall be for the benefit of and enforceable by the Grantor and/or any other person seized or possessed of any part or parts of the lands included in Beach O' Pines Development, the restrictions herein following, which said restrictions shall remain in full force and effect until the first day of August 1962, and the Grantee for himself, his heirs, executors, administrators and assigns further covenants and agrees with the Grantor that he will exact the same covenants with respect to the said restrictions from any and all persons to whom he may in any manner whatsoever dispose of the said lands.

There followed a number of restrictions on the nature and location of buildings on the lots, and then a clause (f) stating that

The lands and premises herein described shall never be sold, assigned, transferred, leased, rented or in any manner whatsoever alienated to, and shall never be occupied or used in any manner whatsoever by any person of the Jewish, Hebrew, Semitic, Negro or coloured race or blood, it being the intention and purpose of the Grantor, to restrict the ownership, use, occupation and enjoyment of the said recreational development, including the lands and premises herein described, to persons of the white or Caucasian race not excluded by this clause.[37]

Fifteen years later Mrs. Annie Maude Noble, widow and heir of an original grantee, decided that she was no longer able to enjoy her Beach O' Pines cottage, and so she sought to dispose of it by sale. The only offer came from Bernard Wolf, like Mrs. Noble a respectable resident of London, Ontario. Mr. Wolf had migrated to Canada from the Ukraine in 1904 at the age of 15, and with his father founded Artistic Ladies Wear which, by 1948, had become a prosperous London enterprise. Wolf's solicitor Edward Richmond, just out of law school, submitted his offer to purchase on 19 April 1948: the agreed price was $6,800, with a $300 down payment enclosed. Mrs. Noble accepted the offer and banked the $300, but Richmond became concerned when he discovered the covenant registered in the title to the cottage lands. On 5 May he wrote to Donald M. Egener, Mrs. Noble's solicitor in London:

Required in view of the fact that the purchaser herein might be considered as being of the Jewish race or blood, we require a release from the restrictions imposed in the said clause (f) and an order declaring that the restrictive covenant set out in the said clause (f) is void and of no effect.[38]

2. COUNTER ATTACK

In the years immediately following World War II, the Canadian Jewish Congress was scouting opportunities to confront discriminatory practices in Canada. Organized first in 1919 with a primary program of assistance to Jewish refugees, the CJC slumbered for 15 years until revived by the Nazi menace and the much greater refugee crisis which resulted. In 1934 the organization represented a different Jewish community, the Canadian-born or -educated generation in transition from the ghetto both physically and mentally. It was much more politically aware, and therefore directed its concern for refugees to the government, employing lobby-group pressure tactics to encourage immigration policy reform. For reasons already described this program was not successful in the 1930s, but the CJC gained experience in political involvement which would be useful later on. The other main thrust of the renewed organization was to counter Nazi propaganda and antisemitism in Canada. To further this particular program the CJC joined with B'nai B'rith, a Jewish fraternal society, to form the Joint Public Relations Committee. The intention was to respond to specific instances of antisemitism and also to engage in broad educational endeavours to overcome negative images and the restrictions that grew from them.[39]

The CJC was bringing a national strategy to bear upon a momentum that had begun individually and regionally. Considering their rejection in so many other areas of daily life, Canadian Jews had achieved remarkable success in politics. Even with the intensified antisemitism of the 1930s Jews were already being elected from constituencies in Montreal, Toronto and Winnipeg, and although they represented areas of Jewish population concentration, Jews formed a majority in none of them. Jewish legislators initiated the movement towards the legal protection of Canadian minorities, and were thus the pioneers of human rights legislation in Canada. Believing that laws both reflect public values and influence public opinion, the leaders of Canadian Jewry regarded the campaign for the passage and subsequent enforcement of protective legislation as an integral part of their educational program.[40]

As early as 1931, provincial member E. Frederick Singer, representing the St. Andrew's riding in Toronto, had raised the question of discriminatory practices in the insurance industry. Some companies charged higher premiums for Jews, or even refused to cover Jews at all, alleging that they presented a greater risk than Christian clients.[41] Under Singer's urging the provincial Superintendent of Insurance wrote to the companies, advising them that nationality and religion were not in themselves acceptable factors on which to assess a risk, but at the same time he assured them that "no company should be required or compelled to provide insurance upon a risk which inquiry dictated to be unsatisfactory." In response Singer's own insurance policy was cancelled without explanation, and so in 1932 he introduced an amendment to the *Insurance Act* to render the practice illegal. Singer's explanations, including examples of Jews forced out of business because they were not able to get fire insurance, were revelatory to his fellow-members, and all participants in the debate denounced this kind of discrimination. In committee the bill was modified somewhat, but nevertheless the Ontario legislature passed an amendment which read: "Any licensed insurer which discriminates unfairly between risks within Ontario because of the race or religion of the insured shall be guilty of an offence."[42] The principles both stated and implicit in this innovative amendment would survive in human rights legislation for an entire generation. Fundamentally it established that since the public issued the licences, the public could set conditions upon their operation. Further, "race" discrimination was declared to be unfair and an offence. Both these principles suggested intriguing notions about public policy and the legislative reflection of common moral values.

Also in 1932, and specifically in response to Adrien Arcand's racist propaganda, Quebec Jewish members Peter Bercovitch and Joseph Cohen introduced in the Assembly a bill "concerning the publication and distribution of outrageous subject matter against any religious sect, creed, class, denomination, race or nationality." The "Bercovitch bill" would enable individuals belonging to a maligned group to take civil action to obtain an injunction to halt publication of libellous materials. As Bercovitch explained to the Assembly:

The object of the bill under consideration is merely to prevent a repeated and systematic publication of libels, not only against Jews, but against any nationality, any religion and any race. . . . [T]he law does not authorize the claiming of damages by the race or nationality that has been libeled nor is there any provision for punishment by imprisonment; it merely gives a judge of the Superior Court the power to issue an injunction to restrain the repeated publication of libel against any nationality or race – in other words, the real object of the law is to give bigotry no sanction, persecution no assistance.[43]

Premier Taschereau was initially sympathetic, but he soon recognized that "public opinion is not ready for such a radical measure."[44] The press, particularly *Le Devoir*, interpreted the bill as another Jewish attempt to gain "special privileges" and a move towards press censorship, and in any case as unnecessary since Jews and other minorities were already protected by "existing law." With government compliance the Bercovitch draft was referred to a committee which dissolved when the Assembly prorogued a few days later, automatically killing the bill.[45]

While the group-libel bill was still under debate, a Lachine fruit merchant, E. Abugov, brought injunction proceedings against Joseph Menard, publisher of Adrien Arcand's antisemitic journals *Le Miroir*, *Le Goglu* and *Le Chameau*. Mr. Abugov alleged that the anti-Jewish statements and the boycotts instigated by the journals had damaged his reputation and cost him his business. The legislature notwithstanding, a precedent seemed to be provided by the Plamondon case in Quebec City. In 1910 Mr. J. Edouard Plamondon delivered a speech containing a vicious attack on Jews, which was subsequently published as a pamphlet. Jewish merchant Benjamin Ortenberg sued Plamondon and the publisher for defamation, claiming that the speech resulted in loss of business and harassment against himself and his family. Justice Malouin decided in 1913 that no defamation was possible since no individual had been named, but this was reversed by the Court of King's Bench in 1915 on the grounds that since the Jewish population of Quebec City comprised only 75 families, Mr. Ortenberg was sufficiently identifiable to suffer individual injury from an attack on the Jewish collectivity.[46] But in September 1932 Justice Ganzalve Desaulniers declared himself unable to reach a similar conclusion. Though he denounced Menard and his malicious antisemitism, Justice Desaulniers regretfully ruled that since the legislature had recently declined to empower the courts to impose injunctions in exactly these circumstances, it was not within his discretion to grant Mr. Abugov's request.[47] Despite this exposure of the inadequacy of "existing law," the Quebec legislature took no steps to correct it in the following session.

A bill similar to Bercovitch's was more successful when introduced in the Manitoba legislature in 1934 by Jewish member Marcus Hyman. Hyman was able to gain the support of the Conservative Bracken administration for his amendment to the *Libel Act*, authorizing individuals to obtain an injunction against publications that libelled the "race" or religion to which they belonged.[48] The law was almost immediately tested in court by Captain W. V. Tobias, a decorated war hero and prominent Winnipeg lawyer. Tobias won an injunction against the *Canadian Nationalist*, run by Arcand associates William Whittaker and Herman and Anna Neufeld, prohibiting the further publication of anti-Jewish allegations, in particular that Canadian Jews practised the ritual murder of innocent Christians.[49]

Encouraged by the Manitoba victory, Ontario Jewish member J. J. Glass announced his intention in 1935 to introduce legislation against racial slander. But in the face of a public and press reaction similar to that in Quebec, to the effect that the law already provided satisfactory protection,[50] Glass did not pursue the idea that session. Two years later, when open antisemitism was increasing and a candidate in the 1937 provincial election campaigned for a boycott of Jewish stores, Glass again announced his intention to bring in protective legislation against group libel or slander. Although entered on the Order Paper, the bill was eventually withdrawn when Premier Hepburn advised Glass that its constitutionality was doubtful.[51] The Manitoba law would remain unique in Canada until 1970.

Parallel to published defamation as a concern for the Jewish community was the issue of discriminatory public signs. In 1932 J. J. Glass, then chair of the Toronto Parks Commission, applied the principle of the Singer amendment to eliminate the ubiquitous "Gentiles Only" warnings that began to appear on the Toronto Island beaches that summer. Since all land on the islands was owned by the city and leased to private individuals for summer cottages and recreation, Glass announced that the public had an interest in how its property was used and he inserted a clause in island leases prohibiting the posting of discriminatory notices.[52] One year later Argue Martin, a Christian member of the Ontario legislature, introduced a bill to outlaw public advertisements and signs that discriminated on the basis of "race" or religion, providing penalties up to $500. Although the Martin bill would have left intact the right of property owners or employers to discriminate, prohibiting only the public advertising of discrimination, the bill was dropped by the Legal Bills Committee on the grounds that the problem of racial discrimination could not be solved through legislation. Instead, the committee presented a resolution to the House condemning such signs.[53]

It would be more than 10 years before a new version of Martin's proposal was debated and passed by the Ontario legislature. Although it became a government measure, the project was inaugurated by Jewish member Joseph Salsberg. In the 1943 provincial election the Communist Salsberg and his colleague Alex MacLeod had made anti-discrimination legislation a campaign issue.[54] The election produced a minority government for Conservative Premier George Drew, making him more open to suggestion from opposition members than he might otherwise have been. Also during 1943 Canadians were becoming increasingly aware of Nazi wartime atrocities, and thus were readier to regard Jewish concerns with sympathy.[55] Within two months of the election Drew made the statement, in the course of a speech denouncing racial prejudice as a threat to democracy, that "the stirring up of such prejudices not only injures those against whom they are directed but in the end weakens the whole social structure."[56] This would be the premier's theme throughout the subsequent debate: everyone suffers when prejudice and discrimination are tolerated; the entire society is undermined.[57]

Prior to the next legislative session Salsberg advised Drew that anti-discrimination legislation was his party's most urgent priority, and Drew invited Salsberg to outline a draft bill on the subject. Salsberg's proposal went considerably beyond public notices, suggesting that discrimination in employment, housing, public accommodations and recreation should all be declared illegal.[58] The Speech from the Throne a few days later promised unspecified "action" against discrimination, but when the government bill was introduced in March 1944 it dealt only with the publicity issue. The bill aroused vehement objections nonetheless. The *Globe and Mail* revived the argument that adequate protection already existed and the bill posed a danger to the freedom of speech; the Toronto *Telegram* insisted that people must have the right to make distinctions among their associates.[59] A public rally at Massey Hall heard representatives from the Orange Lodge and several churches denounce the unseemly interference this law would create in the citizen's right to freedom of expression.[60] Drew was forced to modify an already moderate bill, adding a section that the free expression of opinion was not to be affected. Though it still refused to endorse the bill, complaining that "restrictive laws cannot be a substitute for conscience," the influential *Globe and Mail* at least withdrew its objection.[61] The legislature finally passed the *Racial Discrimination Act* on 13 March 1944, prohibiting the publication or display of signs, notices or symbols expressing racial or religious discrimination in Ontario.[62] The Canadian Jewish Congress, which had lobbied vigorously in support of the Act, regarded it as "a small but significant beginning. As little as it was, it established a precedent of interest and the right of the state to step in and enact laws against racial and religious discrimination."[63]

The *Racial Discrimination Act* was innovative on the Canadian scene, but Ontario was not behaving in total isolation. During the debate George Drew implicitly acknowledged the impact of World War II on the Canadian conscience. He told the legislature: "If you discriminate against any person because of race or creed in respect to their ordinary rights as citizens you deny that equality which is part and parcel of the very freedom we are fighting to preserve."[64] It has often been said that a "paradigm shift" occurred during the War, not just in Canada but throughout much of the world, characterized by the birth of a new concept: human rights. The war against the Nazis and in particular their racist doctrine caused a coalescence of the allied war aims around the notion that every human individual had rights which must not be violated. The Atlantic Charter of 14 August 1941, though it did not yet use the term "human rights," delineated certain rights and freedoms which should belong to everyone regardless of the inclinations of their own particular government. By 1945 the *United Nations Charter* could declare its "faith in fundamental human rights, in the dignity and worth of the human person," and dedicate the new world organization to "promoting and encouraging respect for human rights and fundamental freedoms for all without distinction as to race, sex, language or religion."[65] Then on 10 December 1948 the UN issued the *Universal Declaration of Human Rights*, which set out both the rationale and the direction for human rights programs in the postwar world: "Whereas disregard and contempt for human rights have resulted in barbarous acts which have outraged the conscience of mankind . . . it is essential . . . that human rights should be protected by the rule of law." Included in these rights were equality before the law and the equal protection of the law, freedom from racial or religious discrimination, and, of interest to Bernard Wolf, the right to own property.[66]

At the UN General Assembly the day the *Universal Declaration* was adopted, Canadian delegate Lester Pearson announced on behalf of his government:

we shall, in the future as we have in the past, protect the freedom of the individual in our country, where freedom is not only a matter of resolutions but also of day-to-day practice from one end of the country to the other. The freedoms to which I refer have developed in Canada within the framework of a system of law derived both from statutes and from the judgments of the courts. We have depended for the protection of the individual upon the development of this system rather than upon general declarations. Because this method is in accord with our tradition, we shall continue to depend on it, and to expand it as the need arises.[67]

Professor Frank Scott drew attention to the implications for Canada of these UN instruments: "our Parliament and legislatures will now or later come under an obligation, moral if not legal, to bring our domestic laws into line with these formal statements. International action thus impels us toward national legislation."[68]

In retrospect it can be seen that global factors made the public more receptive, and legislators more inclined, to the legal articulation of human rights in Canada. But in the postwar decade there lingered the notion that morality could not be legislated, and in any case the allegations of discrimination in Canada were really evidence only of the individual's historic right to choose the company he or she might like to keep.[69] Premier Drew, who faced a backlash within his own party over the 1944 Act,[70] explained why his government did not see fit to introduce more legislation of this kind: "The best way to avoid racial and religious strife is not by imposing a method of thinking, but by teaching our children that we are all members of a great human family; that each member has a part to contribute and that we are only one part."[71]

This, then, was the situation faced by the Canadian Jewish Congress as it prepared its postwar counterattack on the remaining bastions of anti-semitism in Canada. The war conscience and the international declarations lent a moral base and a publicly recognizable reference point for a campaign to eliminate racial discrimination; what had to be designed was a specific program of action which would accommodate majority Canadians' reluctance towards legal interference in what were presumed to be private affairs. In January 1946 the Joint Public Relations Committee decided that "This is an auspicious period for basic educational work." While they would continue to react to racist incidents "on an emergency basis," it was acknowledged that "overt acts of anti-semitism are rarer today than they have been." The problem was the myriad distinctions made regularly and legally to the disadvantage of Jews. What was needed was a long-range program to "ensure that the integration of Canadian Jewry into Canadian life is so complete that anti-semitism will be discredited as the impossible nonsense that it is in reality."[72]

Rabbi Abraham Feinberg was chair of the JPRC, and in 1947 Ben Kayfetz became executive director. Together Feinberg and Kayfetz fashioned a strategy. The legislative target would be laws protecting individual rights, the rights of every Canadian individual, under which Jewish rights would automatically be covered. All instances of discrimination must be exposed, not just those perpetrated against Jews, to illustrate the need for protection and to expose the "tacit approval which the absence of law gives to the social pattern of discrimination." Alliances must therefore be forged with other minority organizations and with liberal forces generally in Canada to demonstrate a constituency on behalf of reform and to avoid the impression that "pushy Jews" were merely seeking to enhance their own interests. There was an urgency not to appear as a "special interest": the claim to equality had to be universalized and cast in the most embracing terms. The instruments, according to the circumstances, might be municipal by-laws, court cases to enforce and enhance individual rights, and provincial civil rights legislation. Specifically, the JPRC designed a move against two major areas of concern: employment discrimination and "the iron curtain fabricated by restrictive covenants." Rabbi Feinberg explained this dual selection of priorities to a CJC meeting:

One involves the basic need of livelihood, and the other involves the need of status and self-respect. Both rest on the spiritual truth that there is no second-class citizenship in a democracy, and on the practical truth that the citizens of Canada endorse that proposition.[73]

The Canadian Jewish Congress was therefore poised to respond to Bernard Wolf's problem with a certain property covenant.

3. PRINCIPLES AND POLICIES

A covenant is like a contract, or at least it is treated like one by the courts: a violation gives rise to a cause of action; delinquents can be sued for damages, or an injunction can be obtained.[74] In 1875 Sir George Jessel articulated the prevailing principle in the English legal tradition:

If there is one thing more than any other which public policy requires, it is that men of full age and competent understanding shall have the utmost liberty of contracting, and that contracts, when entered into freely and voluntarily, shall be held good and shall be enforced by courts of justice.[75]

On the other hand a property covenant is a restriction on the sale of land, and an equally valid principle in the English tradition insisted upon the free and unrestrained sale of property. By a statute in 1289-90 known as *Quia Emptores Terrarum*, it was established "That from henceforth it shall be lawful to every freeman to sell at his own pleasure his lands and tenements, or part of them." Certain kinds of restrictions, however, became regarded as acceptable and were deemed not to violate the principle of freedom of alienation. Specifically these were restrictions which could be defined as "partial," for they did not absolutely inhibit the free use and disposal of property, such as restraints or conditions which lasted for only a stipulated length of time, or which applied only to a limited set of people.[76]

But would this mean therefore that in the question of a covenant restraining sale to Jews over a period of thirty years, the sanctity of contract should automatically prevail over the freedom of alienation? "Public interest" could be invoked against it, since to uphold such a covenant the courts would not merely be *condoning* private discrimination but using the law to *impose* discrimination. Furthermore several Canadian judges had previously argued that any restrictions defined exclusively in terms of "race" or colour were contrary to common law.[77] Bernard Wolf's attempt to avoid being bound by a contract he had not himself made therefore entered a debate relating to the role of the courts, the scope of the common law and the nature of the public's interest, as well as to the question of racial discrimination.

By 1948 the direction, if not the actual conclusion, of this debate was reasonably apparent. In 1911 BC Chief Justice Hunter had invalidated a property covenant restraining sale to Chinese and Japanese, but he gave no reasons for his decision.[78] In the 1930 Ontario case *Essex Real Estate v. Holmes*,[79] the plaintiff company sought to enforce a covenant which stated "that the lands shall not be sold to or occupied by persons not of the Caucasian race nor to Europeans except such as are of English-speaking countries and the French and the people of French descent."[80] Despite the apparent intention of the exclusion, Justice Garrow upheld the defendant's right to sell a piece of the covenanted land to a Syrian.

He ruled that the Syrian was a Caucasian and was therefore acceptable under the first criterion, and that he was not a European and therefore was not affected by the restriction against non-English- or non-French-speaking Europeans who were the only Caucasians disqualified by the covenant.[81] Justice Garrow's decision was subsequently confirmed by the Ontario Court of Appeal.[82]

A year later another covenant, apparently more precise, came before the Ontario courts in *Re: Bryers and Morris*.[83] The covenant declared that "none of the lands described herein shall be used or occupied by, let or sold to negroes or Asiatics, Bulgarians, Austrians, Russians, Serbs, Roumanians, Turks, Armenians, whether British subjects or not, or foreign born Italians, Greeks or Jews."[84] Though the aspiring purchaser was a foreign-born Jew, a category specified in the covenant, Justice Hodgins decided that "The evidence before the Court . . . is not sufficient and the inquiry which ought to be made should not be made in chambers." He therefore declined to pronounce upon the validity of the covenant and gave the parties one month to collect sufficient evidence "as may enable the Court to pronounce definitely and finally on this restriction."[85] Justice Garrow's decision could be interpreted as implicitly accepting the validity of a racial restrictive covenant, for he concluded only (albeit inventively) that the covenant in dispute did not apply to the purchaser. Justice Hodgins' message, however, had broader implications. If there was evidence that a purchaser came from a group named in the covenant, and this was not sufficient to enforce it, then it is difficult to think of what further evidence the parties might collect to enable a definitive pronouncement by a court of law. Some other body beyond the courts, Justice Hodgins was implying, must supply the justification for a restrictive covenant.

A step was taken away from this direction in March 1945 by Justice Chevrier in *Re: McDougall and Waddell*.[86] A covenant had been registered in September 1944 restraining "any person or persons other than Gentiles (non-semitic) of European or British or Irish or Scottish racial origin" from owning or using the land.[87] The question put to Justice Chevrier was a narrow one: was the covenant invalid as an offence against the *Racial Discrimination Act*, proclaimed six months before the covenant was made. Justice Chevrier acknowledged that the covenant was discriminatory, but he held that the Act only covered the items specifically enumerated – the publication or display of "any notice, sign, symbol, emblem or other representation indicating discrimination or an intention to discriminate" – and this did not extend to the registration of a covenant or deed in the Registry Office.[88] In an aside Chevrier lamented "the unchristian action of racial discrimination," denounced the Holocaust "inflicted upon certain races and creeds by a satanic direction in this present war," and extended sympathy to the suffering Jewish people. Nevertheless he felt bound to uphold the covenant, for the legislature could have increased the range of the Act but chose to limit it to certain specific instances.[89] An option was, however, available, as an editorial note in the *Dominion Law Reports* suggested, for he could have been guided by Section 1(A) of the Act, which was a general prohibition against publication or display, rather than Section 1(B), which enumerated a set of prohibited examples.[90] Justice Chevrier reopened the possibility of having a covenant enforced by the courts, and demonstrated that Justice Hodgins' impossibly strict conditions need not be met.

The era of permissiveness thus initiated was not to last for long. In October 1945 Justice Keiller Mackay heard the case *Re: Drummond Wren* in the Ontario High Court.[91] The Workers' Educational Association had purchased a lot in East York, intending to build a house on it and then raffle it off for fund-raising purposes. It was, however, discovered that the land was restricted by a covenant pronouncing that it was "not to be sold to Jews or persons of objectionable nationality." This would seriously complicate the raffle, so the WEA applied to have the covenant declared invalid. Four alternative grounds were offered: "first, that it is void as against public policy; secondly, that it is invalid as a restraint on alienation; thirdly, that it is void for uncertainty; and fourthly, that it contravenes the provisions of the *Racial Discrimination Act*."[92] The applicant Drummond Wren, who was general secretary of the WEA, was represented by John Cartwright and Irving Himel, and J. M. Bennett appeared on behalf of the Canadian Jewish Congress, assisted by Jacob Finkelman, Bora Laskin and Charles Dubin. Justice Mackay had notice served upon any other parties interested in this or adjacent lands, but no one appeared in court to oppose the application.

The covenant was declared void on three of the four grounds suggested by counsel. First and most emphatically Justice Mackay found the covenant to be contrary to public policy. Citing English and American authorities he established that any contract, covenant or agreement injurious to public policy could not be supported, and that it was the proper function of the courts to interpret and apply public policy at any given moment. Public policy will fluctuate with circumstances and with time, and in determining what it was in Ontario in 1945 Mackay considered an imaginative range of indicators. Canada had subscribed, for example, to the Atlantic Charter and to the *UN Charter*, committing her to respect human rights without distinction as to "race" or religion. The Ontario legislature had revealed its abhorrence of racial discrimination through the *Insurance Act*, through regulations passed under the *Community Halls Act*, and through the *Racial Discrimination Act*. Supporting statements were enlisted from Franklin Roosevelt, Winston Churchill, Charles De Gaulle and others to show that antisemitism was incompatible with the democratic order installed in Ontario and could be analogous to treason. In Keiller Mackay's stated opinion,

nothing could be more calculated to create or deepen divisions between existing religious and ethnic groups in the Province, or in this Country, than the sanction of a method of land transfer which would permit the segregation and confinement of particular groups to particular business or residential areas, or conversely, would exclude particular groups from particular business or residential areas. . . .

Ontario, and Canada too, may well be termed a Province, and a Country, of minorities in regard to the religious and ethnic groups which live therein. It appears to me to be a moral duty, at least, to lend aid to all forces of cohesion, and similarly to repel all fissiparous tendencies which would imperil national unity.

Conscious that he could be accused of creating a "new head of public policy," Justice Mackay added that in the absence of written constitutional guarantees it was an established feature of the common law courts to employ "the doctrine of public policy as an active agent in the promotion of the public weal." He continued:

I do not conceive that I would be breaking new ground were I to hold the restrictive covenant impugned in this proceeding to be void as against public policy. Rather I would be applying well-recognized principles of public policy to a set of facts requiring their invocation in the interest of the public good.[93]

Considering the other grounds more quickly, Justice Mackay confirmed that the covenant was an improper restraint on alienation. There was no time limitation placed upon the life of the covenant, so it could not be regarded as a "partial restraint."[94] Furthermore the wording was uncertain. The phrase "persons of objectionable nationality" had no legal meaning at all, and even the term "Jews" had been found less than certain in the recent British case *Clayton v. Ramsden*.[95] Finally, though he recognized "considerable merit" in John Cartwright's argument that the registration of a covenant constituted publication and was therefore contrary to the *Racial Discrimination Act*, Mackay deemed it unnecessary to contradict Chevrier's judgment directly in view of the fact that "the public policy applicable to this case in no way depends on the terms of the Racial Discrimination Act, save to the extent that such Act constitutes a legislative recognition of the policy which I have applied."[96]

Justice Mackay's reasoning coincided exactly with the philosophical thrust of CJC strategy after the War: the goal was cohesion, the elimination of barriers, the principle that access should not depend on group membership. Canadian Jews were delighted at the result, and gratified at the part played by the CJC in achieving it. The JPRC prepared a pamphlet publicizing the decision and explaining its impact upon the rights of racial minorities.[97] In the United States, "Negroes, Jews and other racial and religious minorities found it tonic to their interests and so widely advertised it."[98] Even the crusty old *Globe and Mail* was moved to call it a "blow to prejudice" which was "on the noblest level of jurisprudence."[99] From lawyers the *Drummond Wren* decision drew immediate accolades, particularly for its innovative method for the interpretation and application of public policy. In reporting the case *Dominion Law Reports* inserted an enthusiastic editorial note:

The present decision is of importance not merely in breaking new ground of public policy, and as indicating the creative nature of the judicial process, but also in furnishing an instance of a Court ascertaining public policy by analogy to legislative enactment rather than judicial decision. The common, as opposed to the civil, law has been slow to use legislative policy from which to argue to new and unprovided for situations, but the principle seems to accord with accepted ideas of legislative supremacy as well as our democratic form of government.[100]

Other legal commentators have echoed this analysis, praising Keiller Mackay's courage and regarding his decision as the "dawn of a new era" in judicial interpretation. *Drummond Wren* was widely celebrated by scholars in Britain, the United States and Canada; one American law review termed it "a landmark case in the legal order of the entire world, and one that should always be held in honor."[101]

Judges far beyond the direct influence of an Ontario precedent paid tribute by citing *Drummond Wren*. By 1945 every American court which had faced the issue had given its sanction to racial restrictive covenants, finding most typically that in the absence of explicit legislative prohibition they must be upheld.[102] The National Association for the Advancement of Colored People launched a major drive involving political lobbying and court challenges to change public policy, and *Drummond Wren* was embraced as a tactical ally to demonstrate that existing policy already opposed restrictive covenants if only it were intelligently applied.[103] In a signal victory, the Michigan Supreme Court in 1947 relied on the Ontario decision to find a property covenant against blacks to be invalid.[104] When this case, with three others, came before the US Supreme Court in January 1948, Attorney General Tom C. Clark submitted an *amicus curiae* brief citing *Drummond Wren* in opposition to restrictive covenants, and Solicitor General Philip B. Perlman referred to it in his oral presentation.[105] In a unanimous decision issued on 3 May 1948, usually referred to as *Shelley v. Kraemer*, the Supreme Court found all four covenants to be unenforceable since by its nature a covenant requires "the full coercive power of government" to uphold a private agreement to engage in discrimination, and this amounted to an unconstitutional use of the public power.[106]

A decision based on the American constitution had no authority in Canada, though it served as a corroboration of the wisdom of *Drummond Wren*. Meanwhile in Canada there were further indications reinforcing the accuracy of Keiller Mackay's interpretation of public policy. In January 1947 the Toronto skating rink Icelandia refused admission to a Jewish girl, apparently according to its usual practice. In protest the Rev. James Finley, national chair of the Fellowship Of Reconciliation, held a meeting at his Carlton Street United Church where 500 participants passed a unanimous resolution calling for legislation against discrimination.[107] The issue was promptly taken up by Alderman Nathan Phillips. With the support of a public delegation, Phillips convinced the Toronto Board of Police Commissioners to pass unanimously a regulation in February 1947 withholding licences from any operation under the Board's authority – including all places of recreation and amusement – which practised racial or religious discrimination.[108] Also in 1947 the CCF government of Saskatchewan enacted a *Bill of Rights* which provided *inter alia* that "every person or class of person shall enjoy ... the right to acquire by purchase, to own, lease, rent or occupy any property ... without discrimination because of his race, religion, colour, or ethnic or national origin."[109] Furthermore a Gallup Poll released that summer revealed that 64 percent of Canadians would support legislation against discrimination.[110]

Bernard Wolf's application therefore seemed relatively straightforward; the Beach O' Pines covenant must surely not be valid on grounds of public policy. On 6 May 1948 Donald Egener, Mrs. Noble's solicitor, replied to Ted Richmond that "in our opinion the decision rendered in the case of *Re: Drummond Wren* . . . applies to the facts of the present sale, with the result that the Clause (f) objected to is invalid and the vendor and purchaser are not bound to observe it."[111] The cautious Richmond was not, however, satisfied. He wrote back the same day insisting that an order be obtained from the courts to declare the restrictive covenant void and of no effect.[112] Egener thereupon made application under the *Vendors and Purchasers Act*[113] which provided that

A vendor or purchaser of real or leasehold estate or his representative may, at any time and from time to time, apply in a summary way to the Supreme Court or a judge thereof in respect of any acquisition or objection or any claim for compensation, or any other question arising out of or connected with the contract, except a question affecting the existence or validity of the contract, and the Court or judge may make such order upon the application as appears just, and refer any question to a master or other officer for inquiry and report.

He asked on behalf of Mrs. Noble for an order

declaring that the objection to the restrictive covenant made in writing on behalf of the purchaser dated the 5th day of May, 1948, has been fully answered by the Vendor and that the same does not constitute a valid objection to the title *or for such further and other Order as may seem just*.[114]

A solid precedent existed; a friendly and influential jurisdiction had made a parallel decision; the people's representatives had advanced the legislative line against discrimination; the popular will had been tested. Neither Mrs. Noble nor Mr. Wolf had any reason to doubt the successful outcome of their application when it was heard in chambers by Justice Schroeder on 22 May 1948.

4. THE PUBLIC INTEREST

When the other property owners learned that Mrs. Noble had agreed to sell her cottage to a Jew, a meeting was convened of the Beach O' Pines Protective Association to discuss strategy options. First they engaged a London lawyer, John D. Harrison, to approach Ted Richmond with an offer to buy the Agreement of Purchase and Sale at a profit to Mr. Wolf.

This offer was "unceremoniously rejected."[115] The Association then determined to enforce the covenant by more formal means. Six Association members retained Kenneth G. Morden, KC, a prominent Toronto lawyer (and later justice of the Ontario Court of Appeal), to oppose the sale to Mr. Wolf.[116] They were therefore already mobilized for action when a Notice of Motion was sent on 8 May 1948 to the Association and the Frank S. Salter Company, pursuant to the application of Donald Egener, announcing that a hearing would occur in two weeks' time.[117] The Salter Company had passed out of existence, but the Association accepted the challenge on behalf of all the Beach O' Pines property owners. At the hearing Justice Shroeder confirmed this arrangement by directing Mr. Morden to represent the interests of the other landowners as well as the six who had retained him.[118]

Ted Richmond was alerted to the strength of the opposition being raised against this apparently simple property transaction. Bernard Wolf was an old friend of the Richmond family, so Ted visited him at his home in the evening to explain the situation frankly. The young lawyer told his client about *Drummond Wren* and suggested that John Cartwright, victorious senior counsel in that case, might be retained to represent them at the forthcoming hearing. Mr. Wolf was determined to fight, and insisted that Richmond call Cartwright immediately at his home in Toronto. John Cartwright was equally enthusiastic and agreed over the telephone to take the case, asking to have the papers sent to him the next day. Though Mr. Cartwright would appear on the record on behalf of the vendor Mrs. Noble, it was Mr. Wolf who recruited him and agreed to be responsible for all fees and costs associated with the hearing.[119]

Before Justice Schroeder of the Ontario High Court, Mr. Morden argued that over the years since it had been formed in 1935, the Beach O' Pines Protective Association had nurtured a congenial summer community among its members. It had paved and maintained the roads, provided police and fire protection, and undertaken substantial general improvement to the property, to the effect that the Beach had become a desirable location whose value would be diminished by any change to its character. This positive development had occurred under the protective shield of the restrictions contained in the covenant, which each owner had been aware of at time of purchase. Very few changes in ownership had taken place, so that it was a compatible and intimate group of citizens who in 1948 sought to maintain their enjoyment and the value of their property.[120] Mr. Cartwright, assisted by Paul Hess, submitted that the racial clause in the covenant was contrary to public policy, uncertain, and an attempt to restrain alienation of property. For all these reasons it was void and of no effect.[121] In the course of the presentation Justice Schroeder seemed unconvinced by Mr. Cartwright's argument, interrupting on one occasion to state:

What we must keep in mind is that while protecting the rights of minorities, we must not lose sight of the rights of the majorities as well. Let us say that a man does not want Hindus or Orientals as his neighbours, would that be against public policy too?
Mr. Cartwright: Yes, I have no hesitation in saying it would be.

And again the judge interjected:

There is nothing to indicate that Wolf could not buy somewhere else. . . .
Mr. Cartwright: I have been told he would have to walk a long way along Lake Huron before he could find a place to buy.
Mr. Justice Schroeder: I am trying to view the situation as a whole. I'm considering the effect on other people who bought property in this area on the strength of this covenant.

In another revealing comment Schroeder asked:

This is a small restricted area. It prevents people of a certain race from living there. Is such a narrow restriction contrary to public good when there are millions of square miles in the country?
Mr. Cartwright: There is no way for the Court to say it is valid in this small place without saying it is valid everywhere else.

When Cartwright's submission was completed Richmond supported it in its entirely on behalf of Mr. Wolf. Justice Schroeder then announced that he would reserve judgment: "This is a problem of far reaching importance. It is not only this Lake Huron summer colony that is involved but property all over the country. I want to give it study and consideration."[122]

In his judgment issued 11 June 1948, Justice Schroeder considered first the restraint on alienation question. He agreed that freedom of alienation was a "cardinal principle of English and Ontario law," but since the covenant was limited in time to 1 August 1962, and only applied to a "particular class of persons," he concluded that it did not "substantially" deprive Mrs. Noble of her power to sell her property and therefore "comes within the category of partial restraints on alienation." Partial restraints, he reiterated, were valid.[123]

Next Schroeder addressed the more complicated question of certainty. Was it possible to identify absolutely a person of Jewish "race or blood" as stipulated in the covenant? Citing dictionaries and encyclopedias and even St. Paul, the judge found satisfactory evidence that "blood" and "race" could be used interchangeably, and that Jews were both commonly and officially considered to be a "race," for example in the Canadian census. The definition of a Jew, he argued, "must surely be dealt with in a practical way . . . in a broad common sense way." If necessary, an alleged Jew could be "subjected to an examination for discovery, in which questions are directed to him as to his family history and ancestry; evidence may also be available from friends, neighbours, acquaintances or relatives of the person whose racial origin is the subject of investigation." The application of common sense, in Justice Schroeder's opinion, could satisfactorily determine a racial identity. In the British case of *Clayton v. Ramsden*, which John Cartwright had brought up both here and in *Drummond Wren*, the dispute was over a will which insisted that a daughter marry a person of "Jewish parentage" and "Jewish faith" or be disinherited. Since the outcome would be complete forfeiture of the estate, the House of Lords was correct to demand absolute certainty, Schroeder conceded, especially since "Jewish parentage" did not specify whether it meant one or both parents, multiple generations, status by birth or conversion, etc. The unfortunate daughter could never be certain about an intended spouse and no court could enlighten her beforehand, and thus she must either renounce her inheritance or renounce marriage forever. But in a deed or a covenant "quite different considerations apply." The test was the simpler one of constructing "the object which they were designed to accomplish." In *Essex Real Estate v. Holmes*, an Ontario court had decided the issue based on the judge's interpretation of what the terms in the covenant meant, and he had decided that a Syrian was a Caucasian. In Mr. Wolf's case his own solicitor had announced that "he might be considered of the Jewish race or blood." The question in any event was not whether Mr. Wolf was a Jew but whether the terminology of the covenant conveyed the intent of its designers with sufficient clarity for a court to determine who was to be excluded. Justice Schroeder decided that it did.[124]

The major point was of course the public policy definition established by *Drummond Wren*. Justice Schroeder felt that it was inapplicable in the present case because *Drummond Wren* concerned basic shelter whereas in

Noble and Wolf it was the less urgent matter of summer recreation. Also, the covenant in *Drummond Wren* was unlimited in time.[125] But he went beyond these technicalities. Emphasizing that he was not bound by a decision in a court of co-ordinate jurisdiction, Justice Schroeder declared that he could not agree with Keiller Mackay's interpretation of public policy. Pronouncements by allied leaders, the *UN Charter* or any other alleged international obligation had never been given effect by Canadian legislation, and the UN itself had uttered no demand that domestic laws must be overborne by *Charter* provisions. To Justice Schroeder it appeared that his colleague Mackay had created "an entirely novel head of public policy." He continued:

While it may be fairly assumed that the public policy of this country is opposed to the taking of affirmative action by any competent legislative authority which would be inconsistent with the sentiments or ideals expressed in these treaties or enactments, it would, in my view, constitute a radical departure from established principle to deduce therefrom any policy of the law which may be claimed to transcend the paramount public policy that one is not lightly to interfere with the freedom of contract.[126]

His proper function as a judge was "to expound and interpret the law and not to create the law based on any individual notion or opinion of what the law ought to be." A competent legislative body must "determine what is best for the public good" and make a proper enactment. Until the democratically elected representatives of the people had decided upon it, it was not in the province of a judge to do so.[127] All three of John Cartwright's arguments had been rejected, and the covenant was held valid and enforceable. Counsel for Mrs. Noble had not satisfactorily answered the objection raised in Ted Richmond's letter of 5 May, and so the motion for a declaratory order negating the covenant was dismissed and she was ordered to pay the costs of the third parties who intervened.[128]

The day after the decision was announced Cartwright wrote to Richmond:

I must confess that I am gravely disappointed in the result. I was quite prepared to have the Drummond Wren case distinguished insofar as it rested upon the point of restraint of alienation but you will observe that Mr. Justice Schroeder has dealt also with the point of uncertainty and public policy and has flatly disagreed with Mr. Justice Mackay. It is never the part of counsel to urge clients to appeal but I hope that it will be decided to carry the matter to the Court of Appeal.

Inevitably, judicial opinion upon questions of public policy will be unconsciously influenced by the personal views of the individual judges but on this point I think the reasoning of Mr. Justice Mackay is more persuasive than that of Mr. Justice Schroeder. On the point of uncertainty with greatest respect I do not think that the distinctions drawn by Mr. Justice Schroeder between the present case and the Drummond Wren case and Clayton and Ramsden are sound.[129]

Elsewhere the Schroeder judgment was regretted, but the judge himself was treated with more sympathy than Cartwright gave him. Generally speaking the conclusion was that Schroeder had no choice, considering the absence of specific legislation, and that he had properly channelled the problem to the legislature, where it belonged. CCF leader Ted Jolliffe declared that "The time has come for Ontario to clarify the law which guides the decisions of the courts and protect the rights of its citizens," and promised to introduce an appropriate bill in the next session.[130] CCF MPP Harry Walters issued a press release saying that

It is a sad commentary on the laws of this supposedly democratic land, that the judge should be obliged to render such a decision. . . . Laws against discrimination should be so clear and forceful that a decision such as that rendered by Judge Schroeder last week would be impossible.[131]

The call for corrective legislation, spearheaded by the CCF, was taken up by the Canadian Congress of Labour and the Trades and Labour Congress.[132] As Jolliffe wrote privately, "I think it was a mistake to expect too much of the courts. After all, we do not want judges to make law: we want law to be made by the elected representatives of the people. As far as McKay's [sic] judgment is concerned, I have never felt that it served the purpose."[133]

Nevertheless, the parties most directly concerned decided to take Cartwright's advice and seek a judicial solution. Mr. Wolf was a wealthy man. His assets, valued at over $2 million, were clearly adequate in the 1940s to sustain an appeal, and he was convinced that he should continue the battle as a "mission [for] the protection of the rights, freedoms and happiness of all Canadian Jewry."[134] Furthermore, Justice Keiller Mackay had asked to meet Mr. Wolf shortly after the Schroeder judgment appeared and told him that he was "outraged" by the decision,[135] an apparent endorsement of Cartwright's view that an appeal would be successful. Wolf and Richmond went to Cartwright's office in Toronto to announce their decision and to discuss arrangements for the appeal.

Cartwright drafted the Notice of Appeal and Richmond filed it on 21 June 1948, stating as grounds:

1) That the said clause in the restrictive covenant in question is illegal, void, and unenforceable, being contrary to public policy;
2) That the said clause is void and unenforceable for uncertainty;
3) That the said clause is an illegal and void restraint upon the freedom of alienation of the lands thereby affected;
4) That the said clause is void and unenforceable as a restraint upon the alienation, occupancy and user of land because of race or blood, such being a novel restraint unknown to and unrecognized by the Common Law.[136]

In the midst of preparing the Appeal Books shortly thereafter, Richmond had a flash of anxiety. He had been reading the Japanese Canadian deportation case, and was reminded that both the Supreme Court of Canada and the Judicial Committee of the Privy Council had already decided that "race" was a sufficiently certain category for legal enforcement. In early 1945 the federal government had conducted a survey amongst Japanese Canadians, asking them to declare a preference either for "repatriation" to Japan after the war or for relocation in Canada east of the Rockies. In conditions of wartime internment and an atmosphere of intense anti-Japanese sentiment throughout Canada, 6,884 adult Japanese Canadians opted for "repatriation."[137] By the time the war actually ended, however, 4,527 of these people had applied to reverse their earlier decision, but the government utilized the authority of the *War Measures Act*, just two weeks before it was due to expire, to pass orders-in-council on 15 December 1945 providing for the deportation of certain "persons of the Japanese race" regardless of their citizenship or even their birthplace.[138] Following a challenge by the Co-Operative Committee on Japanese Canadians, supported by the attorney general of Saskatchewan, the federal government agreed in January 1946 to refer the deportation orders to the Supreme Court of Canada. John Cartwright and Andrew Brewin argued the case against the deportation claiming, *inter alia*, that

The Orders-in-Council throughout depend upon the persons affected being in fact of the "Japanese race." It would be the duty of the Court on any application for Habeas Corpus to determine the issue as to whether or not any particular individual was "of the Japanese race." . . . The phrase "Japanese race" is so vague as to make the provisions unenforceable.

The textbook authorities ... indicate that the word "race" is not definable in scientific terms and has not any precise meaning. It is a hypothetical group inferred to have existed in the past. Provisions in a will in regard to the "Jewish race" have been held to be void for uncertainty. . . . [139]

Among the seven justices hearing the case, only Chief Justice Rinfret deigned to comment on this argument, and then only summarily to dismiss it:

[T]he question referred to us is whether the Orders in Council are *ultra vires*, and the point that some words or sentences therein are vague does not fall within that question. The Orders in Council would not be *ultra vires* even if some parts thereof were vague.[140]

Upon failing in Ottawa, the Co-Operative Committee appealed to the Privy Council in London, where Andrew Brewin repeated the argument that "the Orders-in-Council which empower the Minister of Labour to make orders for deportation of persons 'of the Japanese Race' are so vague that they are incapable of application to ascertained persons and are therefore inoperative and invalid."[141] To this the Privy Council replied: "It is sufficient to say that in their Lordships' opinion they are not."[142] The "common sense" definition of "race," taken for granted in the orders-in-council, had been explicitly affirmed in the courts. Although the Canadian government decided not to proceed with enforced deportations despite their legal approval, Ted Richmond feared that the Privy Council's dictum would undermine the second ground of the Noble and Wolf appeal based on the uncertainty of racial definitions. John Cartwright, however, did not share this concern, and reassured his junior colleague that "uncertainty" remained an effective ground on which to challenge the covenant. Cartwright's confidence prevailed, and no amendment was made in the appeal case.[143]

It was at this point that the Canadian Jewish Congress became actively involved in the case. Ben Kayfetz called Ted Richmond to inform him of how important this appeal was to the Congress, and to offer assistance. With Cartwright and Richmond's concurrence, the JPRC formed a committee chaired by Bora Laskin to monitor the proceedings and provide advice. At Cartwright's suggestion the CJC retained J. Shirley Denison, KC, a former treasurer of the Law Society of Upper Canada and one of Canada's leading authorities on real estate law, to represent the purchaser, Wolf, and Mr. Norman Borins was engaged to assist him. Cartwright and Hess continued to represent the vendor, Mrs. Noble.[144] Professor Laskin's committee of Jacob Finkelman, S. M. Harris, Lou Herman, Syd Midanik and Dick Shiff, plus Cartwright, Borins, Denison and Hess and with Richmond and Wolf in occasional attendance, repeatedly examined the Schroeder decision for flaws. They were confident that they were properly prepared for the appeal hearing set for 20 September. But the Court of Appeal decided that all the Beach O' Pines property owners must be contacted and given the opportunity to appear, rather than simply those who directly retained Mr. Morden. Eventually 26 of the 35 Beach O' Pines members, 13 American and 13 Canadian, agreed to be represented by Morden, and the others declined the right to be represented at all. Among the Canadians on Morden's list was Judge H. E. Grosch of Chatham. The other Canadians came from London, Toronto and Stratford. All the Americans had Michigan addresses.[145]

With all this delay it was not until 10 January 1949 that the case came before Chief Justice Robertson and Justices Henderson, Hope, Hogg and Aylesworth of the Ontario Court of Appeal.[146] The appeal team met an unanticipated hostility from the bench. Shirley Denison, who joined the appellants' team after the grounds were submitted in June 1948, led the argument with a new objection not raised before: conditions (a) to (e) in the covenant dealt properly with how the land could be *used*, but clause (f), the racial restriction, applied improperly to the *user*. "It is not therefore a covenant that will run with the land, under the rule of Tulk v. Moxhay." According to Mr. Denison, the covenant in question was purely a personal one and as such was binding upon the original signatories alone; only covenants that "ran with the land" were enforceable against a subsequent purchaser. It would be an arbitrary extension of the doctrine "to uphold a covenant which was not a burden on the land, but rather a restraint on the capacity of particular races to own the land." Chief Justice Robertson interrupted frequently, primarily to object that "This is a wholly new point, never argued before in this case." Mr. Denison, then in his seventies, responded with dignity to these intrusions: "If the Court does not want to hear me, I will sit down." The chief justice snapped, "Oh we will hear you, Mr. Denison." Robertson also complained that the intent of the *Vendors and Purchasers Act*, under which this motion was brought before the court, was to settle differences between vendor and purchaser. It was therefore "anomalous" that in this case the vendor and purchaser were in agreement.[147]

Norman Borins followed, and was given a particularly "rough time" by the court.[148] It fell to Borins to elaborate the public policy argument, which he did by indicating that for a hundred years Ontario policy had been contrary to racial distinctions. To reject the covenant would not be to "create" public policy; on the contrary, "To give legal sanction to such a covenant as this would itself be to create a new head." To Borins' argument that specific legislation was not required for the court to recognize a public policy against racial discrimination, the chief justice interjected, "That might involve the abolition of such groups as the St. Andrew's Society and the St. George's Society."[149] It was clearly not a very sympathetic court.

The most complete case against the covenant was developed by John Cartwright, subject though it was to constant interruption from the bench. Fundamentally Cartwright pressed the *Drummond Wren* precedent: "a covenant such as this is against the public good, and hence contrary to public policy." The covenant was also uncertain and therefore unenforceable, following *Clayton v. Ramsden*, and was an invalid restraint on alienation. It was true that "partial" restraints had been upheld before, but those cases had different circumstances from the current matter and were not binding on this court. "I ask the Court at least to say that the right to impose a partial restraint must not be extended beyond the decided cases; a restraint such as the present, excluding particular classes in the community, would be such an extension." Finally Cartwright insisted that the 1944 *Racial Discrimination Act* did apply. "Registration of the covenant is a publication to the world," and was directly contrary to Section 1 of the Act. *Re: McDougall and Waddell* must be overturned.[150]

On behalf of the respondents, Kenneth Morden pointed out that Mrs. Noble had benefited from the covenant for 15 years, enjoying the protected environment it created, and only now raised a doubt about its validity. If the covenant were breached it would affect the value of the properties and therefore would injure the other owners. Their contract not to do so was binding. The 1944 Act favoured the respondents: since the legislature had entered the field and had remained silent on this particular issue, the court could not find a public policy against it. UN and other resolutions opposing discrimination were irrelevant. "This covenant is in effect no more discriminatory than one that requires that a house built on a particular parcel shall be of a prescribed minimum value." Freedom to choose one's associates, as confirmed by *Christie v. York*, made a positive contribution and was in the public interest: it ensured a healthy variety in the community and operated against the "complete regimentation" of society. As a partial restraint the covenant was valid, and *Clayton v. Ramsden* must be distinguished because "A will is a unilateral act, but here there is evidence of mutual intention." The law did recognize a Jewish "race," in the *Statistics Act* for example, so there was no reason why a court must find the term uncertain.[151] If there was ever any doubt about who was a Jew, Morden concluded, it would suffice simply to ask the person in question. Justice Henderson commented gratuitously: "Oh, you don't have to ask, you can tell."[152] Henderson added: "At the moment, I am inclined to think that if we declared this covenant void, we would stir up a good deal more hate in the community than otherwise. It might create hate, ill-will, and probably violence there."[153]

From their verbal interjections during the hearing of the appeal it would seem that the judges' views were fairly well formed, but it was not until five months later, on 9 June 1949, that the written decision appeared. Chief Justice Robertson went through all four issues raised in Richmond's Notice plus the fifth raised orally by Denison. He found that this was a partial, and therefore a valid, restraint upon alienation. "The field of likely purchasers is left largely untouched. There is nothing in any way approaching a general restriction upon alienation." Since many covenants restricted ownership to members of a certain family, "race or blood" had frequently been upheld as a valid criterion. He agreed with Schroeder that rules of certainty were less strict for a covenant than a condition.

The Court is to give the words their usual and ordinary meaning and not a technical one. Further, it is not fatal to a covenant that some part or parts of it are not clear, if the meaning of what remains is clear. . . . The covenant should be declared void only if it is impossible reasonably to give it any meaning.

Denison's submission that the covenant did not run with the land was quickly dismissed as irrelevant to the specific question before the court, which Robertson took to be the simple one of whether Mrs. Noble had answered Mr. Wolf as to the validity of the covenant.[154]

It was Robertson's comments on the public policy issue that attracted most publicity. Meditating upon a pleasant holiday spent in congenial company, the chief justice gave the opinion that

The purpose of clause (f) here in question is obviously to assure, in some degree, that the residents are of a class who will get along well together. To magnify this innocent and modest effort to establish and maintain a place suitable for a pleasant summer residence into an enterprise that offends against some public policy, requires a stronger imagination than I possess. . . . There is nothing criminal or immoral involved; the public interest is in no way concerned.

Then, in an abrupt denial of the opinion expressed by Schroeder, among others, that it was up to the legislature to make explicit rules on the subject, he added:

Doubtless, mutual goodwill and esteem among the people of the numerous races that inhabit Canada is greatly to be desired. . . . To be worth anything, either at home or abroad, there is required the goodwill and esteem of a free people, who genuinely feel and sincerely act upon, the sentiments they express. A wise appreciation of the impotence of laws in the development of such genuine sentiment, rather than mere formal observances, no doubt restrains our legislators from enacting, and should restrain our Courts from propounding, rules of law to enforce what can only be of natural growth, if it is to be of value to anyone.[155]

All four of his colleagues concurred in a unanimous affirmation of the Schroeder decision. Justice Henderson bluntly asserted: "I am of opinion that the judgment in Re Drummond Wren is wrong in law and should not be followed." For Henderson, freedom of contract and freedom of association were absolute, and besides, "people are enabled to exercise a choice with respect to their friends and neighbours." As for the uncertainty argument, Henderson insisted that "a common-sense reading of the covenant makes its interpretation certain and unquestionable. . . . It is common knowledge that the people who inhabit Canada are divided into races or are described as members of one or other particular race. . . . 'A person of Jewish blood' is a phrase thoroughly understood. . . ."[156] Justice Hogg concurred with his colleague in this view. "The classification must necessarily be made having regard to the word 'race' in its ordinary and popular sense. If the language of clause (f) of the covenant is regarded in its ordinary and popular sense, this clause cannot be said to be void for uncertainty. . . ." Hogg also expanded upon the reason for rejecting Denison's "run with the land" argument:

It is true that an appellate Court may allow points of law not taken in the Court of first instance to be raised upon appeal, but, in the present case, not only was the point of law argued by Mr. Denison not involved in the reply to the requisition on title and not raised upon the hearing of the original application, but it was not one of the grounds of appeal to this Court and all of the parties who would be affected by the decision of this Court upon this aspect of the case were not before the Court. For these reasons I do not think the point in question can be considered upon this appeal.[157]

Justice Hope emphasized the "public interest" theme, giving the opinion that "freedom of the individual in and under a democracy has implicit in it, as an absolute, the freedom of association. . . . I can find nothing in the scheme of covenants in the association in this case which could be suggested, with an atom of reason, as being unduly oppressive of the public."[158] There was general agreement that uncertainty was not an issue, that the restraint upon alienation was acceptably partial, and that public policy did not oppose this covenant. The appeal was dismissed with costs against the appellants.[159]

The public reaction was swift. On behalf of the CJC Rabbi Feinberg condemned the decision: "Canadian democracy may never grow beyond a collection of isolated racial units, roped off from one another by a legalized iron curtain of snobbery and barred from the mutual acquaintance and understanding which alone can develop internal unity."[160] The Association for Civil Liberties was equally critical: "The court would appear not to recognize that a war has been fought in which millions were killed for the principles of the four freedoms and the Atlantic Charter."[161] Both national labour organizations drafted resolutions denouncing the judgment on 10 June.[162] The *Hamilton News*, among the great majority opposing the decision, vituperated against "one of the most vicious legal expedients ever to be allowed under the British system of law, namely the restrictive covenant."[163] In the midst of this publicity the Canadian Institute of Public Opinion conducted a poll asking: "If you were buying a home and the neighbours asked you to sign an agreement promising not to sell or rent it later to people of certain races or color, would you be willing or not willing to sign such an agreement?" When the results were announced in July they showed that only 19 percent of Canadians would sign, 13 percent were undecided and 68 percent definitely would not sign.[164] For the *Toronto Star Weekly*, "This finding shows the prevalence of the democratic spirit of tolerance among Canadians. . . . [T]he law clearly is lagging behind enlightened public opinion."[165] The *Toronto Star* demanded legislation to eliminate such undemocratic practices as restrictive covenants, and in the meantime urged an appeal of *Noble and Wolf* to the Supreme Court of Canada.[166]

Editorially, only the *Globe and Mail* approved of what the Robertson court had done. Identifying two basic principles – the right to food and shelter without discrimination and the right to choose one's own associates – the *Globe* contended

In this case it cannot seriously be claimed that basic rights to shelter are being denied by the covenant. But to assert that any group of people should be forbidden to associate themselves in a perfectly lawful manner, would create problems of a far-reaching character with all sorts of dangerous implications. This newspaper does not have to protest its opposition to racial discrimination in social and economic relationships, but it is convinced that to make a law that discrimination should cease would not be the effective way to deal with the problem. . . . It would appear to us that to give any one a legal right to force himself uninvited into an association of people would be the most certain way to add to social tensions. . . . There is much to correct in our treatment of minorities in Canada, but force is not the way to do it.[167]

5. PREPARING FOR THE SUPREME COURT OF CANADA

John Cartwright was distressed but not surprised by the Court of Appeal decision. Nor had he changed his mind about what the outcome should have been. The day the judgment came down he wrote:

I read the reasons with care and I find them particularly unsatisfactory on the question of uncertainty. They deal with this point by saying that the same certainty is not required in a covenant as in a condition of defeasance. They do not attempt to define the test which would have to be applied in determining whether any individual was or was not within the scope of the covenant.

There is always a danger of getting too much convinced of the right and justice of one's own side of a case but I must confess that I hope the clients will decide to take the case further.[168]

But the principals in the case were beginning to doubt the wisdom of proceeding any further. Mr. Wolf had already spent thousands of dollars and was discouraged by the unanimous result at the appeal. Although he could readily afford the financial costs of the proceedings, it was the emotional strain that was taking its toll. In particular his wife was urging him to drop the matter, confessing that she was embarrassed by the whole affair and wanted to retire from it with dignity. And the other necessary partner to the transaction, Mrs. Noble, had never been truly keen on the contest and was becoming anxious that her cottage remained unsold and was probably declining in value because of the controversy.[169] Even the CJC had to consider its options. Fred Catzman, who replaced Rabbi Feinberg as JPRC chair about this time, later said:

we had to make a decision. There were suggestions, vigorously upheld, that the wisest thing would be to drop the proceedings. The case, admittedly, was not the best test case on which to try out the principle of discrimination. It did not concern shelter as the 1945 case did, but summer property. The Court of Appeal ruled in favour of the restrictive covenant without a dissenting opinion. The Bench, we were told, is always reluctant to give a judgment on public policy and some people felt that to base our argument on uncertainty, i.e. on the inability to determine who is not racially a Jew, Negro, or other person, would be a self-contradiction and a poor position for a Jewish organization to place itself in.[170]

Nevertheless the CJC's decision, when it came later in June, was to carry the case to the Supreme Court of Canada. The organization would prepare and finance the appeal; Noble and Wolf would not need to participate beyond lending their names to the motion. To some extent this was a tactical move. Confidence was not 100 percent in a favourable answer, but there could be advantages either way. As Catzman explained: "should the court rule against us, we could then feel that we had gone to the court of highest instance and only then could we resort to the legislature, having used all possible means of redress."[171] A win was a win. A loss would lay the foundation for a legislative campaign. Publicly the JPRC launched the Supreme Court appeal expressing "full confidence that the court would confirm the full civil rights of all citizens, irrespective of race or religion."[172]

Mrs. Noble's doubts were not dispelled. On 28 June her solicitor, D. M. Egener, wrote to Ted Richmond:

You will understand that Mrs. Noble is an elderly woman and that these whole proceedings have been a matter of anxiety and worry to her. . . . [U]nder no circumstances does she care to be involved in any further appeals. . . . [H]er health is being affected by the matter.[173]

Richmond consulted Cartwright by telephone, wondering whether to carry on the appeal only in the name of Wolf. Cartwright was insistent: both names must appear; the case must be presented on the contract made between Mrs. Noble and Mr. Wolf. After sounding Egener out further, Richmond suggested to the CJC that if they would promise to find an alternative buyer and pay any difference in price if the appeal was unsuccessful, Mrs. Noble would acquiesce.[174] Ben Kayfetz replied with an immediate telegram – "Approve of suggestion as your letter June 30th" – and followed it with a letter. "No effort should be spared" to keep Mrs. Noble in the case, Kayfetz urged, and the CJC would guarantee her against any loss in her property value. "We know how cooperative she has been up to now and appreciate the necessity of her further participation."[175]

Frail though she might have been, Mrs. Noble was prepared to fight for the most favourable terms. Mr. Wolf was to pay forthwith the 1948 and 1949 taxes on the cottage, $650 rent for the "use" of the cottage during the court proceedings, and provide "a written guarantee under seal" that regardless of the conclusion in court he would pay the original purchase price plus 5 percent interest from May 1948.[176] A dispirited Bernard Wolf refused to consent to these terms. He was very doubtful about his chances in the Supreme Court, and "personally, would like to wash his hands of the whole matter." He would, however, consent to proceed if the CJC would take up Mrs. Noble's new demands.[177] Cartwright was away on vacation, but Kayfetz contacted him by telephone and reported his conversation to Bora Laskin's legal committee:

Mr. Cartwright feels that in spite of the unanimous verdict there is a better than even chance of the higher court reversing it. His opinion is that there is a strong probability that the court will deal with it on the uncertainty aspect though they will prefer not to consider the point of view of public policy.

He also feels that the case cannot go on successfully without Mrs. Noble's participation in it. While it would be preferable if the case had been brought as an action rather than a motion, he feels that if the case were now allowed to die the Court of Appeal verdict would become a binding judgment.

He feels that while the new terms of Mrs. Noble can be considered onerous, by the addition of the payment of interest, nevertheless they should be met, having in view the importance of the case.[178]

The CJC deliberated over two weeks, no doubt consulting the treasurer as well as the assembled legal experience represented by Laskin and his colleagues, and on 3 August Kayfetz announced that "The consensus of opinion is that we have no choice but to meet Mrs. Noble's terms, unfair as they might be."[179] It took another month to draw up a formula acceptable to Mrs. Noble. Finally on 6 September she and Mr. Wolf signed an agreement to allow the CJC to proceed.[180] On 23 September 1949 leave was granted to appeal to the Supreme Court of Canada.

While *Noble and Wolf* was proceeding from the provincial High Court through to the Supreme Court of Canada, other developments were affecting Ontario public policy towards racial discrimination in general and property covenants in particular. On 7 June 1948 the Ontario electorate returned the Conservative government, but Premier Drew lost his own seat and resigned as leader. After a caretaker period under Premier T. L. Kennedy, the party selected Leslie Frost as leader on 27 April 1949. An Orangeman and a small-town Ontario Tory, still Frost was a new man on the job and a new opportunity for the resumption of the human rights debate.[181] That opportunity was to be taken promptly by the Association for Civil Liberties, formed that spring of 1949 with the express intention of pressing for legislation in the field of "race relations." The secretary and "moving spirit" of the ACL was Irving Himel, junior counsel to John Cartwright in the Drummond Wren case. The chair was Provost Seeley of Trinity College, and on the board were Ben Kayfetz, Bora Laskin, Andrew Brewin, Joseph Sedgwick, Abraham Feinberg, Syd Harris, Syd Midanic, B. K. Sandwell and other representatives of Toronto's progressive "establishment."[182]

Just days after Frost was sworn in as premier on 4 May, Vivien Mahood, chair of the ACL Committee on Group Relations, wrote to him asking for an appointment "to discuss the status of discriminatory practices in Ontario, and the need for corrective legislation."[183] To Attorney General Dana Porter, Himel explained:

The purpose of the delegation is to submit representations to the Premier and the government touching on large areas of discrimination that affect minority groups in the province, and on the need for remedial legislation by the Ontario Legislature designed to eliminate such discrimination and accord fundamental human rights to all residents of the province, regardless of race, colour or creed.[184]

Mahood's committee drafted a brief to present to the premier at their meeting set for 7 June,[185] illustrating instances of discrimination and regretting the ineffectiveness of the 1944 Act. Prominent among the examples cited in the brief were restrictive covenants, and the conflict between the judgments of Mackay and Schroeder. "We believe," the brief continued,

that the time is appropriate to remove the confusion that now prevails with regard to these covenants. To make it perfectly clear that such restrictions have no place in a democracy, we would ask that your government introduce in the next session of the legislature an amendment to the Racial Discrimination Act which will provide that racial restrictive covenants have no legal validity.[186]

To the 35 people attending the presentation the premier said he was "impressed" by what they had revealed and would give "serious consideration" to their request for legislation.[187]

The lack of committal in the premier's response was indicative of his government's attitude at the time, and no legislation was forthcoming. And so in January 1950, in preparation for another session of the legislature, the ACL mobilized another and much more impressive delegation. The brief this time was formally printed and bound, and not just mimeographed as in 1949, and copies were sent to a broad array of organizations for endorsement. Property covenants were again highlighted as "Evidence of the Need for Legislation," and the Court of Appeal's *Noble and Wolf* decision was denounced for placing "the stamp of legality on discrimination."[188] Seventy organizations, many of them with no obvious identification with racial issues such as the Canadian Legion and the Registered Nurses Association, the major religious denominations, several unions and student groups, joined the ACL in sponsoring the brief, and over 300 persons participated in the presentation on 24 January.

Following the formal speeches Premier Frost replied that there was no serious racial problem in Ontario, and such as existed was best handled through voluntary compliance rather than legal coercion. Irving Himel interjected with his own profound disappointment in the premier's attitude, and asked for his response to the specific proposals in the brief. Frost declined, but assured the delegation that he was grateful for their concern and welcomed their advice: "there is no iron curtain around me. Any group of citizens can see me at any time. However I am not prepared to pass on anything you recommend at this time."[189] The Ontario press reacted with considerably more enthusiasm than Premier Frost. The *Toronto Star* immediately and characteristically endorsed the delegation editorially, as did newspapers across the province including the Toronto *Telegram*, which had not been sympathetic to the issue previously.[190] *Saturday Night* magazine, whose editor B. K. Sandwell was an ACL board member, criticized Frost's cool reception of the delegation as a "serious mistake" and reminded the premier: "The great body of voters is at the moment considerably impressed by the world-wide campaign against these discriminatory practices and by the available evidence that Canada is not as free from them as a leading progressive nation ought to be."[191]

Whether it was the almost universal press support, the evidence of widespread popular concern represented in the 24 January delegation, pressure from party colleagues, or an overnight conversion, the premier apparently changed his mind and in the Speech from the Throne on 16 February he inserted a sentence promising to give "consideration to a measure concerning discriminatory covenants in deeds." This simple reference won a front-page banner headline from the *Globe and Mail*: "Ontario Plans to End Bias in Property Deals."[192] The covenants measure, in fact, attracted more attention than anything else in the Throne Speech that year,[193] and to the premier it brought a host of encouraging and congratulatory letters.[194] Provost Seeley expressed the ACL's disappointment that the government program would not address all the problems raised in the brief, but he welcomed the announcement as a promising first step.[195] Vivien Mahood, who had coordinated the campaign for endorsements to the brief, wrote of the Throne Speech:

It is a minor triumph, but a triumph. The papers unqualifiedly give the credit for this move to our delegations, though that alone would not have done it. What is behind it is the steady pounding of labour, the swing of public sentiment so noticeable in the press and in our last delegation to the premier. Some of it undoubtedly springs from the changing American attitude, but nevertheless, I feel our work has been in good part responsible. It is most gratifying. The papers selected this item from the Speech to headline, and that in itself is indicative of the public attitude.[196]

The measure when fully unveiled by the attorney general was, however, of limited effect, for it outlawed only future covenants leaving existing restrictions intact.[197] The CCF opposition demanded that it be made retroactive, but Frost insisted that existing covenants were not really a problem and most would eventually expire, whereas to enact a retroactive ban would disrupt property arrangements across the province. The real benefit from the bill, he maintained, would be that it would free property developers from the restraints imposed by covenants, and therefore encourage more activity and growth to the advantage of all Ontarians. No doubt with his eye on certain of his own more reluctant colleagues on the government benches, Frost asked rhetorically:

What would happen, for instance, if some of these lands up in York County that may be used for housing schemes have restrictions of that sort put on them?

How would you ever plan a community? The thing would be impossible, and I think now is the time to stop that sort of thing.[198]

The bill to amend the *Conveyancing and Law of Property Act* was accordingly passed unanimously, providing that

Every covenant made after this section comes into force which but for this section would be annexed to and run with the land and which restricts the sale, ownership, occupation or use of land because of the race, creed, colour, nationality, ancestry or place of origin of any person shall be void and of no effect.[199]

Exactly one month later the Manitoba legislature amended its *Law of Property Act* with a similar provision.[200]

The Ontario amendment was proclaimed on 24 March 1950, in the midst of the CJC preparations for the presentation to the Supreme Court of Canada. The previous September the "Special Committee on the Restrictive Covenant Case" had added some new members and had debated the basic strategy to be followed in the appeal. John Cartwright, whose views were put to the meeting by Rabbi Feinberg, felt that "there was an even chance on the public policy angle and a good chance on uncertainty." He suggested as well that it did not really matter on what grounds a victory was won, for "the publicity accruing to the voiding of a covenant, even on uncertainty, would leave the main impression that such contracts were illegal." Bora Laskin disagreed, urging that the public policy issue be given most prominence in the pleading to ensure the broadest impact from a positive judgment. The committee decided to recommend that all four points made before the Ontario Court of Appeal be reiterated.[201]

Then three days before Christmas 1949 John Cartwright was appointed to the Supreme Court of Canada by Prime Minister Louis St. Laurent. In gracious letters to Bernard Wolf and Ted Richmond, Cartwright indicated that "I have no greater regret than that I cannot personally finish the presentation of your case."[202] The regrets were no doubt mutual, for the appeal team was losing its most prominent player. Ben Kayfetz consoled Mr. Wolf: "Though Mr. Cartwright will not be able to act as counsel or sit on the Bench which takes your appeal, his name, I understand, will stand on the appeal application which will appear before the Supreme Court."[203] It was the new judge's suggestion to retain as his replacement Mr. Gershom Mason, KC, a leading Ontario counsel and treasurer of the Law Society of Upper Canada. An approach was made to Mr. Mason in February but he declined, stating that previous commitments rendered him unavailable. Instead, following consultations with everyone involved, the CJC engaged John J. Robinette to present the case for Mrs. Noble.[204] It was the day the Speech from the Throne was announced in the Toronto press.

The new legislation provoked a reassessment of strategy. At first it was thought that the legislation might obviate their case entirely; when its limited extent was known, its impact upon and use in their presentation had to be discussed. One point of view wanted the legislation to be used as a clear indication of public policy, encouraging the court to extend that policy to cover covenants already in effect when the new law was proclaimed. Another view felt that the law favoured the respondents, for they could argue that the legislature had spoken and that the public policy thereby enunciated had left the Beach O' Pines covenant legal. Further to this view, the Supreme Court decision would bind all common law provinces, and to rely upon a single provincial measure could be counterproductive. In the end John Robinette settled the matter: there would be no reference to the new legislation in the appellants' case. "The appeal is from the decision of the Ontario Court of Appeal which at the time did not have for consideration the recent Ontario legislation."[205] The argument would be built upon the four points: that the covenant was void on grounds of public policy, for uncertainty, as a restraint on alienation, and, in refinement of this, as an attempt to affect the user rather than the use of the land.

6. NOBLE AND WOLF v. ALLEY

The *factum* for Mrs. Noble, prepared by Robinette and Hess in early May, put the first three points: that the Court of Appeal had erred in holding that clause (f) of the covenant "(1) was not contrary to public policy; (2) was not void and unforceable for uncertainty; [and] (3) was a valid restraint upon the freedom of alienation."[206]

The argument for point one relied upon *Drummond Wren* whose conclusion could best be understood, it was submitted, as declaring that "there was no public interest in Ontario requiring the Court to support a contract aimed at prohibiting the sale of land to Jews." The judgment in the 1948 American Supreme Court covenants case was quoted to illustrate that it was not based exclusively on a piece of legislation peculiar to the United States but, like *Drummond Wren*, on an interpretation of broader indications of public policy. In *Hurd v. Hodge* the American court explained that even if the 14th Amendment had not existed, there are other considerations which would indicate that enforcement of restrictive covenants in these cases is judicial action contrary to the public policy of the United States. . . . The power of the federal courts to enforce the terms of private agreements is at all times exercised subject to the restrictions and limitations of the public policy of the United States as manifested in the Constitution, treaties, federal statutes, and applicable legal precedents. Where the enforcement of private agreements would be violative of that policy, it is the obligation of courts to refrain from such exertions of judicial power.

A 1938 Privy Council decision, *Fender v. Mildmay*, had similarly held that "There are considerations of public interest which require the Courts to depart from their primary function of enforcing contracts, and exceptionally to refuse to enforce them. Public policy in this sense is disabling." The issue could not be cast as a public interest in freedom of contract or freedom of association; truly, enforcement of the covenant would give judicial recognition to "a public interest in the creation of inequality of civil status because of race or blood."

Several English cases had demonstrated the impossibility of giving a definite legal meaning to racial terms. Just as the daughter in *Clayton v. Ramsden* would remain forever single, Mrs. Noble could never sell her land to anyone because no court could define for her which potential buyer was or was not a Jew. The census classified people by "race" but gave no definite legal meaning as could be applied by a court of law. Different dictionary definitions of "race" and "blood" were quoted to show that the terms were wildly imprecise. In concluding its argument on uncertainty, the *factum* added ominously: "An example of an attempt to give definite legal meaning to 'blood' is found in Germany in the Nuremberg Decrees of September 29, 1933 [*sic*]. . . ."

On the alienation issue the *factum* was blunt: the covenant was contrary to freedom of commerce for it inhibited Mrs. Noble's right to sell her land, and it transgressed even further "by attempting to exclude persons because of their race or blood from equal participation in commerce."

Shirley Denison had virtually the entire *factum* of the appellant Bernard Wolf to elaborate upon the fourth ground of appeal. A restriction on the manner in which land might be used was legally transferable from one owner to the next, but a restriction on the user of land, he submitted, is purely a personal one and as such it does not attach to the land, but exists only between the parties who sign the contract. The Frank S. Salter Company, which had inserted the clause in its deeds, had ceased to function and had lost its charter. The contract had therefore expired. That the impugned clause (f) was personal, according to Denison, was proclaimed by the fact that it would prevent members of the excluded "races" from purchasing the land, even as absentee owners, whether they used the land or not. Clearly, therefore, the covenant was not about the use of land at all and by the rule expressed in *Tulk v. Moxhay* it could not run with the land. No restriction survived to prevent Mr. Wolf from buying this land from Mrs. Noble. The *factum* concluded with an endorsement of the arguments presented in the Noble *factum*, with particular emphasis upon the public policy issue.[207]

Kenneth Morden submitted his *factum* for the respondents in the name of W. A. Alley et al., members of the Beach O' Pines Protective Association. Its fundamental contention was that by the exchange of letters between Egener and Richmond in May 1948, the question submitted to the court was whether *Drummond Wren* "applies to the facts of the present sale, with the result that the Clause (f) objected to is invalid and the vendor and purchaser are not bound by it." Morden argued that *Drummond Wren* "was not applicable to the facts of this case, and further, that it was wrongly decided."[208] The lower court decisions were submitted in evidence of this. Public policy recognized only severely limited reasons for voiding a contract. Besides fraud, a contract might be invalidated as "injurious to the state, injurious to the public service [*sic*], tending to pervert justice, contrary to morality, in restraint of marriage, in restraint of trade." None of these "existing heads of public policy" was applicable to this case. Public interest, on the contrary, was served by upholding the covenant, for example the validity of contracts, freedom of association, freedom of commerce, and the monetary interests of the respondents. *Christie v. York* had established "the right of persons to deal with whom they pleased." Pressing an argument raised successfully in the Court of Appeal, Morden insisted that the covenant was socially beneficial:

The Appellants' argument in essence means that we must all think and act in the same way. This would result in a dead level of uniformity in the community which is one of the badges of totalitarianism, whether of the Fascist or Communistic type. Canada is a country of minorities – and every group has brought certain characteristics and traditions which have and are enriching our Canadian heritage. If the Appellants' argument be sound, such groups as St. George's and St. Andrew's Societies, The Knights of Columbus and B'Nai B'Rith would be illegal organizations.

The restraint on alienation was partial, and the meaning sufficiently certain, for the court to have no option but to enforce it.

The atmosphere in the Supreme Court of Canada, where the case was heard from 13 to 16 June 1950, was considerably different from the Ontario Court of Appeal. The judges appeared sympathetic to Robinette and Denison, and this time it was Morden who was subjected to interruptions. For example, when he suggested that his clients' property would depreciate in value if Jews were allowed, Justice Ivan Rand interjected that if Albert Einstein and Arthur Rubinstein purchased cottages there the property values would increase, and the Association "should be honoured to have them as neighbours." To Morden's claim that the covenant upheld "freedom of association," Justice Rand retorted, "freedom of association on a voluntary basis is one thing but it is quite a different thing to say that the law should protect an inclination to disassociate." Morden's plea for the legal protection of cultural diversity was termed by Rand "using the law to enforce a multitude of idiosyncrasies." Finally, Rand challenged Morden to reconcile two legal principles: suppose a Gentile man bought a cottage, then married a Jew and subsequently died. Under Ontario statute the Jewish widow would own the property. Would the covenant be enforceable in this circumstance? A witness to the proceedings later wrote: "This really exploded the case of the Beach O' Pines Association."[209]

A positive judgment was therefore anticipated by the appellants, though its appearance on 20 November 1950 gave only a qualified cause for rejoicing.[210] The result was summarized by the *Dominion Law Reports* as follows:

Held, on appeal, Locke J. dissenting, the covenant was not one which would run against subsequent purchasers of the burdened land since it did not touch or concern the land within the meaning of *Tulk v. Moxhay*. That doctrine requires that the covenant be directed to the land or to some mode of its use. It does not apply to a covenant prohibiting alienation to particular classes of persons. *Held*, further, the covenant was void for uncertainty, since there was nothing in it to enable a Court to say in all cases whether a proposed purchaser was or was not within the prohibited classes. There was no indication of any limits to the lines of race or blood which would or would not disqualify a proposed purchaser. The certainty required in covenants is no different from that required in conditions.[211]

Shirley Denison's argument was given primacy by the court in explaining its decision. To the objection that this was a new ground added to the appellants' case, that was not put before Justice Schroeder and had been explicitly rejected by the Ontario Court of Appeal, acting Chief Justice Patrick Kerwin pointed to "the wide terms of the notice of motion" which had asked the Court for a declaration that the purchaser's objection had been fully answered by the vendor "*or* for such other order as might seem just."[212] Five of the six judges who rejected the covenant gave the *Tulk v. Moxhay* doctrine as their first reason. Indeed, Justice Kerwin, for himself and Robert Taschereau, relied on that interpretation exclusively, stating that "it would be an unwarrantable extension of that doctrine to hold, from anything that was said in that case or in subsequent cases that the covenant here in question has any reference to the use, or abstention from use, of land."[213]

Justice Ivan Rand, delivering the judgment of himself, Roy Kellock and Gerald Fauteux, agreed that "by its language, the covenant here is directed not to the land or to some mode of its use, but to transfer by act of the purchaser." Rand added that "the covenant was unenforceable for uncertainty." *Clayton v. Ramsden* was indistinguishable from the present case, for it was "impossible to set such limits to the lines of race or blood."[214] Justice James Estey was swayed by the latter argument: the language used in the covenant "fails to indicate the intention of the parties as to the amount or degree of the prohibited race or blood that might be permitted. It must, therefore, upon the authorities, be held void for uncertainty."[215] The seventh justice, Charles Locke, would have dismissed the appeal on the ground that the *Tulk v. Moxhay* argument was not raised before Justice Schroeder and the Court of Appeal had declined to consider it; it would therefore be an improper interference in the Court of Appeal procedure for the Supreme Court to consider that argument now. On all the other points raised before the court, Locke stated simply that he agreed "with the learned Chief Justice of Ontario."[216]

Six out of seven is a convincing victory.[217] It was what was left unsaid and uncontested by the decision that caused disappointment, particularly to Bora Laskin and the CJC. The most resounding silence was on the public policy issue. Not a hint was raised by any of the judges, not a challenge or a doubt. In effect this left intact the interpretation of the Ontario Court of Appeal that racial restrictions were not contrary to public policy. Mr. Morden's contention that the covenant was not immoral was not contradicted by the court; his argument that *Christie v. York* upheld the legality of discrimination drew no comment. The Beach O' Pines covenant was not invalidated on the racial principle, but on the fashion of its language.

The Joint Public Relations Committee allowed only a tinge of regret in its generally celebratory report to the CJC.

While we would have preferred to see the decision made on the broader base of public policy which per se would have struck a forceful blow against all discrimination, we nonetheless recognized the great value of the court's view that restrictive covenants were invalid on the basis of a strict reading of law relating to the use of land. . . .

The meaning of decision and [Ontario and Manitoba] legislation is that no further covenants can be registered or, being already written, can be enforced where contested.[218]

The reaction paraded before the public was unstintingly ecstatic. J. Irving Oelbaum, regional CJC president, announced:

All people of goodwill will hail this judgment with deepest satisfaction. It is further evidence that there is no place in Canada for racial and religious intolerance. The judgment gives force of law to a moral principle.

The hearts of all minorities in Canada will beat faster for Canadianism now that they are no longer considered second class citizens. There is one law for all Canadians. The judgment is in keeping with 20th century thinking and its lesson should be taken to heart. This is a landmark in civil liberties.[219]

Rabbi Feinberg hailed the judgment as

a potent weapon in the cold war of ideology between communism and the west. . . .

We had faith that the highest law body in the land would purge our democracy, once and for all, of the Nazi-like moral taint of restrictive covenants. Now, the Supreme Court has justified that trust and given much-needed inspiration and strength to liberal forces throughout the world.[220]

Even Norman Borins told reporters the court had declared that "the discriminatory features of racial restrictive covenants are contrary to the principles of genuine democracy."[221]

Generally the press accepted the judgment accordingly. In an awkward but passionate headline, the *Toronto Star* told its readers "Covenant Rule Seen Proof Canada's Court Freedom's Defender." The accompanying story and an editorial expressed satisfaction that covenants were henceforth illegal, and that the decision would help to "break down race and color prejudice in this country" and "make Canada a land of fair play and equal opportunity for all."[222] The *Telegram*, though expressing itself more moderately, also welcomed the "ruling invalidating restrictive covenants in property deals."[223] One letter to the editor was especially representative of the public's understanding of what had been decided in Ottawa:

With a great struggle going on in the world between opposing ideologies, the decision has struck a great blow for the Western democracies and its effect should be felt beyond the confines of the Dominion. One of the greatest sources of foreign propaganda is the allegation of racial prejudice and bigotry to which minorities in this country are subjected. It is true that we cannot mold the individual mind as to its likes and dislikes. But when the highest legal tribunal in our country upholds the principle of equality and scotches [sic] the doctrine of segregation and the myth of superiority, then indeed it should be a cause of great satisfaction to all liberal-minded and progressive citizens.[224]

Only the *Globe and Mail* put a sober interpretation upon what the judges had actually said.

The large volume of extra-judicial interpretation which has followed the judgment of the Supreme Court of Canada respecting restrictive covenants seems to be confusing the situation rather than clarifying it. . . .

By basing their decision upon the specific circumstances of this case, and by avoiding any reference to arguments heard concerning the general public interest, the Supreme Court bench has quite properly avoided any attempt to impose non-discrimination upon individuals by law. By affirming the right of an individual to dispose of his property as he likes, within the framework of the case before it, the court has left the law just as it always has been.[225]

Who was right? The common view – that racism had suffered a defeat and that all discriminatory covenants were now illegal – at least confirmed the strategy advocated by John Cartwright more than a year previously, when he said that even a technical victory would have the desired impact. Subsequent legal and scholarly opinion has been far less enthusiastic. In an early comment Allan Goldstein reflected that the specific grounds given for judgment

applied only to the facts of this particular case. The position of other types of racial covenants has not been clarified.

The covenant in the Noble Case suffered from two defects: it did not run with the land (five judges) and it was void for uncertainty (four judges). It can safely be said that at the time that the *Noble and Wolf* judgment was handed down, most, if not all racial covenants were void for uncertainty. Apparently this defect could be avoided in the future by careful drafting. It would not be difficult for an ingenious conveyancer to satisfy this requirement.

Goldstein added that since it was its restriction on the transfer of land that had been condemned in the Beach O' Pines covenant, a different wording

which solely prohibits use by a clearly defined class, and does not purport to restrict alienation, would be valid. This would confine the case to a narrow scope and racial covenants running with the land would be operative. . . .

The Supreme Court could have settled it by declaring racial covenants void as offending against public policy. It chose not to do so.[226]

D. A. L. Smout agreed.

[T]he lack of a ruling upon public policy, it is submitted, leads to certain unfortunate results.

If a stipulation should be so phrased as to be definite in its nature, then the reasons of the Supreme Court of Canada indicate that it would accordingly be enforceable by at least the original covenantee. . . .

[T]he effect of the Supreme Court of Canada's decision in Noble and Wolf is not to outlaw the racial or religious stipulation. In provinces where there is no remedial legislation the stipulation may well remain effective.[227]

In a commentary which he left unpublished because the Smout article pre-empted it, Ted Richmond also pointed out that covenants would remain enforceable between the original covenantor and covenantee, and that membership in a religious denomination was "certain" enough to pass the Supreme Court's test.[228]

Several other commentators have lamented the limitations placed upon the scope of their decision by the Supreme Court justices. As C. R. Bourne put it,

One feels some regret that the judges . . . did not see fit to express an opinion upon the public policy issue. There is little doubt that, as matters now stand, lawyers in Ontario will consider the lone decision of Mackay J. in *Re Drummond Wren*, insofar as it relates to public policy, as being thoroughly discredited.[229]

J. R. Shiff asked plaintively, "Shall then the dicta of Chief Justice Robert-son and Mr. Justice Schroeder, to the effect that racial restrictive covenants in no way concern the public interest, remain the actual law on the subject?"[230] A somewhat comforting answer came 25 years later from Walter Tarnopolsky:

It is possible to argue that the Supreme Court decision achieved the same result as did Mackay J. However, one certainly could not look to the decision for any inspiration in attempting to achieve an egalitarian society. Pronouncements of the Supreme Court could and should be looked to for guidance by the public, and should also provide guidance for the representatives of the public in enact-ing legislation. Although *Noble and Wolf v. Alley* was not as unfortunate a deci-sion as either Quong-Wing or Christie, it certainly will not go down in the annals of judicial history as one of the more inspiring judgments of our Supreme Court.[231]

Ian Bushnell, in a more recent commentary, is also more positive toward the decision. "*Noble and Wolf v. Alley* is a significant law-making decision, as well as a significant civil-liberty decision. It was a sister case to *Boucher*." Bushnell goes on to argue, however, that the Court engaged in "some sleight of hand" by relying on a convenient interpretation of *Tulk v. Moxhay* to invalidate the Beach covenant. "The judges appeared to be trying to disguise or hide their reform of the law." Unlike legal critics at the time Bushnell accepts the proposition that *Noble and Wolf* outlawed *all* racial covenants, and indeed he makes the claim that the Ontario and Manitoba legislation on the subject was rendered "completely superflu-ous" by the Supreme Court of Canada decision.[232]

Subsequent generations have their perspective shaped by something unavailable to contemporary commentators: an extended period of his-tory since *Noble and Wolf* when there has not been any reported case involving a racial restrictive covenant in Canada.[233] In practical terms the Supreme Court did continue the impact of *Drummond Wren*, though the absence of a statement on public policy produced other complications as will be discussed below. The technical, property judgment was appar-ently sufficient to eliminate the particular problem raised in the case. Furthermore, as Professor Jim Phillips has pointed out, "there is a long tradition of courts using devices like uncertainty (as well as some others) to strike down conditions of which they probably simply disapprove."[234] It was perhaps circumstantial that the Court's pronouncement about the uncertainty of "race" was in accord with advanced scientific thinking in

1950. And yet by refusing to accept the respondents' contention that "race" was readily ascertainable and legally recognizable, the Court was at least acknowledging that scientific certainty about racial categorization was breaking down.[235]

Though the fundamental principle against racial covenants was settled, in 1950, the case itself did not immediately disappear. Mrs. Noble and Mr. Wolf were awarded costs for both the Ontario Court of Appeal and the Supreme Court itself. Apparently Kenneth Morden raised the objection that since the CJC had in fact paid the Supreme Court costs, and no award had been made to the CJC, his clients should not be held responsible. This argument was rejected by the Taxing Officer in September 1951, but the costs remained unpaid and so in October the sheriff's office was ordered to begin seizing chattels belonging to Alley et al. at the Beach O' Pines resort. The threat had some of the desired effect: in early November Morden negotiated a settlement whereby his clients paid $4,000, something less than half the sum assessed by the Taxing Officer.[236] Mr. Wolf turned over all the money he received to the CJC, adding a personal donation of $1,000, and Mr. Richmond declined to bill for his services.[237] The rest of the shortfall was absorbed by the CJC's operating budget.

By the time this was settled, Bernard Wolf had sold the cottage. He received an offer from one of the other owners in April 1951, but at first hesitated to sell to one of the parties opposing him. Richmond sought the advice of the CJC, explaining that "once the trouble started 3 years ago, he lost all interest in the property as far as using it for a residence was concerned, and from then on it was merely a matter of principle as far as he was concerned."[238] When the CJC was able to suggest no reason why he should continue the struggle any longer, Mr. Wolf announced on 16 October: "I am happy that I was able to dispose of the property without further antagonism or ill feeling toward anyone."[239]

7. *NOBLE AND WOLF* AS PRECEDENT

The various questions and doubts raised by contemporary observers have to a considerable extent been settled by *Noble and Wolf's* subsequent legacy as a precedent. Although not at all widely cited, it has been used in cases involving both property law and racial issues. Later interpretations have extended its significance in property cases, but revealed its weakness as an instrument against racial discrimination.

Noble and Wolf's first appearance as a precedent occurred in a property covenant case in 1959. A group of University of Toronto professors had established a 1,000-acre hunting and fishing retreat in 1898, the Madawaska Club, providing in its charter that the lands could be used only by club members who must be graduates, undergraduates or officials of the university. When club regulations were challenged, it was decided that they related strictly to the kind of person who could use the land and therefore could not "run with the land." In the words of Chief Justice Kerwin, there was "no possible ground for any distinction between a covenant restricting alienation and one .restricting occupation."[240] The fears expressed by Allan Goldstein and others, that *Noble and Wolf* could be avoided by a covenant restricting use of the land by a clearly defined class of persons, were laid to rest by *Galbraith v. Madawaska Club.*

Five years later a second aspect of *Noble and Wolf* invalidated the will of Mr. Frank Schechter, who had left much of his estate to the Jewish National Fund for the establishment of a "Jewish colony." The BC Court of Appeal found the term "Jewish colony" to be even less certain than the "Jewish race or blood" in the Beach O'Pines covenant.[241] Presumably this was not the kind of legacy intended by Bernard Wolf and the CJC, though it did illustrate judicial acceptance of the fact that racial terms were uncertain and unenforceable. This particular benefit was not to last, however. Mr. Torazo Iwasaki, suing for the return of his property confiscated during World War II, contended that the government's orders-in-council authorizing the seizure of property "belonging to any person of the Japanese race" were void for uncertainty and for their basis in the term "race." But because the Supreme Court of Canada and the Privy Council had already upheld the orders in the *Japanese Deportation* case, the Exchequer Court rejected Mr. Iwasaki's claim. Besides, it was noted, since he was born in Japan and had a Japanese name there was sufficient evidence to prove that he was a member of the "race" specified in the orders.[242] Any hope that *Noble and Wolf* would lead to greater sophistication in the use of racial terminology in Canadian law was dashed by this decision.

In 1973 *Noble and Wolf* returned to the restrictive covenant realm when Mr. Michael Sekretov challenged a covenant requiring him to keep his property in its "natural state." Ironically it was Justice Schroeder who delivered the judgment of the Ontario Court of Appeal cancelling the covenant on the grounds that "It is well settled that restrictive covenants must be precise in terms, and if they are vague and indefinite in meaning they will not be enforced."[243] *Sekretov*, with *Madawaska*, confirmed *Noble and Wolf's* role in limiting the application of property covenants, rendering any possible racial variation even less enforceable than the Supreme Court had left it in 1950.

Probably the most significant use of *Noble and Wolf* came in the *Bhadauria* case, whose main outline and implications for the *Christie* legacy have already been described.[244] At the Ontario Court of Appeal level in December 1979 Justice Bertha Wilson had cited *Drummond Wren* to support her decision that public policy could be discerned from the underlying purpose of legislative enactments. Thus, a property covenant could be invalidated by Keiller Mackay because it was contrary to the public policy expressed in the *Racial Discrimination Act*, even though the Act was silent on property covenants. Similarly, referring to the preamble of the *Ontario Human Rights Code*, she found convincing evidence of "what is now, and probably has been for some considerable time, the public policy of this Province respecting fundamental human rights."[245] That preamble reads in part:

Whereas recognition of the inherent dignity and the equal and inalienable rights of all members of the human family is the foundation of freedom, justice and peace in the world and is in accord with the Universal Declaration of Human Rights as proclaimed by the United Nations;

And Whereas it is public policy in Ontario that every person is free and equal in dignity and rights without regard to race, creed, colour, nationality, ancestry or place of origin;

And Whereas these principles have been confirmed in Ontario by a number of enactments of this Legislature;

And Whereas it is desirable to enact a measure to codify and extend such enactments and to simplify their administration. . . . [246]

Justice Wilson was able to conclude that the *Ontario Human Rights Code* recognized rights which were already inherent in the common law, and therefore there must be a common law remedy.[247] On behalf of a unanimous court, Wilson ruled that Dr. Bhadauria could sue Seneca College for racial discrimination, recognizing a tort of discrimination for the first time in Canada.[248]

One week later Justice Linden in the Ontario High Court of Justice followed *Bhadauria* in permitting Abdul Aziz to pursue a civil action for damages against the Toronto Chief of Police, alleging racially discriminatory hiring practices.[249] Justice Linden explained:

By enacting these principles in the preamble of the Code, the Legislature of Ontario has chosen to underscore its commitment to equal rights for all our citizens and its opposition to all forms of discrimination. The Court of Appeal made it clear [in *Bhadauria*], however, that this new tort for discrimination did not depend for its life on the Ontario Human Rights Code, but rather was based on the common law. The public policy against racial and other discrimination existed in Ontario before the enactment of the Ontario Human Rights Code and was not created by the Code. The Code merely recognizes that pre-existing policy in its preamble and then establishes an agency and procedures that seek to eliminate or reduce the number of incidents of discrimination in this province. The Courts of Ontario should cooperate with the Legislature, where possible, in promoting the public policy enshrined in the Ontario Human Rights Code.[250]

Justice Linden went on to indicate some of the positive benefits that would come from recognizing a tort for discrimination, most particularly that the complainant him or herself remained in control of a suit for damages whereas the Human Rights Commission directed procedures following a complaint under the *Code*. The Commission, whose mandate is to effect a settlement, might accept a proposal that the complainant did not find personally satisfactory; the Commission might even decide not to proceed at all. The common law route ensured that every complainant could have his or her "day in court."[251]

But the new tort of discrimination, which had received a mixed reception from the Canadian legal community,[252] was to have a short lifetime. As has already been noted, in 1981 Chief Justice Bora Laskin and a unanimous Supreme Court rejected the Ontario Court of Appeal decision. In the course of doing so it implicitly affirmed the 1939 *Christie* decision, by limiting the application of a "duty to serve" to innkeepers.[253] Much more explicitly, the Laskin court placed a restrictive interpretation upon *Noble and Wolf*. In commenting upon Justice Wilson's use of *Drummond Wren*, which he acknowledged lent "perhaps the strongest support" for her decision, the chief justice pointed out that Wilson had failed to consider *Noble and Wolf*. At the Ontario Court of Appeal, Laskin continued, *Noble and Wolf* had overturned *Drummond Wren*'s pronouncement on public policy, and in *Noble and Wolf v. Alley* the Supreme Court of Canada had left that element of the Appeal decision untouched.[254] The reasoning employed by Justice Wilson, i.e., that *Drummond Wren* would allow an analogous use of the *Ontario Human Rights Code*, was therefore undermined by *Noble and Wolf*, and Wilson's "strongest support" disappeared.

The propriety of the Supreme Court's *Bhadauria* decision has been widely debated, and is of no direct concern here. It is however extremely interesting to find Bora Laskin fulfilling his own prophecy, made when he insisted that the public policy issue must be given primacy in carrying *Noble and Wolf* to the Supreme Court in 1950.[255] At that time Professor Laskin feared that a judgment omitting public policy would be narrowly construed, and nowhere was this more accurately demonstrated than in his own *Bhadauria* decision in 1981. The Laskin argument is especially interesting as an apparent illustration of his approach to the application of judicial precedent, for he admitted that he personally agreed with *Drummond Wren*, but found it "necessary" to follow *Noble and Wolf*.[256] As Harry Kopyto commented, *Bhadauria* "marks a sharp break from, if not a full repudiation of, the *Re Drummond Wren* case."[257] And this from the man who appeared on behalf of the Canadian Jewish Congress in *Drummond Wren* and who headed the CJC's advisory committee on *Noble and Wolf*. A disappointed Ian Hunter, who had advocated the right to choose a common law remedy in discrimination cases, wrote of *Bhadauria*:

One cannot but recall Lord Denning's division of judges into two groups: "timorous souls ... fearful of allowing a new cause of action" and, opposing them, "bold spirits who were ready to allow it if justice so required." One wonders which side our Supreme Court has chosen to take up. For Chief Justice Laskin, the great dissenter, it seems a particularly unaccustomed role since he, above all Canadian jurists, would seem to have deliberately fashioned a judicial career in the Denning mould.[258]

An explanation has been offered by another commentator, Ian McKenna. He has contrasted the "rules-based" model of applying precedents with a "principles-based" doctrine as developed by Ronald Dworkin.[259] According to the Dworkin model, judicial decisions are based upon a contest of principles relevant at the time; their career as precedents would depend upon the continued relevance of the successful principle. McKenna's application of this distinction to *Bhadauria* elicits an assessment of *Noble and Wolf* as precedent:

Basing its judgment on the "rules-based" philosophy of positivism, the Supreme Court in *Bhadauria* was virtually compelled to view *Noble and Wolf* as a rejection of *Re Drummond Wren* and to reject the common law action for discrimination in spite of the fact that the Supreme Court did not disapprove of the approach taken in *Re Drummond Wren*. Had it adopted a "principles-based" theory of law in the

Dworkin mould, the Supreme Court could have viewed *Noble and Wolf* in the context of its era. The Chief Justice could have recognized that, while that decision may have represented a satisfactory balancing of the competing principles of freedom of contract and freedom from discrimination in the early post-war era, it was not necessary that the courts of today be bound by the calculus of the courts of a different era.[260]

A different explanation is possible, focusing upon Bora Laskin's insistance that the enforcement of human rights should be left to Human Rights Commissions. The first *Human Rights Code* case to come before the courts was initiated by Kenneth Bell, who had declined to rent a set of rooms in his own home to Carl McKay, a young Jamaican immigrant. McKay complained to the Ontario Human Rights Commission, but before the board of inquiry prescribed by the *Code* could be held, Bell applied for a motion for prohibition on the grounds that the premises in question were not covered by the *Code*. The prohibition was granted by Justice Stewart in the Ontario High Court, accepting the argument that the rooms did not fall under the category "self-contained unit" described in the *Code*. Justice Stewart added, "It is equally important that the rights of a middle-aged white Canadian homeowner be protected as those of a young, black, Jamaican tenant. Neither more important nor less important. Equally. And perhaps it is time that this was made clear."[261]

The Stewart decision was reversed on appeal. Justice Laskin, then a member of the Ontario Court of Appeal, wrote the unanimous judgment declaring that the Commission had the authority and responsibility to pursue a case through a board of inquiry. If the evidence showed that the *Code* had not been violated, the board should have an opportunity to make that decision without interference from the regular courts. Justice Laskin went on to claim that Mr. Bell's "rights at law," which Justice Stewart had protected, were transformed by the passage of the *Ontario Human Rights Code* in 1962.

[T]he Code has drastically changed the common law position of owners of certain kinds of housing accommodation, as it has changed the position of employers and of operators of places to which the public is customarily admitted. . . . Neither Bell nor any other citizen has any legal immunity from administrative procedures prescribed by a competent Legislature for effectuating a policy which has been translated into substantive statutory prescriptions.[262]

A majority of the Supreme Court of Canada restored the Stewart decision on the grounds that the kind of housing Mr. Bell owned was not included in the *Code* and that he was not compelled to submit to a board of inquiry before seeking to have his rights established in a court of law.[263] The Ontario legislature subsequently enacted the Laskin interpretation when it amended the *Human Rights Code* so that judicial intervention could occur only after the Commission had completed its own hearings.[264] Chief Justice Laskin's *Bhadauria* decision can be recognized as consistent with Justice Laskin's *Bell* decision, since both upheld the integrity of the Human Rights Commission as the only legitimate route to redress in a dispute over racial discrimination. In both decisions Bora Laskin was also acknowledging that the common law before 1962 had condoned discrimination.

The Ontario Court of Appeal took another opportunity to reconsider the public policy implications of *Noble and Wolf* in 1990, though the earlier case received only the briefest reference (along with *Christie v. York*). The case involved a complaint by the Ontario Human Rights Commission against a trust, established in 1923 by Colonel Reuben Wells Leonard, to provide educational scholarships. The terms of the trust excluded from benefit "all who are not Christians of the White Race, and who are not of British Nationality or of British parentage, and all who owe allegiance to any Foreign Government, Prince, Pope or Potentate." In the Ontario High Court Justice McKeown upheld the trust in words reminiscent of Justice Schroeder or Chief Justice Robertson 40 years before:

Is there harm to the Ontario public so obnoxious to the public good that the rules of law governing testamentary trusts cannot have their normal operation? I think not. . . .

I accept that racial and religious discrimination is nowadays widely regarded as deplorable in many respects . . . but I think that it is going much too far to say that the endowment of a charity, the beneficiaries of which are to be drawn from a particular faith or are to exclude adherents to a particular faith, is contrary to public policy. . . .

It is important to remember that the freedom of contract and the freedom of testamentary disposition are firmly rooted in law and are important matters of public policy in their own right.

In further echo of the earlier era, Justice McKeown held that the description in the trust "passes the test of uncertainty" and that "there is a wide field open . . . for the selection of students who manifestly satisfy the qualifications of being white, of Canadian citizenship and of the Protestant faith."[265] This time, however, the Court of Appeal did not agree.[266] Justice Robins for the majority referred first to community standards, indicating that about 30 articles had appeared in the press criticizing the Leonard Foundation terms, and some universities had refused to administer the scholarships because they were discriminatory. Archbishop Ted Scott, Primate of the Anglican Church of Canada (to which Colonel Leonard had belonged) had written to the Foundation in 1986, denouncing its racist criteria as contrary to public policy and not "in keeping with the spirit and intent of the *Canadian Charter of Rights*." The archbishop appealed for a revision of the scholarship terms, arguing that

There is every reason why the good works of the generous benefactor of the Foundation should live on in perpetuity but, in my view, they must be in keeping with the society of today just as what was written those many years ago was, no doubt, although regretfully, in keeping with the society of that day.[267]

All things considered, Justice Robins was able to conclude that

The freedom of an owner of property to dispose of his or her property as he or she chooses is an important social interest that has long been recognized in our society and is firmly rooted in our law. That interest must, however, be limited in the case of this trust by public policy considerations. In my opinion, the trust is couched in terms so at odds with today's social values as to make its continued operation in its present form inimical to the public interest.[268]

In this case, therefore, the public policy against racism took precedence over freedom of contract and of testamentary disposition.

Concurring in that result, Justice Tarnopolsky wrote a separate judgment addressing the Human Rights Commission's claim to exclusive jurisdiction over the case and adding his own reflections on the public policy issue. Canvassing case law and legislation on human rights, parliamentary debates and international conventions ratified by Canada, Justice Tarnopolsky decided: "Clearly this is a charitable trust which is void on the ground of public policy to the extent that it discriminates on grounds of race (colour, nationality, ethnic origin), religion and sex."[269] But Justice Tarnopolsky added a caveat:

This decision does not affect private, family trusts. By that I mean that it does not affect testamentary dispositions or outright gifts that are not also charitable trusts. Historically, charitable trusts have received special protection.... This preferential treatment is justified on the ground that charitable trusts are dedicated to the benefit of the community. It is this public nature of charitable trusts which attracts the requirement that they conform to the public policy against discrimination. *Only where the trust is a public one devoted to charity will restrictions that are contrary to the public policy of equality render it void.*[270]

Justice Robins had implied a similar rationale when he wrote:

While the Foundation may have been privately created, there is a clear public aspect to its purpose and administration. In awarding scholarships to study at publicly supported educational institutions to students whose application is solicited from a broad segment of the public, the Foundation is effectively acting in the public sphere. Operating in perpetuity as a charitable trust for educational purposes, as it has now for over half a century since the settlor's death, the Foundation has, in realistic terms, acquired a public or, at the least, a quasi-public character.[271]

It would seem, therefore, that a private act of discrimination administered without benefit of charitable status would be sufficiently non-public to avoid the public policy veto, even if it were publicly recorded in legal instruments.[272] The legacy of *Noble and Wolf* still haunted Ontario jurisprudence.

And so, apparently, *Noble and Wolf* has been assigned a particular role in Canadian legal history, based on certain assumptions that deserve examination. They are, first, that the Supreme Court's silence on public policy must be taken as an endorsement of the Schroeder and Court of Appeal denunciation of *Drummond Wren* and, secondly, that public policy in 1950 therefore tolerated racial discrimination. Neither assumption is necessary. The tendency to make decisions on the narrowest possible grounds is a characteristic of legendary proportions in the common law judicial system. If a case can be decided on one ground, others need not be considered. Witness even Keiller Mackay's reluctance to declare upon the terms of the *Racial Discrimination Act* since he could decide against the covenant without directly contradicting his colleague Chevrier in *McDougall and Waddell*.[273] Witness as well Bertha Wilson's refusal to answer Dr. Bhadauria's claim that a breach of the *Human Rights Code* gave rise to a civil cause of action, since a sufficient ground existed in the common law.[274] Both Mackay and Wilson limited their reasoning to what was necessary. In *Noble and Wolf* the Supreme Court found the technical arguments to be sufficient. Although there has been much legitimate regret at the failure to comment on public policy, it must be recognized that it was not necessary in the circumstances to do so. This is not to deny that their silence could have been calculated, but rather to question the automatic assumption that it must have been.

With respect to Ontario public policy in 1950, there are indications that it was against discrimination which are at least as compelling as those which suggest the contrary. The reception of *Drummond Wren* was universally positive, including comments made in the Ontario legislature. If the legislators felt that their 1944 Act had been abused they could have said so, or even have passed new legislation. Premier Frost's refusal to make the *Conveyancing Act* amendment retroactive, when challenged during second reading on 22 March 1950, was accompanied by a statement that "the position of this government here and my personal position is one of strongest opposition to racial discrimination of any kind."[275] While there may be a conflicting impression of public policy from the 22 March debate, the government was absolutely direct in the preamble to the *Fair Employment Practices Act*, introduced just three months after the *Noble and Wolf* decision, in which the Universal Declaration of Human Rights was explicitly endorsed and it was declared that racial discrimination was "contrary to public policy in Ontario."[276] Speaking to a Brotherhood dinner at Beth Shalom synagogue in April 1951, Premier Frost expanded on the reasons behind the Fair Employment legislation:

The first is our obligation to the United Nations. . . . [I]n passing such legislation we are making our contribution to the furtherance of the ideals of the Charter to which our Canadian government has subscribed as representing the people of Canada.

Secondly, there is our obligation to ourselves. . . . Our people subscribe to these principles. They believe in them. . . .

I am glad to have played a humble part, in company with my colleagues and with the citizens of Ontario and with the unanimous vote of the Legislature, in placing on our statutes a law which above everything else carries with it our recognition that all men of whatever race, colour or creed must be accorded equality.[277]

A more emphatic confirmation of *Drummond Wren* is hard to imagine.

It is obvious in retrospect that the Supreme Court of Canada could have included an affirmative statement on public policy in *Noble and*

Wolf without fear of contradiction or controversy and without violating the intentions of the Ontario legislature. Had it done so the court would have gained for itself and for the Canadian judiciary a much more significant place in the movement for racial equality that ensued across Canada and the world in the 1950s and 60s. By omitting the public policy issue from its judgment, the Supreme Court consigned *Noble and Wolf* to a much less distinguished legacy in Canadian case law. It also diminished any opportunity to engage other discriminatory government practices, most notably immigration policy, in the courts of Canada.

5

Narine-Singh v. Attorney General of Canada

1. "RACE" AND IMMIGRATION

For a country such as Canada, immigration is undoubtedly the most fundamental policy a government can set. Immigrants provide the raw material for the national identity. The nature of the country itself, and what it is to be in the future, is determined by the kind of people who are allowed to enter. An immigration policy is a conscious screening mechanism enabling the current occupants of the territory to select their partners in the building of the nation. As one-time immigration minister Frank Oliver reminded the House of Commons in 1914:

We are in occupation of the country; we are in control of its affairs, and there is nothing that is of such intimate, immediate and ultimate future concern as the character of the population that goes to make up the country. The country is the people; the people are the country, and it is the first duty of the country, as it is the first duty of the Government, to take such measures as may be right and expedient to prevent, if prevention is necessary, the occupation of this country by population that shall hamper and deter in any material degree the development of those ideals of civilization which we believe ourselves to be here for the purpose of working out to their highest degree.[1]

The notes to this chapter are on pages 411-25.

To this declaration Oliver's leader, Sir Wilfrid Laurier, added: "The people of Canada want to have a white country."[2] Since immigration policy did in fact reflect the core attitudes of the Canadian people, the doctrine articulated by Oliver and Laurier consistently produced restrictions upon the entry of persons who were not white.

On 17 September 1953 a 26-year-old Trinidadian, Harry Singh, entered Canada to visit his uncle Clive Ablack, a Canadian citizen. Under Section 7(c) of the *Immigration Act*,[3] Mr. Singh was granted visitor status until April 1954, but after several months in Toronto and many conversations with his uncle, who had served as a wireless operator in the RCAF during World War II, he decided to enlist in the Canadian forces himself. He sent for his wife Mearl, who arrived from Trinidad on 1 March 1954, and shortly thereafter Harry Singh applied to the army's Toronto recruiting office. As a qualified draftsman he proved attractive to the recruiting officer but, it was explained, he would need the approval of the Immigration Branch. Lieutenant McPherson called the local immigration office to make an appointment for Mr. and Mrs. Singh.[4]

Harry and Mearl presented themselves at the immigration offices on Church Street in Toronto on 5 April 1954. Immigration Officer T. Delaney perceived that this was not to be a routine authorization, for the Singhs appeared to belong to a category whose admission to Canada was restricted. Delaney therefore passed the applicants to Special Inquiry Officer C. Schreiber, who announced that the Singhs must submit to an immediate Board of Inquiry to determine their suitability as immigrants. Harry asked for a postponement and for the right to have a lawyer present, but Mr. Schreiber explained that a postponement would cost him $100 and that although he could have a lawyer present if he wished, it really was not necessary as all he had to do was answer a few questions. Harry and Mearl consulted together for a few minutes, and then decided to proceed with the hearing. Once they were sworn, Mr. Schreiber proceeded to ask a series of questions. He determined both Harry and Mearl's family backgrounds, including the names, maiden names and addresses of their parents in Trinidad, names, ages and marital status of their brothers and sisters, the war record of uncle Clive Ablack, Harry's occupation as a draftsman and Mearl's as a housewife, the routes they followed in travelling to Canada, the state of their health. The core of the Inquiry, however, was more succinct. Harry was asked:

Q. What is the place and date of your birth?
A. April 19, 1928, Trinidad, British West Indies.

Q. Of what country are you a citizen?
A. I am a British subject.
Q. Of what race are you?
A. East Indian. . . .
Q. Of what race is your wife?
A. East Indian.

Schreiber thereupon concluded that Harry did not meet the conditions of Section 20(4) of the Immigration Regulations, which stated that

the admission to Canada of any person is prohibited where in the opinion of a Special Inquiry Officer such person should not be admitted by reason of . . .
(b) his unsuitability, having regard to the economic, social, industrial, educational, labour, health or other conditions or requirements existing, temporarily or otherwise, in Canada or in the area or country from or through which such person comes to Canada.[5]

Harry was consequently ordered to be deported. As his wife, Mearl was automatically ordered deported as well.[6] Harry was further ordered to be detained pending his deportation, but was released conditionally after posting a $100 bond.[7]

Through Mr. Ablack, Harry learned of the Toronto Labour Committee for Human Rights, an organization that was gaining a reputation for intervening in discriminatory immigration cases. When she heard the circumstances of the Singhs' inquiry, the Committee's executive secretary, Donna Hill, telephoned Schreiber to protest. She maintained that Harry had been "tricked" into an official hearing when he had believed that he was merely going for a letter of permission to join the army. Schreiber responded that all British West Indians, except the immediate family of Canadian citizens, were ordered deported under Section 20(4)(b). Ms. Hill indicated that she knew of several West Indians who had been admitted under the "case of exceptional merit" category, and surely this should apply to a skilled craftsman in whom the army had expressed a positive interest. That same afternoon Schreiber called Harry on the telephone and invited him back to the immigration office.[8]

Hopeful once again, Harry Singh appeared at the immigration office on 7 April. Officer Schreiber tore up his deportation notice, but immediately issued a new one which specified that Section 20(2) of the Regulations absolutely barred the Singhs from Canada. The Section stated that the landing in Canada of any Asian is limited to the following classes of person or persons: the wife, the husband or the unmarried children under twenty-one years of age of any Canadian citizen resident in Canada who is in a position to receive and care for his dependents.[9]

Harry protested that he was not an "Asian": his family had been in Trinidad for five generations, and he had never even visited Asia; in fact he had never been anywhere except Trinidad and Toronto. Schreiber insisted that the Singhs were Asian by "race." His only concession was to advise Harry to appeal to the minister of Immigration. The Singhs' appeal was considered by the minister on 29 April, but it was unsuccessful. Harry and Mearl were ordered to leave Canada within 30 days. As soon as she learned the result, Donna Hill enlisted Toronto lawyer Andrew Brewin to launch an appeal through the courts.[10]

2. RESTRICTIVE TRADITION

As early as 1815 the Nova Scotia House of Assembly crystallized the prevailing outlook in a resolution designed to prohibit the arrival of fugitive American slaves. Black people were labelled as total aliens, incapable of adjusting to the physical conditions of British North America, unable to assimilate or even associate with Anglo-Canadians, suitable only for unskilled labouring and service employment and therefore an economic threat to equivalent classes already here.[11] All the elements that would persist for a century and a half are to be found in this resolution. Nevertheless Nova Scotia's declared wish in 1815 was ignored by the British government, emphasizing the fact that until Confederation, immigration to British North America was determined by officials in London. Then by Section 95 of the *British North America Act*, control of immigration was to be shared by the federal and provincial governments, though policy established by the federal Parliament would predominate.[12]

Control of entry to post-Confederation Canada was jealously guarded, being deemed a *sine qua non* for the development of a Canadian nationality. Methodist leader Rev. S. D. Chown was not the only one to believe that "The immigration question is the most vital one in Canada today, as it has to do with the purity of our national life-blood."[13] In Parliament, Frank Oliver expressed the pith and substance of the Canadian position:

To say that we in Canada shall not be able to say who shall join us in the work of building up the country, that we must accept the dictation of other people as to who shall join us in that work, places us in a position not of a self-governing state in a free empire, but in the position of a subordinate dependency not in control of its own affairs.[14]

In this spirit the new dominion had promptly passed its first *Act Respecting Immigration and Immigrants* in 1869.[15] The Act implicitly assumed that the bulk of immigrants would come from Britain with a smaller number from northern Europe. Section 1 declared that immigration agents were to be located throughout Britain, with one on the continent of Europe. Sections 11 and 16 permitted the government to deport handicapped persons or others who might likely become a public charge, but no reference was made to racial qualifications. An 1872 amendment added "criminal or other vicious classes" to the category of those who might be excluded.[16]

Canada was a British dominion in political terms, and it would be a British nation in demographic terms. As a leading intellectual, G. M. Grant, would insist, "Canada is paramountly a British nation: founded on British principles, peopled by sturdy stock from the British Isles, and dedicated to the furtherance and continuation of the British Empire."[17] This was not simply a matter of aesthetic preference or ethnic pride, for in that age of "scientific racism" it was believed that potential immigrants' character and future behaviour could be predicted according to the "race" to which they belonged. Some "races," Anglo-Saxons being the outstanding example, had an instinct for political liberty and democratic government, as well as for material progress. Others were best suited to despotism and were satisfied with meagre material returns in life. To admit the wrong type would be to undermine Canada's free institutions, for certain peoples could not understand constitutional democracy, and material advance would equally be thwarted. "Alien settlers must be assimilated and made acquainted with our institutions," Robert Borden declared at a political rally, and "a national spirit must be created and maintained."[18] But some groups were believed to be biologically unable to assimilate, a view that was supported by orthodox medical opinion as reflected in the mainstream Canadian medical journals. Because of unalterable genetic characteristics and natural antipathies between racial categories, doctors maintained that "public health" demanded a homogeneous population.[19] The consequences of a bad immigration policy could be the destruction of Canada itself.[20] The Great War Veterans' Association was merely uttering the conventional wisdom when in 1927 it supported an admission policy restricted "to such races as are so related to the British and French peoples by blood or tradition as to be readily assimilated and amenable to our traditions, customs and laws."[21]

From Confederation to 1896, fully 90 percent of Canadian immigrants came from Britain. In the fall of that year Clifford Sifton took over the Ministry of the Interior, with responsibility for immigration, and he expanded the recruitment area for Canadian prairie settlers to include central and eastern Europe. He explained to his chief, Prime Minister Laurier:

Our desire is to promote the immigration of farmers and farm labourers. We have not been disposed to exclude foreigners of any nationality who seemed likely to become successful agriculturalists. . . . It is admitted that additions to the population of our cities and towns by immigration [are] undesirable from every standpoint and such additions do not in any way contribute to the object which is constantly kept in view by the Government of Canada in encouraging immigration for the development of natural resources and the increase of production of wealth from these resources. . . . [22]

Sifton concentrated his efforts to attract immigrants upon those European regions he believed would send appropriate prairie farmers. Though only persons perceived to be diseased, criminals, or likely to become public charges were explicitly proscribed, there continued the implicit assumption that all immigrants would be white and European. Sifton's promotional efforts, including free land for prairie settlers, financial incentives for recruiting agents and subsidies for steamship companies, were directed only at Europe.[23]

The government's policy of encouraging immigration met with favour from entrepreneurial and business interests in Canada. Throughout the Laurier era, industry as well as agriculture required increasing supplies of labour, both skilled and unskilled, and so businessmen actively participated in the recruitment of suitable immigrants. Recognizing exactly the same effects from immigration, but regarding them from a different perspective, organized labour was equally inclined to discourage the entry of competitors. The Trades and Labour Congress actually sent an anti-immigration agent to England to counter the claims of Canadian government and business advertising. At home the TLC argued that the privileges and subsidies granted to immigrants would be better spent improving conditions for Canadian labour, and it repeatedly went on record decrying the arrival of more and more workers whose chief impact was to keep wages low.[24]

As has already been described with respect to Chinese immigration to British Columbia,[25] labour resolutions were typically laden with cultural and racial overtones. At its 1904 Convention the TLC complained that "of late, an inferior class of immigrants are arriving from Continental Europe; they do not assimilate, [and] are very slow to adopt our methods of living, herding on the communal plan."[26] The key concept, as always, was assimilation: implying the threat of low wages and unseemly personal characteristics, the label "unassimilable" remained the most devastating charge against any body of immigrants.

A new *Immigration Act*, designed by Sifton just before his departure from the ministry, was enacted in 1906. It granted the government authority to "prohibit the landing in Canada of any specified class of immigrants,"[27] though in 1906 the classes specified were still assumed to be the diseased, the impoverished and the immoral. A scant four years later, a new Act highlighted an increasing recognition that "race" seemed to require equally explicit attention. It was the events in Vancouver in 1907 and the continuing prospect of large-scale Asian immigration that prompted this more careful articulation of what constituted desirability. Section 37 of the *Immigration Act* of 1910 declared that immigrants must "possess in their own right money to a prescribed minimum amount, which amount may vary according to the race, occupation or destination of such immigrant," and Section 38 enabled the government to

(a) prohibit the landing in Canada or at any specified port of entry in Canada of any immigrant who has come to Canada otherwise than by a continuous journey from the country of which he is a native or naturalized citizen, and upon a through ticket purchased in that country or prepaid in Canada; ...
(c) prohibit for a stated period, or permanently, the landing in Canada, or the landing at any specified port of entry in Canada, of immigrants belonging to any race deemed unsuited to the climate or requirements of Canada.[28]

The urges expressed in Nova Scotia's 1815 resolution had finally been actualized: "race" was now designated as an immigration category in a Canadian statute. Also in the 1910 Act, and of significance for Harry Singh's eventual story, was section 23 specifying that

No court, and no judge or officer thereof, shall have jurisdiction to review, quash, reverse, restrain or otherwise interfere with any proceeding, decision or order of the Minister or of any Board of Inquiry, or officer in charge, had, made or given under the authority and in accordance with the provisions of this Act relating to the detention or deportation of any rejected immigrant.

By 1910 those "races" supposed to be genetically incapable of assimilation could be kept out by the decision of immigration officials, not even subject to judicial review. Parallel to this policy were the various enactments denying equal rights to certain "races," as previously described. The unassimilable were to be isolated within Canada, and kept from full participation in Canadian institutions, for to do otherwise would be to risk Canada's survival as a democratic, progressive, British nation. Directed first against the Chinese and then the Japanese in British Columbia, the discriminatory restrictions were amenable for application to any immigrant group that could be identified by racial criteria.

3. SOUTH ASIAN IMMIGRATION

A Colonial Office Minute written in 1897 set out Britain's imperial dilemma in confronting the migration of East Indians to the self-governing white colonies:

The whole subject is perhaps the most difficult we have had to deal with. The Colonies wish to exclude the Indians from spreading themselves all over the Empire. If we agree, we are liable to forfeit the loyalty of the Indians. If we do not agree we forfeit the loyalty of the Colonists.[29]

The colony of Natal in South Africa proved most resourceful in solving this problem with legislation requiring all immigrants to pass a test written in "a European language." Because it did not mention any specific group, the law appeared unbiased and universal in application. In practice the test requirement could be arranged to enable immigration officials to exclude any individual: if the applicant could pass the test in English, it would be administered in Dutch, for example, and so on until the applicant failed. Known as "the Natal Formula," this ingenious device served as a prototype to other anxious British dominions seeking to avoid both Indian immigration and the wrath of Westminster.[30]

At first Canada did not find it urgent to emulate the Natal Formula. Almost no Indians were entering Canada at the turn of the century; in fact there was not even a category for registering arrivals from India. Visitors passed through on occasion – Sikh soldiers en route to London for Queen Victoria's 1897 jubilee and again for King Edward's 1902 coronation, for example – and positive impressions of Canada were apparently circulating amongst the Sikhs of Punjab, but very few came to stay. The first recorded immigrants landed in 1903-4, and once begun the movement increased rapidly so that by 1907-8 over 5,000 persons had immigrated from India. Almost all were Sikh men and most originated in the same small area in the Punjab. Although they had been farmers at home the Sikhs became labourers in Canada, often in the sawmills and lumber camps of British Columbia, where they could earn five times the amount paid for manual labour in India. Among them was a handful of business and professional men.[31] As their numbers increased, the Indians attracted attention: the various restrictions already imposed on Chinese and Japanese in BC were reworded to include Indians as well, and in 1907 natives of India were disfranchised.[32] This new influx from Asia, in particular the arrival in Vancouver harbour of a ship bearing a rumoured 900 Indian migrants, was one of the factors precipitating the Vancouver race riot in September 1907.[33]

Ironically, Indians avoided attack by the Vancouver mob because they did not inhabit the central area where the riot occurred, but they certainly did not avoid the open hostility of both press and public in BC. Not only were they included in the general invective against Chinese and Japanese, they often suffered in comparison with other Asians. They were considered, according to the scientific orthodoxy of the times, to be genetically incapable of assimilation, unsuited to Canadian conditions, a threat to public health, and unfair economic competition in labouring occupations. "They are a case even more apart than the Chinese," complained the Victoria *Colonist*, while the Victoria Trades and Labour Council passed a resolution that

The people of India, in common with all Asiatic races, are reared and nurtured in and under the influence of civilizations and environments that seem to be, in principle, totally opposed to the civilization and environments under which we of the Western civilization are born and reared. In practice they are certainly found to be both unwilling and incapable of assimilating with the people of the western races who have settled and developed this country, and who, for very justifiable reasons, aspire to control the destiny of this broad and fair land, with the hope that civilization in the best and truest sense may advance and develop to a fuller degree than has yet been achieved. But the invitation or admission of these people, the Hindus, would threaten and even make impossible the realization of such hopes.[34]

India was deemed "a hotbed of the most virulent and loathsome diseases," which could be transmitted to Canada, and Indians belonged to "a race of people who can never be of any use to Canada as citizens and whose very existence amongst our people could be a menace to the well-being of the community."[35] A public meeting in Vancouver carried unanimously a resolution "that the influx of Asiatics is detrimental and hurtful to the best interests of the Dominion, from the standpoint of citizenship, public morals, and labour conditions."[36] When a suggestion was made that Sikh veterans of Britain's Indian army might be recruited to the BC militia, it was reported that white militiamen would thereupon resign.[37] Even the saintly J. S. Woodsworth considered Indians to be inappropriate immigrants for both physical and cultural reasons.[38]

It is hardly surprising that the Canadian government should take action against such an unpopular immigration. The restraint of course was that Britain did not wish to give her Indian subjects a legitimate ground of complaint. Colonial Secretary Joseph Chamberlain warned that explicit regulations against Indians would cause "substantial unrest" in India, and would therefore not be acceptable to the Crown.[39] Superintendent of Immigration W. D. Scott conducted a personal investigation in Vancouver and pronounced the Indians "unsuitable" and "unassimilable"; his findings were sent to the government of India to discourage further migration.[40] More dramatically the deputy minister of Labour, W. L. Mackenzie King, went to London to seek an efficient and acceptable method to exclude Indians. In the high reaches of the British government King found "That Canada should desire to restrict immigration from the Orient is regarded as natural, that Canada should remain a white man's country is believed to be not only desirable for economic and social reasons, but highly necessary on political and national grounds."

With classic diplomatic hypocrisy King reported:

it was recognized in regard to emigration from India to Canada, that the native of India is not a person suited to this country, that, accustomed as many of them are to the conditions of a tropical climate, and possessing manners and customs so unlike those of our own people, their inability to readily adapt themselves to surroundings entirely different could not do other than entail an amount of privation and suffering which render a discontinuance of such immigration most desirable in the interests of the Indians themselves.

His recommendations were to publicize throughout India the harsh conditions met by Indians in Canada, to induce steamship companies to exercise caution in carrying Indian immigrants to Canada, to encourage India to enforce a law against the emigration of contract labour, to require intending immigrants to possess a sum of money high enough to serve as a disincentive, and to introduce a "continuous journey" rule. These remedies, King concluded, would preserve the integrity of the British Empire and protect Canada from a "serious disturbance" to her social and economic fabric.[41]

It was in consequence of King's report that the federal cabinet passed orders-in-council in 1908 requiring all "Asiatic" immigrants except those already covered by separate provisions to possess at least $200,[42] and stipulating that immigrants must come to Canada by a continuous journey and on a through ticket from their country of origin.[43] Although Indians were never mentioned in the regulations, Chinese and Japanese were excepted by the existence of separate immigration provisions, leaving Indians as the only "Asiatics" to be affected by the $200 requirement. Furthermore there did not exist any means to make a continuous journey from India to Canada nor were there ticketing arrangements available in India to piece together a journey via Hong Kong. The government of India, nevertheless, pronounced itself "pleased" that Canada had managed to solve its immigration problem "without resorting to invidious legislation aimed particularly at British Indians."[44]

As Mackenzie King had predicted, the impact of the new regulations was immediate: immigration from India declined drastically after 1908 from thousands to only a few dozen per year. Among other things this meant that South Asians already resident in Canada could not bring in their wives and children. Family reunification became the primary campaign theme and the chief moral argument for South Asian organizations over the next several decades. The Khalsa Diwan Society, initiated in 1907 as a Sikh religious organization, led the campaign on behalf of all South Asians. Petitions and delegations were sent to Ottawa and to London, public rallies were staged in Vancouver, and a propaganda organ, an English-language publication entitled *Aryan*, was distributed amongst potential allies including white women's and church groups. The case presented in *Aryan* and in the various petitions and debates was that Indians were British subjects, many had served in the imperial services, separation of families was unnatural and immoral, and besides, Indians were not members of the inferior Asiatic "races" but in fact cousins of the Anglo-Saxons through their Aryan ancestors.[45] Interestingly, the attack on racial discrimination did not deny the validity of racist assumptions, but merely argued that Indians did not belong in the disadvantaged class.[46]

Following the passage of the 1910 *Immigration Act*, whose Sections 37 and 38 belatedly empowered the government to impose the monetary and continuous journey requirements, new orders-in-council were issued stating that

[926] No immigrant of Asiatic origin shall be permitted to enter Canada unless in actual and personal possession in his or her own right of two hundred dollars, unless such person is a native or subject of an Asiatic country in regard to which special statutory regulations are in force or with which the Government of Canada has made a special treaty, agreement or convention;[47]

and that

[920] the landing in Canada shall be and the same is hereby prohibited, of any immigrants who have come to Canada otherwise than by continuous journey from the country of which they are natives or citizens, and upon through tickets purchased in that country or purchased or prepaid in Canada.[48]

This particular wording would bring the government to grief in 1913.

4. REHEARSAL: NARAIN SINGH AND MUNSHI SINGH

On 17 October 1913, 56 South Asians arrived in Victoria; 17 were permitted to land because they had previously established domicile in Canada and were returning after a visit to India, and the remaining 39 were ordered deported under PCs 920 and 926. The detainees' first application for a writ of *habeas corpus* was dismissed on the grounds that Section 23 of the 1910 *Immigration Act* precluded judicial intervention in an immigration board decision, but on appeal to BC Chief Justice Gordon Hunter the result was different.[49]

The issue in the appeal of Narain Singh et al., as stated by attorney J. Edward Bird, was that the Indians were being held illegally because their deportation derived from orders-in-council that were *ultra vires* and, since compliance with the orders was impossible for people in India, the court must intervene to correct a fundamental injustice.[50] Chief Justice Hunter rejected any concern "with questions of expediency or good faith," declaring that if the government wished to ban Indians by a "subterfuge" it had a right to do so. But he did accept Bird's contention that PCs 920 and 926 differed substantially from their enabling legislation and must therefore be found *ultra vires*. Section 37 of the Act permitted the government to require immigrants to "possess in their own right" a prescribed amount of money; PC 926 required Asiatics to be "in actual and personal possession" of the money. An immigrant with sufficient money in a Canadian bank would satisfy the Act but not the order. Section 37 also permitted the government to vary the amount according to the "race" of the immigrant; PC 926 imposed the requirement on "immigrants of Asiatic origin." As the chief justice pointed out, "the word 'origin' includes more than the word 'race.'" A person born in India of British parents would be Asiatic by origin but not by "race." PC 920 required continuous journey "from the country of which they are natives or citizens"; Section 38 of the Act specified "native or naturalized citizen." The difference, Chief Justice Hunter insisted, was that the same hypothetical British child born in India would be a "native" of India but a "citizen" of Great Britain; the order would exclude such a person from Canada while the Act would not. Since the orders exceeded the Act in these various ways they were *ultra vires* and the Indians' deportation notices were cancelled. Article 23 was of no effect because its restriction on judicial interference "applies only to proceedings had under the authority and in accordance with the provisions of this Act," a condition not existing in this instance.[51]

A week after the *Narain Singh* decision, the federal government enacted an order temporarily banning all artisans and labourers from landing in BC ports.[52] In early January 1914 orders 920 and 926 were replaced by PCs 23 and 24, answering Chief Justice Hunter's objections with wording carefully following the terms of the Act.[53] There would be no more loopholes, and no more immigrants from India. But another result of the 1913 decision was that it encouraged one more attempt to challenge Canada's restrictions against South Asians. Gurdit Singh enlisted Indian passengers for a voyage by chartered ship from Hong Kong to Vancouver. The *Komagata Maru* left Hong Kong in April bearing 376 persons, mostly Sikhs, and arrived in Vancouver on 23 May 1914.[54] Immigration agents kept the ship anchored in Burrard Inlet, and the government declared its intention to keep the gates closed. Prime Minister Borden advised the House of Commons:

It is my opinion that the immigration of Oriental aliens and their rapid multiplication is becoming a serious menace to living conditions on the West Coast and to the future of this country in general. This Government shall take immediate action to bring to an end such immigration for residence purposes. Specifically those Sikhs who are presently seeking such admittance in Vancouver shall be barred.[55]

Sir Wilfrid Laurier warned ominously: "I know that if these Hindus are allowed to come into British Columbia, there may be riots on the streets of Vancouver and Victoria."[56] Accordingly, deportation orders were issued to all but 22 of the passengers, the exceptions having established previous domicile in Canada.

The 354 excluded passengers hired J. Edward Bird, recommended by his *Narain Singh* victory just six months previously. It was decided to apply for writs of *habeas corpus* and thereby to challenge the validity of the deportations. The government sought to engage in a single test case, to decide the fate of all the passengers with minimum fuss and publicity. The passengers, naturally, sought individual hearings, but after stalling for a month, with conditions deteriorating on board the *Komagata Maru*, they submitted reluctantly to the government's proposal. Munshi Singh, a Sikh farmer from Punjab, was selected as the representative case. An application on his behalf for a writ of *habeas corpus* was speedily rejected without argument or reasons by Justice Murphy so that the BC Court of Appeal could hear the case without delay.[57]

The arguments put by Bird and his associate Robert Cassidy followed several themes present in the Indians' own campaign for immigration reform, but framed in constitutional terms. The fact that all persons born in British India were British subjects and should therefore enjoy equal rights throughout the Empire was, for example, a frequent claim put by East Indians in Canada. Bird and Cassidy took that point to challenge the constitutionality of the *Immigration Act* itself. Under the *BNA Act* the federal government had control over "aliens," but British subjects were not aliens. Thus the *Immigration Act* provisions for the detention and deportation of British subjects were *ultra vires* and trenched upon the appellant's "civil rights" which belong constitutionally to provincial jurisdiction. The orders issued under the authority of the *Immigration Act* exceeded the powers delegated by the statute. Section 37 permitted a monetary requirement which could "vary" according to the "race" of the immigrant. PC 24 set a $200 sum for "the Asiatic race," but no amounts for any other "race." This was not a "variation," but a specific imposition and a clear case of discrimination. With respect to PC 23 it was argued rather forcedly that Munshi Singh had in fact complied with it: a British subject born in British territory (India) had begun his voyage to Canada from British territory (Hong Kong) and had therefore made a continuous journey. In any case PC 23 and its enabling Section 38 of the Act were *ultra vires* because they banned "any immigrant who has come." This wording made the banning conditional upon arrival, and the government had no authority to establish a condition precedent to the making of a proclamation or order. The constitutionality of PC 897, banning all labourers, was not challenged, but it was argued that Munshi Singh was a farmer, not a labourer. The immigration officials had no evidence that Munshi Singh was a labourer, and so their decision was a violation of the common law principle that "a man shall not be convicted without proof such as would satisfy natural justice."[58] Natural justice was violated, too, as was the *Magna Carta*, by the *Immigration Act*'s denial of appeal to the courts for persons deprived of their freedom by an immigration board order and by the impossibility of an applicant's case being heard by a jury of his peers.[59] The appellants reached beyond constitutional issues as well. Blandishing an encyclopedia, Bird anticipated an argument of the 1950s when he stated that the expression "Asiatic race" used in the orders was "ethnologically incorrect and too indefinite to be capable of application."[60] And, whatever definition was offered for "Asiatic race," it could not include Munshi Singh. The peoples of India to which Munshi Singh belonged were Caucasians, members of the Aryan family, and as such were racially cousins to the English. Munshi Singh was an "alien" neither legally nor racially. He deserved to be admitted to Canada.[61]

But this time it was not Chief Justice Hunter on the bench. All five justices of the Court of Appeal rejected every argument put on Munshi Singh's behalf. Although their language differed, each judge upheld the deportation order and scoffed at the logical and grammatical tactics used by counsel. Chief Justice MacDonald termed them "ingenious" but "absurd."[62] It was held that the *Immigration Act* was constitutional, and that Parliament had the right to ban British subjects including even those born in England of English ancestry. The *BNA Act* gave sovereign power to Canada, specifying power over immigration.[63] The $200 requirement was seen as reasonable, and since the Act made discrimination inevitable the order could not be impeached on that ground.[64] That Hong Kong could be considered Munshi Singh's native country was dismissed as a fallacy.[65] The onus of proof that he was not a labourer fell on Munshi Singh; his failure to convince the immigration officials that he was a farmer did not constitute a denial of justice.[66] And of course he could appeal the deportation decision, not to the courts but to the minister.[67] Parliament, not the courts, was responsible for the establishment of policy. Justice Martin reminded Bird that "A court of law has nothing to do with a Canadian Act of Parliament, lawfully passed, except to give it effect according to its tenor. . . . It cannot be too strongly put that with the wisdom or policy or expediency of an Act, lawfully passed, no Court has a word to say."[68] Or, in the words of Justice McPhillips, "This Court – one of His Majesty's Courts of Justice – is without jurisdiction to hear this appeal, but this in no way indicates there is any refusal of justice. The Courts of law cannot attract to themselves jurisdiction. Jurisdiction must be conferred.[69]

In response to the non-constitutional arguments, the *Encyclopedia Britannica* was quoted as justifying the use of the term "Asiatic races,"[70] and an association called the "Asiatic Society," founded in Calcutta in 1784, was explicitly mandated to examine Indian culture, so that India and the Indians were understood as being Asiatic.[71] In a more sophisticated rejection of the "Aryan family" argument than that given by the United States Supreme Court, who relied on "common understanding" to classify Indians as different from whites, Justice A. E. McPhillips pointed out that what the people of India and of England shared was not their racial attributes but their linguistic roots in the Aryan family of Indo-European languages. "Kindred languages" did not imply any "blood" relationship.[72] On that particular issue Justice McPhillips took extravagant care to indicate that Indians (whom he called Hindus) and Europeans were racially quite distinct, and in doing so he articulated the fundamental principles motivating Canada's immigration policy:

It is plain that upon study of the question, the Hindu race, as well as the Asiatic race in general, are, in their conception of life and ideas of society, fundamentally different to the Anglo-Saxon and Celtic races, and European races in general. . . . The laws of this country are unsuited to them, and their ways and ideas may well be a menace to the well-being of the Canadian people. . . .

The Parliament of Canada – the nation's Parliament – may be well said to be safeguarding the people of Canada from an influx which it is no chimera to conjure up might annihilate the nation and change its whole potential complexity, introduce Oriental ways as against European ways, eastern civilization for western civilization, and all the dire results that would naturally flow therefrom. . . .

In that our fellow British subjects of the Asiatic race are of different racial instincts to those of the European race – and consistent therewith, their family life, rules of society and laws are of a very different character – in their own interests, their proper place of residence is within the confines of their respective countries in the continent of Asia, not in Canada, where their customs are not in vogue and their adhesion to them here only give rise to disturbances destructive to the well-being of society and against the maintenance of peace, order and good government. . . .

Better that peoples of non-assimilative – and by nature properly non-assimilative – race should not come to Canada, but rather, that they should remain of residence in their country of origin and there do their share, as they have in the past, in the preservation and development of the Empire.[73]

Scarcely a month later Canada was at war, and the immigration issue became academic. The war interrupted the greatest movement of people to Canada since overseas settlement began: 400,870 arrived in the peak year of 1913 alone, indicating the welcome Canadians generally extended to immigrants whose origin was deemed suitable. The merest handful came from India, however, and many of these returned to India during the War. By the 1921 census there were only 1,016 East Indians in Canada.[74] Under pressure from Britain and India at Imperial War Conferences, Canadian regulations were changed to permit East Indian men in Canada to apply for the entry of their wives and children, but mechanisms to implement this program were tardy, complicated and unpublicized. In the decade following its passage, when immigration generally was being resumed, only 144 women and 188 children came to Canada from India.[75] Then on 16 September 1930 all previous regulations were replaced with PC 2115, which stated that

the landing in Canada of any immigrant of any Asiatic race is hereby prohibited, except . . . :

The wife or unmarried child under 18 years of age of any Canadian citizen legally admitted to and resident in Canada, who is in a position to receive and care for his dependents,

Provided that this regulation shall not apply to the nationals of any country in regard to which there is in operation a law, a special treaty, or agreement, or convention regulating immigration.[76]

5. WEST INDIAN IMMIGRATION

For nearly a century before Confederation, Maritime merchants enjoyed a flourishing commercial relationship with the British Caribbean colonies. In 1868 Nova Scotian Presbyterians established a mission in Trinidad, aimed particularly at the large East Indian community there (into which Harry Singh would be born in 1928). Canadian missionary activity spread to other British islands and mainland Guiana, soon followed by Canadian financial institutions. During the 1880s and 1890s the Royal Bank of Canada, the Bank of Nova Scotia and the Sun Life Insurance Company began the tradition of Canada's dominant influence in the financial affairs of the British West Indies.[77] Contacts therefore were close at certain levels, and although they largely involved Canadians going to the West Indies, there was always some movement in the other direction. Individual slaves from the West Indies were imported into New France and Nova Scotia,[78] and occasionally free black migrants would appear. The most dramatic migration was the sudden and unannounced arrival in Halifax of over 500 Jamaican "Maroons" in 1796. Following an armed conflict between the Maroons and the British governors of Jamaica, one group of Maroons was sent into exile in Nova Scotia, but they never adjusted and so, in 1800, most of them were removed by the British government to the colony of Sierra Leone in West Africa.[79] During the 19th century there were a few dozen West Indians in Victoria, Toronto and Halifax, admitted by their status as British subjects. They continued to trickle in, brought by ships' captains seeking a return cargo from a voyage delivering Canadian fish or lumber to the Caribbean. The largest number, recruited initially in Barbados, settled in Sydney, Nova Scotia, where they were employed in the coal mines and blast furnaces and would become the founders of a thriving cultural community which remains distinct in Canada.[80] Although these early migrants were economically useful and employers continued to seek more West Indian workers, the government response was to classify them as inadmissible. Superintendent of Immigration W. D. Scott explained to his officials in Nova Scotia:

The government does not encourage the immigration of coloured people. There are certain countries from which immigration is encouraged and certain races of people considered as suited to this [country] and its conditions, but Africans, no matter where they come from are not among the races sought, and, hence, Africans no matter from what country they come are in common with the uninvited races, not admitted to Canada.[81]

In the early 20th century there was a huge demand from middle- and upper-class households for domestic servants, but a limited supply of young Canadian women willing to engage in this poorly paid and demanding work. The answer, clearly, was to import domestic labour: in the decade prior to World War I alone, 129,000 domestic servants entered Canada from overseas.[82] Only a few of these came from the West Indies, despite regular demand from employers and several attempts to increase the supply. In 1910-11, for example, lawyer Joseph Dion devised a scheme to recruit domestics for Quebec homes from the French colony of Guadaloupe. Immigration officials in New York examined the first group to arrive en route to Montreal, and reported that "Taking all things into consideration, they may be classed desirable as domestics. The scarcity of such help in the cities they are going to will no doubt help them in the future to be in a position to secure employment at all times."[83]

But the arrival of the Guadaloupe domestics in Canada attracted attention to West Indian migration just as the movement of African Americans from Oklahoma to the prairies was receiving national publicity and arousing attendant fears. In May 1911 a questionnaire was sent to 96 employers who had received Guadaloupienne servants; of the 55 responses, 49 were overwhelmingly positive, but immigration officials chose to emphasize the few negative comments they received. Superintendent Scott wrote to Minister Frank Oliver in June that "the girls admitted are not all of good moral character, and I think this class of immigration should be discouraged."[84] Scott informed Joseph Dion that his scheme must cease by 30 June 1911, and despite frequent requests from scores of Canadian households in subsequent months the government insisted that West Indian women were physically and morally unfit.[85] One disappointed Canadian family was told: "We do not regard immigration of this sort as desirable and I have no doubt that even you yourself would not like to have Canada filled up with persons of the class you are now seeking to bring into this country."[86]

Under this gaze the already infinitesimal migration of West Indians to Canada shrank even further. The chief Immigration Branch inspector in the Maritimes was asked to conduct an investigation. He suggested that if all other means failed, West Indians could ultimately be rejected under Section 3(g) of the *Immigration Act* as "likely to become a public charge." Scott immediately accepted this advice, and instructed local agents that all West Indian applicants "are to be rejected as LPC."[87] There would be some exceptions made, for example when the Dominion Coal and Dominion Iron and Steel companies were authorized to import needed labourers as a special wartime concession,[88] but more often Canadians seeking West Indian employees were urged to "suffer some little inconvenience" rather than flood Canada with undesirables.[89]

As in the case of the East Indians, the British government grew alarmed that overtly discriminatory policies were being applied against British subjects. In addition, Canadian employers and traders with Caribbean connections protested that exclusionary practices damaged Canada's economic interests. The Canadian government was able to respond that "There are no special regulations governing the entry to this Dominion of British-born subjects coming from the West Indies," but to save embarrassment and gain outside approval it was decided that use of the "continuous journey" order might be most acceptable. Since virtually all ships from the West Indies then stopped at New York or St. John's en route to Canada, PC 23 proved to be almost as total an obstacle for West Indians as for East Indians. As an extra measure, steamship companies were advised that they would be held liable for any costs incurred in detaining and returning inadmissible West Indian passengers. Although demand for agricultural labourers and domestic servants was high in the 1920s, and deliberate efforts were being made to recruit European immigrants throughout the decade, it was decided that West Indians were unsuited to farm labour and that black domestics had already proved themselves unfit for Canadian homes.[90] Finally, by order-in-council in 1923, the Canadian government limited West Indian immigration by the simple expediency of omitting them from the list of British subjects eligible to come to Canada.[91] As the minister stated, to explain why barriers were being created at a time of labour shortage, "there are some would-be immigrants into Canada who are not suited for the Dominion owing to physical, moral, or industrial unfitness or because they belong to races that cannot be assimilated without social or economic loss to Canada."[92] If no genuine economic reason existed, then one could be invented.

6. POLICY SHIFTS, 1945-52

As has already been noted, World War II was a watershed in the flow of Canadian attitudes about the world and its peoples. The specific war aims of the democratic allies made it seem disloyal to espouse openly racist ideals. A war fought against Nazi racism challenged policies and practices based on racial preferences, and this eventually came to include immigration. In introducing an immigration resolution in April 1946, Moose Jaw MP W. R. Thatcher indicated that the first weakness of Canadian policy as it then existed was that "it is based on racial discrimination and outworn prejudices." He continued: "It seems very strange that during the recent war, at the very time Canadians were being urged to enlist to help in eradicating racial intolerance abroad, our own nation was practising similar intolerance at home in selecting its immigrants."[93] Later, another Saskatchewan MP, E. B. McKay, argued that in admitting immigrants "There should not be any preferred races. . . . Canadian boys laid down their lives to defeat militarism promoted by a race which rated itself as supermen. . . . Let us have done with superior races and preferred nations."[94] For, as the member for Winnipeg North, Alistair Stewart, pointed out:

The war taught us there are no superior and inferior races, that the superior races might easily become the inferior races and vice versa, that we are all dependent upon one another for mutual protection, that the old shibboleths are obsolete, that narrow nationalisms must give way to a broader community of nations.[95]

The War provoked a recognition not only that "race" was a dangerous foundation for state policy but that certain Canadian practices were out of step with declared Canadian ideals, and suggested that some reforms were therefore necessary.

To Canada's awakened conscience were added certain external pressures and commitments. Madame Chiang Kai-shek raised the question of Chinese exclusion during a wartime visit to Ottawa,[96] West Indian government representatives complained of barriers against British subjects from the Caribbean,[97] and the leaders of the new India were quick to raise objections about Canada's treatment of people with origins in India.[98] Canadian adherence to the United Nations *Charter* was cited repeatedly in the House of Commons as a moral and legal obligation to eliminate racial selectivity in immigration policy; even more acute feelings were aroused by Canada's membership in a multiracial Commonwealth of supposedly equal members.[99] CCF leader M. J. Coldwell declared: "The time has come, if we are to be regarded as the kind of nation that we hope to be regarded throughout the world, for us to remove every jot and tittle of this discriminatory legislation from the statute books of Canada."[100] Outside parliament, too, it was being recognized that the values espoused by Canada internationally were not reflected in immigration regulations. The Khalsa Diwan Society enlisted the support of the UN *Charter* in a renewed campaign for a non-discriminatory immigration policy.[101] The Ottawa diocesan synod of the Anglican Church passed a resolution at its 1947 convention that "This synod opposes any advantage being given to immigrants of any racial or religious group."[102]

Some of the pressures for change were more materialistic. The Canadian Manufacturers' Association, the Canadian Chamber of Commerce and agricultural associations were all calling on the government to increase the supply of immigrant workers. A low birth rate during the Depression meant a postwar shortage of workers which only immigration could solve. Within two years after the War it became apparent that the transition to a peacetime economy had been accomplished without serious dislocation, and that Canada was engaged in an economic expansion that would require a large increase in population and labour power to sustain.[103] Unions, as well as business, could observe the economic need for more workers and more consumers in the expanding postwar economy. Gradually, organized labour began to modify its anti-immigration stance. As early as 1942 the TLC favoured open immigration within the British Empire and the Americas. In 1944 the TLC called for Canada "to do her share" in receiving postwar refugees from Europe, and the CCL passed a similar resolution the same year.[104]

By 1946, when they were invited before a parliamentary committee on immigration, both the TLC and the CCL favoured an expanded immigration policy as long as it did not introduce a pool of cheap and docile workers into Canada. CCL president A. R. Mosher, in answering a direct question, went so far as to accept Japanese and "Negro" immigration; the TLC, however, reaffirmed its adherence to Article 12 of its Platform of Principles, which demanded "Exclusion of all races that cannot be properly assimilated into the national life of Canada."[105] TLC president Percy Bengough explained his reasoning before the 1947 annual convention:

It must be recognized that there are citizens of other countries who may be good brothers and sisters, internationally, but yet would not be accepted as brothers- and sisters-in-law to Canadians. Experience has clearly demonstrated that because of this fact certain nationals who have in the past been admitted into Canada remain as a distinct race and will remain a problem for future generations. The result of permitting such an immigration policy has been equally unfair to those admitted and to their children, as to the citizens of Canada generally. Organized Labour naturally opposed such immigration for the fact that such immigrants came and for many years remained a reservoir of cheap labour and a menace to Canadian standards of living. Any system of selection must include the suitability of assimilation, and must, in the best interests of all, be rightly adhered to.[106]

Within these limitations there can be recognized a genuine movement away from a historical opposition to immigration, and another powerful member was added to the lobby for policy reform.

The body hearing labour's testimony was the Senate Committee on Immigration and Labour, established in 1946. In over 1,000 hours of testimony, the Committee heard no one "opposed to the general principle of immigration into Canada."[107] Not surprisingly the Committee's final report included recommendations to increase immigration, but within a set of selection criteria. On the one hand, the Committee stated,

There should be no discrimination based on race or religion in the execution of Canadian immigration policy.... Any suggestion of discrimination based on either race or religion should be scrupulously avoided both in the drafting of any future Immigration Act and its administration.

But just a few pages later the impact of this recommendation was modified by the cautionary statement that "As the limitations placed on Asiatic immigration are based, of course, on the realities of effective absorption, such restrictions should continue."[108]

The new postwar attitude, therefore, was encouraging to reform, but few people were asking for revolutionary change. In keeping with public opinion, the government initiated an incremental shift in policy without altering any fundamental principles. The chief immigration policy instruments at war's end were PC 2115 of 1930, covering Asians, and PC 695 of 1931, covering virtually everybody else.[109] Both were characterized by their restrictive nature. The only piece of legislation that was specific to one country was the *Chinese Immigration Act* of 1923. Faced with a well-organized lobby demanding its repeal, and with no real reason to continue it, the government readily withdrew the Chinese Act early in 1947. The result was not the open admission of Chinese immigrants, but merely that Chinese now came under PC 2115 like other Asians. It was anticipated that the number of wives and minor children eligible to enter Canada under PC 2115 would only number in the hundreds: no significant increase in the Chinese-Canadian population was expected.[110]

Pressed during the debate on the Chinese amendment to make a definitive statement on immigration policy, Prime Minister King responded on 1 May 1947 with what has come to be regarded as the "classic" position on postwar immigration. Government policy, the prime minister stated, was to encourage immigration for the purpose of fostering economic growth. Regulations would ensure the careful selection "of such numbers of immigrants as can advantageously be absorbed in our national economy." In the short run, the economic requirements under PC 695 would be interpreted more leniently to allow designated British subjects and American citizens to enter, and the range of relatives admissible from Europe would be broadened. Special measures would be designed for special situations, such as the Displaced Persons in European refugee camps, but individual selection would be maintained to choose "a type likely to make good citizens" and "who can be readily placed in employment." For the longer term, the prime minister promised carefully planned growth, with numbers adjusted annually according to "the absorptive capacity of the country." On the subject of racial discrimination in the selection of immigrants, King had this to say:

I wish to make it quite clear that Canada is perfectly within her rights in selecting the persons whom we regard as desirable future citizens. It is not a "fundamental human right" of any alien to enter Canada. It is a privilege. It is a matter of domestic policy. Immigration is subject to the control of the parliament of Canada. This does not mean, however, that we should not seek to remove from our legislation what may appear to be objectionable discrimination. . . .

There will, I am sure, be general agreement with the view that the people of Canada do not wish, as a result of mass immigration, to make a fundamental alteration in the character of our population. Large-scale immigration from the orient would change the fundamental composition of the Canadian population. Any considerable oriental immigration would, moreover, be certain to give rise to social and economic problems of a character that might lead to serious difficulties in the field of international relations. The government, therefore, has no thought of making any change in immigration regulations which would have consequences of the kind.

I wish to state quite definitely that, apart from the repeal of the Chinese Immigration Act . . . the government has no intention of removing the existing regulations respecting Asiatic immigration unless and until alternative measures of effective control have been worked out. Canada recognizes the right of all other countries to control the entry or non-entry of persons seeking to become permanent residents. We claim precisely the same right for our country.[111]

The necessity to confront "what may appear to be objectionable discrimination" was acknowledged with what appeared to be a reform. No "fundamental alteration" would be made in the "character" of the Canadian population.

Between 1947 and 1950 a series of new orders-in-council gave effect to Mackenzie King's statement. The range of family members eligible for sponsorship by Canadian residents was expanded, the list of acceptable occupations was extended, and the category of approved nationalities was broadened.[112] During 1947 the first Displaced Persons came from Europe, eventually to total over 165,000 people from regions previously considered "non-traditional."[113] In 1948, at the urging of the new prime minister, Louis St. Laurent, France was placed in the preferred category, and in 1950 Germans became admissible.[114] This expansionary trend was, however, an echo of the pre-Depression policies of the 1920s, for it was limited in practical terms to the continent of Europe. The only exception was a regulation adopted on 28 December 1950 which, recognizing that "people of the Asiatic races seldom marry persons of European origin," amended PC 2115 to allow Asian women who were Canadian citizens to bring their Asian husbands to Canada. The age for admissible unmarried children was raised from 18 to 21.[115]

There was a demonstrable movement away from British exclusivity, and the most overt example of discriminatory legislation, the Chinese Act, had been repealed, but prospective immigrants from anywhere except Europe were virtually as restricted as ever. In the early 1950s the Department of Citizenship and Immigration was still routinely sending a standard letter to applicants from southern countries, including Commonwealth territories, which read as follows:

[I]n dealing with applications from persons residing in tropical or sub-tropical countries, consideration must be given to their prospects for becoming readily adapted to the Canadian mode of life. It must also be borne in mind that natives of such countries are more apt to break down in health than immigrants from countries with similar climatic conditions to those of Canada. These points are taken into consideration in conjunction with the circumstances existing in each individual case which is carefully reviewed by the Department. . . .

[A]ll aspects of your case were very carefully reviewed and the conclusion reached was that you cannot qualify under present immigration regulations.[116]

Restrictions against citizens of independent India were an irritant and a complication in Indo-Canadian relations. India regarded Canadian regulations as an insult and a threat to Commonwealth unity; Canada insisted that immigration was a domestic matter, and every nation, India included, must be free to set its own rules. A symbolic compromise was reached in January 1951, when an annual quota of Indian immigrants was set. Apparently the suggestion that a quota be struck came from India, though the Americans had already established a quota in 1946, admitting 100 Indians per year. The 1951 agreement permitted 150 Indians to enter Canada under their own qualifications, in addition to the close family members of Canadian citizens already admissible under PC 2115. Though scarcely significant in numerical terms, the Indian quota signalled a breach in the wall so long maintained against migrants from the southern hemisphere.[117]

7. THE IMMIGRATION ACT, 1952

On 4 July 1952 Immigration Minister Walter Harris rose in the House of Commons to defend his budget of $244,046. Since 1951 had witnessed the largest number of immigrant arrivals in almost 40 years, the minister was careful to assure the House that although liberalization had occurred, immigration policy had remained the same in principle since Mackenzie King's 1947 statement. "That policy," Harris summarized, "is to admit to Canada in numbers not exceeding the absorptive capacity of our country and without altering the fundamental character of our people, such persons as are likely to contribute to our national life."[118] Harris went on to explain the regulations existing in PCs 2856 and 2115, indicating between them "precisely who is admissible from what particular country." He unfolded a set of four layers divided into twelve ranks of admissibility, emanating outward from most to least acceptable. In the first layer were white British subjects and citizens of Ireland, the United States and France, who shared the top rank and who had virtually open access. The next layer held various nationals of northern and western Europe, ranked from Scandinavians to Greeks and Italians, who were eligible if they proposed to work in certain occupations. The qualifying immigrant could bring a spouse, children, siblings, parents, grandparents, fiancé(e) and even orphaned nieces and nephews under 21. Grouped in the third layer were nationals from the rest of Europe, some Middle-Eastern countries, South America and the British West Indies, who needed to be closely related to a legal Canadian resident in order to qualify. "Cases of exceptional merit" were also admissible from these ranks. Finally came Asians and "others" (Africans were the only major group left unnamed) who had to be the spouse or unmarried child under 21 of a Canadian citizen in order to gain immigrant status. It will of course be noticed that the requirements grew systematically tighter as the line moved further away from the Anglo-Celtic core.[119]

This was an extremely candid public pronouncement of Canadian regulations, made in the context of a ministerial report during the annual supply debate. While governments had muttered frequently in the past against specific groups, chiefly people of African and Asian origin, never before had a minister been quite so explicit in describing the intimate details of the ranking system. Naturally, Opposition members took aim. CCF leader M. J. Coldwell decried the discrimination against Commonwealth citizens, particularly Indians. He was joined in this by Conservative leader George Drew. BC Conservative MP Davie Fulton added that East Indians who had immigrated earlier had become valuable Canadian citizens, and so restrictions against their relatives were mistaken. Even BC Liberal MP James Sinclair rose to confess that Canadian-born children of South Asian ancestry had assimilated completely to life in BC.[120] Harris insisted, despite these comments, that it was the clear desire of the Canadian people to favour immigrants from northern Europe, particularly Britain and France.[121]

On the very day that this debate took place Royal Assent was being given to a new *Immigration Act*, reconfirming the priorities outlined by the minister. During the second reading two weeks previously Harris had avoided a full debate, arguing that the bill merely revised administrative procedures. The new legislation "retains the principles [and] follows the pattern of the present [1910] Act which defines those admissible as of right and those prohibited, and vests the governor-in-council authority to make regulations for the admission of others." The major contribution of the bill, Harris claimed, was to "modernize" certain aspects of the 1910 Act and "to vest in the department, the minister and the governor-in-council in some cases, up-to-date powers to deal with problems which are faced by all countries who choose to keep their borders from being entered by undesirable people."[122] The government view, Harris later explained, was that the administrative details and chief policy instruments should continue to be under ministerial discretion and via orders-in-council, and need not be specified in a statute, for

immigration could not possibly become a matter of law and we did not want to get into a system ... whereby we would try to define in law those persons who could be admitted to Canada, so that one could approach the Courts in this country and have a judge decide in an action at law whether an applicant came within the terms of the law.[123]

The *Immigration Act* of 1952[124] did indeed delegate authority over the details of immigration policy to the minister. At the heart of the Act was Section 61:

The Governor in Council may make regulations for carrying into effect the purposes and provisions of this Act and, without restricting the generality of the foregoing, may make regulations respecting. . . .
g) the prohibiting or limiting of admission of persons by reason of
    i) nationality, citizenship, ethnic group, occupation, class or geographical area of origin,
    ii) peculiar customs, habits, modes of life or methods of holding property,

iii) unsuitability having regard to the climatic, economic, social, industrial, educational, labour, health, or other conditions or requirements existing, temporarily or otherwise, in Canada or in the area or country from or through which such persons come to Canada, or

iv) probable inability to become readily assimilated or to assume the duties and responsibilities of Canadian citizenship within a reasonable time after their admission.[125]

Subsection g) was a carte blanche to prohibit anyone the minister happened not to like. Parliament was virtually delegating its legislative authority to the governor-in-council. Parliament also delegated judicial powers to the minister and, more ominously, to officials in his department. Having established that "immigration officers-in-charge are Special Inquiry Officers," Section 11 went on to state that "a Special Inquiry Officer has authority to inquire into and determine whether any person shall be allowed to come into Canada or to remain in Canada or shall be deported." At this inquiry, by Section 27, "the person concerned, if he desires and at his own expense, shall have the right to obtain and be represented by counsel." An unsuccessful applicant could appeal to the minister, but the minister need not conduct another hearing or even give reasons for a decision. And, as in the 1910 Act, Section 39 provided that

No court and no judge or officer thereof has jurisdiction to review, quash, reverse, restrain or otherwise interfere with any proceeding, decision or order of the Minister, Deputy Minister, Director, Immigration Appeal Board, Special Inquiry Officer or immigration officer had, made or given under the authority and in accordance with the provisions of this Act relating to the detention or deportation of any person, upon any ground whatsoever, unless such person is a Canadian citizen or has Canadian domicile.

The Act was essentially exclusionary, reaffirming the principle that no one had a right to immigrate to Canada,[126] and the authority over whom to exclude was left to the Department of Immigration.

One apparently meaningful change from 1910 was that the word "race" was replaced by the more acceptable term "ethnic group" in Section 61(g)(i). By 1952, "race" had come under severe scientific questioning, and few serious scientists gave the term any credibility. Alastair Stewart, CCF MP from Winnipeg North, had quoted UNESCO documents in March 1952 to indicate that racial origin had no effect on the mental abilities or achievements of human beings.[127] During second reading of the immigration bill, Stewart condemned the government for being

prepared to ban people on racial grounds. . . . Experience has shown that ["race"] is a word which had very little scientific validity. . . . But what is the meaning of "race"? . . .

I agree that it is right and proper for Canada to decide who should come to this country, but we have used these racial concepts viciously in the past.[128]

Whether the government accepted this argument, and how meaningful was the word change in Section 61(g), would await further elaboration in the case of Harry Singh.

8. CAMPAIGN FOR IMMIGRATION REFORM

Harry Singh's closest collaborators and financial sponsors in his bid to remain in Canada were members of the Toronto Labour Committee for Human Rights. This body was founded in 1947 at the instigation of the Jewish Labour Committee of Canada, recognizing that organized labour's attitude towards racial and religious minorities required change. Representatives of both the TLC and CCL were involved in establishing the Toronto Committee, whose initial tactics were to attend union meetings and conventions with educational material on the dangers and damages to working people caused by discrimination. It was quickly discovered that political activity was required as well, and so the Toronto Committee began drafting resolutions calling for changes in public policy for adoption at labour gatherings. Close contacts were established with the CCF members of Parliament, who often cooperated in bringing these concerns to public attention.[129]

Early in 1951 the Toronto Committee became aware of the role of immigration policy in the syndrome of Canadian discrimination when two West Indians about to be deported appealed for help. When the Committee's intervention with government officials proved successful, many more West Indians faced with deportation sought their aid. By September 1951, having discovered PC 2856[130] as a source of the problem, the Committee decided "to bring this matter to the attention of the public" and to seek to change the racist features of Canadian immigration policy.[131] One early success occurred at the TLC's 1951 annual convention in Halifax, which unanimously approved a resolution removing Section 12 from the Platform of Principles – which had called for the exclusion from Canada of unassimilable "races" – "as it is in direct contradiction to the established policy of the TLC against racial discrimination."[132] A month later the CCL convention passed a resolution specifically condemning PC 2856 as being racially discriminatory.[133]

At almost exactly the same time, a group of West Indians in Toronto formed the Negro Citizenship Association, primarily to discover why so many of their compatriots were being deported or refused admission to Canada. The letters and documents sent to rejected applicants were worded very generally, and gave no explicit reasons why that individual was not qualified to enter Canada. In the course of their search they too found PC 2856 and the definition of "British subject" that excluded them.[134] The two organizations decided to collaborate in their efforts both to protect West Indians already in Canada and to affect the policy restricting their entry.[135]

"Case work" continued – posting bonds for jailed deportees, making individual inquiries to officials and to the minister – but "political work" became more and more central.[136] Considerable attention was gained in April 1952 when their campaign reached the floor of the Commons. A founder of the Negro Citizenship Association sought to bring his granddaughter from Barbados, and his application drew the typical departmental response. Gordon Milling, executive secretary of the Toronto Labour Committee for Human Rights, wrote to M. J. Coldwell and other CCF MPs describing this case and suggesting a set of questions that could be asked in the House. Joseph Noseworthy, MP for York South, wrote to Harris for information, and received a reply couched in the terms used in departmental letters. The minister wrote:

I have had the case reviewed by the immigration branch to ascertain whether some grounds could not be found for extending favourable consideration. It is quite evident, however, that Miss Braithwaite does not qualify for admission under present regulations and in the circumstances no encouragement can be offered. . . .

[O]ne of the conditions for admission to Canada is that immigrants should be able readily to become adapted and integrated into the life of the community within a reasonable time after their entry. In the light of experience it would be unrealistic to say that immigrants who have spent the greater part of their life in tropical or sub-tropical countries become readily adapted to the Canadian mode of life which, to no small extent, is determined by climatic conditions. It is a matter of record that natives of such countries are more apt to break down in health than immigrants from countries where the climate is more akin to that of Canada. It is equally true that, generally speaking, persons from tropical or sub-tropical countries find it more difficult to succeed in the highly competitive Canadian economy.[137]

Since the minister claimed that these weaknesses were "a matter of record," Noseworthy asked the pre-arranged questions in the House of Commons designed to expose the nature of this alleged record:

1. How many persons of British West Indies origin are at present living in Canada?
2. How many persons have entered Canada from the British West Indies during each of the five years 1947-51, inclusive?
3. How many applicants for entry to Canada from the British West Indies have been refused entry during each of the five years 1947-51, inclusive?
4. For what reasons were these applicants rejected, and how many were rejected for each of these reasons?
5. How many students were admitted to Canada from the British West Indies for the purpose of studying in Canada during each of the years 1947-1951, inclusive?
6. How many of those students applied for permanent residence in Canada?
7. How many of these student applicants were granted permanent residence in Canada?
8. Are any statistics available to show how immigrants to Canada from the British West Indies compare with immigrants from other warm climate countries in the following respects (a) health records; (b) wages or salaries earned; (c) unemployment records; (d) profession and occupation followed; (e) public liabilities?[138]

The minister was not, of course, in a position to answer these detailed questions, and so they were passed as orders for returns. They languished in that state for over a year.

The two Toronto groups meanwhile prepared a brief to the prime minister and cabinet decrying PC 2856 as discriminatory and unjust, and harmful to Canada's reputation as a democratic country. The brief gave a capsule history of blacks in Canada, emphasizing their loyalty and participation in every one of Canada's wars. In recent years they had proven themselves as equals in Canadian society and were therefore "entitled to all the rights, privileges and responsibilities that are inherent in the status of Canadian citizen." They asked, in consequence, for a "fair ratio" of West Indian immigrants and for a change in immigration law to remove its overtly discriminatory features. Copies of the brief were mailed to MPs and cabinet ministers, along with a resolution passed at a public meeting held in Carlton Street United Church calling for changes to PC 2856.[139] The Toronto material arrived in Ottawa in June 1952, about the same time as a brief from the Khalsa Diwan Society asking for the same privileges in bringing relatives to Canada as those enjoyed by Europeans.[140] Both the West Indians and the East Indians made a special point of the fact that fellow citizens of the Commonwealth, if they happened not to be white, had fewer rights than white foreigners. Their arguments obviously had no impact on Walter Harris, whose 4 July summation of immigration policy openly proclaimed the racially based characteristics of Canadian policy.

Organized labour was more responsive. The Ontario Federation of Labour called for a non-discriminatory immigration policy and urged its affiliates to assist immigrants in trouble; the TLC's annual presentation to the federal cabinet included a recommendation to revise immigration policy so as to remove racial discrimination; and the CCL roundly attacked the "degrees of desirability for admission" contained in government policies that were especially unfair to West Indians.[141] The national convention of the CCF, held at Toronto in August 1952, unanimously passed a resolution drafted by Gordon Milling of the Toronto Labour Committee for Human Rights, regretting that

this evidence of a "white supremacy" policy in Canada will inevitably tend to discredit us in the eyes of the non-white peoples of the world, both within the Commonwealth and elsewhere, and must undermine the confidence of minority groups within their own country. . . .

[We] demand an immigration policy that will conform more closely to the principles of the United Nations, with uniform standards and conditions of admission based on the legitimate requirements of the country rather than on groundless prejudices.[142]

The CCF caucus in Ottawa followed through. When Immigration estimates were next discussed, in April 1953, Joe Noseworthy revealed to the House the answers he had just received to his parliamentary questions put a year previously. Reminding the House that, according to the minister, it was "a matter of record" that natives of southern countries could not adapt to the Canadian climate and therefore broke down in health and failed economically, Noseworthy read out the Department's admission that it was unable to answer a single one of his questions because records were not available on the subject. His CCF colleague Angus

MacInnis leapt on the discomfited minister with a new brief from the East Indians in British Columbia, complaining against discriminatory regulations which kept families divided. Then Alistair Stewart attacked Harris' annual report, which continued to list immigrant arrivals by "race" despite the changed wording in the Act. Indicating the headings used in the Department's columns, Stewart declared:

I submit that there is no such thing as a Scottish race or an Irish race, or to take two different examples, the Belgian race or the Swiss. . . . Ethnically the term is outmoded, and I should like to see it removed.[143]

Other Opposition MPs joined the chorus, but it was obviously Noseworthy's revelations that stung the minister most. He issued a statement that the letter to Noseworthy had been mistakenly drafted by department officials, that he had signed it but warned that it not be sent until the matter was reconsidered, but then by error the letter was in fact delivered.[144] Just a month later a new order-in-council was proclaimed, setting out the "Norms of Admissibility to Canada."[145] Notably missing was any reference to "climate," though it appeared in Section 61(g) of the enabling Act. Then in December came another moral boost for the campaign when the Queen's Christmas message was dedicated to the theme of racial equality. Queen Elizabeth pledged "To that new conception of an equal partnership of nations and races I shall give myself heart and soul, every day of my life."[146]

Commonwealth partnership, colonial independence, the judicial assault on American segregation laws in the spring of 1954: these things generated a spirit that came in conflict with Canada's traditional immigration ideals, causing some confusion and some hypocrisy. Shortly after the Queen's message, Walter Harris reiterated in a public speech the Mackenzie King principle and explained that it meant "that the racial background of our people would be maintained within reasonable balance; and that we would avoid an influx of persons whose viewpoint differed substantially from that of the average, respectable, God-fearing Canadian."[147] The *Globe and Mail* wondered editorially from whom Canadians were being protected, "Arabs, Zulus, or what?" "No one," the *Globe* affirmed, "seriously proposed taking immigrants from any part of the world save Western Europe."[148] The Toronto *Star Weekly*, in an editorial praising the Queen's commitment to racial equality, added the comment that "Racial discrimination is an established (and most would say sensible) feature of our immigration policy."[149] In February 1954, during a state visit to New Delhi, Louis St. Laurent advised the Indian Parliament that "The Commonwealth is an association of people of many races and colours and creeds, working together on a basis of mutual respect and complete equality of status."[150] A few weeks after this, in a radio debate with labour representative Eamon Park, Harris denied the charge that Canada discriminated against certain British subjects and Commonwealth citizens. "I must assure you that we are not going to draw any lines which would be contrary to the Canadian understanding of the equality of all people."[151] The Canadian people could be forgiven if they did not entirely understand the position of their government on this most crucial issue.

The Toronto campaigners decided that the time was ripe for another joust at the restrictive policies. Plans were carefully laid for an effective delegation to Ottawa on 27 April 1954.[152] The decision was made to concentrate only on West Indian immigration, leaving Asia and Africa aside for the moment. Kalmen Kaplansky of the Jewish Labour Committee of Canada advised his Toronto colleagues: "If the Immigration Act could be amended whereby West Indians would be treated in the same manner as other British subjects, it would set a precedent, which we could utilize in pressing for the liberalization of the whole Act."[153] Donna Hill, executive secretary of the Toronto Labour Committee for Human Rights, sought a wide range of endorsements for the brief she had helped to prepare. The CCL quickly came on board, agreeing to be part of the delegation as well as signing the brief. The TLC, more cautious as always, declined the invitation to participate. Both the United and Anglican churches formally endorsed the brief, as did the Brotherhood of Sleeping Car Porters, the United Auto Workers, the Universal Negro Improvement Association, and 20 other Canadian organizations. On 27 April the delegation of 35 representatives led by the Negro Citizenship Association steamed into Ottawa to confront Walter Harris.[154]

The written brief, presented by Donald Moore, emphasized the discrimination in PC 2856 against citizens of the Commonwealth West Indies "because it creates two classes of Her Majesty's subjects," dividing white from coloured and instilling "a feeling in these divided groups . . . that there are superior and inferior races." Similar ideas had recently shattered the world, and Canada as a democracy must help to extinguish this threat to global peace. The climate argument against West Indians had been demolished, the brief continued, and as English-speaking citizens of the British Empire, West Indians were already adapted to Canadian customs, habits, modes of life and methods of holding property.

The adjustment required upon arrival in Canada was minimal. The regulations allowed for the admission of "cases of exceptional merit." One would assume this category would include persons whose skills were needed in Canada, "but cases in the last few years indicate that immigration authorities have turned down applications for permanent entry of persons whose skills were most desirable: nurses, draughtsmen, stenographers, and graduates of Canada's leading educational institutions have been rejected." Citing the Queen's Christmas message and the *Universal Declaration of Human Rights*, the brief called upon the government to amend the definition of "British subject" in the immigration regulations to include all peoples who were legally definable as such, to make provisions for the entry of British West Indians "without regard to racial origin," to define the term "persons of exceptional merit," and to establish an immigration office in the British West Indies. Spoken presentations during the meeting were not always so constrained. For example, Stanley G. Grizzle, Toronto president of the Brotherhood of Sleeping Car Porters, gave Harris the figures his own officials had been unable to find: 728 "British Negroes" had entered Canada since the war, an annual average of 104 and ample evidence, for Grizzle, of a "Jim Crow Iron Curtain" in Canadian immigration regulations. "They evince in a hundred ways a determination . . . to keep other races in a position of subordination and inferiority. It is against this very attitude peoples the world over are in revolt."[155]

Harris was gracious in response. He said he would give "serious consideration" to the brief and would see if it were possible to widen the category of admissible relatives. He expressed concern about only one of their recommendations, the entry of British West Indians without regard to racial origin. "You were not thinking of the Chinese?" Harris asked. "These are as big a problem as I have to deal with. If I admit Chinese from the West Indies, how can I exclude Chinese from places other than the West Indies?"[156] In the House of Commons he was less candid and less encouraging. During his annual report and consideration of the estimates in June 1954, he was asked by Joe Noseworthy

what action, if any, the government has taken or proposes to take as a result of the brief presented to him during the latter part of April by the Negro Citizenship Association on behalf of immigrants from the West Indies, those British subjects who, by regulation of the immigration department, are not British subjects.

Harris replied:

Upon receiving the brief we studied it. I examined the statistics with regard to these persons and I found that there had been a steady increase in the numbers of Negroes from the West Indies being admitted to Canada. If we leave the present regulations as they are for the time being I think the numbers will probably increase in any event and that we shall have what I would consider to be a reasonably fair representation of these people in the flow of immigrants to Canada. I could place before the House the shifting changes in the numbers but I assure the hon. members that they are on the increase. In addition to the close relative groups who come in in almost every case I should not say as of right but nevertheless almost so, we have a special merit case and we have been using it with respect to these people.[157]

And once again Harris submitted his report on immigration "by racial origin." Still listed as "races" were Irish, Scottish, Belgian and Swiss, along with Chinese, Japanese and Negro.[158]

Four days later Harris retired and was replaced by his close associate Jack Pickersgill who, on being offered a choice between Transport and Immigration, chose the latter as a "lighter portfolio" so that he could spend more time in his role as special assistant to the prime minister.[159] The change in ministers, not surprisingly, did not imply any change in policy. Pickersgill reconfirmed the government's retention of the Mackenzie King principle and, when asked about restrictions on West Indians and Asians, replied: "We are not going to permit any massive immigration from those areas."[160] A new order-in-council issued in September 1954, PC 1351, carried identically worded "Norms of Admissibility" over from the previous PC 859.[161] Following several letters from Donald Moore, president of the Negro Citizenship Association, the minister finally acknowledged that he had read the brief, but "I can offer no encouragement."[162]

The "lighter portfolio," however, turned out not to be as Pickersgill expected. He was continually on the defensive in the House.[163] The 1955 session of parliament began with a motion of no confidence put by Conservative Davie Fulton: "in the opinion of this house, the immigration policy of the government is not clear, consistent or coordinated; is not in conformity with the needs or responsibilities of Canada; and in its administration denies simple justice to Canadians and non-Canadians alike."[164]

Next to high taxation and unemployment, Fulton contended, immigration was the subject of greatest concern to Canadians. This debate gave Joe Noseworthy and Angus MacInnis another opportunity to raise objections to the restrictions against West Indians, East Indians and Chinese,[165] but not every critic of government policy had the same changes in mind. Toronto Conservative Donald Fleming attempted to identify the source of the public concern noted by his colleague Fulton:

Let us face frankly the fear which immigration has engendered in some Canadians. Those fears have been principally on the grounds of race and employment. On the subject of race I think the government owes a duty to the people of Canada to say, as we Conservatives say and say emphatically, that immigration to this country must never be permitted to have for its purpose disturbance of the fundamental racial composition of Canada. We subscribe most emphatically to that point of view.[166]

No doubt relieved to find a question he could answer in the affirmative, Pickersgill retorted: "Has the hon. member not read the statement made by Mr. King on May 1, 1947, by which we still abide and in which a declaration of this character was made long before the Conservative party had any policy on the subject?"[167]

Over the next several days, the debate grew more specific in supporting the charges made in Fulton's motion. The Canadian Bar Association had struck a subcommittee to examine immigration policy at its 1952 annual meeting. Two of the subcommittee's three members were John R. Taylor of Vancouver and John H. McDonald of Ottawa, prominent immigration lawyers. Their report, submitted to the Association's 1954 annual meeting in Winnipeg, called for the codification of regulations and publication of directives sent to field officers on their interpretation, the implementation of legal appeal procedures, the availability to applicants of non-confidential files concerning their own cases, and "the establishment of a procedure setting forth reasons for rejection in each case, in such a way as to give the rejected party . . . an opportunity of overcoming the department's objections."[168] This report, as one observer has noted, served as the "heavy ammunition" for Opposition MPs attacking the procedural inconsistencies and injustices in current regulations.[169]

The minister was not inclined to take the subcommittee's report quite so seriously. Taylor and McDonald, it seems, collaborated on a number of immigration cases which had been unsuccessful and, according to Pickersgill, they deliberately used the subcommittee to embarrass the department by alleging abuses and irregularities. In his autobiography, Pickersgill explained the background to Fulton's motion:

It turned out that the whole agitation was based upon Chinese Canadian cases handled by Taylor's law firm [for which McDonald was Ottawa agent]. In September 1954 McDonald came to see me and said he and Taylor would call off their campaign against the Immigration officials if I would reverse the decisions made when Harris was Minister refusing a number of specific applications, of which I later learned all but one were from Taylor's clients. I was told, if I did not follow his suggestion, I could expect trouble in Parliament.[170]

However, the case Fulton highlighted as a prime example of departmental inefficiency and even inhumanity, that of Leong Ba Chai, was not represented by Taylor or McDonald.

Leong Hung Hing, a Canadian citizen, had applied for the admission of his son Leong Ba Chai in 1951, when the son was 18 years old. When the young man was investigated in Hong Kong, it was learned that his mother was Leong Hung Hing's second wife, married when the first wife proved to be sterile. The first wife had since deceased, but as she was still alive when Leong Ba Chai was born, immigration officials decided this made the boy illegitimate and therefore ineligible to go to Canada. Though PC 6229 made no reference to legitimacy in allowing Asians to bring in unmarried children under age 21, the department refused to consider him further. Justice Clyne in the BC Supreme Court ordered the department to consider the application on the grounds that PC 6229 was silent on the issue of legitimacy and besides, according to the customs of China where he was born, Leong Ba Chai was legitimate. The department then took the case to the BC Court of Appeal and, upon a second loss, pursued it to the Supreme Court of Canada late in 1953.[171] The department's attempt to hide behind Section 39 of the Act, preventing judicial review, was to no avail. The Supreme Court decided that by not discharging his duty to consider Leong Ba Chai's application under the regulations, the official was liable to review by the courts. The department's appeal was dismissed once more. But "considering" the application took almost another year: x-ray reports took longer than expected; correspondence between father and son had to be translated and studied in Ottawa. On 30 November 1954, Leong Hung Hing died: Leon Ba Chai was no longer the son of a Canadian citizen in a position to receive and care for him. The application was therefore and finally rejected in December 1954.[172]

Leong Ba Chai was notable mostly for the tenacity with which the department fought to keep a single representative of an unwanted "race" from the shores of Canada. If the minister was the least bit embarrassed by the revelations, he did not show it. He later wrote:

Fulton's attack had really boiled down to a single question: did a Canadian citizen whose application for a relative was refused by an immigration officer have a right to appeal to the law courts and, for that purpose, to be told why the relative had been refused?[173]

His short answer was a simple "no." In his parliamentary response, which he assessed as "the most important speech I ever made on immigration,"[174] Pickersgill defended his officials' resistance to having immigration matters aired in the courts.

After all, the purpose of our Immigration Act is to get good immigrants into Canada and not to enter into complicated consideration of marginal cases. . . .

The hon. member for York South (Mr. Noseworthy) [suggested] that these people were being convicted without being heard, and if they could bring in evidence a different judgment might be rendered. . . .

These people are not on trial at all in the sense that someone is on trial in a court. They are people who have applied for entry into this country, which we have a perfect right to deny to anyone who is not a Canadian. . . .

So far as discrimination is concerned, I am more concerned to see that there is no discrimination as between one person and another who is in this country, who had been admitted to this country, than I am about a certain limited discrimination among those whom we admit.[175]

Reporting his departmental statistics a month later, Pickersgill revealed that some of the exposure in Parliament and in court was having an effect: immigrants were categorized for the first time according to their "Last Permanent Residence" rather than "race" as heretofore.[176] But that the change was no more than cosmetic is indicated by an answer he gave to Parliament in May 1955. Asked if a Chinese American was admissible to Canada, Pickersgill explained that the regulations applied to all "persons of the Chinese race," regardless of citizenship.[177] An American citizen of Chinese extraction would be barred. Summarizing government policy at that time, the *Canada Year Book* for 1955 explained that immigrants were admissible "if they are found to be suitable and desirable." The explanation continued:

Suitability and desirability are established in part by social, economic and labour conditions in this country. Prospective immigrants should be of a type that will become readily integrated into the community and that will be able to assume the duties and responsibilities of Canadian citizenship within a reasonable time after admission.[178]

In a confidential memorandum dated 14 January 1955, the director of immigration revealed that "suitability" was interpreted to mean that certain "races" were considered incapable of meeting the demands of Canadian citizenship:

It is not by accident that coloured British subjects other than negligible numbers from the United Kingdom are excluded from Canada. It is from experience, generally speaking, that coloured people in the present state of the white man's thinking are not a tangible asset, and as a result are more or less ostracized. They do not assimilate readily and pretty much vegetate to a low standard of living. Despite what has been said to the contrary, many cannot adapt themselves to our climatic conditions. To enter into an agreement which would have the effect of increasing coloured immigration to this country would be an act of misguided generosity since it would not have the effect of bringing about a worthwhile solution to the problem of coloured people and would quite likely intensify our own social and economic problems. I think that the biggest single argument against increasing coloured immigration to this country is the simple fact that the Canadian public is not prepared to accept them in any significant numbers.[179]

Or in the minister's own folksy idiom, "it is easier to transplant into soil which is similar to that from which you take the plant."[180]

9. THE INEVITABLE: HARRY SINGH IN THE ONTARIO COURTS

The passage of Ontario's *Fair Employment Practices Act* in 1951[181] and its federal counterpart in 1953[182] helped to relieve Canadian labour's fear of competition from cheap immigrant labour. The activists in the Toronto Labour Committee for Human Rights, who had in fact been significant in the Fair Employment campaign as well, were gaining a more positive response in the union constituency for their arguments in favour of immigration policy reform. Both the major labour organizations, the TLC and the CCL, were formally committed to the elimination of "race" as a qualification for entry, and many individual unions had passed equivalent resolutions. The crusaders were poised for an assault on the federal government. The stage was set and the plot was written; all that was missing was a lead character. And then Harry Singh walked into the Toronto Committee's office.

Harry Singh became the test case, the living symbol, the human content in an otherwise faceless movement to change the law. This is not to say that Singh's interests were ignored or that the result in his court appeal could have been different, but it is true that his appearance offered a golden opportunity to link an abstract principle to a man and a woman caught in a personal drama. Sid Blum of the Toronto Labour Committee wrote to president Donald Moore of the Negro Citizenship Association:

the case is very important for two reasons: 1) to show the public the unfair treatment that non-white British subjects are receiving from a Department of the Canadian Government; and 2) to show the Immigration Department that such policies are unfair and that a substantial section of the public feel deeply enough about this injustice to protest against it.[183]

To the CCL's Toronto Council, Blum wrote reminding them of CCL resolutions against discrimination in immigration policy, and adding: "We feel that this is an important issue – and one of the ways we can fight against such injustice is to challenge Singh's deportation in the courts."[184] In his standard letter acknowledging contributions toward Singh's legal expenses, Blum closed with the assurance that "The Committee has high hopes that our fight will result in substantial changes in the Immigration Act – changes in accord with the democratic ideals and aims of the Canadian Labour Movement."[185]

As soon as she learned the circumstances of Harry Singh's new deportation order as an "Asian," Donna Hill knew that she had a case virtually designed to reveal the ridiculous and arbitrary features of Canadian policy.[186] Just before her impending motherhood caused her to vacate her position as executive secretary of the Toronto Labour Committee, Ms. Hill enlisted the CCL leadership and the CCF party in the Singhs' support. MP Alistair Stewart took up the case with Walter Harris, unsuccessfully, and promised to push the matter publicly, but privately he told Donna Hill: "I don't think we are going to get far but at least the facts of the situation certainly demand their being placed on the record."[187] Optimistic still, Hill recruited Andrew Brewin, noted immigration lawyer and social crusader, who agreed to take the case without fee as he was personally convinced that a precedent-setting decision was possible. Ms. Hill issued a press release describing the factual background, while Mr.

Brewin initiated the court challenge.[188] Hill's colleague and successor as executive secretary, Sid Blum, established a Singh Defence Fund and began soliciting donations from union locals and individual workers.[189] He wrote personal notes to reporters at all three Toronto daily newspapers, giving them the human interest story and offering further information as the case progressed.[190]

Certain liberal elements in the press became aroused by Harry Singh's experience. The *Toronto Star* featured a story emphasizing that Harry and Mearl had faced a "surprise hearing before the Immigration Board of Inquiry ... without being warned in advance" and that they were "effectively prevented from having legal counsel."[191] *Saturday Night* magazine carried a front-page editorial denouncing the *Immigration Act* as "well-spattered with gobbledygook" and the Immigration Department as populated by "arrogant little men." The editorial described the Singhs' "surprize hearing" and the absence of a lawyer as "shocking" and openly discriminatory, and concluded:

The present Immigration Act obviously confers arbitrary powers on petty officials and leaves much too much room for discriminatory, unfair treatment of visitors and settlers. It is up to Mr. Harris to present to Parliament amendments to the Act which will make it a clear, just vehicle for the regulation of immigration – and at the same time to ensure that his Department is organized to apply the regulations with courtesy and reason.

An accompanying photograph of Walter Harris bore the caption "A time for spring-cleaning."[192]

These and similar stories prompted the official involved, Mr. C. Schreiber, to demand an apology from Harry Singh, which was immediately forthcoming. In his statement to Schreiber, Harry regretted "all the recent unfavourable publicity" and affirmed that "you did not deceive me." He acknowledged that he had an opportunity to have a lawyer but declined, that Schreiber had informed him that he must appear before a Special Inquiry, and that inferences to the contrary in the Toronto press were incorrect.[193] This experience undoubtedly contributed to a growing doubt on Harry's part of the wisdom of his supporters' course of action. In a conversation with Sid Blum toward the end of May 1954, Singh confessed that he was worried about the publicity and feared that Immigration officials would become biased against him. His employer, a Mr. Fitzgibbons, had tried to interfere on Harry's behalf with some "influential Liberal friends," and had received a letter from Walter Harris warning him that this campaign was connected with "communists or Reds." Harry's relatives in Trinidad, where local papers had picked up the story, were writing in alarm at Harry's notoriety. In a written aide-mémoire recording this conversation, Blum noted:

Singh asked me to try to see that he, and the case, did not attract too much publicity. I tried to persuade him that the right kind of publicity would help his case, but he appeared very frightened and still wanted to have as little to do with the press as possible.

I told him that I would try to help him, but once the case went into court there was little that I could do.[194]

Convinced however of the righteousness of his cause, Blum continued to prod the attention of the press in both Toronto and Trinidad, and issued personal invitations to attend Harry's appearance before Justice Aylen, of the Ontario Supreme Court, scheduled for 29 June 1954.[195]

Andrew Brewin applied for a writ of *habeas corpus* with *certiorari* in aid, to determine the validity of Schreiber's decision. In his submission before Justice Aylen, Brewin directly confronted the racist features of Canadian policy. Using UNESCO materials supplied by Sid Blum, the lawyer argued that "race" theories had no scientific justification, racial discrimination was "odious," and policies based on "race" were "confused and unenlightened and are more in keeping with national socialism in Germany." "Race" had been eliminated as an entrance criterion in the 1952 *Immigration Act*, Brewin continued, so the reference to "Asian" in the regulations, which was not specifically defined there, could not be interpreted as a racial category. Harry's "ethnic group" could not be described as "Asian": in Trinidad, he and his forebears had participated in a composite culture deriving from Africa and Europe as well as Asia, he was born into a Christian family, and he followed no identifiably Asian practices. The only remaining definition of "Asian" was geographical, and Harry had never even been in Asia and had no geographical association with that continent. The Immigration official had operated on the principle that the word "Asian" in the regulations referred to a racial category, and had therefore improperly inquired into Harry Singh's racial background. Since this was an error, the official had not conducted an inquiry in accordance with the provisions of the Act and his decision must be quashed by the court.

Brewin called upon *Leong Ba Chai* as a precedent, for there the Supreme Court of Canada had determined that when an immigration official exceeded his authority and inquired into irrelevant details, the decision must be set aside. He also cited *Samejima v. The King* to indicate that an improper procedure at an immigration inquiry must result in the reversal of a deportation decision.[196] The substitution of a second deportation notice following Donna Hill's complaint, Brewin contended, constituted a procedural irregularity not authorized by the Act.

The Immigration Department's attorney, J. D. Pickup, argued simply that although "race" and "Asiatic" had been eliminated from the Act, the terms had been replaced by "Asian," "ethnic group" and "geographical area of origin," all of which retained the meaning of the previous wording for the purposes of immigration. Asians were not welcome as immigrants under the 1910 Act and they were not welcome under the 1952 Act.[197]

Justice Aylen found the simpler argument more convincing. The omission of "race" from the Act, he pointed out, was accomplished by a revision, not a formal amendment. The intent of the previous wording had not been changed. "Asian" meant the same thing as "Asiatic," and according to both the *Shorter Oxford* and *Murray's New English* dictionaries, an Asian was "a person pertaining to or characteristic of one of the Asian races." The intent of the Act could hardly be geographical, because that would exclude an English person born in Asia and such persons were quite obviously admissible to Canada. The "racial" interpretation was the only sensible one. An immigration officer had to make a practical decision based on any applicant's "predominant characteristics," and if the officer made a mistake the applicant could appeal to the minister. Furthermore, Justice Aylen found the Ontario decision in *Re: Robinson* to be more pertinent as a precedent: if the Board of Inquiry was conducted according to the Act, its decision was immune from judicial interference even if that decision was based on faulty evidence.[198] Harry and Mearl "received a fair and apparently well-conducted hearing," and Schreiber had "acted under the authority and in accordance with the provisions of the Act." There were therefore no circumstances to justify an appeal to the courts. Brewin's application was dismissed.[199]

Blum immediately brought his campaign back into operation, with Brewin's concurrence, for an application to the Ontario Court of Appeal.[200] There was a renewed appeal for funds, and an attempt to gain the endorsement of the TLC as well as the CCL. The secretary of the TLC responded that "the Executive are not unsympathetic to the appeal to a higher court in behalf of Mr. Singh but cannot endorse the appeal to the unions [for funds]. . . ."[201] The ensuing fundraising effort was therefore limited to CCL-affiliated unions and, for practical purposes, to the province of Ontario. Blum also revived his publicity tactics, advising Trinidadian as well as Canadian newspapers of the Aylen decision and the forthcoming appeal to a higher court.[202]

The parties assembled before Justices Hope, Aylesworth and Gibson on 10 September 1954. Mr. Brewin began, as previously, by contending that "The new Immigration Act . . . is substantially different from its predecessor."[203] Previously members of "the Asiatic race" were banned from Canada, under authority of the old Act which permitted restriction by "race"; now "race" was no longer a ground for exclusion, but "Asians," were prohibited under the regulations. "The meaning is not the same," Brewin argued, yet "the word 'Asian' is apparently still interpreted by the authorities as having only a racial significance."[204] Referring to Section 61(g) of the 1952 Act, prohibiting admission by reason of "nationality, citizenship, ethnic group, occupation, class or geographical area of origin," by which Section 20(2) of the 1953 regulations was authorized, he indicated that the only term applicable to Harry Singh was "geographical area of origin," as there was no such thing as Asian nationality, citizenship, ethnic group, occupation or class. And on that basis Harry and Mearl Singh were not "Asians," since they came from Trinidad. Justice Hope intervened at this point to ask whether "origin" did not refer to the applicants' ancestors, to which Brewin replied "that the expression is equivalent to domicile of origin or place of birth."[205] Since the inquiry officer erred in interpreting "Asian" as a "race," his decision was not protected from judicial review by Section 39 of the Act. The officer "declined jurisdiction, or wrongly exercised his jurisdiction, by considering the question of race. The record clearly shows that it was on the basis of race alone that he decided the applicant was an 'Asian,' and Parliament itself had made the question of race extraneous."[206]

On the one hand, then, was the evidence that the Singhs' inquiry was improper; on the other hand there remained the possibility that Section 20(2) was intended to apply to "race," and if so the regulation itself was *ultra vires*.

Parliament has given the Governor in Council the right to define classes to be excluded, but it must be done in a definite way, and show clearly the tests that are to be applied, so that a special inquiry officer can easily determine the nature of the inquiry to be made by him. There must be some reasonable degree of certainty. . . . Parliament has delegated wide power to the Governor in Council, and those powers are to be interpreted liberally, but they do not include the making of Regulations that set up no standards whatever and are too indefinite. The word "Asian" is so vague and indefinite as to be outside what Parliament authorized.[207]

After this frontal attack, Brewin retreated to a technical argument. Section 28(3) of the Act, which authorized Schreiber's order, permitted exclusion of persons "seeking admission to Canada"; the Singhs were already in Canada and were therefore not seeking admission, and Schreiber's order was invalid.[208]

Without calling upon Mr. Pickup to respond to Mr. Brewin's case, Justice Hope delivered the judgment of the court orally. First, they found that Schreiber's inquiry "was not in error procedurally, nor did he err on any principle of law." Therefore the court had no jurisdiction to interfere. Secondly, "Asian" was not vague or indefinite. According to *Murray's New English Dictionary* it meant "pertaining to Asia," and in the case under consideration it would mean "a member of an ethnic group which ordinarily is located in Asia. An 'ethnic group' is defined as, and is well understood to relate to, race or any part of a particular race." Section 20(2) was therefore *intra vires*. Thirdly, Justice Hope dismissed Brewin's technical argument by showing that, as visitors to Canada under Section 7(3), the Singhs were properly considered by an inquiry under Section 28(2)(b).[209] The appeal had failed.

10. ANTICLIMAX: THE SUPREME COURT OF CANADA

Immediately after the Court of Appeal decision, Andrew Brewin wrote to Sid Blum:

In my view it should, if it is at all possible, be appealed to the Supreme Court of Canada.

The issue involved, to put it briefly, was whether the Immigration Officials are entitled to reject prospective immigrants on the sole grounds of racial origin. . . . In 1952 the Parliament of Canada revised the Immigration Act and excluded race as a proper ground for exclusion of immigrants. It is true that they did permit the Cabinet to pass regulations for exclusion on the ground of "Ethnic Group." It seems to me therefore that the Immigration Officials in introducing the element of race are going directly against the intention of Parliament in omitting the terminology of race. The concept of an Ethnic Group is far more precise and reasonable. It also seems to me that the exclusion of people on the broad general ground that they are Asian is offensive and probably illegal. In my view the Law Courts who have rejected our argument have failed to deal with the main argument involved in the case and that is the question of exclusion on racial grounds on the face of the amendment to the Statute of the Immigration Act in 1952.

I am satisfied that we have a good prospective of success on an appeal to the Supreme Court of Canada. The sort of problem that is involved in this case would undoubtedly be received with very much greater sympathy than in the Ontario courts. It will be recalled by way of illustration that in the Ontario Courts they upheld the validity of restrictive covenants based on racial grounds, but were reversed in the Supreme Court of Canada. I am therefore convinced that both on legal merits and as a matter of attempting to remove racial intolerance as a factor in the administration of the Immigration Act, that this case should be appealed if possible.

Brewin added that once again he would "prepare the appeal and argue it in the Supreme Court of Canada without any fee," but funding would be necessary for the $500 bond, for printing the appeal case and *factum*, for travel to Ottawa and for other expenses.[210]

For a third time Blum rallied his troops, planting stories in newspapers and raising funds from union locals.[211] The most successful tactic in the generation of publicity was placing a resolution before the CCL annual convention in Toronto on 27 September 1954, written by Blum and presented by Bromley Armstrong and Dennis McDermott of the United Auto Workers:

Whereas the Canadian Immigration Act contains provisions that provide for discriminatory treatment of non-white British subjects;

And whereas these provisions provide that British subjects in the Commonwealth not be considered British subjects for purposes of Immigration unless they come from Britain, Ireland, Australia, New Zealand or South Africa;

And whereas these provisions enable the Immigration Department to arbitrarily bar British subjects from Canada because of their colour or racial extraction, particularly prospective immigrants from the British West Indies, and thus give the lie to our professions of brotherhood with the rest of the British Commonwealth and the principles of Canadian Democracy;

Be it resolved that we urge the Canadian government to amend the Immigration Act so that British subjects from all Commonwealth countries be treated equally under the Act, regardless of their race, creed, or colour.[212]

In an accompanying report from R. J. Lamoureux, chairman of the CCL's Committee on Human Rights, it was claimed that discriminatory immigration policies were "a blot on Canada's good name" and would drive the countries of Asia and Africa "into the Communist camp." The Toronto press, in attendance for this national meeting, gave prominent attention to the discussion and to the fact that Canadian immigration regulations were racially defined.[213]

The campaign for funds was, considering that this was the third appeal to the same unions, remarkably successful. Predicting that "a favourable decision in the Singh case will help to remove racial intolerance, in the Immigration Department, as well as have widespread effects on other sections of the Government and the Community,"[214] Blum attracted a stream of $5 and $10 donations. In less that two weeks he had raised enough for the $500 deposit.[215] Andrew Brewin was able to proceed with his application to the Supreme Court of Canada "for the issue of a writ of *habeas corpus* and with *certiorari* in aid and by way of *certiorari*."[216]

The Appellant's *Factum* contained no new arguments, and in fact the technical challenge to Section 28 was dropped. In his Grounds of Appeal Brewin claimed the Ontario Court of Appeal was erroneous because the Special Inquiry Officer exceeded his jurisdiction by considering the Singhs' "race," the Singhs were not Asian by geographical origin, and the regulations were *ultra vires*. The written Argument proceeded through the points made in the lower courts, resting on the submission

that the omission of "race" as a possible ground of exclusion must be deemed to have been in pursuance of a deliberate policy of the Parliament of Canada and that it is not open to Immigration Officers to reintroduce the category of race into any consideration of the admissibility or otherwise of prospective immigrants.

Parliament undoubtedly had authority to legislate for the admission of aliens, including on grounds of "race," but had not in fact done so. The concept of "race" was "vague, unscientific and offensive." The term "ethnic groups," used in the 1952 Act, did not mean a "race" but a group of people distinguished by their physical and cultural environment; their membership was demonstrated by their behaviour and practices. Asia contained "almost every conceivable ethnic group," so that the term "Asian ethnic group" was meaningless. To link the Singhs geographically with an Asian origin was tantamount to calling an American Negro "African" or a Canadian Indian "Asian."

The extreme confusion and complication that would ensue if the place of more remote ancestral origin was to be investigated would reduce the concept of the word "Asian" as a test for admission of immigrants or for any other test involving a judicial decision to a high degree of absurdity.

Section 20(2) of the regulations did not indicate which categories from Section 61(g) of the Act were being applied, and it was therefore "so vague and uncertain as not to be a valid exercise of the subordinate legislative power" conferred by the Act and must be *ultra vires*.[217]

The *Factum* of the Respondent was prepared by John D. Pickup with F. P. Varcoe as solicitor for the attorney general. They argued that all the appropriate steps were taken in the Singhs' special inquiry, and so the courts had no right to examine its decision. The regulations were not uncertain. According to the dictionary "ethnic" meant "pertaining to race" and "Asian" was identical to "Asiatic." In Regulation 20(2) "Asian" meant "a person pertaining to or characteristic of one of the races of Asia." The respondents noted that in *Quong Wing*, Justice Duff had ruled that it was the "common understanding" of racial terminology that must be accepted in the courts, and that "as generally used in Canadian legislation" such terms "point to a classification based upon origin, upon racial or personal characteristics and habits, rather than upon nationality or allegiance." Justice Martin's statement from *Munshi Singh* was enlisted to the same effect. "[T]he expression 'Asiatic race'," Martin had found, "must be construed according to the common understanding of the words," and if this were done "there is no uncertainty about its meaning or application. We speak constantly about European, Asiatic and even Latin-American races, and no one doubts what the people at large understand thereby." Finally from that same case the *factum* quoted Justice McPhillips' insistence that the words "Asiatic race" as used in the immigration orders were "in their meaning comprehensive and precise enough" for judicial enforcement. Pickup and Varcoe submitted that the same test of "common sense" must be applied to "Asian" in the 1952 regulations: "The word 'Asian' according to the common understanding of the word refers to a member of an ethnic group which is native of Asia.... As commonly used or understood the word 'Asians'... has a definite and clear meaning." Since Harry Singh was already free on bail, *habeas corpus* was not an available remedy; since the regulations were *intra vires* and the inquiry was conducted properly, *certiorari* did not apply.[218]

The Supreme Court met on 5 April 1955 to consider the Singhs' case, with Chief Justice Patrick Kerwin and Justices Ivan Rand, Roy Kellock, James Estey and John Cartwright in attendance. Andrew Brewin made an oral presentation, and John Pickup and his associate were preparing to present their arguments when the chief justice interrupted to say that a decision had already been reached: the appeal was dismissed.[219] Written reasons for this decision appeared two weeks later.[220] On behalf of the court Justice Kellock wrote that "ethnic" and "race" were equivalent terms, according to the *Oxford Dictionary*, and therefore Parliament had not effected any practical change when the wording in the Act was revised. Asians were restricted by Section 39(c) of the former Act, and they were restricted still by Section 61(g) of the current Act. When Schreiber asked, "Of what race are you?" Harry Singh answered, "East Indian," clearly establishing his identity. The deportation order was authorized by Regulation 20(2), and the Regulation itself was within the statute. There was no reason for judicial interference, and the appeal must fail.[221]

Harry and Mearl Singh were denied entrance to Canada,[222] but Sid Blum and Andrew Brewin did not consider the case a total failure. Blum reported to Kalmen Kaplansky:

Andy feels that he might have misjudged the legal attraction and interest of the case, but in the circumstances it should have been presented to the Supreme Court anyway. As far as its effect on our educational work, he feels that the defeat in Court merely underlines the need for changing the political administration of the Immigration Act. . . .

I feel that the battle was well worth the effort – and the money. These things have to be challenged. It is very easy not to lose battles. Do not fight any. Actually the Court may be quite correct – "ethnic group" can be used as a racial discriminatory feature of the Immigration Act, even though it doesn't contain the word race. As far as future court cases involving racial discrimination – we both feel that the decision in this case covers so narrow an area that it will have no harmful effect.[223]

Far from retreating in defeat, Blum called together a meeting in Toronto of persons committed to the cause of immigration reform, including lawyers Andrew Brewin, Bora Laskin, David Lewis and Sid Midanuk, to consider a strategy for future campaigns.[224] According to Brewin, the *Singh* result "indicates that the remedy for this situation lies in public opinion and legislative action. The case will have served to underline the true situation and bring it to public attention."[225]

And the result did serve a propaganda purpose for the reform cause. The *Toronto Star* carried a major feature by Charles Woodsworth, asking "How many generations does it take before the racial origin or immigrant stock ceased to count...?" Describing the Singhs' experience in detail, Woodsworth concluded, "The case illuminates some points in Canadian immigration policy and the regulations which embody it, that are not too familiar to many Canadians."[226] The Ontario Federation of Labour inserted a paragraph in their annual brief to the Ontario government in April 1955, describing the Singh campaign and claiming that the decision illustrated an unfortunate fact: "If you're white, you're okay. If you're colored, you'll get kicked around."[227] Prompted by *Singh*, the TLC adopted a resolution condemning the racially discriminatory features of immigration policy at its annual meeting in May.[228] Blum felt as well that the publicity had embarrassed immigration officials and helped to soften their attitudes, making them amenable to admit a group of black nurses from the West Indies when similar attempts in the past had been unsuccessful.[229] On 17 August 1955 the *Toronto Star* carried a front-page article reporting a speech by Sid Blum in which he suggested that *Singh* had demonstrated a sorry reality that was virtually ignored by the Canadian people: "race" was still a valid concept in Canadian public policy.[230]

11. CONFIRMATION

Sid Blum had discovered a truth when he decided "the Supreme Court may be quite correct:"[231] Parliament had not intended any meaningful change in Canadian immigration policy after all; "race" and "ethnic group" were meant to maintain the same barriers and achieve the same goal. The revision was cosmetic, to disguise Canadian policies in a Commonwealth and a world increasingly hostile to overt racism. It was the "continuous journey" strategy, updated for the 1950s. In a November speech in Victoria, BC, just months after his department's success in keeping the Singhs out of Canada, Jack Pickersgill insisted:

There is no racial discrimination in Canada's immigration policy despite some public feeling to the contrary. . . . It is not the government's intention to maintain any precise racial balance in the Canadian population, but I believe that we want to attract the bulk of our immigrants from the UK and from those countries in northern and western Europe whose historical traditions and political and social institutions are most like our own.[232]

The minister, too, was correct: "we" – a majority of the Canadian people – did not wish to see any shift away from the "traditional sources" of immigrants; "we" wanted discriminatory regulations kept in place.[233] Confident that his views were widely shared, Pickersgill was quite candid in

Parliament. Asked why Canada had only one immigration agent for all of South Asia, he replied:

As a matter of fact, you know as well as I do, that we do not have an office in India for the purpose of getting immigrants for the sake of increasing the population of Canada. We agreed upon this quota as a gesture for the improvement of Commonwealth relations, and having done so, we have to treat these applicants decently and have enough employees there to answer the letters and deal with the correspondence and the applications which are received. That does not mean, however, that we have any great interest in Indian immigration.[234]

Singh has never been cited in a subsequent case; its legal history was brief. The reason for this brevity is that the regulations challenged in *Singh* were amended a year later, following a return engagement between Messrs. Pickup and Brewin and a reconsideration of some of the same underlying issues by the Supreme Court of Canada. The occasion was the case of Shirley Kathleen Brent, a white American, who was rejected at an immigration inquiry in Toronto in January 1954 under Section 20(4)(b) of the regulations by reason of her "unsuitability, having regard to the economic, social, industrial, educational, labour, health, or other conditions or requirements existing, temporarily or otherwise, in Canada or in the area or country from or through which [she came] to Canada."[235] Ms. Brent asked that the reason she was being judged undesirable be clarified. The officer, C. R. Brooks, merely showed her a copy of the regulations and asked if she could read English. Her appeal to Minister Pickersgill was similarly rejected without indicating the grounds for her deportation. Andrew Brewin took her case before Justice Wilson of the Ontario High Court in July 1954, arguing that she had not received the "full and proper inquiry" required by Section 11 of the Act since she could not respond to the unstated objections of the immigration official. Justice Wilson agreed, finding that an immigration decision must be conveyed to the applicant in an "intelligible form," and that Section 20(4)(b) was so vague that no applicant could ever prove him or herself suitable as an immigrant. The deportation order was quashed.[236]

This result was escalated when the department took the case before the Ontario Court of Appeal in October 1954. In his written decision, issued one day after the *Singh* defeat in the Supreme Court of Canada, Justice Aylesworth agreed with every one of Andrew Brewin's arguments. Not only had Brent failed to receive a "full and proper inquiry"; the regulation was *ultra vires*. Section 20 virtually repeated the language of Section

61 of the Act: in other words, the powers granted by Parliament to the governor-in-council had in turn been handed over directly to immigration officials. This exceeded the authority of the Act, which had intended the governor-in-council to define specific regulations to carry out the general principles stated in Section 61.[237]

The department felt obliged to appeal this to the Supreme Court of Canada. As Pickersgill informed the House, "If the judgment in the Brent case were to stand we would have to give very serious consideration to the whole state of immigration law. It is for this reason . . . that we appeal that case to the Supreme Court of Canada."[238] But stand it did. In February 1956, Chief Justice Kerwin explained:

I agree with Justice Aylesworth . . . that Parliament had in contemplation the enactment of such regulations relevant to the named subject matters, or some of them, as in His Excellency-in-Council's own opinion were advisable and not a wide divergence of rules and opinions, ever changing according to the individual notions of Immigration Officers and Special Inquiry Officers. There is no power in the Governor General-in-Council to delegate his authority to such officers.[239]

The ruling had the impact Pickersgill feared. In his memoirs he wrote:

The Supreme Court decision in effect destroyed the whole administrative basis for the selection, admission, and exclusion of prospective immigrants and visitors. . . . I spent many hours with the officials of the department and with the Deputy Minister of Justice drafting the kind of regulations the government could make that would be within both the letter and the spirit of the law.[240]

When the new regulations were issued on 24 May 1956, they bore the imprint not only of *Brent* but of *Singh* as well. PC 785 did not eliminate discrimination: the familiar pattern of descending acceptability from white British subjects to Asians was maintained.[241] But underlying membership in each category was citizenship "by birth or naturalization." All explicit references to "Asians" or to "race" were dropped, and instead the hierarchy was established on the basis of a legal qualification rather than a personal characteristic. Pickersgill related that

It gave me real satisfaction that the new Regulations removed the offensive provision which excluded prospective immigrants of "Asiatic race." [This wording had, of course, already been removed in 1952.] This change did not mean, nor was it intended to mean, that Canada had adopted an open-door policy in place of selective immigration; but in the new Regulation, geography and citizenship, not race, became the basis of selection.[242]

Then, in an apparent reference to Harry and Mearl Singh, Pickersgill told the House of Commons that the 1956 regulations

removed one anomaly which I must say troubled me a great deal. It was not a very important thing, but it was a source of annoyance to a number of people. For instance, persons of east Indian and Chinese origin who were living, say in Trinidad, found it more difficult to get into Canada than persons of other origins in Trinidad and that did seem rather absurd, especially if the family had been there for several generations. This is no longer true.[243]

On reading this in *Hansard*, Sid Blum wrote to Andrew Brewin: "Your arguments in the Harry Singh case appear to have had a substantial, if delayed, effect on the Immigration Department. . . . While we lost the case, we accomplished the hoped-for change in the regulations."[244]

The crusaders had not, however, accomplished what they hoped. In that same debate, Pickersgill permitted a rather intimate glimpse into the process by which the new regulations had been drafted, revealing that the fundamental principles had not changed at all. The discussion was prompted by a delegation and a written brief from the East Indian Welfare Association, complaining that people from such non-Commonwealth southern countries as Egypt, Lebanon, Turkey and Latin America could bring in a broader range of relatives under the regulations than could Commonwealth South Asians. First, Pickersgill reported to the House, he had told the delegates

that one of the reasons why they have [a] favourable public opinion at the present time is that they have become good Canadian citizens and are accepted in the community. I said to them: "Now let us be completely honest about this and recognize that one of the reasons that this situation exists is that your numbers are comparatively small. . . . We are not going to contribute anything to the welfare of this country if we admit newcomers of any group in such numbers as to create problems, tensions and strains in this country that it would be desirable not to have."[245]

Having acknowledged in this way that racial feeling remained pronounced in the mainstream population, and therefore in government policies, Pickersgill went on to point out that certain countries only *appeared* to be in a more favourable category, but in fact no discrimination would occur. It is impossible to believe that the minister did not recognize the heavy irony in his detailed explanation of why Egypt, Israel, Lebanon, Turkey and Latin America appeared in the more favourable category 20(c) in a set of regulations which he claimed had eliminated racial distinctions.

There are virtually no Egyptians in this country and the applications we do receive from Egypt are almost entirely from people who are not Egyptians but people who happen to be living there and who are English or French or in many cases Armenian in origin. . . .

The same thing applies to Turkey. There are practically no Turks in this country and there is no desire on the part of Turks to come here. But there are Armenians and other communities in Turkey where the people have relatives in this country, and it is just for administrative convenience that these two countries are in this category. . . .

Israel is a country of immigration and the government of Israel is very anxious to keep able-bodied people in that country, and I doubt if there are many members of the house who do not sympathize with their desire, particularly at this time. We do everything we can to discourage applications from these people. . . .

In the case of Lebanon, it is true we have quite a considerable number of Lebanese in this country. . . . In many ways Lebanon is almost more a European country than it is an Asiatic country but again immigration is very small. . . .

So far as the South American and Central American countries are concerned, the same thing is even truer. These countries are also countries of immigration and the local inhabitants very rarely come here as immigrants. . . .

Having made this explanation, I hoped that would satisfy the East Indians that there was no intention to discriminate in these matters in the sense of saying that some people are better than others. It is just an administrative device.[246]

Pickersgill's explanations were more accurate than Blum's enthusiastic outburst. Had Harry and Mearl Singh applied after the 1956 regulations came into effect they would still have been rejected, but the reason would have been their Trinidadian citizenship rather than their Asian "race" that offended the regulations. The "continuous journey" device had been sophisticated once more. There remains little doubt that in the *Singh* decision the justices of the Supreme Court of Canada correctly interpreted the will of Parliament when they concluded: "We therefore think that for present purposes at least, the change in the language of the statutes and the regulations is not of significance."[247] They had also granted a victory to "common sense."

6

Implications

If Canadians imagine a racially defined society, it is probably Nazi Germany or apartheid South Africa that come most readily to mind. In that classic of racist propaganda, *Mein Kampf*, Adolf Hitler described Jews in terms that seem idiosyncratic in their assumption of racial purity and the threat posed by genetic mixing: "With satanic joy in his face, the black-haired Jewish youth lurks in wait for the unsuspecting girl whom he defiles with his blood, thus stealing her from her people. With every means he tries to destroy the racial foundations of the people he has set out to subjugate."[1] According to Hitler, Jews spread disease and economic disorder and were explicitly responsible for prostitution and the white slave traffic. Against the "Jewish threat" the Nazis inaugurated a set of economic restrictions, including a boycott of Jewish shops and exclusion from many employment categories (the practice of law among them), then authorized the barring of Jews from theatres, restaurants and hotels. The 1935 Nuremberg Laws gave precise legal definition to racist terminology, forbade intermarriage between Jews and other Germans, protected "Aryan" women from Jewish violation even to the extent that Jews were not permitted to employ them, and specified that full citizenship in Germany would be limited to "Aryans."[2] In apartheid South Africa there were laws assigning every South African a racial identity, establishing residential segregation, protecting white women from black

The notes to this chapter are on pages 425-28.

sexuality, setting "influx controls" on African migration, keeping blacks and whites apart in restaurants, bars, theatres and beaches and distinguishing employment access on lines of "race."[3] These are the images, perhaps combined with American scenes of southern segregation and northern ghetto violence, against which Canadians have been able to contrast their own experience not only in relative but in absolute terms. And yet the four case studies suggest a startlingly different reality. Many of the restrictions in genuinely racist societies apparently had a Canadian counterpart, including features for the protection of women of the dominant class, employment and other economic disadvantages, limited access to land and services, legalized segregation and even the legal definition of citizens by "race." If the extent and impact of the Canadian legislation was minuscule by comparison, a similar acceptance of the meaning of "race" was recognizable, as was a readiness to use the machinery of the state to regulate relations between "races."

It has become common in recent years to regard "race" as a social construct. Over the half century represented in these case studies, in Canada as elsewhere, "race" was also a legal artifact. And in the process of its formulation, the Supreme Court of Canada was a significant participant, legitimating racial categories and maintaining barriers among them. Even in *Noble and Wolf* the Court allowed the respondents' argument – that racial discrimination was both morally and legally acceptable – to pass without contradiction, and declined to confirm the appellants' assertion that racial distinctions were contrary to public policy. None of the seven judges in the case commented on discrimination per se or its legality so that the law already established on racial discrimination, for example by the *Quong Wing* and *Christie* decisions, was not affected. Then in *Narine-Singh* the Supreme Court positively upheld the legality of "race" as a discernible factor in Canadian public policy. The widespread existence of a racial paradigm in Canada and a legal role in its fashioning are two of the observations one might take from the examined cases.

If these four cases were "telling events," then they should articulate the legal and racial sensibilities of their times. In the sections that follow, some of the more general meanings of the cases will be drawn, and particularly their implications for a better understanding of "race" and "race relations" in Canada, the functioning of the Canadian legal sensibility through the Supreme Court of Canada, and the quest for "keys" to facets of Canadian history which have been locked away.

1. "RACE" AND "RACE RELATIONS"

The evidence examined in the four case studies exposed something that could be called "systemic racism," rather than individual deviancy or pathological personalities. Furthermore, this system was the product of a long and highly complex historical process. Temporary social and economic forces, such as bursts of immigrant numbers or the Depression of the 1930s, were seen to exacerbate the symptoms, but the syndrome persisted regardless of any identifiable "causative" events in Canada. Individualized explanations would require different kinds of evidence; the process here observed formed an intimate aspect of everyday Canadian life, supported by the leading institutions, sustained by high culture and popular belief. It is easy to recognize the heroes in these stories, but more difficult to find individual villains.

Throughout the period under study there were numerous indications that external, even global influences permeated the Canadian experience, and what happened in Canada refracted global patterns. It is indeed tempting to adopt a Geertzian model and find the Canadian "local knowledge" of a universal racist paradigm. Certainly the European overseas expansion and its resulting hierarchies produced an assignment to specific economic and social functions on the basis of "race." M. G. Smith's pluralism is useful in recognizing how European imperialism incorporated the resources and the populations of much of the world, from which emerged differentiated economic and political access distinguishable by membership in a "race." Roles had already been assigned and stereotypes had already been generated, in other words, in an imperial context in which Canada was only a very small player. Thus when certain types of immigrants were specifically admitted to perform certain tasks, an external pluralism was being imported into Canada;[4] Asians and Africans migrated from one part of a pluralized globe to another. That very telling resolution of the Nova Scotia assembly in 1815, defining all African people as "labourers and servants,"[5] did not derive from local experience alone.

A global network of ideas and practices pertinent to "race" was apparent, too, in Canada's deliberate emulation of American, Australian and South African restrictions on Chinese,[6] or the inspiration of the "Natal Formula" as a device for excluding unwanted subjects of the British Empire.[7] The Victoria newspapers assessed the character of the Chinese based on tales emanating from California and Australia.[8] The anxieties rampant in the Edmonton IODE petition crossed the border before the African Americans themselves.[9] The influence of Nazi ideology was evident during the 1930s in the utterances of Adrian Arcand, in campaigns in both Montreal and Toronto for boycotts of Jewish shops, and use of the swastika emblem by vandals and rioters.[10] Operating in a different direction but equally indicative of external influences was the ready adoption in Canada of the rhetoric, and eventually the principles, of wartime and postwar movements against colonial oppression and racial hierarchies across much of the world.[11]

One significant transmitter of global paradigm to local circumstance, indicated by this evidence at least, was the law. Canadians do not need to imagine some hypothetical process translating imperial models for application in Canada; there is a concrete example in the legal system. Law was a channel for bringing imperial experience to Canada directly, through Privy Council decisions, and continuously through the suffusion of English precedents in Canadian courts. Perhaps *Tomey Homma* stands as the paramount example, for it created an authentication for laws cast explicitly in terms of "race" and launched a legal discourse on racial differentiation that resonated through almost every case considered here.[12] The imperial connection could also act as a restraint, as in the moderation of certain immigration policies discriminating against subjects of the Empire or imperial allies, and in the nullification of local laws which violated British treaty commitments.[13] More recently Canada's own adherence to United Nations and other international agreements has shaped domestic law.[14]

Canadian law, then, provided a mechanism for the local manifestation of principles that were broadly current throughout Western civilization, and beyond.[15] Legislative acts and judicial decisions fitted those principles to Canadian circumstances, fixing local needs and preoccupations in legal terms. For example, the Court upheld Saskatchewan's *Female Labour Act* because it dealt with Chinese "as men of a particular race or blood," evidencing not only the Privy Council's *Tomey Homma* authorization but the realities of Canadian federalism which would put Chinese "as aliens or naturalized subjects" under the jurisdiction of the Dominion government.[16] By responding rather precisely to local Canadian concerns, law institutionalized and perpetuated a peculiarly Canadian version of the "race" phenomenon.

Immigration law probably provides the clearest revelation of this process at work. Canadian anxieties provoked by transnational stereotypes and racial doctrines demanded that certain peoples be excluded entirely or, of equal significance, admitted to a narrowly defined function in Canada. "Race" made its explicit debut in the *Immigration Act* of 1910.[17]

To sustain the conditions of admission, and to assuage local concerns about unfair economic competition, legal instruments were introduced restricting employment opportunities of targeted groups. Direct legislation prevented employment in the public service, outlawed occupational categories such as underground mining, denied licences to operate a business. Indirect legal devices imposed contract compliance and leasing agreements upon employers and set differential licensing fees and taxation benefits.[18] Educational disadvantage was legally effected by segregated schools in Nova Scotia and Ontario, with the added touch in Nova Scotia of legislating a limit upon the qualifications of teachers in the black schools.[19] Laws prescribed differential access to civil rights, protections and benefits, including the vote, public office and jury service.[20] The courts upheld an entire network of discriminatory practices in services and accommodation, and in effect not only condoned but extended such practices through the establishment of precedents. The Christie Defence Committee's fear that a negative decision would "encourage further and more open discrimination" was more than realized in its eventual reverberations from Dresden, Ontario, to Calgary and Vancouver.[21] As a result of the law, "race" became an officially meaningful category in Canada, a "factor of legal consequence" as the German ambassador would say.[22] "Race" as discourse was rendered "race" as artifact. Although every Canadian institution has not been examined in this study, and it remains possible that some other factors were even more important, still an instrumental role for the law is recognizable in giving public effect to private beliefs and fears about "race," and in setting the terms of relations among the groups thus designated.

Because of entry restrictions, colour and status became equated. With the legal structuring that occurred in Canada, entry status tended to be perpetuated beyond the immigrant generation. Status, it might be said, had been "racialized," and colour could serve as a marker of status even when no other differences were present. Since "race" coincided with position in society, occupation, educational achievement, residential patterns and social behaviour, local observation confirmed numerous transnational stereotypes. "Race" made the observable distinctions intelligible. "Race" had become common sense. Notice the entirely commonsensical approach taken in the postwar Senate Committee on Immigration: there should be no discrimination based on "race," but restrictions on Asians were based, "of course," on "reality" and should be continued.[23] Or the *Star Weekly* editorial in 1954 praising the Queen's Christmas message calling for racial equality in the Commonwealth and adding, as if without contradiction, "Racial discrimination is an established (and most would say sensible) feature of our immigration policy."[24]

"Race," clearly, had entered the prevailing discourse and became constructed as "truth." Captured within that discourse was a pervading fear, as Tory MP Donald Fleming told the House of Commons in 1955, that different "races" would disturb the welfare of the white majority.[25] One fundamental component, which Fleming identified, was the widely observed phenomenon that persons of colour tended to work for lower wages, threatening employment opportunities of others. Acceptance of a lower standard of living was attributed, by common sense at least, to genetic factors such as a lack of ambition or even lower physical requirements. Other features in the discourse reflected a similar fear towards characteristics believed to be genetically immutable and potentially disruptive. The notion that other "races" were "lawless" had an enduring currency in Canada, as specified in Ontario petitions against the settlement of fugitive American slaves,[26] in BC's 1884 Act restraining Chinese,[27] and in the *Munshi Singh* decision rejecting East Indian immigrants.[28] The most widely perceived threat was probably sexual: lower "races" could not control their basic instincts. Every group covered in this study faced the charge, at some time, of errant sexuality,[29] though the evidence was most indicative of attitudes toward Chinese. The Saskatchewan law was accepted as a protective measure because the Chinese sexual threat was taken for granted. "The control or influence of any Chinaman," the Saskatchewan Supreme Court decided, would "endanger" white women; no actual incidents were offered or demanded.[30] Support for the Chinese restriction from white middle-class women's associations and from organized labour, insisting that Chinese were "a menace to the virtue of white women," appeared not only in Saskatchewan but in every province from Ontario westward, and published innuendo about the Chinese threat had national circulation.[31] An equivalent attitude toward people of African ancestry was exemplified in the 1911 IODE petition and the immigration report that "farmers' wives" in Manitoba were afraid of black men.[32] Cancellation of the scheme to bring domestics from Guadaloupe was explained by the women's "immorality."[33] East Indians, a Vancouver public meeting resolved, were a threat to "public morals."[34]

The presence of people bearing such characteristics was especially disturbing because their differences were attributed to genetics and were therefore assumed to be permanent. The Trades and Labour Congress' long-standing platform principle against the immigration of "unassimil-able races" was one example of a concern echoing through Canadian dis-course until the middle of the 20th century.[35] The racially alien would remain foreign, even those born in Canada; Bora Laskin needed a special letter to vouch for his Canadian loyalties, though he was Canadian-born, and Quebec campaigns against "alien Jews" did not exempt families who had been in Canada for several generations.[36] Segregation was accepted as normal because inherent difference was believed to produce a natural aversion between "races," as part of a racial group's survival mechanism. Justice Mackenzie of Regina could expect "racial antipathy" to preserve the virtue of white women against alien seduction,[37] Justice Pelletier of the Quebec Court of King's Bench announced that "il est prouvé que la présence des noirs . . . empêche d'autres citoyens,"[38] and Chief Justice Robertson of Ontario felt that the purpose of a racially restrictive covenant was "obviously to assure . . . that the residents are of a class who will get along well together."[39] Mackenzie King's fear that Asian migration would "change the fundamental composition of the Canadian population"[40] bore the same underlying assumption that the "wrong" kind of immigration would be disruptive; as a BC court said in 1914, it would endanger "the maintenance of peace, order and good government."[41] The fact that earlier generations had assimilated, or that local experience often denied the validity of transnational stereotypes, was not sufficient to interrupt the momentum. The minister of Immigra-tion felt justified in arguing in 1951 that it was a "matter of record" that people of African heritage broke down in health in Canada, ignoring over 300 years of African Canadian history and, as was shown by Joe Noseworthy, the absence of any such records.[42] Especially poignant was the Canadian military's rejection of African Canadian volunteers in World War I, just when new recruits were most desperately needed. The notion of black unsuitability for warfare was conventional wisdom among the Western allies early in the century, but it was directly contra-dicted by Canadian experience: black soldiers had served with distinc-tion in Canadian and British armies in many wars before their image was changed by the "Scramble for Africa" late in the 19th century.[43]

Each group categorized as a "race" had an appropriate "place," with repercussions that encompassed people's lives as the case studies showed. And yet, despite this clear pattern, majority Canadians consist-ently denied that racial inequality existed in their country. Defence Min-ister Norman Rogers insisted that racial discrimination had no part in the rejection of black volunteers early in World War II;[44] Mayor George

Miller of Vancouver found no racial discrimination in his city's refusal to permit Chinese restaurants to hire white waitresses;[45] Lester Pearson could hold at the United Nations that Canada had no racial discrimination;[46] Leslie Frost could declare in his own legislature that racial discrimination was not practised in Ontario.[47] Especially revealing were apparently blatant contradictions in public utterances on "race." In one article the Toronto *Globe* decried "racial mixing" as "criminally unwise," yet called the female labour laws unfair for failing to distinguish between good and bad Chinese;[48] other newspaper articles and official statements demanded the elimination of racial restrictions yet proposed that Asian exclusion should continue.[49] This may have been simple hypocrisy, but other explanations are possible. If a genuine belief in Western racial doctrine is allowed, and if it is understood that the prevailing definition of equality meant that "likes" should be treated alike (with the corollary that "unlikes" could be treated differently),[50] then the apparent contradiction is reconcilable. One is sceptical of Immigration Minister Walter Harris' radio statement in 1954 – "I must assure you that we are not going to draw any lines which would be contrary to the Canadian understanding of the equality of all people"[51] – until the term "Canadian understanding" is drawn to attention. Under the British rhetoric of maternalistic trusteeship that formed so prominent a part of Canadian discourse until well after World War II, distinctions were justified as long as they were intended for the benefit of the less fortunate and did not differentiate among persons "similarly situated." To deny a restaurant licence was not incompatible with this outlook as long as its purpose was to protect white women. Only if some Chinese were affected, and others not, would the law be classed as inequitable, according to this logic, or if some other party gained an unfair advantage from it. This was *common sense*, and required no hypocrisy from persons declaring it. To receive condemnation from contemporaries, a particular act had to violate prevailing standards of equality. This helps to explain why what was then defined as "racial discrimination" was regarded as pathology, practised by aberrant individuals, while the majority reconciled their racial practices with a commitment to British justice and fair play.[52]

But there was a different interpretation of those Canadian virtues, and it is interesting to see how often the minority challengers turned the same rhetoric on its head to demand "equal" treatment for themselves. That these positions were taken up by entire communities would indicate that a different "common sense" was able to co-exist within Canadian society. For an understanding of Canadian "race relations" it is surely significant that minority groups had not accepted their fate or submitted to the doctrine of their own inferiority, and that their resistance was imbued with a faith that "British justice" would set things right for them. The global human rights "paradigm shift" that allegedly occurred during and after World War II represented at least a shift in sensibility in Canada: public protests against discriminatory businesses, the campaigns against Japanese Canadian deportation and to repeal the Chinese immigration laws, support for Asian enfranchisement, passage of municipal by-laws and provincial fair practices legislation, all represented the development of a new perception among majority Canadians about what was right and fair. At the same time this study cautions against attributing too much to a "paradigm shift." If *Drummond Wren* was most representative of the new era, *Noble and Wolf* demonstrated its limitations and *Narine-Singh* provided a dash of insight into the continued prevalence of the "race" paradigm in Canadian life and public policy. However helpful the global fallout might have been, *Canadian* struggle was required in order to overcome racial disadvantage in Canada.

2. LEGAL SENSIBILITY

For non-lawyers, the four case studies have probably revealed a surprising degree of "judicial creativity" in the legal decision-making process. Despite their incessant denials, judges clearly had a determining influence on public policy, and the impression is that they were "making" law and not simply applying existing rules. In each case the judges had a choice, and there were legally acceptable reasons for deciding more than one way. Only the *Narine-Singh* decision was unanimous; in the other three cases, and in most of the case law examined with them, there were powerful dissenting judgments illustrating an alternative (and usually an opposite) solution to the problem before them. In some of the cases, as well, there was more than one set of reasons for arriving at the *same* decision. On its own "the law," apparently, was not enough to determine a "correct" conclusion. Contradictions and ambiguities abound, both in the case law and in the legislation. In deciding which statutes or precedents to apply, the judges had not only to *find* the law but to assign its *meaning*.

In the various cases considered here, the standard judicial procedures could not be described as rigid or mechanistic. *Stare decisis* offered considerable latitude. To the lay person *Quong Wing* perhaps presents the starkest example: there were reasonable arguments for selecting either of the two Privy Council precedents. The momentum from *Tai Sing* in 1878 to *Bryden* in 1900 was against setting special regulations for Chinese Canadians, but *Tomey Homma* opened a new line of interpretation.[53] In *Christie*, though recent case law had been moving in the direction of the proprietor's right to exclude, still the facts of the case permitted a distinction to be made.[54] It is interesting to find *both* sides in *Noble and Wolf v. Alley* citing *Christie*: for the appellants *Christie* meant freedom of commerce, Mr. Wolf's right to buy and Mrs. Noble's right to sell; for the respondents it meant the freedom to associate with persons or groups of their own choice.[55] Justice Wilson selected *Drummond Wren* as her precedent for *Bhadauria*, without even mentioning *Noble and Wolf* or addressing its relevance for her construction of the case law.[56] Judicial discretion was considerable, and precedents seemed to be used as much to support a particular interpretation as to dictate an automatically discernible conclusion.

In assessing statutes the interpretive role of judges was equally apparent. In *Christie* they had to decide whether the language of the Quebec *Licencing Act* applied to a tavern, and the answer was not always the same.[57] Justice Chevrier in 1945 decided that Ontario's *Racial Discrimination Act* applied only to the specific items listed as examples; though he denounced racial discrimination in his decision and extended sympathy to Jews, he upheld a restrictive covenant. Justice Chevrier was interpreting not only the Act but his own function as a judge, for he declared himself bound by the wording of the Act, yet a *Dominion Law Reports* editorial suggested that he could have followed the Act's general prohibition of discrimination, and Justice Mackay demonstrated in *Drummond Wren* how a judge could find in the same Act the "legislative recognition" of a policy against restrictive covenants.[58] The determination of legislative intent was at the core of the *Narine-Singh* decision as well. Although the decision seems simplistic, with its reference to an ordinary dictionary to establish the meaning of the *Immigration Act*, the judges were in fact declaring that when Parliament changed the *language* of the Act they had not intended to change its *meaning*, and for this insight they could not rely on a dictionary.[59] In each instance more than one plausible meaning was available.

Since the law as written was so often indeterminate, sometimes ambiguous and occasionally contradictory, judges had to look beneath the text to the underlying principles that suffused the law, to what was called its "pith and substance," and to assess the long-term trajectory of the common law against the case in question. To grasp the essential principles in an elusive case, the judges would engage in a diagnostic process to find an analogy to some other principle or body of law. An obvious and often tortured example of this is found in *Christie* and the cases leading up to it, where the analogy to contract law was eagerly adopted. Of Justice Archibald's several reasons for finding in favour of the complainant in *Johnson v. Sparrow*, only the notion that the sale of a theatre ticket was like a contract survived the appeal court. Justice Archibald also offered an analogy to the common innkeeper and stated that the British tradition opposed discrimination among citizens. Had these points been sustained in the appeal court *ratio decidendi*, the subsequent cases of Barnswell, Reynolds, Franklin, Christie, Rogers, Desmond and King would have been entirely different.[60] As this example shows, even when subtextual diagnosis occurred there was still no obvious or correct answer to be found. Consider the debates between Justice Wilson and Chief Justice Laskin or Justice O'Halloran and his BC colleagues over the fundamental and cumulative meaning of equality under the common law.[61] The underlying principles themselves could often be indeterminate, sometimes ambiguous and occasionally contradictory.

Judges were making a choice, and the choices they made, the analogies they drew and the principles they discovered, reflected a set of assumptions and values on the part of the judge him- or herself. It would be difficult to match Justice Archibald's moral fervour in *Johnson v. Sparrow*[62] or Justice Idington's in *Quong Wing*,[63] for both were articulating a moral position recognizable today, yet Chief Justice Fitzpatrick expressly found the Saskatchewan law to be "in the moral interest."[64] Morality, apparently, was a feature in the way judges made their choices. Justice Rinfret's denial on the part of the majority in *Christie* that racial discrimination could be considered immoral is dramatic evidence of the same characteristic.[65] Chief Justice Robertson of Ontario said of a racially restrictive covenant that "There is nothing criminal or immoral involved."[66] Not only was morality a legitimate consideration, but moral outlooks did not always coincide, as reversals and dissents illustrated. Social values, assumptions about what was good and beneficial, were present in every one of the analyzed decisions. Judges considering *Quong Wing* denied themselves any judgment on the wisdom or policy of the Saskatchewan Act, yet that was exactly what they did do: they found not only that the law was within the provincial jurisdiction but that it was "*necessary* to the welfare of women and girls in Saskatchewan"; Justice Idington, opposing, argued that the act was a "breach of *faith*."[67] These comments revealed that the wisdom, justice and policy of the Act were very much under consideration, a process called by Professor Laskin in a 1940 comment on *Christie*, "reading social and economic doctrine into law."[68]

Each case began in a dispute over a "right" or a conflict between "rights," and perhaps no issue is more indicative of a moral and political outlook than how rights are defined. Of particular interest is the way in which these disputes were rendered justiciable. To carry a claim into court, a plaintiff had to contend some legally recognizable "fact"; in examining the claim, the judges cast it as a question amenable to the kind of answer they were able to give. In the terminology of current policy analysis, the courts had to consider the situation as a legal "problematic" before they could solve it. Quong Wing's initial challenge sprang from his claim that the discriminatory Saskatchewan law was unfair. This was rendered justiciable by putting it in terms of federal-provincial jurisdiction, "the only real question for the Court" as the Saskatchewan Supreme Court revealed so tellingly, so that the problematic finally put to the test was the province's "right" to protect white women and girls. Given that question the province's right was upheld, but Quong Wing's question was not answered.[69] Fred Christie's claim that discrimination was wrong was similarly translated into a question the courts of his day were equipped to consider. "We ought to start," Justice Rinfret explained, with the principle of "complete freedom of commerce."[70] Then the question became: was there anything in this case to justify limiting the tavern's freedom? In this translation of the issue the analogy to a business contract was intelligible, and a judge could be found suggesting, in answer to Mr. Christie's contention about racial discrimination, that the tavern's advertisements were not "an offer to sell" but an "invitation to buy," and therefore there was no contract. Even in dissent the best Justice Galipeault could argue was that an implied contract did exist.[71] The distance from the original problem remained glaringly apparent. In court, "race" dropped from view, but in the "real world," as has been described, *Christie* as precedent produced an increase in racial discrimination.[72] The courts had not addressed Fred Christie's problem at all.

In *Noble and Wolf* the contest between the appellants' "equality of civil status" and the respondents' "freedom of association" did receive consideration throughout, though not ultimately in the Supreme Court of Canada decision.[73] The debate at the Ontario Court of Appeal exhibited two fairly explicit views of social harmony, both employing the language of what would now be called multiculturalism. The Beach O'Pines Association, and the Chief Justice of Ontario, held forth on the virtue of cultural variety and the right of every group to preserve its differences; Mr.

Wolf and the Canadian Jewish Congress were arguing for the right, in a multicultural society, of every individual to have access under the law to the same assets and advantages. At the Ontario court the Beach vision prevailed.[74] The closest the Supreme Court of Canada came to this debate, in its written decision, was to declare that group membership in terms of "race" could not be established with legal certainty. Five of the six majority judges expressed their decision on the reasoning that a restrictive covenant, like a personal contract, was valid only between the contracting parties and could not attach to a piece of land. Once Shirley Denison asked the right question, the appellants achieved the result (although not exactly the answer) they had wanted.[75]

A similar process was visible through *Narine-Singh*, but only in hindsight with the benefit of the subsequent *Brent* decision. Andrew Brewin argued in *Narine-Singh* that the immigration regulations were *ultra vires* because in the Act Parliament gave the governor-in-council authority to define the classes to be excluded from Canada, but the regulations were "so vague and uncertain" that no actual standards were set and immigration officials were conducting improper hearings.[76] In this instance it was the vagueness and uncertainty of the terms "Asian" and "race" that were in contention. In its abrupt decision the Supreme Court of Canada found those terms certain enough, and so the *ultra vires* argument failed. Language precision became the justiciable issue, not the structural weaknesses of the immigration regulations. The manner of the *Narine-Singh* decision was misleading – the terse dismissal of Brewin, the failure even to call on the government lawyer to state an argument – for it seemed to suggest that only one answer was obvious and that Brewin had no reasonable case at all. Just months later Mr. Brewin played the same argument again, in a case sharing many pertinent facts. This time the courts decided that the governor-in-council had acted improperly in not setting precise rules for officials to follow, and so the regulations were *ultra vires*.[77] The example in *Brent*, a woman excluded for "unsuitability," displayed sufficient vagueness for the courts to recognize the structural defects in the system. Andrew Brewin finally gained the result, but still not the answer, he had wanted.

The impression gained from the case studies is that judicial decisions were not as simple or mechanistic as they might seem at first glance. But neither were they arbitrary. Infusing each case was a legal sensibility, a notion of what constituted a relevant question, a legitimate analogy, an acceptable argument, as well as an appropriate range of answers. What the judges tried to do was to make sense of the often disconnected facts and conflicting rights before them, to make them coherent as a lawful interpretation and a reasonable resolution of the dispute. These notions were culturally contingent: "sense" and "reason," like "rights" and "justice," were achieved within a context. Judges' oft-noted reluctance to be innovative or to assume an interpretive initiative reflected their legal sensibility, which set a particular meaning on the nature of law and the role of judges. This was not a case of hypocrisy on the part of judges, for they could not avoid being part of the context. The legal sensibility was widely shared across Canadian society: it was part of the prevailing paradigm, the common sense.

It is striking, in the cases under study, how closely the decisions represented the mind of the nation, how contemporary values and priorities were so generally captured. Judges applied what have come to be called "community standards," giving legal effect *within* the paradigm to issues of community concern. Ian Bushnell, in a 1992 comment on *Quong Wing*, wrote: "In an extremely brief judgment that bordered on nonsense, Chief Justice Fitzpatrick characterized the [Saskatchewan] law as being the regulation of places of business in the interest of the morals of females."[78] Assuming (incorrectly) that "Public opinion was silent, since the case was not reported in the newspapers," Bushnell intimated that had public opinion and the press been mobilized in 1914, the *Quong Wing* decision would have been different.[79] The contextual background presented in chapter 2 suggests the opposite: in every corner of society there was concern over immigration, especially Chinese immigration, and the legal sensibility quite obviously accepted the legitimacy of racially specific restriction. The press did report the case at each level from magistrate's court to the Supreme Court of Canada, and there was no hint that the judicial reasoning was considered "nonsense." That the Court accurately interpreted the Saskatchewan legislation was made retroactively clear when, in 1924, a Regina judge did permit Yee Clun to hire white waitresses for his restaurant. Immediately the legislature amended the law to make it easier for local authorities to restrict white female employment by Chinese. Provincial legislatures, municipal councils, trade unions, women's groups, all asserted a need for, and the propriety of, the discriminatory legislation.[80] Anyone reading the *Hansard* debates on immigration during that era could not escape the conclusion that the community demanded protection against Chinese.[81] Then, in 1927-28, when the Ontario law was inadvertently proclaimed and enforced, the *Quong Wing* decision was in effect tested again in the press, in the legislature, in diplomatic exchanges, in public discourse. Although there were a few moderate voices of disapproval, only the Chinese consul labelled it "inconsistent with Anglo-Saxon sense of justice and fairplay."[82] Consul Chow, like the 1992 commentator, did not share the legal sensibility of majority Canadians in the 1910s and 1920s. Evidence at Fred Christie's first court appearance made it equally unmistakable that racial segregation was widespread and acceptable to the majority.[83] Community standards also accepted the right of a proprietor to refuse any customer as consistent with fairness and justice. Injustice in the 1930s would be to *require* a proprietor to serve an unwanted patron. When the deputy minister of Justice wrote to Dresden's Hugh Burnett in 1943 to report that it was lawful for a local restaurant to discriminate on grounds of "race," he explained that a law forcing businesses to serve any member of the public "would be entirely one-sided," and he appealed to Mr. Burnett's common sense to understand.[84] Although Hugh Burnett did not share this particular feature of the paradigm, discriminatory practices during wartime by the National Selective Service and the Canadian armed forces suggest that he held the minority view, and that the Supreme Court in 1939 had resolved the Christie dispute according to the legal sensibility of the times.[85] In this example, common law was indeed common: it operationalized common sense.

For understanding the context of *Noble and Wolf*, there are opinion polls tracking contemporary views on Jews and other minorities and on the acceptability of racial covenants. Although Jews remained unpopular, ranking second to Japanese as undesirable immigrants as late as 1945,[86] by 1947, 64 percent of Canadians approved of legislation to prevent employment discrimination and the approval rate increased when Jews (rather than the more general "race, colour or religion") were specified in the questionnaire.[87] In a 1949 poll, 68 percent declared that they would refuse to sign a racially restrictive covenant, and only 19 percent said they would agree.[88] The Association for Civil Liberties enjoyed widespread endorsement from individuals and community groups in its campaign to restrain private discrimination through the instrument of the law.[89] A resolution passed by the Women's Missionary Society of the United Church of Canada in early 1950 and sent to Premier Frost represented how the pulse of the nation was beating to a different rhythm from less than a decade previously:

Whereas instances of flagrant race discrimination are being reported from all parts of the country, including Ontario; and whereas the essence of a democracy is equal rights for all its citizens; and whereas a fundamental doctrine of Christianity is the belief in the Fatherhood of God and the Brotherhood of man, involving as that does a respect for every human soul and a duty to treat as a brother every person irrespective of colour, race or creed;

Therefore the Executive of the Women's Missionary Society of United Church of Canada calls upon the Government of Ontario to strengthen its legislation in such a way that racial and religious discrimination, particularly in the matters of employment, rental and purchase of property, access to hotels, restaurants and public places, may be eliminated.[90]

The distance from resolutions passed by women's organizations earlier in the century is remarkable.[91]

The same file in Premier Frost's papers bulges with letters and resolutions congratulating the premier on the passage of his legislation against restrictive covenants. Press response to the legislation, and to the Supreme Court of Canada decision eight months later, was overwhelmingly positive.[92] Not only had attitudes towards minorities changed, but so had the public's acceptance of discrimination by private individuals and of the propriety of using the law to enforce majority standards. As was mentioned in chapter 4, the Court could almost certainly have declared discrimination to be contrary to public policy without violating the prevailing sentiment of 1950. It remained true, however, that the limited decision was consistent with the practice of pronouncing only upon the essential points required to resolve an issue, itself an entrenched aspect of Anglo-Canadian legal sensibility, and that a significant portion of the Canadian population still hesitated to see the state interfere in private relationships. As the chief justice of Ontario said, with a frequent echo from the *Globe and Mail*, morality was not an appropriate field for legislation because the law could not change minds or hearts.[93] The *Noble and Wolf* decision rather effectively captured the delicate cusp of this shift in sensibility.

Data from opinion polls also helps to explain the *Narine-Singh* decision. Despite the postwar momentum for immigration reform and statements from churches, parliamentary committees, labour and press opposing racially discriminatory regulations, this position must be examined in the context of a continued belief in the reality of "race" characteristics and a definition of "discrimination" that included only certain kinds of distinction. The *Globe and Mail* was surely correct in its January 1954 editorial: "No one seriously proposed taking immigrants from any part of the world save Western Europe."[94] Parliament's 1956 revision of the regulations, in the wake of *Brent*, left the level of racial discrimination more or less exactly as it had been when the Supreme Court of Canada discerned that no change was intended, and a 1956 opinion poll showed the majority of Canadians satisfied with policies ensuring that immigrants would come from "traditional" source countries.[95] The court had accurately read parliamentary intent, and had recognized "community standards" through an ambiguous public rhetoric denouncing discrimination.

All of which serves to emphasize the overwhelming significance of context for the analysis of a law or legal decision, not just a snapshot of surrounding circumstances but a consideration over time of the interconnections between the legal issue and other manifestations of contemporary culture, the "social dynamics," of which the law forms such an important part. Values, morals and principles found expression in these cases, along with public concern and political expediency, all translated into a meaningful legal rule for people to follow. The question of whether the law was a reflection of what already existed or a vision of what was to come assumes a false dichotomy: the law was a *participant* in the context. As a part of the cultural system, law had a specific function: to render society's norms into a form that could be understood, predicted, respected and enforced. Law was process. As racist doctrine and anxieties about racial degeneration increased, laws to maintain racial separation confirmed and reproduced the motivating forces. As conventional wisdom about "race" began to change, law was engaged to participate in the transformation of structures that were no longer appropriate.

It is frequently remarked that the Canadian Supreme Court has been "passivist" in contrast to the "activist" American Supreme Court. Regarded historically, the way Canadian judges articulated their rulings implied that they were "strictly, even mechanistically, applying established rules and precedents."[96] A leading legal historian has written:

Our courts have tended to express attitudes and values within narrow limits and through results and technical reasoning, and they have not usually made decisions that have a major impact on society. . . . Nor have we used courts much to declare values nor to focus and make apparent problems, especially diffused problems that affect otherwise relatively powerless groups.[97]

The cases included in this study do not support this perspective, for judges openly consulted moral principles, applied social values and diagnosed conflicting trends. The social impact of their decisions, particularly upon "relatively powerless groups," was considerable. A private dispute in a civil law case in Quebec became both public and national as a consequence of the Court's declaration of values in *Christie*. The standard interpretation of a non-active court reflects a "presentist" orientation: since the Court did not *then* advance values and groups that are ascendant *today*, they must have been doing nothing at all.

It is true that the Supreme Court of Canada was not an instrument for civil libertarian reform, and that the social order its judges adhered to was conservative and hierarchical; but it would not be accurate to say that the Court was isolated from majority concerns. Neither does the evidence support the proposition that law was a deliberate instrument to benefit particular interest groups. There was no specific interest being served by *Quong Wing*, for example;[98] although organized labour and a small commercial sector were motivated partly by economic protection, these are not the classes usually associated with control of the judiciary. The concept of "instrumentalism" seems analytically useful only if it is defined sufficiently broadly, as in David Kairys' observation that "The law is a major vehicle for the maintenance of existing social and power relations. . . . The law's perceived legitimacy confers a broader legitimacy on a social system."[99] The Court operated as a "power centre" (as Foucault expressed it), functionalizing the dominant discourse. If this concept is tested against *Christie*, it reveals that the law maintained a property and business orientation, and within that context legitimized the freedom to discriminate for the sake of upholding the "sanctity of contract" and "freedom of commerce."[100] It was also apparent, however, that views inherent in the *Christie* decision were not the exclusive preserve of property or any other identifiable interest. The decision was "instrumental," but it was rendering into law a social and power relationship that permeated every level of Canadian society at that time.

Without denying the influence of personal idiosyncrasy in the decisions under study here, in every example the rules upheld by the Court were already part of the social and moral framework. It exercised its interpretive latitude within the permissible realms of the legal sensibility then existing. As individuals the judges were after all participants in the same general culture as their contemporaries. Renowned jurists such as Lyman Duff and Ivan Rand and even Bora Laskin made decisions that appear less than innovative today, and may seem to restrict present definitions of "rights." This reflection should encourage a respectful understanding that common sense is context-bound, for judges as for every other member of society, and this includes the propriety of selecting one precedent over another. Some, it is true, recognized an "implied Bill of Rights" in both the common and the civil law. In BC, Justices Gray and Crease went beyond the division of powers issue to denounce anti-

Chinese legislation,[101] and Justice O'Halloran bluntly announced that "it is contrary to common law to refuse service to a person solely because of his colour or race."[102] In Quebec, Justice Archibald found that "Our constitution is and has always been essentially democratic, and does not admit of distinctions between races," and Justice Fortin agreed that "In this country the colored people and the white people are governed by the same laws, and enjoy the same rights without any distinction whatever." This was echoed by Justice Carroll – "Tous les citoyens de ce pays, blancs et noirs, sont soumis à la même loi et tenus aux mêmes obligations"[103] – and Justice Galipeault had no difficulty claiming that racial discrimination was "contre les bonnes moeurs, contre l'ordre public, contre le droit et la loi."[104] But these were minority opinions at the time, and none prevailed. Not only was the weight of precedent against them, but so was the expressed wish of the legislatures and the majority population. When change in the law occurred, it was not because a reforming judge decided to break with tradition, but when the social dynamic within which the law existed underwent a shift. In the examples studied in this book, the initiative for reform was taken first by members of the public who perceived a need for change, usually individuals from the affected minority. The evidence considered here suggests that the law did not change itself. Challenge, resistance and struggle were required in court, in Parliament, and in the public discourse. Reform was accommodated only when common sense grew to accept it.

3. HISTORICAL STUDY

The history in Canada of the "race" phenomenon may serve as a reminder for historians that an exclusively national focus in historical explanation has limitations. Canada was very much on the periphery of developments which led to a civilization committed to the principle that "race" was significant in human behaviour, and then to a conviction that it was not. Events within Canada are not sufficient to explain either a *Quong Wing* or a *Noble and Wolf*. Canadian attitudes and practices were so often an apparent fragment of a globally pervasive paradigm, but at the same time local conditions had a defining impact on the specific manifestations of "race" in Canada: federalism, building the railroad, scarcity of labour, stresses of nation building, demographic and settlement patterns, reliance on immigration. An examination of the Canadian events is therefore a useful reminder as well that there were local systems operating within the broader civilization. This kind of analysis can help in the discernment of the "universal" patterns: recognition of how the universal took forms that varied from one society and period to another may clarify the factors involved and contribute eventually to an understanding of the phenomenon itself. Local study conducted from a larger-scale perspective, it would seem, can lend insight into both the particular and the general.

The four cases examined here suggest that, in approaching local study in this way, the works of Clifford Geertz can provide a helpful guide for historians. There *is* meaning in the local devices that are developed to construe the universals, as Geertz demonstrated, and so analytical attention turned to the "construable signs" and "orienting notions" assists in understanding the "conceptual world" that might otherwise remain inaccessible. Of particular benefit for a study such as this one is Geertz's identification of a "legal sensibility" as one of those signs.[105] On the other hand, the cases have indicated the significance of the time dimension, which Geertz did not emphasize. *Quong Wing* could be misconstrued without analysis of the political and legal developments of the 1920s; *Narine-Singh* could be misconstrued in ignorance of *Brent* and the 1956 immigration amendments; none of the cases is isolatable from the ongoing trajectories into which they offered a momentary glimpse. The "location" metaphor, implicit in Geertzian description, does not supply an adequate model for historians. Place *and* time condition the context, and both deserve analytical attention. Frozen in time, something that is "becoming" appears as if it already "is."

When the four cases are viewed from a historical perspective the context is revealed as movement, as a process, and the movement is *dynamic* from universal to local and back again, from one local event to another. Historical change is not unidirectional; it resonates. German "local knowledge" resonated to Canada in the 1930s, intensifying Canadian antisemitism; the *Drummond Wren* decision resonated to the United States and much of the Western world.[106] British imperial interests resonated to Canadian immigration restrictions against people from India; the *Komagata Maru* incident resonated back to India, fostering political unrest against the Empire.[107] Not only were universals manifest in Canada, but Canadian developments helped shape the universals. The fragment's meaning is discernible through its relationship to the whole.

Within this dynamic movement definitions changed. Morality, as was so often demonstrated in these cases, was particularly susceptible to contextual motion. "Rights," despite their frequent description as "universal" and "inalienable," underwent comparable shifts in definition. Rights are what the law says they are, and the law on this point changed dramatically. Perhaps the most fundamental conceptual mutation recorded here was the shift towards state intervention. Restrictions on personal behaviour – even to restrain the public posting of a discriminatory sign – were impossible to legislate in the 1930s and were introduced in the face of a powerful individual rights-based resistance in the 1940s. Society did not necessarily value racial discrimination, but it did value the right of the individual to be free from state coercion. That same rhetoric of individual rights would come to signal the rights of the citizen to be protected by the state against displays of racial discrimination.[108]

South Africans have an anecdote that neatly illustrates this transition. Van der Merwe, the typical slow-witted character in Afrikaans humour, was fined for assaulting a black worker. "What's freedom coming to," he asks the magistrate, "if you can't hit your own *kaffir* on your own farm with your own *sjambok*?"[109] "Freedom" had changed its meaning, in South Africa as in Canada. Common sense itself accommodated the definitional shift, so that the former way of looking at rights became wrong. The discourse conveying the reversal, much to the confusion of Canadians in the 1950s, was engaged in this dynamic, resonating with colonial independence struggles, the decline of hierarchical models, wartime acceptance of unprecedented state controls, stricken conscience. Only in retrospect does the process seem inevitable, with a pre-established direction. Around *Noble and Wolf* and *Narine-Singh* in particular, the discourse can be understood as intercourse, as reverberation and exchange and generation. Historians' accustomed reluctance to subscribe to determinism is justified by the course of these stories.

Evident throughout this study has been the sound of more than one voice at any given time. Minority resistance challenged the hegemony of the prevailing paradigm and revealed the presence of multiple historical trajectories within Canadian society. Minority resistance did not begin with World War II, and it was carried frequently before the majority population in petitions and delegations to legislatures, newspaper campaigns, action in the workplace, and testing through the courts. The majority could ignore it because it was the protest that was considered aberrational according to the common sense of the times, but historians do not need to perpetuate the same mythology by portraying minorities as pliable, passive and content. Nor was it only in a struggle against restriction that minorities displayed historical integrity. These were vibrant communities with religious institutions, newspapers, political and social organizations, a range of cultural expressions, all contributing to a group momentum distinct from the mainstream. These were recognizable entities, subordinate in some respects but in others preserving considerable control over their own lives. This was a history in which people were actively engaged, not as victims or objects, but as participants in the shaping of their own destinies.

A pattern of multiple entities, brought forward in the forceful community efforts described in these cases, contests the concept of "master story" in Canadian history. Numerous "facts" in the conventional interpretation are directly contradicted, particularly those which have contributed to a Canadian identity incorporating an image of generosity toward minorities. Furthermore the wars, elections and migrations which feature in the master story have quite different meaning for different groups. Canada did not "come of age" as a democracy, during World War I, for the men of the No. 2 Construction Battalion.[110] It is not intelligible to define Canadian history according to any one trajectory. On the other hand, to acknowledge multiple trajectories need not mean their pursuit as disconnected group stories. As has been shown, connections were intricate and unavoidable, forming a propelling force in the Canadian social dynamic. Not all of them were vertical lines of oppression and opposition. It is this web of relations that deserves attention from Canada's interpreters. To render those relationships coherent remains a worthy challenge for a new generation of social historians.

In pursuit of this challenge the singled-out case approach has certain advantages. Since the focus is upon a particular "subject," either individual or group, the perspective is forced away from the surrounding society *except* in terms of its relationship to the "subject"; the webs of relations become important and they become apparent. Similarly, societal structures and conceptual trends are presented in terms of personalized experience, involving relations between the "subject" and the contextual environment. There is a further advantage from singling out legal cases for the study of social relations. The law represents organizing principle in Western democratic society; it is the law that orders power relations and rationalizes them according to contemporary sensibility. For the social historian, law grants access to the lines of connection. This is not to suggest that the "rules" hold the key to understanding social relations, but the ways in which rules are designed, applied, explained, avoided and resisted. In the singled-out case, attention moves beyond the political and legislative sphere to the functioning of law in human lives, to the social dynamic in which law participates, to the relationships that are effected and affected.

Although there is an increasing use of criminal case records by social historians in Canada, illustrating one aspect of "history from below,"

Canadian history generally has not considered the law as a route to understanding social conditions or the beliefs and values of an age. The grand interpreters of national history have virtually ignored the law. The case studies presented in this book suggest that law, and case law in particular, does articulate the prevailing principles and paradigms historians seek through research in other sources. Encasing the body of law, as has been seen, is a "legal sensibility" which is part of the "conceptual world" at any given time and is made visible through the way laws are interpreted in the resolution of real disputes in court. The case law examined here exposed some of the "orienting notions" in early 20th-century Canada which can contribute to a historical understanding of their period and especially of the relations that channelled so much in daily life: the function of government, the rules of commerce, individual rights, gender roles, sexual anxieties and stereotypes, the assumptions of common sense. The exploration of "race" as an orienting notion revealed the complexity and range of the relationships infused with this concept. It was more subtle than colour antipathy, more complicated than a capitalistic plot, more pervasive than working-class protectionism. It was a strand in political, economic and moral networks ravelling the social process, and for analytical purposes it cannot be separated from its context. "Race" as a force in the Canadian past does not submit to the common sense of today. The singled-out case method applied to legal cases requires a consideration of context and common sense through the analysis of statutes, evidence, opposing arguments and the judges' resolution. The challenge to conventional wisdom and the separate trajectory, as well as the dominant ideology, are ensnared in the case records. "Presentism," that great barrier to historical understanding which imposes current values on past events, is perhaps more easily avoided in the struggle to explain a legal decision. The fragments will not have meaning, or not the meaning that led to their connection in court, unless they are examined in terms that were recognizable to contemporaries.

Social history practised in this way can bring the legal component into an interpretation of Canadian history generally, and it may also appeal to legal historians. Legal developments are extremely context-connected, so that interpretive models fashioned in other cultures may not be totally transferable. With its insistence upon specific contextual analysis and detailed archival research, the singled-out case approach offers a technique to assess the local characteristics of Canadian law and the cultural framework within which it has taken shape.

Afterword

Prevailing Canadian opinion holds that the Charter of Rights and Freedoms is a powerful weapon on behalf of individual rights;[1] it is widely regarded, in the words of a 1986 CTV special program, as *A Gift of Freedom.*[2] In a celebratory statement launching the Charter, Justice Minister Jean Chrétien expressed a typical expectation:

Now it is not just the politicians who will defend our rights, it will also be the courts. That is better because politicians sometimes tend to just go with the wind. Now, due to the Charter, it is also possible to think about those issues in the courts away from the arena of political debate and where emotions and votes cannot influence you.[3]

Nor was it only Liberals who had such confidence. Conservative Prime Minister Brian Mulroney would say in the House of Commons that it was the Charter that enabled Canadians to "live in the kind of democracy for which we are all grateful."[4] Conventional wisdom accepted that the courts had at last been equipped to fulfil this vital role. The courts, and especially the Supreme Court of Canada, had been "transformed" by the Charter,[5] and a new era had begun in the way Canadians would be governed;[6] a judicial "renaissance," even a "revolution," was in process,[7] introducing a "new paradigm" into the interpretation of Canadian rights

---

The notes to the Afterword are on pages 428-36.

and the judicial function.[8] Chief Justice Antonio Lamer shared this vision of a new dawn in Canadian judicial practice. On the tenth anniversary of the Charter's implementation a Toronto newspaper reported his opinion that "the Charter has changed our job descriptions." Rather than simply applying the law, as had been the case before 1982, the courts now had a responsibility to "judge" the laws themselves, to make value judgments, to become an active participant in public policy. "Now that's a revolution," the chief justice claimed. "That's like introducing the metric system. It is like Pasteur's discoveries. Medicine was never the same after. Like the invention of penicillin, and the laser. It was a great event." An additional consequence of the Charter, the chief justice observed, was that Canadians had become much more rights-conscious since 1982. "The public wants its rights ... And they know if they are correct the court will give it to them."[9]

Within a decade of the Charter's implementation, the four cases studied here seemed consigned to the dustbin of history. No longer viable as precedents or representative of continuing principles in Canadian judicial reasoning, their only further purpose would be as object lessons of what used to be. If *Quong Wing* was the "base-point from which to measure the evolution of egalitarian principles in Canadian law,"[10] then clearly a sincere and profound advancement had been made, to the virtual reversal of trends previously in existence. It was of course not the Charter alone that caused this change. By the early 1980s societal developments, in Canada and internationally, were apparently leading towards a new sensibility, even a new common sense, and it was already being recognized in legislative innovations and in human rights jurisprudence. The Charter was part of a broader process, which can be traced through developments in public policy since the mid-1950s. Positive though it all appears, this new policy direction needs to be tested against actual conditions in the lives of Canadian minorities, and against judicial trends which could have an impact on minority rights. Such an exercise provides grounds for sincere apprehension.

1. DIRECTIONS IN PUBLIC POLICY

At the time when *Narine-Singh* was decided, public policy in Canada still served as a source of discrimination and as an enforcer of discriminatory acts by others. But then during the 1950s positive laws imposing racial distinctions were removed, with the notable exception of immigration regulations, and a solution to the problem of racism was proposed through laws protecting minorities from overt acts of private discrimination.[11] This policy impulse, which might be labelled the "protective shield," continued into the 1960s and 1970s.

The quintessential federal example of the new direction was the *Bill of Rights* passed by the Diefenbaker government in 1960. Although it created no new rights, the Bill was a "manifesto"[12] confirming Parliament's respect for traditional rights and freedoms. Canadians would be protected against violation of those rights, for the Justice Department was required to scrutinize every parliamentary bill and every act already in existence to guarantee compatibility with the bill's declaration of equality before the law.[13] As the deputy minister of Justice who drafted the Bill put it, "the Bill operates prenatally."[14] Action by the courts was not therefore expected to be considerable, but judicial review was explicitly invited to "construe and apply" *every* Canadian law according to the principles contained in the Bill unless – in recognition of parliamentary supremacy – Parliament itself declared that a particular act should operate notwithstanding the *Bill of Rights*. The entire machinery of the state, Parliament, civil service and courts, was enlisted to protect the individual rights of Canadians including in particular "equality before the law and the protection of the law." The *Canadian Bill of Rights* applied only to actions of the federal government, but there was a provincial counterpart. Beginning with Ontario in 1962, each province eventually introduced human rights legislation confirming equality before the law, declaring that public policy was contrary to racial distinctions, and recognizing the state's right to interfere to protect the individual.[15]

Equally significant, and politically more revolutionary, were changes in immigration law during this same era. In 1962 the Conservative government introduced new regulations granting admission to Canada on the basis of an applicant's "education, training, skills or other qualifications."[16] Although the regulations retained one discriminatory feature – sponsorship privileges were broader for Europeans than for Asians and Africans – Immigration Minister Ellen Fairclough explained to the House that from now on "any suitably qualified person from any part of the world can be considered for immigration to Canada, without regard to his race, colour, national origin or the country from which he comes."[17] Orders introduced by the Liberal government in 1967 completed the movement begun by the Conservatives in 1962, establishing a "points system" assigned to applicants on the basis of qualifications.[18] Ostensibly no more than a rationalization of existing policy, the 1967 regulations removed "race" from the text of Canadian immigration law.

A step in the same policy direction was taken on 8 October 1971 when Prime Minister Trudeau announced that Canada was committed to "multiculturalism within a bilingual framework."[19] When the Royal Commission on Bilingualism and Biculturalism was appointed in 1963, it had been instructed to "take into account" "the contribution made by the other ethnic groups to the cultural enrichment of Canada and the measures that should be taken to safeguard that contribution."[20] As a part of the Liberal program to build "national unity" emerging from the *B and B Report*, Trudeau announced his government's dedication to full participation in Canadian society for all individuals whatever their "race" or ethnic background. Cultural diversity was an instrument toward integration rather than a product valued for itself. According to Trudeau, multiculturalism

should help to break down discriminatory attitudes and cultural jealousies. National unity, if it is to mean anything in the deeply personal sense, must be founded on confidence in one's own individual identity; out of this can grow respect for that of others and a willingness to share ideas, attitudes and assumptions. A vigorous policy of multiculturalism will help to create this initial confidence. It can form the base of a society which is based on fair play for all.[21]

Multiculturalism was a part of a broad policy sweep, commencing after World War II, to remove barriers to the effective integration of all Canadians, including those who had earlier been considered unsuitable. As elaborations upon the same theme, there were serious proposals during the 1960s to abolish Indian reserves,[22] and in Nova Scotia the most famous separate black community, Africville, was annihilated and its people relocated in downtown Halifax.[23] The underlying principle was inclusivity, with the power of the government enlisted to guarantee every citizen's right to equal participation.

The same principle was affirmed in a new *Immigration Act* passed in 1976. For the first time immigration legislation explicitly stated that non-discrimination on grounds of "race," national or ethnic origin, colour, religion or sex was a fundamental objective of Canadian admission policy.[24] Coincident with the new *Immigration Act*, the federal government introduced a *Canadian Human Rights Act*,[25] applying the non-discriminatory principles of its provincial counterparts to the federal sphere and declaring Canada's expanding dedication to equality.

The legislative momentum since 1960 was unmistakable: the *Bill of Rights*, human rights codes in every jurisdiction, a national policy of multiculturalism and a non-discriminatory immigration law. Public policy was clearly committed to the path of egalitarianism. The Supreme Court of Canada seemed to share in this momentum. In 1970 it met its first case dealing with "race" since passage of the *Bill of Rights*. At issue in *R. v. Drybones*[26] was a provision in the *Indian Act* that imposed penalties upon an Indian person for intoxication "off a reserve," whereas the regular laws of the Northwest Territories where the offense occurred imposed a milder penalty for non-Indians and only for intoxication in a "public place." The Supreme Court decided that this section of the *Indian Act* violated Mr. Drybones' equality rights because Section 1(b) of the *Bill of Rights*, in the words of Justice Ritchie,

means at least that no individual or group of individuals is to be treated more harshly than another under the law, and I am therefore of opinion that an individual is denied equality before the law if it is made an offence punishable at law, on account of his race, for him to do something which his fellow Canadians are free to do without having committed any offence or having been made subject to any penalty.[27]

However, the limitations of the *Drybones* interpretation of "equality before the law" would soon become apparent. In *AG Canada v. Lavell*[28] another section of the *Indian Act* was challenged, which provided that an Indian woman who married a non-Indian man lost her Indian status and band membership. When an Indian man married a non-Indian woman, on the other hand, he retained his status and his wife actually gained status as an Indian and became a registered band member. In this case the Supreme Court decided that no violation of the *Bill of Rights* had occurred. Beginning with the principle that the *BNA Act* gave the federal Parliament constitutional authority to make laws for "Indians and Indian lands,"[29] the Court maintained that the fulfilment of this function would require distinctions between Indians and non-Indians. Otherwise the *Bill of Rights* would have to be seen as rendering the entire *Indian Act* inoperative, an option the Court rejected as inconsistent with parliamentary intent. Instead "equality before the law" was construed to mean "the equal subjection of all classes to the ordinary law of the land as administered in the ordinary courts."[30] *Drybones* could be distinguished because in that case his "race" subjected him to discriminatory treatment "in the administration and enforcement of the law before the ordinary courts of the land."[31] In *Lavell*, despite the distinctions between Indian men and Indian women and between Indian women and non-Indian women, the

Court ruled that the circumstances did not warrant interference under the *Bill of Rights*. Indian status and band membership, as Justice Beetz later elaborated, were instrumental to the application of the *Indian Act* and indispensable to Parliament's effective control over "Indians and Indian lands." Penal laws, such as was impugned in *Drybones*, were not in the same category.[32]

Clarification of the distinction between *Drybones* and *Lavell* was offered in a subsequent case, *AG Canada v. Canard*. Mrs. Canard objected that an executor had been appointed by the Department of Indian Affairs to administer her late husband's estate, against her wishes and without her knowledge. Non-Indians had the right to administer their deceased spouses' estates, so she claimed discrimination contrary to Section 1 (b) of the *Bill of Rights*. Justice Ritchie rejected her claim because

The civil right said to be denied to Mrs. Canard "that other Canadians not of her race enjoy" is a provincial right which is beyond the scope of the legislative authority of the Parliament of Canada, and which cannot therefore, in my view, be invoked in contra-distinction to the provisions of otherwise valid federal legislation so as to result in a denial . . . of "equality before the law" within the meaning of S. 1 (b) of the *Canadian Bill of Rights*. . . .

This is not a case like *R. v. Drybones* . . . where there was found to be inequality before the law because of the interaction of two federal statutes.[33]

Further clarification was provided in an unrelated case when the Court ruled:

This Court has held that S. 1 (b) of the *Canadian Bill of Rights* does not require that all federal statutes must apply to all individuals in the same manner. Legislation dealing with a particular class of people is valid if it is enacted for the purpose of achieving a valid federal objective.[34]

Within five years of *Drybones*, "equality before the law" had come to mean "equality when brought to face a charge before a judge."

In its direct confrontation with what it defined as racial discrimination in *Drybones*, the Supreme Court clearly stated that restrictions on the basis of "race" contravened the right to equality before the law. To define equality so narrowly as to mean that a law must apply equally only to persons *within* a particular group, the Court declared, would be to justify "the most glaring discriminatory legislation against a racial group."[35] On the other hand the Court was conscious that, by the wording of the bill, the rights and freedoms listed there "have existed and shall continue to exist," meaning that the bill "did not create new rights. Its purpose was to prevent infringement of existing rights."[36] Furthermore, in deference to parliamentary supremacy, the Court decided that even if a government act was discriminatory it could still be acceptable if it fulfilled "a valid federal objective."[37] Justice McIntyre explained in 1980:

The question which must be resolved in each case is whether such inequality as may be created by legislation affecting a special class . . . is arbitrary, capricious or unnecessary, or whether it is rationally based and acceptable as a necessary variation from the general principle of universal application of law to meet special conditions and to attain a necessary and desirable social objective.[38]

To fix the meaning of the law in terms of what is "rational," "necessary" or "acceptable" would seem to deny any meaning at all beyond what the judges felt to be the case at any given moment.[39] As a "protective shield," the *Bill of Rights* was not playing a particularly effective role.

Perceived problems with the *Bill of Rights* had an impact on the conceptualization and the specific wording of the *Charter of Rights and Freedoms*. The Charter was also a product of negotiation and compromise, particularly its keystone Section 15 on equality rights. In the fall of 1980, in the face of provincial reluctance for constitutional reform, Prime Minister Trudeau announced a federal proposal to patriate the constitution unilaterally, and he established a Special Joint Committee to consider the text for a new Canadian constitution, including a Charter of Rights.[40] In that highly politicized atmosphere of 1980-81, with federal and provincial governments competing for moral support, the parliamentary committee's discussions offered an opportunity to insert political programs into an entrenched constitution, and the federal negotiators were at least prepared to listen.[41] The final product read:

15. (1) Every individual is equal before and under the law and has the right to equal protection and equal benefit of the law without discrimination and, in particular, without discrimination based on race, national or ethnic origin, colour, religion, sex, age or mental or physical disability.

(2) Subsection (1) does not preclude any law, program or activity that has as its object the amelioration of conditions of disadvantaged individuals or groups including those that are disadvantaged because of race, national or ethnic origin, colour, religion, sex, age or mental or physical disability.

Racial discrimination headed the list of proscriptions, and the elaborate wording of Section 15 seemed to cover any conceivable operation of the law. The confusions arising under the *Bill of Rights* could no longer occur. A constitutional scholar was able to conclude that "S. 15 should be interpreted as providing for the universal application of every law. When a law draws a distinction between individuals, on any ground, that distinction is sufficient to constitute a breach of S. 15."[42]

One of his colleagues, however, commented more ominously:

Section 15 was developed primarily on public relations grounds as a means of co-opting highly visible and vocal interest groups into supporting the Trudeau government's unilateral constitutional restructuring. The public and legislative discussions concerning it provide little guidance to our judges as to how far or how fast it is desirable to eliminate all forms of discrimination in Canadian society.[43]

Still the Charter did contain another article which could conceivably affect the implementation of Section 15 as a guarantee of racial equality: "27. This Charter shall be interpreted in a manner consistent with the preservation and enhancement of the multicultural heritage of Canadians."

The Charter did not simply prohibit discrimination; it provided a positive guarantee that "everyone has the following fundamental freedoms...," "everyone has the right to life, liberty and security...," "every individual is equal."[44] Taken with Section 15 (2), this kind of wording suggested a readiness to interfere in support of individual rights, to take positive measures in furtherance of the constitutional guarantees. A similar conceptual orientation was displayed in the *Ontario Human Rights Code* when it was rewritten in 1981. In the original 1962 *Code* the preamble had declared: "it is public policy in Ontario that every person is free and equal in dignity and rights without regard to race."[45] In 1981 it became:

it is public policy in Ontario to recognize the dignity and worth of every person and to provide for equal rights and opportunities without discrimination that is contrary to law, and having as its aim the creation of a climate of understanding and mutual respect for the dignity and worth of each person so that each person feels a part of the community.[46]

The old Section 4 stated: "No person shall discriminate...." In 1981 Section 4 began: "Every person has a right to equal treatment...." The philosophical thrust was no longer protection against antisocial acts by aberrant individuals, but the active promotion of an egalitarian community based on the assertion of people's rights. Until this time Ontario's *Code*, and all the others modelled upon it, recognized only direct and deliberate discriminatory practices. By Section 10 in the new *Code*, Ontario added non-deliberate or "systemic" practices which were not intentionally discriminatory but which would have a discriminatory "result."[47] The correction of unequal conditions, rather than punishment of offenders, had become the human rights theme. The duties of a new Race Relations Division, set out in Section 27 of the 1981 *Code*, reflected the movement away from a complaints-based program to something far more proactive. The Division was granted a mandate

to inquire into incidents of and conditions leading or tending to lead to tension or conflict ... and take appropriate action to eliminate the source of tension or conflict;

to initiate investigations into problems ... that may arise in a community and encourage and coordinate plans, programs and activities to reduce or prevent such problems;

to promote, assist and encourage, public, municipal or private agencies ... to engage in programs to alleviate tensions and conflicts.

An examination of existing policy instruments, as Ontario's 1982 *Strategy for Race Relations* reported, had "clearly demonstrated the need for a more active promotion of harmonious race relations."[48]

Numerous other related policies participated in the directional shift towards more positive intervention. A Special Committee on the Participation of Visible Minorities in Canadian Society was formed in 1983 under MP Bob Daudlin as chair. Their 1984 report *Equality Now!*, issued following nationwide public hearings, recommended an assault on systemic discrimination and the active promotion of a hiring program for "visible" minorities.[49] Also in 1983 the federal government appointed Judge Rosalie Abella to conduct a Royal Commission on Equality in Employment. Her 1984 report strongly supported "affirmative action," which she called "employment equity," whose need she demonstrated statistically in existing employment and income discrepancies.[50] A "National Strategy on Race Relations" appeared in 1984, calling upon Canadians to participate in "helping minority groups to overcome barriers to full and equal participation in Canadian society" through "institutional change."[51] When Otto Jellinek launched Canada's "Programme of Action for the Second Decade to Combat Racism and Racial Discrimination" in 1985, he could admit that the existence of Canadian racism had been "well documented" by *Equality Now!* and *Equality in Employment*. "Today the law provides for equality. . . . The task now for our society is to translate these provisions into the reality of everyday life."[52] Another parliamentary report in 1985, *Equality for All*, endorsed the "systemic" or "results-oriented approach" to Section 15 of the Charter.[53] Then, less than two months before Section 15 was to come into effect in April 1985, Parliament amended the *Indian Act* to eliminate the disadvantage faced by Indian women who married non-Indian men, and granted individual bands the right to determine their own membership.[54] In 1986 the Abella Commission's recommendations were enacted as the *Employment Equity Act*,[55] committing the federal government and Crown corporations to affirmative hiring programs and requiring contractors and federally regulated businesses to move towards "proportional representation" in their workforce through "positive policies" and "reasonable accommodation." As a result of the government's response to *Equality Now!*, "visible minorities" were included as a "target group" under the federal Employment Equity program.[56] In 1988 Prime Minister Mulroney announced that an agreement had been reached on "redress" to Japanese Canadians for their World War II dislocation and violation of their rights. This announcement had great symbolic significance, for it recognized a responsibility for past injustice and signalled a determination to remedy its effects.[57]

A discursive change, a shift in sensibility, was evident in the measures of the 1980s, and the new direction was perhaps most explicitly captured in the multicultural policy by which Canadians had come to define themselves as a nation. In 1988 Canada introduced the world's first *Multiculturalism Act*,[58] which made "race relations" its top priority and "institutional change" its method. The *Multiculturalism Act*, along with Section 27 of the Charter, made diversity a central feature in the Canadian vision, an "organizing principle" of Canadian life and law, but a diversity conditional upon equal respect and equal opportunity. Multiculturalism therefore became an instrument to ensure access, with proactive and remedial measures aimed at social structures and systemic disadvantages long considered benign.[59] Discrimination had been redefined, and the policies and agencies designed to address a previous definition were no longer seen as effective. The "protective shield" was being replaced by a "remedial sword" in the struggle against injustice and inequality.

In April 1985 the Supreme Court of Canada gave a ruling exhibiting its concurrence with 1980s definitions of equality,[60] at the same time indicating that the "frozen rights" concept had thawed and that the Court was joining the remedial stream. Rejecting *Bill of Rights* jurisprudence, Justice Dickson on behalf of the majority wrote that

the Canadian Charter of Rights and Freedoms does not simply "recognize and declare" existing rights as they are circumscribed by legislation current at the time of the Charter's entrenchment. The language of the Charter is imperative . . . intended to set a standard upon which present *as well as future* legislation is to be tested.[61]

In proceeding with this analysis, he said, the Court must first determine the *purpose* of the legislation in the broadest sense. Then, if the purpose is deemed constitutionally appropriate, the Court must next examine the law's *effect*. If the effect or impact was discriminatory, even if the purpose was valid, the Court would overturn the law.[62] Justice Wilson agreed with the majority result, but she insisted that a law's purpose was irrelevant in determining its validity. The Charter, she claimed, was "first and foremost an effects-oriented document,"[63] and that was all the Court needed to consider. Interesting, too, was Justice Dickson's contention that "equality" did not mean "identical treatment." "In fact," he concluded, "the interests of true equality may well require differentiation in treatment."[64] Positive "equality," as much as its negative "discrimination," had clearly undergone a redefinition.

In another case that same year the Court clarified its definition of equality and the legal remedies available to create it.[65] "Adverse effect," the Court confirmed, was the only criterion required to prove discrimination. "The proof of intent, a necessary requirement in our approach to criminal and punitive legislation, should not be a governing factor in construing human rights legislation aimed at the elimination of discrimination."[66]

The momentum peaked in the first Charter Section 15 case actually to be argued before the Court. The facts of *Andrews v. Law Society of BC*[67] were deceptively simple: a man who met all the qualifications to be called to the bar of British Columbia except Canadian citizenship laid a complaint under the Charter when his bar application was rejected solely on grounds of citizenship. In response to Mr. Andrews' challenge the members of the Court generated three separate and complex judgments. For the sake of assessing *Andrews'* place in the development of equality rights, however, it is possible to focus on the decision of Justice McIntyre and its interpretation of the meaning of Section 15 (1), for in this all the written opinions generally concurred. Justice McIntyre definitively put aside the protective shield and waved the remedial sword: "The promotion of equality entails the promotion of a society in which all are secure in the knowledge that they are recognized at law as human beings equally deserving of concern, respect and consideration. It has a large remedial component." The old "similarly situated" test of equality, as applied in *Bill of Rights* decisions, was "seriously deficient." "If it were to be applied literally, it could be used to justify the Nuremberg laws of Adolf Hitler."[68] The wording of Section 15 (1), with its "four basic rights," was intended to overcome the defects of the *Bill of Rights*, Justice McIntyre continued, and in doing so it "reflected the expanded concept of discrimination being developed under the various Human Rights Codes." Every Canadian jurisdiction had passed laws attacking discrimination, and the principles developed in those laws and the jurisprudence associated with them created a broad context within which to understand how Section 15 should be applied. The Section guaranteed equality "without discrimination," and on the basis of its historical evolution Justice McIntyre was able to conclude that

discrimination may be described as a distinction, whether intentional or not but based on grounds relating to personal characteristics of the individual or group, which has the effect of imposing burdens, obligations, or disadvantages on such individual or group not imposed upon others, or which withholds or limits access to opportunities, benefits, and advantages available to other members of society. Distinctions based on personal characteristics attributed to an individual solely on the basis of association with a group will rarely escape the charge of discrimination, while those based on an individual's merit will rarely be so classed.[69]

The differences among the justices arose not over the McIntyre interpretation of Section 15, but whether the discrimination in Andrews' particular case was justifiable under Section 1 which recognized that "reasonable limits" could be imposed on Charter rights. Justice McIntyre himself, despite his expansionary views on equality, decided that the restriction against non-citizens was reasonable. The majority decision, written by Justice Wilson, was that Section 1 could not be invoked to save the discriminatory feature in BC's regulation.[70] Mr. Andrews won his case, though in the meantime he had become a Canadian citizen anyway.

One other case from 1985 revealed the direction of Charter jurisprudence. Under the *Immigration Act* of 1976[71] persons already physically present in Canada could not apply for landed immigrant status: either they had to leave the country and apply from elsewhere, or claim special status as refugees. In order to render this process efficient, and to eliminate "unfounded" claims more quickly, the Act permitted the Immigration Appeal Board to reject applicants for refugee status on the basis of written evidence. If the applicant's sworn statement and transcript of an interview with an Immigration official seemed less than convincing, the Board could decide not to proceed to an actual hearing with the applicant. In 1985 the Supreme Court of Canada heard appeals against this procedure brought by seven individuals under a single representative case, *Singh v. Minister of Employment and Immigration*.[72] The Court emphasized that it was not considering the merits of individual claims but the refugee determination procedures by which the claims had been denied. A unanimous Court decided that the *Immigration Act* violated the claimants' rights, but the judges divided three to three on the reasons for their decision. One interpretation, written by Justice Beetz, was that the refugee procedures were contrary to Section 2 (e) of the *Bill of Rights*, which guaranteed that "no law of Canada shall be construed or applied so as to . . . (e) deprive a person of the right to a fair hearing in accordance with the principles of fundamental justice for the determination of his rights and obligations." Since Mr. Singh had been denied a hearing, his rights under the *Bill* were wrongfully restricted.[73] The other view was put by Justice Wilson and was based on Section 7 of the Charter: "Everyone has the right to life, liberty and security of the person and the right not to be deprived thereof except in accordance with the principles of fundamental justice." The Charter argument was perhaps the more interesting. Section 7 guarantees rights to *everyone*, and Justice Wilson found "that the term includes every human being who is physically present in Canada and by virtue of such presence is amenable to Canadian law."[74] In *Singh v. Minister of Employment and Immigration* the "principles of fundamental justice" were held to include a fair hearing, but the even more fundamental principle that the Charter applied to "everyone" would mean that Section 15 equality rights could also be invoked to support an immigration claim.[75] Either by the Bill or the Charter the *Immigration Act* provisions were struck down, and a strong case was made that immigration procedures, would have to operate in full accordance with the Charter guarantees.

Not only had the Charter overcome the weaknesses of the *Bill of Rights*, but in *Singh* the Bill itself was brought into line with the "correctional" mode in rights interpretation. In a few key Charter decisions the Court had amended or rejected the discriminatory principles incorporated in the cases studied in this book, along with many of the judicial practices by which they had been created and maintained. Charter Section 1, requiring the courts to determine limits "as can be demonstrably justified in a free and democratic society," demanded an assessment of methods and alternatives available to the elected representatives. To fulfil this task, as Justice McLachlin has written,[76] judges would have to embrace an expanded definition of acceptable evidence. Intervenors were admitted in increasing numbers – 10 parties intervened in *Andrews*, for example – and there was increasing reference to scholarly interpretation, to the benefits of American experience with entrenched rights, and to international agreements to which Canada was committed.[77]

As a consequence of these more elastic procedures, the courts were beginning to recognize the creativity of the judicial role. *Stare decisis* was no longer considered a restraint, as the explicit rejection of previous decisions had illustrated. Reasons for judgment seemed to display an understanding of the law as an expansive and responsive element in the social fabric. Just before he became chief justice, Brian Dickson wrote that a constitution

is drafted with an eye to the future. Its function is to provide a continuing framework for the legitimate exercise of governmental power and, when joined by a Bill or a Charter of Rights, for the unremitting protection of individual rights and liberties. Once enacted, its provisions cannot easily be repealed or amended. It must, therefore, be capable of growth and development over time to meet new social, political and historical realities often unimagined by its framers. The judiciary is the guardian of the Constitution and must, in interpreting its provisions, bear these considerations in mind. Professor Paul Freund expressed this idea aptly when he admonished the American courts "not to read the provisions of the constitution like a last will and testament lest it become one."[78]

2. APPREHENSIONS

According to the trajectory traced in the previous section of this chapter, "race" should no longer be a consideration in Canadian life or law. Developments from the 1970s and 1980s, of which the Charter was a part, would render the conditions leading to the case studies impossible to repeat, and besides, those four decisions would not fit the common sense (community standards) of the post-Charter era. Turning from legal theories to some indicators of social reality for many Canadians, however, it is apparent that these expectations are not entirely warranted. Opinion surveys on the eve of the Charter revealed that a majority of Canadians would admit to some degree of racial bias, and 16 percent were defined by researchers as "hard-core" racists. Africans and Asians were identified as unwelcome marital partners or in-laws, and about one third of Canadians reported that they might move if many "visible minorities" came to live in their neighbourhood.[79] Surveys conducted later in the 1980s and into the mid-1990s showed little change. In 1986, 42 percent of "Anglo-Saxons" expressed concern about "more and more minorities" moving into their neighbourhood.[80] In 1994, after more than a decade of Charter-consciousness and policy reform, the percentage of a national sample labelled "hard-core" racists remained exactly the same at 16.[81] Especially indicative were studies tracing attitudes toward immigration: survey after survey showed that as many as half of all Canadians believed there were too many immigrants of Asian or African origin, and up to three quarters expressed a concern that immigrants should not change the "character" of Canada and should assimilate to mainstream culture and values.[82] A survey analyst concluded in 1994 that these figures seemed to represent a "retreat" from Canada's "tradition of tolerance and compassion,"[83] though historically no "retreat" was apparent: the figures and the specific concerns were remarkably consistent with previous decades. Meanwhile, surveys among the "victim" groups produced reports that more than half, and sometimes as high as 85 percent, of African, Asian and Jewish Canadians felt that they had been the targets of racial discrimination.[84] Since different surveys asked different questions of different population samples, it is not possible to depict trends over time with any acceptable degree of accuracy. The poll results do, however, suggest that there was no counterpart shift in common sense comparable to the developments in public policy during the same period.

To the impressionistic evidence from survey samples could be added more objective data illustrating the survival of "race" as a meaningful factor in Canadian life. At its most extreme, racial antagonism continued to provoke harassment, vandalism and assault. In 1993, according to B'nai B'rith, there were more "hate crimes" than in any year since records began in 1981, with Jews and African Canadians the most frequent victim groups.[85] More indicative of Canadian reality were census data from 1981, 1986 and 1991 revealing that "visible minorities," and especially African Canadians, had consistently lower-than-average incomes and higher levels of unemployment. Even when qualifications, experience and regional factors were considered, Canadians of African and Asian origin earned less than white Canadians in comparable circumstances.[86] To test the degree to which racial discrimination was responsible for this discrepancy, a study was conducted in 1985 (similar to Pierre Berton's in 1948) to test employer responses to white and visible-minority job applicants. Sending actors with comparable resumes to more than 400 employment interviews, the researchers found that white applicants received three times as many job offers. They also reported that white applicants were treated with greater courtesy during the interviews and when successful were offered higher salaries.[87] A national survey of 672 employment recruiters in 1987 reported that 87 percent of corporate recruiters and 100 percent of employment agencies received explicit requests to discriminate by "race" when selecting personnel; these requests were actually fulfilled by 73 percent of the corporate recruiters and 94 percent of the private agencies.[88] A series of tests run by the Canadian Civil Liberties Association in the 1980s and 1990s into employment agencies showed a consistent 80 percent willing to "screen" applicants according to racial requests from employers.[89] Racial discrimination was widely reported in housing as well, and in one 1986 "test" of apartment rentals in Toronto more than 40 percent of applications were denied on apparently racial grounds.[90] Perhaps most insidious of all, studies by the Toronto Board of Education showed that black school children were streamed into "basic" courses at a rate more than double that for white children, a factor no doubt contributing to a higher drop-out rate for African-Canadian students than for any other identified group.[91]

And so "race" remained a "factor of consequence," determining where some Canadians could live, what they could study in school, how they could earn their living, raising the question of whether human rights and the redefinition of equality had penetrated this dark corner of the Canadian experience. And while "race" had been eliminated in explicit terms from immigration law, many observers still found a racial "effect" in the regulations. For example, a disproportionate number of immigrants admitted under the "Entrepreneur" and "Investor" programs, which grant entry to anyone willing to invest a substantial sum of money in Canada, came from non-European countries, leading one study to describe these programs as a "reinstituted head tax" requiring Asians to buy their way into Canada.[92] Regulations for the unwealthy have meanwhile become more stringent: in 1992 nannies were required to have completed a grade 12 education and a six-month training course. The year before the new regulations, 68 percent of immigrant nannies came from the Philippines and 4.5 percent from Britain; the year following, 7 percent came from the Philippines and 30 percent from Britain.[93] At the same time bonus points for assisted relatives were reduced and the cost of applying for an adult relative under family reunification was $450, non-refundable in case of failure, a situation MP Roy Pagtakhan of Winnipeg, himself of Filipino origin, described as "systemic racism" since its chief impact was felt by Third World applicants.[94] In 1995 a "right of landing" fee was inaugurated by the government, requiring anyone over age 19 seeking permanent residence in Canada to pay a sum of $975. Although presented by the government as a tax-saving measure, by having immigrants pay a share of their own processing costs, immigration advocates noted that the new fee fell heaviest on Third World immigrants.[95] Even refugees faced a kind of "continuous journey" clause, by which they could come to Canada only from their country of origin, and airlines were made responsible for the return passage of immigrants refused entry into Canada. These policies need not imply overt racism, as some commentators suggested,[96] but they did coincide with an anxiety, reflected in public opinion polls, concerning the rate of immigration of people of colour.

Despite profound changes in the law, the "remedial" phase in rights policy beginning around 1980 had limited impact upon "race relations" in Canada. By most measurements, racial minorities were in more or less the same situation more than a decade after the "sword" was unsheathed. Why, then, was the legal reform not being translated into genuine change in people's lives? Had the Charter done nothing better than constitutionalize the racial status quo? Some trends were emerging, as the Charter entered its second decade, suggesting that the courts had not been reequipped to fulfil their new responsibilities.

One problem complicating the relationship between the new values of human rights and the daily experience of many Canadians was that the laws incorporating those values remained ambiguous. Most human rights codes did not define "discrimination," and the same action may be considered discriminatory or non-discriminatory depending on quite arbitrary circumstances. According to one commentator this has created a "legislative mosaic" in which certain practices may or may not be illegal, depending on the precise language of each protective code.[97] On the same day in 1985, the Supreme Court of Canada decided in favour of Theresa O'Malley, a Seventh Day Adventist in dispute with Simpsons-

Sears over Saturday work, and against K. S. Bhinder's claim that the
CNR discriminated against his religion by requiring him as a maintenance electrician to wear a safety helmet over his turban. Both plaintiffs
identified employers' regulations which interfered with the practice of
their religion. The difference in the two cases was the wording of the
human rights laws under which the complaints were laid, the *Ontario
Human Rights Code* for Mrs. O'Malley and the *Canadian Human Rights Act*
for Mr. Bhinder. The CNR's hard-hat rule was definable as a "bona fide
occupational requirement" under the federal *Act*, and so its enforcement
was acceptable.[98] Although the Court reversed its own *Bhinder* decision
in 1990 by deciding that a "bona fide occupational requirement" cannot be
used to excuse "adverse effect discrimination,"[99] the signal from *Bhinder*
and *O'Malley* was that "basic human rights" could vary from case to case.
In a series of decisions on mandatory retirement in 1990, employees covered by the federal Charter could claim discrimination, but those complaining under the *Ontario Human Rights Code* could not because Section 9
(a) defined the protected age range to be from 18 to 65.[100] A "rights
mosaic" derived as well from the power of legislatures to exempt a statute
from human rights protection, making it possible to "treat people differently" and still stay within the law. In 1992 the Supreme Court of Canada
permitted Ontario insurance companies to charge discriminatory rates
according to a customer's age, sex and marital status on the ground that
Section 21 of the *Ontario Human Rights Code* provided an exemption for
insurance contracts.[101] It may be noted that the *Code* addresses only "discrimination that is *contrary to law*," thus allowing legislators to enact discriminatory regulations with full legality.[102] Most human rights codes
contain explicit exemptions for religious, charitable, racial and ethnic associations, permitting them to accept as members or to employ only persons
belonging to an identifiable group.[103] Rights exemptions on grounds of
"race" are of course *intended* for positive purposes, to foster group
integrity or to overcome disadvantages, but they are also entrenching the
concept of differential rights in the law and the public consciousness and
their unintended results in both social and legal terms could be ominous.

Even the precise language of Section 15 of the Charter has not made it
immune to similar ambiguities. The Supreme Court of Canada has
demonstrated a willingness to define equality rights as group rights, so
that they could vary from group to group and result in the restoration of
a "similarly situated" conceptualization of equality. The Charter's intention, or that of its architect, was entirely otherwise. Pierre Trudeau was
confident that the Charter would ensure that every Canadian individual

must "enjoy certain fundamental, inalienable rights and cannot be deprived of them *by* any collectivity (state or government) or *on behalf of* any collectivity (nation, ethnic group, religious group or other)."[104] Walter Tarnopolsky ably articulated the conventional wisdom at the time of the Charter's inception when he pointed out that

an assertion of a human right emphasizes the proposition that everyone is to be treated the same *regardless* of his or her membership in a particular identifiable group. The assertion of group rights, on the other hand, bases itself upon a claim of an individual or a group of individuals *because* of membership in an identifiable group.[105]

There are many group rights recognized in the Charter – language rights in Sections 16-23, aboriginal rights in Section 25, denominational education in Section 29 – but equality rights were not initially among them. Section 15 (1) guaranteed equality to "Every individual . . . *without* discrimination" based on group membership. As Justice McIntyre put it in *Andrews*: "Distinctions based on personal characteristics attributed to an individual solely on the basis of association with a group will rarely escape the charge of discrimination."[106] Section 15 (2) permits certain exceptions so that remedial programs designed to overcome "conditions of disadvantaged individuals or groups" should not be held to violate the individual principle expressed in Section 15 (1). But in 1989 the Court suggested that "discrimination" could occur only when its recipient belonged to a certain kind of group, particularly a "discrete and insular minority."[107] While superficially a benevolent interpretation directing protection towards those suffering "historical disadvantage or vulnerability to political and social prejudice," Justice Wilson's invention in *Turpin* of a concept of "frozen disadvantage" could require Section 15 (1) claims to be cast in terms of group membership. If such an interpretation were to survive, the courts would have to decide which group, in competing circumstances, is most deserving of their sympathetic attention. Since then there has been another apparent shift. In a 1990 minority opinion, Justice McLachlin noted that the rights of a citizen to protection under the Charter were defined differently in the Court's *Andrews* and *Turpin* decisions. "In my view," she stated, "the essential requirements for discrimination under S15 remain as set forth in *Andrews*."[108] Then in 1995 all nine justices of the Supreme Court of Canada endorsed a version consistent with *Andrews* and rejected the "discrete and insular minority" criterion, finding "that membership in such a disadvantaged group is not an essential precondition for bringing a claim under S15 of the Charter."[109] Judicial inconsistency over the meaning of the Charter has provoked confusion and cynicism in the minds of many Canadians.[110] Even more dangerous, however, are the constitutional ghettos that may be created by decisions which confirm legal distinctions, stereotypes and differential treatment based on group membership.

3. REFLECTIONS

These impressions combine to suggest that public policy may not have changed so much as the public seems to believe. There is still the potential for different laws for different people, definitions of equality that vary from group to group in assigning protections and benefits, legally justified discrimination and restricted access, depending on how the judges interpret human rights codes and the Charter. Various (and sometimes conflicting) solutions for this dilemma have been offered by Canadian critics. It has been suggested, for example, that judges could be elected, which would render them accountable for decisions made and provide a mechanism for the expression of the public voice.[111] There could be pre-appointment hearings, as occurs in the United States, to ascertain a prospective judge's views on issues of current concern.[112] Judges may be deliberately appointed to represent certain groups or points of view in society,[113] or there could be post-appointment seminars to sensitize judges to selected issues.[114] Decisions could be opened up to a wider range of influences and points of view through extending the definition of admissible evidence to give the courts more information to apply to a question in dispute,[115] through expert research explicitly commissioned by the courts to provide the non-legal information that is so often vital to Charter decisions,[116] through encouraging interventions by groups with a special interest or knowledge in a given case.[117]

What this variety of criticisms suggests is a recognition that rights issues are not yet settled in Canada, but the implicit confidence that procedural reform can make law precise and scientific, or achieve an immediate social transformation, seems misplaced. If there is a final impression from the historical case studies, it is probably that "race," rights and law are imbued in a broad cultural sensibility. This would help to explain why changes in the past have rarely been accomplished through direct frontal attacks in the courts. Even *Noble and Wolf*, the single "victory" examined here, participated in a much wider shift in consciousness. Courtroom struggle bore fruit only when it was accompanied by struggle in the legislatures, the press, academic research, and public conversation; that is, the sensibility itself had to shift, and not just one of its instruments. History does not necessarily repeat itself, but there appears to be good reason to believe that this general condition remains substantially true.[118]

Is the Canadian dream then an illusion? No doubt many of the dream's underpinnings have been challenged in this book, as they relate to a presumed tradition of tolerance and equality, and yet its very survival represents something significant, something "real," about Canadians. We would not select these characteristics for ourselves, even link them to our national identity, unless we held them to be valuable. The national dream indicates that Canadians want a tolerant nation, a legal system that promotes equality, a national history that makes sense of ourselves as a multicultural people. Left as undisturbed illusion, the dream can perpetuate inequality by denying the very existence of racial disadvantage; put forward as an unrealized ambition, the dream can become a force for social change. Experience suggests that a new sensibility will emerge to reconcile the quest for equality with standards of fairness, but its precise nature cannot be predicted or taken for granted. Its direction may very well be influenced by the way our national dream is interpreted. As has been the case throughout our history, a shift in sensibility will involve something more than proclamations by courts, commissions and legislatures; it is a broader process, akin to a national conversation, testing attitudes against realities and assessing the way our law represents our ambitions. It can benefit from a genuine reflection upon our past, to learn how our institutions have neglected reality for many Canadians, how common sense has shifted its ground over time. To understand 1914 or 1939 or the 1950s in their own context leads to an appreciation for how context operates, how "orienting notions" actually do orient people's perceptions of what is right or what needs attention, what is achievable and who should do it. What was true for previous generations remains true for our own. We are not nearly so unique as we sometimes like to think, and this is a profound lesson to be taken from historical study. Clifford Geertz put a similar sentiment with unmatchable eloquence:

To see ourselves as others see us can be eye-opening. To see others as sharing a nature with ourselves is the merest decency. But it is from the far more difficult achievement of seeing ourselves amongst others, as a local example of the forms human life has locally taken, a case among cases, a world among worlds, that [comes] the largeness of mind, without which objectivity is self-congratulation and tolerance a sham.[119]

Notes

The following abbreviations are used throughout the Notes.

Archives

CJC   Canadian Jewish Congress, National Archives
DND   Department of National Defence
NA   National Archives of Canada
OJA   Ontario Jewish Archives
OPA   Ontario Public Archives
PABC Provincial Archives of British Columbia
PANS Public Archives of Nova Scotia
SAB   Saskatchewan Archives Board

Case Reports

AC   *Appeal Cases, Judicial Committee of the Privy Council*
BCR   *British Columbia Reports*
CA   *Cour d'appel, Québec*
CCC   *Canadian Criminal Cases*
CCLT *Canadian Cases on the Law of Torts*
CLJ   *Canadian Law Journal*
CPR   *Canadian Patent Reporter*
CR   *Criminal Reports*
CS   *Rapports judiciares de Québec, cour supérieure*
CSP   *Cours des Sessions de la paix*
DLR   *Dominion Law Reports*
ER   *English Reports*
MPR   *Maritime Provincial Reports*
NSR   *Nova Scotia Reports*
OLR   *Ontario Law Reports*
OR   *Ontario Reports*
OWN   *Ontario Weekly Notes*
QKB   *Quebec Court of Appeal, King's Bench*
SCR   *Supreme Court Reports*

SC   *Rapports judiciares de Québec, Superior Court*
UCQB *Upper Canada Court of Queen's Bench*
US   *United States Supreme Court*
WLR   *Western Law Reporter*
WLT   *Western Law Times*
WWD *Western Weekly Digest*
WWR *Western Weekly Reports*

Statutes

BS   *British Statutes*
SA   *Statutes of Alberta*
SBC   *Statutes of British Columbia*
SC   *Statutes of Canada*
SM   *Statutes of Manitoba*
SNB   *Statutes of New Brunswick*
SNS   *Statutes of Nova Scotia*
SO   *Statutes of Ontario*
SQ   *Statutes of Quebec*
SS   *Statutes of Saskatchewan*
SUC   *Statutes of Upper Canada*

INVITATION

1 For example, in a discussion of the Yonge Street "race riot" of 4 May 1992, Austin Clarke commented that despite recent troubles, Canada "is still *north* of the border of America and of racism" (*Public Enemies: Police Violence and Black Youth* [Toronto: HarperCollins, 1992], 18).
2 Canadian Press, 1 April 1991, reporting a survey conducted by Goldfarb for the Heritage Project of the C. R. Bronfman Foundation.
3 *Maclean's*, 3 July 1989.
4 For example, in a 1955 essay on *American and Canadian Viewpoints* (Washington, DC: American Council on Education, 1955), Dennis H. Wrong wrote: "Canadians are today perhaps more aware of the differences in their attitudes toward the law than of anything else distinguishing them from Americans" (38). Things had not changed 40 years later, when Bronwyn Drainie could write in the *Globe and Mail*, 7 September 1995: "Fairness is one of the great Canadian virtues, and when it comes to managing a social and legal nightmare like the Bernardo trial, citizens of this country can look with a certain grim satisfaction at the fair and measured way that case was handled by our court system. The shenanigans surrounding the O. J. Simpson trial, running concurrently in the United States, could not have presented a more eloquent example of the cultural difference between our two countries."
5 *Globe and Mail*, 1 July 1995.
6 *Hansard*, 19 February 1981, 7474-76.
7 When case files are 60 years old they are transferred to the National Archives.
8 The *Female Labour Act* for *Quong Wing* and the *Immigration Act* for *Narine-Singh*.

9 The Consolidated Chinese Benevolent Association for *Quong Wing*, the Canadian Jewish Congress for *Noble and Wolf* and the Jewish Labour Committee and the Ontario Labour Committee for Human Rights for *Narine-Singh*. Some local records from the ad hoc committee in support of Fred Christie were also found in private hands in Montreal.

1 ORIENTATION

1 Quoted in Michael Banton, *Racial Theories* (Cambridge: Cambridge University Press, 1987), vii.
2 Quoted in Carl Berger, *The Sense of Power: Studies in the Ideas of Canadian Imperialism, 1867-1914* (Toronto: University of Toronto Press, 1970), 230-31.
3 For example, see Frank M. Snowden, Jr., *Before Color Prejudice: The Ancient View of Blacks* (Cambridge, MA: Harvard University Press, 1983).
4 Pierre Bourdieu, *In Other Words: Essays Towards a Reflexive Sociology* (Stanford: Stanford University Press, 1990), 52.
5 Clifford Geertz, *Local Knowledge: Further Essays in Interpretive Anthropology* (New York: Basic Books, 1983), 10-11.
6 For example, see Mariana Valverde, *The Age of Light, Soap and Water: Moral Reform in English Canada, 1885-1925* (Toronto: McClelland and Stewart, 1991), esp. chap. 5, "Racial Purity, Sexual Purity and Immigration Policy."
7 James S. Woodsworth, *Strangers within Our Gates, or Coming Canadians*, with an introduction by Marilyn Barber (Toronto: University of Toronto Press, 1909; rpt. ed. 1972), 76, 84, 102, 108-9, 116, 132, 155, 158, 164, 181-82, 230-32.
8 Quoted in R. Bruce Shepard, "Plain Racism: The Reaction Against Oklahoma Black Immigration to the Canadian Plains," *Prairie Forum*, 10 (1985): 375. The petition was endorsed by Boards of Trade in Strathcona, Morinville, Fort Saskatchewan and Calgary, Alberta, Yorkton and Saskatoon, Saskatchewan and Winnipeg, Manitoba.
9 Quoted in Kay J. Anderson, *Vancouver's Chinatown: Racial Discourse in Canada, 1875-1980* (Montreal and Kingston: McGill-Queen's University Press, 1991), 90.
10 *Hansard*, 27 March 1903, 597-600.
11 *Hansard*, 16 December 1907, 700.
12 Ibid., 722.
13 Ibid., 732-38.
14 Ibid., 738.
15 *Hansard*, 8 May 1922, 1510, 1514, 1515, 1516.
16 Ibid., 1555-56, 1562, 1564.
17 For example, Robert E. Park, *Race and Culture* (Glencoe, IL: Free Press, 1950).
18 Gunnar Myrdal, *An American Dilemma: The Negro Problem and Modern Democracy*, 2 vols. (New York: Harper & Row, 1944).
19 John Murray Gibbon, *Canadian Mosaic: The Making of a Northern Nation* (Toronto: McClelland and Stewart, 1938), v.

20 W. Burton Hurd, "Racial Origins and Nativity of the Canadian People," *Census of Canada, 1931*, Vol. 13 (Ottawa: Supply and Services, 1942), vii.

21 Ibid., 567-68.

22 Ibid., 571, 636, 685, 693, 700.

23 Ibid., 827.

24 *Hansard*, 12 February 1936, 151.

25 *Hansard*, 17 February 1938, 570.

26 John Dollard, *Caste and Class in a Southern Town* (Garden City, NY: Doubleday, 1937).

27 T. Adorno, E. Frenkel-Brunswick, D. Levinson and R. Sanforo, *The Authoritarian Personality* (New York: Harper & Row, 1950).

28 For example, see Gordon Allport, *The Nature of Prejudice* (Cambridge, MA: Addison-Wesley, 1954); Thomas F. Pettigrew, "Personality and Sociocultural Factors in Intergroup Attitudes: A Cross-National Comparison," *Journal of Conflict Resolution*, 2 (1958): 29-42.

29 Franz Boas, "History and Science in Anthropology," *American Anthropology*, 38 (1936): 140.

30 For a clause-by-clause discussion of the UNESCO document, see Ashley Montagu, *Statement on Race* (New York: Oxford University Press, 1951).

31 *Hansard*, 17 July 1944, 4925-26.

32 Ibid., 4929.

33 Ibid., 4935.

34 "Chinatown! Time was when that foreign quarter . . . had an aura of wickedness for the Vancouver consciousness. . . . How it has changed! Or perhaps, how we, under the impact of World War Two have changed. China is now our ally, and visitors look at Chinatown through new eyes" (Vancouver *Sun*, 1 May 1943, quoted in Anderson, *Vancouver's Chinatown*, 177).

35 *Hansard*, 2 June 1952, 3079.

36 Norman J. Berrill, "The Myth of White Supremacy," *Saturday Night*, 27 October 1956.

37 Quoted in Ian Bushnell, *The Captive Court: A Study of the Supreme Court of Canada* (Montreal and Kingston: McGill-Queen's University Press, 1992), 56. Justice Anglin's views were reflected as well in the United States Supreme Court in the early years of the 20th century, where "the common law was recognized as the distinct subject matter of legal science – as that body of doctrine that emerged when prior judicial decisions were systematically studied with a view to their principled coherence" (Paul W. Kahn, *Legitimacy and History* [New Haven: Yale University Press, 1992], 110).

38 For example, see Donald E. Fouts, "Policy-Making in the Supreme Court of Canada, 1950-1960," in Glendon Schubert and David Danelski, eds., *Comparative Judicial Behavior: Cross-Cultural Studies of Political Decision-Making in the East and West* (New York: Oxford University Press, 1969), 257-91; Mark R. MacGuigan, "Precedent and Policy in the Supreme Court," *Canadian Bar Review*, 45 (1967): 627-65; Patrick J. Monahan, "Judicial Review and Democ-

racy: A Theory of Judicial Review," *UBC Law Review*, 21 (1987): 87-164, and "Commentary," 165-206; Paul Weiler, *In the Last Resort: A Critical Study of the Supreme Court of Canada* (Toronto: Carswell Methuen, 1974); Bertha Wilson, "Decision-Making in the Supreme Court," *University of Toronto Law Journal*, 36 (1986): 227-48.

39 A. V. Dicey, *The Law of the Constitution*, 10th ed. (London: Macmillan, 1965), 39.

40 *British Statutes* (BS) 1867 c. 3, s. 91 and 92.

41 *AG Ontario v. AG Canada (Reference Appeal)*, [1912] AC 571.

42 Peter W. Hogg, *Constitutional Law of Canada*, 2nd ed. (Toronto: Carswell, 1985), 257-59.

43 Ibid., 88-89. In the early years after Confederation, Hogg explains, the federal government dominated the provinces "akin to a colonial relationship." But Privy Council decisions, aided by tendencies within Canada toward decentralization, "elevated the provinces to coordinate status with the Dominion." This was especially true under the tutelage of Lord Watson (1880-99) and Lord Haldane (1911-28).

44 Bora Laskin, "An Inquiry into the Diefenbaker Bill of Rights," *Canadian Bar Review*, 37 (1959): 77-78. F. R. Scott, *Civil Liberties and Canadian Federalism* (Toronto: University of Toronto Press, 1959), argued that "if we go back to our constitutional roots in English history we find several notable formulations of rights and liberties, from Magna Carta in 1215 down to the Bill of Rights of 1689. . . . The theoretical sovereignty of the British Parliament has tended to blind us to the reality of the limitations upon that sovereignty residing in the theory of government these documents proclaim. . . . Parliament is restrained in England by certain principles of government almost as effectively as if they were written into a binding constitution" (14-15). Scott further identified "the established rule that all statutes should be strictly interpreted if they limit or reduce the rights of the citizen. Parliament must always be presumed to have intended the least interference with our freedom, not the most" (26). As will be shown in subsequent chapters, there were Canadian judges who accepted this tradition of a common law guarantee of equality.

45 W. R. Riddell, *The Constitution of Canada in Its History and Practical Working* (New Haven: Yale University Press, 1920), 98-100. In the first two paragraphs quoted here, Riddell was repeating verbatim comments from his own judicial decisions in 1909 and 1908, respectively.

46 National Archives (NA), RG 25, G-1, Vol. 1875, file 558, H. U. Granow to O. D. Skelton, 14 March 1938. I am grateful to Myron Momryk of the National Archives for bringing this file to my attention.

47 Ibid., reply, 27 June 1938.

48 S. 91 ss.25; S. 92 ss.13.

49 Canada, Parliament, Sessional Papers, Vol. 36, No. 13, 1902, No. 54, *Report of the Royal Commission on Chinese and Japanese Immigration*, including appen-

dices; Robert Huttenback, *Racism and Empire: White Settlers and Colored Immigrants in the British Self-Governing Colonies, 1830-1910* (Ithaca: Cornell University Press, 1976).

50 *Statutes of British Columbia* (SBC) 1872 c. 39; 1895 c. 20; 1907 c. 16; *Statutes of Saskatchewan* (SS) 1908 c. 2. For a list of the disadvantages deriving from disfranchisement, see Canada, Parliament, Senate, *Proceedings of the Special Committee on Human Rights and Fundamental Freedoms* (Ottawa, 1950), 277-79.

51 For example, *Statutes of Canada* (SC) 1885 c. 41. Originally "an Indian normally resident on an Indian reservation" was disqualified from voting. In 1948 the *Dominion Elections Act* was amended to read "For the purpose of this provision 'Indian' means any person wholly or partly of Indian blood who is entitled to receive any annuity or other benefit under any treaty with the Crown" (SC 1948 c. 46, s. 6 ss. f).

52 For more detail see James W. St. G. Walker, " 'Race' and Recruitment in World War I: Enlistment of Visible Minorities in the Canadian Expeditionary Force," *Canadian Historical Review*, 70 (1989): 1-26.

53 For example, SC 1879 c. 34, s. 7 and 8; SC 1880 c. 28, s. 95 and 96.

54 For example, Anderson, *Vancouver's Chinatown*, 90.

55 SBC 1884 c. 2; 1899 c. 39; 1900 c. 18; 1908 c. 3; 1910 c. 30.

56 Ken Adachi, *The Enemy That Never Was* (Toronto: McClelland and Stewart, 1976), 142-45; Patricia Roy, "Educating the 'East': British Columbia and the Oriental Question in the Interwar Years," *BC Studies*, 18 (1973): 51-52; W. Peter Ward, *White Canada Forever: Popular Attitudes and Public Policy toward Orientals in British Columbia* (Montreal: McGill-Queen's University Press, 1978), 119-23.

57 NA, MG31 E55, Tarnopolsky Papers, Vol. 43, file 4; SBC 1885 c. 30; 1902 c. 39; 1908 c. 50; 1912 c. 34; *Hansard*, 9, 10 and 23 March 1911, 4930-31, 5038-39, 5941-48; Public Archives of Nova Scotia (PANS), "Colored Cooks, Stewards and Firemen," file of correspondence concerning Canadian National Steamships.

58 Howard Palmer, *Patterns of Prejudice: A History of Nativism in Alberta* (Toronto: McClelland and Stewart, 1982), 145-48.

59 Chief Joe Mathias and Gary R. Yabsley, "Conspiracy of Legislation: The Suppression of Indian Rights in Canada," *BC Studies*, 89 (1991): 39.

60 *Statutes of Nova Scotia* (SNS) 1884 c. 29; 1918 c. 9; *Revised Statutes of Ontario* (RSO) 1960 c. 368; NA, Tarnopolsky Papers, Vol. 44, file 5; V. Carter and W. Akili, *The Window of Our Memories*, Vol. 1 (St. Albert, AB: Black Cultural Research Society of Alberta, 1981), 55; Patricia E. Roy, *A White Man's Province: British Columbia Politicians and the Chinese and Japanese Immigrants, 1858-1914* (Vancouver: University of British Columbia Press, 1989), 15, 24-27.

61 SC 1869 c. 10; 1885 c. 71; 1900 c. 32; 1903 c. 8; 1907 c. 50; 1910 c. 27; 1923 c. 38; *Hansard*, 8 and 14 June 1900, 7052-57, 7406-15, 27 March 1903, 597-612, 23 March 1923, 1443-54; Sessional Papers, 1902, No. 54; Ward, *White Canada Forever*.

62 Howard Sugimoto, "The Vancouver Riots of 1907: A Canadian Episode," in H. Conroy and T. Miyakawa, eds., *East Across the Pacific: Historical and Sociological Studies of Japanese Immigration and Assimilation* (Santa Barbara, CA: American Bibliographic Center-Clio Press, 1972), 92-126; NA, MG26 G1(a), Laurier Papers, Vol. 477, correspondence and reports on the riots; Vol. 489, Confidential Report by the Hon. Rodolph Lemieux on his visit to Japan.

63 The final version of this order is found in PC 32, 1914.

64 NA, RG76 Vol. 192, file 72552, "Immigration of Negros [*sic*] from the United States to Western Canada"; *Hansard*, 2, 22 and 23 March and 3 April 1911, 4470, 4471, 5911-13, 5941-48, 6523-28; PC 1324 and 2378, 1911; Shepard, "Plain Racism," 365-82; Harold Troper, "The Creek-Negroes of Oklahoma and Canadian Immigration, 1909-11," *Canadian Historical Review*, 53 (1972): 272-88.

65 Treaties and Historical Research Centre, Indian and Northern Affairs, *The Historical Development of the Indian Act* (Ottawa, 1978), 5-8.

66 Statutes of the Province of Canada 1857 c. 26; BS 1867 c. 3 (*British North America Act*), s. 91 ss. 24; SC 1869 c. 6.

67 SC 1876 c. 18.

68 Ibid., ss. 86-94.

69 For example, see Vic Satzewich and Linda Mahood, "Indian Affairs and Band Governance: Deposing Indian Chiefs in Western Canada, 1896-1911," *Canadian Ethnic Studies*, 26 (1994): 40-58; SC 1869 c. 6, s. 10; SC 1880 c. 28, s. 72.

70 For example, Kathleen Jamieson, "Sex Discrimination and the Indian Act," in J. Rick Ponting, ed., *Arduous Journey: Canadian Indians and Decolonization* (Toronto: McClelland and Stewart, 1986), 112-36. SC 1869 c. 6, s. 6, said: "Any Indian woman marrying any other than an Indian shall cease to be an Indian within the meaning of this Act."

71 For example, Tina Loo, "Dan Cranmer's Potlatch: Law as Coercion, Symbol, and Rhetoric in British Columbia, 1884-1951," *Canadian Historical Review*, 73 (1992): 125-65; SC 1884 c. 27, s. 3; SC 1895 c. 35, s. 6; SC 1914 c. 35, s. 8.

72 For example, John Tobias, "Protection, Civilization, Assimilation: An Outline History of Canada's Indian Policy," in Ian Getty and Antoine Lussier, eds., *As Long as the Sun Shines and Water Flows* (Vancouver: University of British Columbia Press, 1983), 39-55; SC 1894 c. 32, s. 11.

73 *Historical Development of the Indian Act*, 114-15, 124; SC 1920 c. 50; SC 1922 c. 26; SC 1933 c. 42.

74 For example, James S. Frideres, *Native Peoples in Canada: Contemporary Conflicts* (Scarborough, ON: Prentice Hall, 1988), chap. 2, "The Indian Act," 25-38; *Historical Development of the Indian Act*, 23-25, 61. S. 3 ss. 3 of the 1876 Act defined an Indian as "Any male person of Indian blood reputed to belong to a particular band; Any child of such person; Any woman who is or was lawfully married to such person."

75 For example, Mathias and Yabsley, "Conspiracy of Legislation," 34-45; Howard E. Staats, "Some Aspects of the Legal Status of Canadian Indians," *Osgoode Hall Law Journal*, 3 (1964): 36-51; *Historical Development of the Indian Act*.

76 Sarah Carter, *Lost Harvests: Prairie Indian Reserve Farmers and Government Policy* (Montreal and Kingston: McGill-Queen's University Press, 1990).

77 Kenneth Coates, "Best Left as Indians: The Federal Government and the Indians of the Yukon, 1894-1950," in Robin Fisher and Kenneth Coates, eds., *Out of the Background: Readings on Canadian Native History* (Toronto: Copp Clark Pitman, 1988), 236-55.

78 Department of National Defence (DND), file HQ 61-4-10, "Sorting Out Coloured Soldiers"; Canada, Parliament, House of Commons, Special Committee on Orientals in British Columbia, *Report and Recommendations* (Ottawa, 1940); NA, RG24 Vol. 2765, file 6615-4-A, Vol. 5, correspondence and committee minutes on enlistment of "Asiatics"; RG27 Vol. 130, file 601-3-4, "Conscription of East Indians for Canadian Army."

79 NA, RG27 Vol. 1486, file 2-153-1, petitions; DND, file HQ 504-1-7-1, Vol. 1, "Organization and Administration. Enlistment of Chinese"; Douglas MacLennan, "Racial Discrimination in Canada," *Canadian Forum*, October 1943, 164-65.

80 Adachi, *Enemy*, 199ff.; Peter Ward, "British Columbia and the Japanese Evacuation," *Canadian Historical Review*, 57 (1976): 289-308; Carol Lee, "The Road to Enfranchisement: Chinese and Japanese in British Columbia," *BC Studies*, 30 (1976): 54-60; *Hansard*, 17 July 1944, 4911-38; SC 1944-45 c.26.

81 Donna Hill, ed., *A Black Man's Toronto, 1914-1980: The Reminiscences of Harry Gairey* (Toronto: Multicultural History Society of Ontario, 1981), 56-57; F. J. McEvoy, "'A Symbol of Racial Discrimination': The Chinese Immigration Act and Canada's Relations with China, 1942-1947," *Canadian Ethnic Studies*, 14 (1982): 34-35; NA, Tarnopolsky Papers, Vol. 32, file 13 and Vol. 36, file 5; RG25 Vol. 1539, file 178, "Immigration to Canada of Chinese," petitions; SC 1946 c. 15.

82 SC 1951 c. 29; SC 1960 c. 39.

83 NA, MG30 A53, Kaplansky Papers, Vols. 20 and 21, "Reports of Activities for Improved Human Relations, 1946-1956"; Tarnopolsky Papers, especially Vols. 36, 40, 41 and 45.

84 Walter Tarnopolsky, "The Iron Hand in the Velvet Glove: Administration and Enforcement of Human Rights Legislation in Canada," *Canadian Bar Review*, 46 (1968): 565-90, "The Canadian Bill of Rights from Diefenbaker to Drybones," *McGill Law Journal*, 17 (1971): 437-75, *Discrimination and the Law in Canada* (Toronto: R. de Boo, 1982); T. C. Hartley, "Race Relations Law in Ontario," *Public Law* (1970): Part 1, 20-35, Part 2, 175-95; P. V. MacDonald, "Race Relations and Canadian Law," *University of Toronto Faculty of Law Review*, 18 (1960): 115-27; Mark MacGuigan, "The Development of Civil Liberties in Canada," *Queen's Quarterly*, 72 (1965): 270-88.

85 PC 2115, 1930; *Hansard,* 11 February, 1 May 1947, 307-45, 2644-47.
86 *Hansard,* 24 April 1952, 4351-53; SC 1952 c. 42; NA, MG28 V75, Jewish Labour Committee of Canada Papers, especially Vols. 41 and 42.
87 Sec. 101.
88 *Hansard,* 18 March 1870, 507.
89 George Adams and Paul J. Cavalluzzo, "The Supreme Court of Canada. A Biographical Study," *Osgoode Hall Law Journal,* 7 (1969): 61-86; Bushnell, *The Captive Court;* Fouts, "Policy-Making in the Supreme Court of Canada"; Bora Laskin, "The Supreme Court of Canada: A Final Court of and for Canadians," *Canadian Bar Review,* 29 (1951): 1038-79, "The Supreme Court of Canada: The First One Hundred Years. A Capsule Institutional History," and "The Role and Functions of Final Appellate Courts: The Supreme Court of Canada," *Canadian Bar Review,* 53 (1975): 469-81; MacGuigan, "Precedent and Policy in the Supreme Court"; Frank MacKinnon, "The Establishment of the Supreme Court of Canada," *Canadian Historical Review,* 27 (1946): 258-74; Peter McCormick and Ian Greene, *Judges and Judging* (Toronto: J. Lorimer, 1990), chap. 7; Peter H. Russell, *The Supreme Court of Canada as a Bilingual and Bicultural Institution* (Ottawa: Royal Commission on Bilingualism and Biculturalism, 1969), 1-11, 26-27, 33-37; Snell and Vaughan, *Supreme Court of Canada;* Weiler, *In the Last Resort,* chap. 1; Wilson, "Decision-Making in the Supreme Court."
90 *The Supreme Court and Exchequer Court Act,* SC 1875 c. 11.
91 [1935] SCR 378, at 381. Over the years various practices in interpreting statutes have been designated as "rules" which elaborate upon the meaning to be assigned to a disputed piece of legislation. For summaries of these rules, see Elmer A. Driedger, *The Composition of Legislation* (Ottawa: Queen's Printer, 1957), especially chap. 13, "Rules of Interpretation Applied to Drafting" and chap. 19, "Statutory Interpretation," and John Willis, "Statute Interpretation in a Nutshell," *Canadian Bar Review,* 16 (1938): 1-27.
92 Carl Baar and Ellen Baar, "Diagnostic Adjudication in Appellate Courts: The Supreme Court of Canada and the Charter of Rights," *Osgoode Hall Law Journal,* 27 (1989): 1-25; Bushnell, *The Captive Court;* J. A. Corry, "The Use of Legislative History in the Interpretation of Statutes," *Canadian Bar Review,* 32 (1954): 624-37; E. A. Driedger, "The Preparation of Legislation," *Canadian Bar Review,* 31 (1953): 33-51; Fouts, "Policy-Making in the Supreme Court of Canada"; D. G. Kilgour, "The Rule Against the Use of Legislative History: 'Canon of Construction' or 'Counsel of Caution'?" *Canadian Bar Review,* 30 (1952): 769-90.
93 Supreme Court of British Columbia, *Reasons for Judgment of the Hon. Chief Justice Allan McEachern* (Victoria, 1991); (1991) 79 DLR (4th) 185. Besides the usual attention from legal commentators, *Delgamuukw* has attracted critics from other disciplines and from those engaged in native issues in Canada. Of particular interest is a special number of *BC Studies,* 95 (1992), including Robin Fisher, "Judging History: Reflections of the Reasons for Judgment in

Delgamuukw v. BC," 43-54, and Bruce G. Miller, "Common Sense and Plain Language," 55-65. For a collaborative discussion by an anthropologist and a legal scholar, see Michael Asch and Catherine Bell, "Definition and Interpretation of Fact in Canadian Aboriginal Title Litigation: An Analysis of *Delgamuukw," Queen's Law Journal*, 19 (1994): 503-50.

94 DLR, at 201.

95 Ibid., at 251.

96 For example, see James W. St. G. Walker, "The Indian in Canadian Historical Writing," Canadian Historical Association, *Historical Papers 1971* (Ottawa, 1971), 21-51.

97 Bruce G. Trigger, "Early Native North American Responses to European Contact: Romantic Versus Rationalistic Interpretations," *Journal of American History*, 77 (1991): 1195-1215; Sarah Carter, *Lost Harvests: Prairie Indian Reserve Farmers and Government Policy* (Montreal and Kingston: McGill-Queen's University Press, 1990).

98 E. H. Carr, *What Is History?* (Harmondsworth, Middlesex: Penguin, 1964), 87, 103.

99 For example, see Richard T. Vann, "The Rhetoric of Social History," *Journal of Social History*, 10 (1976), 224, 230-31; Lloyd S. Kramer, "Literature, Criticism, and Historical Imagination: The Literary Challenge of Hayden White and Dominick LaCapra," in Lynn Hunt, ed., *The New Cultural History* (Berkeley: University of California Press, 1989), 100; Allan Megill, "Recounting the Past: 'Description', Explanation and Narrative in Historiography," *American Historical Review*, 94 (1989): 627.

100 *English Social History* (London: Longmans, Green, 1944), vii.

101 Peter N. Stearns, "Social History and History: A Progress Report," *Journal of Social History*, 19 (1985): 319; Hunt, *The New Cultural History*, "Introduction," 1, 4; Lynn Hunt, "History Beyond Social Theory," in David Carroll, ed., *The States of 'Theory': History, Art, and Critical Discourse* (New York: Columbia University Press, 1990), 95. For a considerably less positive reaction to this conquest see Gertrude Himmelfarb, *The New History and the Old: Critical Essays and Reappraisals* (Cambridge, MA: Belknap, 1987).

102 Trian Stoianovich, *French Historical Method: The Annales Paradigm* (Ithaca: Cornell University Press, 1976).

103 Harvey J. Kaye, *The British Marxist Historians* (Cambridge: Polity Press, 1984).

104 Fernand Braudel, *The Mediterranean and the Mediterranean World in the Age of Philip II*, 2 vols., English translation (New York: Harper & Row, 1972). Quotation is from Vol. 1, 21. See also "Preface" to the same volume, and Fernand Braudel, *On History*, English translation (Chicago: University of Chicago Press, 1980), especially "The History of Civilizations," 177-218.

105 For example, especially Thompson, *The Making of the English Working Class* (New York: Pantheon Books, 1964), and *Whigs and Hunters: The Origin of the Black Act* (New York: Pantheon Books, 1975).

106 Peter N. Stearns, "Coming of Age," *Journal of Social History*, 10 (1976), and "Social History and History: A Progress Report."

107 For example, Bernard S. Cohn, "History and Anthropology: The State of Play," *Comparative Studies in Society and History*, 22 (1980): 198-221; Ian McKay, "Historians, Anthropology, and the Concept of Culture," *Labour/Le Travailleur*, 8/9 (1981/82): 185-241; Roger Chartier, "Intellectual History or Sociocultural History? The French Trajectories," in D. LaCapra and S. Kaplan, eds., *Modern European Intellectual History: Reappraisals and New Perspectives* (Ithaca: Cornell University Press, 1982), 30; E. Somekawa and E. A. Smith, "Theorizing the Writing of History or, 'I can't think why it should be so dull, for a great deal of it must be invention'," *Journal of Social History*, 20 (1988): 149-61; Peter N. Stearns, "Social History Update: Encountering Postmodernism," *Journal of Social History*, 24 (1990): 449-52.

108 *Foucault Live: Interviews 1966-84* (New York: Semiotext(e), 1989), 80. Foucault styled himself "an historian of culture."

109 *L'histoire de la folie* (Paris: Gallimard, 1961).

110 *Foucault Live*, 295.

111 Ibid., 296.

112 Mark Poster, "Foucault and History," *Social Research*, 49 (1982): 128; Larry Shiner, "Reading Foucault: Anti-Method and the Genealogy of Power-Knowledge," *History and Theory*, 21 (1982): 382-97; Patricia O'Brien, "Michel Foucault's History of Culture," in Hunt, ed., *New Cultural History*, 23-46.

113 *Foucault Live*, 139.

114 Michel Foucault, "Nietzsche, Genealogy, History," in Donald Bouchard, ed., *Language, Counter-Memory, Practice. Selected Essays and Interviews* (Ithaca: Cornell University Press, 1977), 139-64.

115 *Local Knowledge*, 3, 6.

116 Clifford Geertz, *The Interpretation of Cultures* (New York: Basic Books, 1973), 29.

117 *Local Knowledge*, 4, 19-35.

118 Ibid., 186-87, 232-33.

119 Ibid., 4.

120 Ibid., 233; *Interpretation of Cultures*, 18-19.

121 Ibid., 14.

122 Ibid., 27.

123 Ibid., 24.

124 *Local Knowledge*, 6.

125 *Interpretation of Cultures*, viii.

126 Ibid., 21, 23.

127 *Local Knowledge*, 186-87.

128 *Interpretation of Cultures*, 5.

129 Kramer, "Literature, Criticism, and Historical Imagination," 100.

130 Lawrence W. Levine, "The Unpredictable Past: Reflections on Recent American Historiography," *American Historical Review* 94 (1989): 677.

131 Irmline Veit-Brause, "Paradigms, Schools, Traditions – Conceptualizing Shifts and Changes in the History of Historiography," *Storia Della Storiografia*, 17 (1990): 50-65; Hunt, "History Beyond Social Theory," 102-3; Elizabeth Fox-Genovese and Eugene Genovese, "The Political Crisis of Social History," *Journal of Social History*, 10 (1976): 216; Himmelfarb, "Reflections on the New History," 669.

132 Natalie Zemon Davis, "The Shapes of Social History," *Storia Della Storiografia*, 17 (1990): 28, 31.

133 Karin J. MacHardy, "Crises in History, or: Hermes Unbounded," *Storia Della Storiografia*, 17 (1990): 5-27; Davis, "The Shapes of Social History," 28; Veit-Brause, "Paradigms, Schools, Traditions," 53; Hunt, "Introduction," *New Cultural History*, 12; Jean-Luc Nancy, "Finite History," in Carroll, ed., *The States of 'Theory'*, 149.

134 See, for example, the special issues of the *American Historical Review*, 94 (1989), and *Storia Della Storiografia*, 17 (1990), and the publications by Himmelfarb, *The New History and the Old* (1987), Hunt, ed., *The New Cultural History* (1989), and Carroll, ed., *The States of 'Theory'* (1990). One observer, noting that the participants are clearly enjoying themselves, has labelled the current historiographical debate a "tournament" (Caroline Walker Bynum, *Fragments and Redemption: Essays on Gender and the Human Body in Medieval Religion* [New York: Zone Books, 1992], 21, 24).

135 Herbert Butterfield, *The Whig Interpretation of History*, rev. ed. (London: Bell, 1976).

136 This background is described most thoroughly in Robert W. Gordon, "J. Willard Hurst and the Common Law Tradition in American Historiography," *Law and Society Review*, 10 (1976): 9-55. See also Ernst-Wolfgang Bockenforde, *State, Society and Liberty: Studies in Political Theory and Constitutional Law* (New York: Berg, 1991), especially chap. 1, "The School of Historical Jurisprudence and the Problem of the Historicity of Law," 1-25; H. L. A. Hart, "Positivism and the Separation of Law and Morals," *Harvard Law Review*, 71 (1958): 593-629; Graham Parker, "The Masochism of the Legal Historian," *University of Toronto Law Journal*, 24 (1974): 279-317; W. Wesley Pue and Barry Wright, *Canadian Perspectives on Law and Society: Issues in Legal History* (Ottawa: Carleton University Press, 1988), especially chaps. 1 and 2; Barry Wright, "Towards a New Canadian Legal History," *Osgoode Hall Law Journal*, 22 (1984): 349-74.

137 Gordon, "Hurst and the Common Law Tradition," 11, 20.

138 Parker, "Masochism of the Legal Historian," 284.

139 *The Growth of American Law: The Law Makers* (Boston: Little, Brown, 1950), *Law and the Conditions of Freedom in the Nineteenth Century United States* (Madison: University of Wisconsin Press, 1956), *Law and Economic Growth: The Legal History of the Lumber Industry in Wisconsin 1836-1915* (Cambridge, MA: Belknap Press, 1964). Gordon, "Hurst and the Common Law Tradition," is an altogether admiring account of Hurst's contribution. Flaherty,

"Writing Canadian Legal History," 6-7, and "An Approach to American History: Willard Hurst as a Legal Historian," *American Journal of Legal History*, 14 (1970): 222, matches Gordon. Parker's awe is more restrained in "Masochism of the Legal Historian," 313-16.

140 For a thorough and often amusing critique of this theoretical school see Robert W. Gordon, "Historicism in Legal Scholarship," *Yale Law Journal*, 90 (1981): 1017-56, and "Critical Legal Histories," *Stanford Law Review*, 36 (1984): 57-125. One particularly vapid example of "adaptationism" quoted by Gordon explains that "the evolution of the right of privacy was a response to the increasing complexity and interdependence of modern society" ("Critical Legal Histories," 64).

141 Morton Horwitz, *Transformation of American Law* (Cambridge, MA: Harvard University Press, 1977). Horwitz' work is discussed in D. G. Bell, "The Birth of Canadian Legal History," *UNB Law Journal*, 33 (1984): 318; Flaherty, "Writing Canadian Legal History," 13-14; Gordon, "Critical Legal Histories," 98ff.; Wright, "New Canadian Legal History," 363-65.

142 "The Historical Contingency of the Role of History," *Yale Law Journal*, 90 (1971): 1082.

143 "The Conservative Tradition in the Writing of American Legal History," *American Journal of Legal History*, 7 (1973): 276.

144 *Local Knowledge*, 215.

145 Ibid., 173.

146 Ibid., 16.

147 Ibid., 216-18, 230-32.

148 Ibid., 232.

149 Ibid., 182.

150 Ibid., 218-19, 232.

151 Ibid., 215.

152 *Discipline and Punish: The Birth of the Prison* (London: A. Lane, 1977), 23. Foucault was referring specifically to the criminal law and to forms of punishment, but his compatibility with Geertz is apparent.

153 *The Poverty of Theory* (New York: Monthly Review Press, 1978), 96.

154 For example, see Alan Hunt, "The New Legal History: Prospects and Perspectives," review essay, *Contemporary Crises*, 10 (1986): 201-8.

155 Gordon explains that his title "Critical Legal Histories," 57, is intended to suggest that the label covers several different historiographical practices.

156 There is a lively and growing literature describing and debating Critical Legal Studies. Some of the more accessible items informing the present discussion, besides those already mentioned in footnotes, would include Andrew Altman, *Critical Legal Studies: A Liberal Critique* (Princeton: Princeton University Press, 1990); Richard Delgado, "The Ethereal Scholar: Does Critical Legal Studies Have What Minorities Want?" *Harvard Civil Rights – Civil Liberties Law Review*, 22 (1987): 301-22; Ronald Dworkin, *Law's Empire* (Cambridge, MA: Belknap Press, 1986); William Ewald, "Unger's Philoso-

phy: A Critical Legal Study," *Yale Law Journal*, 97 (1988); P. Fitzpatrick and A. Hunt, eds., *Critical Legal Studies* (London: B. Blackwell, 1987); Robert W. Gordon, "Critical Legal Studies as a Teaching Method, Against the Background of the Intellectual Politics of Modern Legal Education in the United States," *Legal Education Review*, 1 (1989): 59-83; Alan Hunt, *Explorations in Law and Society: Toward a Constitutive Theory of Law* (New York: Routledge, 1993); Allan C. Hutchinson and Patrick J. Monahan, "Law, Politics, and the Critical Legal Scholars: The Unfolding Drama of American Legal Thought," *Stanford Law Review*, 36 (1984): 199-245; David Kairys, ed., *The Politics of Law* (New York: Pantheon Books, 1982), especially Robert Gordon, "New Developments in Legal Theory," Elizabeth Mensch, "The History of Mainstream Legal Thought," and Kairys' own introduction; Mark Kelman, *A Guide to Critical Legal Studies* (Cambridge, MA: Harvard University Press, 1987); David Trubek, "Where the Action Is: Critical Legal Studies and Empiricism," *Stanford Law Review*, 36 (1984); Mark Tushnet, "Critical Legal Studies: An Introduction to Its Origins and Its Underpinnings," *Journal of Legal Education*, 36 (1986): 505-17; Tushnet, *Red, White and Blue: A Critical Analysis of Constitutional Law* (Cambridge, MA: Harvard University Press, 1988); Roberto Unger, *The Critical Legal Studies Movement* (Cambridge, MA: Harvard University Press, 1986); see also Unger, "Critical Legal Studies Movement," *Harvard Law Review* 96 (1982): 561-675; Cornell West, "Critical Legal Studies and a Liberal Critic," *Yale Law Journal*, 97 (1988).

157 Gordon, "Critical Legal Histories," 109, 111. See also Bockenforde, *State, Society and Liberty*; Hunt, *Explorations in Law and Society*, esp. chap. 13, "Law as a Constitutive Mode of Regulation."

158 Gordon, "Critical Legal Histories," 75, 118.

159 Ibid., 114.

160 The most convenient entry to Critical Race Theory is offered by Richard Delgado, ed., *Critical Race Theory: The Cutting Edge* (Philadelphia: Temple University Press, 1995). Delgado has also produced, with Jean Stefancic, "Critical Race Theory: An Annotated Bibiography," *Virginia Law Review*, 79 (1993): 461, and an early update, "Critical Race Theory: An Annotated Bibliography – 1993, a Year of Transition," *University of Colorado Law Review*, 66 (1995): 159. Other useful compilations are in symposia in the *California Law Review*, 82 (1994): 741, and the *University of Illinois Law Review* (1992): 945. Most of the journal articles are written by proponents of the theory, but see Douglas E. Litowitz, "Some Critical Thoughts on Critical Race Theory," *Notre Dame Law Review*, 72 (1997): 503.

161 For example, Viscount James Bryce, *The Relations of the Advanced and Backward Races of Mankind* (Oxford: Clarendon Press, 1902).

162 For example, Oliver Cox, *Caste, Class and Race: A Study in Social Dynamics* (New York: Doubleday, 1948).

163 For example, A. Davey, *Learning to Be Prejudiced* (London: Edward Arnold, 1983).

164 Michael Banton, *Racial and Ethnic Competition* (Cambridge: Cambridge University Press, 1983), 75, 136.

165 For example, John Rex and David Mason, eds., *Theories of Race and Ethnic Relations* (Cambridge: Cambridge University Press, 1986).

166 M. G. Smith, *The Plural Society in the British West Indies* (Berkeley: University of California Press, 1965); M. G. Smith and L. Kuper, eds., *Pluralism in Africa* (Berkeley: University of California Press, 1969); Leo Kuper, *Race, Class and Power: Ideology and Revolutionary Change in Plural Societies* (London: Duckworth, 1974). A concise statement of the theory can be found in M. G. Smith, "Pluralism, Race and Ethnicity in Selected African Countries," in Rex and Mason, eds., *Theories of Race and Ethnic Relations*, 187-225.

167 Robert Blauner, *Racial Oppression in America* (New York: Harper & Row, 1972).

168 *Internal Colonialism: The Celtic Fringe in British National Development, 1536-1966* (Berkeley: University of California Press, 1975), 30.

169 "The Past, Present, and Future of Split Labor Market Theory," in C. B. Marrett and C. Leggon, eds., *Research in Race and Ethnic Relations* (Greenwich, CN: JAI Press, 1979), Vol. 1, 18.

170 Edna Bonacich, "A Theory of Ethnic Antagonism: The Split Labor Market," *American Sociological Review*, 37 (1972): 547-59.

171 Davis, "The Shapes of Social History," 28-34.

172 One of the most influential demonstrations of this technique is Natalie Zemon Davis, *The Return of Martin Guerre* (Cambridge, MA: Harvard University Press, 1983).

2 QUONG WING V. THE KING

1 *Statutes of Saskatchewan* (SS) 1912 c. 17.

2 Regina *Morning Leader*, 5 March 1912.

3 Moose Jaw *Evening Times*, 29 April 1912.

4 Regina *Morning Leader*, 14 May 1912. The 1894 *Treaty of Commerce and Navigation* between Britain and Japan was given effect in Canada by the *Japanese Treaty Act*, SC 1907 c. 50. Article 1 guaranteed British and Japanese subjects "full liberty to enter, travel or reside in any part of the dominions and possessions of the other Contracting Party, and . . . full and perfect protection for their person and property."

5 SS 1912-13 c. 18; *Census of Canada, 1911*, Vol. 2; National Archives (NA), RG 25 Vol. 1142, file 308, Pope to Borden, 10 March 1914; Saskatchewan Archives Board (SAB), Scott Papers, Hori to Scott, 30 April 1914, reply, 1 May, Hori to McLeod, 7 May 1914; Saskatoon *Daily Star*, 14, 15 and 21 August 1912. Two other prosecutions were reported in the *Daily Star*, of restaurant owners identified only as "a Jap and a Chinaman," who like Mr. Yoshi were fined $10 plus $10 costs by Saskatoon's Magistrate Brown (15 and 21 August).

6 Moose Jaw *Evening Times*, 1 May 1912; Regina *Leader*, 13 May 1912; NA, RG 25 Vol. 1142, file 308, Yang Shu-Wen to Charles Doherty, 4 February 1914, Pope to Borden, 28 February, Newcombe to Pope, 6 March, Pope to Borden, 10 March; Yang Shu-Wen to Borden, 22 June 1914, E. Blake Robertson, memo, 29 June 1914, Canada, Department of External Affairs, *Documents on Canadian External Relations*, Vol. 1, 1909-18 (Ottawa, 1967), 651-53.

7 SS 1918-19 c. 85; SAB, Scott Papers, J. A. Allens to Martin, 5 December 1918, Yang Shu-Wen to Martin, 31 January 1919; *Regina Daily Post*, 17 and 18 January 1919.

8 For example, see Mark Berlin and William Pentney, *Human Rights and Freedoms in Canada* (Toronto: Butterworths, 1987), 11-13; Douglas Schmeiser, *Civil Liberties in Canada* (London: Oxford University Press, 1964), 259-60; Walter Tarnopolsky, "The Supreme Court and Civil Liberties," *Alberta Law Review*, 14 (1976): 61; Walter Tarnopolsky, *Discrimination and the Law in Canada* (Toronto: R. de Boo, 1982), 9-14; "The Control of Racial Discrimination," in R. St.J. MacDonald and John P. Humphrey, eds., *The Practice of Freedom: Canadian Essays on Human Rights and Fundamental Freedoms* (Toronto: Butterworths, 1979) 292.

9 For a thorough discussion of the Chinese "problem," and of Quong Wing's lower-court experiences, see Constance Backhouse, "White Women's Labour Laws: Anti-Chinese Racism in Early 20th Century Canada," *Law and History Review*, 14 (1996): 315-68.

10 *Census of Canada, 1911*, Vol. 2; Moose Jaw *Evening Times*, 8 August 1911; Saskatchewan, Royal Commission on Immigration and Settlement, 1930, *Report*.

11 Moose Jaw *Evening Times*, 6 September 1913; SAB, Project Integrate, "An Ethnic Study of the Chinese Community of Moose Jaw" (1973), 8, 9, 17, 18, 22, 24, 26; W. S. Chow, "The Chinese Community in Canada Before 1947 and Some Recent Developments," in Frances Henry, ed., *Ethnicity in the Americas* (The Hague: Mouton, 1976), 128; Peter S. Li, "Chinese Immigrants on the Canadian Prairie, 1910-47," *Canadian Review of Sociology and Anthropology*, 19 (1982): 533; Peter S. Li, *The Chinese in Canada* (Toronto: Oxford University Press, 1988), 53; Edgar Wickberg, ed., *From China to Canada: A History of the Chinese Communities in Canada* (Toronto: McClelland and Stewart, 1982), 79, 91.

12 Quoted in James Gray, *Red Lights on the Prairies* (Toronto: Macmillan, 1971), 77. Another contemporary observer quoted by Gray remarked: "Moose Jaw isn't a city or a municipality or even a geographic location! Moose Jaw is a goddam virus that has permanently afflicted Regina and for which there is no known cure!" (76).

13 Ibid., 75-80; James Gray, *The Roar of the Twenties* (Toronto: Macmillan, 1975), 269. There were frequent newspaper accounts of raids and arrests in Chinatown, e.g., *Evening Times* 31 October 1911, 18 December 1911, 14 March 1912. An allegation that Chief Johnson personally appropriated the gambling stakes during such raids was reported in the *Evening Times*, 11 May 1912.

14 Regina *Morning Leader*, 27 February, 2 and 5 March 1912.
15 Project Integrate, "Chinese Community of Moose Jaw," 10; Wickberg, *From China to Canada*, 120; David Chuenyan Lai, *Chinatowns: Cities within Cities in Canada* (Vancouver: University of British Columbia Press, 1988), 93-94. Lai is apparently inaccurate in alleging that "The case was widely publicized by local newspapers." There was one report of an alleged assault on a school-girl in a Chinese restaurant in Moose Jaw, but the charge was quickly dismissed following evidence that the child's aunt had prompted her to lay a false complaint (*Evening Times*, 1 and 30 September 1911).
16 NA, RG 25 Vol. 1142, file 308, Yang Shu-Wen to Doherty, 4 February 1914. Misspelling is in the original.
17 *Statutes of Manitoba* (SM) 1913 c. 19.
18 *Statutes of Ontario* (SO) 1914 c. 40, s. 2(1).
19 NA, RG 25 Vol. 1142, file 308, Pope to Borden, 28 February 1914; SAB, Scott Papers, Allan to Martin, 5 December 1918.
20 *Porcupine Advance*, 2 July 1915, quoted in Kwok B. Chan and Lawrence Lam, "Chinese in Timmins, Canada, 1915-1950: A Study of Ethnic Stereotypes in the Press," *Asian Profile*, 14 (1986): 573.
21 *Statutes of British Columbia* (SBC) 1919 c. 63.
22 Provincial Archives of British Columbia (PABC), Attorney General's Papers, file 2060, 1181, copy in NA, MG 31 E55, Tarnopolsky Papers, Vol. 43, file 5, Parsons to Attorney General, 16 August 1922.
23 SBC 1923 c. 76.
24 Chuen-Yan Lai, "The Chinese Consolidated Benevolent Association in Victoria: Its Origins and Functions," *BC Studies*, 15 (1972): 53; W. Peter Ward, *White Canada Forever: Popular Attitudes and Public Policy Toward Orientals in British Columbia* (Montreal: McGill-Queen's University Press, 1978), 16, 23; W. E. Willmott, "Some Aspects of Chinese Communities in British Columbia Towns," *BC Studies*, 1 (1968-69): 28-29; W. E. Willmott, "Approaches to the Study of the Chinese in British Columbia," *BC Studies*, 4 (1970): 44. The most thorough account of Chinese in British Columbia during this period is to be found in Patricia Roy, *A White Man's Province: British Columbia Politicians and Chinese and Japanese Immigrants, 1858-1914* (Vancouver: University of British Columbia Press, 1989), esp. chap. 1.
25 Gunter Baureiss, "Ethnic Resilience and Discrimination: Two Chinese Communities in Canada," *Journal of Ethnic Studies*, 10 (1982): 73; Gunter Baureiss, "Discrimination and Response: The Chinese in Canada," in Rita Bienvenue and Jay Goldstein, eds., *Ethnicity and Ethnic Relations in Canada* (2nd ed.; Toronto: Butterworths, 1985), 243; Elizabeth Comack, " 'We Will Get Some Good Out of This Riot Yet': The Canadian State, Drug Legislation and Class Conflict," in Stephen Brickey and Elizabeth Comack, eds., *The Social Basis of Law: Critical Readings in the Sociology of Law* (Toronto: Garamond Press, 1986), 70-71; Lai, "Chinese Consolidated Benevolent Association," 54; Li, "Chinese Immigrants on the Canadian Prairie," 530, 532-33; Li, *Chinese in Canada*, 51;

Paul L. Voisey, "Two Chinese Communities in Alberta: An Historical Perspective," *Canadian Ethnic Studies*, 2 (1970): 17-18; Ward, *White Canada Forever*, 15-16, 36; Willmott, "Approaches to the Study of the Chinese," 38-39, 42.

26 Anthony B. Chan ("Orientalism and Image Making: The Sojourner in Canadian History," *Journal of Ethnic Studies*, 9 [1981]: 37-46) argues that the Chinese workers really intended to settle permanently in Canada, and that the "sojourner myth" is a later invention by Euro-Canadians. His chief evidence is that contemporary Chinese-language sources did not use the Chinese characters for "sojourners" or "temporary migrants" in referring to these men. J. A. Chapleau, one of the Royal Commissioners examining Chinese residents in 1884-85, offered some contrary evidence, claiming that the Consul-General of China told him "we are laborers who have come out here to work, and when it is done, we go back to our own country" (*Hansard*, 2 July 1885, 3010).

27 The *Victoria Gazette* for 31 March 1859 is cited in Ward, *White Canada Forever*, 25, and Anderson, *Vancouver's Chinatown*, 37. For a full discussion of the anti-Chinese measures taken in the other British colonies see Robert A. Huttenback, *Racism and Empire: White Settlers and Colored Immigrants in the British Self-Governing Colonies, 1830-1910* (Ithaca and London: Cornell University Press, 1976).

28 *Hansard*, 12 May 1882, 1477.

29 Andrew L. March, *The Idea of China: Myth and Theory in Geographic Thought* (New York: Praeger, 1974); Edward W. Said, *Orientalism* (New York: Pantheon, 1978).

30 Lai (*Chinatowns*, 55) suggests that the young Chinese worker could earn 10 to 20 times more in Canada than in China.

31 Gillian Creese, "Working Class Politics, Racism and Sexism: The Making of a Politically Divided Working Class in Vancouver, 1900-1939," PhD dissertation, Carleton University, 1986, 63-75; Bruce Ryder, "Racism and the Constitution: The Constitutional Fate of British Columbia Anti-Asian Immigration Legislation, 1884-1909," *Osgoode Hall Law Journal*, 29 (1991): 638; Vic Satzewich, "Racisms: The Reactions to Chinese Migrants in Canada at the Turn of the Century," *International Sociology*, 4 (1989): 312-19.

32 Senate, *Debates*, 21 May 1886, 680.

33 Cited in John A. Munro, "British Columbia and the 'Chinese Evil': Canada's First Anti-Asiatic Immigration Law," *Journal of Canadian Studies*, 6 (1971): 42. See also Ward, *White Canada Forever*, 33.

34 Comack, "Drug Legislation and Class Conflict," 73; Mary E. Hallett, "A Governor-General's Views on Oriental Immigration to British Columbia, 1904-1911," *BC Studies*, 14 (1972): 56.

35 For example, Gillian Creese, "Exclusion or Solidarity? Vancouver Workers Confront the 'Oriental Problem,'" *BC Studies*, 80 (1988-89): 24-51.

36 Cited in ibid., 33-34.

37 Donald Avery and Peter Neary, "Laurier, Borden and a White British Columbia," *Journal of Canadian Studies*, 12 (1977): 31; Peter S. Li, "A Historical Approach to Ethnic Stratification: The Case of the Chinese in Canada, 1858-1930," *Canadian Review of Sociology and Anthropology*, 16 (1979): 325; Li, *Chinese in Canada*, 46; Ward, *White Canada Forever*, 38; Willmott, "Approaches to the Study of the Chinese," 45; *Hansard*, 2 July 1885, 3008.

38 SBC 1884 c. 2, 3 and 4.

39 SBC 1884 c. 4.

40 CPR contractor Andrew Onderdonk and the railway's president, George Stephen, warned the federal government that unless the BC legislation was "promptly disallowed" completion of the railway would be delayed for a year. Patricia Roy, "A Choice between Evils: The Chinese and the Construction of the Canadian Pacific Railway in British Columbia," in H. A. Dempsey, ed., *The CPR West: The Iron Road and the Making of a Nation* (Vancouver: Douglas and McIntyre, 1984), 32; Ryder, "Racism and the Constitution," 654-55.

41 Canada, Parliament, Sessional Papers, 1885, Vol. 18, No. 54A, Royal Commission on Chinese Immigration, *Report*, 1885, "Statement of the Knights of Labor, Nanaimo," Minutes of Evidence, 156. Each of the commissioners submitted a separate report. Chapleau's was paginated i-cxxxiv, and Gray's i-cii. Minutes of Evidence were appended in pages numbered 1-487. In subsequent references the Chapleau and Gray reports will be identified with the commissioner's name.

42 Ibid., Evidence, 75.

43 Ibid., 103.

44 Ibid., Gray, lxix.

45 Ibid., Evidence, 97.

46 Ibid., Chapleau, cxxx.

47 Ibid., Gray, lxix.

48 *Hansard*, 2 July 1885, 3009.

49 *Report*, 1885, Chapleau, xciv; *Hansard*, 2 July 1885, 3006.

50 *Hansard*, 2 July 1885, 3010.

51 *Report*, 1885, Evidence, 72.

52 *Statutes of Canada* (SC) 1885 c. 71. Exempted from the head tax were diplomats, tourists, merchants and students, none of whom would expect to stay in Canada. According to Commissioner Chapleau, the head tax device was adopted from the Australian colony of Queensland (*Hansard*, 2 July 1885, 3004).

53 *Hansard*, 4 September 1891, 5059.

54 *Hansard*, 7 July 1899, 6846.

55 Canada, Parliament, Sessional Papers, 1902, Vol. 13, No. 54, Royal Commission on Chinese and Japanese Immigration, *Report*, 1902, 97-127.

56 Ibid., 79.

57 Satzewich, "Reactions to Chinese," 319.

58 *Report*, 1902, 278.

59 *The Canadian Annual Review*, 1902, 335, cited in K. Paupst, "A Note on Anti-Chinese Sentiment in Toronto Before the First World War," *Canadian Ethnic Studies*, 9 (1977): 55.

60 *Saturday Night*, 8 September and 27 October 1906. Certain classes did continue to argue for access to Chinese labour. In 1907 a petition was submitted by wealthy Vancouver women seeking repeal of the $500 tax because it made it difficult to find Chinese house-servants. This brought a response from the Vancouver TLC that reverberated with assumptions concerning class, "race" and gender in that era: "The women of the working class do their own work and when they need help, they employ their own race. Let these ladies who now waste their time . . . [in] useless functions emulate the example of their poorer sisters and do a little of their own domestic work. If, however, they claim immunity from work, let them pay the price, or modify the conditions of service in such a manner as will secure for them girls of their own race. It is, we think, absurd that the working class of Canada should run the risk of having its standard of living degraded to the level of a Chinese coolie merely to gratify the whim of an aristocratic lady for a Chinese servant" (Vancouver TLC Minutes, 21 March 1907, cited in Creese, "Vancouver Workers Confront the 'Oriental Problem,' " 33).

61 Emily Murphy, *The Black Candle* (Toronto: T. Allen, 1922), 109.

62 H. Glynn-Ward, *The Writing on the Wall* (Vancouver, 1921; rpt. Toronto: University of Toronto Press, 1974); Robert E. Wynne, "Reaction to the Chinese in the Pacific Northwest and British Columbia," PhD dissertation, University of Washington, 1964, 182.

63 *Calgary Herald*, 4 October 1910, cited in Gunter Baureiss, "The Chinese Community in Calgary," *Alberta Historical Review*, 22 (1974): 6.

64 Vancouver *World*, 10 February 1912, cited in Anderson, *Vancouver's Chinatown*, 97.

65 T. L. Chapman, "The Anti-Drug Crusade in Western Canada, 1885-1925," in D. J. Bercuson and L. A. Knafla, eds., *Law and Society in Canada in Historical Perspective* (Calgary: University of Calgary, 1979), 91-109; Voisey, "Two Chinese Communities," 21.

66 Valverde, *Light, Soap and Water*, 57; Regina *Morning Leader*, 28 May 1912.

67 Chapman, "Anti-Drug Crusade," esp. 91-94, 97, 98, 101, 109; Voisey, "Two Chinese Communities," 21.

68 Valverde, *Light, Soap and Water*, 97-98.

69 Quoted in *Globe and Mail*, 11 June 1994.

70 Murphy, *Black Candle*; Glynn-Ward, *Writing on the Wall*. Each devoted an entire chapter to the theme of entrapment.

71 Cited in Paupst, "Anti-Chinese Sentiment," 58.

72 Cited in Huttenback, *Racism and Empire*, 137-38.

73 Chapman, "Anti-Drug Crusade," 103; Shirley J. Cook, "Canadian Narcotics Legislation, 1908-1923: A Conflict Model Interpretation," *Canadian Review of Sociology and Anthropology*, 6 (1969): 43.

74 Murphy, *Black Candle*, 188-89.
75 Baureiss, "Chinese in Calgary," 8; Baureiss, "Discrimination and Response," 251, 257-58; Li, "Chinese on the Prairie," 534; Patricia E. Roy, "British Columbia's Fear of Asians, 1900-1950," *Histoire sociale/Social History*, 13 (1980): 161-72; Roy, *White Man's Province*, 13-36; Ward, *White Canada Forever*, 49, 62-64; Edgar Wickberg, "Chinese and Canadian Influences on Chinese Politics in Vancouver, 1900-1947," *BC Studies*, 45 (1980): 53; Anderson, *Vancouver's Chinatown*, 90-91; David Chuenyan Lai, "The Issue of Discrimination in Education in Victoria, 1901-1923," *Canadian Ethnic Studies*, 19 (1987): 47-67; Timothy J. Stanley, "White Supremacy, Chinese Schooling, and School Segregation in Victoria: The Case of the Chinese Students' Strike, 1922-1923," *Historical Studies in Education/Revue d'histoire de l'éducation*, 2 (1990): 287-305.
76 Baureiss, "Chinese in Calgary," 3; Chan and Lam, "Chinese in Timmins," 580; Howard Palmer, "Anti-Oriental Sentiment in Alberta 1880-1920," *Canadian Ethnic Studies*, 2 (1970): 31; Patricia E. Roy, "The Preservation of the Peace in Vancouver: The Aftermath of the Anti-Chinese Riot of 1887," *BC Studies*, 21 (1976): 44-59. For a thorough analysis of the American pattern in this same period see John R. Wunder, "Anti-Chinese Violence in the American West, 1850-1910," in John McLaren et al., eds., *Law for the Elephant, Law for the Beaver. Essays in the Legal History of the North American West* (Regina and Pasadena: Canadian Plains Research Centre and Ninth Judicial Circuit Historical Society, 1992), 212-36.
77 NA, MG 26 G1(A), Laurier Papers, Vol. 477, correspondence and reports on the riots; Canada, Royal Commission to Investigate Losses Sustained by the Japanese Population of Vancouver, *Report*, 1908; Canada, Royal Commission to Investigate Losses Sustained by the Chinese Population of Vancouver, *Report*, 1908; Comack, "Drug Legislation and Class Conflict," 79-83; Hallett, "Governor-General's Views on Orientals," 57, 63; Roy, *White Man's Province*, 185-226; Howard Sugimoto, "The Vancouver Riots of 1907: A Canadian Episode," in H. Conroy and T. Miyakawa, eds., *East Across the Pacific: Historical and Sociological Studies of Japanese Immigration and Assimilation* (Santa Barbara: American Bibliographical Center-Clio Press, 1972), 92-126; Howard Sugimoto, *Japanese Immigration, the Vancouver Riots, and Canadian Diplomacy* (New York: Arno Press, 1978); Ward, *White Canada Forever*, 67-74.
78 The phrase is from Ryder, "Racism and the Constitution," 631. Constance Backhouse offers a detailed canvas of immigration restrictions and other anti-Chinese legislation produced across Canada in "Gretta Wong Grant: Canada's First Chinese-Canadian Female Lawyer," *Windsor Yearbook of Access to Justice*, 15 (1996): 3-46.
79 *BNA Act* s. 95 states: "any law of the Legislature of a Province relative to ... Immigration shall have effect in and for the Province as long and as far only as it is not repugnant to any Act of the Parliament of Canada."
80 Confirmed by the Canadian government in SC 1907 c. 50.
81 *Hansard*, 27 March 1903, 603.

82 See chap. 1, sec. 1.

83 Ryder, "Racism and the Constitution."

84 SBC 1872 c. 37, s. 13; SBC 1872 c. 26, s. 22. As their numbers came to warrant the attention, Japanese and East Indians were disfranchised in 1895 and 1907 respectively. SBC 1895 c. 20; SBC 1907 c. 16.

85 SBC 1903-4 c. 17, s. 3.

86 *Hansard*, 4 May 1885, 1582.

87 SS 1908 c. 2, s. 11.

88 H. F. Angus, "The Legal Status in British Columbia of Residents of Oriental Race and their Descendants," in Norman MacKenzie, ed., *The Legal Status of Aliens in Pacific Countries* (London, 1937; rpt. New York: Kraus, 1975), 77-88.

89 SBC 1877 c. 15, s. 46(33).

90 SBC 1890 c. 33, s. 4. Restrictions on the employment of women and children in mining were becoming commonplace in Canada at that time. Ontario's *Mines Act*, for example, stated "No boy under the age of 15 shall be employed ... below ground; and no girl or woman shall be employed at mining work or allowed to be for the purpose of employment at mining work in or about any mine." SO 1892 c. 9, s. 54. For discussion of the context in which such restrictions were developed see below, sec. 5, "Defending the Family." The addition of a racial restriction was unique to British Columbia.

91 SBC 1897 c. 1; SBC 1898 c. 28; SBC 1900 c. 14; SBC 1902 c. 38; SBC 1903 c. 14; SBC 1905 c. 30.

92 PABC, Attorney-General's Papers, file 2060-17-18, 27, Orders-in-Council 245 and 275, 26 May and 16 June 1902, copies in NA, Tarnopolsky Papers, Vol. 43, file 4; *In Re The Japanese Treaty Act 1913*, (1920) BCR 136.

93 SBC 1902 c. 39.

94 SBC 1908 c. 50.

95 (1904) 10 BCR 408, at 424-26.

96 *Edmonton Journal*, 27 March 1918.

97 SBC 1885 c. 21, s. 11; Baureiss, "Chinese in Calgary," 5; Huttenback, *Racism and Empire*, 277-78; Palmer, "Anti-Orientalism in Alberta," 37; Lee Wai-Man, "Dance No More: Chinese Hand Laundries in Toronto," *Polyphony*, 6 (1984): 33; Edgar Wickberg, "Some Problems in Chinese Organizational Development in Canada, 1923-1937," *Canadian Ethnic Studies*, 11 (1979): 94.

98 SM 1916 c. 4.

99 (1878) 1 BCR 101.

100 Ibid., at 104.

101 Ibid., at 110-12.

102 (1885) 1 BCR 150, at 151. The case was brought on a writ of *certiorari*.

103 Ibid., at 157 and 162. The preamble to the 1884 Act is quoted in sec. 2 above.

104 Ibid., at 163. Alan Grove and Ross Lambertson ("Pawns of the Powerful: The Politics of Litigation in the Union Colliery Case," *BC Studies*, 103 [1994]: 3-31) point out that Judge Crease was identified with the business class who had an interest in the continued immigration and exploitation of Chinese

labour. Before the Royal Commission just months previously, Crease had claimed that Chinese competition with white labour was healthy and their exclusion would "create the worst of all monopolies, next to that of capital: the tyranny of labour." (*Report*, Evidence, 143.) It is possible therefore that the judge was simply being consistent with a business bias in his *Wing Chong* decision. On the other hand, attorney Drake, who introduced the question of Chinese rights into the argument, had spoken *against* Chinese immigration to the Royal Commissioners (*Report*, Evidence, 153-54) and was known as an exclusionist (Grove and Lambertson, 12-13). Class was apparently not the only consideration for the parties in this case. It may be noted that Crease could have overturned the Act without elaborating upon its injustice; his denunciation of discrimination therefore has a ring of conviction. John P. S. McLaren discusses *Tai Sing* and *Wing Chong* along with three other cases decided between 1878 and 1886 in the BC courts. While he confirms the class interest of the judges involved, McLaren demonstrates that Chief Justice Begbie and Justices Gray and Crease had an interpretation of the "rule of law" which incorporated the right of all subjects to equality before the law, including Chinese in Canada, and this right had to be protected by the courts even against encroachment by the legislature. McLaren argues as well that they had a pro-federalist inclination and a distrust of mass democracy which prompted them to disallow discriminatory acts passed by the BC legislature. In the absence of Canadian or English precedents dealing with comparable legislation, they followed examples set by "activist" judges in the United States, until the Privy Council established a pattern favouring provincial jurisdiction and a narrower role for judicial creativity (John P. S. McLaren, "The Early British Columbia Supreme Court and the 'Chinese Question': Echoes of the Rule of Law," *Manitoba Law Journal*, 20 [1991]: 107-47, and "The Early British Columbia Judges, the Rule of Law and the 'Chinese Question': The California and Oregon Connection," in McLaren, et al., eds., *Law for the Elephant, Law for the Beaver*, 237-73).

105   (1897) 5 BCR 306.

106   Ibid., at 316.

107   Ibid., at 317.

108   Ibid., at 318-19. Emphasis added. Grove and Lambertson ("Pawns of the Powerful," 23) comment: "The exclusionist politicians had now become exclusionist judges."

109   [1899] AC 580. Justice Drake heard the case first, and his decision in favour of Bryden was appealed to the full BC Supreme Court in August 1898 where Drake again delivered the judgment. Since the purpose in this entire strategy was for Bryden to lose, and thus permit Union Colliery to continue employing Chinese, Bryden's victory necessitated an appeal to the Privy Council. For a thorough discussion of the background of this case and its surrounding issues as it worked its way through the BC courts, see Grove and Lambertson, "Pawns of the Powerful."

110 AC, at 581.

111 Ibid., at 585.

112 Ibid., at 587.

113 Grove and Lambertson, "Pawns of the Powerful," 31.

114 RSBC 1897 c. 67.

115 (1901) 7 BCR 368.

116 Ibid., at 372. Once again, a BC judge was including a statement not entirely necessary to the decision at hand, but which suggested the propriety of recognizing equal rights for all British subjects in Canada regardless of "race."

117 (1901) 8 BCR 76.

118 [1903] AC 151.

119 Ibid., at 155-56.

120 Ibid., at 157.

121 Ibid., at 156.

122 Ibid.

123 Ibid., at 157.

124 Constance Backhouse, "'Pure Patriarchy': Nineteenth-Century Canadian Marriage," *McGill Law Journal*, 31 (1986): 312; Catherine L. Cleverdon, *The Woman Suffrage Movement in Canada* (2nd ed.; Toronto: University of Toronto Press, 1974), Introduction by Ramsay Cook, xiii; John McLaren, "The Canadian Magistracy and the Anti-White Slavery Campaign 1900-1920," in W. Wesley Pue and Barry Wright, eds., *Canadian Perspectives on Law and Society: Issues in Legal History* (Ottawa: Carleton University Press, 1988), 329-53; James G. Snell, "'The White Life for Two': The Defence of Marriage and Sexual Morality in Canada, 1890-1914," *Histoire sociale/Social History*, 16 (1983): 111-13.

125 Murphy, *Black Candle*, 235.

126 Veronica J. Strong-Boag, *The Parliament of Women: The National Council of Women of Canada, 1893-1929* (Ottawa: National Museums of Canada, 1976), 7; Alison Prentice et al., *Canadian Women: A History* (Toronto: Harcourt, Brace Jovanovich, 1988), 179-80, 211; Graeme Decarie, "Something Old, Something New . . . : Aspects of Prohibitionism in Ontario in the 1890s," in Donald Swainson, ed., *Oliver Mowat's Ontario* (Toronto: Macmillan, 1972), 166-67; Cook, Introduction to Cleverdon, xii.

127 Quoted in Strong-Boag, *Parliament*, 81.

128 Veronica Strong-Boag, "'Setting the Stage': National Organization and the Women's Movement in the Late 19th Century," in Susan Mann Trofimenkoff and Alison Prentice, eds., *The Neglected Majority: Essays in Canadian Women's History* (Toronto: McClelland and Stewart, 1977), 103.

129 Prentice, *Canadian Women*, 180-84; Decarie, "Prohibitionism"; Snell, "Defence of Marriage"; Karen Van Dieren, "The Response of the WMS to the Immigration of Asian Women 1888-1942," in Barbara K. Latham and Roberta J. Pazdro, eds., *Not Just Pin Money: Selected Essays on the History of Women's Work in British Columbia* (Victoria: Camosun College, 1984), 80-89, Valverde, *Light*,

Soap and Water, 116; Naomi Griffiths, *The Splendid Vision: Centennial History of the National Council of Women of Canada 1893-1993* (Ottawa: Carleton University Press, 1993).

130 Murphy, *Black Candle*, 17; Carol Lee Bacchi, *Liberation Deferred? The Ideas of the English-Canadian Suffragists, 1877-1918* (Toronto: University of Toronto Press, 1983), 112-13; Constance B. Backhouse, "Nineteenth Century Prostitution Law Reflection of a Discriminatory Society," *Histoire sociale/Social History*, 18 (1985): 387-423; Judy Bedford, "Prostitution in Calgary 1905-1914," *Alberta History*, 29 (1981): 1-11; Graham Parker, "The Legal Regulation of Sexual Activity and the Protection of Females," *Osgoode Hall Law Journal*, 21 (1983): 187-244.

131 In "White Women's Labor Laws," Constance Backhouse explores the tensions generated by the women's reform movement and majority Canadians' racial identity, and their impact upon the Chinese immigrant community. On this issue more generally, see Valverde, *Light, Soap and Water*, chap. 5; Prentice, *Canadian Women*, 193; Bacchi, *Liberation Deferred*, 52-53, 104; Strong-Boag, *Parliament*, 247. The National Council of Women convention in London, Ontario, in 1912, for example, passed resolutions on child welfare, prevention of tuberculosis, pure milk, playgrounds, training of women teachers, Chinese and Japanese "houses of ill-fame," and the international white slave traffic (Regina *Morning Leader*, 28 May 1912).

132 Strong-Boag, "Setting the Stage," 90.

133 Decarie, "Prohibitionism," 164.

134 Ibid.; Prentice, *Canadian Women*, 173.

135 Strong-Boag, *Parliament*, 247-48; Bacchi, *Liberation Deferred*, 53; Carol Bacchi, "Race Regeneration and Social Purity: A Study of the Social Attitude of Canada's English-Speaking Suffragists," *Histoire sociale/Social History*, 11 (1978): 461.

136 Backhouse, "Prostitution Law"; Bedford, "Prostitution in Calgary"; Snell, "Defence of Marriage"; Strong-Boag, *Parliament*, 429-31.

137 Backhouse, "Prostitution Law," 395.

138 Cook, Introduction to Cleverdon, xiii.

139 *In Times Like These* (rpt. ed.; Toronto: University of Toronto Press, 1972), 48.

140 Prentice, *Canadian Women*, 150.

141 Valverde, *Light, Soap and Water*, 109.

142 Prentice, *Canadian Women*, 227; Ruth Frager, "No Proper Deal: Women Workers and the Canadian Labour Movement, 1870-1940," in Linda Briskin and Lynda Yanz, *Union Sisters. Women in the Labour Movement* (Toronto: Women's Press, 1983), 46; Janice Acton et al., eds., *Women At Work: Ontario, 1850-1930* (Toronto: Canadian Women's Educational Press, 1974), 5.

143 Frager, "No Proper Deal," 51-52.

144 Quoted in Susan Wade, "Helena Gutteridge: Votes for Women and Trade Unions," in Barbara Latham and Cathy Kess, eds., *In Her Own Right: Selected Essays on Women's History in BC* (Victoria: Camosun College, 1980), 193.

145 Quoted in Marie Campbell, "Sexism in British Columbia Trade Unions, 1900-1920," in Latham and Kess, *In Her Own Right*, 175-76.
146 Campbell, "Sexism in British Columbia," 177.
147 *The Ontario Factories Act*, SO 1884 c. 39, for example, set a 10-hour day and 60-hour week for women factory workers, insisted that they be allowed a full hour for lunch in a suitable room away from the machinery, prevented women from being assigned to clean machinery while it was in motion, and stated generally that "It shall not be lawful to employ in a factory any child, young girl or woman, so that the health ... is likely to be permanently injured."
148 NA, RG 25 Vol. 1524, file 867, "Canadian Laws Governing the Employment of Women," enclosed in H. H. Ward, deputy minister of Labour, to L. Beaudry, Department of External Affairs, 28 September 1928.
149 For example, *Ontario Shops Regulation Act*, SO 1888 c. 33.
150 "Canadian Laws Governing the Employment of Women." This Canadian legislation evolved in a continental context, as American states passed similar laws. See Alan Brinkley, "For Their Own Good," *New York Review of Books*, 26 May 1994, 42. The Canadian background is given in Margaret E. McCallum, "Keeping Women in Their Place: The Minimum Wage in Canada, 1910-25," *Labour/Le Travail*, 17 (1986): 29-56, and Gillian Creese, "Sexual Equality and the Minimum Wage in British Columbia," *Journal of Canadian Studies*, 26 (1991-92): 120-40.
151 Snell, "Defence of Marriage," 121. Again, a parallel process was apparent in the United States. For example in 1910 Congress passed the *Mann Act*, providing a five-year federal jail term for any man who *intended* to commit an immoral act with a woman who had crossed a state line either with him or to visit him. See David J. Langum, *Crossing Over the Line: Legislating Morality and the Mann Act* (Chicago: University of Chicago Press, 1994).
152 *Saturday Night*, 15 August 1925. In the absence of explicit laws the responsible authorities often followed their "common sense" in preventing marriage between members of different "races." Magistrate Emily Murphy recounted the story of a Chinese man "whose morals were as oblique as his eyes" brought before her by some nuns who wanted him deported to stop a marriage to a white domestic servant (*Black Candle*, 236-37). The Regina *Morning Leader*, 5 September 1912, told of a clergyman who had abruptly refused to marry a Chinese man and white woman. Stories commenting upon intermarriage, always negatively, frequently appeared in the Canadian press during this period. See also the terrifying case of Ira Johnston and Isabella Jones in chap. 3, sec. 2. One interesting aspect of their dilemma was their extreme difficulty in finding a clergyman willing to marry them.
153 Strong-Boag, *Parliament*, 186.
154 For example, Van Dieren, "Response of the WMS."
155 Lai, *Chinatowns*, 54; Stanley, "White Supremacy, Chinese Schooling, and School Segregation in Victoria," 290.

156 W. L. Mackenzie King, *Report on the Need for the Suppression of the Opium Traffic in Canada*, 1908; SC 1908 c. 50; Chapman, "Anti-Drug Crusade," 93-95; Comack, "Drug Legislation and Class Conflict," 67-89; Cook, "Canadian Narcotics Legislation," 37, 39; Melvyn Green, "A History of Canadian Narcotics Control: The Formative Years," *University of Toronto Faculty of Law Review*, 37 (1979): 42-43; G. E. Trasov, "History of the Opium and Narcotic Drug Legislation in Canada," *Criminal Law Quarterly*, 4 (1962): 276; Neil Boyd, "The Origins of Canadian Narcotics Legislation: The Process of Criminalization in Historical Context," in R. C. Macleod, ed., *Lawful Authority. Readings on the History of Criminal Justice in Canada* (Toronto: Copp Clark Pitman, 1988), 192-218; Anderson, *Vancouver's Chinatown*, 99; C. Mosher, "The Legal Response to Narcotic Drugs in Five Ontario Cities, 1908-1961," PhD dissertation, University of Toronto, 1992; C. Mosher and J. Hagan, "Constituting Class and Crime in Upper Canada: The Sentencing of Narcotics Offenders circa 1908-1953," *Social Forces*, 72 (1994): 613-41.

157 *Hansard*, 26 January 1911, 2518-2553; SC 1911 c. 17; Boyd, "Origins of Canadian Narcotics Legislation," 205; Chapman, "Anti-Drug Crusade," 95, 96, 104; Comack, "Drug Legislation and Class Conflict," 86; Cook, "Canadian Narcotics Legislation," 37-39; Hallett, "Governor-General's Views on Orientals," 70; Huttenback, *Racism and Empire*, 188. Discussing the 1923 Opium Bill, Senator Wellington B. Willoughby of Moose Jaw declared that he knew "personally" of opium being planted on a Chinese suspect with police connivance (Senate, *Debates*, 27 April 1923, 347).

158 TLC, *Reports of the Proceedings of the Annual Convention*.

159 TLC, *Report*, 1912, 107.

160 Glen Makahonuk, "Craft Unionism and the 1912 Strike Wave," *Saskatchewan History*, 44 (1992): 59-67.

161 TLC, *Report*, 1912, 30-32; Regina *Morning Leader*, 7 February 1912.

162 Regina *Morning Leader*, 5 September 1912.

163 Moose Jaw *Evening Times*, 6 September 1913, 21 and 24 February 1914.

164 TLC, *Report*, 1912, 32-34, 107.

165 TLC, *Report*, 1914, 22-24, 33-36, 76, 119. British Columbia was at first unresponsive, and Alberta hinted that it would act after the Quong Wing case was settled in the courts. TLC, *Report*, 1915, 41-46, 110.

166 For example, Chan and Lam, "Chinese in Timmins," 579; Miriam Yu, "Human Rights, Discrimination, and Coping Behaviour of the Chinese in Canada," *Canadian Ethnic Studies*, 19 (1987): 114-24.

167 *Census of Canada, 1921*.

168 Royal Commission, *Report*, 1885, Gray, xi.

169 *Census of Canada, 1911*.

170 Royal Commission, *Report*, 1902, 236.

171 Ibid., 65.

172 Wickberg, *From China to Canada*, esp. chaps. 3, 6, 8 and 12, gives a very thorough description of Chinese organizations in Canada. For further elaborations,

not always in agreement, see Gunter Baureiss, "Chinese Organizational Development – A Comment," *Canadian Ethnic Studies*, 12 (1980): 124-30; Gunter Baureiss and Leo Driedger, "Winnipeg Chinatown: Demographic, Ecological and Organizational Change, 1900-1980," *Urban History Review*, 10 (1982): 11-24; Anthony B. Chan, "'Orientalism' and Image Making: The Sojourner in Canadian History," *Journal of Ethnic Studies*, 9 (1981): 37-46; Chan and Lam, "Chinese in Timmins"; Peter S. Li, "Immigration Laws and Family Patterns: Some Demographic Changes among Chinese Families in Canada, 1885-1971," *Canadian Ethnic Studies*, 12 (1980): 58-73; Li, *Chinese in Canada*, esp. part II; Wickberg, "Chinese Organizational Development"; Wickberg, "Chinese Politics in Vancouver"; Edgar Wickberg, "Chinese Organizations and the Canadian Political Process: Two Case Studies," in Jorgen Dahlie and Tissa Fernando, eds., *Ethnicity, Power and Politics in Canada* (Toronto: Methuen, 1981); W. E. Willmott, "Some Aspects of Chinese Communities in British Columbia Towns," *BC Studies*, 1 (1968-69): 27-36.

173 Representative of this perspective is the work of Peter S. Li, particularly "Historical Approach to Ethnic Stratification," "Chinese on the Prairie," and *Chinese in Canada*, chap. 3, "Occupations and Ethnic Business." A non-"victim" interpretation of the same phenomenon, attributing it rather to the tradition of entrepreneurism and upward mobility in Chinese peasant society, is given by Paul Yee, "Business Devices from Two Worlds: The Chinese in Early Vancouver," *BC Studies*, 62 (1984): 44-67.

174 Yee, "Business Devices from Two Worlds," 45-47.

175 Most of the items mentioned in the three preceding footnotes contain references to the CBA. In addition see Lai, "Chinese Consolidated Benevolent Association," and Chuen-Yan Lai, "Chinese Attempts to Discourage Emigration to Canada: Some Findings from the Chinese Archives in Victoria," *BC Studies*, 18 (1973): 33-49.

176 Baureiss, "Chinese in Calgary," 5; Baureiss, "Discrimination and Response," 256-57; Ivan L. Head, "The Stranger in Our Midst: A Sketch of the Legal Status of the Alien in Canada," *Canadian Yearbook of International Law*, 2 (1964): 131; Lai, "Chinese Consolidated Benevolent Association," 59; Stanley, "White Supremacy, Chinese Schooling, and School Segregation in Victoria," 289; Ward, *White Canada Forever*, 33; Wickberg, "Chinese Organizational Development," 94-95; Wickberg, "Chinese Politics in Vancouver," 47, 53; NA, Tarnopolsky Papers, Vol. 43, file 5. A special issue of *Canadian Ethnic Studies*, 19, 3 (1987) is devoted to the topic "Coping with Racism: The Chinese Experience in Canada." Of particular interest to the discussion here are Gunter Baureiss, "Chinese Immigration, Chinese Stereotypes, and Chinese Labour," Gillian Creese, "Organizing Against Racism in the Workplace: Chinese Workers in Vancouver Before the Second World War," David Chuenyan Lai, "The Issue of Discrimination in Education in Victoria, 1901-1923," and Jin Tan, "Chinese Labour and the Reconstituted Social Order of British Columbia."

177 Moose Jaw *Evening Times*, 1 and 28 May 1912; Regina *Morning Leader*, 10 May 1912; Regina *Daily Province*, 13 and 16 May 1912.

178 SAB, Collection R 1267, file #474, docket 192/12, "R. v. Quong Wing," Information and Complaint of W. P. Johnson, 21 May 1912.

179 SAB, Naturalization Certificate, Quong Wing, 7 December 1905. The name of the restaurant appears variously in different sources: CER, C and R, CNR, CPR. The form "CER" was used in the local magistrate's court documents, and is the one adopted here.

180 *Census of Canada*, 1911; Moose Jaw *Evening Times*, 5 July 1913.

181 SAB, Examination of Witnesses, 27 May 1912; Docket 191, "R. v. Quong Sing," Naturalization Certificate, Quon Sing [*sic*], 6 December 1901.

182 SAB, "R. v. Quong Wing," Naturalization Certificate; Deposition of Witnesses; Conviction.

183 Moose Jaw *Evening Times*, 28 May 1912.

184 The discussion of who or what was "white" received more attention in the trial of the restaurant owner Yoshi in Saskatoon less than three months later. In that case the three waitresses involved were not English but Russian and German, and the defence asked whether they should be included in the category "white woman or girl" set out in the statute. The Crown attorney asked the magistrate to "give these words the meaning which is commonly applied to them; that is to say the females of any of the civilized European nations." Magistrate Brown however decided to adjourn the trial while he considered the issue. It took him a week to decide that while "he did not think it necessary to go into the classification of the white race," still it was possible to include "Germans and Russians" as "members of the Caucasian race." Mr. Yoshi was thereupon convicted, along with two other Saskatoon restaurateurs, one Japanese and one Chinese, whose names and circumstances were not reported. See above chap. 2, sec. 1; Saskatoon *Daily Star*, 14, 15, 19 and 21 August 1912. The Yoshi case is discussed in Constance Backhouse, "White Female Help and Chinese-Canadian Employers: Race, Class, Gender and Law in the Case of Yee Clun, 1924," *Canadian Ethnic Studies*, 26 (1994): 37-38.

185 *The Canadian Parliamentary Guide* (Ottawa: Mortimer, 1919) described Mr. Willoughby as a bencher of the Law Society of Saskatchewan, Opposition leader from 1912 to 1917, prominent Anglican layman and Masonic Past Grand Master. In 1917 he was appointed to the Senate of Canada.

186 SAB, "R. v. Quong Wing," Affadavit and Receipt.

187 SAB, Affadavit, 1 November 1912; Order to Magistrate, 5 November and reply, 9 November 1912.

188 SAB, Judgment Roll, No. 191 (Quong Sing) and 192 (Quong Wing), 9 July 1913.

189 (1913) 12 DLR 656; (1913) 4 WWR 1135; 21 CCC 326; 49 CLJ 593. Subsequent references are to DLR.

190 DLR, at 657. By "coloured" the chief justice obviously meant anyone of Asian or African descent or a native Canadian.

191 Ibid., at 660, 661.

192 Ibid., at 662.

193 Ibid., at 666.

194 Ibid., at 667.

195 Ibid., at 668-69.

196 F. W. G. Haultain sat in the Saskatchewan legislature as Leader of the Opposition from 1905 to 1912. Following his Conservative party's resounding defeat in the July 1912 election, Haultain was appointed chief justice of Saskatchewan. His close association with Wellington Willoughby, his successor as Conservative leader, may have made him more attentive to the arguments put on behalf of Quong Wing and against the Act passed by his political opponents. Regina *Morning Leader*, 12 July 1912; Stanley Gordon, "Sir Frederick Haultain," *The Canadian Encyclopedia* (2nd ed.; Edmonton: Hurtig, 1988), 967. (Haultain was knighted in 1916.)

197 That is, not recorded in the Saskatchewan or National Archives.

198 NA, RG 125 Vol. 340, file 3389, Registrar's Certificate; Lai, "Chinese Consolidated Benevolent Association," 59.

199 TLC, *Report*, 1912, 30-32.

200 TLC, *Report*, 1914, 76.

201 SAB, Affadavit, 13 August 1913.

202 NA, RG 125 Vol. 340, file 3389, Case on Appeal.

203 Ibid., Case File 3389, Appellant's *Factum*.

204 Ibid., Respondent's *Factum*.

205 (1914) 39 SCR 440 at 444. Other reports are found in (1914) 18 DLR 121; 23 CCC 113; (1914) 6 WWR 270. Subsequent references are to SCR.

206 SCR, at 445.

207 Ibid.

208 Ibid., at 448-49.

209 Ibid., at 447-48.

210 Ibid., at 449-50.

211 Ibid., at 465-66.

212 Ibid., at 463-65. Emphasis added.

213 Ibid., at 451.

214 Ibid., at 452.

215 Ibid., at 453-54.

216 Ibid., at 456.

217 Ibid., at 440, and Case File. The application was made on 16 April and rejected on 19 May 1914.

218 SCR, at 457.

219 TLC, *Report*, 1915, 56.

220 Tarnopolsky, *Discrimination and the Law*, 14-16; Tarnopolsky, "Supreme Court and Civil Liberties," 68-70.

221 "1. The Canadian Charter of Rights and Freedoms guarantees the rights and freedoms set out in it subject only to such reasonable limits prescribed by law as can be demonstrably justified in a free and democratic society."

222 Wickberg, *From China to Canada*, 120.

223 Project Integrate, "Chinese Community of Moose Jaw," 10; Lai, *Chinatowns*, 93-94.

224 Moose Jaw *Evening Times* 5 March 1912.

225 Ibid., 1 and 30 September 1911.

226 Sec. 8 above.

227 Wickberg, *From China to Canada*, 120, acknowledges the "moral concern" but concludes that "economic reasons were paramount" and the true aim was to exclude Chinese from the restaurant business.

228 TLC, *Report*, 1915, 56.

229 This explanation has virtually become standard among analyses of the Chinese situation in BC. For a particularly effective articulation see Ryder, "Racism and the Constitution." A sophisticating nuance has, however, been inserted into the debate by Ross Lambertson: "The state is not so much an instrument of class rule as an arena of class struggle, a struggle without any preordained outcome, although the dice are heavily weighted in favour of the interests of Capital" ("After *Union Colliery*: Law, Race, and Class in the Coalmines of British Columbia," in H. Foster and J. McLaren, eds., *Essays in the History of Canadian Law*, Vol. 6: *British Columbia and the Yukon* [Toronto: Osgoode Society and University of Toronto Press, 1996], 405).

230 Makahonuk, "Craft Unionism."

231 In February 1914, two years after the *Female Labour Act* was introduced, owners of two steam laundries in Regina asked for a $500 annual tax on all laundries in the city, with the intention of forcing the small Chinese operators out of competition (Moose Jaw *Evening Times*, 21 February 1914).

232 Backhouse writes: "Although the legislation did not directly bar Asian entrepreneurs from operating restaurants, laundries or other businesses, it enjoined them from hiring white women, something which was *intended* to have significant economic consequences" ("Yee Clun," 35, emphasis added).

233 Quoted in (1922) 65 DLR 577, at 582.

234 [1920] 3 WWR 997; (1920) BCR 136.

235 (1922) 63 SCR 293; (1922) 65 DLR 577.

236 DLR, at 586-87.

237 [1923] AC 450.

238 *Hansard*, 8 May 1922, 1509.

239 SC 1923 c. 38.

240 Senate, *Debates*, 26 June 1923, 1121.

241 Ibid., 1123.

242 SC 1923 c. 22.

243 Murphy, *Black Candle*, 138.

244 Ibid., 96.

245 *Regina Daily Post*, 17 January 1919.
246 Regina *Morning Leader*, 8 August 1924. For a scholarly account of this case see Backhouse, "Yee Clun."
247 Regina *Morning Leader*, 12 and 13 August 1924.
248 Ibid., 13 August, 24 September 1924.
249 Ibid., 20 August 1924.
250 Ibid., 8 October 1924.
251 Ibid., 22 October 1924; [1925] 3 WWR 714.
252 Ibid., at 715-16.
253 Ibid., at 716-17.
254 Ibid., at 717-18.
255 It is tempting to discern a mischievous motive in Justice Mackenzie's interpretation of the 1919 amendment. Or perhaps he was conscientiously applying the canons of statutory construction to infer the intent from the text of the law rather than from the minds of the legislators.
256 SS 1925-26 c. 53.
257 NA, Tarnopolsky Papers, Vol. 43, file 5.
258 Ibid.
259 Ibid.
260 SO 1914 c. 40, s. 2(2).
261 TLC, *Report*, 1914, 24 and 76.
262 Backhouse, "Yee Clun," Appendix B, reports a deliberate proclamation of the Act by an unpublished order-in-council dated 2 November 1920 "upon the recommendation of the Honourable the Minister of Labour." Since it was not published there was no program to enforce the law.
263 NA, RG 25 Vol. 1524, file 867, Chow Kwo Hsien to Ferguson, 31 August 1928.
264 Ibid., Chow to Ernest Lapointe, acting prime minister of Canada, 2 October 1928.
265 Ibid., Chow to W. Stuart Edwards, deputy minister of Justice, 7 September 1928.
266 Ibid., Edwards to Edward Bayly, deputy attorney general of Ontario, 7 September 1928.
267 Ibid., Bayly to Edwards, 15 September 1928.
268 Ibid., G. N. Gordon to Lapointe, 24 September 1928.
269 8 September 1928.
270 2 October 1928.
271 Anne Elizabeth Wilson, "A Pound of Prevention – or an Ounce of Cure? A Plea for National Legislation on a Growing Problem," *Chatelaine*, December 1928, 12, 13, 55.
272 NA, RG 25 Vol. 1524, file 867, Memorandum initialled "JC" to Edwards, 5 October 1928. Premier Ferguson apparently would have welcomed federal interference, but Mr. Lapointe was reluctant to do so (memorandum initialled "HLK" to O. D. Skelton, 27 February 1929).

273 Ibid., W. C. Chen to Sir Austen Chamberlain, British foreign secretary, 11 January 1929, forwarded without comment to Ottawa, 4 February 1929.
274 Ibid., H. H. Ward, deputy minister of Labour, to Laurent Beaudry, External Affairs, 28 September 1928.
275 Ibid., Chow to Lapointe, 2 October 1928.
276 SO 1929 c. 72, s. 5.
277 NA, RG 25 Vol. 1524, file 867, O. D. Skelton to Chen Kwong Gow, 23 May 1929.
278 Ibid., Li Tchuin to D. C. Draper, 24 October 1929, and to H. W. Walker, 30 October 1929.
279 Gray, *Roar of the Twenties*, 267-73; Robert Moon, *This Is Saskatchewan* (Toronto: Ryerson Press, 1953), 45-47. The Klan did accomplish the dismissal of Chief Walter Johnson, whose River Street connections were widely known. The chief returned to public life at the age of 77 in 1939, elected as mayor of Moose Jaw on a platform of financial reform (Gray, *Roar of the Twenties*, 270-71; *Red Lights*, 85). For background on the KKK in the Canadian West, see Patrick Kyba, "Ballots and Burning Crosses – The Election of 1929," in Norman Ward and Duff Spafford, eds., *Politics in Saskatchewan* (Toronto: Longmans, 1968), 105-23; Tom M. Henson, "Ku Klux Klan in Western Canada," *Alberta History*, 25 (1977): 1-8.
280 *Census of Canada, 1931*. Tables 49 and 69 in Vol. 7 give a detailed breakdown for the gainfully employed in 1921 and 1931.
281 SAB, Charter and Act to Incorporate the Eastern Club, 1915.
282 NA, Case File, Affidavit sworn by Jasper Fish, 31 May 1916. Quong Wing did, however, pay the respondent's costs in the Supreme Court of Canada, amounting to $482.94.
283 Quoted in Anderson, *Vancouver's Chinatown*, 113; Patricia E. Roy, "British Columbia's Fear of Asians, 1900-1950," *Histoire sociale/Social History*, 13 (1980): 171.
284 *Report*, 193.
285 [1920] 3 WWR 937; (1922) 65 DLR 577; (1922) 63 SCR 293.
286 *Regina v. Millar*, (1953-54) 10 WWR (NS) 145.
287 *Morgan et al. v. Attorney-General for Prince Edward Island*, (1973) 42 DLR (3d), 603; *Richard Alan Morgan and Alan Max Jacobson and The Attorney General for the Province of Prince Edward Island*, [1976] 2 SCR 349.
288 *McNeil v. Nova Scotia Board of Censors and Attorney General of Nova Scotia*, (1978) 25 NSR (2d) 128.
289 *R. v. Thrifty Foods Limited et al.*, (1981) 3 WWR 626.
290 *Corporation professionelle des médecins du Québec c. Richard Riverin*, [1984] CSP 1124.
291 *R. v. Laybolt and Laybolt*, (1985) 54 Nfld & PEIR 51.
292 [1976] 2 SCR 349, at 363. The American appellants in the PEI property case had cited *Bryden* as a precedent to deny the provincial government authority to pass a law restricting aliens.
293 SM 1940 c. 35; SO 1947 c. 102, s. 1; SBC 1968 c. 53, s. 29; SS 1969 c. 24, s. 73.

3 *CHRISTIE V. YORK CORPORATION*

1 [1940] SCR 139; [1940] 1 DLR 81.
2 Interviews: Mr. Edward Packwood and Mrs. Ann Packwood, Montreal, 13 June 1988; Dr. Harold Potter, Montreal, 14 June; Mrs. Ann Packwood, 15 June.

   In court Mr. Hazen Hansard, counsel for the York Tavern, entered a curious exchange with Mr. Christie.

   Q. Of course, I want you to understand, as far as my personal feelings in this matter are concerned, they do not count, but it is the fact that you, Mr. Christie, and Mr. King, are of the coloured race?
   A. Yes. . . .
   Q. Are you a full blooded negro?
   A. Yes.
   Q. I notice your complexion is not extraordinarily dark. That is the reason I ask you?
   A. Well, that is a question.
   Q. I just merely want it on the record that you are not extraordinarily black?
   A. As far as I know.
   Q. And similarly I notice Mr. King is not extraordinarily black, is he?
   A. No.
   (Supreme Court, Case File #6684, "Evidence on Discovery.")

3 Ibid.; interview: Dr. Harold Potter.
4 Supreme Court, Case File #6684, "Deposition of René St. Jean," waiter. Fred Christie insisted that he had been served in the new location, but the waiter claimed that African Canadians had not been admitted since the York opened in the Forum.
5 Supreme Court, Case File #6684, "Evidence on Discovery."
6 Interviews: Mrs. Martha Griffiths, Montreal, 13 June 1988; Mr. and Mrs. Packwood.
7 Supreme Court, Case File #6684.
8 J. Cleland Hamilton, "Slavery in Canada," *Magazine of American History*, 25 (1891): 238.
9 Older accounts of Canadian slavery include T. Watson Smith, "The Slave in Canada," *Collections of the Nova Scotia Historical Society*, 10 (1899), entire issue; W. R. Riddell, "Slavery in Canada," *Journal of Negro History*, 5 (1920): 261-377; W. R. Riddell, "Notes on the Slave in Nouvelle France," *Journal of Negro History*, 8 (1923): 316-30; M. J. Viger and L. H. Lafontaine, "De l'esclavage en Canada," *Mémoires et documents relatifs à l'histoire du Canada* (Montreal: La Société historique de Montréal, 1859), 1-63; F. W. Harris, "The Black Population of the County of Annapolis," in C. I. Perkins, ed., *The Romance of Old Annapolis* (Annapolis Royal: N.p., 1925), 60-68. The definitive study of slavery in New France is Marcel Trudel, *L'esclavage au Canada français* (Quebec: Presses universitaires Laval, 1960), to which has been

added his *Dictionnaire des esclaves et de leurs propriétaires au Canada français* (Lasalle: Hurtubise, 1990), which contains an entry on almost every slave and slave owner in French Canada. Other recent discussions are found in Robin Winks, *The Blacks in Canada: A History* (Montreal: McGill-Queen's University Press, 1971), 1-60; James W. St. G. Walker, *A History of Blacks in Canada: A Study Guide for Teachers and Students* (Ottawa: Minister of State, Multiculturalism, 1980), 19-27; David Bell, "Slavery and the Judges of Loyalist New Brunswick," *UNB Law Journal*, 31 (1982): 9-42; Barry Cahill, "Slavery and the Judges of Loyalist Nova Scotia," *UNB Law Journal*, 43 (1994): 73-134, and "Habeas Corpus and Slavery in Nova Scotia: R. v. Hecht Ex Parte Rachel, 1798," *UNB Law Journal*, 44 (1995): 179-209; Gary Hartlen, "Bound for Nova Scotia: Slaves in the Planter Migration, 1759-1800," in Margaret Conrad, ed., *Making Adjustments: Change and Continuity in Planter Nova Scotia, 1759-1800* (Fredericton: Acadiensis Press, 1991), 123-28; Michael Power and Nancy Butler, *Slavery and Freedom in Niagara* (Niagara-on-the-Lake: Niagara Historical Society, 1993), Part 1, "Simcoe and Slavery," 9-39. A summary of the legal provisions applicable to Canadian slavery is provided by Helen T. Catterall, *Judicial Cases Concerning American Slavery and the Negro*, Vol. 5: *Canadian Cases* (New York: Octagon Books, 1968), 340-48.

10 Nova Scotia, House of Assembly, *Journals and Proceedings*, 1808, 155, 156, 159, 272, 281, 295. The Bill was twice examined by a Committee of the Whole and twice deferred.

11 C. Vann Woodward, *The Strange Career of Jim Crow* (New York: Oxford University Press, 1955), 8. According to Woodward, "The origin of the term 'Jim Crow' applied to Negroes is lost in obscurity. Thomas D. Rice wrote a song and dance called 'Jim Crow' in 1832, and the term had become an adjective by 1838" (7). Stuart Berg Flexner dates the term to the 1730s, when African slaves were first called "crows," and Rice's song to 1828 (*I Hear America Talking: An Illustrated Treasury of American Words and Phrases* [New York: Van Nostrand Reinhold, 1976], 39). Rice, the alleged originator of blackface minstrelsy in the United States, designed his dance after seeing a slave with a physical disability jumping and wheeling to a song with the words "Weel a-bout and turn a-bout / And do just so / Every time I weel a-bout / I jump Jim Crow" (Lerone Bennet Jr., *Before the Mayflower* [Baltimore: Penguin, 1966], 220). Rice's song and dance routine became a hit and popularized the use of the term "Jim Crow" as a noun to refer to African Americans and as an adjective to the separate facilities set apart for black use, such as those described by Vann Woodward, and the laws enforcing them. Benjamin Quarles, *The Negro in the Making of America* (3rd ed.; New York: Collier, 1987), 73, identifies the Jim Crow dance as a "favorite" among the slaves when celebrating Christmas or July 4th. Since slave dances at such celebrations were often surreptitious mockeries of their masters' dancing styles (Lynne F. Emery, "Dance," in R. M. Miller and J. D. Smith, eds., *Dictionary of American Slavery* [Westport, CN: Greenwood Press, 1988], 173-74) and since "old Mr. Crow" was a term sometimes

used by slaves to mean slave owner (Bennet, *Before the Mayflower*, 221), it is possible that Rice's Jim Crow dance was a satire upon a satire.

12 James W. St. G. Walker, *The Black Loyalists* (2nd ed.; Toronto: University of Toronto Press, 1992).

13 John N. Grant, *The Immigration and Settlement of the Black Refugees of the War of 1812 in Nova Scotia and New Brunswick* (Dartmouth, NS: Black Cultural Centre for Nova Scotia, 1990); William Spray, "The Settlement of the Black Refugees in New Brunswick, 1815-1836," *Acadiensis*, 6 (1977): 64-79.

14 Donald G. Simpson, "Negroes in Ontario from Early Times to 1870," PhD dissertation, University of Western Ontario, 1971; Jason H. Silverman, *Unwelcome Guests: Canada West's Response to American Fugitive Slaves, 1800-1865* (Millwood, NY: Associated Faculty Press, 1985); James Pilton, "Negro Settlement in British Columbia, 1858-71," MA thesis, University of British Columbia, 1951; Crawford Kilian, *Go Do Some Great Thing: The Black Pioneers of British Columbia* (Vancouver: Douglas and McIntyre, 1978); James W. St. G. Walker, "On the Record: The Testimony of Canada's Black Pioneers, 1783-1865," in A. W. Bonnett and G. L. Watson, eds., *Emerging Perspectives on the Black Diaspora* (Lanham, MD: University Press of America, 1990), 79-119. Until recently a figure of 30,000 to 40,000 has generally been accepted for the number of American fugitives who came into Canada. Michael Wayne ("The Black Population of Canada West on the Eve of the American Civil War: A Reassessment Based on the Manuscript Census of 1861," *Histoire sociale/Social History* 28 [1995]: 465-85) suggests a total of only about 20,000 to 23,000, most of whom remained in Canada following the Civil War.

15 Harold Troper, "The Creek-Negroes of Oklahoma and Canadian Immigration, 1909-11," *Canadian Historical Review*, 53 (1972): 272-88; R. Bruce Shepard, "Black Migration as a Response to Repression: The Background Factors and Migration of Oklahoma Blacks to Western Canada, 1905-1912," MA thesis, University of Saskatchewan, 1976; Judith Hill, "Alberta's Black Settlers: A Study of Canadian Immigration Policy and Prejudice," MA thesis, University of Alberta, 1981; Howard and Tamara Palmer, *Peoples of Alberta: Portraits of Cultural Diversity* (Saskatoon: Western Producer Prairie Books, 1985), 365-93. Bruce Shepard has published a number of articles related to his thesis topic: "Diplomatic Racism: Canadian Government and Black Migration from Oklahoma, 1905-1912," *Great Plains Quarterly*, 3 (1983): 5-16; "Plain Racism: The Reaction against Oklahoma Black Immigration to the Canadian Plains," *Prairie Forum*, 10 (1985): 365-82; "Origins of the Oklahoma Black Migration to the Canadian Plains," *Canadian Journal of History*, 23 (1988): 1-23; "North to the Promised Land: Black Migration to the Canadian Plains," *Chronicles of Oklahoma*, 66 (1988): 306-27, and has related the entire episode in *Deemed Unsuitable* (Toronto: Umbrella Press, 1997).

16 Nova Scotia, House of Assembly, *Journals and Proceedings*, 1815, 107.

17 William Pease and Jane Pease, "Opposition to the Founding of the Elgin Settlement," *Canadian Historical Review*, 38 (1957): 202-18; Harold Potter, "Negroes in Canada," *Race*, 3 (1961): 45; Walker, *History of Blacks in Canada*, 79-83.

18 Allen P. Stouffer, "'A Restless Child of Change and Accident': The Black Image in Nineteenth Century Ontario," *Ontario History*, 76 (1984): 128-50.

19 W. D. Scott, "The Negro," in Adam Shortt and Arthur Doughty, eds., *Canada and Its Provinces*, Vol. 7 (Toronto: Publishers' Association of Canada, 1914), 531.

20 28 April 1911, quoted in Colin Thomson, *Blacks in Deep Snow: Black Pioneers in Canada* (Don Mills, ON: Dent, 1979), 82-83.

21 NA, RG 76 Vol. 192, J. Bruce Walker to W. D. Scott, 21 August 1908.

22 Ibid., George Clingan to J. Bruce Walker, 21 Aug. 1908.

23 NA, MG 26 G1(A), Laurier Papers, Ada Knight, secretary, Edmonton IODE, to Frank Oliver, 31 March 1911, and enclosure.

24 Carol Lee Bacchi, *Liberation Deferred? The Ideas of the English-Canadian Suffragists, 1877-1918* (Toronto: University of Toronto Press, 1983), 53.

25 *Edmonton Capital*, 27 March 1911, quoted in Thomson, *Blacks in Deep Snow*, 81-82.

26 *Hansard*, 2, 22 and 23 March 1911, 4470-71, 5911-13, 5943-47.

27 *Hansard*, 3 April 1911, 6523-28.

28 Robin Winks, "Negro School Segregation in Ontario and Nova Scotia," *Canadian Historical Review*, 50 (1969): 164-91; Hildreth H. Spencer, "To Nestle in the Mane of the British Lion: A History of Canadian Black Education, 1820 to 1870," PhD dissertation, Northwestern University, 1970; Jason Silverman and Donna Gillie, "'The Pursuit of Knowledge under Difficulties': Education and the Fugitive Slave in Canada," *Ontario History*, 74 (1982): 95-112.

29 *Statutes of Nova Scotia* (SNS) 1836 c. 92, s. 5.

30 *Revised Statutes of Nova Scotia* (RSNS) 1884 5th ser. c. 29, s. 3 ss. 10.

31 Ibid., s. 13.

32 *Statutes of Upper Canada* (SUC) 1850 c. 48, s. 19.

33 (1854) 11 UCQB 569.

34 *Hill v. Camden and Zone*, 11 UCQB 573.

35 (1861) 21 UCQB 75.

36 *Re Stewart and School Trustees of Sandwich East*, (1864) 23 UCQB 634.

37 *Statutes of Ontario* (SO) 1964 c. 108, s. 1

38 SNB 1842 c. 37.

39 V. Carter and W. L. Akili, *The Window of Our Memories* 2 vols. (St. Albert, AB: Black Cultural Research Society of Alberta, 1981, 1990), Vol. 1, 55; R. Bruce Shepard, "The Little 'White' Schoolhouse: Racism in a Saskatchewan Rural School," *Saskatchewan History*, 39 (1986): 81-93.

40 Proceedings of a Meeting of Toronto Blacks, 13 January 1838, in C. Peter Ripley, ed., *The Black Abolitionist Papers*, Vol. 2: *Canada 1830-1865* (Chapel Hill: University of North Carolina Press, 1986), 69.

41 Ida Greaves, *The Negro in Canada* (Orillia, ON: Packet-Times Press, 1930), 63.

42 For an excellent account of the situation in the 1920s, see Greaves, *The Negro in Canada*, chap. 8. A representative list of restrictions during that period is given in Winks, *Blacks in Canada*, 325-26.

43 3 November 1855, quoted in Daniel G. Hill, *The Freedom Seekers* (Agincourt: Book Society of Canada, 1981), 105.

44 Palmer Research Files, J. Miller, Calgary City Clerk, letter dated 13 April 1920. I am grateful to the late Howard Palmer and Tamara Palmer Seiler for having allowed me to photocopy the research notes for their chapter on "The Blacks" in *Peoples of Alberta*.

45 In March 1919, Vancouver city council passed a motion asking the city solicitor to design a system of legal segregation confining "Asiatics" to "some well defined given area of the city." After an extensive search undertaken by the city solicitor with the assistance of the Retail Merchants' Association of Canada, council was informed in 1923 that municipalities did not have the power to restrict "Orientals" in this way (Anderson, *Vancouver's Chinatown*, 126-27).

46 Calgary *Herald*, 27 April, 29 April, 30 April, 1 May 1920; Calgary *Albertan*, 27 April, 30 April, 1 May, 21 May 1920.

47 For example, *Hansard*, 9, 10 and 23 March 1911, 4930, 5040-41, 5941-42, 5946.

48 Peter Gallego to Thomas Rolph, 1 November 1841, *Black Abolitionist Papers*, 87-94.

49 *Saturday Night*, 25 August 1888.

50 *Edmonton Capital*, 9 April 1912, quoted in Thomson, *Blacks in Deep Snow*, 82.

51 *Saturday Night*, 1 August 1936.

52 Winks, *Blacks in Canada*, 283-84; Ralph Weber, "Riot in Victoria, 1860," *Journal of Negro History* 56 (1971): 141-48.

53 Lyle E. Talbot, "Black and Canadian: Inside Looking In," unpublished ms., 56.

54 Greaves, *The Negro in Canada*, 62.

55 Winks, *Blacks in Canada*, 420.

56 Charles R. Saunders, *Share and Care: The Story of the Nova Scotia Home for Colored Children* (Halifax: Nimbus, 1994).

57 Interview: Mr. Calvin Ruck, Dartmouth, NS, 12 October 1993.

58 Don Clairmont and Fred Wien, "Blacks and Whites: The Nova Scotia Race Relations Experience," in Douglas Campbell, ed., *Banked Fires: The Ethnics of Nova Scotia* (Port Credit, ON: Scribbler's Press, 1978), 157.

59 NA, RG 24 Vol. 1206, file 297-1-21, John T. Richards to the Duke of Connaught, 4 October 1915.

60 Ibid., George Morton to Gen. Sir Sam Hughes, 7 September 1915.

61 Ibid., John Richards to Military Secretary to the Governor General, 20 November 1915. See also RG 24 Vol. 4739, file 448-14-259.

62 NA, RG 24 Vol. 1206, file 297-1-21, C. G. Henshaw to Brigade Major, 23rd Infantry, 7 December 1915.

63 Ibid., District Officer Commanding Military District No. 11, Victoria, to Secretary, Militia Council, 9 December 1915.

64 Ibid., W. H. Allen, Halifax, to 6th Division HQ, 14 December 1915.

65 NA, RG 24 Vol. 4387, various letters contained in file 34-7-141.

66 NA RG 24 Vol. 1206, file 297-1-21, C. S. MacInnes, memo to the Secretary, 25 March 1916.

67 NA, RG 24 Vol. 1206, file 297-1-21, Memorandum, 13 April 1916.
68 Ibid., Militia Council Minutes, 19 April 1916.
69 NA, RG 24 Vol. 1469, file 600-10-35, Mobilization to Gwatkin, 19 February 1917, and reply, n.d.; memo to Naval Secretary, 21 February 1917, and reply, 23 February.
70 NA, RG 9 III Vol. 1698, file E-186-9, Vol. 1, OC No. 9 District to Director of Timber Operations, 19 August 1918; RG 9 III Vol. 4645, Assistant to Director of Chaplain Services, report, 20 February 1918; RG 9 III Vol. 5010, War Diaries, No. 2 Construction Company, Vol. 13, 1918.
71 NA, RG 9 III Vol. 1709, file D-3-13, Collier to OC Canadian Troops, Kinmel Park, 10 January 1919.
72 *Toronto Daily Star*, 1 March 1930; Toronto *Globe*, 1 and 3 March 1930. The second *Globe* story includes the Klan's own statement on the course of the evening's events.
73 Toronto *Globe*, 3 March 1930; *Toronto Daily Star*, 1 and 24 March, 17 April 1930; *Dawn of Tomorrow*, 24 March 1930; *Canadian Forum*, April 1930, 233; *Rex v. Phillips* (1930) 55 CCC 49. The young lovers continued to try to find a minister who would marry them. Late on the night of Saturday 22 March, they went to the home of Rev. Frank Burgess, the native Indian pastor of the United Church on the New Credit Six Nations reserve. Though his wife "pleaded with her husband not to take the chance of defying the Klan," Mr. Burgess finally agreed and Ira and Isabella were married in the pastor's kitchen with Mrs. Burgess as witness. When the Klan learned of the marriage a spokesman said the matter was now closed. "We will not put asunder what God hath joined together" (*Star*, 24 March 1930).
74 For example, see *Globe and Mail*, 8 December 1990.
75 The most succinct account of the escape, recapture and execution of Marie-Joseph-Angélique is in Trudel, *Dictionnaire des Esclaves et de leurs Propriétaires au Canada Français*, 113-14. A very brief reference is in the *Dictionary of Canadian Biography*, Vol. 2 (Toronto: University of Toronto Press, 1969), 457-58, written by André Vachon. Another high-profile slave was Mathieu Léveillé, purchased in 1733 by the government of New France from his owner in Martinique to serve as public executioner in Quebec. Léveillé grew "melancholy" in the pursuit of his profession, so in 1742 Intendant Hocquart purchased a wife for him in the West Indies. Before they could be married Léveillé died and his fiancée, baptized as Angélique-Denise, was sold by the Intendant as no longer useful to the government (André Lachance, "Léveillé, Mathieu," *Dictionary of Canadian Biography*, Vol. 3 [Toronto: University of Toronto Press, 1974], 398-99). The position of executioner was considered dishonourable in New France, and government authorities turned to the purchase of a slave because no free white man could be found for the job. Léveillé's frequent illness in Quebec suggested the inappropriateness of this solution, and he was replaced after his death by a white man. Apparently Léveillé was not involved in the execution of Marie-Joseph-Angélique in 1734.

76 Viger et LaFontaine, "De l'Esclavage en Canada," 4-5.
77 Ibid., 5-6, 17-18.
78 Ibid., 8-9.
79 Ibid., 9, Vaudreuil to Belestre, 9 September 1760.
80 Catterall, *Judicial Cases Concerning American Slavery and the Negro*, Vol. 5, 341-45. The case was *Charlotte v. Chouteau*, heard before Judge Richardson in 1857. At issue was the legal existence of slavery in Montreal where the plaintiff's mother had been born in 1768. The argument was that since slavery did not exist the mother was born free, and consequently the plaintiff was also free. Judge Richardson canvassed the French and British laws to conclude that slavery had in fact been legal in both French and English Canada.
81 Riddell, "Slavery in Canada," 276.
82 Ibid., 303.
83 Viger et LaFontaine, "De l'Esclavage en Canada," 27-28, citing Assembly *Journal*, 28 January, 26 February, 8 March and 19 April 1793.
84 David C. Este, "The Emergence and Development of the Black Church in Canada with Special Emphasis on Union Church in Montreal, 1907-1940," cognate essay, University of Waterloo, 1979, 50-51.
85 Wilfred E. Israel, "The Montreal Negro Community," MA thesis, McGill University, 1928, 227ff.; Harold H. Potter, "The Occupational Adjustment of Montreal Negroes, 1941-48," MA thesis, McGill University, 1949, Appendix A, "The Sleeping Car Porter," 143-52; Agnes Calliste, "Sleeping Car Porters in Canada: An Ethnically Submerged Split Labour Market," *Canadian Ethnic Studies*, 19 (1987): 1-20.
86 *Census of Canada, 1911*, Vol. 2, Table 14, *1931*, Vol. 2, Table 34. In 1931 there were 634 black men and 568 black women in Montreal. During the Depression the male population declined as African-Canadian men sought greater employment opportunities in the United States.
87 In 1917 the Eureka Association introduced a program of communal property purchase for resale or rental to black Montrealers. It undertook this initiative, a pamphlet explained, because "The housing situation among Negroes in Montreal gives no hope of improvement in the future. We are still forced to live in unsanitary houses, to pay high rentals and suffer humiliation from landlords whilst endeavoring to procure suitable residences" (quoted in Dorothy W. Williams, *Blacks in Montreal, 1628-1986: An Urban Geography* [Montreal: Editions Yvon Blais, 1989], 37).
88 Israel, "Montreal Negro Community," 1-2, 175; Potter, "Occupational Adjustment," 6-15; Este, "Union Church in Montreal," 54, 56, 59; Greaves, *The Negro in Canada*, 65; interviews: Mrs. Griffiths, 13 June 1988; Mr. and Mrs. Packwood, 13 June; Mrs. Packwood, 15 June.
89 Greaves, *The Negro in Canada*, 55-56.
90 Israel, "Montreal Negro Community," 77-78; Potter, "Occupational Adjustment," 15-16; Este, "Union Church in Montreal," 55.

91 Potter, "Occupational Adjustment," 29. A trained and experienced black stenographer, bilingual in English and French, could find work only as a domestic (Potter, "Negroes in Canada," 49-50).

92 Potter, "Occupational Adjustment," 118-19.

93 Israel, "Montreal Negro Community," 230ff.; Greaves, *Negro in Canada*, 54-55.

94 Potter, "Occupational Adjustment," Appendix A, 143ff.; Calliste, "Sleeping Car Porters."

95 Interview: Mr. Eddie Packwood, 13 June 1988.

96 Mason Wade, *The French Canadians, 1760-1960* 2 vols. (rev. ed.; Toronto: Macmillan, 1968), Vol. 2, 862ff.; Everett C. Hughes, *French Canada in Transition* (Chicago: University of Chicago Press, 1943), 219; Susan Mann Trofimenkoff, ed., *Abbé Groulx: Variations on a Nationalist Theme* (Toronto: Copp Clark, 1973), introduction, 15; Fernand Ouellet, "The Historical Background of Separation in Quebec," in Ramsay Cook, ed., *French Canadian Nationalism: An Anthology* (Toronto: Macmillan, 1969), 15; Michael Oliver, *The Passionate Debate: The Social and Political Ideas of Quebec Nationalism, 1920-1945* (Montreal: Vehicule Press, 1991).

97 Howard Palmer, *Patterns of Prejudice: A History of Nativism in Alberta* (Toronto: McClelland and Stewart, 1982); John Higham, *Strangers in the Land* (New York: Atheneum, 1963), 264-99. Although the first Canadian branch of the Ku Klux Klan appeared in Montreal in 1921, the Klan's greatest success was in the West and particularly in Saskatchewan, as described above, chap. 2, sec. 10.

98 Cook, *French Canadian Nationalism*, especially Pierre Elliott Trudeau, "Quebec on the Eve of the Asbestos Strike," 33-34; Jean-C. Bonenfant and Jean-C. Falardeau, "Cultural and Political Implications of French Canadian Nationalism," 21-22; Ouellet, "Historical Background of Separatism," 61. See also W. D. K. Kernaghan, "Freedom of Religion in the Province of Quebec, with Particular Reference to Jews, Jehovah's Witnesses and Church-State Relations 1930-1960," PhD dissertation, Duke University, 1966, 58, 146.

99 Lionel Groulx, "French Canadian Nationalism," in Trofimenkoff, ed., *Abbé Groulx*, 87, 94; Susan Mann Trofimenkoff, *Action Française: French Canadian Nationalism in the Twenties* (Toronto: University of Toronto Press, 1975), 90.

100 Quoted in Wade, *French Canadians*, Vol. 2, 869.

101 Trofimenkoff, *Action Française*, 77ff.; Lionel Groulx, *L'Appel de la Race* (5th ed.; Montréal: Fides, 1962).

102 Kernaghan, "Freedom of Religion," 83.

103 Hughes, *French Canada in Transition*, 135.

104 Pierre Anctil, *Le Rendez-vous Manqué. Les Juifs de Montréal face au Québec de l'entre-deux-guerres* (Québec: Institut Québécois de Recherche sur la Culture, 1988), 135.

105 André Laurendeau, *Witness For Quebec*, English trans. (Toronto: Macmillan, 1973), 71-72. Emphasis added.

106 Interview: Mr. Eddie Packwood, 13 June 1988. "Race relations" in anglophone Montreal are the background for Morley Callaghan's novel, *The Loved and the Lost* (Toronto: Macmillan, 1951). Though it occurs after World War II, the novel describes a world of restriction and rejection for black people in Montreal.

107 Williams, *Blacks in Montreal*, 45.

108 Israel, "Montreal Negro Community," 151-64; Este, "Union Church in Montreal," 60-61; interview: Mrs. Packwood, 15 June 1988.

109 Israel, "Montreal Negro Community," 98, 99, 106, 108-9, 168-88, 227; Potter, "Occupational Adjustment," 143ff.; Greaves, *Negro in Canada*, 55; interview: Mrs. Packwood, 15 June 1988.

110 Leo W. Bertley, "The Universal Negro Improvement Association of Montreal, 1917-1979," PhD dissertation, Concordia University, 1979; Israel, "Montreal Negro Community," 111, 204-7; Este, "Union Church in Montreal," 69-72; interviews: Dr. Leo Bertley, Montreal, 14 June; Mrs. Packwood, 15 June 1988.

111 Este, "Union Church in Montreal"; Israel, "Montreal Negro Community," 281ff.; Potter, "Occupational Adjustment," 19; Robert Tremblay, "Les Noirs d'Ici," *Parti Pris*, 5 (1967-68): 17-23; interviews: Mr. Buddy Jones, Montreal, 13 June 1988; Mr. and Mrs. Packwood, 13 June; Ms. Dorothy Williams, Montreal, 13 June; Dr. Bertley, 14 June; Mrs. Packwood, 15 June.

112 Interview: Mrs. Griffiths, 13 June 1988.

113 Interviews: Mr. Packwood, 13 June 1988; Mrs. Griffiths, 13 June; Dr. Potter, 14 June; Mr. Clarence Este, 14 June. Mr. Packwood has in his possession a list of donors and a file of *Free Lance* issues from the period of the Christie crusade. The quotation is from 9 July 1938.

114 NA, RG 24 Vol. 1206, file 297-1-21, W. Stuart Edwards to E. A. Stanton, 31 January 1916.

115 For a full discussion of the issue see Henry L. Molot, "The Duty of Business to Serve the Public: Analogy to the Innkeeper's Obligation," *Canadian Bar Review*, 46 (1968): 612-42.

116 Cited in Molot, "Duty of Business," 632, and in Douglas A. Schmeiser, *Civil Liberties in Canada* (London: Oxford University Press, 1964), 269.

117 Cited in Molot, "Duty of Business," 637, and Schmeiser, *Civil Liberties in Canada*, 271.

118 (1899) 15 CS 104. In 1994 the Centre de Recherche-Action sur les Relations Raciales announced "Le Prix Frederick Johnson" to be awarded annually to a group or individual making an outstanding contribution to the struggle against racial inequality in the Province of Quebec. The two categories under which awards are made, both of which commemorate Mr. Johnson's initiative almost a century previously, are "sensibilisation et pression" and "contestation judiciaire." CRARR press release.

119 CS, at 106.

120 Ibid., at 107-8.

121 Ibid., at 108-10.

122 (1899) 8 QKB 379.

123 Ibid., at 383.

124 Ibid., at 384.

125 Ibid., at 379-80.

126 Greaves, *The Negro in Canada*, 62, citing as her source a personal letter from the deputy attorney general of Ontario.

127 (1914) 21 BCR 435; (1915) 31 WLR 542 (BCCA). I am grateful to Mr. Paul Winn of Vancouver for sending me the reports on *Barnswell*.

128 BCR, at 436.

129 Ibid., at 438.

130 Israel, "Montreal Negro Community," 108-11; Este, "Union Church in Montreal," 57-58.

131 *Montreal Gazette*, 5 March 1919; (1921) 30 QKB 459. The newspaper dated the incident as occurring on 26 January 1919; Justice Carroll, hearing the appeal on 29 December 1919, apparently mistakenly said it had occurred on 26 January 1918, QKB at 461.

132 *Montreal Gazette*, 5 March 1919.

133 Ibid. Since it was apparently Mr. Reynolds who had purchased all four tickets, Justice Fortin might have decided that the damages were his alone, but this reason was not mentioned in the newspaper account of the trial.

134 (1921) 30 QKB 459, at 462.

135 Ibid., at 463.

136 Ibid., at 466-67.

137 Ibid., at 460-61.

138 Ibid., at 464.

139 *Dawn of Tomorrow*, 2 and 9 February 1924; (1924) 55 OLR 349.

140 OLR, at 350.

141 *Dawn of Tomorrow*, 16 February 1924. Misspelling in original.

142 OLR, at 350.

143 Ibid., at 350-51.

144 Ibid., at 352. The *Dawn of Tomorrow* gave a curiously erroneous report on the case, 16 February 1924: "Damages were awarded W. V. Franklin, of Kitchener, in his suit against Alfred Evans at the Middlesex assizes last Saturday before Justice Haughton Lenox. It is alleged that the defendent refused to serve him food on account of his (Franklin's) color. It took the jury only 20 minutes to decide that Mr. Franklin should be awarded damages." Misspelling in original.

145 Lowell C. Carroll, *Landlord and Tenant in the Province of Quebec* (Montreal: Southam Press, 1934), also *Marriage in Quebec: The Conditions of Validity* (Montreal: H. S. Oakes, 1936). He later edited *The Quebec Statute and Case Citator, 1937* (Montreal: Kingsland, 1937), and *Commercial Law of Quebec* (Toronto: Sir I. Pitman and Sons, 1938).

146 *Canadian Law List, 1936*.

147 Supreme Court, Case File #6684.

148 RSQ 1925 c. 25, s. 33.

149 (1937) 75 SC 136, at 138.

150 *Gazette*, 25 March 1937.

151 (1938) 65 QKB 104. Ad Hoc Justice Pratte joined the majority but on the exclusive ground "that the appellant's refusal herein complained of was made under circumstances such that it could not cause any damage to the respondent" (at 105).

152 Ibid., at 107.

153 Ibid., at 121.

154 Ibid., at 105.

155 RSQ 1925 c. 37.

156 QKB, at 106-7, 109-10, 113-14, 122-24.

157 Ibid., at 114-15.

158 Ibid., at 110.

159 Ibid., at 111, 117-19.

160 Ibid., at 111, 120.

161 Ibid., at 110-11, 116-17.

162 F. R. Scott, "The Bill of Rights and Quebec Law," *Canadian Bar Review*, 37 (1959): 145.

163 QKB, at 117, 124.

164 Ibid., at 124-25.

165 Ibid., at 105, 112, 124.

166 Ibid., at 115, 120.

167 Ibid., at 112.

168 Ibid., at 123, 125.

169 Ibid., at 137-38.

170 Ibid., at 128.

171 Ibid., at 128-30.

172 Ibid., at 131.

173 Ibid., at 132.

174 Ibid., at 135.

175 Ibid., at 133.

176 Ibid., at 134.

177 Ibid., at 135-36.

178 Ibid., at 136.

179 Ibid., at 136-37.

180 Ibid., at 137-39.

181 Ibid., at 137, 139.

182 Ibid., at 105.

183 *Free Lance*, 9 July 1938.

184 Ibid.

185 RSC 1927 c. 35.

186 [1939] 4 DLR 723; Supreme Court, Case File #6684.

187 Ibid., Appellant's *Factum*.

188 Ibid., Respondent's *Factum*.
189 Walter S. Tarnopolsky, "The Supreme Court and Civil Liberties," *Alberta Law Review*, 14 (1976): 65. See also Gerald Le Dain, "Sir Lyman Duff and the Constitution," *Osgoode Hall Law Journal*, 12 (1974): 261.
190 [1940] SCR 139.
191 Ibid., at 141.
192 Ibid., at 142.
193 Ibid., at 142-43.
194 Ibid., at 143-44.
195 Ibid., at 144-45.
196 Ibid., at 145.
197 Ibid., at 146.
198 Ibid., at 147-48.
199 SQ 1921 c. 24, then RSQ 1925 c. 37.
200 SCR, at 148-49.
201 SQ 1921 c. 25, then RSQ 1925 c. 38.
202 SCR, at 150.
203 (1902) 1 KB 296.
204 SCR, at 152.
205 Ibid., at 152-53.
206 Supreme Court, Case File #6684. Respondent's costs were $594.43.
207 Interview: Mrs. Griffiths, 13 June 1988.
208 *Montreal Standard*, 9 December 1939, and the *Gazette*, 11 December, reported the basic facts of the Supreme Court decision on inside pages without comment. The *Gazette's* heading was "Negro Loses Suit Against Tavern."
209 [1940] 1 DLR 81.
210 Bora Laskin, "Tavern Refusing to Serve Negro – Discrimination," *Canadian Bar Review*, 18 (1940): 314-16.
211 Schmeiser, *Civil Liberties in Canada*, 274.
212 Molot, "Duty of Business," 612, 641.
213 Tarnopolsky, "Supreme Court and Civil Liberties," 76.
214 Ian A. Hunter, "The Origin, Development and Interpretation of Human Rights Legislation," in R. St.J. MacDonald and John P. Humphrey, *The Practice of Freedom: Canadian Essays on Human Rights and Fundamental Freedoms* (Toronto: Butterworths, 1979), 79.
215 Frank R. Scott, *The Canadian Constitution and Human Rights* (Toronto: Canadian Broadcasting Corporation, 1959), 37.
216 Scott, *Civil Liberties and Canadian Federalism*, 36.
217 (1921) 30 QKB 459, at 465-66.
218 Ibid., at 464. Emphasis added.
219 Ibid., at 460-61. Emphasis added.
220 Ibid., at 463-64. Emphasis added.
221 Ibid., at 466.
222 Ibid., at 459. Emphasis added.

223 (1924) 55 OLR 349, at 350.

224 Ibid.

225 Ibid.

226 SCR, at 144.

227 Justice Galipeault had merely ridiculed the idea that the York would lose business by serving blacks, since in a tavern the customers were not required to associate intimately ([1938] 65 QKB 104, at 136-37).

228 NA, MG 26 J13, Mackenzie King Diary, 30 June 1940.

229 Douglas MacLennan, "Racial Discrimination in Canada," *Canadian Forum* (October 1943), 164-65. Potter, "Occupational Adjustment," has extensive evidence of NSS discrimination (see esp. 69-75, 93, 122). "Report of the Audit Committee to the Windsor Interracial Council" (mimeograph, 1949).

230 MacLennan, "Racial Discrimination," 165; Potter, "Occupational Adjustment," 70, 93; Canadian Jewish Congress archives, reel 1, File 78, NSS Circular 81, 7 November 1942.

231 *The King's Regulations and Orders for the Royal Canadian Air Force*, 1924, Paragraph 275.

232 *King's Regulations for the Royal Canadian Air Force*, 1943, Article 171.

233 Potter, "Occupational Adjustment," 106-8, 130-31; Potter, "Negroes in Canada," 47; interview: Mr. James Braithwaite, Toronto, 17 June 1990.

234 *Regulations and Instructions for the Royal Canadian Navy*, 1942, chap. 7, Article 144(2), amended by PC 4950, 30 June 1944.

235 For example, *Montreal Gazette*, 8 December 1939.

236 Department of National Defence, Directorate of History (DND, DHist), HQ 61-4-10, Norman Rogers to F. Barrington Holder, 20 January 1940.

237 Ibid., "Coloured Troops. Remarks," Halifax, n.d. (September 1939).

238 Ibid., H. E. Boak to Secretary, DND, 7 September 1939; Boak to Holder, 22 September.

239 Ibid., C. E. Connolly to Secretary, DND, 25 May 1941.

240 Ibid., C. W. Clarke, Memorandum, "Enlistment – Coloured Personnel," 5 June 1941.

241 Segregated hair-care facilities for both men and women were common in Canada, particularly in Nova Scotia and southwestern Ontario (*Clarion*, 15 December 1947; Winks, *Blacks in Canada*, 294, 325; interview: Mr. Calvin Ruck, Dartmouth, NS, 12 October 1993). The *Globe and Mail* reported, on 26 February 1947, the predicament of Marguerite Bradley of Toronto, who was accepted by letter as a student at the Marvel Hairdressing School but rejected when she appeared in person. Marvel manager Arthur Ready told the *Globe* "You realize it would be impossible to have a colored girl here with so many students and business connections. There would be a natural objection by the students." The Marvel attitude was apparently widespread. Viola Desmond was establishing a beauty school in Halifax where black women could learn hairdressing skills, and used her tours around the province to recruit potential students.

242 PANS, RG 39C Vol. 937, file SC 13347, *R. v. Desmond*, "Affadavit of Viola Irene Desmond," "Record" and "Conviction"; Halifax *Chronicle*, 30 November 1946; Toronto *Star*, 30 November 1946; *Clarion*, 1 December 1946; interviews: Mr. Jack Desmond, Halifax, 19 February 1990; Dr. Carrie Best, New Glasgow, 20 February 1990; telephone interview, Mr. Henry MacNeil, New Glasgow, 14 October 1993; confidential interview with a Desmond relative, 19 June 1995. Mr. MacNeil agreed to continue our discussion in a personal interview on 15 October 1993, but this was prevented by his daughter who said that the affair "was not a proud moment in Pictou County history and should be left alone." Mr. MacNeil himself insisted that the incident was "an unfortunate sequence of coincidences" and he was "glad of an opportunity to set the record straight." He maintained, for example, that Mrs. Desmond grew violent and slapped the policeman's face when he politely asked her to move. Mrs. Desmond's injuries were treated by a Halifax doctor on Tuesday 12 November, the delay caused by the 11 November public holiday. Her knee soon recovered, but she was still receiving treatment for her hip when interviewed by the Halifax *Chronicle* on 30 November. Her husband and another relative confirmed that the hip pain persisted for the rest of her life. Apparently Mrs. Desmond was scarcely more than five feet tall, and weighed only about 100 pounds. Reports from those who knew her intimately testify to her sense of absolute shock at what had happened to her in New Glasgow. A detailed account of Mrs. Desmond's ordeal in New Glasgow can be found in Constance Backhouse, "Racial Segregation in Canadian Legal History: Viola Desmond's Challenge, Nova Scotia, 1946," *Dalhousie Law Journal*, 17 (1994): 299-362.

243 PANS, RG 39C Vol. 937, File SC 13347, "Notice of Motion," "Judgment of Justice Archibald"; 20 MPR 297, at 298-99.

244 MPR at 300. The editors of *Criminal Reports* added a "practice note" to their report of the Desmond appeal, explaining the application of *certiorari* (4 CR 200): "Ordinarily *certiorari* is applicable where there is (a) a total want of jurisdiction in the tribunal (e.g., where the subject-matter is not within its jurisdiction); (b) a defect in the jurisdiction of the tribunal (e.g., where an essential step preliminary to its exercise is omitted); (c) an excess of jurisdiction (e.g., where a penalty is imposed beyond that authorised by law); (d) an irregularity of substance appearing on the face of the proceedings; and (e) exceptional circumstances (e.g., fraud or perjury in procuring the conviction of accused)." D. C. M. Yardley later summarized the grounds for *certiorari* as "(i) defect of jurisdiction, (ii) breach of natural justice, and (iii) error of law on the face of the record." Yardley described the features of natural justice to be that the judicial officer must hear both sides of the story, and the accused must be accorded a fair opportunity of replying to a charge; the deciding official must have no interest or any other cause for bias in the outcome; the proceedings must be reasonable; there must be no fraud involved ("The Grounds for Certiorari and Prohibition," *Canadian Bar Review*, 37 [1959]: 298-99, 310-21).

245   MPR, at 297; 89 CCC 278; 4 CR 200; [1947] 4 DLR 81.

246   MPR, at 307. Justice Hall's contention that Mr. Bissett made an error in proceeding by way of *certiorari* rather than an appeal demonstrates the assumptions prevailing on the Nova Scotian court. Since Mr. Bissett was challenging the right of the magistrate to make the decision in the first place, an appeal from the decision itself would implicitly have accepted the propriety of the method used in reaching it. He denied not Magistrate MacKay's jurisdiction to hear a case brought under the *Theatres, Cinematographs and Other Amusements Act*, but the validity of using the Act to prosecute Mrs. Desmond. Mr. Bissett's error was perhaps that he was too subtle in presenting his case as a "denial of natural justice," since a bench schooled in the normalcy of Jim Crow failed to grasp his point that it was more than the fine and the guilty verdict that were being challenged. In the only contemporary published comment on the case, J. B. Milner accepted the "technical" accuracy of the *Desmond* decision, but he also raised a question which suggests support for Bissett's argument: "The function of the court is to administer justice under the law. If there appears before a magistrate a person who is being prosecuted for improper reasons by misuse of a statute, it is surely the magistrate's duty to explore that misuse. The magistrate has no jurisdiction until an informant lays an information and, if a private informant misuses a statute and improperly lays an information, then is the magistrate acting without jurisdiction?" ("Civil Liberties – Theatre Refusing to Admit Negro Person to Orchestra Seat – Violation of Tax Law – Summary Conviction – Certiorari – Abuse of Legal Process," *Canadian Bar Review*, 25 [1947]: 920). On the other hand a recent analysis of the Desmond case clearly faults Bissett's *certiorari* tactic. Constance Backhouse ("Racial Segregation in Canadian Legal History") appears to accept the judges' interpretation that Bissett used this method in order to have the case reconsidered at the Supreme Court level because he had missed the opportunity to lodge an appeal.

247   15 April 1947.

248   The NSAACP went further, and claimed that the *Desmond* decision had "eliminated Jim Crow" from Nova Scotia theatres. Presumably this was based on an exaggerated interpretation of William Hall's comment. PANS, NSAACP Membership Committee, *The Nova Scotia Association for the Advancement of Coloured People: Nova Scotia's No. 1 Human Rights Organization*, n.d. (recruitment and fund-raising pamphlet). Colin Thomson, *Born with a Call: A Biography of Dr. William Pearly Oliver, CM* (Dartmouth: Black Cultural Centre for Nova Scotia, 1986), 83-84, makes a similar error and compounds it by locating the final victory for Mrs. Desmond in the Supreme Court of Canada.

249   1 and 15 August 1947.

250   NA, MG 30 A 53, Kaplansky Papers, Vol. 20, file 3, 170; Harry Gairey, *A Black Man's Toronto, 1914-1980* (Toronto: Multicultural History Society of Ontario, 1981), 26-27; interview: Mr. Harry Gairey, Toronto, 22 February 1992. Inter-

estingly this was the solution recommended by Bora Laskin in his 1940 comment on *Christie*, when he wrote "Administrative oversight by a licensing authority of discriminatory practices by imposing conditions upon the grant of a licence or by exercising a right to refuse renewal is a possible method of dealing with the question raised by the principal case" ("Tavern Refusing to Serve Negro – Discrimination," *Canadian Bar Review* 18 [1940]: 316).

251 NSAACP, recruiting and fund-raising pamphlet.

252 *Calgary Herald*, 22 February, 22 March, 23 April 1947; Palmer Research Files, Alberta Hotel Association to Mayor J. C. Watson, 15 March 1947; City Clerk to City Solicitor, 18 March, to Legislative Committee, 1 April; City Solicitor to City Clerk, 28 March, 8 April 1947; interview: Mr. Ted King, Vancouver, 27 November 1993.

253 *Calgary Herald*, 24 August 1948. Mr. Ted King reported (interview: 27 November 1993) that until the late 1930s he and other black children had been allowed to swim in the pool.

254 *Calgary Herald*, 8 May 1951.

255 Canadian Press, 20 December 1949.

256 Dresden Town Hall, Council Minutes, 8 November 1949; *Dresden Times*, 8 December 1949.

257 SO 1954 c.28.

258 Arnold Bruner, "The Genesis of Ontario's Human Rights Legislation," *University of Toronto Faculty of Law Review*, 37 (1979): 236-53; Hunter, "Origin, Development and Interpretation of Human Rights Legislation," 77-109; Tarnopolsky, *Discrimination and the Law*, 25-37.

259 SQ 1963 c. 40, s. 8.

260 Tremblay, "Les Noirs d'Ici," 17-23; *Montreal Star*, 20 November 1968; "Being Black in Montreal," *Maclean's* (December 1968), 46-47; Rosemary Brown, *Being Brown: A Very Public Life* (Toronto: Random House, 1989), esp. 23-40.

261 Dennis Forsythe, ed., *Let the Niggers Burn! The Sir George Williams University Affair and Its Caribbean Aftermath* (Montreal: Black Rose Books, 1971); P. Kiven Tungten, "Racism and the Montreal Computer Incident of 1969," *Race*, 14 (1973): 229-40.

262 Doug Collins, "Fear and Loathing in the Canadian Mosaic," *Weekend Magazine*, 11 September 1976, 8-10. The new generation of black Montreal appears to have forgotten Fred Christie as well. Williams, *Blacks in Montreal, 1628-1986* (1989), does not even mention the Christie case.

263 [1940] 3 DLR 583.

264 RSBC 1936 c. 160.

265 DLR, at 585-86.

266 Ibid., at 588.

267 Ibid.

268 (1920) SC 805.

269 DLR, at 588-92.

270 Ibid., at 594.

271 Ibid., at 592-93.

272 *Canadian Bar Review*, 17 (1940): 730-32.

273 Schmeiser, *Civil Liberties in Canada*, 265-72.

274 Raleigh Township Centennial Museum, National Unity Association papers, F. P. Varcoe, deputy minister of Justice, to Hugh Burnett, 3 August 1943.

275 Palmer Research Files, City Solicitor to City Clerk, 8 April 1947.

276 [1940] 1 DLR 81.

277 T. Rinfret, "Reminiscences from the Supreme Court of Canada," *McGill Law Journal*, 3 (1956): 2, cited in Peter H. Russell, *The Supreme Court of Canada as a Bilingual and Bicultural Institution* (Ottawa: Royal Commission on Bilingualism and Biculturalism, 1969), 30.

278 Calgary District Court, file CO9863, Examination for Discovery of Theodore Stanley King, 6 August 1959; Palmer Research Files, interview: Mrs. Hazel Proctor Ostler, 30 May 1979.

279 Examination for Discovery of Theodore Stanley King; (1960) 31 WWR 451; *Calgary Herald*, 26 October 1959; *Calgary Albertan*, 27 and 28 October 1959; interview: Mr. Ted King, Vancouver, 27 November 1993.

280 WWR at 452-59; personal communication from Mr. Ted King, 13 November 1993; interview: 27 November. Judge Farthing was apparently not alone in resenting the kind of press attention provoked by Mr. Palmer. The *Globe and Mail*, 21 April 1995, described Ontario Chief Justice Charles Dubin as "not enamoured of lawyers who put their case to the reporters before putting it to the judge," and quoted a speech by the chief justice in which he said: "I think one of the most serious threats to professionalism is the increased resort by some members of our profession to argue their cases in the media."

281 (1961) 35 WWR 240; interview, 27 November 1993.

282 SA 1961 c. 40, s. 2.

283 [1966] CS 436.

284 (1921) 30 QKB 459, at 460-61.

285 [1940] SCR 139, at 142.

286 *Adrian Messenger Services v. The Jockey Club Ltd.*, [1972] 2 OR 369.

287 *Philippe Beaubien et Cie v. Canadian General Electric Co*, (1977) 30 CPR (2d) 100.

288 Ibid., at 145.

289 (1979) 27 OR (2d) 142; (1979) 105 DLR (3d) 707. When the plaintiff's husband ran for Parliament in the 1993 federal election the family name was spelled Bhaduria.

290 (1703) 2 Ld. Raym. 938; 92 ER 126.

291 [1945] OR 778.

292 DLR, at 714-16.

293 (1981) 17 CCLT 106.

294 Ibid., at 120.

295 Ibid., at 119-20.

296 Ibid., at 119.

297 Ibid., at 116. Emphasis added.

4 NOBLE AND WOLF V. ALLEY

1 Pierre Berton, "No Jews Need Apply," *Maclean's*, 1 November 1948.
2 National Archives of Canada (NA), MG 28 I 173, Ontario Labour Committee for Human Rights Papers, Vol. 6, Vivien Mahood to Kalmen Kaplansky, 1 December 1948.
3 (1832) 1 Wm IV c. 57.
4 Richard Menkis, "Antisemitism and Anti-Judaism in Pre-Confederation Canada," in Alan Davies, ed., *Antisemitism in Canada: History and Interpretation* (Waterloo: Wilfrid Laurier University Press, 1992), 11-38; Gerald Tulchinsky, "The Contours of Canadian Jewish History," in Robert J. Brym et al., eds., *The Jews in Canada* (Toronto: Oxford University Press, 1993), 5-21; Gerald Tulchinsky, *Taking Root: The Origins of the Canadian Jewish Community* (Toronto: Stoddart, 1997), parts 1 and 2; Bernard Vigod, *The Jews in Canada* (Ottawa: Canadian Historical Association, 1984), 3-4; Irving Abella, *A Coat of Many Colours: Two Centuries of Jewish Life in Canada* (Toronto: Lester and Orpen Dennys, 1990), 27-30; Louis Rosenberg, *Canada's Jews: A Social and Economic Study of the Jews in Canada* (Montreal: Canadian Jewish Congress, 1939), 303; Stephen A. Speisman, *The Jews of Toronto: A History to 1937* (Toronto: McClelland and Stewart, 1979), 117-19.
5 The *shtetl* were the villages, and the *ghettos* the restricted urban areas, where the largely impoverished and persecuted Jews had resided in eastern Europe.
6 There were some Jewish agricultural settlements on the Canadian prairies, but none lasted beyond the first decade of the 20th century (Yossi Katz and John C. Lehr, "Jewish Pioneer Agricultural Settlements in Western Canada," *Journal of Cultural Geography*, 14 [1994]: 49-67; Abraham Arnold, "The New Jerusalem: Jewish Pioneers on the Prairies," *Beaver*, 74 [August-September 1994]: 37-42). The overwhelming majority of the Canadian Jewish population has remained urban in every census since Confederation. Life in the Canadian Yiddish community in the early years of the century is brilliantly evoked in the novels of Adele Wiseman.
7 22 September 1924, cited in Stephen Speisman, "Antisemitism in Ontario: The Twentieth Century," in Davies, ed., *Antisemitism in Canada*, 118.
8 Michael Brown, "From Stereotype to Scapegoat: Anti-Jewish Sentiment in French Canada from Confederation to World War I," in ibid., 39-66; Speisman, "Antisemitism in Ontario," 113-33; Dennis H. Wrong, "Ontario's Jews in the Larger Community," in Albert Rose, ed., *A People and Its Faith* (Toronto: University of Toronto Press, 1959), 45-59; Irving Abella, "Anti-Semitism in Canada in the Interwar Years," in Moses Rischin, ed., *The Jews of North America* (Detroit: Wayne State University Press, 1987), 235-46; Tulchinsky, "Contours of Canadian Jewish History," 5-21; Tulchinsky, *Taking Root*, parts 3 and 4.
9 Cited in Lita-Rose Betcherman, *The Swastika and the Maple Leaf: Fascist Movements in Canada in the Thirties* (Toronto: Fitzhenry and Whiteside, 1975), 103. The Quebec journal *L'Action Catholique* claimed that of 15 Communist lead-

ers in Canada, 13 were Jewish and 2 English, 11 May 1935, cited in W. D. K. Kernaghan, "Freedom of Religion in the Province of Quebec with particular reference to the Jews, Jehovah's Witnesses and Church-State Relations," PhD dissertation, Duke University, 1966, 118.

10 Betcherman, *Swastika and the Maple Leaf*, esp. chap. 4; Lita-Rose Betcherman, "The Early History of Canada's Anti-Discrimination Law," *Patterns of Prejudice*, 7 (1973): 19-20; Irving Abella and Harold Troper, "Canada and the Refugee Intellectual, 1933-1939," in J. C. Jackman and C. M. Borden, eds., *The Muses Flee Hitler: Cultural Transfer and Adaptation* (Washington: Smithsonian Institution Press, 1983), 262; Abella, *Coat of Many Colours*, 186; Rosenberg, *Canada's Jews*, 302.

11 David Rome, *Clouds in the Thirties: On Antisemitism in Canada 1929-1939*, sec. 2 (Montreal: Canadian Jewish Congress, 1977), 26-27, and sec. 7 (Montreal: Canadian Jewish Congress, 1979), 37-48; Pierre Anctil, *Le Rendez-vous Manqué. Les Juifs de Montréal face au Québec de l'entre-deux-guerres* (Montreal: Institut Québécois de Recherche sur la Culture, 1988), 131-38; Pierre Anctil, "Interlude of Hostility: Judeo-Christian Relations in Quebec in the Interwar Period, 1919-39," in Davies, ed., *Antisemitism in Canada*, 140-49; Kernaghan, "Freedom of Religion," 101-2; Sheldon M. Schreter, "French-Canadian Anti-Semitism," *Strobe*, 3 (1969): 94-97; Michael Oliver, *The Passionate Debate: The Social and Political Ideas of Quebec Nationalism, 1920-1945* (Montreal: Vehicle Press, 1991), 186, 189-91; Martin Robin, *Shades of Right: Nativist and Fascist Politics in Canada, 1920-1940* (Toronto: University of Toronto Press, 1992), 108.

12 Rome, *Clouds*, sec. 7, 48.

13 Abella, *Coat of Many Colours*, 218; *Globe and Mail*, 27 July 1989. In the same period a reference written on behalf of the American Jewish scholar Oscar Handlin assured the recipient that "he has none of the offensive traits which some people associate with his race." Quoted in Joan Wallach Scott, "History in Crisis? The Others' Side of the Story," *American Historical Review*, 94 (1989): 684.

14 Rosenberg, *Canada's Jews*, 304; Abella, *Coat of Many Colours*, 180-81; Speisman, *Jews of Toronto*, 120-21; Betcherman, *Swastika and the Maple Leaf*, 48-49.

15 Vigod, *Jews in Canada*, 13.

16 Betcherman, *Swastika and the Maple Leaf*, 51, 100; Rome, *Clouds*, sec. 2, 29; Wrong, "Ontario's Jews," 52; Ontario Jewish Archives, Toronto (OJA), Box, Fair Employment Practices Legislation, 1943-63, Oscar Cohen to J. J. Glass, 29 August 1938, C. G. Faris to T. B. McQuesten, 8 August 1939; OJA, Minutes of the Executive Committee, 22 June 1939; interview: Mr. Allan Grossman, Toronto, 25 July 1989.

17 Kernaghan, "Freedom of Religion," 104-6; Schreter, "French-Canadian Anti-Semitism," 100-1; Oliver, *The Passionate Debate*, 190-94; Mordecai Richler, *Oh Canada! Oh Quebec! Requiem for a Divided Country* (Toronto: Viking Penguin, 1992), 100. In *The Apprenticeship of Duddy Kravitz* (Boston: Little, Brown, 1959), Richler describes the postwar expansion of Jewish summer properties

in the Ste. Agathe region, presumably the trend being resisted in the late 1930s.

18 Rome, *Clouds*, sec. 7, 5; sec. 2, 19.

19 The most thorough account of this topic is Irving Abella and Harold Troper, *None Is Too Many: Canada and the Jews of Europe 1933-1948* (Toronto: Lester and Orpen Dennys, 1983). The same authors have written a concise version of the story, " 'The Line Must Be Drawn Somewhere': Canada and Jewish Refugees, 1933-9," *Canadian Historical Review*, 60 (1979): 178-209.

20 *Hansard*, 30 January 1939, 428.

21 Anctil, "Interlude of Hostility," 149-53; Anctil, *Rendez-vous Manqué*, chap. 4; Robin, *Shades of Right*, 110; Bernard Vigod, *Quebec before Duplessis: The Political Career of Louis-Alexandre Taschereau* (Kingston and Montreal: McGill-Queen's University Press, 1986), 156-60.

22 Anctil, "Interlude of Hostility," 153-58; Robin, *Shades of Right*, chap. 5; Betcherman, *Swastika and the Maple Leaf*; Rome, *Clouds*.

23 Anctil, *Rendez-vous Manqué*, 34.

24 Quotation from Schreter, "French-Canadian Anti-Semitism," 74, and see 84-88 on "Achat chez nous" and mainstream antisemitism generally. See also Everett C. Hughes, *French Canada in Transition* (Chicago: University of Chicago Press, 1943), 135, 212-19; Robin, *Shades of Right*, 108-12, 320-21; Kernaghan, "Freedom of Religion," 83-87; Oliver, *The Passionate Debate*, 187; Susan Mann Trofimenkoff, *Action Française: French Canadian Nationalism in the Twenties* (Toronto: University of Toronto Press, 1975), 78-79; Esther Delisle, *The Traitor and the Jew: Anti-Semitism and the Delirium of Extremist Right-wing Nationalism in French Canada from 1929-1939* (Montreal: R. Davies, 1993), 111, 135, 138, 148, 166; Richler, *Oh Canada! Oh Quebec!*, 78-90, 210-11, 245-49.

25 See especially Betcherman, *Swastika and the Maple Leaf*; Rome, *Clouds*; Cyril Levitt and William Shaffir, *The Riot at Christie Pits* (Toronto: Lester and Orpen Dennys, 1987); Robin, *Shades of Right*, chap. 5; Speisman, "Antisemitism in Ontario"; Abella, "Anti-Semitism in the Interwar Years."

26 Abraham Feinberg, "Those Jews," *Maclean's*, 1 March 1945.

27 Richler, *Oh Canada! Oh Quebec!*, 80.

28 On the original order dated 7 November 1942, Circular 81, see above, "Christie v. York," sec. 7. A copy of the corrective Circular 81A, 9 December 1943, is located in the Canadian Jewish Congress National Archives, Montreal (CJC), Reel 1, File 78, "Discrimination against Jews in Employment."

29 *Census of Canada*, 1941, Vol. 1, "Racial Origin," 219.

30 Cited in Berton, "No Jews."

31 CJC, Reel 1, File 78, "Discrimination against Jews in Employment," Survey of Application Forms, Survey of Business Schools and Employment Agencies; NA, Ontario Labour Committee Papers, Vol. 9, "Association for Civil Liberties, 1949," Brief in Respect to Legislation Dealing with Expressions of Racial and Religious Discrimination in Ontario, first draft, 1949. The ap-

plication form for the A. C. Nielsen Co. of Toronto asked bluntly: "Race: Jewish ___ Gentile ___."

32 OJA, "Fair Employment Practices Legislation," 1951; NA, Ontario Labour Committee Papers, Vol. 7, Milling to Kaplansky, 6 September 1951.

33 Cited in Berton, "No Jews."

34 CJC, Reel 1, Survey of Summer Resorts, 1947; NA, Ontario Labour Committee Papers, Vol. 39, 1950.

35 NA, MG 31 E55, Tarnopolsky Papers, Vol. 43, file 6 and Vol. 46, file 5 contain examples of restrictive covenants from different parts of Canada. From Pictou County, NS, 1940: Peter and Viola Thomson sell a lot of land to Christina Cox on condition "that the said Grantee her heirs or assigns covenants and agrees that they shall not at any time sell or transfer the said land to any one of colored or Negro blood." From West Vancouver, 1946: British Pacific Properties sell lots with the condition that "No person of the African or Asiatic race or of African or Asiatic descent (except servants of the occupier of the premises in residence) shall reside or be allowed to remain on the premises."

36 OJA, Box, Joint Public Relations Committee, "Restrictive Covenants." This covenant came to public attention when one of the lots was donated by Conservative MP Joseph Murphy to the Sarnia branch of the Canadian Legion for a lottery prize in 1949. A Sarnia member was selling tickets in Windsor, and referred to the restriction as a positive virtue. A Windsor Legion member thought otherwise, and protested to the Toronto Legion office against the organization's involvement in discrimination of this kind since all "races" had fought together in the Canadian forces during the War. Toronto agreed, and Sarnia branch was ordered to cancel the lottery.

37 Supreme Court, Case File #7594.

38 NA, MG31 E53, Richmond Papers, "Correspondence, 1948"; *Time* magazine, 4 December 1950; Supreme Court, Case File #7594, "Appeal Case"; Edward Richmond, "More Thoughts on Wolf Property Case," *Canadian Jewish News*, 19 February 1987.

39 CJC, "Summary of Activities of the National Joint Public Relations Committee of the Canadian Jewish Congress and B'nai B'rith," n.d. (1946); OJA, "Review of Congress Activities," September 1938; OJA, Fred M. Catzman Papers, file 5445; *Congress Bulletin*, October 1951.

40 For example, see OJA, Catzman Papers, Memo, Kayfetz to Catzman, 25 October 1951.

41 This was apparently a widespread stereotype in Canada. According to *Le Patriote* of 7 December 1933: "The Jew has used sneaky and fraudulent means to get hold of our commerce. The fires . . . , the numerous bankruptcies, the robberies in the middle of the night in their own stores by accomplices to collect theft insurance, have been for the Jews weapons to ruin the honest commerce of others." Cited in Robin, *Shades of Right*, 320-21. In the Plamondon case, discussed below, it was alleged that Jews deliberately set fire to their own shops in order to collect insurance.

42 SO 1932 c. 24, s. 4; Rome, *Clouds*, sec. 2, 52-54; Herbert A. Sohn, "Human Rights Legislation in Ontario: A Study of Social Action," Doctor of Social Work, University of Toronto, 1975, 40-44; Betcherman, *Swastika and the Maple Leaf*, 50, and "Anti-Discrimination Law," 20.

43 Cited in Robin, *Shades of Right*, 132.

44 Cited in Vigod, *Quebec Before Duplessis*, 160.

45 Rome, *Clouds*, sec. 2, 42-50; Betcherman, "Anti-Discrimination Law," 19; Robin, *Shades of Right*, 128-35; Kernaghan, "Freedom of Religion," 99.

46 (1915) 24 QKB 69; Robin, *Shades of Right*, 312-13; Kernaghan, "Freedom of Religion," 52-54; Schreter, "French-Canadian Anti-Semitism," 79; Rosenberg, *Canada's Jews*, 302. Justice Henry-George Carroll, who dissented in favour of Sol Reynolds in the Loew's Theatre case, wrote the majority decision granting Mr. Ortenberg $50 damages against Mr. Plamondon and $25 against publisher René Leduc.

47 The judgment was unreported, but was printed in the Montreal *Gazette*, 14 September 1932. Rome, *Clouds*, sec. 2, 71-72; Kernaghan, "Freedom of Religion," 99-101; Robin, *Shades of Right*, 136-37, 329-30.

48 "1. The publication of a libel against a race or creed likely to expose persons belonging to the race or professing the creed to hatred, contempt or ridicule, and tending to raise unrest or disorder among the people, shall entitle a person belonging to the race or professing the creed to sue for an injunction to prevent the continuation and circulation of the libel; and the Court of King's Bench is empowered to entertain the action. 2. The action may be taken against the person responsible for the authorship, publication, or circulation of the libel. 3. The word 'publication' used in this section shall be interpreted to mean any words legibly marked upon any substance or object signifying the matter otherwise than by words, exhibited in public or caused to be seen or shewn or circulated or delivered with a view to its being seen by any person" (SM 1934 c. 23, s. 13A).

49 Rome, *Clouds*, sec. 2, 89-95; Betcherman, "Anti-Discrimination Law," 21-22; Rosenberg, *Canada's Jews*, 303; Robin, *Shades of Right*, 203-4.

50 In 1935 Mr. A. J. Freiman won a defamatory libel case against Arcand's Ottawa associate Jean Tissot, who wrote pamphlets accusing Jewish merchants of using dishonest business practices and conspiring to drive Christians out of business. The distinguishing feature of this case was, however, that Mr. Freiman was named in Tissot's publications, allowing him to sue for personal not group libel (Robin, *Shades of Right*, 158-59).

51 OJA, Executive Committee Minutes, 23 November 1937; Rome, *Clouds*, sec. 2, 57; Betcherman, "Anti-Discrimination Law," 22-23.

52 Rome, *Clouds*, sec. 2, 54-55; Sohn, "Human Rights Legislation," 44.

53 Rome, *Clouds*, sec. 2, 54-56; Sohn, "Human Rights Legislation," 45; Betcherman, "Anti-Discrimination Law," 20-21.

54 Interview: Mr. Joseph Salsberg, Toronto, 26 July 1989.

55 On 17 December 1942 the UN issued a declaration confirming the claim by Polish Jews that the Germans were engaged in a program of extermination against the Jews of Europe (Yehuda Bauer, *The Holocaust in Historical Perspective* [Seattle: University of Washington Press, 1978]; Walter Laqueur, *The Terrible Secret: The Suppression of the Truth about Hitler's "Final Solution"* [Boston: Little, Brown, 1980]). On Canadian awareness, see Marilyn F. Nefsky, "The Shadow of Evil: Nazism and Canadian Protestantism," in Davies, ed., *Antisemitism in Canada*, 203, 214.

56 *Globe and Mail*, 15 October 1943.

57 For accounts of the progress of the bill see Sohn, "Human Rights Legislation," 50-57, and John C. Bagnall, "The Ontario Conservatives and the Development of Anti-Discrimination Policy, 1944-1962," PhD dissertation, Queen's University, 1984, 18-65.

58 *Globe and Mail*, 14 February 1944; *Toronto Star*, 14 February 1944; interview: Mr. Salsberg, 26 July 1989.

59 *Globe and Mail*, 10 March; *Telegram*, 9 March 1944.

60 *Telegram*, 31 March 1944.

61 *Globe and Mail*, 13 March 1944.

62 SO 1944 c. 51:

S.1. No person shall –

a) publish or display or cause to be published or displayed; or

b) permit to be published or displayed on lands or premises or in a newspaper, through a radio broadcasting station or by means of any other medium which he owns or controls, any notice, sign, symbol, emblem or other representation indicating discrimination or an intention to discriminate against any person or any class of persons for any purpose because of the race or creed of such person or class of persons.

S.2. This Act shall not be deemed to interfere with the free expression of opinions upon any subject by speech or in writing and shall not confer any protection to or benefit upon enemy aliens.

S.3. Every one who violates the provisions of section 1 shall be liable to a penalty of not more than $100 for a first offence nor more than $200 for a second or subsequent offence and such penalties shall be paid to the Treasurer of Ontario.

S.4.(1) The penalties imposed by this Act may be recovered upon the application of any person with the consent of the Attorney General, to a judge of the Supreme Court by originating notice and upon every such application the rules of practice of the Supreme Court shall apply.

(2) The judge, upon finding that any person has violated the provisions of section 1 may, in addition to ordering payment of the penalties, make an order enjoining him from continuing such violation.

(3) Any order made under this section may be enforced in the same manner as any other order or judgment of the Supreme Court.

63 OJA, Catzman Papers, Memo, Kayfetz to Catzman, 25 October 1951.

64 *Debates*, 7 March 1944.

65 *United Nations Charter*, Preamble and Article 1.
66 *Universal Declaration of Human Rights*, Preamble and Articles 2, 7 and 17.
67 Cited in J. R. Shiff, "Public Policy and the Restrictive Covenant," *Obiter Dicta*, 25 (1951): 9-10.
68 F. R. Scott, "Dominion Jurisdiction Over Human Rights and Fundamental Freedoms," *Canadian Bar Review*, 27 (1949): 498.
69 A *Globe and Mail* editorial, 15 March 1951, encapsulates the position which that newspaper, among others, supported throughout this period: "The elimination of discrimination will not be accomplished by a law. . . . The reasons some people have for associating or not associating with other members of the community are sometimes deplorable, but their right of choice in such relationships is absolute." Even employment discrimination was preferable to government "compulsion," according to a *Globe* editorial on 16 April 1953. "People have an innate right to choose their associates and, by extension, their employees."
70 Sohn, "Human Rights Legislation," 92.
71 *Globe and Mail*, 2 September 1948.
72 CJC, Summary of Activities of the National Joint Public Relations Committee of the Canadian Jewish Congress and B'nai B'rith (1946).
73 OJA, "Fair Employment Practices Legislation," speech by Rabbi Feinberg to CJC Plenary Session, 24 October 1949; OJA, Catzman Papers, Report of the National Joint Public Relations Committee, October 1951; interview: Mr. Ben Kayfetz, Toronto, 24 July 1989.
74 A restrictive covenant may in fact be regarded as more binding than a contract, since "it can give rise to a property right that stays with the land" (Prof. Jim Phillips, private communication, 24 July 1995).
75 Cited in D. A. L. Smout, "An Inquiry into the Law on Racial and Religious Restraints on Alienation," *Canadian Bar Review*, 30 (1952): 867.
76 Ibid., 865-67; Clement E. Vose, *Caucasians Only: The Supreme Court, the NAACP, and the Restrictive Covenant Cases* (Berkeley and Los Angeles: University of California Press, 1959), 2-3, 20.
77 For example Justices Archibald, Fortin, Carroll, Demers, Galipeault, Davis and O'Halloran, as described above in chapter 3. These were, of course, minority opinions or decisions overturned on appeal, but they were evidence of a particular interpretive orientation existing on the Canadian bench.
78 Smout, "Racial and Religious Restraints," 868; Allan Goldstein, "Racial Restrictive Covenants," *University of Toronto Faculty of Law Review*, 9 (1951): 35.
79 (1930) 37 OWN 392.
80 Ibid.
81 Ibid., at 393.
82 (1930) 38 OWN 69.
83 (1931) 40 OWN 572.
84 Ibid., at 572-73.
85 Ibid., at 573.
86 [1945] OWN 272; [1945] 2 DLR 244.

87 DLR, at 245.

88 Ibid., at 247.

89 Ibid., at 247-48.

90 Ibid., 245.

91 [1945] OR 778; [1945] 4 DLR 674.

92 DLR, at 675.

93 Ibid., at 678-79.

94 Ibid., at 681.

95 [1943] 1 A11 ER 16.

96 DLR, at 682.

97 Sohn, "Human Rights Legislation," 87-88.

98 Vose, *Caucasians Only*, 134.

99 Cited in Arnold Bruner, "The Genesis of Ontario's Human Rights Legislation: A Study in Law Reform," *University of Toronto Faculty of Law Review*, 37 (1979): 245.

100 DLR, at 674.

101 For example, Shiff, "Public Policy and the Restrictive Covenant," 10; C. E. Bourne, "International Law – Unimplemented Treaties – Their Effect on Municipal Law – Public Policy," *Canadian Bar Review*, 29 (1951): 969-72; Mark MacGuigan, "The Development of Civil Liberties in Canada," *Queen's Quarterly*, 72 (1965): 270; Ian Bushnell, *The Captive Court: A Study of the Supreme Court of Canada* (Montreal: McGill-Queen's University Press, 1992), 302.

102 Vose, *Caucasians Only*, 23-38.

103 Ibid., 50-73.

104 *Sipes v. McGhee*, 316 Mich 614 (1947), discussed in Vose, *Caucasians Only*, 122-50.

105 Ibid., 191; Smout, "Racial and Religious Restraints," 873-75.

106 *Shelley v. Kraemer* and *McGhee v. Sipes*, 334 US 1 (1948); *Hurd v. Hodge* and *Urciolo v. Hodge*, 334 US 24 (1948).

107 *Telegram*, 14 January; *Globe and Mail*, 18 January 1947. This was not the first time Icelandia had aroused protest. In November 1945 University of Toronto students and others had picketed the rink when it denied admission to a black boy (*Globe and Mail*, 23 November 1945).

108 *Globe and Mail*, 22 February 1947; OJA, JPRC Report of Activities, n.d. (1947); NA, MG 30 A53, Kalmen Kaplansky Papers, Vol. 20, file 3, 170; Bagnall, "Anti-Discrimination Policy," 74, 81-82; Sohn, "Human Rights Legislation," 74, 83-84.

109 SS 1947 c. 35, Sec. 14(1).

110 CJC, *Information and Comment*, August 1947.

111 Supreme Court, Case File #7594, "Appeal Case."

112 As Mr. Richmond later explained, "A precedent can be overturned but an order is an order" (interview: Mr. Ted Richmond, London, ON, 15 August 1992).

113 RSO 1937 c. 168, s. 3.

114 Supreme Court, Case File #7594, "Appeal Case." Emphasis added.

115 Ted Richmond, "Racially Restrictive Covenants and the Judiciary in Canada," unpublished ms., 2; interview: Mr. Richmond, 15 August 1992.
116 Affidavit of James B. Book, secretary, Beach O' Pines Protective Association, Supreme Court, Case File #7594.
117 Ibid., Notice of Motion.
118 [1948] 4 DLR 123; [1948] OR 579.
119 Richmond, "More Thoughts on Wolf Property Case"; OJA, Box 3, JPRC, 1944-48, Agreement between Annie Maud Noble and Bernard Wolf; interview: Mr. Richmond, 15 August 1992.
120 OR, at 580-82.
121 Ibid., at 583.
122 *Toronto Star*, 22 May 1948; Richmond, "Racially Restrictive Covenants," 5-6.
123 OR, at 583-84.
124 Ibid., at 585-90.
125 Ibid., at 591.
126 Ibid., at 597.
127 Ibid., at 597-98.
128 Ibid., at 598.
129 NA, Richmond Papers, Cartwright to Richmond, 12 June 1948.
130 *Toronto Star* 21 June; *Telegram*, 21 June 1948.
131 NA, Kaplansky Papers, Vol. 20, File 6, Report, June 1948.
132 NA, MG 28 V75, Jewish Labour Committee of Canada Papers, Vol. 13, Minutes of the Canadian Congress of Labour National Committee for Racial Tolerance, 15 June 1948; Vol. 15, Trades and Labour Congress of Canada, *Report*, 1948; Ontario Labour Committee Papers, Vol. 6, Correspondence, Jewish Labour Committee, 1948.
133 NA, Richmond Papers, Jolliffe to Richmond, 23 June 1948. Since Jolliffe was obviously sympathetic to Mr. Wolf's case, his preference for a legislated solution is a significant indication of the prevailing attitude towards the role of the courts in effecting legal reform.
134 NA, MG 31 H20, Bernard Wolf Papers, "Correspondence, Clippings 1948-1949," statement by London B'nai B'rith, 18 June 1948; Richmond Papers, Cartwright to Richmond, 18 June 1948; interview: Mr. Richmond, 15 August 1992.
135 Richmond, "Racially Restrictive Covenants," 9.
136 NA, Richmond Papers, "Notices, Motions, Orders, Affidavits 1948," Notice of Appeal, 21 June 1948.
137 Ann Gomer Sunahara, "Deportation: The Final Solution to Canada's 'Japanese Problem,'" in J. Dahlie and T. Fernando, eds., *Ethnicity, Power and Politics in Canada* (Toronto: Methuen, 1981), 254-78.
138 PC 1945-7355, 7356 and 7357. The first order stated: "Whereas during the course of the war with Japan certain Japanese nationals manifested their sympathy with or support of Japan by making requests for repatriation to

Japan and otherwise; And whereas other persons of the Japanese race have requested or may request that they be sent to Japan; And whereas it is deemed desirable that provisions be made to deport the classes of persons referred to above. . . .

(1) Every person of sixteen years of age or over . . . who is a national of Japan resident in Canada and who, (a) has, since the date of declaration of war by the Government of Canada against Japan, on December 8, 1941, made a request for repatriation; or (b) has been in detention at any place in virtue of an order made pursuant to the provisions of the Defence of Canada Regulations . . . may be deported to Japan.

(2) Every naturalized British subject of the Japanese race of sixteen years of age or over resident in Canada who has made a request for repatriation may be deported to Japan; Provided that such person has not revoked in writing such request prior to midnight the first day of September, 1945.

(3) Every natural born British subject of the Japanese race of sixteen years of age or over resident in Canada who has made a request for repatriation may be deported to Japan; Provided that such person has not revoked in writing such request prior to the making by the Minister of an order for deportation.

(4) The wife and children under sixteen years of age of any person for whom the Minister makes an order for deportation to Japan may be included in such order and deported with such person."

139 Supreme Court, Case File #7594, *Factum* of the Co-Operative Committee on Japanese Canadians. This line of argument apparently originated with John Cartwright. In a private letter Andrew Brewin wrote that "An interesting possibility . . . was suggested to me by Mr. Cartwright, namely, that the words 'Japanese race' are almost meaningless, and that it might be impossible for the Crown to prove that any particular individual was of the Japanese race. We might refer in this connection to Clayton vs. Ramsden, 1943 AC 320. We are advised that Anthropologists are not at all agreed as to what is the proper test" (NA, MG32 C26, Brewin Papers, Vol. 1, file 7, Brewin to Arnold Campbell, 5 January 1946).

140 [1946] SCR 248, at 267. Every individual judgment throughout the Supreme Court decision made reference to "Japanese race" without further explanation.

141 In the Privy Council, Case for the Appellant, Co-Operative Committee on Japanese Canadians.

142 [1947] AC 87, at 109.

143 NA, Richmond Papers, Cartwright to Richmond, 14 July, Richmond to Cartwright, 19 August 1948; interview: Mr. Richmond, 15 August 1992.

144 OJA, Box 3, JPRC 1944-48, Report of Activities, n.d. [1948], Kayfetz to Richmond, 29 September; Catzman Papers, speech notes, 1951; Richmond, "More Thoughts on Wolf Property Case"; interview: Mr. Richmond, 15 August 1992.

145 NA, Richmond Papers, Morden to Cartwright, 28 October, Cartwright to Richmond, 5 November, Cartwright to Richmond, 30 November 1948; interview: Mr. Richmond, 15 August 1992.

146 [1949] 4 DLR 375; [1949] OR 503.

147 OR, at 505; interview: Mr. Richmond and Mrs. Marion Richmond, 15 August 1992. Mrs. Richmond was also in court for the appeal hearing.

148 Richmond, "More Thoughts on Wolf Property Case."

149 OR, at 506-7.

150 Ibid., at 507-9.

151 Ibid., at 509-12.

152 Richmond, "Racially Restrictive Covenants," 10-11; interview: Mr. and Mrs. Richmond, 15 August 1992.

153 *Globe and Mail*, 11 January 1949.

154 OR, at 520-22. The request had actually been for a declaration on Mrs. Noble's answer "or for such further and other Order as may seem just" (Supreme Court, Case File #7594, "Appeal Case").

155 OR, at 522-23.

156 Ibid., at 523-25.

157 Ibid., at 526-36.

158 Ibid., at 525-26.

159 Ibid., at 536. Justice Aylesworth agreed with Chief Justice Robertson.

160 *Toronto Star*, 10 June 1949.

161 *Globe and Mail*, 11 June 1949.

162 NA, Ontario Labour Committee Papers, Vol. 6.

163 *Hamilton News*, 12 July 1949. Copies of this and numerous other press responses are in the Wolf Papers, clipping file.

164 Copy of poll and results in the Richmond Papers.

165 *Star Weekly*, 27 August 1949.

166 *Toronto Star*, 13 June 1949.

167 *Globe and Mail*, 11 June 1949.

168 NA, Richmond Papers, Cartwright to Richmond, 9 June 1949.

169 Ibid., Richmond to Cartwright, 24 June 1949; OJA, Box 3, JPRC, 1944-48, Memo, Harry C. to Kayfetz, 17 June 1949.

170 OJA, Catzman Papers, notes for a speech, 1951.

171 Ibid.; see also Richmond Papers, Richmond to Cartwright 24 June 1949.

172 OJA, JPRC Report, February 1951.

173 NA, Richmond Papers, Egener to Richmond, 28 June 1949; copy in OJA, Box 3, JPRC, 1944-48.

174 NA, Richmond Papers, Richmond to Kayfetz, 30 June 1949.

175 Ibid., Kayfetz to Richmond, telegram 30 June, letter 5 July 1949.

176 Ibid., Egener to Richmond, 11 July 1949.

177 Ibid., Richmond to Kayfetz, 19 July 1949.

178 Ibid., Memo, Ben Kayfetz, 19 July 1949.

179 Ibid., Kayfetz to Richmond, 3 August 1949.

180 Ibid., Richmond to Cartwright, 6 September 1949; OJA, Box 3, JPRC 1944-48, "Agreement between Annie Maude Noble and Bernard Wolf," n.d. (6 September 1949).

181 Roger Graham, *Old Man Ontario: Leslie M. Frost* (Toronto: University of Toronto Press, 1990).

182 NA, Ontario Labour Committee Papers, Vol. 9, "Association for Civil Liberties," includes minutes of meetings, membership lists, correspondence; CJC, Reel 6, File 8, "Association for Civil Liberties, selected correspondence"; interview: Mr. Irving Himel, Toronto, 28 July 1989.

183 Ontario Public Archives, RG 3, Frost Papers, General Correspondence, Box 6, File 11-G, "Association for Civil Liberties," Mahood to Frost, 13 May 1949; interview: Mrs. Vivien Mahood Batke, Waterloo, ON, 11 July 1989.

184 OPA, Frost Papers, Himel to Porter, 27 May 1949.

185 NA, Ontario Labour Committee Papers, Vol. 9, Association for Civil Liberties, circular letters, 26 May, 1 June; Murphy to Himel and Mahood, 1 June 1949.

186 Ibid., Brief in Respect to Legislation Dealing with Expressions of Racial and Religious Discrimination in Ontario, 7 June 1949.

187 Ibid., Vol. 6, Mahood to Kaplansky, 10 June 1949; *Globe and Mail*, 8 June, *Toronto Star*, 8 June 1949.

188 A Brief to the Premier of Ontario, Association for Civil Liberties, January 1950; interview: Mr. Himel, 28 July 1989.

189 *Toronto Star*, 24 January; *Telegram*, 24 January; *Globe and Mail*, 25 January 1950.

190 *Star*, 27 January; *Telegram*, 30 January 1950. OJA, Box 3, File 7 contains a file "Press Comment on Anti-Discrimination Law," with clippings from many provincial newspapers.

191 *Saturday Night*, 7 February 1950.

192 *Globe and Mail*, 17 February 1950.

193 NA, Wolf Papers, "Correspondence, Clippings 1950"; interview: Mrs. Batke, 11 July 1989.

194 OPA, Frost Papers, Box 48, file 87-G.

195 Ibid., Box 6, file 11-G, Seeley to Frost, 17 February; *Globe and Mail*, 18 February 1950.

196 NA, Ontario Labour Committee Papers, Vol. 7, Mahood to Kaplansky, 17 February 1950.

197 *Debates*, 28 February 1950.

198 Ibid., 22 March 1950.

199 SO 1950 c. 11, s. 20A.

200 SM 1950 c. 33, s. 6A: "Every covenant made after this section comes into force that, but for this section, would be annexed to and run with land and that restricts the sale, ownership, occupation, or use, of land because of the race, colour, nationality, ancestry, place or origin, or creed of any person shall be void."

201 OJA, JPRC Minutes, 27 September 1949; Box 3, JPRC 1944-48, sub-committee minutes, 29 September 1949.
202 Wolf Papers, Cartwright to Wolf, 11 January 1950. Similar letter in Richmond Papers, Cartwright to Richmond, 19 January 1950.
203 Richmond Papers, Kayfetz to Wolf, 4 January 1950.
204 OJA, JPRC Minutes, 1 February; JPRC Box, "Restrictive Covenants," Kayfetz to Richmond, 17 February 1950.
205 NA, Richmond Papers, Richmond to Kayfetz, 18 February; Richmond to Borins, 5 May; Hess to Richmond, 9 May; Borins to Richmond, 9 May 1950.
206 Supreme Court, Case File #7594, *Factum* of the Appellant Annie Maud Noble.
207 *Factum* of the Appellant Bernard Wolf.
208 *Factum* of the Respondents W. A. Alley et al.
209 Richmond, "More Thoughts on Wolf Property Case"; interview: Mr. and Mrs. Richmond, 15 August 1992. Mr. Robinette later commented to Mr. Richmond that it was surprising that no members of the talented legal team ranged on behalf of Noble and Wolf had thought of the simple but conclusive example of the hypothetical widow supplied by Justice Rand.
210 [1951] SCR 64; [1951] 1 DLR 321.
211 DLR, at 321-22.
212 Ibid., at 303. Emphasis added.
213 Ibid., at 325.
214 Ibid., at 326-27.
215 Ibid., at 331.
216 Ibid., at 334, 336.
217 Chief Justice Rinfret and of course Justice John Cartwright were absent.
218 OJA, Report of the National Joint Public Relations Committee, October 1951.
219 *Globe and Mail*, 21 November 1950.
220 Ibid.
221 Ibid.
222 *Toronto Star*, 21 November 1950.
223 *Telegram*, 21 November 1950. Other examples from Canadian newspapers can be found in NA, Bernard Wolf papers, "Clippings, 1950," and OJA, JPRC Box, "Restrictive Covenants."
224 Phillip E. Band to the editor, *Toronto Star*, 23 November 1950.
225 *Globe and Mail*, 22 November 1950.
226 Allan Goldstein, "Racial Restrictive Covenants," *University of Toronto Faculty of Law Review*, 9 (1951): 34-35.
227 D. A. L. Smout, "An Inquiry into the Law on Racial and Religious Restraints on Alienation," *Canadian Bar Review*, 30 (1952): 877, 880.
228 NA, Richmond Papers, correspondence with Smout and article typescript. Mr. Richmond has also demonstrated the dissonance between the Ontario legislation and the Supreme Court of Canada decision, concluding that the

conveyancing amendment, with its exclusive and explicit reference to covenants which "run *with* the land," had been rendered meaningless by *Noble and Wolf v. Alley*.

229 C. R. Bourne, "International Law – Unimplemented Treaties – Their Effect on Municipal Law - Public Policy," *Canadian Bar Review*, 29 (1951): 974.

230 J. R. Shiff, "Public Policy and the Restrictive Covenant," *Obiter Dicta*, 25 (1951): 131.

231 Walter Tarnopolsky, "The Supreme Court and Civil Liberties," *Alberta Law Review*, 15 (1976): 76-77.

232 Bushnell, *The Captive Court*, 307-10. Aimé Boucher was a Jehovah's Witness charged with seditious libel for distributing tracts describing the Quebec government and the Roman Catholic Church as enemies to God. The case was heard in the Supreme Court of Canada in June 1950, immediately prior to *Noble and Wolf*, and resulted in a 5-4 decision dismissing the charge against Mr. Boucher. In Bushnell's opinion (296), "The Boucher case contained the most overt statement of judicial creativity yet found in the decisions of the Supreme Court of Canada."

233 Property covenants, however, are an increasingly popular device in Canadian real estate transactions. In the 1951-54 period, 5.2 percent of development plans in the city of Kitchener, ON, contained restrictive covenants, and in 1985-91 it was 65.7 percent. The figures for the adjacent city of Waterloo were 0 in 1951-54 and 71.0 percent in 1985-91. Covenants are legally enforceable within the covenanting group, and when private covenants conflict with public zoning regulations the courts have usually opted in favour of the covenant. One consequence has been the disruption of municipal and provincial zoning plans (Pierre Filion, "The Impact of Restrictive Covenants on Affordable Housing and Non-Single-Family Uses of Homes: A Waterloo Region Case Study," Report to the Canadian Mortgage and Housing Corporation, 1993, 2, 6-8, 26-27 and 44).

234 Private communication, 24 July 1995.

235 For example, the *UNESCO Statement on Race*, 18 July 1950. See above, chap. 1, sec. 1.

236 NA, Richmond Papers, correspondence between Borins and Richmond, 25 July-9 November 1951; interview: Mr. Richmond, 15 August 1992. Judge Grosch, one of the Beach O' Pines litigants, was not a popular man among attorneys in southwestern Ontario because of his reputation as a courtroom bully. Since each person on the Respondents' list was liable for the full amount of the costs, it was suggested that the bill should be immediately served to Grosch.

237 NA, Wolf Papers, Wolf to Kayfetz, 16 October 1951; OJA, Box 5, JPRC, 1952-54, Richmond to Borins, 14 January 1952.

238 NA, Richmond Papers, Richmond to Kayfetz, 11 April 1951.

239 NA, Wolf Papers, Wolf to Kayfetz, 16 October 1951.

240 *Galbraith v. Madawaska Club*, (1959) 18 DLR (2d) 424, (1960) 23 DLR (2d) 6, (1961) 29 DLR (2d) 153. Quotation at 166.

241 *Re Schechter Estate*, (1963) 41 WWR 392, *Royal Trust and Jewish National Fund v. Richter et al*, (1964) 46 WWR 577 (BCCA).

242 *Iwasaki v. The Queen*, (1968) 2 DLR (3d) 241. Justice Sheppard distinguished *Noble and Wolf* because the rules of certainty applicable to a covenant do not apply to a statute or statutory order. Even an obscure law must be interpreted by the courts rather than rejected outright.

243 *Re Sekretov and City of Toronto*, [1972] 3 OR 534, [1973] 2 OR 161, quotation at 168. Nevertheless it was his *Noble and Wolf* decision that pursued Justice Schroeder for the rest of his life. On his death in 1983, the *Globe and Mail* headed his obituary "Judge Upheld Racial Pact," and gave the details of the *Noble and Wolf* case (1 June 1983, cited in Bushnell, *The Captive Court*, 552).

244 Chap. 3, sec. 8.

245 (1980) 27 OR (2d) 142; (1979) 11 CCLT 121; (1980) 105 DLR (3d) 707, 714-15.

246 SO 1961-62 c. 93.

247 The rule, usually summarized as *ubi jus, ibi remedium*, was articulated in the 1703 English case *Ashby v. White*: "If the plaintiff has a right, he must of necessity have a means to vindicate and maintain it, and a remedy if he is injured in the exercise or enjoyment of it; and indeed it is a vain thing to imagine a right without a remedy; for want of right and want of remedy are reciprocal" ([1703] 92 ER 126).

248 DLR, at 715-16.

249 (1979) 11 CCLT 134.

250 Ibid., at 138.

251 Ibid., at 139-40. This argument was put in greater detail by Ian Hunter in "Civil Actions for Discrimination," *Canadian Bar Review*, 55 (1977): 106-30, which Justice Linden quoted in his judgment.

252 For example, Dale Gibson, "The New Tort of Discrimination: A Blessed Event for the Great-Grandmother of Torts," (1979) 11 CCLT, 141-51; Maureen E. Baird, "Pushpa Bhadauria v. The Board of Governors of The Seneca College of Applied Arts and Technology: A Case Comment," *University of Toronto Faculty of Law Review*, 39 (1981): 97-111. The press gave the Appeal decision an adulatory response. In a front page story the *Globe and Mail* claimed the Wilson judgment gave human rights the full protection of the common law, quoting Joseph Pomerant that "It is the most important decision for the little guy in the street in the history of this country." Alan Borovoy of the Canadian Civil Liberties Association told the *Globe* it was "a creative and progressive application of the best public policy principles in the development of the common law" (13 December 1979). But in his book *When Freedoms Collide* (Toronto: Lester and Orpen Dennys, 1988), Mr. Borovoy shows a less positive attitude: "I urge a policy of caution. There are potential risks as well as benefits to any approach that divests the commissions of their control over human rights enforcement. . . . The experience with the judiciary should deter human rights activists from making such proposals. So often when the courts have been drawn into these matters,

they have wound up rendering unduly conservative decisions. There is a risk that more of these decisions will become precedents which could encumber human rights work" (224).

253 See above, chap. 3, sec. 8.

254 17 CCLT 106, at 117-18.

255 See above, sec. 5.

256 CCLT, at 117-18.

257 Harry Kopyto, "The Bhadauria Case: The Denial of the Right to Sue for Discrimination," *Queen's Law Journal*, 7 (1981): 146.

258 Ian A. Hunter, "The Stillborn Tort of Discrimination: Bhadauria v. Board of Governors of Seneca College of Applied Arts and Technology," *Ottawa Law Review*, 14 (1982): 226.

259 Ian B. McKenna, "A Common Law Action for Discrimination in Job Applications," *Canadian Bar Review*, 60 (1982): 122-37.

260 Ibid., 132.

261 (1969) 6 DLR (3d) 576.

262 (1970) 11 DLR (3d) 658.

263 (1971) 18 DLR (3d) 1. Human rights advocates regarded the Supreme Court's *Bell* decision as a setback, preferring the decision of the Ontario Court of Appeal. David Baker, "The Changing Norms of Equality in the Supreme Court of Canada," *Supreme Court Law Review*, 9 (1987): 524; R. Brian Howe, "The Evolution of Human Rights Policy in Ontario," *Canadian Journal of Political Science*, 24 (1991): 793.

264 SO 1974 c.73, s. 5.

265 *Re: Canada Trust and Ontario Human Rights Commission*, (1987) 42 DLR (4th) 263, at 281-83.

266 *Canada Trust v. Ontario Human Rights Commission*, (1990) OR (2d) 481.

267 Ibid., at 490-91.

268 Ibid., at 495.

269 Ibid., at 513.

270 Ibid., at 515. Emphasis added.

271 Ibid., at 494.

272 For case comment on *Canada Trust* see Jim Phillips, "Anti-Discrimination, Freedom of Property Disposition, and the Public Policy of Charitable Educational Trusts," *The Philanthropist*, 9 (1990): 3-42; J. C. Shepherd, "When the Common Law Fails," *Estates and Trusts Journal*, 9 (1989): 117-31; L. A. Turnbull, "Case Comment: Canada Trust," *Estates and Trusts Reports*, 38 (1990): 47-52.

273 See above, sec. 3.

274 For discussion see above, chap. 3, sec. 8.

275 *Debates*, 22 March 1950.

276 SO 1951 c. 24.

277 Notes for the speech are in OPA, Frost Papers, Subject Files, Box 2, "Discrimination Acts, 1951, 1954."

5 NARINE-SINGH V. ATTORNEY GENERAL OF CANADA

1 *Hansard*, 1 June 1914, 4562.
2 Ibid., 4565.
3 RSC 1952 c. 325.
4 Supreme Court, Case File #8299. In official court documents the Singhs' last name appeared as Narine-Singh.
5 PC 1953-859.
6 *Immigration Act*, Sec. 5 (O).
7 Supreme Court, Case File #8299.
8 NA, MG 25 V 75, Jewish Labour Committee of Canada Papers, Vol. 41, file 16, Donna Hill to Kalmen Kaplansky, 4 May 1954.
9 PC 1953-854.
10 NA, Jewish Labour Committee Papers, Hill to Kaplansky, 4 May 1954, F. B. Cotsworth to Harry Singh, 4 May 1954; Supreme Court, Case File #8299, Appeal Case Book; interview: Mrs. Donna Hill, Don Mills, ON, 20 July 1989.
11 For an account of this resolution and a discussion of its implications, see above, chap. 3, sec. 2.
12 BS 1867 c. 3, s. 95: "In each Province the Legislature may make Laws in relation to Agriculture in the Province, and to Immigration into the Province; and it is hereby declared that the Parliament of Canada may from time to time make Laws in relation to Agriculture in all or any of the Provinces, and to Immigration into all or any of the Provinces; and any Law of the Legislature of a Province relative to Agriculture or to Immigration shall have effect in and for the Province so long and as far only as it is not repugnant to any Act of the Parliament of Canada."
13 Undated address, cited in Mariana Valverde, *The Age of Light, Soap and Water: Moral Reform in English Canada, 1885-1925* (Toronto: McClelland and Stewart, 1991), 106.
14 *Hansard*, 1 June 1914, 4563.
15 SC 1869 c. 10.
16 SC 1872 c. 28, s. 10.
17 Quoted in Douglas C. Nord, "Strangers Unto Our World: Asian Immigration and the Evolution of Canadian Immigration Policies," MA thesis, Duke University, 1976, 146.
18 "Speech Delivered by Mr. R. L. Borden at Vancouver, 24th September 1907," published as a pamphlet [Vancouver, 1907].
19 Zlata Godler, "Doctors and the New Immigrants," *Canadian Ethnic Studies*, 9 (1977): 6-17.
20 *Canada Year Book, 1957-8* (Ottawa: Dominion Bureau of Statistics, 1958), 168, "Restrictions Relating to Assimilability." See also Carl Berger, *The Sense of Power: Studies in the Ideas of Canadian Imperialism, 1867-1914* (Toronto: University of Toronto Press, 1970), 349ff., Valverde, *The Age of Light, Soap and Water*, chap. 5.

21 *Saskatoon Star*, 11 June 1927, cited in Martin Robin, *Shades of Right: Nativist and Fascist Politics in Canada, 1920-1940* (Toronto: University of Toronto Press, 1992), 51-52.

22 Memo, Sifton to Laurier, 15 April 1901, quoted in Mabel F. Timlin, "Canada's Immigration Policy, 1896-1910," *Canadian Journal of Economics and Political Science*, 26 (1960): 518.

23 Ibid., 517-32.

24 For example, see Donald Avery, "Canadian Immigration Policy and the 'Foreign' Navvy, 1896-1914," Canadian Historical Association, *Historical Papers 1972* (Ottawa, 1972), 135-56; David C. Corbett, *Canada's Immigration Policy: A Critique* (Toronto: Canadian Institute for International Affairs and University of Toronto Press, 1957), 5ff.; William Petersen, "The Ideological Background to Canada's Immigration," in B. R. Blishen et al., eds., *Canadian Society: Sociological Perspectives* (3rd ed.; Toronto: Macmillan, 1968), 60ff.

25 See above, chap. 2, sec. 2.

26 Trades and Labour Congress of Canada, *Report*, 1904.

27 SC 1906 c. 19, s. 30.

28 SC 1910 c. 27.

29 Quoted in Robert L. Huttenback, *Racism and Empire: White Settlers and Colored Immigrants in the British Self-Governing Colonies 1830-1910* (Ithaca, NY: Cornell University Press, 1976), 144.

30 Ibid., 139ff.

31 Norman Buchignani and Doreen M. Indra, *Continuous Journey: A Social History of South Asians in Canada* (Toronto: McClelland and Stewart, 1985), 5-14; Hugh Johnston, *The East Indians in Canada* (Ottawa: Canadian Historical Association, 1984), 3-6; Brij V. Lal, "Political Movement in the Early East Indian Community in Canada," *Journal of Indian History*, 58 (1980): 193-94; Nord, "Strangers Unto Our World," 51-63; W. Peter Ward, *White Canada Forever: Popular Attitudes and Public Policy Toward Orientals in British Columbia* (Montreal: McGill-Queen's University Press, 1978), 79-81; S. Chandrasekhar, "A History of Canadian Legislation with Respect to Immigration from India," *Plural Societies*, 16 (1986): 259-64.

32 SBC 1907 c. 16.

33 Buchignani, *Continuous Journey*, 17-27; Howard Sugimoto, "The Vancouver Riots of 1907: A Canadian Episode," in H. Conroy and T. Miyakawa, eds., *East Across the Pacific* (Santa Barbara: American Bibliographical Center – Clio Press, 1972), 92-126.

34 Quoted in Ward, *White Canada Forever*, 83-84.

35 George Gray to W. D. Scott, 15 October 1906, quoted in Huttenback, *Racism and Empire*, 175.

36 NA, MG 31 E 55, Tarnopolsky Papers, Vol. 43, file 6.

37 Huttenback, *Racism and Empire*, 178.

38 James S. Woodsworth, *Strangers Within Our Gates* (Toronto: Missionary Society of the Methodist Church of Canada, 1909), 188-89.

39 Nord, "Strangers Unto Our World," 64.

40 Huttenback, *Racism and Empire*, 176.

41 *Report by W. L. Mackenzie King on the Subject of Immigration to Canada from the Orient and Immigration from India in Particular* (Ottawa, 1908).

42 PC 1908-1225.

43 PC 1908-27.

44 Quoted in Huttenback, *Racism and Empire*, 190.

45 NA, Tarnopolsky Papers, Vol. 43, file 6; Buchignani, *Continuous Journey*, 36-43; N. Buchignani and D. Indra, "The Political Organization of South Asians in Canada, 1904-1920," in Jorgen Dahlie and Tissa Fernando, eds., *Ethnicity, Power and Politics in Canada* (Toronto: Methuen, 1981), 202-32; Lal, "Political Movement," 195-210.

46 Parallel developments were occurring in the United States. Canadian immigration restrictions deflected Indian migrants to the American West coast, provoking public hostility and official exclusion. On 5 September 1907, on the very eve of the Vancouver riot, a violent white mob in Bellingham, WA, forced about 700 East Indians to flee across the border into Canada. Under American law "white" immigrants could apply for naturalization. Indians argued that since they were "Caucasians" they should be considered white and therefore eligible for naturalization, but the 1910 US census listed them as "other" on the grounds that "the popular conception of the term 'white'" applied only to "Caucasians of European origin" and not to their distant cousins in Asia. With few exceptions federal officials denied citizenship to Indian applicants, but the issue was not settled until 1923 when a unanimous US Supreme Court ruled in *US v. Bhaghat Singh Thind* that according to the "understanding of the common man" East Indians were not white and therefore could not become American citizens (Gary R. Hess, "The Forgotten Asian Americans: The East Indian Community in the United States," *Pacific Historical Review*, 43 [1974]: 580-81, 588-92; Joan M. Jensen, *Passage from India: Asian Indian Immigrants in North America* [New Haven: Yale University Press, 1988], 246-69).

47 PC 1910-926.

48 PC 1910-920.

49 (1913) 18 BCR 506.

50 Ibid., at 507-8.

51 Ibid., at 509-10.

52 PC 1913-2642, renewed the following March by PC 1914-897.

53 PC 1914-24, "No immigrant of any Asiatic race shall be permitted to land in Canada unless such immigrant possess in his own right money to the amount of at least two hundred dollars." PC 1914-23, "The landing in Canada ... is hereby prohibited of any immigrant who has come to Canada otherwise than by a continuous journey from the country of which he is a native or naturalized citizen and upon a through ticket purchased in that country or prepaid in Canada."

54 For a full discussion of this interesting episode, see Hugh Johnston, *The Voyage of the Komagata Maru: The Sikh Challenge to Canada's Colour Bar* (2nd ed.;

Vancouver: University of British Columbia Press, 1989). Jensen, *Passage from India*, chap. 6, has a succinct account of the Komagata Maru "challenge," while Robie L. Reid, the immigration department employee who wrote the official report on these events, offered a contemporary's perspective (and defense of the government's actions) in "The Inside Story of the Komagata Maru," *British Columbia Historical Quarterly*, 5 (1941): 1-23.

55 Quoted in Nord, "Strangers Unto Our World," 1.

56 *Hansard*, 1 June 1914, 4565.

57 (1914) 20 BCR 243. Chief Justice Gordon Hunter of the BC Supreme Court was not held in great respect by the provincial government. Unable to replace him, the BC government created a Court of Appeal in 1909 which was superior to Hunter's Supreme Court. See Johnston, *Voyage of the Komagata Maru*, 21, and fn. 11, 140.

58 In the BCR account, the constitutional arguments of Bird and Cassidy are summarized at 249-53. In their judgments the five justices commented upon additional arguments raised by Bird and Cassidy, as cited below.

59 BCR, at 275, 280.

60 Ibid., at 272.

61 Ibid., at 289-90.

62 Ibid., at 256-57.

63 Ibid., at 255, 258, 259, 260, 262, 263, 265, 266, 275, 282, 283, 286, 287.

64 Ibid., at 256, 261, 272, 273, 274, 285.

65 Ibid., at 267, 277.

66 Ibid., at 258, 262, 268.

67 Ibid., at 263, 264, 265, 269, 270, 271.

68 Ibid., citing Lord Chancellor Loreburn, (1912) 81 LJ, PC 210, at 213.

69 BCR, at 280.

70 Ibid., at 272, 289.

71 Ibid., at 289.

72 Ibid., at 290. This was the same Justice McPhillips who sided with the Empress Theatre in its refusal to admit Mr. Barnswell in April 1915. See above, chap. 3, sec. 4. On the American decision see *US v. Bhaghat Singh Thind*, 261 US 204 (1923).

73 BCR, at 290-92.

74 Johnston, *East Indians in Canada*, 16.

75 PC 1919-641; Buchignani, *Continuous Journey*, 65-74; Buchignani and Indra, "Political Organization of South Asians," 218, and 230, n. 86; Emmaline E. Smillie, "An Historical Survey of Indian Migration Within the Empire," *Canadian Historical Review*, 4 (1923): 230.

76 PC 1930-2115.

77 For example, James J. Guy, "Canada and the Caribbean: How 'Special' the Relationship," *The Round Table*, 304 (1987): 435-36; Mona S. Henry, "Canada-West Indies Economic Relations, 1884-1925," MA thesis, University of Water-

loo, 1978; Brinsley Samaroo, "The Politics of Disharmony: The Debate on the Political Union of the British West Indies and Canada, 1884-1921," *Revista/ Review Interamericana*, 8 (1977): 50; Robin Winks, *Canada-West Indian Union: A Forty-Year Minuet* (London: Athlone Press, 1968). East Indians were brought to the British West Indies as indentured labourers after the abolition of slavery in 1834 created a labour shortage in plantation agriculture.

78 Including Mathieu Léveillé, from Martinique, who served as public executioner in Quebec from 1733 to 1743, and his fiancée Angélique-Denise. See above, chap. 3, sec. 3.

79 Mavis C. Campbell, *The Maroons of Jamaica, 1655-1796* (Granby, MA: Bergin and Garvey, 1988); Mavis C. Campbell, ed., *Nova Scotia and the Fighting Maroons. A Documentary History* (Williamsburg, VA: College of William and Mary, 1990); C. R. Dallas, *The History of the Maroons from Their Origin to the Establishment of their Chief Tribe at Sierra Leone*, 2 vols. (1803; rpt. London: Cass, 1968).

80 *Census of Canada, 1911*, Vol. 2, 384-85; Elizabeth Beaton, "Religious Affiliation and Ethnic Identity of West Indians in Whitney Pier," *Canadian Ethnic Studies*, 20 (1988): 112-31; Agnes Calliste, "Race, Gender and Canadian Immigration Policy: Blacks from the Caribbean, 1900-1932," *Journal of Canadian Studies*, 28 (1993-94): 134-40. Several hundred African Americans had been recruited to work in the blast furnaces by the Dominion Iron and Steel Company in 1901-2, but most of these workers and their families returned to the United States within two or three years.

81 NA, RG 76 Vol. 566, file 810666, Scott to Pickford and Black, 14 November 1914, cited in Calliste, "Blacks from the Caribbean," 135-36.

82 Genevieve Leslie, "Domestic Service in Canada, 1880-1920," in J. Acton et al., eds., *Women at Work: Ontario, 1850-1930* (Toronto: Canadian Women's Educational Press, 1974), 95. See also Marilyn Barber, "The Women Ontario Welcomed: Immigrant Domestics for Ontario Homes, 1870-1930," *Ontario History*, 72 (1980).

83 NA, RG 76 Vol. 475, file 731832, J. Stafford to W. Klein, 7 April 1911.

84 Ibid., memo, Scott to Oliver, 2 June 1911. Scott went on to explain that people of African descent were not "congenial" to Canada in any case.

85 Ibid., Scott to Dion, 16 June 1911, Scott to Gilbert, 28 July.

86 Ibid., Scott to G. Boudrias, 4 August 1911.

87 Ibid., L. Fortier to Scott, 27 and 30 June 1914, Scott to Fortier, 2 and 27 July.

88 Ibid., Scott to Fortier, 10 Aug. 1916.

89 Ibid., Scott to Knight, 25 April 1916.

90 John Schultz, "White Man's Country: Canada and the West Indian Immigrant, 1900-1965," *American Review of Canadian Studies*, 12 (1982): 58-60; Calliste, "Blacks from the Caribbean," 140-45.

91 "Restrictions Relating to Assimilability," *Canada Year Book, 1957-38*, 168-70.

92 Cited in Peter S. Li and B. Singh Bolaria, "Canadian Immigration Policy and Assimilation Theories," in John A. Fry, ed., *Economy, Class and Social Reality: Issues in Contemporary Canadian Society* (Toronto: Butterworths, 1979), 419.

93 *Hansard,* 3 April 1946, 525.

94 *Hansard,* 2 May 1947, 2732.

95 *Hansard,* 4 February 1947, 114.

96 *Hansard,* 12 July 1943, 4683.

97 Vic Satzewich, "The Canadian State and the Racialization of Caribbean Migrant Farm Labour 1947-1966," *Ethnic and Racial Studies,* 11 (1988): 288, noting pressures from Barbados and Jamaica as early as 1947.

98 *Hansard,* 11 February 1947, 324; *Globe and Mail,* 25 February 1947.

99 For example, *Hansard,* 11 February 1947, 319, 332; 5 May 1947, 2754-57; 24 March 1952, 714, 728-30; 4 July 1952, 4260-62.

100 *Hansard,* 11 February 1947, 332.

101 NA, RG 76, file 536999, part 17, petition, 3 March 1947.

102 *Ottawa Journal,* 1 May 1947; *Hansard,* 3 May 1947, 2732.

103 *Canada Year Book, 1957-58,* 157-58, 164; Corbett, *Canada's Immigration Policy,* 11; Alan G. Green, *Immigration and the Postwar Canadian Economy* (Toronto: Macmillan, 1976), 35; *Hansard,* 3 April 1946, 525-28; Constantine Passaris, "Immigration to Canada in the Post Second War Period: Manpower Flows from the Caribbean," in A. Marks and H. Vessuri, *White Collar Migrants in the Americas and the Caribbean* (Leiden: Royal Institute of Linguistics and Anthropology, 1983), 85; Petersen, "Ideological Background," 64-65; Satzewich, "Caribbean Migrant Farm Labour," 283-89; Harold Troper, "Canada's Immigration Policy since 1945," *International Journal,* 48 (1993): 258-59.

104 Corbett, *Canada's Immigration Policy,* 7-9, 48; *Hansard,* 3 April 1946, 526-27; Petersen, "Ideological Background," 60-64; M. F. Timlin, "Canadian Immigration Policy: An Analysis," *International Migration,* 3 (1965): 53.

105 *Hansard,* 11 February 1947, 317.

106 TLC, *Report,* 1947, 31-32.

107 Senate Committee on Immigration and Labour, *Proceedings,* August 1946, 310.

108 Ibid., 1949, 17, 23.

109 PC 1931-695. This order, issued in March 1931, permitted the entry of British subjects born or naturalized in Great Britain, Northern Ireland, Newfoundland, New Zealand, Australia or South Africa, and American citizens, who had the means to support themselves until they found employment, wives and unmarried children under 18 of Canadian residents who could support them, and farmers with sufficient capital to establish a farm. Asians were excluded from PC 695, being already covered by PC 2115.

110 *Hansard,* 11 February 1947, 308ff.

111 *Hansard,* 1 May 1947, 2644-47.

112 The changes were consolidated in PC 1950-2856.

113 *Canada Year Book 1955* (Ottawa: Dominion Bureau of Statistics, 1955), 165.

114 PC 1948-4186; PC 1950-4364.

115 PC 1950-6229, amending PC 1930-2115 to extend admissibility to Asians who were "The wife, the husband, or the unmarried child under twenty-one

years of age, of any Canadian citizen legally admitted to and resident in Canada, who is in a position to receive and care for his dependents."

116 NA, Jewish Labour Committee Papers, Vol. 41, P. T. Baldwin, Chief, Admission Division, Department of Citizenship and Immigration, to Mr. R. L. Anderson, 17 August 1951. For a virtually identical letter see W. R. Baskerville, District Superintendent, to Mrs. Rachel Mills, 10 September 1951, in Donald Moore, *Don Moore: An Autobiography* (Toronto: Williams Wallace, 1985), 90-91.

117 Subsequently the quota was extended to 100 citizens of Pakistan and 50 citizens of Ceylon (Sri Lanka), *Canada Year Book 1952-53*, 164. The Indian quota was doubled by PC 1958-7.

118 *Hansard*, 4 July 1952, 4263.

119 Ibid., 4270-71. The actual ranks laid out by Harris (grouped by norms of admission) were:

(1) Great Britain and Northern Ireland, Australia, New Zealand, Union of South Africa, Ireland, the United States, France;

(2) Belgium, Luxembourg, Norway, Denmark, Sweden, Switzerland;

(3) Holland;

(4) Germany, Austria, Greece, Finland;

(5) Italy;

(6) Israel, Turkey, Syria, Lebanon, Iran;

(7) all other European countries;

(8) South America;

(9) British West Indies;

(10) India, Pakistan, Ceylon;

(11) all other Asian countries;

(12) all other countries.

120 Ibid., 4260, 4261, 4262, 4272, 4278, 4279.

121 Ibid., 4269.

122 *Hansard*, 10 June 1952, 3074-76.

123 *Hansard*, 26 June 1954, 6832.

124 SC 1952 c. 42.

125 Subsections a) to f) of Section 61 gave the minister authority to determine

"a) the terms and conditions under which persons who have received financial assistance to enable them to obtain passage to Canada or to assist them in obtaining admission to Canada may be admitted to Canada;

b) literacy, medical and other examinations or tests and the prohibiting or limiting of admission of persons who are unable to pass them;

c) the terms, conditions and requirements with respect to the possession of means of support or of passports, visas or other documents pertaining to admission;

d) the admission to Canada of persons who have come to Canada otherwise than by continuous journey from the countries of which they are nationals or citizens;

e) the prohibiting or limiting of admission of persons brought to Canada by any transportation company that fails to comply with any provision of the Act or any regulation, order or direction made under it;

f) the prohibiting or limiting of admission of persons who are nationals or citizens of a country that refuses to readmit any of its nationals or citizens who are ordered deported; and"

[g) as quoted].

126 J. W. Pickersgill, *My Years with Louis St. Laurent* (Toronto: University of Toronto Press, 1975), 233.

127 *Hansard*, 24 March 1952, 728.

128 *Hansard*, 10 June 1952, 3079.

129 The Committee's original name was the Toronto Joint Labour Committee Against Racial and Religious Intolerance. The change occurred in 1953 at the suggestion of Donna Hill (interview: Donna Hill, 20 July 1989).

130 S. 1 of PC 2856 (issued 9 June 1950) stated that "for the purpose of this Regulation the term 'British subject' shall mean a person born or naturalized in the United Kingdom of Great Britain and Northern Ireland, Australia, New Zealand or the Union of South Africa, or a citizen of Ireland who has become a citizen of the United Kingdom." British subjects from elsewhere in the Commonwealth were not admissible to Canada under this Regulation.

131 NA, Jewish Labour Committee Papers, Vol. 41, Milling to Kaplansky, 1951 "Report of Progress"; NA, MG 30 A 53, Kaplansky Papers, Vol. 20, "Report of Activities for Improved Human Relations in the Labor Field, submitted to the Joint Advisory Committee on Labor Relations," March 1951, 5-7, April, 8, May, 8, September, 7-8. Gordon Milling was the executive secretary of the Toronto Labour Committee for Human Rights, and Kalmen Kaplansky the executive director of the Jewish Labour Committee of Canada.

132 NA, Kaplansky Papers, Vol. 20, Report, September 1951, 2-3.

133 NA, Jewish Labour Committee Papers, Milling to Kaplansky, 1951 Report.

134 Moore, *Autobiography*, 87-89; *The Canadian Negro*, June 1953; interview: Mr. Don Moore, Toronto, 25 July 1989. The African Methodist Episcopal church at its annual conference in the summer of 1949 passed a unanimous resolution expressing "deep concern" that British West Indians were not included as British subjects in immigration regulations, and urging the federal government to grant them "equal rights and privileges" with all other British subjects. PC 2856 had not yet been issued, but the West Indies had been omitted from the admissible British category in many previous orders-in-council. NA, RG76 Vol. 244, file 165172, Rev. W. Constantine Perry to Louis St. Laurent, 25 August 1949.

135 NA, Jewish Labour Committee Papers, Vol. 41, Milling to Kaplansky, 1951 Report.

136 Ibid., Milling to Kaplansky, 28 April 1952, 19 June 1952, 26 February 1953; NA, Kaplansky Papers, Vol. 20, Report, April 1953, 8.

137 *Hansard*, 24 April 1953, 4351-52; NA, Jewish Labour Committee Papers, Vol. 41, Milling to Kaplansky, 3 March 1952.

138 *Hansard*, 9 April 1952, 1400.

139 The brief is enclosed in NA, Jewish Labour Committee Papers, Vol. 41, Milling to Kaplansky, 20 June 1952. See also Milling to Kaplansky, Report, January 1952, Milling to Kaplansky, 4 February 1952; Moore, *Autobiography*, 100-3; *The Canadian Negro*, June 1953; NA, Kaplansky Papers, Vol. 20, Report, June 1952, 6-7; RG 76 Vol. 244, file 165172, "Resolution," 22 June 1952.

140 *Hansard*, 4 July 1952, 4279.

141 NA, RG 76 Vol. 244, file 165172, Norman Dowd, executive secretary of the CCL, to Walter Harris, 14 November 1951; Kaplansky Papers, Vol. 20, Report, February 1952, 2, March, 1-3, September, 8-9; Jewish Labour Committee Papers, Vol. 41, Toronto Committee Report for April-June 1952.

142 Contained in NA, Jewish Labour Committee Papers, Vol. 41.

143 *Hansard*, 24 April 1953, 4324-26, 4346, 4351-54.

144 Corbett, *Canada's Immigration Policy*, 54.

145 PC 1953-859 (26 May).

146 *Toronto Star Weekly*, 16 January 1954.

147 *Globe and Mail*, 14 January 1954.

148 Ibid.

149 Editorial, "The Queen Backs Race Equality," *Toronto Star Weekly*, 16 January 1954.

150 NA, MG 28 I 173, Ontario Labour Committee for Human Rights Papers, Vol. 15, file: "Immigration - general policy and problem of immigrants," text of St. Laurent address, 23 February 1954.

151 Ibid., transcript of CFRB radio debate, 12 April 1954.

152 Interviews: Mr. Stanley G. Grizzle, Toronto, 10 July 1988; Mrs. Donna Hill, 20 July 1989; Mr. Don Moore, 25 July 1989; Mr. Harry Gairey, Toronto, 22 February 1992.

153 NA, Jewish Labour Committee Papers, Vol. 41, Kaplansky to Hill, 9 April 1954.

154 Ibid., Moore to MacDonald, 12 April, Hill to Wismer, 12 April, Hill to Andras, 12 April, Kehoe to Hill, 27 April 1954.

155 NA, Ontario Labour Committee Papers, Vol. 19, file: "Negro Citizenship Association," "Brief Presented to the Prime Minister, the Minister of Citizenship and Immigration, and Members of the Government of Canada by the Negro Citizenship Association, 27 April 1954"; "Statement of Stanley G. Grizzle regarding Canadian Immigration Act and PC 2856."

156 *The Canadian Negro*, April-May 1954; Moore, *Autobiography*, 115.

157 *Hansard*, 26 June 1954, 6816, 6826.

158 Ibid., 25 June 1954, 6776-77.

159 Pickersgill, *My Years*, 231.

160 *The Canadian Negro*, December 1954.

161 PC 1954-1351 (17 September).

162 Moore, *Autobiography*, 119-20.

163 Pickersgill, *My Years*, 231.

164 *Hansard*, 15 February 1955, 1158. Mr. Fulton's own perspective had already been revealed to the House in an earlier debate, when he said: "We want to take our country as we have it now and we want to develop it, we do not want to change it. These limitations, that we must not bring in people faster than we can absorb them, in either a physical or cultural sense, are I think agreed upon by everyone in the House" (*Hansard*, 24 April 1953, 4337-38).

165 *Hansard*, 15 February 1955, 1171, 1192.

166 Ibid., 1196.

167 Ibid.

168 Ibid., 1165-66, 1241. The third member was Halifax MP John H. Dickey.

169 Freda Hawkins, *Canada and Immigration: Public Policy and Public Concern* (2nd ed.; Kingston: McGill-Queen's University Press, 1988), 108-9.

170 Pickersgill, *My Years*, 234.

171 [1952] 4 DLR 715; [1953] 2 DLR 766; [1954] 1 DLR 401. On PC 6229 see above, n. 107.

172 *Hansard*, 17 February 1955, 1243.

173 Pickersgill, *My Years*, 235.

174 Ibid.

175 *Hansard*, 17 February 1955, 1248, 1250.

176 *Hansard*, 24 March 1955, 2331.

177 *Hansard*, 6 May 1955, 3527.

178 *Canada Year Book, 1955*, 166.

179 NA, RG 76 Vol. 830, file 552-1-644, part 2, C. E. S. Smith to G. McInnes with enclosure, director to deputy minister, "A Review of Immigration from the British West Indies," 14 January 1955. A virtually identical version of this memo had been written in 1949. The Rev. Constantine Perry wrote to Prime Minister St. Laurent on 24 September 1949 following up his letter of 25 August (above, n. 134). In the new letter Rev. Perry declared his amazement that the *Immigration Act* continued to discriminate against West Indians, though St. Laurent had promised to eliminate racial inequality during the recent election campaign. The letter was sent to Director of Immigration Jolliffe to draft a reply. Jolliffe advised against any government reply. "In substance," he wrote to the minister's private secretary J. G. Levy, "there is only one answer to give Dr. Perry: to recognize that the present regulations as they apply to British subjects are deliberately restrictive and give reasons for them. It is not by accident. . . ." (RG76, Vol. 244, file 165172, 12 October 1949). According to Jolliffe's advice no such response was sent to Rev. Perry, but obviously Smith had Jolliffe's memo in hand when writing his "Review" five years later.

180 *Hansard*, 8 August 1956, 7219.

181 SO 1951 c. 24.

182 SC 1953 c. 28.

183 NA, Ontario Labour Committee Papers, Vol. 19, file: "Harry Singh," Blum to Moore, 18 June 1954.

184 Ibid., Blum to Toronto and Lakeshore Labour Council, 28 June 1954.

185 Ibid., Blum to Miss Ruth Gordon, 24 June 1954.

186 NA, Jewish Labour Committee Papers, Vol. 41, Hill to Kaplansky, 4 May 1954.

187 NA, Ontario Labour Committee Papers, Vol. 19, file: "Harry Singh," Hill to Andras, 7 May 1954, Alistair Stewart to Andras, 18 May 1954.

188 NA, Jewish Labour Committee Papers, Vol. 41, press release, May 1954; Supreme Court Case File #8299.

189 NA, Ontario Labour Committee Papers, Vol. 38, file: "Singh Defense Fund," numerous letters.

190 NA, Ontario Labour Committee Papers, Vol. 19, file: "Harry Singh," Blum to Ron Haggart, *Globe and Mail*, to Fred Jones, *Telegram*, to Pat McNenly, *Toronto Star*, all 19 May 1954.

191 *Toronto Star*, 29 May 1954.

192 *Saturday Night*, 22 May 1954.

193 Copy of letter is in Supreme Court Case File #8299.

194 NA, Ontario Labour Committee Papers, Vol. 19, file: "Harry Singh," Blum, "Conversation with Harry Singh, May 26, 1954, 5 PM."

195 For example, ibid., Blum to reporters at the *Globe and Mail*, *Star* and *Telegram*, 22 June 1954.

196 [1932] 4 DLR 246. Munetaka Samejima entered Canada in September 1928 to be the domestic servant of J. Uyeno of Nanaimo, but Uyeno had gone bankrupt and was unable to employ him and he could find no other domestic work. In April 1931 he was ordered deported, but the order did not state the reason and so Justice Fisher quashed the deportation as improper. Immigration officials then issued a new order, stating the reason that his entry application as a domestic servant was a misrepresentation. The Supreme Court of Canada decided that Samejima had not had an opportunity to reply to this charge, and that his original deportation having been quashed it could not later be amended.

197 [1954] OR 784; *Toronto Star*, 30 June 1954; *Globe and Mail*, 30 June; NA, Jewish Labour Committee Papers, Blum to Kaplansky, 30 June 1954.

198 [1948] OR 487. An American trade union officer, H. Reid Robinson, had been deported as someone who advocated the violent overthrow of the government. His appeal to the courts was dismissed because S. 3 (n) and (o) of the *Immigration Act* permitted advocates of violence to be deported. The fact that the Board's evidence was incomplete at the time of the immigration hearing was not sufficient cause to invoke judicial interference: Robinson's proper course of appeal was to the minister, not the courts.

199 [1954] OR 784, at 786-789; *Globe and Mail*, 13 July 1954.

200 NA, Jewish Labour Committee Papers, Vol. 41, Blum to Kaplansky, Report for July 1954.

201 Ibid., Blum to Kaplansky, 6 August 1954.
202 Ibid., Blum to "All Ontario Local Unions CCL," 14 August 1954, Blum to R. J. Lezama, Port-of-Spain, Trinidad, 3 August 1954; *Trinidad Guardian*, 21 July 1954.
203 [1954] OR 789.
204 Ibid., at 789-90.
205 Ibid., at 790. Mr. Bromley Armstrong reports a piece of homely wisdom injected by one of the judges during this exchange, intended to refute Mr. Brewin's argument: "If a cat had her kittens in an oven, that wouldn't make them cookies" (interview with Mr. Armstrong, 25 July 1989).
206 OR, at 790-91.
207 Ibid., at 791.
208 Ibid., at 792.
209 Ibid., at 792-93.
210 NA, Jewish Labour Committee Papers, Vol. 41, Brewin to Blum, 10 September 1954.
211 Ibid., Blum to Kaplansky, 22 September 1954.
212 Copy of resolution contained in NA, Ontario Labour Committee Papers, Vol. 38, file: "Singh Defense Fund."
213 *Telegram*, *Star*, *Globe and Mail*, all 28 September 1954. The *Telegram* story was a page-wide spread with pictures, one of which showed a poster with a black and a white figure applying for Canadian citizenship, one marked "admitted" and one marked "barred," with the caption "Discrimination in Immigration!"
214 NA, Jewish Labour Committee Papers, Vol. 41, mimeograph, "Report on the Singh Immigration Case to Ontario CCL Local Unions," October 1954.
215 NA, Ontario Labour Committee Papers, Vol. 38, file: "Singh Defense Fund," Brewin to Blum, 22 September 1954, Blum to Kaplansky, 22 September.
216 Supreme Court, Case File #8299, Appellant's *Factum*.
217 Ibid.
218 Ibid., *Factum* of the Respondent.
219 Canadian Press, 5 April 1955; NA, Jewish Labour Committee Papers, Vol. 41, Blum to Kaplansky, 5 April 1955.
220 [1955] SCR 395.
221 Ibid., at 397-98. Dictionaries are not the most suitable sources upon which to rely for legal application. As Raymond Williams has demonstrated, dictionary definitions encapsulate the "presuppositions of orthodox opinion" from the period in which the dictionary is compiled, as well as the ideology of its editors. He notes that even the *Oxford English Dictionary*, created between the 1880s and the 1920s, "is not so impersonal, so purely scholarly, or so free of active social and political values as might be supposed." *Keywords: A Vocabulary of Culture and Society* (rev. ed.; New York: Oxford University Press, 1985), 18. By employing the *Oxford Dictionary* the Supreme Court of Canada was resurrecting an "orthodox opinion" and perpetuating it in Canadian law.

222 I tried to locate Harry and Mearl Singh or some of their relatives, in order to provide an ending to their story from their own perspective. During a visit to her native Trinidad Ms. Pat Craton of Waterloo, ON, placed advertisements in local newspapers and launched inquiries in the Trinidad Asian community hoping to find someone who knew the Singhs' whereabouts, but she received no response. I am extremely grateful to Ms. Craton for undertaking this mission on my behalf.

223 NA, Jewish Labour Committee Papers, Vol. 41, Blum to Kaplansky, 5 April 1955.

224 Ibid., Blum to Kaplansky, 15 April 1955.

225 NA, Ontario Labour Committee Papers, Vol. 38, file: "Immigration: Harry Singh Case," memo, Andrew Brewin, 6 April 1955.

226 Undated clipping found in NA, Ontario Labour Committee Papers, Vol. 19, file: "Harry Singh."

227 NA, Ontario Labour Committee Papers, Vol. 13, Ontario Federation of Labour brief.

228 NA, Kaplansky Papers, Vol. 20, Report, May 1955, 2.

229 NA, Jewish Labour Committee Papers, Vol. 41, Blum to Kaplansky, 15 April 1955.

230 *Toronto Star*, 17 August 1955.

231 NA, Jewish Labour Committee Papers, Blum to Kaplansky, 5 April 1955.

232 *The Canadian Negro*, December 1955.

233 1956 Gallup Poll, cited in Winks, *Blacks in Canada*, 436.

234 Canada, Parliament, House of Commons, Special Committee on Estimates, *Minutes and Proceedings of Evidence*, No. 11, 301, 14 March 1955.

235 [1954] OR 706.

236 Ibid., at 707-12.

237 [1955] OR 480.

238 *Hansard*, 29 April 1955, 3299-300.

239 [1956] SCR 318, at 321.

240 Pickersgill, *My Years*, 240.

241 PC 1956-785:

"20. Landing in Canada of any person is prohibited except where the person falls within one of the following classes of persons who may be landed in Canada if such person meets the requirements of the Act and of these regulations:

(a) a person who is a British subject by birth or by naturalization in the United Kingdom, Australia, New Zealand, or the Union of South Africa, a citizen of Ireland, a citizen of France born or naturalized in France or in St. Pierre and Miquelon Islands, or a citizen of the United States of America if such person has sufficient means to maintain himself in Canada until he has secured employment therein;

(b) a person who is a citizen by birth or by naturalization of Austria, Belgium, Denmark, the Federal Republic of Germany, Finland,

Greece, Iceland, Italy, Luxembourg, the Netherlands, Norway, Portugal, Spain, Sweden or Switzerland or who is a refugee from a country of Europe, if such person undertakes to come to Canada for placement under the auspices of the Department or, if the Department has given its approval thereto, for establishment in a business, trade or profession or in agriculture;

(c) a person who is a citizen by birth or by naturalization of Egypt, Israel, Lebanon, Turkey, or of any country of Europe or of a country of North America, Central America or South America if such person is the husband, wife, son, daughter, brother, sister, as well as the husband or wife and the unmarried children under 21 years of age of any such son, daughter, brother or sister, as the case may be, the father, the mother, the grandparent, the unmarried orphan nephew or niece under 21 years of age, the fiancé or fiancée, of a Canadian citizen or of a person legally admitted to Canada for permanent residence who is residing in Canada and who has applied for any such person and is in a position to receive and care for any such person; or

(d) a person who is a citizen of a country other than a country referred to in paragraphs (a), (b) or (c) or in section 21, if such person is the husband, the wife or the unmarried child under 21 years of age, the father where he is over 65 years of age, or the mother where she is over 60 years of age, of a Canadian citizen residing in Canada who has applied for and is in a position to receive and care for any such person, but no such child shall be landed in Canada unless his father or his mother, as the case may be, is landed in Canada concurrently with him.

21.   The Government of Canada having entered into an agreement with the Government of India, the Government of Pakistan and the Government of Ceylon with respect to the admission to Canada of 150, 100 and 50 persons annually from such countries, respectively, the landing in Canada of persons from any such country is, notwithstanding section 20, limited accordingly to such numbers of persons respectively, and in addition to the husband, the wife or the unmarried child under 21 years of age, the father where he is over 65 years of age or the mother where she is over 60 years of age, of a Canadian citizen residing in Canada who has applied for and is in a position to receive and care for such person.

242 Pickersgill, *My Years*, 240.
243 *Hansard*, 8 August 1956, 7207.
244 NA, Jewish Labour Committee Papers, Vol. 42, Blum to Brewin, 19 September 1956.
245 Canadian Press, 12 July 1956; *Hansard*, 8 August 1956, 7205.

246 Ibid., 7205-6.
247 [1955] SCR 395, at 398.

6 IMPLICATIONS

1 Adolf Hitler, *Mein Kampf*, translated by Ralph Manheim (New York: Houghton Mifflin, 1943), 325.
2 "Reich Citizenship Law" and "Law for the Protection of German Blood and Honour," 15 September 1935, in R. S. Landau, *The Nazi Holocaust* (Chicago: I. R. Dee, 1994), Appendix E, 310-12.
3 Respectively, the *Population Registration Act* (1950), *Group Areas Act* (1950), *Immorality Amendment Act* (1950), *Bantu Act* (1952), *Separate Amenities Act* (1953) and *Bantu Labour Act* (1953).
4 Note Sir John A. Macdonald's insistence before the House of Commons in 1882 that Chinese were admissible only as labourers for the railway (chap. 2, sec. 2).
5 Chap. 3, sec. 2.
6 Chap. 2, sec. 3.
7 Chap. 5, sec. 3.
8 Chap. 2, sec. 2.
9 Chap. 3, sec. 2.
10 Chap. 4, sec. 1 and 2.
11 See especially the rhetorical line proceeding through Ontario's anti-discrimination legislation in 1944 and the *Drummond Wren* decision (chap. 4, sec. 2 and 3), and the "New Commonwealth" references throughout the debate on immigration reform (chap. 5, sec. 6 and 8).
12 Chap. 2, sec. 4.
13 Chap. 2, sec. 4; chap. 5, sec. 3 and 5.
14 In case law *Drummond Wren* would serve as a useful example. Ontario's *Fair Employment Practices Act*, passed in 1951, overtly incorporated the UN Charter and Declaration of Human Rights (see chap. 4, sec. 3 and 7).
15 Note, for example, that in *Munshi Singh* the appellant accepted the doctrine of racial hierarchy, denying only that Indians were in the inferior category (chap. 5, sec. 4).
16 Chap. 2, sec. 8.
17 Chap. 5, sec. 2.
18 For example, chap. 2, sec. 3.
19 Chap. 3, sec. 2.
20 Chap. 2, sec. 3.
21 Chap. 3, sec. 6 and 8.
22 Chap. 1, sec. 2.
23 Chap. 5, sec. 6.
24 Chap. 5, sec. 8.
25 Chap. 5, sec. 8.

26 Chap. 3, sec. 2.
27 Chap. 2, sec. 3.
28 Chap. 5, sec. 4.
29 Evidence in the case studies did not implicate Jews in this respect, though Jewish sexuality and designs upon Christian women featured in Nazi lore.
30 Chap. 2, sec. 7.
31 Chap. 2, sec. 5 and 9.
32 Chap. 3, sec. 2.
33 Chap. 5, sec. 5.
34 Chap. 5, sec. 3.
35 Chap. 5, sec. 8.
36 Chap. 4, sec. 1.
37 Chap. 2, sec. 9.
38 Chap. 3, sec. 4.
39 Chap. 4, sec. 4.
40 Chap. 5, sec. 6.
41 Chap. 5, sec. 4.
42 Chap. 5, sec. 8.
43 Chap. 3, sec. 2.
44 Chap. 3, sec. 7.
45 Chap. 2, sec. 9.
46 Chap. 4, sec. 2.
47 Chap. 4, sec. 5.
48 Chap. 2, sec. 9.
49 Chap. 5, sec. 6 and 8.
50 A clear judicial articulation of this interpretation of equality is found in the comment of Justice Tysoe in *R. v. Gonzales* ([1962] 37 BCR 56), a case of a native Indian charged with possession of an intoxicant off the reserve. "Equality before the law" was construed to mean "a right in every person *to whom a particular law relates or extends*, no matter what may be a person's race, national origin, colour, religion or sex, to stand on an equal footing with every other person to whom that particular law relates or extends." Emphasis in the original.
51 Chap. 5, sec. 8.
52 Or American justice: throughout the period under study "separate but equal" was an established legal doctrine in the United States.
53 Chap. 2, sec. 4.
54 Chap. 3, sec. 4. F. R. Scott regarded *Christie* as an effective illustration of "the important role the judges must play in selecting which of two alternative views they will adopt" (*Civil Liberties and Canadian Federalism* [Toronto: University of Toronto Press, 1959], 36).
55 Chap. 4, sec. 6.
56 Chap. 4, sec. 7.
57 Chap. 3, sec. 5.

58 Chap. 4, sec. 3.
59 Chap. 5, sec. 10.
60 Chap. 3, sec. 4, 7 and 8.
61 Chap. 3, sec. 8 and chap. 4, sec. 7.
62 Chap. 3, sec. 4.
63 Chap. 2, sec. 8.
64 Ibid.
65 Chap. 3, sec. 6.
66 Chap. 4, sec. 4.
67 Chap. 2, sec. 8. Emphasis added.
68 Chap. 3, sec. 6.
69 Chap. 2, sec. 7.
70 Chap. 3, sec. 6.
71 Chap. 3, sec. 5.
72 Chap. 3, sec. 7 and 8.
73 Chap. 4, sec. 6.
74 Chap. 4, sec. 4.
75 Chap. 4, sec. 6.
76 Chap. 5, sec. 9 and 10.
77 Chap. 5, sec. 11.
78 Ian Bushnell, *The Captive Court: A Study of the Supreme Court of Canada* (Montreal and Kingston: McGill-Queen's University Press, 1992), 197.
79 Ibid., 199-200.
80 Chap. 2, sec. 9.
81 For example, especially the debate on the Chinese immigration bill, *Hansard*, 8 May 1922, 1509ff.
82 Chap. 2, sec. 9.
83 Chap. 3, sec. 5.
84 Chap. 3, sec. 8.
85 Chap. 3, sec. 7. After the War Hugh Burnett founded the National Unity Association of Dresden, Chatham and North Buxton to combat the rampant racial discrimination of the region. It took a decade: the first African Canadians were served in Dresden restaurants in 1956.
86 Chap. 4, sec. 1.
87 Canadian Jewish Congress, *Information and Comment*, No. 6, August 1947.
88 Chap. 4, sec. 4.
89 Chap. 4, sec. 5.
90 Public Archives of Ontario, Frost Papers, Box 48, file 87-G.
91 Chap. 2, sec. 5; chap. 3, sec. 2.
92 Chap. 4, sec. 6.
93 Chap. 4, sec. 4.
94 Chap. 5, sec. 8.
95 Chap. 5, sec. 10.

96 Jennifer Nedelsky, "Judicial Conservatism in an Age of Innovation," in David H. Flaherty, ed., *Essays in the History of Canadian Law*, Vol. 1 (Toronto: Osgoode Society and University of Toronto Press, 1982), 281, endorsed by James G. Snell and Frederick Vaughan, *The Supreme Court of Canada: History of the Institution* (Toronto: Osgoode Society and University of Toronto Press, 1985), xi.

97 R. C. B. Risk, "A Prospectus for Canadian Legal History," *Dalhousie Law Journal*, 1 (1973): 236.

98 Chap. 2, sec. 9.

99 David Kairys, ed., *The Politics of Law* (New York: Pantheon Books, 1982), introduction, 5-6.

100 Chap. 3, sec. 5.

101 Chap. 2, sec. 4. Note also the federal trade minister's acknowledgement in 1885 that racially based immigration regulations "may be ... opposed to British practice" (chap. 2, sec. 2).

102 Chap. 3, sec. 8.

103 Chap. 3, sec. 4.

104 Chap. 3, sec. 5.

105 Chap. 1, sec. 4.

106 Chap. 4, sec. 1 and 3.

107 Chap. 5, sec. 3.

108 Chap. 4, sec. 2.

109 A version of this anecdote is in Allister Sparks, *The Mind of South Africa* (New York: Alfred A. Knopf, 1990), 78. "Kaffir" is a derogatory term for African people. A "sjambok" is a rawhide whip.

110 Chap. 3, sec. 2.

AFTERWORD

1 National Angus Reid/Southam News poll, 11 April 1992, cited in Patrick Monahan and Marie Finkelstein, "The Charter of Rights and Public Policy in Canada," *Osgoode Hall Law Journal*, 30 (1992): 503.

2 Ian Bushnell, *The Captive Court: A Study of the Supreme Court of Canada* (Montreal and Kingston: McGill-Queen's University Press, 1992), 159-60.

3 Jean Chrétien, "The Negotiation of the Charter: The Federal Government Perspective," in Joseph M. Weiler and Robin M. Elliot, eds., *Litigating the Values of a Nation: The Canadian Charter of Rights and Freedoms* (Toronto: Carswell, 1986), 10.

4 *Hansard*, 10 May 1985, 4611.

5 Carl Baar and Ellen Baar, "Diagnostic Adjudication in Appellate Courts: The Supreme Court of Canada and the Charter of Rights," *Osgoode Hall Law Journal*, 27 (1989): 1.

6 Alan Cairns and Cynthia Williams, "The State and Human Rights," in James Curtis et al., eds., *Social Inequality in Canada: Patterns, Problems and Policies* (Scarborough: Prentice-Hall, 1988), 388.

7 Peter McCormick and Ian Greene, *Judges and Judging* (Toronto: J. Lorimer, 1990), 196, 247.

8 Lynn Smith, "A New Paradigm for Equality Rights," in Lynn Smith, ed., *Righting the Balance: Canada's New Equality Rights* (Saskatoon: Canadian Human Rights Reporter, 1986); Patrick J. Monahan, "Judicial Review and Democracy: A Theory of Judicial Review," *UBC Law Review*, 21 (1987): 88; Beverly McLachlin, "The Charter of Rights and Freedoms: A Judicial Perspective," *UBC Law Review*, 23 (1989): 579-80.

9 *Globe and Mail*, 17 April 1992.

10 Chap. 2, sec. 1.

11 Chap. 1, sec. 2.

12 Walter S. Tarnopolsky, *The Canadian Bill of Rights* (Toronto: Carswell, 1966), 92.

13 "Section 1: It is hereby recognized and declared that in Canada there have existed and shall continue to exist without discrimination by reason of race, national origin, colour, religion or sex, the following human rights and fundamental freedoms, namely,

a) the right of the individual to life, liberty, security of the person and enjoyment of property, and the right not to be deprived thereof except by due process of law;

b) the right of the individual to equality before the law and the protection of the law;

c) freedom of religion;

d) freedom of speech;

e) freedom of assembly and association; and

f) freedom of the press."

Section 2 was more operational, advising the courts that "Every law of Canada shall, unless it is expressly declared by an Act of the Parliament of Canada that it shall operate notwithstanding the *Canadian Bill of Rights*, be so construed and applied as not to abrogate, abridge or infringe or to authorize the abrogation, abridgment or infringement of any of the rights or freedoms herein recognized and declared."

Section 3 set out administrative detail, ensuring that every proposed federal regulation or piece of legislation would be consistent with the "purposes and provisions" of the Bill.

14 Elmer A. Driedger, "The Meaning and Effect of the Canadian Bill of Rights: A Draftsman's Viewpoint," *Ottawa Law Review*, 9 (1977): 304, 310.

15 SO 1961-2 c. 93; Ian Hunter, "The Development of the Ontario Human Rights Code: A Decade in Retrospect," *University of Toronto Law Journal*, 22 (1972): 237.

16 PC 1962-86.

17 *Hansard*, 19 January 1962, 9-12.

18 PC 1967-1616.

19 *Hansard*, 8 October 1971, 8545-46.

20 Canada, Report of the Royal Commission on Bilingualism and Biculturalism, *The Cultural Contribution of Other Ethnic Groups* (Ottawa, 1969), Book 4, 3.

21 *Hansard*, 8 October 1971, 8545-46.
22 Sally Weaver, *Making Canadian Indian Policy: The Hidden Agenda, 1968-1970* (Toronto: University of Toronto Press, 1981).
23 Donald H. Clairmont and Dennis W. Magill, *Africville: The Life and Death of a Canadian Black Community* (Toronto: Canadian Scholars' Press, 1987).
24 SC 1976-77 c. 52; L. W. St. John-Jones, "Canadian Immigration," in T. E. Smith, ed., *Commonwealth Migration: Flows and Policies* (London: Macmillan, 1981), 77-83; John R. Wood, "East Indians and Canada's New Immigration Policy," *Canadian Public Policy*, 4 (1978): 547-67.
25 SC 1977 c. 33.
26 [1970] SCR 282.
27 Ibid., at 297.
28 (1973) 38 DLR (3d) 481.
29 *BNA Act*, s. 91 (24).
30 DLR, at 495.
31 Ibid., at 499.
32 *AG Canada v. Canard*, (1975) 52 DLR (3d) 548, at 576-77.
33 Ibid., at 563.
34 *Prata v. Minister of Manpower and Immigration*, (1975) 52 DLR (3d) 385, at 387.
35 *Drybones*, SCR, at 297.
36 *R. v. Burnshine*, [1975] 1 SCR 693, at 705.
37 This concept is articulated especially clearly in *R. v. Burnshine*.
38 *MacKay v. The Queen*, [1980] 2 SCR 370, at 406.
39 For example, see W. S. Tarnopolsky, "The Supreme Court of Canada and the Canadian Bill of Rights," *Canadian Bar Review*, 53 (1975): 671, where Prof. Tarnopolsky writes: "To sum up my views on the interpretation of section 1(b) of the Bill of Rights, may I state that the majority views in the cases since the *Drybones* case, with their reference to 1960 definitions, merely camouflage the fact that the judges are giving their *own* interpretations of the words used, instead of following the rules of statutory interpretation to see *what Parliament intended*." Emphasis in the original.
40 Chrétien, "Negotiation of the Charter," 5-11; Michael R. Hudson, "Multiculturalism, Government Policy and Constitutional Enshrinement – A Comparative Study," in *Multiculturalism and the Charter: A Legal Perspective* (Toronto: Carswell, 1987), 72ff.; Ian Greene, *The Charter of Rights* (Toronto: J. Lorimer, 1989), 40ff.
41 Keith Banting and Richard Simeon, eds., *And No One Cheered: Federalism, Democracy and the Constitutional Act* (Toronto: Methuen, 1983), 5ff. and 254ff.; Roy Romanow, John Whyte and Howard Leeson, *Canada . . . Notwithstanding: The Making of the Constitution 1976-1982* (Toronto: Carswell-Methuen, 1984), 220ff.; Dale Gibson, *The Law of the Charter: Equality Rights* (Toronto: Carswell, 1990), 42; Baker, "Changing Norms of Equality," 499; Smith, "New Paradigm," 387, n. 27; Greene, *Charter of Rights*, 40ff.; Robert Sheppard and Michael Valpy, *The National Deal: The Fight for a Canadian Constitution*

(Toronto: Fleet Books, 1982), 135ff.; Hudson, "Multiculturalism," 73ff.; Cairns and Williams, "The State and Human Rights," 390.

42 Peter Hogg, *Constitutional Law of Canada* (2nd ed.; Toronto: Carswell, 1985), 800.

43 Peter H. Russell, "The Effect of a Charter of Rights on the Policy-making Role of Canadian Courts," *Canadian Public Administration*, 25 (1982): 26.

44 1. The Canadian Charter of Rights and Freedoms guarantees the rights and freedoms set out in it subject only to such reasonable limits prescribed by law as can be demonstrably justified in a free and democratic society.

2. Everyone has the following fundamental freedoms:
a) freedom of conscience and religion;
b) freedom of thought, belief, opinion and expression, including freedom of the press and other media of communication;
c) freedom of peaceful assembly; and
d) freedom of association.

7. Everyone has the right to life, liberty and security of the person and the right not to be deprived thereof except in accordance with the principles of fundamental justice.

45 SO 1961-2 c. 93.

46 SO 1981 c. 53.

47 S. 10 was in fact codifying some important decisions already made under the previous *Code* applying to non-direct practices (private communication from Mr. Doug Ewart, May 1996). A discussion of the genesis of s. 10 can be found in Judith Keene, *Human Rights in Ontario* (Toronto: Carswell, 1983), 99-130.

48 Ontario Ministry of Labour, Race Relations Division, *Working Together: Strategy for Race Relations in Ontario* (Toronto, 1982), 5.

49 Canada, House of Commons, Special Committee on the Participation of Visible Minorities in Canadian Society, *Equality Now!* (Ottawa, 1984).

50 Rosalie Abella, *Report of the Royal Commission on Equality in Employment* (Ottawa, 1984).

51 Multiculturalism Canada, *National Strategy on Race Relations* (Ottawa, n.d. [1984]), 1.

52 Multiculturalism Canada, *Programme of Action for the Second Decade to Combat Racism and Racial Discrimination* (Ottawa, 1985), 5.

53 *Equality for All: Report of the Parliamentary Committee on Equality Rights* (Ottawa, 1985), 5.

54 Bill C-31, 1985. See Kathleen Jamieson, "Sex Discrimination and the Indian Act," in J. Rick Ponting, ed., *Arduous Journey: Canadian Indians and Decolonization* (Toronto: McClelland and Stewart, 1986), 128-35.

55 SC 1986 c.31.

56 Multiculturalism Canada, *Equality Now! Progress Report* (Ottawa, 1986), 7-8.

57 Audrey Kobayashi, "The Japanese-Canadian Redress Settlement and its Implications for 'Race Relations,'" *Canadian Ethnic Studies*, 24 (1992): 1-19.

58 SC 1988 c.31.

59 For overviews of multicultural policy evolution, see Augie Fleras and Jean Leonard Elliott, *Multiculturalism in Canada* (Toronto: Nelson, 1992), and Hudson, "Multiculturalism," 59-122. Neither the Act nor s. 27 contained specific remedial measures, but they declared a set of goals and values for Canadians and their institutions. S. 3(1) of the Act announced the government's commitment to "recognize and promote" such things as "racial diversity," "full and equitable participation of individuals and communities of all origins" and "equal treatment and equal protection under the law."

60 *R. v. Big M Drug Mart*, [1985] 1 SCR 295; (1985) 18 DLR (4th) 321.

61 SCR, at 359. Emphasis in original. Justice Dickson became chief justice after the *Big M* hearing but before the case report was published.

62 Ibid., at 359-60.

63 Ibid., at 372.

64 Ibid., at 362.

65 *O'Malley v. Simpsons-Sears*, [1985] 2 SCR 536.

66 Ibid., at 551.

67 [1989] 1 SCR 143.

68 Ibid., at 166.

69 Ibid., at 174.

70 Justice La Forest wrote a separate concurring judgment.

71 SC 1976-77 c.52.

72 [1985] 1 SCR 177; (1985) 17 DLR (4th) 422.

73 DLR, at 430.

74 Ibid., at 456.

75 One consequence has been that Immigration officials now try to intercept potentially illegal immigrants before they arrive in Canada. In the summer of 1996 an elaborate operation involving Immigration, Foreign Affairs and the RCMP tracked a group of 96 Indian Sikhs through the forests of Gambia and Senegal to prevent them from boarding a ship bound for Canada. Had they landed here, a spokesperson explained, their claims to refugee status could have taken months or years to determine in the courts and cost thousands of taxpayer dollars in the process (*Globe and Mail*, 28 September 1996). *Singh* did not therefore have the effect of liberalizing Canadian policy towards refugee claimants.

76 McLachlin, "A Judicial Perspective," 579-90.

77 Robert J. Sharpe, "Judicial Development of Principles in Applying the Charter," in Neil R. Finkelstein and Brian M. Rogers, eds., *Charter Issues in Civil Cases* (Toronto: Carswell, 1988), 3-27; A. Wayne MacKay and Dianne Pothier, "Developments in Constitutional Law: The 1988-89 Term – The Approach to Section 15: Articulating Equality," *Supreme Court Law Review*, 1 (2d) (1990): 81-106; Alan Pratt, "The Supreme Law in the Supreme Court: The First Seven Charter Cases," *Advocates Quarterly*, 409-32; Address by Chief Justice Dickson to Canadian Bar Association, Edmonton, 2 February 1985, cited in Smith, "New Paradigm," 395, n. 73.

78 *Hunter v. Southam*, [1984] 2 SCR 145, at 155.
79 For example, J. Berry, R. Kalin and M. Taylor, *Multiculturalism and Ethnic Attitudes in Canada* (Ottawa: Ministry of State for Multiculturalism, 1977); Ontario Human Rights Commission, *Life Together* (Toronto, 1977); Peter Pineo, "The Social Standing of Ethnic and Racial Groupings," *Canadian Review of Sociology and Anthropology*, 14 (1977): 147-57; Walter Pitman, *Now Is Not Too Late: Report of the Task Force on Human Relations* (Toronto: Task Force on Human Relations, 1977); J. S. Frideres, "British Canadian Attitudes Toward Minority Ethnic Groups in Canada," *Ethnicity*, 5 (1978): 20-32; Frances Henry, *The Dynamics of Racism in Toronto* (Ottawa: Department of the Secretary of State, 1978); Cardinal Carter, *Report to the Civic Authorities of Metropolitan Toronto and Its Citizens* (Toronto: Metropolitan Toronto Council, 1979); Peter S. Li, "Prejudice Against Asians in a Canadian City," *Canadian Ethnic Studies*, 11 (1979): 70-77; "Gallup Omnibus Study" conducted for the secretary of state for Multiculturalism, November 1981; John McAlpine, *Report Arising Out of the Activities of the Ku Klux Klan in British Columbia* (Victoria: BC Ministry of Labour, 1981); Frances Henry, *Race Relations Research in Canada Today: A "State of the Art" Review* (Ottawa: Canadian Human Rights Commission, 1986). See also the "Situation Reports" prepared in 1982 on 11 Canadian cities for the secretary of state for Multiculturalism.
80 *Toronto Star, Minority Reports* (Toronto, 1986), 61.
81 Ekos Research Associates poll, reported in the *Globe and Mail*, 10 March 1994.
82 For example, *Maclean's*, 13 October 1986; *Globe and Mail*, 17 September 1987, 23 January 1988, 28 August 1988; *Maclean's*, 3 July 1989; *Kitchener-Waterloo Record*, 23 February 1990; *Globe and Mail*, 21 March 1990; Angus Reid Group, "Multiculturalism and Canadian Attitude Study," August 1991; *Kitchener-Waterloo Record*, 14 December 1993; *Globe and Mail*, 14 December 1993, 10 March, 11 March 1994. Recall Prime Minister King's 1947 declaration that "the people of Canada do not wish, as a result of mass immigration, to make a fundamental alteration in the character of our population" (chap. 1, sec. 2).
83 *Globe and Mail*, 10 March 1994.
84 Henry, *Race Relations Research*, 14-15; *Toronto Star, Minority Reports*, 11, 47, 53-54, 63; Wilson Head, *The Black Presence in the Canadian Mosaic: A Study of Perception and the Practice of Discrimination Against Blacks in Metropolitan Toronto* (Toronto: Ontario Human Rights Commission, 1975) and *Adaptation of Immigrants: Perceptions of Ethnic and Racial Discrimination* (Toronto: York University, 1981); Y. Frenette, *Perception et vécu du racisme par des immigrantes et des immigrants haitiens au Québec* (Montreal: Centre de Recherches Caraïbe, Université de Montréal, 1985).
85 *Globe and Mail*, 17 and 25 February 1994.
86 *Census of Canada*, 1981, "Canada's Immigrants," 1986, "Profile of Ethnic Groups," 1991, "Ethnic Origin" and "Immigration and Citizenship"; J. Reitz et al., "Ethnic Inequality and Segregation in Jobs," *Ethnic Pluralism in an Urban Setting*, Paper No. 4 (Toronto: Centre for Urban and Community Stud-

ies, University of Toronto, 1981); Leon Muszynski and Jeffrey Reitz, *Racial and Ethnic Discrimination in Employment* (Toronto: Social Planning Council of Metropolitan Toronto, 1982); Rosalie Abella, *Equality in Employment: A Royal Commission Report*, (Ottawa, 1984); "Discrimination in Employment," *Currents: Readings in Race Relations*, special issue, 2, 4 (Winter 1984-85), and "Racial Minorities and Access to Employment," special issue, 5, 4 (March 1990); Peter S. Li, *Ethnic Inequality in a Class Society* (Toronto: Wall and Thompson, 1988); Hill Sloan Associates, "Visible Minority Youth Employment and Training Policies," Ontario Ministry of Citizenship, October 1989; Statscan, Employment Equity Program, *Comparison of 1981 and 1986 Census Counts of Visible Minorities in Canada* (Ottawa, 1989); *Globe and Mail*, 20 August 1992; John Kralt and Avril Allen, "Overview of Black Canadians in Toronto CMA" (Ottawa; unpublished, 1992); Marc S. Mentzer and John L. Fizel, "Affirmative Action and Ethnic Inequality in Canada: The Impact of the Employment Equity Act of 1986," *Ethnic Groups*, 9 (1992): 203-17; Carl Raskin, *De Facto Discrimination, Immigrant Workers and Ethnic Minorities: A Canadian Overview* (Geneva: International Labour Organization, 1993); Krishna and Ravi Pendakur, *The Colour of Money: Earnings Differentials Among Ethnic Groups in Canada* (Ottawa: Strategic Research and Analysis, Department of Canadian Heritage, 1996).

87 F. Henry and E. Ginzberg, *Who Gets the Work? A Test of Racial Discrimination in Toronto* (Toronto: Urban Alliance on Race Relations and Social Planning Council of Metropolitan Toronto, 1985).

88 Canadian Recruiters' Guild, *A Survey of Employment Discrimination in Canada* (Ottawa, 1987).

89 *Globe and Mail*, 21 January 1991; Canadian Civil Liberties Association, occasional reports and newsletters.

90 Frances Henry, *Housing and Racial Discrimination in Canada* (Ottawa: Multiculturalism and Citizenship, 1988). See also W. Kalbach, "Ethnic Residential Segregation and Its Significance for the Individual in an Urban Setting," *Ethnic Pluralism in an Urban Setting*, Paper No. 4.

91 Maisy Cheng et al., *The Every Secondary Student Survey, Fall 1987* (Toronto: Toronto Board of Education, 1989).

92 K. W. Taylor, "Racism in Canadian Immigration Policy," *Canadian Ethnic Studies*, 23 (1991): 4.

93 *Globe and Mail*, 23 January 1993.

94 *Globe and Mail*, 28 June 1993.

95 *Globe and Mail*, 1 March 1995.

96 *Globe and Mail*, 10 March 1994.

97 Ivan F. Ivankovich, "The Religious Employee and Reasonable Accommodation Requirements," *Canadian Business Law Journal*, 13 (1987-88): 313.

98 *Ontario Human Rights Commission and O'Malley v. Simpsons-Sears* [1985] 2 SCR 536; *Bhinder v. Canadian National Railway Co.*, [1985] 2 SCR 561.

99 *Central Alberta Dairy Pool v. Alberta (Human Rights Commission)*, [1990] 2 SCR 489.

100 *McKinney v. University of Guelph*, [1990] 3 SCR 229.

101 *Zurich Insurance Co v. Ontario Human Rights Commission* [1992] 2 SCR 321.

102 *Ontario Human Rights Code*, 1981, "Preamble" and s. 28(a). Emphasis added. Note also the "notwithstanding" provision in s. 46(2).

103 For example, *Ontario Human Rights Code*, s. 17 and 21, *Quebec Charter of Rights*, s. 20. Every province except Newfoundland and New Brunswick has some human rights code exemption for charitable and community organizations. In 1996 the Canadian Civil Liberties Association launched a campaign against the practice of the Roman Catholic separate school system to hire only Roman Catholics as teachers (CCLA, *Newsletter*, October 1996). The Association argued that since the separate schools were publicly funded they must adhere to public regulations on equality in employment.

104 Pierre Elliott Trudeau, "The Values of a Just Society," in Thomas S. Axworthy and Pierre Elliott Trudeau, eds., *Towards a Just Society* (Markham, ON: Viking, 1990), 363. Emphasis added.

105 Walter S. Tarnopolsky, "The Equality Rights," in Walter S. Tarnopolsky and Gerald-A. Beaudoin, *The Canadian Charter of Rights and Freedoms: Commentary* (Toronto: Carswell, 1982), 437.

106 SCR, at 174-75.

107 *R. v. Turpin*, [1989] 1 SCR 1296.

108 *R. v. Hess*, [1990] 2 SCR 906, at 941-43. Chief Justice Lamer, on the other hand, seemed to perpetuate a *Turpin* orientation when he referred to "the overall purpose of Section 15 – namely, to remedy or prevent discrimination against *groups* subject to stereotyping, historical disadvantage and political and social prejudice in Canadian society." Quoted in the *Globe and Mail*, 14 July 1993. Emphasis added. The same orientation was echoed by Justice Allen Linden of the Federal Court of Appeal: "Advantaged *groups* have more power in our society; accordingly, it is assumed that distinctions that disadvantage them are not discriminatory." Quoted in the *Globe and Mail*, 13 July 1993. Emphasis added.

109 *Miron v. Trudel*, [1995] 2 SCR 418. Quotation is from Justice Gonthier writing for Chief Justice Lamer and Justices La Forest and Major, at 436. Although they were not agreed in the results of this particular case, the entire Court accepted a definition of discrimination contrary to s. 15 similar to Justice McIntyre in *Andrews*. Justice McLachlin wrote for Justices Sopinka, Cory and Iacobucci (see 485), and Justice L'Heureux-Dubé wrote independently (see 470).

110 For example, these headings in the *Globe and Mail*: "Equal-rights law raises confusion," "Definition of disadvantaged seems to rely on stereotypes," "The Supreme Court's motto: Give me liberty, or give me a good excuse," "Order in the Supreme Court! Ad-hockery is running wild," 17 April, 25 September, 9 October 1995.

111　Andrew Petter and Allan C. Hutchinson, "Rights in Conflict: The Dilemma of Charter Legitimacy," *UBC Law Review*, 23 (1989): 546-47.

112　F. L. Morton, Peter H. Russell and Michael J. Withey, "The Supreme Court's First One Hundred Decisions: A Statistical Analysis," *Osgoode Hall Law Journal*, 30 (1992): 46.

113　*Canadian Human Rights Advocate*, 6 (February 1990), 1-2.

114　Morton et al., "First One Hundred Decisions," 46-47; F. L. Morton, "The Charter Revolution and the Court Party," *Osgoode Hall Law Journal*, 30 (1992): 638.

115　Baar and Baar, "Diagnostic Adjudication," 19-21; McLachlin, "A Judicial Perspective," 586; Wilson, "Decision-Making," 243.

116　Baar and Baar, "Diagnostic Adjudication," 24; Greene, *Charter of Rights*, 220; Marilyn T. MacCrimmon, "Developments in the Law of Evidence: The 1990-91 Term: Social Science, Law Reform and Equality," *Supreme Court Law Review*, 3 (2d) (1992): 269-345. Chief Justice Lamer appeared to endorse this notion while "thinking out loud" about social policy decisions during a conference in Israel. "It may be . . . that in some areas we need to get away from a strictly adversarial process and allow the courts themselves to retain appropriate expertise and perhaps to conduct court-ordered investigations" (*Globe and Mail*, 10 February 1995).

117　Wilson, "Decision-Making," 242.

118　The location of law within a legal sensibility and a cultural framework was poignantly illustrated in the Ontario election of June 1995, when "employment equity" as a legal device for creating equality fell before the force of an appropriately named "common-sense revolution." There was an apparent paradox: Canadians overwhelmingly approved of the equality principles proclaimed in the Charter and human rights codes, yet specific laws purporting to implement those principles were often found "unfair." Rights rhetoric had reached beyond the common-sense view of "justice."

119　*Local Knowledge: Further Essays in Interpretive Anthropology* (New York: Basic Books, 1983), 16.

Index

PUBLICATIONS OF THE OSGOODE SOCIETY
FOR CANADIAN LEGAL HISTORY

1981   David H. Flaherty, ed., *Essays in the History of Canadian Law*, Vol. 1

1982   Marion MacRae and Anthony Adamson, *Cornerstones of Order: Courthouses and Town Halls of Ontario, 1784-1914*

1983   David H. Flaherty, ed., *Essays in the History of Canadian Law*, Vol. 2

1984   Patrick Brode, *Sir John Beverley Robinson: Bone and Sinew of the Compact*
David R. Williams, *Duff: A Life in the Law*

1985   James Snell and Frederick Vaughan, *The Supreme Court of Canada: History of the Institution*

1986   Paul Romney, *Mr Attorney: The Attorney General for Ontario in Court, Cabinet and Legislature, 1791-1899*
Martin Friedland, *The Case of Valentine Shortis: A True Story of Crime and Politics in Canada*

1987   C. Ian Kyer and Jerome Bickenbach, *The Fiercest Debate: Cecil A. Wright, the Benchers, and Legal Education in Ontario, 1923-1957*

1988   Robert Sharpe, *The Last Day, the Last Hour: The Currie Libel Trial*
John D. Arnup, *Middleton: The Beloved Judge*

1989   Desmond Brown, *The Genesis of the Canadian Criminal Code of 1892*
Patrick Brode, *The Odyssey of John Anderson*

1990   Philip Girard and Jim Phillips, eds., *Essays in the History of Canadian Law*, Vol. 3: *Nova Scotia*
Carol Wilton, ed., *Essays in the History of Canadian Law*, Vol. 4: *Beyond the Law: Lawyers and Business in Canada 1830-1930*

1991   Constance Backhouse, *Petticoats and Prejudice: Women and Law in Nineteenth-Century Canada*

1992   Brendan O'Brien, *Speedy Justice: The Tragic Last Voyage of His Majesty's Vessel Speedy*
Robert Fraser, ed., *Provincial Justice, Upper Canadian Legal Portraits from the Dictionary of Canadian Biography*

1993   Greg Marquis, *Policing Canada's Century: A History of the Canadian Association of Chiefs of Police*
F. Murray Greenwood, *Legacies of Fear: Law and Politics in Quebec in the Era of the French Revolution*

1994   Patrick Boyer, *A Passion for Justice: The Legacy of James Chalmers McRuer*
Charles Pullen, *The Life and Times of Arthur Maloney: The Last of the Tribunes*
Jim Phillips, Tina Loo and Susan Lewthwaite, eds., *Essays in the History of Canadian Law*, Vol. 5: *Crime and Criminal Justice*
Brian Young, *The Politics of Codification: The Lower Canadian Civil Code of 1866*

1995 David R. Williams, *Just Lawyers: Seven Portraits*
Hamar Foster and John McLaren, eds., *Essays in the History of Canadian Law*, Vol. 6: *British Columbia and the Yukon*
W. H. Morrow, ed., *Northern Justice: The Memoirs of Mr. Justice William G. Morrow*
Beverley Boissery, *A Deep Sense of Wrong: The Treason, Trials and Transportation to New South Wales of Lower Canadian Rebels after the 1838 Rebellion*
1996 Carol Wilton, ed., *Essays in the History of Canadian Law*, Vol. 7: *Inside the Law: Canadian Law Firms in Historical Perspective*
William Kaplan, *Bad Judgment: The Case of Mr. Justice Leo A. Landreville*
F. Murray Greenwood and Barry Wright, eds., *Law, Politics and Security Measures, 1608-1837*, Canadian State Trials Series, 1
1997 James W. St. G. Walker, *"Race," Rights and the Law in the Supreme Court of Canada: Historical Case Studies*
Lori Chambers, *Married Women and Property Law in Victorian Ontario*
Patrick Brode, *Casual Slaughters and Accidental Judgments: Canadian War Crimes and Prosecutions, 1944-1948*
Ian Bushnell, *A History of the Federal Court of Canada, 1875 to 1992*